Praise for Ian Kershaw's
Fateful Choices

"Superb . . . Kershaw does an excellent job of synthesizing a great deal of scholarship and therefore helping to further our understanding of this epic struggle—as well as of the role of contingency in the making of history." —Max Boot, *The New York Times Book Review*

"Kershaw writes with deep command of his material, weaving together the consequences that each decision had on those that followed. . . . [A] thoughtful, far-reaching examination of events that echo down to today." —*The Washington Post*

"In the end, this book is less about the fateful choices [World War II] leaders made than about the factors that constrained them. That is precisely what lifts it out of the rut of ordinary military history and puts it into a class of its own." —*The Nation*

"The lessons that pour from Ian Kershaw's reenactment of the planet's plunge into World War II offer a sobering reminder of the constraints that limit choice in even the direst circumstances. . . . Fascinating." —*The New Leader*

"An absolutely first-rate scholarly study of a series of vital, inter-related political choices by one of the leading historians of the age." —Tony Judt, author of *Postwar*

"So intelligent, compelling and illuminating that it feels as if this vital history has been made new again." —*Sunday Herald* (U.K.)

PENGUIN BOOKS

FATEFUL CHOICES

Ian Kershaw is Professor of Modern History at the University of Sheffield. For services to history he was given the German award of the Federal Cross of Merit in 1994. He was knighted in 2002 and awarded the Norton Medlicott Medal by the Historical Association in 2004.

He was the historical advisor to three BBC series: *The Nazis: A Warning from History*, *War of the Century* and *Auschwitz*.

His most recent books are *Hitler 1889–1936: Hubris* and *Hitler 1936–1945: Nemesis*, which received the Wolfson Literary Award for History and the Bruno Kriesky Prize in Austria for the Political Book of the Year, and was joint winner of the inaugural British Academy Book Prize, and *Making Friends with Hitler: Lord Londonderry and Britain's Road to War*, which won the Elizabeth Longford Prize for Historical Biography in 2005.

IAN KERSHAW

Fateful Choices

Ten Decisions that Changed the World,
1940–1941

PENGUIN BOOKS

PENGUIN BOOKS

Published by the Penguin Group

Penguin Group (USA) Inc., 375 Hudson Street, New York, New York 10014, U.S.A.
Penguin Group (Canada), 90 Eglinton Avenue East, Suite 700, Toronto,
Ontario, Canada M4P 2Y3 (a division of Pearson Penguin Canada Inc.)
Penguin Books Ltd, 80 Strand, London WC2R 0RL, England
Penguin Ireland, 25 St Stephen's Green, Dublin 2, Ireland (a division of Penguin Books Ltd)
Penguin Group (Australia), 250 Camberwell Road, Camberwell,
Victoria 3124, Australia (a division of Pearson Australia Group Pty Ltd)
Penguin Books India Pvt Ltd, 11 Community Centre,
Panchsheel Park, New Delhi – 110 017, India
Penguin Group (NZ), 67 Apollo Drive, Rosedale, North Shore 0632,
New Zealand (a division of Pearson New Zealand Ltd)
Penguin Books (South Africa) (Pty) Ltd, 24 Sturdee Avenue,
Rosebank, Johannesburg 2196, South Africa

Penguin Books Ltd, Registered Offices:
80 Strand, London WC2R 0RL, England

First published in Great Britain by Allen Lane 2007
Published in Penguin Books (UK) 2008
Published in Penguin Books (USA) 2008

1 3 5 7 9 10 8 6 4 2

ISBN 978-0-14-311372-0
CIP data available

Printed in the United States of America

Contents

CONTENTS

List of Illustrations

Photographic acknowledgements are given in parentheses.

1 French infantry soldiers surrender, May 1940 (akg-images)
2 Allied troops, Dunkirk, 1940 (Alinari Archives)
3 Churchill with Lord Halifax in Downing Street, 1940 (akg-images/ ullstein bild)
4 Grand Admiral Erich Raeder (akg-images)
5 Hitler and Franco at a French border station, October 1940 (akg-images/ullstein bild)
6 Molotov with Ribbentrop in Berlin, 1940 (akg-images)
7 Japanese Panzer tanks in southern China, 1941 (akg-images/ullstein bild)
8 Prince Konoe Fumimaro (akg-images)
9 The signing of the Tripartite Pact in Berlin, September 1940 (Alinari Archives)
10 Rally at the Italian entry into the war, June 1940 (akg-images)
11 Mussolini, Hitler, Ciano and Ribbentrop, October 1940 (akg-images/ ullstein bild)
12 Italian artillery fire on Greek positions, March 1941 (akg-images/ ullstein bild)
13 Roosevelt talking to Cordell Hull, 1940 (akg-images)
14 George C. Marshall and Henry L. Stimson (Time Life Pictures/Getty Images)
15 Stalin and Molotov (akg-images)
16 Captured Soviet soldiers, June 1941 (Roger-Viollet/Topfoto)
17 Stranded Soviet tanks, summer 1941 (Topfoto)
18 Franklin D. Roosevelt and Sir Winston Churchill aboard HMS *Prince of Wales*, August 1941 (AP/Empics)
19 General Tojo Hideki (Bettmann/Corbis)

List of Maps

Map 1 Western Europe, 1940

NORWAY

SWEDEN

DENMARK

IRELAND

Dublin •

GREAT
BRITAIN

London •

Berlin •

THE NETHERLANDS

Brussels •

Dunkirk •

BELGIUM

THE
GERMAN
REICH

Lille •

Paris •

LUXEMBURG

ATLANTIC
OCEAN

OCCUPIED FRANCE

F R A N C E

• Bern

SWITZERLAND

Vichy •

• Milan

VICHY FRANCE

I T A L Y

Hendaye •

Florence •

PORTUGAL

Madrid •

Corsica

Rome •

Lisbon •

S P A I N

Balearic Islands

Sardinia

Mediterranean   Sea

SICILY

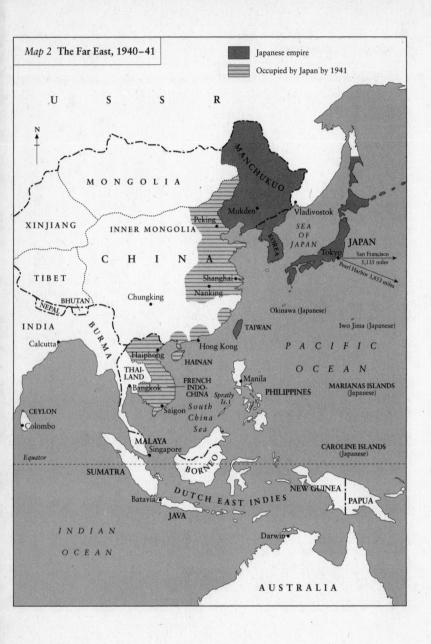

Map 2 **The Far East, 1940–41**

▨ Japanese empire

▤ Occupied by Japan by 1941

N

U S S R

MONGOLIA

XINJIANG

INNER MONGOLIA

MANCHUKUO

Mukden•

Vladivostok

SEA
OF
JAPAN

JAPAN

TIBET

C H I N A

Peking•

KOREA

Tokyo•

San Francisco
5,135 miles

Pearl Harbor 3,853 miles

BHUTAN

NEPAL

Chungking•

Shanghai•

Nanking•

Okinawa (Japanese)

Iwo Jima (Japanese)

INDIA

BURMA

TAIWAN

P A C I F I C

Calcutta•

Hong Kong•

Haiphong•

HAINAN

O C E A N

THAI-
LAND

FRENCH
INDO-
CHINA

Manila•

PHILIPPINES

MARIANAS ISLANDS
(Japanese)

Bangkok•

Spratly
Is.

CEYLON

•Colombo

Saigon•

South
China
Sea

MALAYA

Singapore•

BORNEO

CAROLINE ISLANDS
(Japanese)

Equator

SUMATRA

NEW GUINEA

PAPUA

DUTCH EAST INDIES

Batavia•

JAVA

INDIAN

Darwin•

OCEAN

AUSTRALIA

Map 3 **The Balkans, 1940–41**

THE GERMAN
REICH

•Budapest

HUNGARY
(Nov. 1940)

The dates in brackets
indicate the spread of
Axis influence

N

•Zagreb

ROMANIA
(Nov. 1940)

Trieste
Fiume

Belgrade•

YUGOSLAVIA
(April 1941)

Adriatic Sea

BULGARIA
(March 1941)

Sofia•

Tirana•
Durazzo•

ALBANIA

ITALY

•Naples

Tarranto•

Salonika•

Corfu

GREECE
(April 1941)

Aegean Sea

Ionian Sea

Athens•

SICILY

Mediterranean   Sea

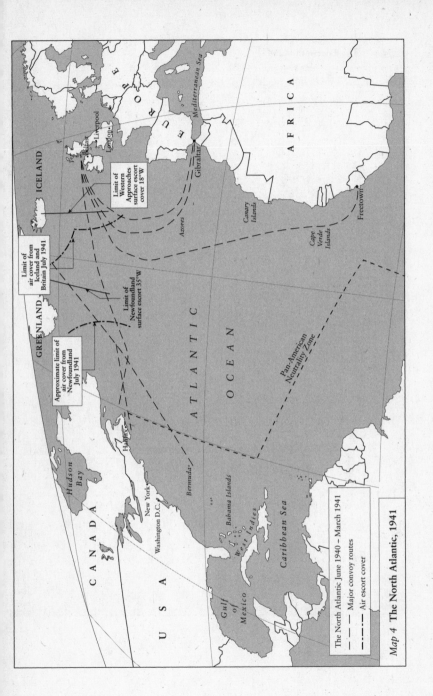

Map 4 The North Atlantic, 1941

ICELAND

GREENLAND

CANADA

Hudson
Bay

U S A

Washington D.C.
New York

Halifax

Gulf
of
Mexico

West Indies

Bahama Islands

Bermuda

Caribbean Sea

ATLANTIC

OCEAN

E U R O P E

Liverpool
London
Dublin

Mediterranean Sea

Gibraltar

Azores

AFRICA

Canary
Islands

Cape
Verde
Islands

Freetown

Limit of
Western
Approaches surface escort
cover 18°W

Limit of
air cover from
Iceland and
Britain July 1941

Limit of
Newfoundland
surface escort 35°W

Approximate limit of
air cover from
Newfoundland
July 1941

Pan-American
Neutrality Zone

The North Atlantic June 1940 – March 1941
—— Major convoy routes
—·—·— Air escort cover

Map 5 The Eastern front, 1941

N

SWEDEN

BALTIC SEA

• Tallinn
ESTONIA
Novgorod •

• Riga   LATVIA

LITHUANIA
Dvinsk •
• Polostk
• Kaunas   Smolensk •
• Vilna

Danzig •   Königsberg •
Pomerania
Danzig-West   East
Prussia   Prussia   • Minsk
Chelmno •   BELORUSSIA
Wartheland   • Bialystok
• Posen   U   S   S   R
Lodz •   Warsaw •
                  Bresz •   Gomel •
Breslau •   P O L A N D
              Lublin •
Upper   General
Silesia   Government
Auschwitz •   • Krakow
                  • Kiev
              Lvov (Lemberg) •
SLOVAKIA   U K R A I N E
              Ternopol •

• Budapest
H U N G A R Y
                              Odessa •
R
O
M
A
N
I
A
Bucharest •   BLACK SEA

The boundary between Germany
and Russia, 28 September 1939–
26 June 1941

to 9 July 1941
to 1 September 1941
to 9 September 1941

Acknowledgements

A chance conversation in our kitchen gave me the idea for this book. Laurence Rees had come up to Manchester to discuss with me the concept for what would become the television series *Auschwitz. The Nazis and the 'Final Solution'* – the third series on which we had collaborated. While we were waiting for the kettle to boil, Laurence happened to mention that, were he a historian, he would want to write a book about the year 1941 – in his view, the most momentous year in modern history. The thought stuck. But it was obvious that the crucial events of 1941 – most obviously the German invasion of the Soviet Union (which triggered the rapid descent into full-scale genocide against the Jews), the Japanese attack on Pearl Harbor and the entry of the United States into the European war – were the logical consequence of a number of vital decisions that had flowed from Hitler's astonishing triumph in western Europe in spring 1940. A study of the interlocking key decisions by the leaders of the major powers during those extraordinary months between May 1940 and December 1941 started to take embryonic shape in my mind. So my first warm thanks are owing to Laurence for the initial impulse to undertake this book.

As usual, numerous other debts of gratitude have been incurred along the way and my brief acknowledgement here can only offer a cursory expression of my thanks. It is right, however, to single out the Leverhulme Foundation, for whose generosity I am once more deeply grateful. Much of the book was written during the final year of a wonderfully generous award which freed me from university commitments.

Finding my way through the less familiar territory that I had to traverse in the research and writing was greatly eased through being able to call upon the expertise of colleagues. I am extremely grateful to David Reynolds, who made very helpful comments on the typescript and shared with me some of his profound knowledge of Churchill and of British relations with the United States. Patrick Higgins kindly let me see his unpublished paper on R. A. Butler, and offered valuable comments on the May crisis of 1940.

ACKNOWLEDGEMENTS

MacGregor Knox, beyond his own superb work on Fascist Italy, not only answered some detailed queries about the Italian armed forces but also, most generously, made available photocopies of the unpublished Roatta letter-diaries. The late Derek Watson (especially), Robert Davies, Robert Service, Moshe Lewin and, in Moscow, Sergei Slutsch were of enormous help on Stalin and the Soviet Union. Patrick Renshaw, Richard Carwardine and Hugh Wilford answered queries about the workings of the Roosevelt administration. In Tokyo Maurice Jenkins and Ms Owako Iwama were extraordinarily helpful in locating materials I required. I also received useful advice from Ken Ishida and, closer to home, Sue Townsend and Gordon Daniels. On more familiar terrain, Otto Dov Kulka in Jerusalem offered, as always, valuable reflections on the harrowing subject of the Nazi onslaught on the Jews. I profited, too, from a discussion about the emergence of the 'final solution' with Édouard Husson, a younger French historian of Nazi Germany, whose fine work will surely soon become more widely known. I also benefited greatly from discussions, during a stay in Freiburg, with Gerhard Schreiber, Jürgen Förster and Manfred Kehrig. To all these colleagues and friends I offer my sincere thanks. Naturally, they have no responsibility for any errors or flaws in what I have written.

Part of Chapter 2 appeared as a contribution to Jeremy Noakes' *Festschrift* (*Nazism, War and Genocide*, Exeter, 2005), and I am grateful to the editor, Neil Gregor, and the University of Exeter Press for their agreement to its inclusion here.

Lack of linguistic competence was a severe shortcoming and enormous frustration in researching the chapters on the Soviet Union, Japan and, to some extent, also Italy (where Latin and French helped with the gist, but not with a refined understanding). So I am extremely grateful to my good friend Constantine Brancovan (under great pressure of time) and to Christopher Joyce, who willingly and ably stepped in to help, for translating important documents from Russian for me; to Darren Ashmore for providing translations of some works in Japanese; and to Anna Ferrarese for speedily translating some Italian material I needed.

The staff of Sheffield University Library, and especially of the Inter-Library Loans section, who had to labour under my numerous requests, offered, as always, extremely friendly as well as efficient help. I also encountered only the best possible service at the Public Record Office (now renamed the National Archives), the British Library and the London School of Economics Library, the Churchill Centre in Cambridge, the Borthwick Institute in York, Birmingham University Library, the Politisches

Archiv des Auswärtigen Amtes in Berlin, the Bundesarchiv/Militärarchiv in Freiburg and the Institut für Zeitgeschichte in Munich.

I would like to thank my colleagues, academic and secretarial, in the excellent Department of History at the University of Sheffield for their continued collegial support. Quite especially, it is a great pleasure to express my gratitude once more to Beverley Eaton, my long-standing (and long-suffering) Personal Assistant, who helped greatly in locating obscure and arcane works as well as dealing, with legendary courtesy and efficiency (if not always legendary patience), with an array of matters which would otherwise have proved most time-consuming. In addition, and a very big help, she took it upon herself to compile the List of Works Cited for me.

I would also like once more to thank my agent, the remarkable Andrew Wylie, for his constant and invaluable help and advice, and the wonderful team at Penguin, both in London and in New York, who make publishing under this particular imprint something special. I am grateful to Cecilia Mackay for her work in locating the illustrations. And my editors, Simon Winder in London and, in New York, Scott Moyers, stand proxy for all those involved in the publication process, but deserve especial thanks for both their constant encouragement and for their sharp, vigilant criticism.

Finally, as always, the last thanks go to my family. Without them, writing books on history would give me no satisfaction at all. So my deepest thanks – as well as my love, of course – go to Betty, to David, Katie, Joe and Ella, and to Stephen, Becky and Sophie for all that they have done and continue to do to help in my work but, above all, for giving me a constant reminder of a proper sense of priorities.

Ian Kershaw
Manchester/Sheffield, November 2006

Dramatis Personae

Only the principal players of the major countries in the unfolding drama are listed here, with a brief indication of their position and standing during the crucial events of 1940–41.

GREAT BRITAIN

Attlee, Clement. Leader of the Labour Party from 1935; Lord Privy Seal in Churchill's War Cabinet.

Cadogan, Sir Alexander. Permanent Under-Secretary in the Foreign Office (head of the diplomatic staff).

Chamberlain, Neville. Prime Minister from 1937 until his resignation on 10 May 1940; thereafter Lord President of the Council and member of the War Cabinet until serious illness forced his resignation from government (and from the leadership of the Conservative Party) a few weeks before his death on 9 November 1940.

Churchill, Winston. Appointed Prime Minister on 10 May 1940 after a decade in the political wilderness; also took on the responsibilities of Minister of Defence. Leader of the Conservative Party following Chamberlain's resignation.

Cripps, Sir Stafford. Ambassador to the USSR from May 1940.

Greenwood, Arthur. Deputy Leader of the Labour Party since 1935; Minister without Portfolio, responsible for economic affairs, in Churchill's War Cabinet.

Gort, Field Marshal Lord. Commander-in-Chief of the British Expeditionary Force, who took the decision in May 1940 to withdraw to Dunkirk for evacuation.

Halifax, Lord. Foreign Secretary from 1938 until his appointment as British ambassador to the United States in January 1941.

Lloyd George, David. Former Prime Minister (1916–22), seen by some (including himself) in 1940 as the likely head of government if peace terms with Germany could be attained.

Lothian, Lord. British ambassador to Washington; exposed Britain's financial plight to the Americans in November 1940, prompting the moves that led to lend-lease; died the following month.

Sinclair, Archibald. Chairman of the Parliamentary Liberal Party from 1935; Secretary of State for Air in the Churchill government; participated in the War Cabinet deliberations in late May 1940.

GERMANY

Brauchitsch, Field Marshal Werner von. Commander-in-Chief of the army from 1938 until December 1941.

Dönitz, Rear Admiral Karl. Commander of the German U-boat fleet.

Eichmann, Adolf. Head of the Jewish Affairs Desk in the Reich Security Headquarters; responsible to Heydrich for organizing the deportation of the Jews; in effect, 'manager' of the 'final solution'.

Frank, Hans. Governor General of occupied Poland.

Goebbels, Joseph. Reich Minister for People's Enlightenment and Propaganda since March 1933.

Göring, Hermann. Commander-in-Chief of the Luftwaffe; head of the Four-Year Plan (since 1936); Hitler's designated successor.

Greiser, Arthur. Provincial head of government, and of the Nazi Party, in the annexed region of western Poland centring on Posen, known as the 'Warthegau'.

Halder, Colonel-General Franz. Chief of the General Staff of the army, responsible for army strategic planning.

Heydrich, Reinhard. Directly subordinate to Himmler; head of Reich Security Headquarters; in charge of the implementation of the 'final solution of the Jewish Question'.

Himmler, Heinrich. Head of the SS since 1929; appointed chief of the German police in 1936; in addition, since October 1939, Reich Commissar for the Consolidation of German Nationality (giving him sweeping powers over the programme of population resettlement in eastern Europe).

Hitler, Adolf. Leader of the Nazi Party since 1921; Reich Chancellor (head of the German government) from January 1933; head of state from August 1934; in supreme and direct control of the newly created High Command of the Wehrmacht from February 1938; addressed officially only as 'Führer' ('Leader') from 1939; at the height of his powers following the victory over France in 1940.

Jodl, General Alfred. As head of the Wehrmacht Operations Staff, responsible for overall strategic planning; Hitler's main adviser on military strategy and operations; strong Hitler loyalist.

Keitel, Field Marshal Wilhelm. Head of the High Command of the Wehrmacht since February 1938, though completely subservient in that position to Hitler.

Müller, Heinrich. Head of the Gestapo since 1937; directly responsible to Heydrich.

Ott, General Eugen. Ambassador in Tokyo since 1938.

Raeder, Grand Admiral Erich. Commander-in-Chief of the German navy.

Ribbentrop, Joachim von. Reich Foreign Minister since February 1938.

Rosenberg, Alfred. Reich Minister for the Occupied Eastern Territories from July 1941.

Schulenburg, Count Friedrich Werner von der. Ambassador in Moscow since 1934.

Warlimont, Major-General Walter. Head of the National Defence Department of the Wehrmacht Operations Staff since November 1938; directly subordinate to Jodl.

Weizsäcker, Ernst von. State Secretary in the German Foreign Office since March 1938; head of the diplomatic staff; had a tense relationship with Ribbentrop.

JAPAN

Hirohito. Emperor since succeeding his father, Yoshihito, in 1926; deified symbol of the 'Showa' era, meaning 'illustrious peace'.

Kido Koichi, Marquis. As Lord Keeper of the Privy Seal from 1 June 1940, the Emperor's closest counsellor.

Konoe Fumimaro, Prince. Prime Minister in 1937, when the war against China began; resigned in January 1939, but reappointed as premier in July 1940; resigned again (nominally) along with the entire government in July 1941; immediately reappointed as Prime Minister for the third time; final resignation at the failure of his policies on 16 October 1941.

Kurusu Saburo. Former ambassador to Germany, sent to Washington as a special emissary in November 1941 to assist Nomura explore the possibilities of staving off war.

Matsuoka Yosuke. Strongly pro-Axis and mercurial Foreign Minister from July 1940 to July 1941, when he was effectively forced out of office.

Nagano Osami, Admiral. Chief of the navy General Staff.

Nomura Kichisaburo. Ambassador to the United States from April 1941.

Oikawa Koshiro, Admiral. Navy Minister between September 1940 and October 1941.

Oshima Hiroshi. Pro-Axis ambassador to Germany, 1938–9, and took up the position again in February 1941.

Shimada Shigetaro. Succeeded Oikawa as Navy Minister in October 1941.

Sugiyama Gen, General. Army Minister in 1937; later chief of the army General Staff.

Togo Shigenori. Former ambassador to Berlin and Moscow; appointed Foreign Minister in Tojo's government in succession to Toyoda in October 1941.

Tojo Hideki, General. Former chief of staff of the Kwantung Army; Army Minister in Konoe's second administration; appointed Prime Minister in October 1941.

Toyoda Teijiro. Navy Vice-Minister in 1940; successor to Matsuoka as Foreign Minister between July and October 1941.

Yamamoto Isoroku, Admiral. Former Navy Vice-Minister; mastermind behind the plan to attack Pearl Harbor; commander of the attack fleet.

Yonai Mitsumasa, Admiral. Konoe's predecessor as Prime Minister between January and July 1940.

Yoshida Zengo, Admiral. Navy Minister between July and September 1940 (when he resigned on grounds of ill-health).

ITALY

Alfieri, Dino. Ambassador to Berlin from May 1940; more acceptable to the German leadership than Attolico.

Attolico, Bernardo. Ambassador to Berlin from 1935 until his anti-interventionist stance prompted Hitler to request his recall in late April 1940.

Badoglio, Marshal Pietro. Commanded the victorious Italian army in Abyssinia in 1935–6; chief of the Supreme Command of the armed forces since 1925; in this capacity, Mussolini's main military adviser; resigned in December 1940 in the wake of the debacle in Greece.

Cavagnari, Admiral Domenico. Chief of staff of the navy, and Navy Under-Secretary until his dismissal in December 1940.

Ciano, Count Galeazzo. Foreign Minister from 1936; married to Mussolini's daughter, Edda.

Graziani, Marshal Rodolfo. Former viceroy of Abyssinia; army chief of staff, 1939–41; Italian commander in north Africa, 1940–41.

Jacomoni, Francesco. Governor of Albania from 1939.

Mussolini, Benito. Leader of the Fascist Party since 1919; head of government since 1922; in addition, in control of the armed forces as War, Navy and Air Minister since 1933; popularity and hold over the Italian state – bolstered by the artificially manufactured Duce cult – at their height after the victory over Abyssinia in 1936; in foreign affairs by 1940, however, increasingly under the shadow of Hitler.

Pricolo, General Francesco. Chief of staff of the air force, 1939–41.

Roatta, General Mario. Deputy chief of the army staff from 1939 to 1941.

Soddu, General Ubaldo. Under-Secretary for War since 1939 and deputy chief of the Supreme Command of the armed forces from June 1940; Mussolini's most trusted military adviser; replaced Visconti Prasca as commander in Albania in November 1940, but soon revealed his own inadequacies in the Greek campaign; resigned on health grounds in January 1941.

Victor Emmanuel III, King of Italy. Sovereign since 1900; also Emperor of Abyssinia and King of Albania; head of state to whom, ultimately, Mussolini, too, was responsible (as the latter's removal from power and arrest in July 1943 were to show).

Visconti Prasca, General Count Sebastiano. Incompetent military commander of Albania, sacked in November 1940 as one of the scapegoats for the failure of the offensive in Greece.

THE UNITED STATES OF AMERICA

Grew, Joseph C. Long-standing, highly experienced and skilful ambassador to Japan; one of the strongest advocates of attempts to defuse the growing crisis in 1941.

Hopkins, Harry. Hugely energetic 'fixer' for Roosevelt, despite serious illness; close to the President, a member of his regular 'inner circle', and sometimes entrusted with especially important missions as a personal envoy.

Hornbeck, Stanley K. Chief adviser to Cordell Hull on the Far East, and an outright 'hawk' in his views on the threat from Japan.

Hull, Cordell. Secretary of State since 1933; a strong believer in the principles of self-determination and international cooperation laid down by President Woodrow Wilson at the end of the First World War, but increasingly drawn into a hard line in protracted negotiations with Japan in 1941.

Ickes, Harold L. Secretary of the Interior and a strong interventionist.

Knox, Frank. Secretary of the Navy from June 1940; alongside Stimson, and a fellow Republican, he pushed for a more assertive defence policy than Roosevelt was prepared to pursue.

Marshall, General George C. Army chief of staff since 1939; superb organizer, who pushed for and presided over a huge and rapid increase in the size of the army between the start of the European war and Pearl Harbor.

Morgenthau, Henry. Secretary to the Treasury; strong proponent of economic assistance for Great Britain; given the task of organizing war production.

Roosevelt, Franklin D. Inaugurated as President in March 1933; re-elected 1936; elected again for an unprecedented third term in November 1940; concerned in the main with domestic recovery from the Depression until the late 1930s, but then, increasingly anxious about the threat from Germany and Japan, commissioned the start of what would prove an immense armaments programme.

Stark, Admiral Harold. Chief of Naval Operations since 1939; a key advocate of according planning priority to the Atlantic over the Pacific.

Steinhardt, Laurence. Ambassador to the Soviet Union since 1939.

Stimson, Henry L. Secretary of War from June 1940; a strong proponent of American interventionism in the war.

Welles, Sumner. Under-Secretary of State and close to Roosevelt, which led to some antagonism in his relations with Hull.

THE SOVIET UNION

Beria, Lavrenti. Chief of the NKVD (the secret police) from 1938; in charge of internal security.

Dekanozov, Vladimir. Soviet ambassador to Germany from December 1940.

Golikov, General Filip. Head of Soviet military intelligence.

Malenkov, Georgi. Stalin's right hand in the General Secretariat of the Communist Party, and manager of the party's bureaucracy; following the German invasion, put in charge of the evacuation of industrial production to the east, and of supplies for the Red Army.

Maisky, Ivan. Ambassador to London since 1932.

Merkulov, Vsevolod. Commissar for State Security (head of the network of foreign intelligence, which was separated in February 1941 from Beria's NKVD and remained distinct from the organization of military intelligence).

Mikoyan, Anastas. Member of Stalin's 'inner circle' in the Politburo; responsible for foreign trade.

Molotov, Vyacheslav. Commissar for Foreign Affairs since May 1939 and, until 5 May 1941, chairman of the Council of People's Commissars (Prime Minister of the state government).

Oumansky, Konstantin. Ambassador to the United States since 1939.

Stalin, Joseph. General Secretary of the Communist Party; from 5 May 1941 chairman of the Council of People's Commissars; unchallenged supreme ruler of the Soviet Union, in control of all the main levers of power, political and military.

Timoshenko, Marshal Semion. Defence Commissar from May 1940; held responsibility for the organization and training of the Red Army.

Voroshilov, Marshal Kliment. Defence Commissar until May 1940; long-standing adviser to Stalin on military matters.

Zhukov, Marshal Georgi. Came to prominence as commander during the conflict with Japanese forces in Mongolia in 1939; chief of the Soviet General Staff from January 1941.

Fateful Choices

Forethoughts

The Second World War recast the twentieth century in ways that are still felt today. And that war – the most awful in history – took its shape largely from a number of fateful choices made by the leaders of the world's major powers within a mere nineteen months, between May 1940 and December 1941. These two thoughts underlie the chapters that follow.

The nearer the twentieth century came to its end, the more it became evident that its defining period had been that of the Second World War. Of course, the First World War was the 'original catastrophe'.[1] It shattered political regimes (the Russian, Austrian and Ottoman empires all fell in its wake), destroyed economies and left a searing mark on mentalities. But the highly unstable, volatile societies and political structures that emerged proved to be of short duration. The immense social, economic and political cost of the seemingly pointless four-year-long carnage meant that a further great conflagration was always probable and gradually became inescapable. The Second World War was in obvious ways the unfinished business of the First. But this second great conflict was not only even more bloody – costing upwards of fifty million lives, between four and five times the estimated death toll of the war of 1914–18 – and more truly global; it was also more profound in its lasting consequences and its reshaping of the world's power structures.[2]

Both in Europe and in the Far East, previous power pretensions – those of Germany, Italy and Japan – collapsed in the maelstrom of destruction. A combination of national bankruptcy and resurgent anti-colonial movements put paid to Great Britain's world empire. Mao's China was a prime legatee of the demise of Japan and the upheavals of the war-torn Far East. And, above all, the two new superpowers, the United States and the Soviet Union, neither of them very super before 1939, now held each other at bay with nuclear arsenals in a Cold War that would last until the final decade of the century. The constellation of power left by the Second World War did not lead to a third cataclysmic conflict – to the surprise and relief of many contemporaries of the early Cold War years – but provided the framework for the phoenix-like recovery both of the European continent and of the Far East with, astonishingly, the defeated countries of Germany (at least its western half) and Japan as the economic driving forces.[3] Only with the unpredictably peaceful (in the main) end of the Soviet bloc in 1989–91 did the world enter its post-postwar era. The impact of the Second World War had, then, been huge, lasting and defining.

The Second World War also left humanity with a new, horrible word which also relates to what has increasingly come to be seen as a defining characteristic of the century: genocide.[4] And, though it was lamentably far from the only instance in that benighted century, what later came to be known as 'the Holocaust' – the planned attempt by Nazi Germany to wipe out a targeted eleven million Jews, a genocidal project unprecedented in history – left the most lasting and fundamental mark on future decades. In terms of power-politics, the legacy of the Holocaust ensured, and gave legitimacy to, the foundation of the state of Israel, supported by much of the world but ferociously attacked by the new country's neighbours who had lost land, and inevitably leading to unending, even increasing, turmoil in the Middle East, with huge implications for the rest of the world. And in terms of mentalities, the ever greater preoccupation with the Holocaust, the further it recedes into history, has profoundly affected views about race, ethnicity and the treatment of minorities. The context for the killing of the Jews had been the Second World War. But, more than just context, the murder of the Jews had been an intrinsic part of the German war effort. This inbuilt genocidal component of the Second World War has come to play an increasingly important part in shaping historical consciousness during subsequent decades.

Before May 1940 two separate wars, in separate continents, had broken out. The first was the bitter war raging in China, following the attack by the Japanese in 1937. The second was the European war which had commenced in 1939 with Germany's attack on Poland, followed two days later by the declarations of war on Germany by Great Britain and France. Terrible atrocities – by the Japanese in China, and by the Germans in Poland – had already become hallmarks of both wars. But at this stage, spring 1940, the genocidal onslaught which was soon to take place in eastern Europe was still in the future. And, although the war in the Far East was of vital concern to the European powers and to the United States, it remained down to this point distinct from the European war, which itself had not geographically extended (apart from Albania, under Italian rule since the invasion of April 1939) beyond parts of central and eastern Europe held down by German arms. The war in Europe was, conversely, alerting eager eyes in Japan to the possibilities opening up of rich pickings in east Asia at the expense, especially, of the biggest imperial power, Great Britain. But the expansion, as Japan's leaders well understood, presaged a possible showdown, not only with Britain, but, even more dangerously, with the United States. In Europe, too, the war was set to widen. In the autumn Mussolini set the Balkans aflame with his attack on Greece. And by the end of the year, Hitler's determination to invade the Soviet Union the following spring was translated into a firm military directive. Meanwhile, American aid for the beleaguered Britain was increasing. The entire world was being rapidly drawn into a single gigantic war.

The chapters that follow examine a number of interlinked political decisions with immense and dramatic military consequences, between May 1940 and December 1941, that transformed the two separate wars in different continents into one truly global conflagration, a colossal conflict with genocide and unprecedented barbarism at its centre. Of course, by December 1941 the war still had far to run. Many vagaries were still to occur over the course of the war. Obviously, other crucial decisions, though mainly strategic and tactical, were yet to be taken. And towards the war's end, with Allied supremacy now assured, the geopolitical framework of the postwar settlement – the basis of the Cold War soon to emerge – was laid down in the Yalta and Potsdam conferences. But the remaining three and a half years of the war would, nevertheless, essentially play out the consequences of the decisions taken between May 1940 and December 1941.[5] These were indeed fateful decisions – decisions that changed the world.

The choices made by the leaders of Germany, Great Britain, the Soviet Union, the United States, Japan and Italy – countries with very different political systems and different decision-making processes (two Fascist, two democratic, one Communist, one bureaucratic authoritarian) – fed from and were interwoven with each other. How were these decisions reached? Each chapter seeks primarily to answer this question. But related questions arise straight away. What influences were brought to bear on those responsible for the decisions? How far were decisions pre-formed by government bureaucracies, or shaped by competing power-groups within the ruling elites?[6] How rational were the decisions – and they were decisions that meant *war* – in terms of each regime's aims and in the light of the intelligence it was receiving? What role was played by the individuals at the centre of the decision-making process, and how greatly did this differ within the varying political systems? What freedom did the war leaders have in reaching their decisions? How significant, in contrast, were external and impersonal forces in conditioning and limiting the decisions? To what extent did the room for manoeuvre in making decisions diminish over the months in question? How far, in other words, did the scope for alternatives narrow, or even disappear altogether, over the nineteen months in question? And what consequences, short and long term, did the decisions have? These are some of the considerations in mind in what follows.

In retrospect, what took place seems to have been inexorable. In looking at the history of wars, perhaps even more than at history generally, there is an almost inbuilt teleological impulse, which leads us to presume that the way things turned out is the only way they could have turned out. It is part of the purpose of this book to show that this was not the case. The war is viewed in each chapter as if from behind a separate leader's desk, with only indistinct notions of enemy plans available, the future open, options to be faced, decisions to be taken. A decision implies that there were choices to be made, alternatives available. To the actors concerned, even the most ideologically committed (or blinkered), vital considerations were at stake, crucial assessments to be made, big risks to be taken. There was no inexorable path to be followed. In each case, therefore, the book asks why a particular option rather than an alternative was chosen, posing in most instances explicitly the question of what might have followed had the alternative option been taken up.

This is *not* counter-factual or virtual history of the type which makes an intellectual guessing-game of looking into some distant future and projecting what might have happened had some event not taken place. There are always far too many variables in play to make this a fruitful line of enquiry, however fascinating the speculation. Nevertheless, it could fairly be claimed that historians implicitly operate with short-range counter-factuals in terms of alternatives to immediate important occurrences or developments. Otherwise, they are unable fully to ascertain the significance of what actually did take place. So the alternatives discussed here are not advanced as long-term projections or musings on 'what ifs', but as realistic short-term, but different, possible outcomes to what was in fact decided. Putting it another way, assessing the options behind a particular decision helps to clarify why, exactly, the actual decision was taken.

Ten decisions are explored. Three, with arguably the most far-reaching consequences of all, were those of Hitler's regime: to attack the Soviet Union, to declare war on the United States and to murder the Jews. The extensive consideration of these decisions reflects the predominant role of Germany as the chief driving force in the crucial course of events that we are following. As a dynamic power triggering events, Japan was second only to Germany, something which the two chapters devoted to Japanese decisions seek to emphasize. The essentially reactive decisions of Great Britain, the Soviet Union and, in a different way (with self-destructive consquences), Italy are taken up in single chapters, though the increasingly vital part played by the United States warrants two chapters. Other decisions than those under consideration here, for example those of Franco's Spain or of Vichy France to refuse to join the war on the Axis side – were, compared with the momentous decisions examined below, of a distinctly lesser order of importance.

It could, of course, be claimed with some force that what shaped the postwar world most fundamentally was a decision taken almost at the end, rather than close to the beginning, of the Second World War: the decision to drop atomic bombs on the Japanese cities of Hiroshima and Nagasaki. Even here, however, a prior decision – to commission the atom bomb – had been necessary, one which also dates back to the fateful months of 1940 and 1941. Following preliminary work and increased research funding after the fall of France in the summer of 1940, American scientists, aided by the findings of refugee physicists in Britain, established by autumn 1941 the fundamental framework for building a bomb. At huge cost, and necessitating the involvement of large numbers of the most talented American scientists, President Franklin D. Roosevelt decided to go ahead with its construction on the day before Japanese bombs rained down on the American warships anchored in Pearl Harbor. Without the decision then, the bomb would not have been available to President Harry S. Truman to use in the final days of the war, in August 1945.[7] When the commission to research an atomic bomb was issued, however, its ultimate use was scarcely even a distant vision.

Each decision in the following chapters had consequences which informed the next and subsequent decisions. So, as the story moves from one country to another, there is a logical sequence of 'knock-on' events and implications as well as an unfolding chronological pattern. The book opens with Great Britain's decision in May 1940 to stay in the war. Far from being the obvious, even inevitable, decision subsequent events (and some persuasive historical writing) have made it seem,[8] the War Cabinet seriously deliberated the choices for three days, with a new Prime Minister still tentatively feeling his way, the British army seemingly lost at Dunkirk, no immediate prospect of help from the United States and a German invasion in the near future presumed to be very likely. The decision eventually taken, not to seek a negotiated settlement, had direct and far-reaching consequences not just for Britain, but also for Germany.

That single decision, in fact, placed in jeopardy Hitler's entire war strategy. With Britain refusing to see sense (as he saw it), with the war in the west not ended, and with the spectre of the United States in the background but looming ever more prominently, Hitler felt compelled already in July 1940 to begin preparations to risk a war on two fronts through an invasion of the Soviet Union the following year. But it was only six months later that the contingency plans were turned into a concrete war directive. In the interim, there was no straight path to the Russian war. Even Hitler seemed vacillating and uncertain. The intervening period saw a range of strategic possibilities explored, but eventually discarded. These options in the summer and autumn of 1940, viewed from behind Hitler's desk and evaluated in the eyes of his advisers, form the subject of Chapter 2.

The extraordinary German victory over France and the perceived likely collapse of Great Britain alerted the Japanese leadership to chances to be taken without delay through expansion in south-east Asia. In Chapter 3, the scene switches, therefore, to the Far East, and to the decision for the southern advance that would inevitably risk conflict with the United States and presaged, therefore, the road to Pearl Harbor directly embarked upon the following year.

The rapidity of France's fall also had immediate and far-reaching consequences in Europe. The next chapter considers the choices facing the Italian leadership as Mussolini exploited the destruction of France to take his country into the war, and then plunged the Balkans into turmoil with the disastrous decision to attack Greece. The crucial position of the United States is explored in Chapter 5; how Roosevelt walked a tightrope between isolationist opinion and interventionist pressure, deciding, out of American self-interest, not only to assist Great Britain with all possible means short of war, but to prepare with maximum speed for America's direct engagement in the war.

This is followed by a chapter dealing with one of the most puzzling episodes of the war, with near fatal consequences for the Soviet Union: Stalin's decision to defy all warnings and the explicit findings of his own secret intelligence of the imminent German invasion, leaving his country unprepared and in disarray when the strike came on 22 June 1941.

From here, the route into global war was short, but not without further twists. Chapter 7 examines the decision of the American administration to wage in provocative fashion an 'undeclared war' in the Atlantic, taking advantage of Hitler's unwillingness to retaliate while embroiled in Russia. This is followed (Chapter 8) by an examination of Japan's extraordinary decision to attack the United States, despite full recognition of the immensity of the risk, aware that the long-term chances of final victory were low if an immediate and total knock-out blow were not attained. This had direct causal impact on Hitler's decision to declare war on the United States, taken in the immediate aftermath of Pearl Harbor and long regarded as one of the strangest of the Second World War. With this decision, explored in Chapter 9, the world was aflame.

But one further decision – or set of decisions – of a different kind, though inextricably entwined with the war itself and intrinsic to it, remains to be examined: the decision, gradually but inexorably reached over the summer and autumn months of 1941, to kill the Jews. The complex process of the transition from partial and limited genocidal actions into total genocide, a process of interlocking impulses from the centre of the Nazi regime and its agencies 'on the ground' in the killing fields of eastern Europe, unfolding in the early months of 1942 into the full-scale 'final solution', is taken up in the last chapter.

By the end of 1941, nineteen months after the German offensive in western Europe was launched, the conflict had become global and genocidal. The war was at this juncture on a knife-edge. The German advance, it is true, had been stymied by the first major Soviet counter-offensive. But the Wehrmacht was withstanding the worst the Red Army and the ferocious Russian winter could inflict on it (for the time being) and was soon starting to regather its strength, poised to make further great inroads down to the autumn of 1942. In the Atlantic, German U-boats would meet with unprecedented success in the first half of 1942. The Allies looked for a time as if they were losing the war at sea. In Europe and in the Far East, the Axis powers still had vital economic resources in their grasp.[9] And, much to Stalin's continued vexation, the Anglo-Americans were still nowhere near opening their promised second front. The full might of the United States' industrial power was still to be converted into weaponry on a scale to defeat both Germany and Japan. Japanese forces had meanwhile made brutal progress in the Far East, and would in February 1942 capture Singapore, long viewed as the bastion of British strength in south-east Asia. The way to the conquest of India, the heart of the British Empire, appeared to lie open. The Axis powers still seemed in the ascendancy. Only in retrospect can it be seen that their colossal gamble was already on the verge of failure, that they had overstretched their capacities, and that with the full engagement in the contest of the might of the United States, now allied with the extraordinary tenacity of the Soviet Union and the last major show of resilience of Great Britain and the British Empire, their eventual defeat would gradually be ensured.[10]

To reach the point, in 1945, when first Hitler's suicide was swiftly followed by a devastated Germany's surrender, then Imperial Japan was crushed into submission, there was a long, tortuous way to go. Millions of lives would be lost in the process; destruction wrought on a scale never known in history. The end was far away. But the path towards it had been laid out by the fateful choices made in 1940 and 1941.

I

London, Spring 1940

Great Britain Decides to Fight On

The P[rime]M[inister] disliked any move towards Musso. It was incredible that Hitler would consent to any terms that we could accept, though if we could get out of this jam by giving up Malta and Gibraltar and some African colonies he would jump at it. But the only safe way was to convince Hitler that he couldn't beat us ... Halifax argued that there could be no harm in trying Musso and seeing what the result was. If the terms were impossible we could still reject them.

Diary of Neville Chamberlain, 26 May 1940

'Future generations may deem it noteworthy that the supreme question of whether we should fight on alone never found a place upon the War Cabinet agenda. It was taken for granted and as a matter of course by these men of all parties in the State, and we were much too busy to waste time upon such unreal, academic issues.'[1] This was Winston Churchill writing his memoirs of the Second World War. These were hugely influential in shaping the way the war came to be seen, and in fashioning the myth that Great Britain, alone, in great adversity, but with indomitable will, had never for a moment flinched in the determination to carry on the struggle against a mighty, triumphant and imminently threatening Germany. It is generally hard, knowing the end of a story, to avoid reading history backwards from the outcome. Given the power of Churchill's narrative and the unique role he played, it is particularly difficult to ignore what came later – national defiance epitomized in the grandiose rhetoric of his speeches in summer 1940, victory in the 'Battle of Britain', the 'hands across the Atlantic' in ever increasing American aid. But Churchill knew full well that it had not been like that in the darkest days of May 1940. History viewed 'from the front' rather than 'the back' sometimes reveals surprises. At any rate, it is often less clear-cut, more 'messy' or confused than subsequently appears to have been the case. And so it was in the middle of May 1940.

It was a deeply anxious time. The British Expeditionary Force in northern France and Belgium was apparently lost, the once mighty French army was reeling under the German onslaught, no possibility existed of immediate help from the United States or, in a direct and practical sense, the overseas Empire, and defences at home were in a fragile state as the prospect of invasion became a distinctly real one. In these circumstances, it would have been extraordinary had the British government indeed regarded the question of whether the country could or should fight on as an 'unreal, academic' issue not warranting discussion. And in fact, though Churchill omitted any reference to it, there was the most grave and prolonged deliberation in the War Cabinet about precisely this question: should Britain fight on, or should she acknowledge that in her current plight the best avenue was to explore what terms could be attained to arrive at a settlement?[2] This was the fateful choice that confronted Britain's leaders over a crucial three-day period in late May 1940. The outcome had profound consequences not only for Great Britain, but for the wider course of the war over the following years.

I

How Britain found herself in such a predicament that the question arose of whether to seek terms from a position of great weakness – which would, in effect, have come close to an acknowledgement of defeat – has, of course, been extensively examined and analysed ever since. Already in 1940, a widely read and influential polemic, *Guilty Men*, laid the blame squarely on those in the British government who had chosen the dangerous, and ultimately self-defeating, road to appeasement of Hitler during the 1930s.[3] Leading characters in the cast of the guilty were the austere, prim, but sharp and incisive Neville Chamberlain, Prime Minister between May 1937 and May 1940, and the extremely tall, somewhat humourless Foreign Secretary, Lord Halifax – a former Viceroy of India and seasoned diplomat, known, for his combination of religious piety and enthusiasm for fox-hunting, as the 'Holy Fox' – who retained his post in Churchill's adminis-tration. History has never forgiven them. The shame of 'Munich' in 1938, when Britain, and her French ally, bowed to Hitler's bullying and handed him a substantial part of Czechoslovakia, has remained forever associated with Chamberlain. It is often conveniently forgotten that appeasement, down to Munich, had been widely popular in Britain, even among those who in the light of subsequent events came to be among its chief detractors and most severe critics. The British government, in seeking to appease Hitler, undoubtedly made grave errors of judgement. Even so, these have to be located within the framework of the barely surmountable problems besetting Britain as the looming danger posed by Hitler gradually came to be recognized.

Britain's debilitating structural problems in the interwar period revolved around the interlinked triad of the economy, the Empire and rearmament. Between them, they ensured that when the dictators began to flex their muscles, an enfeebled Britain was in poor shape to contest their growing might.

Britain emerged from the First World War still a great power – though, mainly beneath the surface, a weakened one. Still a world creditor, with loans on paper outstanding to the Empire and her war allies of £1.85 billion in 1920, her debts to America nevertheless totalled $4.7 billion. It was an indicator of a shift in the financial balance of power which would only over time reveal Britain's growing dependency upon her transatlantic cousin. Even the Royal Navy, still the world's largest, now had to reckon with a future rival in the rapidly growing navy of the United States. And difficulties in India, Egypt and, closer to home, Ireland were stretching limited military resources.[4] With the Dominions of Canada, Australia, New Zealand and South Africa also showing signs of growing independence, the Empire was starting to crumble.

The magnitude of the problems was in good measure concealed during the 1920s, as recovery from the wartime trauma gradually took place despite numerous buffetings. Even so, beneath the surface all was not well.[5] The key industries which had formed the basis of Britain's prewar prosperity – coal, iron and steel, shipbuilding, textiles – were all struggling to combat long-term decline. Unemployment was relatively high throughout the decade. Britain was importing more and exporting less.[6] Still, alongside the stagnation or decline there were signs of new industries taking root, and outside the run-down industrial towns and cities the later 1920s saw an all too brief upsurge of hope, confidence and relative prosperity.[7]

The onset of the world economic crisis in 1929 was rapidly to change all that. It brought economic growth in the industrial world to a juddering halt. Social misery and political turmoil followed. In Britain, the repercussions of the Wall Street stock-market crash of October 1929 ushered in political crisis and lasting economic depression. But indirectly the global consequences were to prove far more threatening. In the Far East, the swift emergence after 1931 of Japanese nationalism, militarism and imperialism, and in Europe the rise of Nazism between 1930 and 1933, were both, in no small measure, products of the economic crisis. Both posed for Britain, herself in an economically weakened state, immense new strategic dangers to add to the potential threat in the Mediterranean, not as yet materialized, emanating from Mussolini's Italy.

The new, thrusting authoritarian powers in Europe and the Far East – Germany, Italy and Japan – had a vested interest in challenging and 'revising' (or overthrowing) the international order established in the wake of the First World War. Each of them had the feeling, with all its attendant resentment, of a 'have-not nation', insistent and determined upon attaining its rightful 'place in the sun'. Each looked at Britain, France and other imperial powers and wanted its own share of empire, the political dominance that went with coveted great-power status and national pride; the economic area of self-sufficiency that, in a fundamental crisis of capitalism which highlighted the uncertainties and the inbuilt unfairness of an international trading economy, appeared to offer the only solution to sustained national prosperity. Other countries were unlikely to offer voluntarily the territorial acquisitions necessary for the formation of the new empires. So like the old, those of Britain and other major powers, they would have to be taken by force – 'by the sword', as Hitler repeatedly put it.

Britain's interests were exactly the opposite. As a supreme 'have nation', her key concern was in upholding her world Empire. This meant adherence to the postwar order, which Britain had been a main party to creating. It meant, too, an emphasis upon international cooperation to maintain security, and the diplomatic negotiation of problems that arose. Above all, it meant a premium on peace. International safeguards and commitment to disarmament would prevent the world once more collapsing into the carnage of 1914–18. The recent and searingly painful memory of the dead millions of the war alone demanded no less.

From the position of a victorious, and still prosperous, world power, demands for a new order based upon liberal freedoms, international agreements and external trade were not difficult to advance. From the vantage-point of the 'have-not nations', precisely this new order was both disadvantageous and, in political terms, humiliating. The memory of the war dead, in the eyes of growing numbers of their citizens, demanded not supine acceptance of the victors' terms, not compliance with economic rules stacked against them, not the weakness that came from disarmament, and not peace, but war – for national glory, for territory to establish lasting future prosperity, and to rectify perceived past humiliation and current injustice.

Britain, together with her most important Continental ally, the war-stricken France, and, across the Atlantic, the burgeoning new world power, the United States, saw the postwar settlement, therefore, through one set of lenses, Italy, Japan and Germany through quite a different set. Moreover, the postwar settlement, framed around the Versailles Treaty of 1919 (and the subsequent Treaties of Saint-Germain and Trianon) in Europe and the Washington Nine Power Treaty of 1922 for the Far East, looked fragile. The refusal of the United States of America to underpin the settlement in Europe by joining the League of Nations, the body established to ensure international cooperation, did nothing to encourage optimism about its longevity. In both the Far East and Europe, however, the settlement none-theless lasted during the 1920s. Japan, a member of the League of Nations, offered no threat to European and American interests in the Far East and 'appeared willing to play by western rules'.[8] Churchill himself outrightly dismissed the prospect of war against Japan. 'I do not believe there is the slightest chance of it in our lifetime,' he wrote in December 1924. 'Japan is at the other end of the world. She cannot menace our vital security in any way.'[9] In Europe, too, the signs were improving. The postwar settlement was strengthened through the Treaty of Locarno of 1925, fixing by inter-national agreement the western borders of the German Reich, and by Germany's accession to the League of Nations the following year. Both were inspired by the outstanding international statesman of the 1920s, the German Foreign Minister Gustav Stresemann.[10] But appearances deceived. The Depression blew apart the optimism. Soon, both in the Far East and in Europe, the postwar settlement would be in shreds.

In the Far East, British weakness was soon demonstrated by the first manifestations of Japanese belligerence, in the occupation of Manchuria in 1931 and attacks on Shanghai the following year. The chiefs of staff of the British armed forces pointed out the danger to British possessions and dependencies, including India, Australia and New Zealand. Sir Robert Vansittart, the powerful Permanent Under-Secretary at the Foreign Office, recorded in early 1932 that 'we are incapable of checking Japan in any way if she really means business', meaning that 'we must eventually be done for in the Far East unless the United States are eventually prepared to use force'.[11] The United States were not – resorting to largely counterproductive denunciations of Japanese actions, but little else. British policy, in fact, favoured Japan over China, though it tried to square the circle by placating the Chinese and the Americans while not alienating the Japanese and at the same time upholding the League of Nations.[12] In early 1934, with Britain still in the throes of severe economic depression, imposing deep constraints on spending for the armed forces (which in any case faced the obstacle of opposition to rearmament in all the major political parties, and in public opinion), the Chancellor of the Exchequer, Neville Chamberlain, stipulated that the friendship of Japan was more important to Britain than that of the United States or the goodwill of China and the friends of the League of Nations.[13] The course for appeasement in the Far East was set. By this time, Japan was no longer a member of the League, and a new, closer and graver danger could not be ignored.

In the crucial early phase when the Nazi regime was establishing its complete control over Germany, Foreign Office officials could not make up their minds about Hitler. Was he the demon of *Mein Kampf*, whose rule meant not just diplomatic disturbance but, ultimately, war? Or would the firebrand eventually cool down into a 'normal' politician as far as foreign affairs were concerned? While they were still trying to decide, Hitler exploited insuperable differences between Britain and France about German rearmament to take his country out of the League of Nations. Like Japan in the Far East, Germany, the wildest card in the European pack, then no longer even paid lip-service to the League's doctrine of collective security. Disarmament, to which British policy and public mood had been wedded, was dead. It was obvious that Germany was rearming as rapidly as possible in secret, and it was recognized that the growing German strength posed a threat greater than that of either Japan or Fascist Italy. But in Britain complacency merged with financial exigency and the political difficulties of proposing rearmament in the face of hostile public opinion. It led to inaction, drift and a policy of 'hope for the best'.

The inertia was ended only with the German announcement in March 1935, in breach of the Versailles Treaty, of an air force and plans for a huge army; then the startling news brought back by the British Foreign Secretary, Sir John Simon, and Lord Privy Seal, Anthony Eden, from their visit to Berlin later that month that Germany's air strength was already on a par with that of Britain. Hitler had exaggerated for effect. But the shock running through Whitehall, and in the public at large when the news came out, was palpable. Belatedly, the urgency of rearmament – something that hitherto only Churchill and one or two lone and derided voices had been clamouring for – was recognized, if still widely opposed in Labour and Liberal circles, as it would be until 1938. In air power, however, acknowledged as the new key to military strength and where the enemy threat was seen to be at its most lethal, it would be years before the lost ground could be made up, if at all. This was the weakness that underlay the entire attempt to appease Hitler.

Stretched by her global commitments, and struggling to overcome lasting economic depression, Britain, it was increasingly evident, could not match, let alone outstrip, German military might. It became equally evident that Britain faced the prospect within only a few years of a new war with Germany. But it was recognized that the British armed forces would be in no position to fight such a war until a lengthy armaments programme had been undertaken, perhaps not before 1942 or so.[14] Even then, building up an air force and reinforcing the navy came at the expense of funding for the army (which would leave its mark in 1940) as attempts were made to keep rearmament costs in line with the demands of a balanced budget and economic recovery from the Depression.[15]

As Britain's military weakness was exposed, her diplomatic strength suffered a calamitous setback in late 1935 in the attempt, together with her ally France, to buy off the aggressor Mussolini at the cost of his victim, Abyssinia. The League of Nations never recovered from the debacle. Profiting from the diplomatic disarray, Hitler sent his troops over the demilitarized line into the Rhineland in March 1936. The German hand was now even mightier. One Conservative Member of Parliament, Robert Boothby, summed up much public opinion, as well as the government's stance, when he stated: 'Nobody feels that we can apply very strong or stringent measures against Germany because she has put troops into the Rhineland.'[16] The British Foreign Secretary, Anthony Eden, confining the response to diplomatic protest, reasserted the government's peaceful objective: 'It is the appeasement of Europe as a whole that we have constantly before us.'[17] Three months later, in early July 1936, the Cabinet acknowledged that Britain could do nothing to help eastern Europe and that only force used against the Empire or parts of western Europe would be resisted.[18]

When he replaced Stanley Baldwin as Prime Minister in May 1937, Neville Chamberlain inherited a foreign policy shaped by confusion, uncertainty and inaction, increasingly compelled to come to terms with Britain's military weakness and her incapacity to do other than respond, often feebly, to events shaped by Europe's dictators. Chamberlain now sought starkly to face up to the cold reality and to devise a practical policy on the basis of recognition of this weakness. This meant active steps to accommodate – or 'appease' – Germany's interests. Realistic about Britain, Chamberlain deluded himself about German aims. Like most observers of the international scene, he presumed that these were purely nationalist in character. He imagined, as did so many, that Hitler was no more than an extreme proponent of territorial claims in central and eastern Europe which were not altogether devoid of legitimacy and could, with goodwill and peaceful objectives on both sides, be settled by negotiation. If German nationalist aims were met, he thought, war could be avoided. Buying Hitler off was the price of peace. It was, for Chamberlain, a price well worth paying.

The saga of 1938, as the Czech crisis culminated in Chamberlain's dramatic flights to Germany to attempt to reach a settlement with Hitler, ending in the Munich Agreement at the end of September, unfolded on this premise. Whether another way out of the crisis, short of war, could have been found is doubtful. But none was tried. Churchill, whose attacks on government defence and foreign policy had mounted with increasing forcefulness since the mid-1930s, was the chief advocate of a 'grand alliance' with France and the Soviet Union to deter Hitler and to resist by force, if need be, any aggression against Czechoslovakia (linked by treaty with both countries). The idea had much support on the Left, and in public opinion, but not in the government. For Chamberlain and his Foreign Secretary, Lord Halifax, detestation for Bolshevism was mixed with deep distrust of Stalin's motives and contempt for the Red Army. They ruled out any alliance.

Conceivably, nothing would have come of the 'grand alliance' even if it had been engineered. The Soviet dictator claimed that his troops were ready to march if Hitler invaded. It was bluff more than intention. No preparations for military action were made by a Red Army reeling from Stalin's purges, and its passage through Poland and Romania would almost certainly have been refused.[19] In the west, in any case, France was looking to wriggle out of her treaty commitments to the Czechs, and Britain was anxious not to be tied to backing any French involvement. Chamberlain was warned that rearmament was insufficient to engage in a major war, and that nothing could be done militarily to save Czechoslovakia. War, he was certain, would endanger the Empire. British interests in the Far East were already threatened by Japan's war against China, expanding since it began the previous summer. (The following summer an initially minor incident in Tientsin, in north China, leading to a stand-off lasting weeks between Britain and Japan, forced a British acknowledgement that, as Lord Halifax put it, 'there seemed little we could do in the Far East unless the United States joined in with us'.[20]) In the Mediterranean, Fascist Italy and the growing likelihood of a Franco victory in the Spanish Civil War, raging since the summer of 1936, posed a mounting danger to British strength. Chamberlain later suggested that he was left with no choice. Britain was not ready for war; he had to gain time. 'Any way and whatever the outcome it is clear as daylight that if we had had to fight in 1938 the results would have been far worse,' he wrote to one of his sisters, months after war had eventually begun. 'It would be rash to prophesy the verdict of history, but if full access is obtained to all the records it will be seen that I realised from the beginning our military weakness and did my best to postpone if I could not avert the war.'[21]

Whether Chamberlain genuinely believed he was gaining time through the surrender of part of Czechoslovakia to Hitler, or whether he genuinely believed that he had taken a major step to securing 'peace for our time', is even now disputed.[22] It is also impossible to be sure whether the squandered opportunity to combat Hitler in the summer of 1938 was better than that which occurred the following year, when war had to be undertaken anyway, and whether a defiant stance over Czechoslovakia might even have resulted in Hitler's fall through an internal coup. The most likely speculation is in both cases a negative one: that a better chance was not lost, and that Hitler would not have been toppled from within. In all probability, Czechoslovakia would have been rapidly overrun, as war games suggested would be the case, and Britain and France would either have come to terms in recognition of a fait accompli or would have been embroiled in war from a militarily weaker starting point than in 1939. In either case, an armed triumph of German might would have been a distinct possibility. And it must be doubted whether the embryonic German opposition would have been sufficiently well organized to act against Hitler before he could have disarmed resistance through victory over Czechoslovakia while keeping the western powers at bay. Whatever the surmises, the truth was, as Churchill vehemently expressed it in the House of Commons, that, through the Munich Agreement, 'we have suffered a total and unmitigated defeat'[23] – though it was one born out of long-standing military weakness and the extremely overdue recognition of the need to rearm with all speed, for which successive British governments, not Chamberlain alone, had to carry the responsibility. At least now, at last, rearmament was sharply accelerated. By September 1939 Britain was still not strong, but she was militarily in a somewhat better position, relative to the strength of German arms, than at the time of Munich.

Once Hitler had shown his true colours in March 1939 by reneging on Munich and invading what remained of Czechoslovakia, the realization dawned on the British government that war was inevitable. The guarantee to Poland at the end of that month effectively ensured that war was unavoidable by leaving Britain's fate in Polish and German hands. The concatenation of events in the dramatic summer of 1939 followed inexorably.

Chamberlain and Halifax only late in the day, and reluctantly, accepted the necessity of broaching the possibility of an alliance with Stalin. They were upstaged yet again by Hitler. The notorious Hitler–Stalin Pact of 23 August 1939 meant that war was not only inevitable, but imminent. It began with the German invasion of Poland little over a week later, on 1 September 1939. The British and French declarations of war on Germany, turning the German–Polish conflict into general European war, followed within two days. Chamberlain reckoned on a long conflict, but was confident that Britain would eventually prevail.

It was an assessment based in good measure upon the superior economic resources at Britain's disposal, which it was presumed would tell in a lengthy war, and upon a perceived critical instability in the German economy. Little dented such underlying optimism during the months of military inaction in western Europe that followed – until spring 1940, when it was blown away within the course of a few days.

II

The thunderclap finally burst on 10 May 1940. For the western Allies, Great Britain and France, the heavy, threatening atmosphere of the 'phoney war' that had lasted since the previous autumn now gave way to the predicted mighty storm. It had been brewing for a month, ever since early April when Hitler's troops had invaded Denmark and Norway. As dawn broke that May morning, German artillery on the Belgian border opened fire. The long-awaited western offensive had begun.

Advancing with breathtaking pace, ruthlessly violating Dutch and Belgian neutrality, the German advance reached the French coast by the night of 20 May, having covered 150 miles in ten days. The Allied forces, split in two by the speed and surprise of the 'sickle-cut' of the German army as it swept through southern Belgium and northern France, were retreating in disarray towards the coast. The last Allied hopes of a counter-offensive proved on 24 May to be illusory. Boulogne fell to the Germans. Calais came under siege. By 25 May the only port still open to the Allies was Dunkirk. Next day, practically the whole of the British Expeditionary Force and most of the French troops still fighting – in all, close to 340,000 men – had started to fall back on Dunkirk and its environs, where they found themselves pinned down between the sea and the German front line.

As the fates would have it, on 10 May, the very day that Hitler opened his western offensive, the man who was to prove one of his toughest adversaries, Winston Churchill, entered office as Prime Minister of the United Kingdom of Great Britain and Northern Ireland. Churchill had been out in the political cold throughout the 1930s. Despite his extensive ministerial experience, dating back to the First World War, he was regarded by the leaders of successive administrations of the 'National Government' (which had first come into office in 1931 during the economic crisis as a coalition of the major political parties, and was dominated by his own party, the Conservatives) as too unreliable and too independent-minded for high office. Remembered and disliked as a reactionary on the political Left, he was regarded as something of a maverick adventurer by much of his own side. His responsibility for the disaster at Gallipoli during the First World War had not been forgotten. Nor had his earlier political inconstancy, when he had deserted the Conservative Party and joined the Liberals before, years later, rejoining the fold. 'I've ratted twice,' he apparently said later, 'and on the second rat Baldwin', the Prime Minister, 'made me Chancellor.'[24] As Chancellor of the Exchequer he was not a great success. His 'years at the treasury', it has been claimed, 'were indeed the weakest in his varied career. His erratic finance' – he was seen as too impatient to master the close detail of financial management – 'discredited him in the eyes of more sober politicians and left the treasury weaker to face a period of real economic difficulty.'[25] That he was 'unsound' seemed once again demonstrated by his outspoken opposition in the early 1930s to his party's policy of limited constitutional reform in India and his strong support for King Edward VIII during the Abdication Crisis in December 1936.

The sense that Churchill, despite his manifold talents, was not to be trusted in political judgement ran through much of the Conservative Party. More than a few would have agreed with the private verdict of Stanley Baldwin, then Prime Minister: 'When Winston was born lots of fairies swooped down on his cradle gifts – imagination, eloquence, industry, ability, and then came a fairy who said "No person has a right to so many gifts", picked him up and gave him such a shake and twist that with all these gifts he was denied judgement and wisdom.'[26] Churchill's supposed untrustworthiness long swayed views within his own party. As late as July 1939, four-fifths of Conservative backbench Members of Parliament did not want Churchill in the Cabinet.[27]

Churchill had indeed been of independent mind. He had freely used his many contacts, his rhetorical and journalistic skills, and his parliamentary standing to denounce, regularly and with increasing effect, British defence and rearmament policy. His warnings about the re-emerging danger from

Germany had proved prophetic. His implacable enmity towards Nazism, consistent since Hitler's takeover of power, had made him a strong opponent of appeasement, one of the few in his party. His condemnation of the ignoble and humiliating Munich Agreement had contrasted strongly with Chamberlain's hapless concession to Hitler's demands. As Hitler's destruction of what remained of Czechoslovakia in March 1939 finally opened British eyes to the fact that he was not seeking to incorporate ethnic Germans into a Greater German Reich, but was set upon imperial conquest, with war in Europe a certainty, Churchill had again vainly advocated, as he had done during the growing crisis the previous year, a 'grand alliance' uniting Britain with the Soviet Union as well as France as the last chance to head off a new great conflagration.[28] When, despite all the appeasers had tried, war nonetheless came, Churchill had been proved right. His return to the Cabinet, to his old office as First Lord of the Admiralty, on 3 September 1939, the day of the British declaration of war on Germany, was, therefore, welcomed in many quarters, even among his own former political opponents. Churchill was back in the inner circles of political power. It seemed to offer some reassurance.

It would be well, however, not to exaggerate Churchill's power-base at this time. Chamberlain remained firmly in control and was still hugely popular within his own party during what he called the 'twilight war'. During these months, Britain's war aims, beyond getting rid of Hitler, were left undefined. There were exaggerated hopes that internal economic crisis or a power-struggle would bring Hitler down. The way would then be open, it was optimistically imagined, for a restoration of borders and an end to the conflict. Chamberlain was, even so, more realistic than many in reckoning with a long war: three years or so, he thought. He doubted that there would be outright victory. But he did not think Hitler could win in the long run, and hoped he would be toppled from within when the German people came to full realization of this. There were those who wanted to end the conflict before it began in earnest by negotiating with the Hitler government. In autumn 1939 Chamberlain received thousands of letters from individuals wishing to stop the war through a negotiated peace.[29] Though there was no 'peace party' as such, disparate individuals – mostly Conservative, and a number of peers of the realm with good contacts to persons in high places – voiced hopes of a negotiated settlement.[30] But the government showed no readiness to go down this route; the 'peace offer' made by Hitler on 6 October 1939, following his triumph in Poland, was turned down without hesitation.[31]

So the 'sinister trance' (as the restless Churchill later called it) of the shadowy war continued over the dark winter months.[32] The strange optimism of the British government that Hitler would in the end fall from power or be defeated – at any rate would not ultimately prevail – continued. But there was also an underlying unease, a sense that the eerie calm would be followed by a great storm. Hitler's next move, it was felt, could not be long in coming. When it did, in April 1940, it was to pre-empt British plans, which Churchill had repeatedly pressed, to mine Scandinavian waters. On 4 April Chamberlain had tempted fate by announcing that in not invading France and Britain by this time Hitler had 'missed the bus'.[33] The foolish boast immediately backfired. Five days later the Germans invaded Denmark and Norway. The disastrous British campaign in Norway followed. The main responsibility lay with Churchill, but it was Chamberlain who paid the political price. The knives were now sharpened for the Prime Minister who had tried to appease Hitler. Churchill, whose warnings from the wilderness now appeared so prophetic, had gained in stature. By early May much of Chamberlain's own party had lost confidence in him as the leader Britain needed in war. The opposition parties were adamant that they would not work with him in a war cabinet. On 10 May, after faring badly in a vote of confidence in the House of Commons, he resigned.

The two contenders to succeed him were Churchill and Lord Halifax, the Foreign Secretary and, since 1937, the leading figure in the Cabinet after the Prime Minister himself. Chamberlain favoured Halifax. So privately (since they had no constitutional opinion in the matter) did King George VI and Queen Elizabeth. Parliament, too, would apparently have backed a Halifax premiership. To move from the House of Lords to the Commons, which would probably have been necessary, was awkward, though it would not have posed an insuperable problem. But Halifax declined. There has been speculation about his reasons.[34] Most likely, the depth of animosity shown towards Chamberlain at the point of his resignation encouraged the recognition in Halifax that he, too, was not temperamentally equipped to be a war leader. Thus the path was clear for the more pugnacious, more dynamic, more determined and more strong-willed – though more unpredictable – Churchill. What the future would have held had Halifax accepted the premiership that was his for the taking is impossible to say. But without doubt his decision to stand back at this point was of enormous importance for the British prosecution of the war. By the evening of 10 May, Winston Churchill was Prime Minister. In his perhaps overdramatized reflections some years later, Churchill described his emotions: 'At last I had the authority to give directions over the whole scene.

I felt as if I were walking with destiny, and that all my past life had been but a preparation for this hour and for this trial.'[35]

The magnitude of the trial would rapidly become clear as, within a fortnight, the fate of France hung in the balance while almost the entire British Expeditionary Force was in the deepest peril, on the verge of captivity or destruction. With his premiership scarcely begun, Churchill was faced with the most serious threat to his country in the whole of her long history. The impending danger now forced upon the War Cabinet one of the most momentous decisions the British government had ever taken: whether to open up channels leading to a negotiated peace with Hitler, or whether to fight on. There was no shortage of opinion, some of it in influential quarters, which looked, reluctantly, to a negotiated settlement based upon honourable peace terms as the only sensible course of action for Britain in such a grave situation.[36] The outcome of the War Cabinet's deliberations was far from obvious in the days that the bulk of the British army was stranded on the Dunkirk beaches.

III

It is not easy to imagine, in the light of later events, how insecure Churchill's position was in the middle of May 1940. His hold on authority, soon to become unchallengeable, was still tenuous. No raptures on the Conservative benches greeted his first appearance in the House of Commons as Prime Minister on 13 May. The cheers that day, apart from those from the opposition side, were for Chamberlain, not Churchill.[37] The latter's speech that day, later seen as epitomizing Churchillian rhetoric, promising 'blood, toil, sweat and tears', met with a cool reception among Conservatives. The distrust remained. Some thought it would be a short-lived premiership.[38] Many Conservatives would have been happy to see Chamberlain back in office. Churchill himself recognized that, with only the conditional backing of his party, he could not afford to alienate his predecessor, still the Conservative Party leader.[39]

Churchill brought a number of leading Labour figures into government, though, with some reshuffling of offices, most of the old faces remained. The War Cabinet was a more radical departure. It was reduced in size to only five members. Three were Conservatives. Churchill himself also took on responsibility for the Ministry of Defence. Neville Chamberlain was given the title of Lord President of the Council, effectively overseeing domestic policy. And Lord Halifax was still retained as Foreign Secretary.

They were joined by two Labour representatives. Clement Attlee, leader of the party since 1935, in his late fifties, a small, dapper, undemonstrative man, unusual among socialists as a former officer in the war, was appointed Lord Privy Seal. His deputy, Arthur Greenwood, aged 60, an affable York-shireman with, like Churchill, something of a fondness for alcohol, whose brief experience in government just before the Depression had shown him to be a competent though undistinguished Minister of Health, became Minister without Portfolio. Churchill was soon to dominate the War Cabi-net, his position greatly strengthened through his control of defence. But there was no such dominance in May 1940, as the crisis worsened. Churchill could not override or impose his will on the other members of the War Cabinet. He recognized his dependence, in particular, on Chamberlain and Halifax. As Chamberlain had written privately of his successor the day after he took office: 'I know that he relies on Halifax and me and as he put it in a letter "My path depends largely on you." '[40]

The magnitude of the crisis facing Churchill's War Cabinet became more evident with every day that passed. The speed of the German advance was breathtaking. Every report indicated that a calamity of major proportions was unfolding. There was increasing concern for the fate of France. With that went the worry, often unspoken, that Britain might be unable to carry on the war if her ally were to fall. Though he later steadied, Chamberlain expressed precisely such an anxiety on the very day that the German offensive began.[41] A few days later, Sir Samuel Hoare, a member of Cham-berlain's War Cabinet but now on the point of departure to take office as British ambassador in Madrid, remarked that the former Prime Minister was 'completely knocked out. Everything finished. The USA no good. "We could never get our army out, or if we did, it would be without any equipment." '[42] The gloom did not stop with Chamberlain. Observers spoke of 'a mood of panic'[43] and 'defeatism' among London's upper classes,[44] while General Sir Edmund Ironside, Chief of the Imperial General Staff, feared the onslaught would mean 'the end of the British Empire'.[45] Air Chief Marshal Hugh Dowding, Commander-in-Chief of Fighter Command, expressed the view on 16 May that if an adequate fighter force were kept within the country, and the navy remained in existence, Britain could continue the struggle. But if fighter squadrons were sent across the Channel, as the French wanted, then defeat for France would also mean the final defeat of Britain.[46] Churchill, initially reluctant to accept the message relayed to him on 15 May by the French Prime Minister, Paul Reynaud, that 'we are beaten', was left in no doubt of the scale of the disaster and of the desperation felt in Paris after he had flown there next day to meet

French leaders.[47] The British Prime Minister gave a bravura performance, impressing upon his hosts the intention of Britain to fight on until the United States came to her aid and Germany was defeated.[48] At the same time, however, through a fog of cigar smoke and deep into the night, he conjured up 'an apocalyptic vision of the war', seeing himself 'in the heart of Canada, directing, over an England razed to the ground by high explosive bombs and over France whose ruins were already cold, the air war of the New World against the Old dominated by Germany'.[49] 'French evidently cracking, and situation awful', noted Sir Alex Cadogan, head of the Foreign Office, on hearing of Churchill's account of his visit. By 21 May Cadogan was confiding to his diary: 'A miracle may save us: otherwise we're done.'[50]

Those who did not share the insights into high politics and have access to the depressing reports of military leaders – the mass of the ordinary people – were in no position to grasp the full gravity of the situation.[51] There was general calm, at least on the surface. Many heads were simply buried in the sand. Chamberlain recounted his own impressions of the public mood in a letter to his sister Hilda on 17 May: 'The public don't in the least realise the gravity of the situation. Walking round the lake [in St James's Park] today it was heartbreaking to see the people enjoying the sunshine as they lolled in their chairs or watched the little ducklings darting about in the water. We shall try and bring them a little nearer to a sense of reality, though I daresay events will do more towards that end than anything we can think of.'[52] Chamberlain's surmise was accurate. Bland reportage on the BBC or in newspapers could not disguise the threat posed by the German advance, or the weakness of the Allied forces to halt it. There was mounting and most justifiable anxiety about events across the Channel. Stiff upper lips did not altogether conceal the worry just below the superficial calm.[53]

Churchill's faith in the ability of the French to hold out had been badly shaken by his visit to Paris on 16 May. A second visit, on 22 May, left him momentarily more optimistic at the prospects of a counter-offensive which he had urged upon the French.[54] But alternative plans had to be made for the possibility, perhaps likelihood, of failure. In such an event Churchill, as he explained to the King on the morning of 23 May, would have only one course of action: to order the British Expeditionary Force to return home. All its arms would have to be left behind. Immense loss of life was to be expected.[55] By nightfall on 23 May, a quarter of a million British troops were caught in the tightening German vice. Calais was unlikely to hold out for long, and meanwhile the forward spear of German tanks was heading closer to Dunkirk, the last accessible port in Allied hands.

When Hitler visited the headquarters of his western commander, Colonel-General Gerd von Rundstedt, on the morning of 24 May, the panzers of the German spearhead were no more than fifteen miles to the south of Dunkirk. After reviewing the military situation with Rundstedt, Hitler gave the order that the advance should be halted at that point and not proceed towards Dunkirk itself. The decision soon came to be regarded as a crucially missed chance to finish off the defeated forces of the British army. Attempting to justify an evident major military error, Hitler later suggested that he had not wanted to destroy the British army, the backbone of the Empire.[56] This was no more than a face-saving rationalization. In fact, he was merely following the military advice of his field commander, Rundstedt, who had wanted to preserve his motorized units for the final push to the south to conclude the campaign. Far from wanting to preserve the British army, Hitler was led to believe by Göring, Commander-in-Chief of the German air force, that the Luftwaffe would finish it off.[57]

Back in London, the War Cabinet was preoccupied with the fate of British troops in Calais, now under siege; and with the likely capitulation in the near future of the Belgians. Boulogne had by then already fallen, and the last remaining British troops there, about a thousand in all, had been taken off by sea. Churchill was adamant, however, that the troops encircled at Calais should continue to fight, to hold up the Germans as long as possible. Any gain in time would be valuable, either for the proposed counter-offensive (which, though Churchill did not know it at this point, was 'never more than a paper scheme',[58] already given up by French military leaders prepared, even at this stage, to consider capitulation[59]), or for evacuation of as much as possible of the British Expeditionary Force. As yet, on 24 May, no British troops had been sent to Dunkirk, where the port was still functioning, though there was a sizeable garrison there of French troops.[60]

The counter-offensive never started. It had simply not been a feasible proposition. Instead, there was a withdrawal of British troops, followed by misunderstandings and recriminations between Paris and London about blame for the fiasco. Once the offensive was finally abandoned on the evening of the 25th, and with Belgian capitulation imminent, the commander of the British Expeditionary Force, General Lord Gort, decided (on his own initiative, later approved in London) to withdraw to the coast, form a bridgehead around Dunkirk and seek to evacuate as many troops as possible. Dunkirk was a name little known to the British public at this stage. Very soon it would be upon everyone's lips.

For the War Cabinet, the increasingly probable fall of France, and with it the likelihood of the loss of the vast majority of British troops within the German encirclement, had to be reckoned with. General Ironside, admittedly given to pessimism, wrote gloomily on 23 May: 'I cannot see that we have much hope of getting any of the B[ritish] E[xpeditionary] F[orce] out.'[61] Two days later he still thought it would be possible to evacuate only 'a minute proportion' of the army. And all the equipment, in such short supply, would have to be abandoned.[62] The British commander, General Lord Gort, agreed that 'a great part of the B.E.F. and its equipment will inevitably be lost even in best circumstances'.[63] On 26 May, the day that the evacuation from Dunkirk, 'Operation Dynamo', was ordered, there was talk of rescuing no more than about 45,000 men.[64] The loss of almost the entire British Expeditionary Force would have been a fearful blow.[65] There was no army to speak of at home ready to replace them. There would have been little to fend off a German invasion which, British intelligence was indicating, could be imminent.[66] In such bleak circumstances, it was scarcely surprising that some thoughts were turning to the options facing Britain if the worst were to happen.

IV

Italy was seen by some, in London as well as in Paris, as the last hope. It was not worth placing too much on the bet, but the attempt had to be made, it was thought, at least to keep Italy – still neutral at this stage – out of the war. Beyond this, there was the related but separate notion that Mussolini might even at this point be persuaded to serve as a conduit to his friend Hitler to help to stave off a widening conflict and the ruination of Europe. Mussolini had, after all, intervened on the side of peace in 1938, even if the shameful Munich Conference had been the result. And Italy could not altogether rest easily at the prospect of a Europe completely dominated by a victorious Germany. Moreover, in any settlement he could broker, Mussolini was certain to gain significant territorial concessions for Italy around the Mediterranean. Enhanced power, new prestige and prosperity for his country in a peaceful Europe were the carrots dangled before him. There were few, if any, other inducements to offer the Italian dictator, certainly nothing to tempt him from the allure of militaristic grandeur, from the prospect of triumph in a war that he imagined was already largely won. Mussolini understood threats, particularly if backed by a big stick. But suggestions that he had 'put his money on the wrong horse', or that Italy was a 'light-weight' in a boxing match with the heavyweight western democracies, which would eventually win a long-drawn-out contest[67] – points aired before Hitler's western offensive had brought France to her knees and left Britain in deep peril – were unlikely to impress him. Mussolini's tone, in his dealings with both France and Britain, had remained belligerent. He had reminded both the French Prime Minister, Paul Reynaud, and Churchill of his determination to remain both politically and militarily the ally of Germany.[68]

At the height of the crisis, however, an approach to Mussolini remained a possible last resort. Édouard Daladier, the French Minister of Defence (and former Prime Minister), proposed trying to 'buy off' Mussolini. He suggested an approach to the Italian dictator through the American President, Franklin Delano Roosevelt, informing him that the Allies would be ready to consider his claims if Italy were to remain out of the war. Italy was also to be promised a seat at the peace conference as if she had been a belligerent. The British Foreign Office signalled its agreement on 25 May.[69] The suggestion that 'we should offer to discuss [the] Mediterranean with Italy' had been put the previous day to the former powerful head of the Foreign Office, Sir Robert Vansittart, who had given it his blessing. So had his successor, Sir Alexander Cadogan, 'if it will stave off war with Italy for a few days'.[70] The immediate aim of the French initiative, and of the British agreement to it, it is clear, was a limited one: to keep Mussolini out of the war in order to buy time. Mention of Italy's role in a prospective peace conference, however, indicates that the suggestion implicitly went further than this. No less than a negotiated end to the conflict was in mind. But this had to involve Germany. And in any peace conference, it was obvious, Hitler would have a great deal to say.

Neville Chamberlain had noted in his diary as early as 16 May 'that if the French collapsed our only chance of escaping destruction would be if Roosevelt made an appeal for an armistice', though he thought it unlikely that the Germans would respond.[71] Churchill also wanted the help of the Americans, but not for negotiating an armistice. In the first of what would turn into a voluminous correspondence with the American President, he struck a defiant tone: 'If necessary, we shall continue the war alone,' he wrote on 15 May, adding three days later: 'We are determined to persevere to the very end, whatever the result of the great battle raging in France may be.' However, he left Roosevelt under no illusions of Britain's perilous plight were France to fall. 'If this country was left by the United States to its fate,' he openly stated in his second letter, 'no one would have the right to blame those then responsible if they made the best terms they could for the surviving inhabitants.'[72] It was an attempt, through laying bare Britain's danger, to push Roosevelt to an open avowal of support, with the hope of practical action to follow. But the later much vaunted 'special relationship' was not so special at this point. Churchill himself was to remark only a few days later, with a tinge of bitterness, that 'the United States had given us practically no help in the war, and now that they saw how great was the danger, their attitude was that they wanted to keep everything which would help us for their own defence'.[73]

Roosevelt was cordial, but non-committal. He had public opinion at home, much of it isolationist, to consider. And he had to ponder whether American backing for Britain at this juncture would not be supporting a lost cause. For, at the height of the crisis, he held out little hope of British survival. On 24 May he had so little confidence in Britain's ability to hold out that he thought Canada and the Dominions ought to urge Churchill to send the British fleet across the Atlantic before Hitler could include its surrender in his peace terms.[74] But at least Roosevelt was prepared to offer what leverage he might have (it turned out, predictably, to be little) to intercede with Mussolini on behalf of the Allies.

On the day that Roosevelt was seeking to have Churchill send the British fleet out of harm's way, Lord Halifax was recommending to the Cabinet acceptance of the French proposal for the President's mediation to try to prevent Italy entering the war. He did not think much would come of it, but approved of the attempt to acquire, via Roosevelt, Italy's terms for staying out of the conflict. Halifax added that it might be useful to suggest at the same time that Roosevelt should convey to Mussolini the gist of the last part of a 'statement which the Prime Minister had proposed to make and had then cancelled'. This was 'that the Allies were ready to consider reasonable Italian claims at the end of the war, and would welcome Italy at a Peace Conference on equal terms with the belligerents'.[75] This was effectively the French proposal that had emanated from Daladier. Churchill evidently had second thoughts about making such a statement himself at this juncture. He and the other members of the War Cabinet, however, were ready to endorse Halifax's suggestion of seeking Roosevelt's intercession not merely to keep the Italians out of the war, but to open the door to Mussolini's participation in a peace conference, presumably to follow an early armistice on the British as well as French side.

About this time – the precise date is not clear – Halifax, who had voiced his view to the Cabinet some months earlier that Britain would not be able to continue alone if France were to make peace with Germany, drafted a telegram for Churchill to send to Roosevelt which, in the event, was not dispatched. It amounted to a plea to Roosevelt to intervene, should Hitler, following the fall of France, offer Britain unacceptable terms 'destructive of British independence', such as involving the surrender of the fleet or the air force. Roosevelt was to make plain, in such a dire eventuality, that this would 'encounter US resistance', and that the United States would give Britain full support.[76] Probably the inherently weak, pessimistic tone did not endear itself to Churchill, who was keen to avoid intimations of desperation. In any case, it was a faint hope, though the unsent telegram shows the way at least one important member of the British government was thinking.

Following the visit of Paul Reynaud to London on 26 May, an Anglo-French request to Roosevelt was finally made. It was thought preferable to approaching Mussolini directly, which might have suggested weakness.[77] That same day, Roosevelt informed Mussolini of his willingness to act as an intermediary. He was prepared, he said, to pass on to the Allies 'Italian aspirations in the Mediterranean zone', and guaranteed Italy's participation on an equal footing with the belligerent powers in any peace negotiations at the end of the war. The price was Mussolini's agreement not to enter the war. The request was unceremoniously turned down the following day.[78]

Meanwhile, however, the possibility of a more immediate and direct avenue to the Italians by the Allies themselves had opened up. It was around this possibility that, for three days, the issue of whether to seek terms or fight on centred.

On 20 May, in a conversation with Lord Phillimore, well known for his Fascist sympathies, the Italian ambassador in London, Count Giuseppe Bastianini, had appeared enthusiastic about the prospects of a British approach to Germany through the intermediacy of Italy. Phillimore duly passed on the message to the Foreign Office, that even now Hitler would listen to Mussolini. Soon after this, Sir Robert Vansittart was invited to meet the press attaché at the Italian embassy, Gabriele Paresci, who implied that an approach to Italy would not be rejected.[79] Halifax relayed this to the War Cabinet on 25 May, mentioning that, after consulting the Prime Minister, he 'had been authorised to pursue the matter further'. Vansittart had meanwhile been invited to a second meeting with Paresci. Halifax cautiously suggested the line to be taken: that 'we were now, as always, willing to enter into discussions with the Italian Government with a view to putting an end to the difficulties and misunderstandings which blocked the path of friendship between the two peoples'. Churchill had no objection, as long as the meeting was not made public.[80]

It was a Saturday, an unusual day for diplomatic meetings, but Halifax was anxious to lose no time in view of the critical military situation. The situation was becoming increasingly grave. The news filtering through was dire. Lingering hopes of a British counter-attack, in tandem with the French, to stave off the German advance were abandoned later that day. The desperate retreat to Dunkirk had begun. German forces were positioned no more than ten miles or so from the port. The prospects for the British army were bleak. 'Everything is complete confusion,' Cadogan, at the heart of the Foreign Office, recorded; 'no communications and no one knows what's going on, except that everything's as black as black. Boulogne taken, Calais heavily besieged. Dunkirk more or less open, and that's the only exit for our B.E.F., if they can ever be extricated. Meanwhile they have little food and practically no munitions ... Every day that passes lessens our chances.'[81]

Late that afternoon, Halifax met Bastianini. Though the usual diplomatic rules of a cautious fencing game were applied, the meeting soon went beyond the limited objective of keeping Italy out of the war. Bastianini widened the issue when he said that it had 'always been Signor Mussolini's view that the settlement of problems between Italy and any other country should be part of a general European settlement'. Halifax replied that in building a peaceful Europe, 'matters which caused anxiety to Italy' – code for her extensive territorial ambitions in the Mediterranean and north Africa – 'must certainly be discussed as part of a general European settlement'. Bastianini enquired whether the British government contemplated discussion of 'general questions' involving 'other countries' as well as Italy and Great Britain. Halifax avoided an answer by saying that such wide discussion was difficult to envisage while war was continuing. But Bastianini countered by saying that once such a discussion had begun, 'war would be pointless'. Mussolini was concerned, the ambassador continued, 'to build a European settlement, that would not merely be an armistice, but would protect European peace for a century'. Halifax stated that 'the purpose of His Majesty's Government was the same, and they would never be unwilling to consider any proposal made with authority that gave promise of the establishment of a secure and peaceful Europe'. The Foreign Secretary agreed when Bastianini suggested informing Mussolini 'that His Majesty's Government did not exclude the possibility of some discussion of the wider problems of Europe in the event of the opportunity arising'.[82]

Halifax was preparing to go to church next morning, Sunday, 26 May, when he received news that Churchill had called a meeting of the War Cabinet, the first of three that day, for 9.00 a.m., prior to the visit of the French Premier, Paul Reynaud. At the meeting, the Foreign Secretary reported on his discussion with the Italian ambassador. He prefaced his comments by stating: 'On the broader issue, we had to face the fact that it was not so much now a question of imposing a complete defeat upon Germany but of safeguarding the independence of our own Empire, and if possible that of France.' No one demurred at the suggestion, sounding most realistic in the desperate circumstances, that survival, not victory, was at stake. Implicit in what Halifax was saying was that at some point, perhaps earlier rather than later, with or – increasingly likely – without France, Britain would have to negotiate an end to the war. Bastianini 'had clearly made soundings as to the prospect of our agreeing to a conference', and had indicated that Mussolini's wish was to secure peace in Europe. Halifax had replied that peace and security were also Britain's objective, 'and we should naturally be prepared to consider any proposals which might lead to this, provided our liberty and independence were assured'. Churchill did not let this pass without comment. He retorted that peace and security might be achieved under German domination of Europe. But Britain's aim was to 'ensure our complete liberty and independence', and he opposed 'any negotiations which might lead to a derogation of our rights and power'.[83] This was not, however, to rule out negotiations at all.

Bastianini had requested a further meeting at which he might have further proposals. There was no disagreement, however, with Attlee's suggestion that any further deliberations had to await the arrival that day of the French Prime Minister, Paul Reynaud, and the report of the chiefs of staff on Britain's prospects of holding out if the French collapsed.

This report, 'British Strategy in a Certain Eventuality', dated 25 May (though not considered in detail by the War Cabinet until 27 May), looked dispassionately at Britain's situation following a projected French capitulation. Accepting the loss of most of the British Expeditionary Force and all its equipment, and Italian intervention in the war against Britain, but reckoning with American financial and economic support (and possibly eventual participation in the war), the report concluded that air superiority was the crux of Britain's hopes, without effective allies, of holding out against possible invasion over the next few months. The report offered grounds, therefore, for cautious optimism even in the face of such adversity.[84]

Reynaud lunched alone with Churchill on 26 May. In his report to the War Cabinet on their discussion, Churchill mentioned the neutralization of Gibraltar and the Suez Canal, the demilitarization of Malta and the limitation of naval forces in the Mediterranean as probable Italian demands. Churchill had told Reynaud, he said, 'that we were not prepared to give in on any account. We would rather go down fighting than be enslaved to Germany. But in any case we were confident that we had a good chance of surviving the German onslaught.' The War Cabinet moved on to the question of whether any approach to Italy should be made. Halifax was in favour. He thought the last thing Mussolini wanted was a German-dominated Europe, and would be anxious 'to persuade Herr Hitler to take a more reasonable attitude'. Churchill 'doubted whether anything would come of an approach to Italy', but left the matter for subsequent consideration by the War Cabinet.[85]

After the second meeting of the War Cabinet that day, at 2 o'clock, Halifax went back to continue the discussions with Reynaud. They were later joined by Churchill, Chamberlain and Attlee, in talks that lasted until Reynaud had to leave, about 4.30 p.m. Reynaud put to the British ministers his hope that 'some formula' might be found to 'satisfy Italian self-esteem in the event of an Allied victory, on condition that Italy did not enter the war'. He told them of the suggestion made a few days earlier by M. André François-Poncet, the French ambassador in Rome, that to have any hope of success the Allies would have to be prepared to deal with the status of Gibraltar, Malta and Suez from the British side and Djibouti and Tunisia from the French. Reynaud thought Halifax was struck by his arguments. The British Foreign Secretary, he later recalled, 'expressed his willingness to suggest to Mussolini that, if Italy would agree to collaborate with France and Britain in establishing a peace which would safeguard the independence of these two countries, and was based on a just and durable settlement of all European problems, the Allies would be prepared to discuss with him the claims of Italy in the Mediterranean and, in particular, those which concerned the outlets of this sea'. But Reynaud recognized that Churchill 'was in principle hostile to any concessions to Mussolini', as were Chamberlain ('with some reservations') and Attlee.[86]

The mood, as the discussions with Reynaud took place, among those fully aware of the dramatic events across the Channel, was distinctly gloomy. Neville Chamberlain's diary entry speaks of 26 May as 'the blackest day of all'. Belgian forces, under heavy attack all day, were close to collapse. Leopold, King of the Belgians, was preparing to capitulate. The French, too, Cadogan learned, were 'in a very bad way' and, according to Churchill's military representative in Paris, Major-General Sir Edward Spear, 'talking about capitulating'. The French Commander-in-Chief, General Maxime Weygand, had stated that 'he had only 50 divisions against 150 German. He would fight to the end if ordered to do so but it would be useless. Paris would fall in a few days.' Chamberlain was not exaggerating in writing of 'a terrible position for France and ourselves, the most terrible in our history'.[87]

Outside the inner circles of government, others were reading the runes. Fears of a German invasion were growing. One Member of Parliament told his wife that they should each try to obtain suicide tablets so that 'if the worst comes to the worst there are always those two little pills'.[88]

According to Chamberlain's diary account of the meeting with Reynaud, the French Prime Minister, through buying off Italian entry into the war by an appeal to Mussolini, accompanied by territorial concessions, hoped to release ten divisions to throw into the defence against the Germans. The British ministers pointed out that this was unlikely to make any real difference to the military position. Reynaud suggested, however, that Mussolini's own self-interest in safeguarding Italian independence in the event of a French and British collapse might predispose him towards a proposal for a European settlement. Chamberlain suspected that Mussolini might indeed look to a four-power conference, though only once Paris had fallen. Churchill made plain his opposition to any appeal to the Italian dictator. 'The P[rime]M[inister] disliked any move towards Musso,' noted Chamberlain. 'It was incredible that Hitler would consent to any terms that we could accept, though if we could get out of this jam by giving up Malta and Gibraltar and some African colonies he would jump at it. But the only safe way was to convince Hitler that he couldn't beat us. We might do better without the French than with them if they tied us up to a conference which we should enter with our case lost beforehand.' Halifax disagreed, arguing 'that there could be no harm in trying Musso and seeing what the result was. If the terms were impossible we could still reject them.' Chamberlain supported Halifax, but had the impression that Attlee, though he said little, favoured the Prime Minister's position. There was evident division within the War Cabinet. Views were still not hard and fast. Chamberlain, despite voicing support for Halifax's proposal, inclined towards Churchill's view that 'it would be best for us to fight on in the hope of maintaining sufficient air strength to keep the German at bay till other forces can be mobilised[,] perhaps in U.S.A.' And Churchill, whatever his own preference, was ruling nothing out at this stage. He told Reynaud, as the French Prime Minister prepared to depart, that 'we would try to find some formula on which Musso would be approached but we must have time to think'.[89]

After Reynaud's departure, what was described as a short 'informal Meeting of War Cabinet Ministers', without the presence of the Cabinet Secretary, took place. This was probably to brief the fifth member of the War Cabinet, Arthur Greenwood, who had not been present at the deliberation with Reynaud, on what had taken place.[90] Then the War Cabinet formally reconvened. It was, noted Halifax, 'a discursive meeting'. The Prime Minister was 'rather jumpy, secretaries kept coming in with messages, and the general atmosphere was like Waterloo Station: very difficult to do business'.[91] The discussion, if not always sharply focused, still centred around the question of whether or not to approach Mussolini. The differences, as they had been in Reynaud's presence, were most plainly articulated by Churchill and Halifax. Churchill emphasized that Britain still possessed powers to resist, which the French did not. He also pointed out that France was likely to be offered decent terms by Germany, whereas 'there was no limit to the terms which Germany would impose upon us if she had her way'. He was anxious to avoid being 'forced into a weak position in which we went to Signor Mussolini and invited him to go to Herr Hitler and ask him to treat us nicely'. Halifax attached, he said, 'more importance than the Prime Minister to the desirability of allowing France to try out the possibilities of European equilibrium' – a somewhat optimistic concept in the circumstances. The Foreign Secretary emphasized that there should be no suggestion of any terms which might jeopardize British independence. But he repeated the suggestion that a Mussolini alarmed at the prospect of German hegemony in Europe might be prepared to look to the balance of power. 'At any rate,' he said, 'he could see no harm in trying this line of approach.' Greenwood saw no objection to the course proposed by Halifax, though he imagined Mussolini had little scope for action independent of Hitler, and thought demands affecting British security would soon enough be raised. Chamberlain, too, was ready to discuss Italian demands with Mussolini, but only if the Italian leader were 'prepared to collaborate with us in getting tolerable terms', pointing out, however, Reynaud's view that a specific offer, not generalities, would be demanded. Churchill wanted no decision until it was seen how much of the army could be brought home from France.[92]

At this point Halifax read out the communiqué, agreed with the French, to the United States, seeking Roosevelt's intercession, and also his account of his interview the previous day with Bastianini. While the former was uncontentious, Churchill once more voiced his opposition to any direct British approach to Mussolini. What Halifax had suggested, he stated, 'implied that if we were prepared to give Germany back her colonies and to make certain concessions in the Mediterranean, it was possible for us to get out of our present difficulties'. This option was, in his view, not open, since 'the terms offered would certainly prevent us from completing our re-armament'. Halifax rejoined that, if so, the terms would be refused. Churchill repeated his earlier point that Hitler, apparently holding the whip-hand, had to be shown that he could not conquer Britain. At the same time, the minutes noted, 'he did not raise objection to some approach being made to Signor Mussolini'. Despite the opposition to such a move that he had voiced at every turn so far, Churchill was still not closing the door on the possibility of an overture to the Italian leader. At the very least, his comment implied that he did not at this juncture feel confident enough to override his colleagues, particularly Halifax, in pressing his own preference.

Greenwood then made a telling point. He reckoned, like others, that Mussolini would demand Malta, Gibraltar and Suez. (Chamberlain thought he might also want Somaliland, Kenya or Uganda.) Greenwood added his certainty that negotiations would break down; 'but Herr Hitler would get to know of them, and it might have a bad effect on our prestige'. Halifax argued that this was a good reason not to mention particulars in the approach, but 'that if we got to the point of discussing the terms of a general settlement and found that we could obtain terms which did not postulate the destruction of our independence, we should be foolish if we did not accept them'. Greenwood pointed out that by the time discussions were undertaken Paris was likely to have fallen, and asked whether, therefore, there was any real chance that negotiations would serve a purpose. At this, the meeting ended inconclusively with adjournment to the following day. Archibald Sinclair, Secretary of State for Air and leader of the Liberal Party, who despite political differences had been a friend of Churchill since serving as his second-in-command during the First World War and had supported his condemnation of the Munich Agreement, was invited to attend. Halifax was asked to circulate for discussion the draft of a possible communication to Italy along with a record of his discussion with Bastianini the previous evening.[93]

The draft 'Suggested Approach to Signor Mussolini', prepared by Halifax and circulated on 26 May to the War Cabinet, summarized the proposal advanced by Reynaud earlier that day. It emphasized the difficulty for Mussolini, should the Germans establish European domination; that Great Britain and France would fight to the end to preserve their independence; that if Mussolini would cooperate 'in securing a settlement of all European questions which safeguard[s] the independence and security of the Allies', they would seek to accommodate his interests; and that if he secretly specified his precise wishes in 'the solution of certain Mediterranean questions', they would try to satisfy them.[94] Though seemingly Reynaud's proposals, in practice they accorded closely both in the idea of Italian mediation and even in their wording with what Halifax had been saying, also to the Italian ambassador, *before* the visit of the French Prime Minister. In other words, the proposals, especially the third one opening up the prospect of a general European settlement, were at least in part Halifax's more than they were Reynaud's.[95]

The first of two War Cabinet meetings next day, 27 May, was predominantly concerned with the appalling military situation.[96] The German air force had started pounding the beaches in Dunkirk. Around the coast of southern England, hastily improvised flotillas of small ships, trawlers, tug boats, tiny motor launches – anything that was serviceable – were being assembled and setting sail to try to do their bit in rescuing the stranded army.[97] But the chances of a large-scale evacuation of troops from the port looked remote. Four British divisions, cut off near Lille, looked unlikely even to reach Dunkirk. Belgium, it was clear, was close to surrender. Later that day the news indeed came through that King Leopold had asked for a cessation of hostilities.[98] The mood in Whitehall was very grim. 'See very little light anywhere,' Cadogan jotted down after the Cabinet meeting. 'Position of B.E.F. quite awful, and I see no hope for more than a tiny fraction of them.'[99] Churchill's private secretary, John Colville, had gleaned something of the tense debates in Cabinet, perhaps from some indiscretion of the Prime Minister. Noting the serious fear now of French collapse, he added: 'The Cabinet are feverishly considering our ability to carry on the war alone in such circumstances, and there are signs that Halifax is being defeatist. He says that our aim can no longer be to crush Germany but rather to preserve our own integrity and independence.'[100]

The second meeting, late that afternoon, concentrated on the suggested approach to Mussolini. According to Halifax's diary entry, there was 'a long and rather confused discussion about, nominally, the approach to Italy, but also largely about general policy in the event of things going really badly in France'.[101]

Halifax began by mentioning that the French ambassador in London, M. Charles Corbin, had been to see him that morning, on instructions from Reynaud, to press for the inclusion of 'geographical precision' in the approach. Halifax had pointed out the opposition of his colleagues to anything beyond a general approach. The Foreign Secretary mentioned the view of the British ambassador in Rome, Sir Percy Loraine, that 'nothing we could do would be of any value at this stage, so far as Signor Mussolini was concerned'. Chamberlain agreed 'that the proposed French approach to Signor Mussolini would serve no useful purpose', but was willing to go ahead with it to prevent France subsequently claiming that Britain had been unwilling even to allow the chance of negotiations with Italy. Churchill's caustic summary of this argument was 'that nothing would come of the approach, but that it was worth doing to sweeten relations with a failing ally'.

Sinclair also took the view that an approach to Italy would prove futile. Any sign of weakness would be an encouragement to the Germans and Italians, and would undermine morale at home and in the Dominions. 'The suggestion that we were prepared to barter away pieces of British territory', Sinclair declared, 'would have a deplorable effect and would make it difficult for us to continue the desperate struggle which faced us.' He thought it was better to await the outcome of Roosevelt's attempted mediation.

Attlee and Greenwood also opposed any Anglo-French approach. Attlee declared that 'the approach suggested would inevitably lead to our asking Signor Mussolini to intercede to obtain peace-terms for us'. Following the French suggestion of geographical precision would simply prompt Mussolini to ask for more; and if Britain refused, it would appear she was letting down her allies. Greenwood thought the approach 'would put us in the wrong', and if word leaked 'that we had sued for terms at the cost of ceding British territory, the consequences would be terrible'. He concluded that 'it would be heading for disaster to go any further with those approaches'.

Churchill's line was similar. He was 'increasingly oppressed', he said, 'with the futility of the suggested approach to Signor Mussolini, which the latter would certainly regard with contempt'. The integrity of Britain's fighting position would be ruined by such an approach. Even avoiding geographical precision would not help; it would be obvious which territories were meant. The best help to Reynaud, argued Churchill, was 'to let him feel that, whatever happened to France, we were going to fight it out to the end'.

Churchill became more vehement in his forceful opposition to Halifax's proposal:

At the moment our prestige in Europe was very low. The only way we could get it back was by showing the world that Germany had not beaten us. If, after two or three months, we could show that we were still unbeaten, our prestige would return. Even if we were beaten, we should be no worse off than we should be if we were now to abandon the struggle. Let us therefore avoid being dragged down the slippery slope with France. The whole of this manoeuvre was intended to get us so deeply involved in negotiations that we should be unable to turn back. We had gone a long way already in our approach to Italy, but let us not allow M. Reynaud to get us involved in a confused situation.

He drew his conclusion: 'The approach proposed was not only futile, but involved us in a deadly danger.'

Chamberlain intervened in a conciliatory manner. Though he agreed that the proposed approach would not serve any useful purpose, he thought 'that we ought to go a little further with it, in order to keep the French in a good temper'. He favoured temporizing until the outcome of Roosevelt's approach was known. This met with some agreement. But Churchill looked no further than fighting it out as an example. 'If the worst came to the worst,' he stated, 'it would not be a bad thing for this country to go down fighting for the other countries which had been overcome by the Nazi tyranny.'

Halifax had been quiet to this point. But he recognized the increasing signs of his isolation in the War Cabinet, and Churchill's strident tones now prompted his intervention. 'He was conscious', the Foreign Secretary said, 'of certain rather profound differences of points of view'. Halifax thought it would have been of value to have the French government declare that they would fight to the end for their independence. Moreover, he could see no resemblance between what he was proposing and the suggestion 'that we were suing for terms and following a line which would lead us to disaster'. He hinted, correctly, that Churchill had changed his mind since the previous day, when he had indicated that he would be thankful to get out of the current difficulties on terms, as long as they did not affect the independence of the country, even if it meant cession of some territory. Now, said Halifax, 'the Prime Minister seemed to suggest that under no conditions would we contemplate any course except fighting to a finish'. He agreed that acceptable terms were unlikely. But if it were to prove possible to attain a settlement which would not impair Britain's fundamental interests, he could not accept Churchill's view, and 'would think it right to accept an offer which would save the country from avoidable disaster'.

Churchill was dismissive. The issue was most unlikely to arise. 'If Herr Hitler was prepared to make peace on the terms of the restoration of German colonies and the overlordship of Central Europe, that was one thing,' Churchill declared, in a mooted concession striking in itself. 'But it was quite unlikely', he went on, 'that he would make any such offer.' Halifax, undeterred, offered a hypothetical scenario. Would the Prime Minister be prepared to discuss terms which Hitler, 'being anxious to end the war through knowledge of his own internal weaknesses', might offer to France and England? The old, misplaced optimism in Hitler's presumed internal problems – thought to be serious and imminent economic crisis[102] – reared its head once more in the question. Churchill replied that he would not join France in asking for terms; but he would consider them if he were told what they were. Chamberlain once more defused the heated exchange between Foreign Secretary and Prime Minister. The dispute closed with agreement that Churchill's reply to Reynaud should be along the lines that Chamberlain had earlier suggested – not complete refusal, but no commitment either, in awaiting the outcome of Roosevelt's approach.[103]

The discussion had been more heated than the official minutes suggested. Halifax noted in his diary that he 'thought Winston talked the most frightful rot, also Greenwood, and after bearing it for some time', he went on, 'I said exactly what I thought of them, adding that if that was really their view, and if it came to the point, our ways would separate'. From the invariably calm, unruffled Halifax, these words, implying that he threatened resignation, were strong indeed. He repeated his threat privately to Churchill after the meeting, but by then the Prime Minister had 'mellowed', as Halifax put it, and 'was full of apologies and affection'. It had been a clash of personalities, as well as a disagreement about substance. Churchill's emotional temperament was the antithesis of Halifax's instinctive cool rationality. According to Halifax, 'it does drive me to despair when he works himself up into a passion of emotion when he ought to make his brain think and reason'.[104] Halifax agreed with Churchill, and the other members of the War Cabinet, that an approach to Mussolini was almost certain to prove fruitless. But he was still not prepared to dismiss the attempt. And what he had been unable to stomach was Churchill's apparent insistence that it would be better to go down fighting, even if Britain were to be devastated in the process, than to contemplate any possible negotiated settlement which might save the country from disaster.[105]

At ten o'clock that evening the War Cabinet was summoned for its third meeting that day. Churchill presented it with the dismal news that Belgium was on the verge of capitulation. The consequences, not just for the chances of prolonged French military resistance, but also for the prospects of evacuating the British Expeditionary Force, were grave in the extreme. 'Of course we did not expect that the Belgians would hold out indefinitely,' Chamberlain noted in his diary, 'but this sudden collapse opens our flank and makes it unlikely that any substantial number of the B.E.F. will get away. I confess I had not much hope of extricating them but there was a chance which has now almost vanished.'[106]

Meanwhile, too, it had become clear that Roosevelt's attempt to intercede with Mussolini had been peremptorily rebuffed. In fact, Mussolini had declined even to receive the American ambassador in Rome, who sought to present the President's message verbally. Nor was any reply forthcoming.

The contempt with which the approach was received could not have been more clearly expressed. Roosevelt's message was conveyed to Mussolini by the Italian Foreign Minister, Count Galeazzo Ciano, who told the ambassador straight away that it would be rejected.[107] 'Roosevelt is off the track,' Ciano said. 'It takes more than that to dissuade Mussolini. In fact, it is not that he wants to obtain this or that; what he wants is war, and, even if he were to obtain by peaceful means double what he claims, he would refuse.'[108]

By the time the War Cabinet resumed its deliberations on a possible approach to Mussolini on the afternoon of the following day, 28 May, therefore, the British ministers knew of the rejection of Roosevelt's intercession and were confronted with the sombre news of the Belgian capitulation, which had taken place in the early hours. This had left British troops retreating to Dunkirk dangerously exposed, as Chamberlain had recognized. It was now a desperate struggle to hold off the Germans so as to allow the retreat to continue. 'Prospects of the B.E.F. look blacker than ever,' Cadogan noted. 'Awful days!'[109] All day, as Churchill later recalled, 'the escape of the British Army hung in the balance'. For many of the French troops also trying to reach Dunkirk it was too late. Cut off and encircled west of Lille, they were forced to surrender.[110]

The members of the War Cabinet now had to consider a request from Paris for a new Anglo-French approach to Mussolini. At Daladier's suggestion, the French Council of Ministers, reacting in a somewhat panicky late-night session to the news of Belgium's surrender, had agreed to make concrete, and unilateral, proposals to Rome in a desperate attempt to keep Italy out of the war. The French government then thought better of a unilateral proposal and postponed an approach until London had been consulted.[111] This was the proposal now facing the British War Cabinet, prompting what Chamberlain described as a 'rather sharp discussion'.[112]

The alternatives sharply voiced by Churchill and Halifax the previous day remained in the foreground.[113] Halifax had learned, he reported, that he had made no progress in his meeting with Bastianini three days earlier, 'and that the position was hopeless'. However, Sir Robert Vansittart, whose initiative had led to that meeting, had subsequently discovered that the Italian embassy had had in mind 'a clear indication that we should like to see mediation by Italy'. Churchill immediately retorted that 'the French were trying to get us on to the slippery slope' of having Mussolini act as an intermediary between Britain and Hitler, and 'he was determined not to get into this position'. The situation would be entirely different, he added, once Germany had made an unsuccessful attempt to invade Britain.

Chamberlain was veering closer to Churchill's position, though, unlike the Prime Minister, he viewed the continuation of the war not as the path to ultimate victory, but as the basis to attain a better compromise peace.[114] Privately regarding the French proposal as 'derisory in itself and inopportune',[115] he pointed out to his Cabinet colleagues that any concessions made to Italy, such as Malta and Gibraltar, could only form part of a general settlement with Germany. Concessions to Italy which left Germany in the war would have no value to Britain. Greenwood and Sinclair concurred in Chamberlain's scepticism about acceptable terms coming from any mediation by Mussolini. Halifax did not disagree, and indeed remarked in his diary on the futility of any further approach to the Italian dictator.[116] But, even if the 'hypothesis was a most unlikely one', he repeated to the War Cabinet his suggestion of the previous day, that if Mussolini 'wished to play the part of mediator, and that he could produce terms which would not affect our independence, he thought that we ought to be prepared to consider such terms'. He went on to suggest that Britain 'might get better terms before France went out of the war and our aircraft factories were bombed, than we might get in three months' time'.

At this juncture, Churchill read out a draft reply to Reynaud, expressing his own views.[117] It was clear to him that Reynaud wanted to use Mussolini's mediation 'to get us to the Conference-table with Herr Hitler'. But if Britain once began negotiations, 'we should then find that the terms offered us touched our independence and integrity. When, at this point, we got up to leave the Conference-table, we should find that all the forces of resolution which were now at our disposal would have vanished.' Chamberlain, increasingly in harmony with the Prime Minister, spoke in agreement with Churchill's draft, though he suggested some wording amendments to make it more acceptable to the French. The main thrust of his suggestion was, nevertheless, along the lines that Churchill had proposed: that Britain felt she could hold out, and, if so, would obtain better terms than if she became involved in negotiations with Mussolini from a position of weakness.

With the tide in the War Cabinet now flowing strongly in his favour, Churchill returned forcefully to the essence of his argument. 'Signor Mussolini,' he said, 'if he came in as mediator, would take his whack out of us. It was impossible to imagine that Herr Hitler would be so foolish as to let us continue our re-armament. In effect, his terms would put us completely at his mercy. We should get no worse terms if we went on fighting, even if we were beaten, than were open to us now.'

It was a powerful point. Halifax intervened, somewhat weakly, to say 'that he still did not see what there was in the French suggestion of trying out the possibilities of mediation which the Prime Minister felt was so wrong'. Chamberlain, for his part, did not see what there was to lose by openly stating that Britain would fight to the end to preserve her independence, but 'would be ready to consider decent terms if such were offered to us'. He pointed out, however, 'that the alternative to fighting on nevertheless involved a considerable gamble'. Churchill declared, with more feeling than reason, 'that the nations which went down fighting rose again, but those which surrendered tamely were finished', and said 'that the chances of decent terms being offered to us at the present time were a thousand to one against'. Chamberlain, again cautiously and somewhat ambivalently, agreed with Halifax's basic assertion on obtaining terms, but added that an offer of decent terms was so unlikely that Britain should not follow Reynaud's suggestion of an approach to Mussolini. He was keen, however, not to reject the French proposal outright, since he did not want France to give up the struggle, and thought there was a possibility of circumstances changing, even within a short time, that might alter the British stance. After more than two hours of discussion, the meeting adjourned at 6.15 p.m. for three-quarters of an hour.

It was an important interval. Churchill took the opportunity to address the ministers who were not members of the War Cabinet. He referred to the meeting in his memoirs. He had seen little of his colleagues outside the War Cabinet since the formation of his government, and now thought it proper to give them an account of the course of events and state of the conflict. Whether, beyond this, he had arranged the meeting to outflank the opposition in the War Cabinet and gain wider support for the uncompromising position he had adopted on the question of an approach to Mussolini is not clear. But that is, in the event, what he attained. After the difficult discussions in the War Cabinet he was now able to advance, unfettered and in full rhetorical flourish, his own convictions, and in front of an audience already at least in part predisposed to accept them.[118]

Twenty-five or so ministers of varying political persuasion, by no means all fervent or long-standing supporters of the Prime Minister, crowded around the table in Churchill's room in the House of Commons. Even if they lacked detailed information, all were aware of the depth of the crisis unfolding across the Channel. They sensed what was at stake. The tension was palpable. Churchill lost no opportunity of exploiting the heightened atmosphere. One of those present, the Minister for Economic Warfare and senior Labour figure, Hugh Dalton, thought Churchill 'magnificent' at the meeting: 'the man, and the only man we have, for this hour.' It was a splendid, morale-boosting speech, even though Churchill still reckoned with bringing back only around 50,000 soldiers from Dunkirk and thought the rescue of 100,000 would be 'a magnificent performance'. Dalton recalled a key point made by Churchill, one he would make in the War Cabinet: 'It was idle to think that, if we tried to make peace now, we should get better terms from Germany than if we went on and fought it out. The Germans would demand our fleet – that would be called "disarmament" – our naval bases, and much else. We should become a slave state, though a British government which would be Hitler's puppet would be set up – "under Mosley or some such person".'[119]

Towards the end of his address, Churchill declared: 'Of course, whatever happens at Dunkirk, we shall fight on.' He knew how bleak the news still was from Dunkirk. By the end of that day, 28 May, a mere 17,000 troops had been rescued. (Only in the following days did the numbers swell to over 50,000 a day.) But his resilience appealed to his attentive audience. He was taken by surprise by the reaction of the experienced parliamentarians from different points on the political spectrum.

Quite a number seemed to jump up from the table and come running to my chair, shouting and patting me on the back. There is no doubt that had I at this juncture faltered at all in the leading of the nation I should have been hurled out of office. I was sure that every Minister was ready to be killed quite soon, and have all his family and possessions destroyed, rather than give in. In this they represented the House of Commons and almost all the people.[120]

Within the hour, he was reporting back to the War Cabinet on the reaction. His colleagues, he said, had 'expressed the greatest satisfaction when he had told them that there was no chance of our giving up the struggle'. He did not recall, he said, 'having ever before heard a gathering of persons occupying high places in political life express themselves so emphatically'. While Halifax and Chamberlain had been preparing the new draft reply to Reynaud, Churchill had been garnering support for his stance. He had now won the day. There was no further opposition from Halifax. Churchill expressed himself content with the draft reply to Reynaud which Chamberlain read out. But when Halifax raised the question of an appeal to President Roosevelt, which Reynaud had also wanted the Allies to make, Churchill was firm. He thought an appeal to the United States at the present time would be 'altogether premature'. Once more, his political reasoning followed psychological instinct. 'A bold stand against Germany' would command the admiration and respect of the United States; 'but a grovelling appeal, if made now, would have the worst possible effect.'[121]

Later that evening the reply went off to Reynaud. The wording had been redrafted by Chamberlain and Halifax, and agreed by all the War Cabinet.[122] Its sentiments were, however, those of Churchill himself. As Chamberlain had advocated, the reply did not rule out the possibility of an approach to Mussolini 'at some time', though it explicitly did so in the current situation.[123] It saw improvement coming only through continuing the struggle, which would 'at once strengthen our hands in negotiations and draw admiration and perhaps the material help of the U.S.A.' If Britain and France continued to hold out, it concluded, 'we may yet save ourselves from the fate of Denmark and Poland'.[124]

In fact, despite the British rejection of an approach to Mussolini, the French government decided to make their own, unilateral offer. It was treated with outright contempt in Rome.[125] Mussolini was set on war, not peaceful negotiation. France was on the verge of defeat, at the hands of Germany. Mussolini wanted the easiest and cheapest route to his share of the glory and the spoils. He duly declared war on France on 10 June (a decision that will be explored fully in Chapter 4 below). The French ambassador in Rome, M. François-Poncet, aptly described it, when being given the news by the Italian Foreign Minister, Count Ciano, as 'a dagger-blow at a man who has already fallen'.[126] A week later, France capitulated.

The British government had reckoned since the middle of May with the prospect of having to continue the fight in the face of French defeat, in the hope of holding out until the United States might decide to help (of which there was no guarantee at all). But what it had not expected was 'the miracle of Dunkirk'. The loss of almost all the British Expeditionary Force had been taken into every calculation in late May. It was under this presumption that the crucial political decision, whose making we have followed, was taken. Only once that decision had been arrived at did it gradually become clear, over the following days, that the armada of small boats – hundreds of them – which had shuttled backwards and forwards across the English Channel had succeeded beyond anyone's hopes in what had seemed an impossible mission. Despite their exposure for days to relentless bombing, practically the whole of the British army (and many Allied soldiers) that had served in northern France had been rescued from the beaches and harbour of Dunkirk – by 4 June 224,301 British and 111,172 French and Belgian troops.[127] That day Churchill was able to tell the House of Commons of the 'miracle of deliverance' at Dunkirk in a stirring speech, reaching its rhetorical climax in his famous, ringing declaration: 'We shall fight on the beaches, we shall fight on the landing grounds, we shall fight in the fields and in the streets, we shall fight in the hills; we shall never surrender . . .'[128] The warmth and enthusiasm with which his patriotic address was received, in the wake of a colossal military calamity that the 'deliverance of Dunkirk' had managed to turn into even a sort of triumph, was an important moment in the elevation of Churchill's public standing, and the regard for his qualities as an indomitable wartime leader.

The Churchill who emerged from the Dunkirk crisis now stood head and shoulders above his colleagues in the War Cabinet. On 6 June he could tell them with unchallengeable authority that 'in no circumstances whatsoever would the British Government participate in any negotiations for armistice or peace'.[129] This had not been the case during the political crisis to determine Britain's war strategy during the very days when the fortunes of the army stranded at Dunkirk seemed at their darkest.

V

In one sense, the outcome of the vital, intense and occasionally heated deliberations of those few days from 25 to 28 May was to alter nothing. Britain was already at war with Hitler's Germany, and now simply continued to stay in the fight. It was a choice, nonetheless: indeed, a most crucial choice to reject an alternative, that of a pathway to negotiations with Hitler which would have taken Britain out of the war with untold but profound consequences.

To be sure, not even Lord Halifax, the main spokesman for exploring the possibilities of Italian mediation towards a peace settlement, contemplated Britain's capitulation, or a settlement on terms which would have been harmful to the country's independence. Halifax was as adamant as Churchill, whatever their differences, that Britain's freedom must be preserved. This objective was shared by all members of the War Cabinet. How to attain that end was what divided the Prime Minister and his Foreign Secretary.

Nor was it a matter of patriotic defiance and Churchillian 'bulldog spirit' prevailing over weakness and defeatism. Halifax was no less a patriot. And he was prepared to fight on, if that was the only way. But his reasoned position was that fighting on, with the unquestionably high sacrifices that would entail, did not necessarily amount to the only course of action available to Britain. He was, therefore, impatient with Churchill's talk of going down fighting when alternatives had not been explored. For all that Churchill spoke with passion and emotion, however, and in ways that irritated the more coldly rational Halifax, his case was nevertheless underpinned by reason and logic. The other members of the War Cabinet, most notably Chamberlain, were ultimately brought behind the Prime Minister's position, rather than that of Halifax, because Churchill had the better arguments.[130]

Halifax wanted to test the waters, to see whether Italian mediation might pave the way for a general settlement. He thought it unlikely; but he did not wish to see the possibility left untried. Any attempt would in reality have been significantly to overestimate Mussolini's influence on Hitler. This had waned greatly since his intervention had paved the way for the Munich Agreement in 1938. Churchill himself would apparently not have been opposed, as he indicated during the sessions of the War Cabinet, to an attempt to buy off Italy at the cost of some British possessions in the Mediterranean, or even, so he said at one point, to settle for German supremacy in central and eastern Europe if it would get Britain 'out of the mess'.[131] But especially once Roosevelt's overture on behalf of the Allies had been so contemptuously rebuffed, he thought any approach to Mussolini was futile. Worse than that, it would leave Britain on 'a slippery slope'. Chamberlain, as the crisis wore on the key figure in the divide between the Prime Minister and Foreign Secretary,[132] accepted this, as did Attlee and Greenwood. Once an opening to negotiations – meaning not just with Mussolini, but also with Hitler – had been made, it had consequences, for Britain's international standing, and for morale at home. Hitler's position, given the mighty inroads his army had made in France, was extremely strong. He would make demands, almost certainly stretching beyond the return of former German colonies, which would leave Britain seriously weakened and her independence as a power threatened.

Halifax's view was that, in such an eventuality, Britain could withdraw from negotiations. Churchill, backed increasingly by the other members of the War Cabinet, pointed to the irreparable damage that would already have been done, even by the readiness to contemplate the inevitable concessions which entry into negotiations meant. It would be as good as impossible to resuscitate fighting morale among the population when it had been realized that the government had been prepared to entertain terms. And the concessions, as Churchill pointed out, would not merely be confined to a few pieces of territory, though satisfying Mussolini's demands alone would have severely weakened Britain's position in the Mediterranean and Middle East. A puppet government would be set up within the country. Britain's effective disarmament would unquestionably also be a condition. The navy would probably have to be given up, or placed under German tutelage.[133] There would be no possibility of rebuilding defences in the air or on land. Britain would consequently, even retaining nominal independence, be at Germany's mercy; subordinated without putting up a fight. Even if the navy were to be spirited away to Canada, and the royal family and government into exile, the likelihood of the United States rushing to Britain's aid would have been much diminished, and the focus of the Empire's resistance to Hitler removed. Churchill could persuasively argue, therefore, that no terms which Hitler was likely to offer Britain would be acceptable. They would not be worse if Britain had fought and lost than if she had not fought at all. Hence, he could reach the conclusion that to fight courageously and be defeated had few, if any, disadvantages, and the distinct advantage that it would provide moral encouragement to Britain's friends in the world, in the Empire and Dominions, and in the United States, to continue the fight.

Ultimately, these arguments were seen by the other members of the War Cabinet, apart from Halifax, to be convincing. And even Halifax concurred in the wording of the telegram sent on the evening of 28 May to Reynaud, which stated the position Churchill had set out, though the final wording was shaped largely by Chamberlain, with assistance from the Foreign Secretary himself.

Three days, from Halifax's meeting in the late afternoon of the 25th to the agreement reached on the telegram to Reynaud on the evening of the 28th, were needed to arrive at the decision. It was a *collective* agreement, with Halifax finally bowing to the wishes of the other members of the War Cabinet and in so doing indicating his own binding commitment to the decision (a point of no small importance in demonstrating the government's unity to Parliament and to the country). It had been reached by reasoned discussion among five ministers (occasionally with a sixth, Sinclair, joining the deliberations). Of these, Churchill held primacy, though not outright dominance. He won his case by reason, not power and browbeating. The military case for reasoned hope, advanced by the chiefs of staff, had also contributed to the growing mood of resilience. Churchill had instinctive backing from Attlee and Greenwood. But the member of the War Cabinet whose support was most valuable was Chamberlain, who, as always, dissected all points of the argument with precision, before his initial ambivalence gave way to firm backing for the Prime Minister's stance. By this time, Halifax had little option (beyond a resignation which would have been as damaging as it was futile, and was never more than a fleeting thought) but to yield to the position adopted by all his colleagues.

Striking about the way the decision was reached was how few individuals were involved in it, and how limited, in a parliamentary democracy, was the number of those who had any inkling of what was at stake. Only the small circle of the War Cabinet knew. Beyond those few ministers, as good as nothing filtered out. The members of the wider Cabinet remained largely in the dark. Only the highest level of officialdom within the Cabinet and Foreign Office was aware of what was happening. The general public had, of course, no notion of the momentous decision facing the War Cabinet, and, in fact, only gradually grasped the enormity of what was taking place so close to home, on the other side of the English Channel, a situation scarcely imaginable in today's society of global television and near-instant coverage of wars taking place thousands of miles away.

History, too, cast a veil over what had taken place. Neither Churchill nor Halifax enlightened the readers of their postwar memoirs about the short-lived proposal to use Italian mediation to come to terms with Hitler. Churchill had, in fact, included in a draft of his war memoirs a reference to Halifax's willingness to placate a 'dangerous enemy', mentioning his meeting with Bastianini, but bowed to encouragement that he should use discretion, and omitted it from the published version.[134] Only when the public records were released, thirty years after the events, did it become fully apparent how vital the deliberations of those May days of 1940 had been to Britain's future.[135]

What would have happened had Halifax's alternative strategy been adopted naturally remains in the realm of speculation and conjecture. We have already seen something of what Churchill and the other members of the War Cabinet thought it would imply, however, and we know enough of German plans (to be explored in the next chapter) to have an idea what might have awaited Britain had she sued for peace.[136]

A first German prerequisite of any negotiations would surely have been a change of government in London. Churchill, long seen as the arch-exponent of an anti-German, warmongering faction (which Nazi warped thinking associated with Jewish influence), and his supporters would have been forced out of office. Germany would have insisted upon a government more attuned to the interests of the Reich, and more prepared to make significant concessions in the interests of European peace than ever could have been expected under Churchill's leadership. Churchill himself imagined, as we have seen, that the Germans would have insisted upon a puppet government led by Oswald Mosley, the British Fascist leader.[137] More probable would have been an attempt to install as the head of a new administration, dependent on the favour of Berlin, David Lloyd George, Britain's Prime Minister during the First World War, admired by Hitler and a great admirer, in turn, of the German dictator when he had met him at Berchtesgaden in 1936.

Churchill had, in fact, wanted Lloyd George in his Cabinet and had asked him on 13 May to become Minister of Agriculture. Lloyd George declined, prompted by his unwillingness to serve with Chamberlain. He was by this time in his late seventies. He thought that Britain could not win the war, and would have to seek a negotiated settlement at some point.[138] But he still had great stature, and remained influential, abroad as well as in Britain. With the situation looking so bleak towards the end of May, Churchill spoke to Chamberlain about including Lloyd George in the government. Chamberlain replied frankly. He did not trust Lloyd George, and could not work with him. Churchill, he said, would have to choose between them. The Prime Minister immediately backed down, adamant that he wanted Chamberlain to stay. They were serving together and 'would go down together', Churchill remarked, somewhat elliptically. He himself did not know Lloyd George's mind, he stated, or whether he would prove defeatist.[139] This did not prevent him approaching Lloyd George on a number of further occasions, though all attempts to bring him into the Cabinet foundered on the mutually bitter enmity between him and Chamberlain.

Lloyd George was no outright defeatist. In the summer of 1940 he took the view that peace terms should not be undertaken immediately, but only once Britain had fended off the German onslaught and could therefore bargain from a better position. But Churchill and Chamberlain were right not to trust him. In autumn 1940 Lloyd George envisaged himself as a peace-making Prime Minister, once Britain's survival was assured but it had been acknowledged that total victory against Germany was impossible. He would 'wait until Winston is bust', he told his secretary in October 1940.[140] Before then, in June and July, as stories of peace-feelers became practically a daily occurrence, rumours had reached Berlin that Lloyd George would soon replace Churchill as Prime Minister.[141] He would most probably have been acceptable to Hitler as the British equivalent of Marshal Philippe Pétain at the head of a Vichy-style government, conceivably under a restored King Edward VIII.[142]

Once embarked upon the 'slippery slope' of negotiations, as Churchill had put it, such a government would have been compelled from its position of weakness to concede territory and armaments to Germany. Though Hitler later on numerous occasions stated that he had wanted to preserve the British Empire, it is unthinkable that this meant preserving it in a position of any independent power. As we shall see in the next chapter, there would certainly have been heavy pressure coming from some parts of his regime, especially from the German navy, to make serious territorial gains at the expense of Britain, as well as ending once and for all any military threat from the Royal Navy.

Of course, an exiled British government would probably have continued the struggle from some part of the Dominions. It might also have been possible to get the fleet out and to the security of friendly harbours abroad. But it is hard to see how Britain could have emerged from any peace dealings to which it had committed itself in the late spring or summer of 1940 in anything other than a perilously enfeebled position.

With Britain supportive of Germany, or at least benevolently neutral towards the Reich, Roosevelt's leanings towards providing material and military backing would have been stopped in their tracks. As it was, the case for supporting Britain was not easy to articulate for a public opinion still extremely cautious about overseas interventionism even when it was not outrightly isolationist. And with western Europe secured and any threat from the United States a distant one, Hitler would have been able to turn his full attention to fighting the war for 'living space' against the Soviet Union, but now with British backing.

The decision taken in late May 1940 not to seek peace terms had, then, the most profound implications, and not just for Britain. A negotiated settlement to Germany's advantage with a severely weakened Britain, followed or accompanied by the crushing military defeat of France, would have left Hitler victorious in the whole of western Europe. The British decision to fight on meant that Hitler was unable to end the war in the west. This at once greatly magnified the enormous gamble he had taken. He would now have to contemplate attacking the Soviet Union, the ideological arch-enemy, in the war that he had always intended to fight for 'living space' and to destroy 'Jewish Bolshevism', with the war in the west unfinished. And behind Britain stood the might of the United States, with the likelihood that American aid for the British war effort would be increasingly forthcoming. As Hitler saw it, time was not on Germany's side. Germany had to remove Britain from the war before the Americans were ready and willing to enter it. If this were to take place before Germany had the complete mastery of Europe and all the Continent's material resources at its disposal, the chances of final victory would be seriously diminished and, in the long run, perhaps altogether undermined. The British decision to stay in the war, therefore, imposed a new sense of urgency on Hitler. If the British government would not come to terms, he saw only two options: impose military defeat on Britain; or force her to acknowledge German supremacy on the Continent through defeating the Soviet Union in a rapid campaign, with the ultimate effect of keeping the Americans out of the war.

Hitler was unaware of the crucial deliberations of the British War Cabinet in the last week of May. Only after the British government's swift rejection of his final, and lukewarm, 'peace-offer' in his Reichstag speech of 19 July, following his triumph over the French, was it plain that Britain was categorically set on rejecting all possibility of a negotiated end to the war. By then, with the British army safely brought back from Dunkirk, tentative steps were being taken in London and Washington to engineer the vital American aid. Hitler had to face his own critical decision. It was not long in coming.

2

Berlin, Summer and Autumn 1940

Hitler Decides to Attack the Soviet Union

The Führer is greatly puzzled by Britain's persisting unwillingness to make peace. He sees the answer (as we do) in Britain's hope on Russia, and therefore counts on having to compel her by main force to agree to peace.

Franz Halder, chief of the army General Staff,
diary entry for 13 July 1940

'With Russia smashed, Britain's last hope would be shattered. Germany then will be master of Europe and the Balkans. Decision: Russia's destruction must therefore be made a part of this struggle. Spring 1941 . . . If we start in May 1941, we would have five months to finish the job.'[1] With these astonishing sentences, Adolf Hitler announced to his generals, meeting on 31 July 1940 at his Alpine retreat, the Berghof, in the mountains high above Berchtesgaden, his most fateful choice of the Second World War. It ushered in the bloodiest conflict in history, a titanic struggle in eastern Europe that would cost the lives of over thirty million Soviet and German citizens and leave vast areas of unprecedented destruction, ending nearly four years later with the German dictator's suicide in the Berlin bunker and the Soviet Union dominant over half of the European continent for the following four and a half decades.

The magnitude of what Hitler was proposing appears, in the light of what happened, sheer madness. Napoleon had once tried it, and the campaign in 1812 had brought an ignominious end to the *grande armée* and to the Emperor's own imperial dreams. In Hitler's case, the gamble had even more catastrophic consequences. The decision looks like a death-wish for himself and his nation. Why, then, did he take it? Was it purely the delusory sense of infallibility in military judgement that the extraordinary triumph in the defeat of France had created, or perhaps just magnified? Was it the logical culmination of a wholly illogical ideology, an irrational lunacy aimed at the destruction of 'Jewish-Bolshevism'? If the decision was madness, why did the leaders of the armed forces go along with it? Was this simply an instance of the dictator imposing his own warped views on an unwilling following? Were other options available, only to be peremptorily rejected? Or, as his opening words suggested, did strategic imperatives lie behind the strange decision, imperatives that left Hitler less free in his choice than might at first appear to have been the case?

Hitler's road to war has been exhaustively explored. But before we try to find some answers to the questions just posed, we need briefly to remind ourselves of some salient points in the prehistory of the fateful decision to attack the Soviet Union.

I

June 1941 was not the first time that German troops had invaded Russian soil or occupied huge tracts of eastern Europe. This had already happened during the First World War. In the latter half of 1915 the German army had overrun the parts of Poland ruled by Russia and occupied enormous swathes of territory along the Baltic coast. Two years later, in further advances, the Germans moved into Belorussia and the Ukraine.[2] The harsh Treaty of Brest-Litovsk, forced on the new Bolshevik regime on 3 March 1918, conceded German influence over Poland, Finland, Latvia, Lithuania, Estonia, Belorussia and the Ukraine.[3] It was a treaty that Hitler praised for providing the 'land and soil' needed to sustain the German people.[4] And when, many years later, he outlined to his military leaders his political objectives on invading the Soviet Union – the establishment of buffer states in the Ukraine, the Baltic, Finland and White Russia (Belorussia) – they bore a distinct resemblance to the terms of Brest-Litovsk.[5]

The images the Germans gleaned of the country they were occupying in 1918 had a lasting impact, helping to shape the mentalities that fed into the second, far more vicious occupation a generation later. 'Deepest Russia, without a glimmer of Central European *Kultur*', one officer noted. 'Asia, steppe, swamps, claustrophobic underworld, and a godforsaken wasteland of slime.'[6] Led by such impressions, the occupiers intended to create a German military state in the Baltic region to impose order and introduce *Kultur*. The key figure in the utopian planning of the military state was General Erich Ludendorff, the most dynamic of the German army leaders in the second half of the war.[7] In the early 1920s he was to come into close contact with Hitler, and to join him in the fiasco of the attempted beerhall putsch in November 1923.

In all probability, Ludendorff was among those who exercised some influence upon Hitler's changing views on Russia in the early 1920s. It was during this time that the early, conventional Pan-German focus of Hitler's ideas on foreign policy – with a main emphasis on restoring Germany's 1914 borders, recovering the lost colonies and eventual revenge against the French and British victors of the war responsible for the hated Treaty of Versailles – gradually gave way to a new concentration on eastward expansion to gain territory at the expense of Russia, with the corollary of a policy of friendship towards Britain. In his first known statement of this view, in December 1922, Hitler stated: 'the destruction of Russia with the help of England would have to be attempted. Russia would give Germany sufficient land for German settlers and a wide field of activity for German industry.'[8] By 1924 the doctrine was fixed in Hitler's mind, and he came to state it unequivocally towards the end of the second volume of his treatise, *Mein Kampf*, published in 1926: 'We National Socialists consciously draw a line beneath the foreign policy tendency of our prewar period. We take up where we broke off six hundred years ago. We stop the endless German movement to the south and west, and turn our gaze towards the land in the east ... If we speak of soil in Europe today, we can primarily have in mind only Russia and her vassal border states.'[9] Once formed, this doctrine of 'living space' (*Lebensraum*) remained unchanged, and was crucial to Hitler's 'world-view' down to the Berlin bunker.

It was not an original idea. In fact, it had been a common strand of nationalist-imperialist thinking since the 1890s and had later been 'intellectualized' by influential geopolitical theorists, most notably Karl Haushofer, a Munich professor who had taught Hitler's private secretary, Rudolf Hess. The idea drew on crude economics: that only increased territory for settlement allowed for the population growth essential to the strength and vitality of a great power. Germany's borders were seen as too confined to allow for the necessary population expansion. Therefore, she needed to gain new territory. And whereas the British Empire, whose power Hitler admired and envied, had been built upon territory gained by overseas conquest and colonial exploitation, Germany's had to be found closer to home, in eastern Europe.

Since no country, state or people would be prepared to give up its land, war for territorial gain was intrinsic to the *Lebensraum* idea. In this it was not just imperialist, but implicitly social Darwinist and racist, believing that the strong had the right to survive, while the weak deservedly went to the wall, and that the more vital, creative races should properly triumph over inferiors. Hitler himself, however, added a further vital racial component to it: antisemitism. Again, there was nothing original in Hitler's antisemitic views, however vicious. He shared them with countless others – though the depth of his anti-Jewish paranoia was certainly unusual. But there *was* an originality in the way in which Hitler combined his pathological antisemitism with the notion of *Lebensraum* – the twin components of his singular world-view.[10] This was by regarding Bolshevism as Jewish rule, a view he had formed by 1920, probably under the influence of his publicist associate Alfred Rosenberg, who hailed from the Baltic, and the rabid antisemitic and anti-Bolshevik tirades of Russian exiles which fed into the German right-wing press.[11] In the passage already quoted, Germany's need for land in the east was directly linked to the eradication of Jewish rule there. 'For centuries,' wrote Hitler, 'Russia drew nourishment from [the] Germanic nucleus of its upper leading strata. Today it can be regarded as almost totally eliminated and extinguished. It has been replaced by the Jew . . . He himself is no element of organization, but a ferment of decomposition. The giant empire in the east is ripe for collapse. And the end of Jewish rule in Russia will also be the end of Russia as a state.'[12] 'Living space' in Russia would, in other words, be synonymous with the destruction of the power of Jewry there.

Hitler returned to the theme of 'living space' in innumerable speeches in the later 1920s, and in an unpublished tract of 1928, where he expounded upon his ideas of foreign policy at greater length than in *Mein Kampf*. In this tract, he defined foreign policy as 'the art of securing for a people the necessary quantity and quality of *Lebensraum*'.[13] For Germany, this meant a single goal, and 'in the one and only place possible: space in the East'.[14] Such ideas were in 1928 still idiosyncratic. Few Germans entertained such notions, and even those who did must have thought them little more than pipe dreams. Hitler headed a fringe party in the political doldrums, with the backing of under 3 per cent of the population at the last Reichstag election, and with no obvious prospect of ever gaining political power. Mainstream politics looked very different from Hitler's vision. The German Foreign Office under Gustav Stresemann was wedded to Locarno and the collective security of the League of Nations. And, despite antipathy towards Bolshevism, relations with the Soviet Union had been, in fact, good since 1922, when the Treaty of Rapallo established a basis of mutually beneficial economic cooperation which helped the Reichswehr bypass the restrictions of the Versailles Treaty and undertake some clandestine steps towards rearmament.[15]

During the Nazi movement's meteoric rise to power, as the Depression caught hold of Germany, Hitler had relatively little to say about 'living space'. A struggle, sometime in the dim and distant future, to acquire land for settlement and entailing war against the Soviet Union, was scarcely a vote-catcher. Most people had the failures of their own government and the everyday worries of trying to cope with the economic misery on their minds. These, and the prospect of a new start under National Socialism, offering unity and strength, were the themes that Hitler hammered home ceaselessly. But although he played down the 'living space' theme, he did not discard it. Meanwhile, his relentless exploitation of the travails of Weimar democracy gained him the dramatic increase in popularity that culminated in Reich President Paul von Hindenburg appointing him to the Reich Chancellorship on 30 January 1933. From now on, his views on foreign policy were no longer those of a fringe-party hothead, but carried the weight of the most important figure in the government, backed by a huge mass movement.

In the beginning, however, neither the attainment of 'living space' nor, indeed, any defined goal in foreign policy was laid down. What Hitler initially set out to do was to overcome Germany's weakness in the international arena. Crucial to this was to restore Germany's armed strength. He wasted no time in establishing the outright priority of rearmament. This was naturally music to the ears of his generals, whom he addressed only four days after taking office. Many of them had long been hoping, and secretly planning, for the day when the shackles would be removed from rearmament; and when, with democracy overthrown, Germany could once more regain strength and power to become, over time, the dominant force in central Europe, even on the European continent. So Hitler's expressed determination on 3 February 1933 to build up the armed forces was sure of a favourable response. He went on to hint at the direction of future foreign policy. Perhaps more exports could be won, he suggested. But the suggestion was raised only to pour doubt on it. 'Perhaps – and probably better – conquest of new living space in the east and its ruthless Germanization' was posed as the alternative.[16] It was a cautious reassertion of his dogma of the 1920s. Most who heard it probably took it to mean no more than a vague allusion to expansionism at some future point to win back territories lost at Versailles and establish German supremacy in central and eastern Europe – something that few disapproved of fundamentally – but scarcely saw it as a concrete foreign-policy aim. Nor was it, at this stage. But it implied, nevertheless, a *direction* to Hitler's thinking on foreign policy, and one that was unchanged from the views he had developed a decade earlier. That is, Hitler's actions over the following years, as Germany came increasingly to force the developments that culminated in war, should not simply be seen as opportunism, as he adapted to the vagaries of international politics. Certainly, he exploited the chances that arose. But the opportunism was ideologically driven.

Hitler's dominance over the German government was already complete by summer 1933. He now controlled not only a huge party, but had the advanced apparatus of bureaucratic state administration at his disposal as well as, not least, the modern machinery of coercion and repression. A year later he had established total supremacy in the state. The brutal massacre of the stormtroopers' leaders in June 1934 removed the one remaining threat to his rule. And with the death of the aged Reich President Hindenburg shortly afterward, the only lingering source of potential alternative loyalty was gone. Hitler now became not just head of government, but head of state. The main beneficiary from the ruthless destruction of his own paramilitary organization had been the German army. This cemented its backing for Hitler, already grounded on his support for a massive rearmament programme. Meanwhile, business and industry, drawn by the scope they were given to maximize profit, had also largely fallen in behind the new regime.

Decision-making in the Nazi regime, once the dust had settled on the upheavals of 1933–4, bore little resemblance to the way democratic states operated. Indeed, it was bizarre even in comparison with other forms of authoritarian rule. Hitler disliked the potential check to his authority posed by any collective body. Hence, the Cabinet, the highest organ of collective government, started to atrophy as soon as Hindenburg was dead. Its meetings became more infrequent as legislation was devised in the main through circulation of drafts among relevant government ministers. After February 1938 Cabinet meetings ceased altogether. Remarkably, therefore, there was now no collective body of government. Meanwhile, the dualism of party and state was left without clear demarcation lines, resulting in a good deal of governmental confusion. This was intensified by Hitler's readiness to create plenipotentiary bodies, backed by his personal support and often party–state hybrids, to overcome blockages or obstacles in government, while at the same time leaving the original government ministry intact. The basic Nazi social Darwinist philosophy of support for the strong and powerful encouraged unbridled competition and use of 'elbow power'. So positions on paper often meant little or nothing in reality as power resided with those individuals who could fight their way to the top and had immediate access to Hitler. Heinrich Himmler, head of the SS, in control from

1936 onwards of the huge police and security apparatus, though nominally subordinate to the weakly placed Reich Minister of the Interior, Wilhelm Frick, and Hermann Göring, head of the Four-Year Plan after 1936, which largely supplanted the still existing Reich Ministry of Economics, were among the most important examples.

In these myriad competing agencies and this administrative anarchy, Hitler's position was supreme. He remained largely aloof from internal policy. To speak of his decision-making would for the most part be inaccurate. 'Decisions' could be no more than an informal utterance picked up by a minister or party functionary at Hitler's regular lunchtime gatherings and then going its way as an 'order of the Führer'. As long as developments were taking shape along the lines he wanted, he seldom intervened in the prewar years (later it was different) unless he was called in to arbitrate, which he was in practice often reluctant to do. But at key junctures, where a crisis point or a fork in the road requiring a new direction was reached, his intervention was needed and was crucial. The crisis in provision of raw materials for rearmament in 1936, which prompted the introduction of the Four-Year Plan to intensify industrial production and make the German economy ready for war, led to perhaps the most crucial such intervention in the early period of the regime.

If he did little more before the war than lay down 'directions for action'[17] in domestic affairs, there can be no doubt that the big decisions of foreign policy from 1933 onwards, down to and including the decision to risk European war by attacking Poland in 1939, were his.[18] Here too, however, he shunned the collective decision-making of a Cabinet. As central government fragmented, he consulted, for the most part on an individual basis, those whose views he needed to sound out, before taking the decision himself. At a crucial meeting with his armed forces' leaders and his Foreign Minister in November 1937, at which he expounded upon the need for expansion and war, he began by stating that the matter under discussion was far too important to be brought before the Reich Cabinet.[19] In part this reflected a characteristic preoccupation with secrecy, not in itself unreasonable in restricting knowledge of risky steps in foreign policy (or, later, vital military operations). In January 1940 he would have hung in the room of every military office his 'Basic Order' stipulating that: 'No one: no office, no officer may learn of something to be kept secret if they don't absolutely have to have knowledge of it for official reasons.' Even then, only limited necessary information, and no earlier than was needed, should be given.[20] But it went beyond concern for secrecy. Hitler's understanding of his position as Führer meant a sense of absolute power and responsibility that brooked no interference; he alone could take the crucial decisions; and, while he might choose to listen to the opinion of a military commander or relevant government minister, he had to be free and unconstrained by the views of others to decide as he chose. The decision was then simply announced to those who needed to know. Opposition was, accordingly, extremely difficult, if not impossible, to articulate publicly, while reservations privately expressed to Hitler had to contend with the possibility of a high-decibel tirade in response. Moreover, Hitler could always reckon on high levels of support within the ruling elites, most importantly in the leadership of the armed forces. When in the summer of 1938 General Ludwig Beck, the chief of the General Staff, fundamentally opposed Hitler's decision to attack Czechoslovakia that autumn (later postponed because of the western powers' intervention at the Munich Conference), he found himself completely isolated within the army leadership and his resignation from office in despair had no effect whatsoever on policy.

As had been the case before 1933 in dealing with his political opponents, Hitler had highly developed antennae when it came to recognizing weakness in others. His successes in foreign policy down to 1938 derived in the main from this bully's intuition, coupled with his instinctive gambler's willingness to take risks for high stakes. Hitler's first major step in determining Germany's new, assertive course in foreign policy, the withdrawal from the Disarmament Conference and the League of Nations in October 1933, was fully in accordance with the wishes of the Foreign Ministry and army leadership. The timing was his, but the move was one which would probably have followed under any nationalist government at the time. Hitler took a more independent line in driving forward a deterioration in relations with the Soviet Union and pushing through a non-aggression treaty with Poland in January 1934, in both cases despite Foreign Ministry preferences. He gradually became more confident, and, with that, bolder. In March 1935 he correctly divined that the western democracies would do nothing if he faced them with a major breach of the Versailles Treaty and announced the existence of a German air force and the introduction of conscription to a mass army. He consulted neither military leaders nor ministers in arriving at his decision.[21] In early 1936 he again correctly presumed that the weakness of the western democracies, laid bare by the Abyssinian crisis, offered an excellent opportunity to remilitarize the Rhineland – another step that would have been on the agenda of any nationalist government. A surprisingly wide circle in the Foreign Ministry and the military leadership were aware of what was pending, as Hitler hesitated over a period of about a month, deliberating the issue with a number of advisers, some of whom opposed action as too risky. Hitler listened. But he took the decision alone, ignoring advice to the contrary. His triumph prompted the statement, made for propaganda effect though reflecting his now boundless self-confidence: 'I go with the certainty of a sleepwalker along the path laid out for me by Providence.'[22]

The path was, however, not a straight one. Since the mid-1920s he had wanted Great Britain as a friend and ally, not an enemy, in the war he envisaged, and desired, against 'Jewish-Bolshevism'. But hints of an alignment, such as the naval treaty between Britain and Germany concluded in 1935, offered only a false dawn. The alienation grew, and remained even when the British Prime Minister, Neville Chamberlain, bent over backwards to 'appease' Hitler in 1938. Long before then, Hitler had realized that he had to number Britain among Germany's foes. He knew, too, that Britain, with a world Empire behind her, was starting, if belatedly, to rearm with urgency. Beyond this, across the Atlantic, lay the vast potential of America, still untapped, to be sure, as the country lay locked in isolationism, but a likely future enemy to be viewed with the utmost seriousness, one whose intervention had sealed Germany's fate in the First World War. Time, in other words, was not on Germany's side. She had built up an advantage with her early and speedy rearmament programme. But the advantage would not last. This fed into Hitler's gambler temperament. The risk, he invariably argued, would be greater by waiting than by acting.

The imperative for early action was driven by another factor: economics. The entire rearmament drive, once past the initial stages, could only be undertaken at reckless cost to state finances and an ordered running of the economy. Germany simply lacked the resources to produce or import all she needed, for arms manufacture and to sustain a modest standard of living for her growing population.[23] Money for arms meant less for food. Guns *and* butter were possible only for a limited time. By the later 1930s that time was starting to run out. Alarm bells were starting to be heard across the economy. War, when it came, was not the result of economic crisis. Rather, the looming economic crisis was a result of ideological imperatives to restructure the economy for war.[24] But it did mean that, by the later 1930s, Hitler was under pressure to act, both because he felt Germany would before many more years be in a far inferior international position, and because an overstretched and overheated economy could not be indefinitely sustained.

Not that Hitler acted only under the constraints of external pressures. Rather, these pushed him in the direction which he wanted to go anyway. Although anti-Bolshevism had played little overt role in shaping Hitler's foreign policy during the early years of the regime, this began to change from 1936 onwards. The beginning of the Spanish Civil War in the summer of that year put Bolshevism back in the spotlight from Hitler's vantage point. Hitler decided alone, and for ideological reasons (to combat the threat of Bolshevism taking over in Spain, then France), to offer German military aid to General Francisco Franco, leader of the nationalist rebellion against the Spanish Republic.[25] Later that summer, his memorandum for the Four-Year Plan rested on the premiss that 'the showdown with Russia is inevitable'.[26] By 1937, Hitler was expecting major war within Europe in the next five or six years, thought Stalin was 'sick in the brain', and spoke of Bolshevism as 'the danger that we will have to knock down sometime'.[27] Hitler, therefore, never lost sight of the ideological aim he had developed in the 1920s, even if adjustments to the changing constellation of practical foreign policy in the years preceding the war meant that it faded for the time being into the background. In August 1939 Hitler made the ultimate adjustment when he overturned, in a move of breathtaking cynicism (shared by Stalin), the antagonism towards the Soviet Union embedded in Nazi ideology to conclude a non-aggression pact with the arch-enemy.[28] Even then, days before this dramatic pact, he allegedly remarked to the Swiss Commissioner to the League of Nations, Carl Burckhardt: 'Everything that I undertake is directed against Russia. If those in the West are too stupid and too blind to understand this, then I shall be forced to come to an understanding with the Russians to beat the West, and then, after its defeat, turn with all my concerted force against the Soviet Union.'[29]

By this time, war in Europe was a certainty. Hitler, more than any other individual, had seen to that. As a combination of determinants – ideological, military-strategic and economic – accelerated the tempo and greatly reduced the timescale for war that he had previously entertained, imagining that it would be around 1943, so his room for manoeuvre in avoiding more imminent conflict with the western powers diminished. In 1938 Britain and France had been so anxious to avoid war that they had given in to Hitler's aggression at Munich, at the cost of Czechoslovakia. Hitler expected them to do the same in Poland, when the stakes, satisfying his claim on Danzig and the Corridor, seemed smaller. This was his miscalculation. His own action in occupying what remained of Czechoslovakia in March 1939, ignoring the deal with the west which he had concluded only six months earlier, had destroyed the backing for appeasement. He thought until the end of August that Britain and France would still, at the last moment, yield, and that he could destroy Poland without their intervention. But two days after his troops had invaded Poland, he finally – if not at the moment of his choosing – had his war with the west. For the time being the war he really wanted, against the Soviet Union, would have to wait.

A one-sided military campaign in Poland brought overwhelming victory in little more than three weeks. But Hitler had no expectation that the half-hearted offer of peace on his terms, made in a speech to the Reichstag on 6 October, would be taken up in London or Paris. He was already plotting his next move. The sense that time favoured his enemies, and that to strike early meant to seize the initiative, to retain the whip-hand – as we have noted, a constant feature of Hitler's psychology – left him impatient with the easy triumph in Poland. He was now anxious to attack the west without delay. With Poland defeated and the Soviet Union, his new-found ally, posing no danger for the time being, Germany was secure in the east. The western front lay open. The circumstances could never be better. The opportunity had to be taken while it lasted to impose a crushing defeat upon France and force Britain to acknowledge her weakness and come to terms. With the war in the west then effectively won, he could turn his attention to preparing for the war he had always wanted to fight: the showdown in the east with 'Jewish-Bolshevism', to destroy Stalin's Russia and to secure Germany's long-term future by acquiring 'living space' and unlimited material resources. This was Hitler's thinking in autumn 1939.

His generals recoiled at the dangers of such a risky early strike against the west, magnified by the imminent onset of bad weather. To brush aside the weak and antiquated Polish army in a brief campaign was one thing. To launch a major offensive against France, its huge army shielded by the elaborate defences of the Maginot Line, and joined in powerful alliance with Great Britain and the British Empire, was quite another. The generals knew that the armed forces were in no fit state for a full-scale, probably long-drawn-out, conflict against powerful enemies. Even the brief Polish campaign had left half the German tanks and motorized vehicles out of action. An immediate continuation of the war by an attack in the west was, in their eyes, unthinkable.

Hitler fumed at their hesitancy and caution. But perhaps he sensed that they were right. At any rate, he bowed to their worries about bad weather conditions and transport difficulties to accept delay after delay – twenty-nine in all – to the launch of the western offensive. Detailed operational planning was not worked out until February of 1940. Then the need to intervene in Scandinavia, where German troops had invaded Denmark and Norway in April, took precedence. The postponements proved invaluable in building up the armed forces. And they eventually resulted in the tactically bold and brilliant plan to attack where least expected, by scything through the wooded Ardennes region of southern Belgium and into lowland France towards the coast. The plan had initially been the tactical brainwave of Lieutenant-General Erich von Manstein but had been seized upon and turned into military directives by Hitler, impatient at the uninspired and conventional ideas of his army High Command. This was the plan behind the attack that eventually commenced on the early morning of 10 May.[30]

The offensive was a stunning success, greater than even Hitler had expected. The Dutch surrendered after five days. The Belgians, their neutrality violated by German troops for the second time in a generation, held out longer, until almost the end of the month. But though the small Belgian army fought gallantly, it was swiftly broken by German might. And, whatever their strength on paper, the French army, ineptly led, badly equipped and poor in morale, proved no match for the Wehrmacht. The fabled fortifications of the Maginot Line, built to fend off any possible third assault within a lifetime from across the Rhine, served little practical purpose in the event. They were incapable of halting the main German thrust, which simply bypassed them. Defiance crumbled. On 14 June, less than five weeks after the offensive had been launched, German troops entered Paris. Hitler was exultant as the news was brought to him three days later that the French had sued for peace. His revenge over the French was complete – or would be once the armistice was signed in his presence on 21 June in the self-same railway carriage in which the Germans had been compelled to capitulate in 1918. The scale of the triumph took his incipient megalomania onto a new plane. And his self-glorification (embracing a sense of infallibility) was magnified by the plaudits of his generals, who had, sometimes reluctantly, to concede not only the magnitude of what had been possible under Hitler, but also his direct role in the extraordinarily successful strategic plan of attack. Only the British, Hitler thought, now stood between him and complete victory in the west. Surely they would see sense, and come to terms?

II

On 6 July 1940 Hitler returned in triumph to Berlin to celebrate before a vast, adoring public the spectacular victory over France and the conclusion of the astonishing western campaign. It was his greatest ever homecoming. To the hundreds of thousands who had waited for hours along the flower-strewn streets of the Reich capital, it seemed as if the end of the war was close at hand. Only Great Britain now appeared to stand in the way of final victory. Few among the cheering crowds imagined that she would pose much of a lasting obstacle to the mighty Wehrmacht. Even in the full flush of the crushing defeat of the French, however, Hitler's military advisers and even the dictator himself were less than sure that Britain's resistance would be swiftly overcome. Behind Britain, too, lay the shadow, if still indistinct, of the United States. Though as yet the sentiment was seldom spoken out loud, the lingering fear was there nonetheless: should the United States mobilize her colossal might and wealth to enter the war, as in 1917, the chances of German total victory would rapidly recede. The twin problem: how to *get* Britain out, and how to *keep* America out of the war, loomed large, therefore, in the thoughts of Hitler and the German military leadership during the immediate weeks following the capitulation of France. The outright priority was to persuade (or, failing that, compel through military force) Britain to negotiate a settlement.[31] Removing Britain from the war would both deter America from engagement in Europe and free Germany's rear to allow Hitler to engage upon the war he had wanted to fight since the 1920s: the war to destroy 'Jewish-Bolshevism' and gain an enormous eastern empire at the expense of the Soviet Union.

But within an hour of Hitler's speech to the Reichstag on 19 July, the first press reports were telling him of Britain's icy response to his 'appeal to reason' to come to terms with Germany and avoid the destruction of her Empire.[32] On 22 July a broadcast speech by the British Foreign Secretary, Lord Halifax, made public what Hitler already knew, that Britain would not entertain the possibility of a negotiated settlement and was determined to fight on.[33] Even before Halifax's speech, Hitler had acknowledged the categorical rejection of his 'appeal' and on 21 July raised with his commanders-in-chief the prospect of invading the Soviet Union that very autumn.

His underlying reasons were ideological, as they had been for almost two decades. Through an attack on the Soviet Union he would destroy the power of the Jews, embodied in his world-view by the Bolshevik regime, and at the same time gain 'living space' for German settlement. Victory would make Germany masters of Europe and provide the base for a racially purified empire which would be equipped eventually to challenge the United States for world domination. But it was now obvious that the war to destroy Bolshevism would not be fought as he had envisaged it, with Britain's support (or at least tolerance). Britain was refusing even at this stage to fit into the concept he had devised all those years ago. Somehow, she had to be compelled to do so, or at least removed from the equation as a hostile force. 'The Führer is greatly puzzled by Britain's persisting unwillingness to make peace,' the army chief of staff, Franz Halder, had noted on 13 July. 'He sees the answer (as we do) in Britain's hope on Russia, and therefore counts on having to compel her by main force to agree to peace.'[34] However strong the ideological motivation, therefore, the urgency implicit in the startling suggestion that the Soviet Union should be attacked that autumn was not ideological but military-strategic. And that was how Hitler presented it to his commanders-in-chief on 21 July.

'No clear picture on what is happening in England', Hitler declared. 'Preparations for a decision by arms must be completed as quickly as possible.' He refused, he said, to let the military and political initiative slip. Germany had won the war, he brashly claimed. Britain's position was hopeless, but she continued because of the expectation of American help over time, and because she 'puts hope in Russia'. This could come from Russia stirring up the Balkans, with the effect of cutting off German fuel supplies, or by Britain inciting the Soviet Union to act against Germany. Stalin, he suggested, was 'flirting with Britain to keep her in the war and tie us down, with a view to gaining time and taking what he wants, knowing he could not get it once peace breaks out'. Hitler concluded that 'Britain must be reduced by the middle of September, at the time when we make the invasion'. But he was less certain than he sounded about this prospect. He thought the crossing of the Channel 'very hazardous', and stipulated that invasion was 'to be undertaken only if no other way is left to reach terms with Britain'. The way to force the issue, in his view, was to destroy the Soviet Union. 'Our attention must be turned to tackling the Russian problem and prepare planning,' he stated. The object was 'To crush [the] Russian army or at least take as much Russian territory as is necessary to bar enemy air raids on Berlin and Silesian industries'. It would take four to six weeks to assemble an invading army. 'If we attack Russia this autumn, pressure of the air war on Britain will be relieved.'[35]

He was ready, therefore, to plunge Germany for a short time (he thought) into war in the east with the war in the west still not conclusively won, raising the spectre of the war on two fronts, dreaded by military strategists and the general public alike. When General Alfred Jodl, head of the Wehrmacht Operations Staff and Hitler's main adviser on military strategy, told his immediate subordinates on 29 July of the intention to launch an eastern campaign, the prospect of a war on two fronts prompted an hour of worried argument. Jodl, whether from conviction or not, countered objections with the case advanced by Hitler: the showdown with Bolshevism was inevitable, so it was better to have it now, while German military power was at its height; and by autumn 1941 the Luftwaffe, strengthened by victorious deployment in the east, would again be ready to be let loose on Britain.[36] Hitler himself was dismissive of anxieties about a war on two fronts. Intoxicated by the grandeur of the victory in the west, he had told his chief military advisers at the time of the French capitulation that 'a campaign against Russia would be child's play'.[37]

Hitler justified the war as necessary to remove Britain's last possible major ally on the Continent. He claimed, too, that the Soviet Union was 'the Far Eastern sword of Britain and the United States, pointed at Japan'.[38] The implication was that victory over the Soviet Union would free Japan to undertake her ambitious southern expansion without fear of Soviet power in the rear, with the combined effect of undermining British power in the Far East, tying down the United States in the Pacific and deterring her involvement in the Atlantic and in Europe. The projected short eastern campaign offered, therefore, the prospect not only of complete hegemony on the European continent, but even of overall final victory in the war. After that, at some indeterminate future date, would come the showdown with the United States. There was no contradiction between ideology and military-strategic considerations in Hitler's thoughts of invading the Soviet Union. They went hand in hand. The essential motivating force, as ever, was ideological. But in the actual decision-making, the strategic imperative dominated.[39]

When the prospect of attacking the Soviet Union that autumn was rapidly ruled out as impractical, he postponed it until May 1941. This was the date he had fixed in his meeting with Jodl on 29 July, and which he announced to his military leaders two days later. It was a momentous decision, perhaps the most momentous of the entire war. And it was freely taken. That is, it was not taken under other than self-imposed constraints. It was not taken in order to head off an immediate threat of attack by the Soviet Union. There was no suggestion at this time – the justificatory claim would come later – of the need for a pre-emptive strike. Hitler himself had acknowledged ten days earlier that the Russians did not want war with Germany.[40] Nor was the decision taken in response to pressure from the military, or from any other lobby within the power-echelons of the regime. In fact, even on 30 July, the day before Hitler's pronouncement, the Commander-in-Chief of the army, Field Marshal Werner von Brauchitsch, and the chief of the General Staff of the army, Colonel-General Halder, agreed that 'it would be better to be on terms of friendship with Russia'. They preferred to concentrate the military effort on the possibilities of attacking British positions in the Mediterranean (particularly Gibraltar) and the Middle East, saw no danger in Russian engagement in the Balkans and Persian Gulf, and envisaged helping the Italians create a Mediterranean empire and even cooperating with the Russians to consolidate the German Reich in northern and western Europe, from which basis a lengthy war against Britain could be contemplated with equanimity.[41]

The pressure upon Hitler was subjective: his sense that no time could be lost before striking at the Soviet Union if the overall initiative in the war, based on the balance of power and armed might, were not to drain away from Germany towards Britain and, ultimately, the United States.[42] This subjective pressure was, however, reinforced by the economic logic of Germany's war. This in turn was rooted in the ideology of 'living space' and the closely related notion of *Großraumwirtschaft*: sphere of economic domination. When the euphoria following the victory over France started to die down, it was realized that Germany's expectations of economic dominance on the European continent had an Achilles heel: the Soviet Union. In fact, in the summer of 1940 Germany was profiting handsomely from Soviet deliveries of food and raw materials under the economic agreements that flowed from the Hitler–Stalin Pact.[43] Even so, Hitler was made aware by the Ministry of Economics that, to equip herself for a long war against Britain and, with growing certainty, the United States, Germany now needed vastly more than she was currently receiving from the Soviet Union. Even though, in the short term, Stalin would probably, to gain time, be prepared to bow to demands for increased supplies, there would inexorably be a growing dependence on the Soviet Union, too precarious a prospect for Hitler to tolerate. He agreed with his Economics Minister, Walther Funk, that the German 'economic sphere' (*der 'großdeutsche Wirtschaftsraum'*) could not be 'dependent upon forces and powers over whom we have no influence'.[44] This view was widely shared in leading sectors of the Wehrmacht, big business and the ministerial bureaucracy. It meant Hitler's decision for war against the Soviet Union was likely to find a good deal of support in all those vital groupings.[45]

Whatever the misgivings of some generals about the venture, Hitler's decision was neither opposed nor contested in the military leadership. In fact, sensing what was coming, the army's General Staff had already begun to prepare feasibility studies weeks before Hitler announced his intention to strike at the Soviet Union.[46] His military leaders were as aware as he was of the strategic position. They put forward no alternative strategy for attaining final victory, assuming that Britain could not be invaded or bombed into submission.[47] Moreover, like Hitler, they grossly underestimated the Red Army (particularly since its poor showing in the 'Winter War' against Finland some months earlier), and they shared his detestation of Bolshevism, some of them even his identification of the Soviet regime with the power of the Jews. But it is doubtful in the extreme whether they would have of themselves come to recommend a decision, within a few weeks of the defeat of France, to prepare urgently for an invasion of the Soviet Union. That decision was Hitler's, and his alone.

The immensity of the catastrophe which he thereby invited would unfold ever more plainly from the autumn of 1941 onwards, once the German advance on Moscow stalled as the terrible Russian winter closed in. However, the question at issue here relates not to the attack itself, but to the decision to launch it, taken the previous year. Did Hitler, even as the logistics for what would come to be known as 'Operation Barbarossa' were being worked out, have options which might have given him a better chance of ending (or even curtailing) the threat to Germany posed by Britain's continuation of the war and America's presumed eventual entry? Germany's navy leadership thought so. And, for a while, so did the Foreign Ministry.

The decision, effectively taken on 31 July 1940, to attack the Soviet Union the following spring was not turned into a war directive until 18 December.[48] Even that directive, of course, did not mean in itself that an invasion had to be launched. But in December the points were switched irreversibly onto the track that led to that invasion. In the four months that intervened between July and December 1940, by contrast, Hitler seemed, in matters determining German strategy, strangely vacillating, unsure which way to turn, hesitant, indecisive, weak even, at the height of his power in his external dealings with lesser dictators (Mussolini and Franco), and the leader of defeated France (Marshal Pétain). He appeared at times to entertain military and foreign-policy suggestions which stood in contradiction to the war in the east. But by the late autumn it was clear that he had returned to the chosen path from which he had never seriously wandered: attacking the Soviet Union at the earliest opportunity with the strategic aim of attaining final victory in the war by conquering London via Moscow. It was a fateful choice of immense magnitude.

Choice presupposes options. What strategic possibilities lay open to the German leadership in the summer of 1940? That an alternative – militarily far more promising – strategy was available, but was squandered through Hitler's insistence on attacking the Soviet Union, was not infrequently claimed in the postwar years.[49] It offered an exculpatory device for some military leaders, all too keen to look no farther than Hitler himself as the cause of 'the German catastrophe'.[50] Later historical research has usually been far more sceptical, invariably concentrating upon Hitler's ideological imperative for the war in the east.[51]

Hitler decided strategy. On that there is no doubt. Moreover, his sensitivity to the prestige invested in his position as supreme Leader demanded that decisions be taken imperiously, without detailed soundings of advice, let alone prolonged debate and discussion. Critical assessment of policy options partly depends in no small measure upon the effectiveness of mechanisms within a governmental system to shape and present them to the leadership. Given the nature of government in the Third Reich, the potential for presenting Hitler with judiciously framed alternatives was not high. Whereas the British War Cabinet reached a collective decision, after three days of intensive debate, to stay in the war, Hitler simply announced to his generals on 31 July (without prior consultation other than with his immediate military advisers, who had had the first contingency plans drawn up) the decision to prepare for war with the Soviet Union the following spring. No one in the Reich's civil administration was informed of the decision.

As we have noted, the fragmentation of government below Hitler was greater even than in any other dictatorship at the time. Once the Reich Cabinet had met for the last time, at the beginning of 1938, even the remnants of collective government no longer existed. At that same point, in early 1938, Hitler had concentrated the leadership of the armed forces in his own hands. But the High Command of the Wehrmacht, set up as the vehicle of Hitler's own control, did not function as a collective advisory body on military strategy in the way that the meetings of the chiefs of staff did for the British War Cabinet. Consequently, there was little or no coherent planning devised collectively by the three branches of the armed forces – army, air force and navy. These largely operated alongside each other, their commanders-in-chief dealing in the main bilaterally with Hitler.

Quite different strategic priorities emerged, therefore. Among them were the German navy's own strategic preferences, which differed markedly from those of Hitler. Did they offer a workable option, ignored by Hitler, which offered a more promising prosecution of the war and could have avoided the debacle in the east?

III

Strategic thinking among the leaders of the German navy – competing in what was usually an uphill struggle with the army and air force for status, influence and resources – had from the outset run along different lines to that of Hitler, though it was no less aggressive and no less global in its ambitions for territorial expansion and eventual world domination. Where Hitler had wanted to harness British friendship to destroy the Soviet Union, looking to build a huge land empire in eastern Europe and impregnable strength from which at some distant future date Germany could engage in a showdown with the United States, the navy saw the destruction of British world power as the central war aim. It demanded a big and powerful fleet, capable of taking on and defeating the Royal Navy in a classic naval war. Accompanied by the construction of an enormous German colonial empire, this would provide the basis to challenge and defeat the United States in the contest for world domination. Attacking Bolshevik Russia did not figure prominently in this thinking. Bolshevism was, of course, accepted as an evil to be confronted and destroyed at some point. But it was taken for granted that it could be contained, then smashed at a later date, once German pre-eminence had been established.

Naval thinking in the Third Reich was, in essence, an updated and amended variant of that of Tirpitz's time.[52] It drew on one of the two main strands of German imperialism, that of the overseas colonial empire. Hitler's ideas (and those of the Nazi Party) arose from the alternative strand of imperialism, also with deep roots in the Wilhelmine period, that looked to expansion and conquest in eastern Europe.[53] For the army, though not the navy, this latter version, with its inbuilt demands for a large land force to ensure Continental mastery, had evident attractions. But the maritime and Continental alternatives could easily stand alongside each other in the prewar years. Though army, navy and air force competed for resources, there was no need to choose between the alternatives. With the decision in 1939 to construct a large surface fleet, envisaged in the Z-Plan, it even appeared for a time as if the navy was getting its way.[54]

But the navy's conception of preparing for a major struggle by the mid-1940s was completely upturned when the Polish crisis led to war between Germany and Great Britain in September 1939. In a remarkable memorandum of 3 September 1939, the very date that Britain and France declared war on Germany, the Commander-in-Chief of the navy, Grand Admiral Erich Raeder, coming close to criticizing Hitler for taking Germany into war prematurely, admitted that the navy, which according to the Z-Plan was arming for a war 'on the ocean' at the turn of the year 1944–5, was still in autumn 1939 nowhere near sufficiently armed for the 'great struggle with England'.[55]

By the spring and early summer of 1940, however, this initial gloom had given way to unbounded optimism. In the wake of the part played by the navy in the Scandinavian conquests in April, then especially the stirring events during the western campaign in May and June, culminating in the dramatic victory over France, naval leaders had worked out their utopian vision of the future world power of Germany resting on the strength of the navy to protect its overseas possessions.[56] Huge territorial annexation was envisaged. According to a memorandum of 3 June, composed by Rear Admiral Kurt Fricke, Denmark, Norway and northern France were to remain as German possessions, safeguarding the Reich's north-western seaboard. A contiguous swathe of territories, mainly to be taken from France and Belgium, added to some returned former German colonies, and others exchanged with Britain and Portugal, would establish a large colonial empire in central Africa. Islands off the African east coast, most notably Madagascar, would offer protective bases.[57]

Admiral Rolf Carls, head of naval command in the Baltic and for long seen as Raeder's likely successor, went even further. Parts of Belgium and France (including Normandy and Brittany) would become German protectorates, based on the Czech model. The French colonial empire would be broken up in favour of Germany, Italy and to some extent Spain. South Africa and Southern Rhodesia would be removed from the British Empire and become an independent state, while Northern Rhodesia would come into German possession as a bridge to link its east- and west-African territories. All British rights in the Persian Gulf, most notably the oilfields, would pass to Germany. Britain and France were to be excluded from any control over the Suez Canal. British mandates in the Middle East would be taken away. Germany would take over the Shetlands and the Channel Islands. Strategic bases were to be established on the Canary Islands (probably in an exchange of territory with Spain), in Dakar on the African west coast (at the expense of France) and on Madagascar, Mauritius and the Seychelles in the Indian Ocean. Carls admitted the vision might seem 'fantastic', though he advocated its realization in order to 'secure Germany's claims of its part of the globe once and for all'.[58]

Yet another memorandum, dated 11 July, imagined the great battle-fleet necessary to defend a large colonial empire and wage war against the United States when Britain had been totally defeated and its once-mighty Empire had broken up. Coastal defences would be massively extended. Bases on the Azores, the Canaries and the Cape Verde Islands would offer security against attack from across the Atlantic. Taking possession of New Guinea as well as Madagascar would offer protection against attack in the Indian Ocean. Links between Germany and its colonies could be upheld without difficulty by dominance in the Indian Ocean, Red Sea and Mediterranean.[59]

It was a breathtakingly grandiose vision, and further testimony to a hubris in the German elite that was far from confined to Hitler.

However, such memoranda fell well short of anything resembling coherent strategic thinking. They remained no more than megalomaniac pipe dreams composed in the intoxication of seemingly imminent final victory. In fact, without the defeat of Britain, which was their underlying premiss, even the first steps towards their realization were out of the question. And they did nothing to prepare the navy for the strategic choice which, by the summer of 1940, Hitler had effectively made: the invasion of the Soviet Union by spring the following year. The dictator's interest remained, as it had done throughout, focused on the prospects of empire in the east of Europe, not in central Africa. For him, in contrast to the navy, building a colonial empire in Africa would only come *after*, not before, the defeat of Bolshevism and formed part of the inevitable future confrontation with the American continent.[60]

For its own part, the naval leadership, when it descended from utopian dreams to practical planning, was preoccupied with the immediate task which had been thrust upon it only weeks earlier: preparing the operational plans for the invasion of Britain by the autumn, aimed at removing British involvement in the war and freeing Germany's rear for the attack on the Soviet Union.

Though preliminary naval contingency planning for a possible invasion of Britain had been undertaken as early as November 1939,[61] serious operational consideration did not begin until June 1940. On the very day that the French sued for peace, 17 June, Major-General Walter Warlimont, who as head of the National Defence Department of the Wehrmacht Operations Staff was close to the very centre of military thinking, told Raeder that Hitler had expressed no intention of attempting a landing in England 'since he fully saw the extraordinary difficulties of such an undertaking'. Accordingly, the High Command of the Wehrmacht had made no preparations for such a move. Warlimont also indicated the evident divergence in Hitler's thinking from the underlying strategic preferences of the naval leadership. He confirmed that Hitler did not want totally to destroy Britain's world Empire, since this would only be 'to the disadvantage of the white race'. He preferred to reach peace with Britain, following the defeat of France, 'on the condition of return of colonies and renunciation of English influence in Europe'.[62]

Nevertheless, within a fortnight General Jodl, as head of the Wehrmacht Operations Staff Warlimont's immediate superior and Hitler's closest military adviser, had devised a strategy for forcing Britain to capitulate, if she could not be persuaded to agree to terms. This involved the prospect of a landing, but also 'war on the periphery', aimed at limited military support for those countries – Italy, Spain, Russia and Japan – which had an interest in benefiting from the undermining of the British Empire. An Italian attack on the Suez Canal and the capture of Gibraltar were specifically mentioned.[63] The 'peripheral strategy' remained under consideration throughout the summer and autumn, and aspects of it coincided with the thinking of the navy leadership.

The idea of an invasion of Britain, on the other hand, had only a brief lifespan. Hitler evidently saw this as a last resort and was highly sceptical from the outset about its practicality.[64] He had emphasized German mastery of the skies as the most important prerequisite for a landing. Raeder fully agreed. But the navy leadership was not only dubious that this could be attained, but also by mid-July expressing its extreme anxiety about transport difficulties and, not least, the worry that, even if German troops could be landed on British soil, the intervention of the Royal Navy could prevent further landings and cut them off, leading to the 'extraordinary endangering of the entire deployed army'.[65] Moreover, the intended completion of preparations for the landing by mid-August rapidly proved illusory.[66] The necessary rescheduling of completion to the middle of the following month[67] meant that only the briefest of opportunities was left until the vagaries of the weather in the English Channel ruled out an attempt before the following spring. By the end of August it was plain to the navy leadership that preparations for transport could not be completed by the new date set, 15 September.[68] Even before the end of July, the Naval Warfare Executive (*Seekriegsleitung*) had, in fact, been advising against trying to carry out the operation in 1940, and putting it off until May the following year at the earliest. On 31 July Raeder conveyed the arguments to Hitler, who acknowledged the difficulties, but deferred a final decision until the Luftwaffe had been given the opportunity to bomb England for eight consecutive days.[69] The order for the indefinite postponement of 'Operation Sealion' was not actually given until 17 September.[70] But in reality, Hitler had always had cold feet about the prospect of a landing in Britain, and possibly accepted as early as 29–31 July, long before the decisive phase of the 'Battle of Britain' was reached, that it would not be possible to go through with the invasion.[71] The decision to attack Russia had swiftly taken the place of the decision to attack Britain. It was seen as less risky.

Grand Admiral Raeder had already left the gathering of military leaders at the Berghof on 31 July 1940, when Hitler announced his decision to prepare for war against the Soviet Union the following spring.[72] But nothing in the announcement could have been unexpected. Raeder had been present ten days earlier when Hitler had first spoken of a possible attack on the Soviet Union.[73] And three days before the announcement, plainly aware of what was in the air, the chief of staff of the Naval Warfare Executive, Rear Admiral Fricke, composed a memorandum outlining his views on conflict with Russia, which Raeder read the following day, 29 July. Fricke accepted that Bolshevism was 'a chronic danger' which had to be 'eliminated one way or the other', and posed no objection to the envisaged German attack, other than acknowledging the sectional disadvantage that naval interests would take a back seat to those of the army and Luftwaffe.[74] At the time of the crucial decision by Hitler on 31 July to prepare for the war against Russia, therefore, the navy raised no objection and had no clearly devised strategic alternative on offer.

Over the following months, however, this was to change. The emergence of a Mediterranean strategy fitted in with the notion of 'war on the periphery' which Jodl had indicated in his memorandum of 30 June. Gradually, a military alternative emerged, though one which demanded a more active diplomacy targeted at Spain, Italy and Vichy France. Meanwhile, however, the operational planning for an attack on Russia was taking shape. This was the sword of Damocles hanging over the timing of any proposed alternative.

During the late summer and the autumn months, the navy's ideas on strategy, as they developed, had much in common with the thinking in Hitler's headquarters. The rapidly fading prospects of an invasion of Britain prompted consideration of other ways to break British resistance. For Jodl, in charge of overall Wehrmacht operational planning, the 'peripheral strategy' he had devised was a crucial concern.[75] But it did not stand in contradiction to an attack on Russia. Rather, it was aimed ideally at forcing Britain to agree to terms and freeing Germany's back for the war on Russia, or, failing that, tying Britain down until victory in the Soviet Union compelled her to yield. For the naval leadership, on the other hand, the 'peripheral' (or Mediterranean) strategy was no temporary solution to facilitate the war in the east. It offered an alternative to that war.

By mid-August, Hitler had agreed on plans (which he thought would meet with Franco's approval) for an operation to take Gibraltar by early 1941 and to support an Italian thrust to the Suez Canal around the same time.[76] Shortly afterwards, the first serious consideration by the navy of a strategy focused on the Mediterranean was signalled by an analysis by Admiral Gerhard Wagner on 29 August of how war against Britain could best be waged, assuming that 'Operation Sealion' was not to take place.[77] Bombing raids and the war in the Atlantic to cut off supplies would not, he took for granted, force a decision over the next months. And by the following spring, British defensive capacity would have improved, perhaps with American support. The best way to attack Britain, he concluded, would be to weaken its Empire through war in the Mediterranean, in tandem with the Italians.

Taking up the thinking in the Wehrmacht High Command, Admiral Wagner pointed out that it would be possible to capture Gibraltar, with Spanish support, and to block the Suez Canal by an offensive thrusting from Libya through Egypt. The result would be to force Britain out of the Mediterranean, which would then be entirely in the hands of the Axis powers. In turn, this would safeguard shipping in the whole of the Mediterranean, ensuring unthreatened imports from north Africa. The position of the Axis powers in the Balkan region would in the process also be greatly strengthened. Turkey would no longer be able to remain neutral, and would fall within their orbit. The raw materials of the Arab countries, Egypt and the Sudan would be available to the Axis. There would be a good platform to weaken British positions in the Indian Ocean through attacks on colonies in east Africa and posing an obvious threat to India itself. The loss of Gibraltar would deprive Britain of one of her most important bases for the war in the Atlantic. Even were Britain to acquire a foothold in the Azores, Madeira or the Canaries, it would scarcely provide compensation. German mastery in the western Mediterranean would enable pressure to be exerted on French north-African colonies and prevent them going over to the Gaullists, and hence to the British side. At the same time, British bases on the west coast of Africa would be endangered.

The Italian navy would, as an additional advantage, be freed to support the German war effort outside the Mediterranean, in the Indian Ocean and the Atlantic, while the Italian army and air force could make further advances against the British, above all in east Africa. A final benefit would be the entry of Spain into the war (seen as implicit in the taking of Gibraltar), thereby widening significantly the basis for German naval warfare in the Atlantic. The memorandum concluded

that the mastery of the Mediterranean will be of decisive strategic significance for the continuation of the war. The operations envisaged for this purpose go well beyond 'interim actions', as they were previously described. Not only will an effective strengthening of the German-Italian war potential and a greatly improved basis for the last decisive struggle against the English Motherland and the sources of strength of the English Empire be attained. [But] since the most sensitive points of the English world empire will be attacked or threatened, there is even the possibility that England will feel compelled to give up further resistance.[78]

This would be all the more likely if American support had been negligible to that point. There was, therefore, no time to be lost. The strategy was in the interests of the navy, Wagner pointed out, ending with the expectation that Raeder would put the proposals to Hitler.

Four days before Raeder could put the case, in his briefing on 6 September, the United States had agreed to provide Great Britain with fifty ageing destroyers. This decision (to which we will return more fully in Chapter 5) was of far greater symbolic than direct military importance, signalling to the German leadership the increased likelihood of a British-American coalition in the not too distant future.[79] Following Raeder's highlighting of the danger to the Portuguese and Spanish islands in the Atlantic and to the French colonies in west Africa which would be posed by American involvement in the war, Hitler gave instructions to prepare for the occupation of the Azores, the Canaries and the Cape Verde Islands to prevent any possible landing by the British and Americans (though naval analysts working on the logistics over the following weeks were not persuaded of the value of such an operation).[80] In the light of the growing 'Problem USA', and asking somewhat disingenuously what Hitler's political and military directives might be in the event of 'Sealion' not taking place, Raeder indeed pressed the argument for a Mediterranean strategy, along the lines of Wagner's memorandum, not as an 'interim' but as a 'main action against England'. He asked for preparations to begin immediately so that they could be implemented before the United States could intervene. Hitler gave orders to that effect. This did not mean, however, that he was signalling approval for a Mediterranean strategy *instead* of the intended strike at the Soviet Union. The proposed Russian campaign – at this time code-named 'Problem S' – came up later in the briefing. When it did, Raeder raised no objections, merely observing that the most suitable time for the navy would be as the ice melted. He added, a point immediately agreed by Hitler, that 'Sealion' should not be attempted at the same time.[81]

By the time of Raeder's briefing with Hitler on 26 September, the case for the Mediterranean strategy had taken on a new urgency in the light of the attack by British and Free French troops (supporters of General Charles de Gaulle) on Dakar a few days earlier. French Morocco, Algeria and Tunisia were endangered as the Vichy regime lost ground to the Gaullist movement in French Equatorial Africa. This concentrated German minds.

Raeder had asked to speak alone with Hitler – a quite exceptional occurrence – and had begun by expressing his wish to go beyond his specific remit in commenting on the progress of the war. He pressed for a more conciliatory approach to the Vichy regime, wishing to upturn previous relations by incorporating the French as full allies in the war against Britain. Waging war together with the French would, argued Raeder, offer the possibility not only of securing the French possessions and their raw materials, but also of forcing Britain out of central Africa and depriving her of the port of Freetown on the western coast, thus causing significant problems for convoy traffic from the south Atlantic, from Latin America and South Africa. It would constitute a big step towards pushing the British out of the Mediterranean. Even before turning to north-west Africa, Raeder had urged Hitler to concentrate on 'waging the struggle against E[ngland] by all available means and without delay, before America can intervene'. The British, he stated, had always regarded the Mediterranean as the key to their world position. He concluded, therefore, that 'the Mediterranean question must therefore be cleared up over the winter'. Gibraltar had to be taken, and even before that the Canaries secured by the Luftwaffe. German support was necessary to help the Italians take the Suez Canal. From there, he saw an advance through Palestine and Syria – which Hitler said would depend upon the French but ought to be possible – as far as Turkey. 'When we reach that point, Turkey will be in our power. The Russian problem will then appear in a different light. Russia basically fears Germany. It is questionable whether an attack on Russia from the north will then be necessary.'[82]

It would have been difficult for Raeder to have been more explicit about the navy's preferred strategy.[83] The Naval Warfare Executive was keen to establish the fact that Hitler had even indicated his basic agreement with the ideas expressed.[84] Two problems nevertheless surfaced at the briefing, if only implicitly.

The first was the size of the fleet. Raeder pointed out (and Hitler concurred) that the fleet was currently too small for the tasks awaiting it if the Mediterranean strategy were to be implemented, particularly if the war were to acquire a global dimension through the entry of the United States. But shipbuilding capacity did not allow for any extension to existing commitments. Obviously, therefore, a maritime strategy was severely hampered from the outset if the fleet was too small to implement it and resources did not allow for any rapid expansion.

The second was the implication for foreign policy, which Hitler touched upon. He told Raeder that after concluding the Tripartite Pact with Japan (which was to be signed the very next day, 27 September), he would have talks with Mussolini and Franco, and would have to decide whether to go with France or Spain. He thought that France was the more likely choice since Spain demanded a great deal (French Morocco) but offered little in return. Britain and the United States had to be excluded from north-west Africa. That much was clear. But France would have to comply with certain territorial demands of Germany and Italy before agreement could be reached on the extent of her African colonial possessions. Though Hitler did not stress the point, this plainly weakened the attractiveness to France of any arrangement with Germany. Moreover, Hitler was cool about Raeder's hopes of engaging the French fleet on Germany's side. He was unprepared to move on this without the approval of his Axis partner Mussolini, who was unlikely to be enamoured of any strengthening of Italy's rival, France, in the Mediterranean. Meanwhile, if Spain were to join the war on the Axis side, the Canaries and perhaps also the Azores and the Cape Verde Islands would have to be secured by the Luftwaffe.[85] In effect, therefore, while agreeing to the Mediterranean strategy in principle, Hitler was making its execution dependent upon the outcome of his negotiations with Mussolini, Franco and Pétain. He was well aware that pleasing all of them would be no easy matter. He recognized, cynically, that squaring the circle of the competing interests would only be possible through 'grandiose fraud'.[86] This would prove beyond even Hitler.

At the time, in late September, the navy's ideas on directing Germany's war effort at the Mediterranean corresponded quite closely to the notion developed in the Foreign Ministry of a 'Continental bloc' of countries formed into a powerful alliance against Britain.[87] The Foreign Minister, Joachim von Ribbentrop himself, no less, had been keen to build up a powerful worldwide alliance, incorporating both the Soviet Union and Japan, which would be ranged against Britain, at the same time neutralizing the United States.[88] Within this grand concept, a western 'Continental bloc' incorporating Vichy France and Spain, alongside Italy, formed a smaller, but vital, component.[89] In military terms, the 'peripheral strategy' as it had developed by early autumn 1940 involved – apart from trying to block British imports – three strands: an Italian-German Middle East offensive; the taking of Gibraltar; and extension of German control over the African coast and the Atlantic islands.[90] Clearly, as had emerged from the Raeder briefing on 26 September, the military potential of such a strategy rested upon important breakthroughs in diplomacy: quite specifically, upon Hitler's ability to come to satisfactory agreements with the leaders of Spain and Vichy France. And this was precisely where they would founder.

IV

As summer turned into autumn, it was still not clear to those close to the hub of power in Germany – including for a while, it seems, Hitler himself – which variant of military strategy should be followed. The setting of different priorities was still possible. That is to say, options were still apparently open.

Hitler's own preference, both ideological and military, was obviously for an early strike on the Soviet Union. That had been plainly established at the end of July. Nothing in the interim indicates that he had changed his mind. But his interest in the 'peripheral strategy' was not simply a ruse. The Russian campaign, which he had initially hoped to launch that autumn, could not take place until spring at the earliest. Meanwhile, however, the worry had deepened that America might join in the war on the British side sooner rather than later.[91] Clearly, Hitler was no less anxious than earlier in the summer to prevent this happening. The most obvious way was to force Britain out of the war. With 'Sealion' now shelved (and effectively, if not nominally, abandoned), a military and diplomatic focus on the Mediterranean offered the best opportunity. Variants of such a strategy were supported, as we have seen, by Jodl (and his deputy Warlimont) in the Wehrmacht Operations Staff, by Raeder and the Naval Warfare Executive and by Ribbentrop, the Foreign Minister. Hitler was prepared for a while to give his backing to the search for a diplomatic opening on the 'periphery' and continued to promote the military planning which would depend upon the success of such a breakthrough. But whereas for Raeder, for Warlimont (if not for Jodl) and even for Ribbentrop the 'peripheral strategy' was viewed as an alternative to the invasion of Russia, for Hitler it was merely a prelude to secure Germany's rear before engaging on the showdown with the Soviet Union which was, in his eyes, both inevitable and alone capable of deciding the final outcome of the war. Hitler's heart was never in the 'peripheral strategy', therefore, as an end in itself. In part at least, this probably explains why his diplomatic effort in the October tour he made to engage in talks with Mussolini, Franco and Pétain proved so unfruitful. He went into them with few illusions.

The central purpose of Hitler's meeting with Mussolini on the Brenner on 4 October was (though he came only slowly to the point) to sound out the Duce about the possibility of bringing France and Spain to a 'common line' and in this way to create 'a Continental coalition against England'.[92] Mussolini had no objections. But both dictators clearly saw that Spain's territorial demands as a price for entering the war – the gain of Morocco and Oran from France as well as Gibraltar from Britain, only the last posing no problem – would be impossible for the French to meet, and would pave the way to Gaullist success (in turn meaning the penetration of British interests) in the vital area of north Africa. Since Mussolini took the opportunity to remind Hitler of Italian demands for French territorial concessions, it was plain that the potential for finding a diplomatic solution which would satisfy the three Mediterranean powers, Italy, France and Spain, was extremely limited. Moreover, Hitler was clearly going to undertake nothing which might damage relations with his Axis partner. So, though friendly, the talks produced nothing tangible to assist the creation of the 'Continental coalition'.[93]

The meeting with Franco at Hendaye on 23 October lacked all promise from the outset.[94] Hitler's bargaining position was weak. He wanted Spain in the war primarily to ease the planned attack on Gibraltar and to bolster the defence of the Atlantic islands off the Iberian coast. But he was not prepared to pay the exorbitant price which he was well aware that Spain would demand: huge supplies of armaments and foodstuffs, and satisfaction of her territorial claims not only on Gibraltar (which was easy to concede) but on Morocco and Oran as well. Hitler's view was probably much the same as the private verdict confided to his diary by Ernst von Weizsäcker, State Secretary in the Foreign Ministry: 'Gibraltar is not worth that much to us.'[95] Germany could not contemplate meeting Franco's material demands. And the territorial concessions, as Hitler had made clear to Mussolini, were out of the question on account of the serious threat they would pose, through the weakening of Vichy France's position, to the hold of the Axis in north Africa. So Hitler had nothing to offer Franco, other than Gibraltar itself. Desirable though the acquisition of Gibraltar was to the Spaniards, it was available only at what, from their point of view, was the high risk of involvement in a war which Franco, despite Hitler's posturing, seriously doubted was as good as won by the Axis. Hitler came away empty-handed.

He fared little better the next day with Pétain, even if the talks were more cordial.[96] Agreement on closer 'cooperation' between France and Germany fell well short of an outright French commitment to join the war against Britain. Discussion remained at the level of generalities. Once again, Hitler's hands were effectively tied, and he had nothing concrete to offer the French. Though Vichy France's entry into the war on Germany's side (and on her terms) made military and strategic sense from the German point of view, it was difficult to make this proposition attractive if mention were made of the mooted tampering with French colonial territory in north Africa in a peace-treaty between the two countries, let alone the expropriation of Briey and Calais on the coast of France itself, as well as Alsace-Lorraine, which the Germans had in mind.[97] Moreover, and a key point for Hitler, closer relations with France would certainly cause Italian hackles to rise, something he wanted at all costs to avoid. In any case, it seems doubtful that Hitler really wanted the French as fully fledged allies.[98] So the talks with Pétain amounted to no more than shadow-boxing.

In short, Hitler could not satisfy Spain without antagonizing France, and could not accommodate the French without upsetting his 'friend' Mussolini. Meanwhile, by the time the two dictators met again, in Florence on 28 October, his 'friend' had, to Hitler's fury, begun his ill-fated invasion of Greece, putting a further sizeable spanner in the works of any strategy revolving around German-Italian military cooperation in the Mediterranean.

Already on his way back from his meetings with Franco and Pétain, Hitler had indicated to his pliant head of Wehrmacht High Command, Field Marshal Wilhelm Keitel, and Jodl that the war against Russia had to take place in the coming year.[99] Soon afterwards, on 4 November, while offering his military leaders a *tour d'horizon* of all current strategic possibilities which concentrated on the Mediterranean and Middle East, Hitler nevertheless remarked that Russia remained the 'great problem of Europe' and that 'everything must be done to be ready for the great showdown'.[100] Evidently, his failure to accomplish any breakthrough in engineering even a limited west-European 'Continental bloc' ranged against Great Britain had confirmed his own prior instinct that the only way to achieve final victory was through attacking and rapidly defeating the Soviet Union. The taking of Gibraltar (together with the Canaries and Cape Verde Islands) was still high on the agenda, and Hitler continued to cherish hopes of Franco joining in the war. If it came to occupying the Azores (in Portuguese possession), and Lisbon demurred, he was prepared if need be, he said, to threaten to send troops into Portugal. But Mussolini's Greek adventure meant that the Italian offensive in Libya had to be deferred, and in consequence also the deployment of German troops in north Africa and the drive to Suez. It was the first clear sign of Hitler's lack of trust in the military capability of his Italian partner.[101]

As Vyacheslav Molotov, the Soviet Commissar for Foreign Affairs, made his way to Berlin for talks with Hitler on 12–13 November, German war strategy was still unclear and undetermined. On the very day that discussions with Molotov began,[102] Hitler put out a military directive which ranged widely over potential fields of combat. The taking of Gibraltar to drive the British from the western Mediterranean and prevent them gaining a foothold on the Iberian peninsula or the Atlantic islands was the dominant item. Political efforts to bring Spain into the war were in train. France would for the time being provide cooperation short of full military engagement in the war against Britain. Deployment of German troops to support the planned Italian offensive against Egypt was put on hold. 'Operation Sea-lion', the invasion of Britain, was not formally abandoned, but no longer figured as anything remotely resembling a military priority. Thanks to Mussolini, preparations had to be undertaken for the occupation of Greece north of the Aegean. But perhaps the most crucial consideration came towards the end of the directive: 'Political discussions with the aim of clarifying Russia's position in the near future are in progress. Whatever the results of these discussions, all preparations already verbally ordered for the east are to be continued.'[103] Though no military option had been closed off by this point, there is every indication that Hitler had become so sceptical about progress in the Mediterranean that he was returning, his ideas confirmed, to the strategy he had already favoured in the summer: the attack on the Soviet Union. The unease prompted in his mind by the Molotov visit was the final determinant.[104]

Raeder's renewed plea, on 14 November, for priority to be given to the Mediterranean, and to a push on Suez, could only fall, therefore, on deaf ears. Hitler made it plain that he was still inclined to press forward with the showdown with Russia. Raeder's recommendation to postpone this until victory over Britain had been attained was by now whistling in the wind. And when Raeder advised caution to obviate a possible occupation of the Portuguese Atlantic islands by the British or Americans, Hitler's reply was characteristic. He was not thinking of the Azores primarily in a defensive, but in an *offensive*, capacity, to allow the stationing of bombers capable of reaching America and therefore compelling the United States to build up air defences rather than providing aid to Britain.[105] It was an indication that the Iberian peninsula and the Spanish and Portuguese Atlantic islands now figured in his thinking as a deterrent to Anglo-American intervention while he was engaged in the east, rather than – as earlier in the summer – as part of a strategy aimed primarily at getting Britain to the conference table.[106]

Only a brief time afterwards, Hitler dispatched his adjutants to find a field headquarters in East Prussia.[107] On 5 December he told Brauchitsch and Halder to prepare the army for an attack on Russia at the end of the coming May.[108] Three days later he heard that renewed attempts to win over Spain had failed. Franco had decided categorically to keep Spain out of the war. Hitler promptly called off preparations to take Gibraltar 'since the political conditions are no longer available'.[109] The operation was abandoned on 9 January, even if Hitler dreamed for some while longer of its possible resurrection.[110] Long before this, the eastward direction of German strategy had been fixed with Hitler's formal directive on 18 December for 'Operation Barbarossa', with the expressed aim, even before the war against Britain was won, 'to crush Soviet Russia in a rapid campaign'.[111] The decision reached in principle on 31 July was now enshrined in a military directive. There would be no turning back. The possibility of an alternative strategy which had briefly presented itself in the late summer and autumn could now definitively be ruled out.[112]

V

Did Hitler, in making his fateful choice in 1940, miss the opportunity of following an alternative course of action which could have led to victory or, at the very least, avoided the calamitous path to defeat that was to follow?

In the light of what we have seen, the question has perhaps to be approached in different ways. The first and most important consideration relates to Hitler's own thinking. *He*, after all, determined policy. Others might seek to influence him. But, ultimately, he decided. Hitler certainly did not think he had missed a chance. In his eyes, despite testing a number of possibilities in the late summer and autumn of 1940, none proved a practicable alternative to the course which he had already regarded by July as the most promising strategy – an attack on the Soviet Union to attain rapid victory before the winter, laying the ground for the wider struggle against Britain and America. This of course fitted his long-established and unchanging ideological convictions. But strategic considerations were paramount in determining the timing.

The United States, he thought, would be ready to enter the war on Britain's side by 1942.[113] He was convinced, therefore, that time was not on Germany's side. Continental dominance, the end of the European war and the impregnability that this would bring had to be attained during 1941 before any conflict with the United States ensued. There is no indication that he considered postponing, let alone cancelling, the invasion of Russia that he had envisaged for spring 1941. The preparations set in train at the end of July 1940 were never halted. By containing Great Britain and deterring the United States, the 'peripheral strategy' offered for him a device for paving the way for the attack on the Soviet Union, not a replacement for it. There is little doubt that he was serious in his support for both the military and diplomatic moves centring on the Mediterranean and the Iberian peninsula. But from his perspective there was nothing to be done during the war to reconcile or overcome the serious differences of interest which separated the main powers in the region, Italy, France and Spain. And since the necessary political framework could not be established, a military strategy for the Mediterranean was unlikely to pay a high dividend.

Without Spain's entry into the war, an assault on Gibraltar, the key to the western Mediterranean, became a different proposition. It could be achieved.[114] But the cost, militarily and politically, would be high. It was no wonder, therefore, that it was called off, once Franco made it clear that Spain would remain neutral. The other main prong of the Mediterranean military strategy, the push to Suez, depended upon the Italians, who soon proved themselves to be the weakest link in the military chain. Once Mussolini had invaded Greece – immediately and unsurprisingly branded by Hitler as an act of stupidity[115] – the prospects of Italian success in north Africa vanished. But with the weakened and stretched Italians up against it in Libya, the push for Suez obviously could not take place. Finally, there was little to be done with France. Until the end of 1940, when Italy's Greek venture had created such difficulties that Mussolini would have welcomed a German-French agreement, the Italians had been reluctant to see any rebuilding of French strength in the Mediterranean and north Africa.[116]

For Hitler, therefore, an alternative to his chosen strategy never posed itself. And what he was aiming for – a prop for his chosen strategy – could not be accomplished. From his point of view, there was, therefore, no chance that was missed.[117]

Did others, close to the heart of strategic planning, think a chance had been missed? The clearest alternative, as we have seen, was thought out by the navy, and it was put before Hitler by Grand Admiral Raeder on more than one occasion. We noted that Raeder did attempt, if not forcefully, to dissuade Hitler from pressing ahead with the attack on Russia. Hitler even agreed with Raeder's proposals for a Mediterranean strategy (though not in place of an eastern campaign). But he changed his tune again, and definitively, in the autumn, particularly following Molotov's visit. There was no question in his eyes about the threat to Germany posed by the Soviet Union. So Raeder, for the reasons already adduced, had no serious prospect of persuading Hitler to change his plans. Hitler never deviated from his conviction that destruction of the Soviet Union in a lightning campaign was the only route to overall victory. Moreover, Raeder, though he favoured another route, did not actually *oppose* the invasion of Russia, even if he was lukewarm about it. And by the time the navy's preferred Mediterranean strategy had taken shape – leaving aside the grandiose utopian dreams of a vast colonial empire that had temporarily seemed so attractive in the wake of the defeat of France – both the political and military framework for its accomplishment were crumbling, leaving the force of Hitler's argument for the Russian option difficult to counter.

In the High Command of the Wehrmacht, the most outspoken advocate of a Mediterranean strategy was Jodl's deputy in the Wehrmacht Operations Staff, and head of its strategic planning section, General Warlimont. But his advancement of proposals to focus Germany's military effort on the drive through north Africa became increasingly futile as the autumn progressed. Warlimont had little support from Jodl, his immediate superior and Hitler's closest adviser on strategic matters. Despite the fact that he himself had put forward the 'peripheral strategy' at the end of June, Jodl, as we have noted, viewed this as the basis for facilitating the strategic goal which Hitler had established: the attack on Russia.[118] Though Jodl was little involved before December 1940 in the detailed preparations for the war in the east, which were the province of the army's High Command, not the Wehrmacht Operations Staff, he did not question Hitler's fundamental decision to attack the Soviet Union. Uncritical belief in Hitler as a military genius, greatly magnified since the triumph over France, ruled out any conceivable opposition from this quarter,[119] and even more so if anything from the toadying Keitel. Whatever the initial doubts of Brauchitsch and Halder, the leaders of the army (which was evidently the key branch of the Wehrmacht in the forthcoming assault on Russia), they were quickly quelled. Both rapidly saw preparation for the war in the east as the outright priority. As Halder had noted on 13 July, they, like Hitler, saw Britain's hopes of Russia as the key to her refusal to come to terms.[120] No serious consideration was given to any alternative, and certainly no alternative strategy could be expected from a Luftwaffe whose leadership was more pro-Nazi than that of the army, and whose Commander-in-Chief was Göring, fearful of losing favour with Hitler and not least for that reason committed to support for an eastern campaign.[121]

The divided organizational structure of the German armed forces in itself hindered the promotion of any serious alternative to Hitler's own plans. As we have already noted, the chiefs of staff of the army, navy and air force, and the chief of the Operations Staff of the Wehrmacht High Command (responsible for overall strategic planning) did not meet in a body to devise strategy. Nor did the commanders-in-chief come together, except in Hitler's domineering presence when genuine discussion was as good as impossible.[122] So the axis of common interest briefly forged between Warlimont's office and naval command both lacked support elsewhere within the armed forces and had no outlet to argue the case for an alternative which could have been put as a reasoned strategy in opposition to Hitler's. Structurally, therefore, it was impossible to construct a coherent alternative strategy. None was ever available to be put forward for consideration. But without that coherent alternative, it is difficult to argue that a chance was missed.[123]

But even if Hitler did not see any other chance, and the armed forces were not capable of presenting a compelling alternative, is it possible, finally, to posit a *theoretical* chance, an option which could have won Germany the war, or at least have prevented such a disastrous outcome, if only the leadership had not been blind to it? Here, of course, we leave historical terrain – that which happened and the actual strategic considerations at the time – and move to the realm of counter-factual speculation. Given the number of possible variables to take into consideration, this rapidly degenerates into little more than an academic guessing game. But, staying with the thought-experiment for a moment, it is possible to imagine that a full German commitment to war in the Mediterranean and north Africa – demanding also a tougher policy towards the Italians, as well as the Spaniards, and full acceptance of the French as fighting allies – at the expense of preparation for a war in the east could have paid dividends in at least the short to medium term, would have given the overall war a different complexion and another possible outcome, and might have avoided the total calamity that came to befall Germany.

The Mediterranean was, it must be admitted, not as vital to Britain's global Empire as Raeder had claimed. Nevertheless, loss of control of the Mediterranean, followed by deprivation of possessions and oil in the Middle East, would unquestionably have been a grave blow. Britain and her Empire would certainly have been seriously weakened, especially if national independence movements in the Middle East and India had, as most probably would have been the case, gained in strength and confidence as a result of British military setbacks. And it is far from certain that the United States, where even as it was Roosevelt had to struggle for months against strong isolationist tendencies, would have rushed to support a weakened Britain. The Japanese would doubtless have shown little hesitation in exploiting British discomfiture in the Far East, so that the Americans, instead of seeing the Atlantic as the main concern, might have found their attention diverted towards the Pacific at an earlier stage than was historically the case.

Whether, given such a bleak scenario, Britain would have continued to hold out, or would have discarded the Churchill government and looked for peace terms with Germany is a moot point. With Britain subordinated, the European continent and north Africa under German control and the Americans preoccupied with Japan, the 'Russian question' would have been seen in a different light. There would have been less urgency, less immediate strategic necessity, to crush the Soviet Union in 1941. The detestation of Bolshevism would have remained. But Stalin's regime would have appeared less of a threat, more capable of containment, and, therefore, perhaps not worth a dangerous military gamble in a lightning war of aggression, thus weakening Hitler's own case for the eastern war in the eyes of his military leaders.

But a Mediterranean strategy, even if followed through, would probably still have led at some point to the war of the continents which Hitler envisaged. Most likely this would have come sooner rather than later, with Germany, holding down massive imperial conquests by little more than brute force and tyranny, still unable to contend in the long run with the immensity of American resources. Conceivably, if circumstances had become favourable, the Soviet Union would have taken the opportunity to join in on the Allied side. Germany would have then faced the feared war on two fronts after all. A race to build nuclear weapons would have taken place and, as indeed happened, would most probably have been won by American scientists (some of German descent). An imaginable outcome of such a contest would have been the dropping of American atom bombs on Berlin and Munich, rather than Hiroshima and Nagasaki.

In the real world of Hitler, rather than the counter-factual world of fantasy and imagination, it seems clear that no chance was missed in 1940. Given the leadership which Germany had, and the very reason she was facing a strategic dilemma in the summer and autumn of 1940 in the first place, the attack on the Soviet Union was indeed the only practicable way open. It was Hitler's decision, though the blame for it does not stop at his door, as some postwar apologetics would have had it. It goes beyond him and ranges widely. The regime's military elite, though with extensive backing both among other power-groupings and within the German population, had supported the policies of a leader who had taken Germany into a gamble for world power with the odds in the long run stacked heavily against her and without a 'get-out clause'. By 1940, unable to end the war, the only option for Hitler, and for the regime which had helped to put him in that position, was to gamble further, to take, as always, the bold, forward move, one that would sweep over the Russians 'like a hailstorm' and make the world 'hold its breath'.[124] It was madness, but there was method in it.

3

Tokyo, Summer and Autumn 1940

Japan Decides to Seize the 'Golden Opportunity'

Seize this golden opportunity! Don't let anything stand in the way!   Hata Shunroku, Army Minister, 25 June 1940

Never in our history has there been a time like the present, when it is so urgent to plan for the development of our national power . . . We should grasp the favourable opportunity that now presents itself.   Statement of the army's position, 4 July 1940

In the Far East another war altogether was raging. It had started in July 1937, more than two years before the European war, and had seen barbarities inflicted by Japanese troops on the Chinese civilian population that matched in their appalling inhumanity those suffered by Poles at the hands of the conquering Germans from autumn 1939. 'The China Incident', as the Japanese invariably called the war with China, was completely separate from the European war that began with the German invasion of Poland on 1 September 1939. However, the interests of the European 'great powers' and the United States in China inevitably meant that the bitter conflict had grave international implications from the outset. No end to this war was in sight by spring 1940, when the German western offensive overran the Low Countries and France and brought Great Britain almost to her knees. It was in the wake of Hitler's astonishing military triumphs in western Europe that Japan, seeking to exploit the weakness of those countries, took the fateful decisions to expand into south-eastern Asia (where Britain, France and the Netherlands held significant colonial possessions) and to forge a pact with the Axis powers, Germany and Italy. In so doing, over these crucial months Japan made choices which greatly increased the risk of her involvement in armed conflict not only with the European powers, but also with the United States. The road to Pearl Harbor was as yet far from being a one-way street. But summer 1940 was the time when the Japanese leadership took vital steps that would lead eventually to blending the two separate wars in Europe and in China into one huge global conflagration.

I

The war with China, which embroiled Japan ever more from 1937 onwards, lay at the heart of the course of action that would culminate in her willingness to risk all by attacking the United States of America. The immediate prehistory of this war went back six years, to the Japanese attack on Chinese troops in Manchuria in September 1931 – the 'Mukden Incident', in Japanese parlance – which not only marked a turning point in international relations in the Far East, but also signalled the changing basis of power within Japan.

There was, however, a longer prehistory. This was rooted in Japan's ambitions to become a great power in the Far East, with the trappings of a colonial empire and enhanced international status. Such ambitions dated back to the late nineteenth century, as Japan, under Emperor Meiji, was undergoing rapid modernization, accommodating western methods to Japanese culture. Wars, in each case started by Japanese aggression, against China in 1894–5 and Russia in 1904–5, had established Japan's position as the dominant power in east Asia. Within Asia, Japan's successes were frequently interpreted as blows against western domination of the region. In reality, Japan was laying the foundations for her own imperialist quest for mastery. Japan had gained possession of Korea, Taiwan, the southern part of the island of Sakhalin, and important leasehold rights together with control of a 700-mile stretch of railway in southern Manchuria. Japan had also, in 1901, been granted the right to keep troops in Peking and a number of other cities in China, ostensibly to protect diplomats and the Japanese minority population in such areas. China, its centralized government in an advanced state of disintegration, later extended the concessions to Japan in southern Manchuria. During the First World War, which she had entered on the Allied side with an eye to gaining German possessions in the Far East, Japan exploited China's weakness and political disorder to gain recognition of her position in southern Manchuria and the adjacent region of eastern Inner Mongolia, and to extend her leasehold and railway rights. Japan even went so far as to demand, in 1915, the establishment of joint Chinese-Japanese police forces in China and the acceptance of Japanese advisers in political, economic and military affairs. China would as a consequence have been effectively reduced to the status of a Japanese colony.

Through allied support for China, it was fended off on this occasion. But it left smouldering resentment and animosity among the Chinese population, and it foreshadowed Japan's attempt to dominate China some twenty years later.

In 1917 Japan reached an agreement with the United States, accepting the principle of the 'Open Door' (established in 1899 to allow all nations equal access to trading ports in China) in return for American recognition of her 'special interests' in China. There was ambiguity in the agreement, but the Japanese took it to mean American acquiescence in Japan's position in southern Manchuria. By the time the war ended, Japan had extended her influence in the region – one rich in mineral resources – and emerged strengthened. Meanwhile, any semblance of centralized state control in an enfeebled China had collapsed. The country was wracked by political disorder.

A combination of international pressure and internal opposition to Japanese rule in Korea and encroachments in China encouraged Japan, however, to adopt a more conciliatory approach in the 1920s. The framework for the interwar international order in the Pacific region was laid down in 1921–2, at the Washington Conference. A nine-power treaty – signed, apart from Japan and China, by Britain, France, Italy, Belgium, the Netherlands, Portugal and the United States – upheld China's independence and integrity.[1] China, it was hoped, would evolve through international cooperation to a stability which would reduce tension in the region and be of economic advantage to the western powers. The 'Washington system', as it was dubbed, by and large worked during the 1920s. Japan retained her moderate course. In 1928 Chinese nationalists, under Chiang Kai-shek, were able to establish a central government in Nanking, and, through foreign (mainly American) capital, started to build transport and communications networks. China, despite her continuing travails, was on the way to incorporation in an international economic order based upon the 'Open Door' principle which the western powers, most of all the United States, had a vested interest in upholding.

Within Japan, however, the voices of those who saw the 'Washington system' as a threat to the country's future were becoming more voluble, and gaining greater public support. Mounting social unrest, as the world economic crisis prompted by the Wall Street Crash in October 1929 began to bite, provided the backdrop to anti-western feeling. Ideas of autarky – maximizing economic self-sufficiency to reduce dependence on western capitalism – were nourished.[2] At the same time, boycotts of Japanese goods instigated by Chiang Kai-shek's nationalist regime in China, and infringements of the economic rights in Manchuria acquired by Japan since 1905, inflamed animosity towards the Chinese within Japan. Anger rebounded onto the Japanese government. Radical voices demanding stronger government and a more assertive foreign policy gained support. Within the military, too, dissatisfaction with what was seen as a compliant stance in international affairs, harmful to Japanese interests, had intensified. The discontent and restlessness were most evident among younger, middle-ranking officers, who were becoming increasingly difficult to control by the army General Staff in Tokyo.

Some of the most radical adherents of change, aiming to break the constraints imposed on Japan's foreign policy by her dependence upon the western powers and their liberal-capitalist principles, were to be found among the officers of the Kwantung Army, which since its creation in 1906 had guarded Japan's Manchurian possessions. On 18 September 1931, with tension running high, some of these officers engineered an attack by Japanese troops on night manoeuvres on local Chinese forces at Mukden in southern Manchuria.[3] Though the attack had not been ordered by the Japanese government, it rapidly gained retrospective sanction in Tokyo, an early indication not only of how little control the civilian government could now exert over the army, but also of its readiness to back arbitrary and dangerous initiatives, and thereby to accede in the dynamic set in train by autonomous actions on the part of the military.

What initially seemed a minor incident proved a turning point. It ended the postwar cooperation in the Far East embedded in the 'Washington system', began Japanese international isolation, and inflamed still further both anti-Chinese and anti-western feeling within Japan. Chinese appeals for international help against Japan fell on deaf ears. In the throes of the Depression, western countries looked to their own interests. The League of Nations failed its first major test. No sanctions were imposed upon Japan. It was an early manifestation of the weakness that was soon to be fully exposed, both in east Asia and in Europe. The United States, not a member of the League, concurred in avoiding denunciation of Japan. Encouraged, the Kwantung Army extended their aggression, retrospectively backed, as earlier, by the Tokyo government and public opinion within Japan. The bombing of Chinchow in south-west Manchuria, on the border with China proper, on 8 October 1931 finally stung the Council of the League of Nations into action – but only as far as setting up a commission, headed by Lord Lytton, a British peer, to examine the causes of the conflict and arrive at recommendations for a settlement. By the time the Lytton Commission reported in September 1932, condemning the Japanese action but also exhorting China to acknowledge Japan's interests in the region, a puppet government had been installed in Manchuria. The newly named Manchukuo was only nominally an independent state. In reality, it was totally under Japanese control.

Amid widespread international condemnation and refusal to accept the status of Manchukuo, Japan left the League of Nations in March 1933. This sealed her isolation. At home, the aggression in Manchuria and establishment of Manchukuo had been greeted with much rejoicing, both among the general population and within the elites. Japan's international isolation fed resentment and defiance. Propaganda had no difficulty in persuading the general public of the justness of Japan's cause and the unfairness of western attitudes (though ironically the Japanese were modelling their own imperialist claims in no small measure on the British Empire they so resented). Politically, the country moved further to the right. Ideologies emphasizing 'national renovation', solidarity, devotion to the Emperor (portrayed as a 'living god') and traditional Japanese culture and mythology gained ground. Parliamentary government had been ended in May 1932, and a Cabinet of national unity formed, mostly comprising military leaders and bureaucrats. Increasingly, the military (though there were significant internal divisions within the army) were forcing the pace, while civilian representatives of government, their effective power reduced, for the most part reacted, usually in compliant fashion, to the pressure.

The Kwantung Army remained at the forefront of the radicalizing drive.[4] Fighting with Chinese troops continued. By May 1933, the borders of Manchukuo had been extended to the Great Wall, little more than forty miles from Peking. Two years later, Chiang Kai-shek's national government felt compelled to withdraw its troops from the border areas south of the Great Wall, including from Peking itself. Puppet governments under Chinese warlords were installed to control the region. By this juncture, Japanese policy was focused upon consolidation of the gains in Manchukuo and stabilization of relations with Chiang Kai-shek's nationalist government in its capital of Nanking. However, the potential for further conflict remained close to the surface.

By the middle of 1936 the Japanese government was ready to define the 'Fundamental Principles of National Policy', along revised lines.[5] The definition lacked precision at this stage, and attempted to incorporate, without resolving their possible tensions and contradictions, the competing aspirations of the army and navy. The underlying consideration was the need to undermine the 'policy of aggression' by the great powers in east Asia. This was to be done by securing Japan's power on the east Asian continent, by fortifying defences and economic strength in Manchukuo to eliminate 'the menace of the Soviet Union', and by expansion into the South Seas. This was the first time that southern expansion had been expressed as a policy guideline. Though still no more than a vague expression of intent, this reflected the growing stridency within the navy, which had retained its high status since the war with Russia in the early years of the century and had successfully pressed in December 1934 for the abrogation of the naval arms limitation treaty signed with Great Britain and the United States in 1922 and renewed in 1930. The aims of foreign policy, as laid out in the summer of 1936, were to be attained peacefully. But army forces were to be built up in Manchukuo and Korea to the level where they could 'deliver the initial blow to Soviet forces in the Far East at the outbreak of hostilities'. Naval rearmament would enable 'command of the Western Pacific against the United States Navy' to be secured. The need for good relations with Great Britain was emphasized, as long as Britain recognized the Japanese vital interest in China and avoided joining the United States, the Soviet Union and China in applying pressure upon Japan. At the same time, particularly on account of her anti-Communist stance, good relations with Germany were to be built up.

Despite the expressions of peaceful intentions, a possible collision course with Britain and the United States was implicit in Japanese policy. The army, meanwhile, stayed wedded to the need for preparation for a war against the Soviet Union, to remove the threat from the north. Japan had by now plainly turned her back on the limitations of the 'Washington system' of 1922. As if to advertise the fact, and clearly indicating the desire for good relations with Germany, the country which had torn up the postwar order in Europe, Japan joined the Anti-Comintern Pact in November 1936, agreeing that neither she nor Germany would provide any assistance to the Soviet Union, should either country become involved in war with her.

By 1937 the need for a common front against Japan, reflecting heightened anti-Japanese feeling, temporarily superseded the bitter divisions between nationalists and Communists in China. Within Japan, the army backed away from the prospect of war with China, while the civilian government reverted, for a short period, to considerations of solving its economic problems not through further territorial expansion, but through a policy promoting industrialization, external trade and international cooperation. Such views could not prevail. They ran counter to the thinking, by now deeply embedded, and not just in the military, that Japan's future lay in economic autarky secured by force of arms. Interference by the army, or groups within it, in the running of government had mounted since the 'Mukden Incident'. An attempted coup of army militants, who murdered several government ministers, had failed in February 1936 and brought severe punishment of those involved.[6] But the consequence was further government instability. The hand of the army in internal affairs had nonetheless emerged still further strengthened.[7] Policy towards China was at the root of its increasing influence. In January 1937 military pressure forced the government to resign. Its replacement lasted only a few months before giving way to the formation in June of a new Cabinet, now headed by a Prime Minister, Prince Konoe Fumimaro, who had good connections to the military and favoured a policy on the Asian continent requiring control of land and natural resources, seen as justified for a 'have-not' nation fighting for its survival.[8] This was the climate in which a minor and unplanned incident – in itself no more than a skirmish – on the night of 7 July 1937, near the Marco Polo bridge south of Peking, when shots were fired by Chinese soldiers on Japanese troops, marked the opening of what would soon develop into full-scale war between Japan and China.[9]

Some senior figures in the army General Staff tried to contain the incident. Their concern was that any escalation leading to prolonged Japanese involvement in China would hinder rearmament to counter the Soviet Union. Briefly, it looked as if the incident might indeed peter out without the danger expanding. But in the prevailing circumstances a truce locally agreed on 11 July had little chance of succeeding. Both in China and in Japan, the governments were under pressure to act from nationalist sentiment which they themselves had stirred up and manipulated. Chiang Kai-shek saw the Japanese aggression as an opportunity he could exploit to expand western support for his cause. For their part, weighty factions in the Japanese military portrayed the incident as a chance to defeat and subjugate China through swift and powerful action. The Army Minister, Sugiyama Gen, and chief of the Imperial Staff, Prince Kan'in Kotohito, told the Emperor that a war with China could be successfully concluded within two or three months.[10] Such opinion prevailed.

The civilian government backed a decision to expand the conflict. Towards the end of July, major troop reinforcements were sent to China. Within two days Peking and Tientsin in the north of the country were occupied. A horrific atrocity in Tungchow, where Chinese troops slaughtered more than two hundred Japanese and Korean civilians, many of them women and children, on 29–30 July, then sparked predictable fury within Japan. The Emperor's brother, Prince Takamatsu, commenting on the army's mood, noted in his diary: 'we're really going to smash China so that it will be ten years before they can stand up straight again.'[11]

By the middle of August, the fighting had spread to Shanghai, where Japanese troops, planes and ships were bombed by Chinese aircraft. Heavy Japanese reinforcements were sent to the area. The Japanese Army Minister now spoke of 'total war'. The government started to refer to the conflict with China as 'holy war'.[12] Konoe, the Prime Minister, spoke of the 'spiritual mobilisation' of the nation.[13]

By early November, as their demoralized troops started to withdraw from Shanghai in the direction of Nanking, the nationalist capital, almost a quarter of a million Chinese civilians (including many women and children) had been killed in the city.[14] Japanese dead and wounded totalled around 40,000. Japanese troops pursued the fleeing Chinese army and civilian refugees to Nanking. When the city fell on 13 December, prompting great celebration in the streets of Tokyo, Japanese soldiers went on the rampage. At least 200,000 Chinese civilians and prisoners of war were murdered in six weeks. Foreign observers put the number of rapes of women and girls of all ages at around a thousand per day.[15]

Reports of the orgy of killing and rape shocked the world. As the horror of Nanking was beginning, revulsion at Japanese behaviour had already been aroused by the shelling of Chinese refugees, then the bombing by trigger-happy Japanese pilots of an American gunboat, the *Panay*, anchored on the Yangtze river north of Nanking, with diplomats and journalists on board. Japanese soldiers had even fired on the last lifeboat making its way to shore from the burning ship. The government in Tokyo rapidly apologized for such a grave error and agreed to pay substantial reparations. But lasting damage was done. Public opinion in the west, quite especially in America, became intensely anti-Japanese. Sympathy with China, unsurprisingly, grew in response. There had always been an idealistic component of American commercial exploitation of Chinese markets through the 'Open Door' policy. Japanese atrocities now intensified the feeling in the United States that support for China was a moral cause.[16]

Not that this translated at this stage into much more than symbolic gestures. Moral condemnation of Japan went hand in hand with political inaction.[17] President Roosevelt associated the United States with the League of Nations' denunciation of Japanese aggression, but vetoed proposals of economic sanctions against Japan. He did, however, take the first steps towards coordinating the exchange of intelligence between the American and British navies in the Pacific, a sign that the Japanese threat was now regarded as serious.

The Japanese government had shown through its swift attempt to make amends for the *Panay* incident that it was anxious at this stage to avoid confrontation with the United States. But this did not go so far as tempering its policy in China. Extremely harsh terms, effectively imposing Japanese control over China, were offered to Chiang Kai-shek after the fall of Nanking.[18] He could not possibly accept them. Japan's stance now hardened still further. Diplomatic relations with the Chinese nationalist government were severed in January 1938. The Japanese Prime Minister, Prince Konoe, chillingly announced the intention to 'eradicate' Chiang Kai-shek's regime.[19]

During the following months, the Japanese army greatly extended its control in China – and in highly brutal fashion. Huge swathes of the country were now under Japanese rule. But by the end of 1938, with 600,000 troops based in China, Japanese resources were stretched. Casualties were mounting. More than 62,000 Japanese soldiers had been killed since the start of the conflict.[20] And Chiang, who had moved his capital to Chungking in the west of China, was bowed but far from defeated. The cruelty of the occupying army saw to it that nationalist resistance stiffened rather than diminished, helped by material aid from America, Britain, France and the Soviet Union. For Japan, the high water mark of the war had been reached. It was now stalemate.

In November 1938 the Japanese government had reformulated its war aims. The basic objective was stipulated as the creation of 'a new order for ensuring permanent stability in East Asia'.[21] The uncompromising stance adopted the previous January was partially modified. Cooperation with Chinese nationalists was now seen as possible. But the price was recognition of Manchukuo, cessation of anti-Japanese activities, collaboration in the defence against Communism (meaning, in effect, the acceptance of Japanese troops within China) and acknowledgement of Japanese economic exploitation of northern China and Inner Mongolia. It was an initiative directed at splitting the nationalist camp by winning over Chiang Kai-shek's rival, Wang Ching-wei, to the Japanese side. Wang, who broke with Chiang Kai-shek in December 1938, was ready to collaborate, advocating peace with Japan on the basis of a united and strong anti-Communist policy. He would eventually be installed, by March 1940, as head of a Japanese client government based in Nanking. But, unsurprisingly, Chiang remained implacable. Chinese nationalists continued overwhelmingly to support him. Unable to attain complete victory, and equally unable to extract itself from the conflict, Japan was bogged down in a political and military quagmire of her own making.

Relations with the United States had meanwhile deteriorated still further. Responding in November 1938 to a protest at the infringement of American rights on the basis of the 'Open Door' in China, the government in Tokyo explicitly rejected the principles of the 'Washington system'.[22] Soon afterwards, a loan – the first of many to come – of $25 million by the United States signalled the American determination to prop up the nationalist regime of Chiang Kai-shek. On 26 July 1939, following numerous protests at Japanese actions in China, the United States announced the abrogation of a vital commercial treaty with Japan, dating back to 1911 and due to lapse in 1940. Since almost a third of Japan's imports came from the United States, this was a serious matter.[23] It gave warning that economic sanctions could be the consequence of further aggression. Japan depended quite especially upon the import of scrap metal and oil from America. If these were to be cut off, Japan's war effort could hold out for no more than six months.[24]

Japanese actions were also harming relations with the European powers. The occupation of strategic bases in the South China Sea – Hainan Island, off the southern coast of China, in February 1939, then, a month later, the uninhabited Spratly Islands, a remote archipelago several hundred miles still further south – gave an indication of Japan's intention to extend her influence southwards. The islands were nominally Chinese possessions, but the move was plainly of concern to Britain, France and the Netherlands, each possessing colonial interests in the region.[25] The Dutch colonial regime in the East Indies responded by reducing imports from Japan. Britain and France were further alienated by a Japanese blockade of their concession in Tientsin in June. Soon afterwards, Japanese forces became involved in serious clashes with Soviet troops, arising from skirmishes near Nomonhan, in the north-west of Manchukuo, on the border with Outer Mongolia. The outcome was a notable military setback, and a warning to Japan not to underrate the Red Army. By the time the fighting ceased, with a truce in mid-September, the Kwantung Army had lost around 17,000 men.

One possible way out of the growing international isolation would have been to form an alliance with Germany. Influenced by Ribbentrop, Hitler's regime had in early 1938 reversed its earlier backing for China, and voiced its support for Japan.[26] The presumption that Japan would win the war in China, and her fervent opposition to the Soviet Union, were important determinants of the change of policy. Recognition of Manchukuo in May followed as a tangible indicator of the new German position. But, wary of alienating the western democracies by casting in their lot with Nazi Germany, the Japanese government avoided overtures to convert the Anti-

Comintern Pact into a full alliance. Since in practice Japan did nothing to reduce the antagonism with the west, but avoided cementing closer ties with Germany, the diplomatic isolation continued. It worsened dramatically towards the end of August 1939 with the announcement of the sensational Nazi–Soviet Pact. In an instant, Japan saw her only powerful would-be friend in Europe in alliance with her arch-enemy to the north. Marquis Kido Koichi, a leading courtier and soon to become the Emperor's closest counsellor as Lord Privy Seal, recorded in his diary that he was 'astonished at this extremely treacherous act'.[27] In bewilderment at the 'inexplicable new conditions' in Europe, the Japanese government resigned en bloc.[28] A few days later, Europe was at war.

The European war inevitably affected Japan, despite her neutrality. Some, both in the army and in the civilian government, favoured a reversal of previous policy by seeking a pragmatic arrangement with the Soviet Union, as Germany had done. They presumed the moment for a new world order, overthrowing the previous dominance by the European democracies and the United States, was dawning. The major powers in Europe were likely to be Germany, Italy and the Soviet Union. It was in Japan's interests, they argued, to ally herself with both Germany and the Soviet Union. As regards the war in China, an alliance with the Soviet Union, it was suggested, could eliminate Soviet supplies to China.[29]

Advocates of a new policy towards the Soviet Union still remained, however, in a minority. Dominant opinion in the government preferred an attempt to improve relations with the United States, conscious that the European war might bind America and Britain more closely together. But since Japan was unwilling to make any serious concessions in her demands on China, this course promised little success. In fact, American policy towards Japan was hardening. Increased aid to China was seen as a way of weakening Japan and reducing the possible threat in the Pacific.

China remained, therefore, the linchpin. As long as the war with China continued, Japanese resources and manpower would be stretched to the maximum. And deteriorating relations with the United States posed a sharp threat to the oil and scrap metal necessary to continue the war. But as long as Japan remained wedded to her territorial conquests and domination, there could be no end to the war, therefore no improvement in relations with the United States, and no diminution of the continued threat to raw materials. With the United States fully backing Chiang Kai-shek and the Japanese government supporting Wang Ching-wei's puppet regime, the impasse was set to continue. This was the position when Hitler's conquest of Denmark and Norway in April, then the overrunning of the Netherlands and Belgium in May, culminating in the remarkable victory over France in June, transformed the scene in Europe. With only Britain, of the major belligerent powers, still withstanding Hitler – and that, apparently, likely to be of short duration – the Japanese government saw new opportunities to resolve her own problems.

II

Japan by 1940 was neither a democracy nor a dictatorship. Perhaps factionalized authoritarianism – not the contradiction in terms that it might at first sight seem to be – could serve as an abstract label. But it conveys little of the complexity and convoluted character of governance as it had developed since the beginning of constitutional rule in 1889 and as it had been transformed in the 1920s and 1930s under the impact of mass politics, domestic turbulence, diplomatic pressures and war. The popular image of a monolithic system of rule under the command of the Emperor greatly distorts reality.[30]

The system of government that had emerged in the late nineteenth century, as Japan was rapidly modernizing, retained strong oligarchic and bureaucratic traits. The constitution of 1889 looked to Europe (and particularly Germany) for its models. It established a parliament comprising an elected House of Representatives with three hundred seats and a House of Peers consisting of five hundred titled court, government and military officials. At the same time, the Emperor held – at least in theory – full personal power. As in Germany, government ministers were appointed by the Emperor and were responsible to him, not to parliament. Frequently, they were not drawn from the political parties. Of notable significance, the military General Staff were specifically granted an independent 'right to supreme command', and were responsible directly to the Emperor. Parliament, elected at first by only about 1 per cent of the population, was able to pass legislation and to approve or veto the state budget, but it could exercise only weak controls over the executive powers of the government and the military. The old oligarchic families, owning much of the country's land and wealth, retained great influence.[31]

Even so, once instituted, mass politics and constitutional representation were unstoppable. As in Europe, they grew in importance, particularly after the First World War. Political parties, the more conservative Seiyukai and the more liberal Minseito, came to represent the vast majority of voters: all males over 25, following a franchise reform of 1925. But communist, socialist and fascist ideologies, imported from Europe into a Japanese setting, also found supporters as economic crisis, social unrest and political violence (which saw the assassinations of two prime ministers and other prominent figures in government and business alongside a number of leading intellectuals in the early 1930s) afflicted interwar Japan.[32] Reflecting the domestic turbulence, governments were unstable and of short duration, with fifteen changes of Prime Minister between November 1921 and June 1937.[33]

The impact of the 'Manchurian Incident' after 1931 and the rapid recovery from the Depression, mainly through major state stimulation of steel, chemical and construction industries and a huge expansion in the military budget (taking up three-quarters of government expenditure by 1937[34]), was to curtail the role of parliamentary parties and pluralist politics. Governments now usually had a majority of Cabinet members representing no political party.[35] Above all, the influence of the military grew sharply. Once the war in China had begun, better coordination of the civilian and military input into decisions became necessary. In late 1937, two types of meeting, Liaison Conferences and Imperial Conferences, were instituted to try to achieve this.

Liaison Conferences were held every few days and, in foreign affairs, effectively supplanted the Cabinet, which now mainly dealt with domestic matters. Key members of the Cabinet – the Prime Minister, Foreign Minister, War Minister and Navy Minister, and occasionally other ministers whose expertise was specifically required – joined the army and navy chiefs of staff and their deputies from the Supreme Command. The meetings took place in a small conference room. Participants sat in a circle of armchairs around the Prime Minister. No one, however, presided in any directive sense, and discussion tended often to be diffuse, a feature of a specifically Japanese way of using often oblique language in a lengthy process of edging towards a decision in which great emphasis was attached to unanimity.[36] For a while, the Conferences were discontinued and replaced by Four- or Five-Minister Conferences involving merely leading government ministers. The problem of lack of coordination returned. The absence of the chiefs of staff proved an inevitable handicap, and the Liaison Conferences were re-established in 1940.

Important decisions reached by a Liaison Conference had to be ratified by an Imperial Conference. The same personnel attended, though were now joined by the President of the Privy Council, and the meeting took place in the presence of the Emperor. Documents registering the decisions of the Liaison Conference lay before the Imperial Conference. They had been prepared by General Staff officers, then circulated to the various ministries for revision and amendment prior to approval by the leading figures in the Liaison Conferences. Now, in front of the Emperor, the Prime Minister and each of the other ministers, then the chiefs of staff, read prepared statements. The Emperor did not usually speak a word, though questions on his behalf were raised by the President of the Privy Council. The Imperial Conference, if largely ceremonial in procedure, was of importance. Once the Emperor felt able to give his sanction to the course of action proposed, thereby legitimating it, the decision was seen as binding on all those present. This made it extremely difficult to alter.[37]

Decisions, particularly those related to foreign policy and war, did not, then, bear the clear stamp of the individual's will, as was the case in the German, Italian and Soviet dictatorships. But nor could the central body of civilian government, the Cabinet, decide, as happened in parliamentary democracies. As we have noted, the Cabinet, itself appointed by the Emperor and not dependent upon parliament, could not take key decisions without accommodating (and, increasingly, acceding to) the wishes of the military staffs. And these, responsible only to the Emperor, had wide-ranging autonomy of action. The inclusion in the Cabinet of senior military officers serving as War and Navy Ministers did not diminish this independence. They themselves had the right of direct report to the Emperor if they wished to bypass the Prime Minister. In any case, their responsibilities were chiefly concerned with personnel and administrative aspects of the armed forces. The crucial areas, strategic and operational planning, were the prerogative of the Supreme Command – army and navy chiefs of staff, whose authority derived from the Emperor alone.[38]

In practice, the military seldom spoke with one voice. Its wishes and demands mainly reflected the often different and competing interests of factions within the army and navy. Ultimately, therefore, decisions on weighty matters of foreign policy arose from 'group bargaining' – the outcome of 'inducing coalitions in support of preferred options'. There was extensive discussion, debate and 'bargaining' – with greater 'leverage' deployed by military spokesmen than others – before a decision emerged, almost by a process of osmosis.[39] But great emphasis was laid upon the eventual 'consensus' behind the decision, which, with the Emperor's approval, then became effectively sacrosanct.

Whatever the factional differences, variants of weighting, political disagreements or alternative strategies, by 1940 a large degree of ideological consensus had come to prevail among Japan's power-elites. During the 1930s, arising from the domestic divisions and disunity of the previous decade, and to the backcloth of the 'Manchurian Incident' then the China War, a new nationalism had been forged that bears more than a passing resemblance, though in Japanese cultural guise, to contemporary European fascisms. Its 'spiritual' focus was the Emperor, as embodiment of the Japanese nation. Its vehicle was militarism.

From the accession to the imperial throne of the 25-year-old Emperor Hirohito in 1926, and especially in the wake of the lavish and spectacular celebrations of his ritual enthronement and 'deification' two years later, the cult of the Emperor was elevated to the keystone of the new doctrine. Hirohito's reign was designated that of the 'Showa' Emperor, symbolizing, ironically in the light of what was to follow, the 'illustrious peace' of the new era. The reign of his father, Emperor Yoshihito, between 1912 and 1926 (during which Hirohito had acted as regent since 1920) had been associated with westernization and democratization. A sense of national decadence had gained ground as domestic crises beset Japan. Democracy and party politics, as in Weimar Germany, were seen by increasing numbers only to indicate a weak and divided nation. Commitment to the 'Washington system' of international politics, the chief beneficiaries of which were seen as the western imperialist powers, merely confirmed the weakness. At its centre, the feebleness was epitomized by the frail and ill figure of the Taisho Emperor (Yoshihito). Hirohito's reign was portrayed as the inauguration of an era which would revert to and build upon the heroic age of his grandfather, Emperor Meiji, who from 1867 to 1912 had presided over the creation of modern Japan, the great triumphs over China and Russia between 1895 and 1905 and the beginnings of overseas Japanese dominance in east Asia.

The essence of the new nationalist doctrine was the so-called 'imperial way' (kodo), which envisaged a Japan returning to the 'true values' of the nation's long (and legendary) history, overcoming the subjugation to western influence and realizing her destiny and mission, as a superior people and culture, to dominate east Asia.[40] It offered the justification for naked imperialist conquest whose underlying aim, pared of its dogma, was the elevation of Japan to a great power with lasting domination based upon the securing of raw materials in Manchuria and north China, then throughout south-east Asia. The manipulation of public opinion through heavy propaganda, coupled with the ruthless suppression of open opposition, meant that elite doctrines became transmitted to the population. It was not difficult to whip up nationalist and imperialist fervour during the crises in Manchuria, then China. The manufactured chauvinism then applied its own pressure to the actions of the elites. Perhaps of greatest importance, the values of the new nationalism permeated down into the officer ranks, and from there to the rank and file, of the army and navy. For the most part at lower levels than that of the High Command itself, a leaven of overt, highly aggressive and risky militarism was being formed beneath the ideological umbrella of the 'imperial way'. By 1940, therefore, nationalist-imperialist ideas had developed into an ideology of supremacy and expansion which, at both elite and popular levels, in the civilian population and, quite notably, in the middle ranks of the military, had become hegemonic. That is to say, whatever operational or tactical differences existed, no other ideology offered serious competition.

There were, of course, those who opposed the new ideological and political trends. The Emperor's long-standing trusted adviser Saionji Kinmochi, a cultured, old-style liberal-conservative who had earlier in his life spent ten years living in Paris where he studied law at the Sorbonne, was one who strongly counselled preserving close ties with Great Britain and America, favoured coming to terms with Chiang Kai-shek and abhorred the growing proximity to Germany and Italy.[41] But Saionji had been born in 1849. He was not only old (he would die before 1940 was out), but, as he realized, out of tune with the dominant currents of ideology. So were some in the army and navy – military politicians such as General Abe Nobuyuki, who served briefly as Prime Minister in 1939–40, and his short-lived successor in office, Admiral Yonai Mitsumasa, or the Foreign Minister in the Abe Cabinet, Admiral Nomura Kichisaburo. Each of these favoured some form of accommodation with the United States and opposed closer relations with the Axis powers, though each also supported Japan's special rights in Manchuria and northern China and her search for a 'new order' in east Asia.[42] That they were able to attain high office indicates that significant divisions of opinion on Japan's future course still existed. That they were so quickly ousted from office demonstrates that they could not withstand the dominant political and ideological forces, particularly represented in the middle echelons of the army and navy, which were now driving Japanese politics.

The leading statesman who had emerged – if only as first among equals – from the morass of Japanese politics by the time of the outbreak of the war against China was Prince Konoe Fumimaro, who became Prime Minister for the first time in June 1937, and was to play a central part in the fateful events of 1940–41. Born in 1891, Konoe became, on his father's death in 1904, the head of Japan's most prestigious noble family below the imperial house itself, with which it had intimate connections. From his early years, he was groomed for high office and regarded as a rising political star.

Even in his late twenties, he was given a place on the Japanese delegation to the Paris Peace Conference in 1919, at the end of the First World War. Months earlier, as the war was ending, he had publicly expressed views which would remain essentially unchanged and fundamental to his thinking. He was critical of Japanese leaders at the time for accepting unreservedly the peace pronouncements of British and American politicians. He accused them of not perceiving 'the conscious and unconscious ways in which the democracy and humanitarianism put forward by Anglo-American spokesmen provide a mask for their own self-interest'. The peace proposed, he added, 'amounts to no more than maintaining a status quo' that suited the Anglo-American interests. Konoe was presenting a case which would become widespread among the up-and-coming sectors of the Japanese elite, and also among younger officers in the army and navy, that Japan was disadvantaged by being a 'have-not' nation. The First World War, argued Konoe, had been 'a struggle between those nations that benefit by maintaining the status quo and those nations which would benefit by its destruction. The former call for peace, and the latter cry for war. In this case pacifism does not necessarily coincide with justice and humanity. Similarly, militarism does not necessarily transgress justice and humanity.' Japan's position, he continued, was similar to that of Germany before the war. He castigated the 'height of servility' with which Japanese leaders were ready to accept the League of Nations 'as if it were a gift from heaven', when in fact it was a device which would 'let the powerful nations dominate the weak nations economically and condemn the late-coming nations to remain for ever subordinate to the advanced nations'. If the policies of the Anglo-American powers should prevail through a League of Nations upholding their own interests through maintenance of the status quo, he concluded, 'Japan, which is small, resource-poor, and unable to consume all her own industrial products, would have no resort but to destroy the status quo for the sake of preservation, just like Germany'.[43]

Konoe repeated the sentiments, in part almost word for word, in a speech in November 1935, less than two years before he became Japan's Prime Minister. He saw two basic causes of war: the unfair distribution of territories, and the maldistribution of resources, among nations. Lasting peace could only come about by rectifying the imbalance among leading nations. But the postwar settlement had sought to eradicate war while doing nothing about the underlying injustice which brought it about. He rejected the principle of peace simply to uphold this situation. 'Our leaders', he declared, 'cannot seem to come out and declare the need for territorial expansion by acquisition, unlike German and Italian politicians. We have been so brainwashed by the virtually sacred Anglo-American idea of a peace structure based on the status quo that we defended our action in the Manchurian Incident like the accused standing before a judge. World peace can no longer be guaranteed by this peace structure. Japan and the other late-coming nations should have demanded a worldwide "new deal" long ago.'[44] It was a political philosophy that would ultimately drive Japan, like Germany, down the road to perdition.

In June 1937 Konoe became Prime Minister, a position he would eventually hold three times. He enjoyed great popularity at the time. He cut an imposing figure – tall, elegant, suave, urbane and at 45 years of age youthful for a Japanese Prime Minister (though he would later come to suffer so badly from piles that he sometimes had to sit on an inflated rubber tyre for comfort).[45] Enormous hopes were invested in him. The army, too, welcomed his appointment, confident that his popularity would help to further its own interests.[46] Within a month the war in China began. Konoe soon found himself presiding over the escalation of a conflict which Japan could not end. He proved in practice to be a weak and ineffectual individual, unable to offer a clear lead to the Cabinet, given to helpless hand-wringing, resigned apathy and lamentations at his inability to shape events.[47] Towards the end of his life, just before his suicide in December 1945, Konoe would seek to portray himself as the helpless victim of an army out of control. But while he certainly did voice private misgivings about the imbroglio in China, he never distanced himself either from the policy aimed at Japanese domination or from the terrible cruelties perpetrated by the army, most notably in Nanking. And his own government, as we have seen, attempted to impose extremely harsh terms on China in December 1937, just prior to breaking off diplomatic relations with Chiang Kai-shek's regime and the expansion of the war in 1938.[48] By the end of that year Konoe had engineered the arrangement with the would-be puppet leader of China, Wang Ching-wei. But dejected, unable to conclude the war and increasingly feeling himself to be the victim of the military forces he had been instrumental in mobilizing, Konoe resigned in January 1939.

In a memorandum written the following year, Konoe revealed that, if the course of the war in China gave him great anxiety, he accepted its necessity. His views were no different from those he had expressed in 1918. The policies of the great powers, he claimed, were threatening Japan through economic blockade, depriving the country of overseas markets and raw materials. The 'Manchurian Incident' had broken this blockade, and the 'China Incident' was destined to lead ultimately to the 'Greater East Asia Co-Prosperity Sphere' – a term invented in 1940 to mean Japanese dominance in the entire east Asian region, seen as Japan's necessary *Lebensraum*.[49]

The inventor of the phrase was Matsuoka Yosuke, appointed Foreign Minister in the new Cabinet which Konoe, returning as Prime Minister, formed in July 1940, a time of high excitement in Japan following the dramatic events in Europe. Small, thickset, a flamboyant personality with a rate of verbal output that had him dubbed 'the Talking Machine',[50] as head of the Japanese delegation Matsuoka had led Japan out of the League of Nations in March 1933. His dramatic defiance of the League turned him into a national hero within a jubilant Japan. It also established his reputation as a proponent of an assertive foreign policy. As a former President of the South Manchuria Railway, Matsuoka was well known for his advocacy of revisionism.[51] He was a forceful individual, given to bursts of temper, self-promoting, arrogant, keen to occupy the limelight. One prominent figure thought Matsuoka had 'the good point of coming up with splendid ideas, but ... the fault of recklessly advancing in the wrong direction'.[52] His prima-donna tendencies made him a fractious colleague. But he was a skilled negotiator, combining shrewdness with single-mindedness. The American Secretary of State, Cordell Hull, thought he was 'as crooked as a basket of fishhooks'.[53] On the other hand, Joseph Grew, who as American ambassador in Tokyo had frequent personal dealings with Matsuoka, thought, initially at least, that he was 'a loose talker but ... a man who is patently straightforward and sincere according to his lights'.[54] At this critical juncture, Matsuoka was the army's choice.[55] The day before he took office, he gave a little-noticed interview to an American journalist in which he made no attempt to conceal his future expectations and political preferences: 'In the battle between democracy and totalitarianism the latter adversary will without question win and will control the world. The era of democracy is finished and the democratic system bankrupt.'[56] He thought it a 'historical inevitability' that Japan and the United States, the two leading Pacific powers, would collide.[57] Such certainties determined Matsuoka's actions and policy recommendations in 1940 and 1941.

A third member of Konoe's second Cabinet, in July 1940, would also play a fateful role in events during those years, and during the war that followed (when, for most of the time, he served as Prime Minister). This was General Tojo Hideki, born in 1884, hard as nails, an experienced military administrator known as 'the razor', former commander of the military police then chief of staff of the Kwantung Army, a leading spokesman of the uncompromisingly expansionist faction in the army, a man of few words, but an outspoken advocate of Japan's imperialist ambitions, and now given a key role as Army Minister.[58]

Beyond the offices held by Konoe, Matsuoka and Tojo, the most important Cabinet position in arriving at the key decisions in the summer of 1940 was that of the Navy Minister. In any southern advance, the role of the navy was self-evidently crucial. But the navy's accord with the broader strategy under contemplation was also vital. And when Admiral Yoshida Zengo, appointed Navy Minister in July 1940, found himself, despite his commitment to expansion, out of step with the dominant forces keen to forge a military alliance with Germany and Italy he soon had to make way for a more pliant successor, Admiral Oikawa Koshiro.[59]

III

The Konoe Cabinet, formed on 19 July 1940, lost no time in responding to the drastically changed situation in Europe. But in fact the ground had already been laid during the preceding administration, headed by Admiral Yonai Mitsumasa. Yonai's Cabinet had been more conciliatory towards the west. Yonai, and his Foreign Minister, Arita Hachiro, who had come into office on 16 January 1940, had opposed the closer ties with the Axis powers which the army favoured. Arita was keen to improve relations with Britain and the United States, a policy which drew the ire of the dominant groups in the army. An essential contradiction in Arita's approach was, in any case, the strong advocacy by the Yonai administration of the 'new order' in east Asia, which the Americans were determined to block.[60] Arita also hinted more than once at Japan's readiness to exploit any change in the status of the Dutch East Indies. But while wanting to avoid damaging relations with the western powers, the Yonai government was starting to contemplate the 'southern advance' which would do precisely that.[61] There was, therefore, no disagreement among the Japanese power-elites about the need to establish a 'new order', aimed at securing the raw materials of east Asia for the Japanese Empire and ending the dominance in the region of Britain, America, France and the Netherlands. The disagreement was about how to achieve these goals.

Even before Konoe had formed his second Cabinet, therefore, the impact of the upheaval in Europe was reshaping Japanese thinking on expansion.[62] The chance had opened up of attaining self-sufficiency through conquest in south-east Asia and destroying the hold of the European colonial powers there. It was seen as too good to miss. Excited by the events in Europe, the manipulated mass media pressed the case. The heavily censored press 'spewed out adjectives in defence of Japan's "just cause" and buried news under mountains of mystical philosophising in an attempt to beautify the underlying opportunism of Hirohito's national programme'.[63] The corollary, however, was the need to adjust Japan's relations with her old enemy, the Soviet Union. A war on two fronts, while still tied down in China, was unthinkable. So for the first time, the prospect of a non-aggression pact with the Soviet Union started to gain favour among army leaders. Alongside this, the feeling rapidly gathered strength that a military alliance with the new force in Europe, Germany, was desirable.

A decisive shift in policy began to take shape even as Hitler's army was advancing through the Low Countries and northern France. In late May the Yonai government had already exerted pressure upon the authorities in the Dutch East Indies to guarantee supplies of tin, rubber, petroleum, scrap iron and nine other vital raw materials.[64] Then, following France's surrender on 17 June, the Japanese forced the beleaguered French and British governments to suspend the supply of vital aid to Chinese nationalists through Indochina, Burma and Hong Kong, a temporary, but humiliating, admission of weakness by the western powers.[65] The French surrender also prompted heated debates in the army about exploiting the opportunity to expand to the south. On 25 June the Army Minister, Hata Shunroku, told his staff members: 'Seize this golden opportunity! Don't let anything stand in the way!' Some, riding the wave of an excitedly chauvinist public opinion, called for immediate preparations for a drive to the south. One senior spokesman, though a lone voice at this time, pressed for a surprise attack on Singapore. Wiser counsels prevailed. No agreement was reached.[66]

But Japan's military leaders ran war games and came up with draft contingency plans for establishing airbases in Indochina and Thailand and carrying out a lightning attack on the Dutch East Indies.[67] The navy's war games led to the disconcerting conclusion that an attack on the Dutch East Indies would ultimately result in war against the United States, Britain and the Netherlands. It was also concluded that, without imports of oil from the United States, and unless the oil of the Dutch East Indies could be captured, safely transported and exploited, Japan would only be able to fight a war for four months. Even with the oil, 'should the war continue beyond a year, our chances of winning would be nil'.[68] It was little wonder that the navy leadership was still hesitant about plunging into a high-risk expansionist drive to the south, even though planning for such an eventuality dated back to 1936 and even though strident voices had been advocating that the time was ripe for it since the beginning of the European war in September 1939.[69] But section chiefs within the naval General Staff carried much weight in shaping policy, and by April 1940, even before the German offensive in western Europe, they were claiming that 'the time has come to occupy the Dutch East Indies'. Orders to prepare an increased state of readiness were issued to the fleet. The chief of staff, Prince Fushimi Hiro-yasu, told the Emperor that five to six months would be needed to prepare the navy for war.[70] Events in Europe then greatly bolstered the optimism of those who thought that a military occupation of the Dutch East Indies might be possible without involving Japan in conflict with either a weakened Britain or an indecisive United States. The hawks were gaining ground.

This was the case in the army, too. By the last weeks of June, the army authorities – the navy General Staff had earlier that month been informed of their thinking[71] – were drafting a policy statement on an advance to the south. They worked fast, under the heady influence of the German victories in Europe. They were confident that Britain's defeat by Germany was imminent, and that Japan would be the beneficiary in south-east Asia. Driven by this confidence, they undertook no careful analysis of Japan's material capability of sustaining a major southern expansion.[72] The pre-sumption was that military conquest would itself provide the necessary resources. By 3 July the draft had reached the stage where it could be adopted by the Army Ministry and the General Staff under the rubric: 'Outline of the Main Principles for Coping with the Changing World Situation'. It was an important document, determining the thrust of army policy, and eventually that of the government, down to the beginning of the Pacific War in December 1941.[73]

The preamble indicated the priorities of settling the 'China Incident' as quickly as possible and seizing the most opportune time 'to solve the problem of the south'. It held out the possibility that southern expansion could take place even if the war in China had not been ended. Whether or not that was the case, 'preparations for war should be completed generally by the target date of the end of August'. In foreign policy, the emphasis was placed upon 'strengthening Japan's political solidarity with Germany and Italy' and 'improving rapidly its relations with Soviet Russia'. The imperative of closing off routes providing aid for Chiang Kai-shek was underlined. The resources of the Dutch East Indies were vital for Japan, and to be attained by force if diplomacy failed. The concluding section struck a belligerent note. Japan would use the right moment for military action in the south. 'It will attack Hong Kong and the Malay peninsula, restricting insofar as possible its operations to Britain alone.' War with the

United States was to be avoided. However, the statement ended ominously, 'anticipating that in the end it will resort to the use of force against the United States if the situation requires, Japan will make the necessary military preparations'.[74]

The 'Outline' was presented to navy representatives the following day. The army spokesmen pressed the case for action to be taken without delay, before the European conflict ended, to free Japan from her dependence on Britain and the United States by establishing 'a self-sufficient economic sphere' with its core in Japan, Manchuria and China, but stretching from the Indian Ocean to the South Seas north of Australia and New Zealand. 'Never in our history has there been a time like the present,' the army's statement read, 'when it is so urgent to plan for the development of our national power ... We should grasp the favourable opportunity that now presents itself.' There was no time to lose. Japan should not miss her golden opportunity.[75]

The navy came up with some amendments, and a second joint conference on 9 July arrived at fundamental agreement. Far from diluting the army's blueprint for aggression, the navy's intervention reinforced it. Though aware from its war games that southern expansion would lead to conflict with the United States, the navy now advocated a firmer approach to the possibility of war with America. In the section dealing with Hong Kong, for example, the navy, while agreeing that a military offensive should be avoided as far as possible, proposed that 'if the situation permits, an offensive will be carried out with a firm resolution for war against Britain (or even against the United States)'. And the army's concluding statement, stressing the avoidance, if possible, of war with the United States was hardened into the formulation: 'While operations should be structured so that no war against the United States results, sooner or later military action against the United States may become inevitable.' Moreover, the earlier pessimism about Japan's long-term chances should it come to war with America had now given way to increasing confidence among navy officers that, providing due preparations were made, Japan would prove victorious.[76] The view marked the triumph of hope over reason.

The shift in the army's position from its traditional focus upon Russia in the north to expansion in the south had, therefore, coincided with the navy's long-standing interest in a southern strategy which obviously necessitated a major expansion of the fleet. From the navy's perspective, the principle of the new policy, 'northern defence and southern advance', could only be welcomed. The alternative scenario, avoiding war with the United States in order to target the Soviet Union, would have meant, inevitably, sacrifice of the naval budget to the needs of the army.[77] In any case, that would have left the decisive issue of Japan's dependence upon the western powers for its raw materials still unresolved. On this issue rested not only Japan's potential for fighting a war against the Soviet Union, but also for a successful outcome to the war in China – an unending drain on resources and on morale. The marriage of convenience, therefore, swiftly concluded to transcend the traditional rivalry between army and navy interests, was held together by a massive gamble that a Japanese offensive which would most likely involve war with America would prove victorious.

A first step in the new accord between army and navy was to arrange a more suitable political environment for the high-risk expansionism. The Yonai government, with its continued hankering after improved relations with the western powers, did not fit the bill. So the army proposed replacing it. The navy concurred. A Prime Minister more in tune with the new thinking was required. 'Now when a political change may be unavoidable within the next four or five days, and the military have been perfecting preparations to meet the abrupt changes in the latest world situation, the character of the Yonai Cabinet is not at all suitable for making negotiations with Germany and Italy and it might even cause a fatal delay,' reported the Vice-War Minister Anami Korechika. 'The conclusion is that a Cabinet change is inevitable in order to face this grave situation. The army unanimously will support Prince Konoye's [= Konoe] candidacy.'[78]

The engineered resignation of Yonai took place on 16 July 1940. The next day, Kido, wholly in tune with the national 'renovationist' spirit that had established itself during the 1930s, and prominent in attuning the imperial court to the dominant thinking in the military, presided over a meeting of six former prime ministers (including Konoe) and the President of the Privy Council. Their task of nominating the next Prime Minister was accomplished in only half an hour – record time. Predictably, the army's favourite, Prince Konoe, thought also to command public support 'at this time when the end of the China Incident is gradually approaching',[79] was entrusted with the formation of a new Cabinet.[80] He would soon, as had been the case in his first administration when he presided over the extension of the war in China, again prove himself the weak and vacillating, but compliant, tool of expansionist forces in the military.

These forces now had prominent representatives in the government. The army had indicated that it wanted Tojo Hideki as Army Minister and Matsuoka Yosuke as Foreign Minister.[81] These duly occupied their places in the new Cabinet, which took office on 22 July. The following day, Konoe told the Japanese people in a radio address that the old world order was collapsing. Japan had to be ready to welcome the new world order.[82] The same day, the German ambassador in Tokyo reported to his Foreign Ministry that the new Konoe Cabinet was certain to follow a policy of seeking closer alignment with the Axis.[83] The way was now open to cement the shift in policy. It did not take long to make the fateful choice.

IV

Even before his new Cabinet was formed, Konoe arranged a meeting with the key figures – Matsuoka, Tojo and Yoshida (who were to take over the Foreign, Army and Navy Ministries) – at his villa in Ogikubo, a suburb of Tokyo. Matsuoka, the most forceful personality in what Konoe came to call the 'Four Pillars Conference', prepared a draft statement and played the dominant role. The participants reached an informal agreement on the shape of future foreign policy. They accepted that, to establish the 'new order' in east Asia, Japan would strengthen ties with the Axis powers and conclude a non-aggression pact with the Soviet Union for the following five to ten years (building up her own military forces in the north to become impregnable to any subsequent possible Soviet attack once the pact had expired). At the same time, Japan would 'draw into' the 'New Order' the western colonial possessions in east Asia. And, though conflict was to be avoided if possible, Japan would 'resist armed intervention by the United States related to the establishment of the New Order in East Asia'.[84] The meeting stopped short of endorsing a military alliance with Germany and Italy. The Navy Minister, Yoshida, was still opposed to such a step. The army, however, made plain that it now favoured converting cooperation with the Axis powers into a formal tripartite military pact. 'We should resolve to share our fate with Germany and Italy,' was how the vice-chief of the army General Staff, Sawada Shigeru, put it in mid-July.[85] The recourse to 'fate' was redolent of Matsuoka's rhetorical flourish more than three years earlier, just after the conclusion in November 1936 of the Japanese-German Anti-Comintern Pact, when he had stated: 'It is characteristic of the Japanese race that, once we have promised to cooperate, we never look back or enter into an alliance with others. It is for us only to march side by side, resolved to go forward together, even if it means committing "double suicide".'[86]

The deliberations in the 'Four Pillars Conference' at Ogikubo were soon formalized as policy. Noting that the world was 'at a major turning point', the new Konoe Cabinet laid down the framework of its foreign policy on

26 July in its 'Outline of a Basic National Policy' (which had been drafted in the Army Ministry). It envisaged Japan building 'a new order in Great East Asia', resting upon the 'three solidly united' nations of Japan, Manchukuo and China (naturally, under Japanese leadership). At the same time, Japan was to be converted into a 'national defence state' ready for war.[87]

Keen to coordinate the civilian and military arms of government in the interests of building a national consensus behind the shift in foreign policy, Konoe resurrected the Liaison Conference, which had fallen into abeyance two and a half years earlier. On 27 July the Liaison Conference adopted the 'Main Principles for Coping with the Changing World Situation', which in effect enshrined as government policy the strategy devised in the discussions between the army and navy leaders earlier in the month.[88] This decision now confirmed, even if the wording remained vague, the two crucial shifts in policy: the southern advance and the strengthening of relations with the Axis powers.[89]

'Political unity with Germany and Italy', the document ran, 'will be strengthened immediately in an attempt to effect readjustment of diplomatic relations with Soviet Russia.' Preparations for the southern advance were to be accelerated, though timing would depend upon exploiting the changing circumstances to best advantage. A deterioration in relations with the United States was accepted as inevitable, though friction was to be avoided where possible. Pressure was to be exerted on French Indochina to cease supplies to Chiang Kai-shek and to provide Japan with supplies, use of airfields and troop passage. Measures would be adopted 'to eliminate immediately the antagonistic attitude of Hong Kong', and Burma would be blockaded to prevent aid reaching the Chinese nationalists. Diplomatic efforts would be made to obtain important resources from the Dutch East Indies. Wherever diplomacy failed, it was made clear, armed strength would be deployed, if circumstances demanded it.

The resolution of the 'China Incident' through elimination of aid to Chiang Kai-shek and the 'immediate subjugation of the Chungking regime by every possible means' still underpinned the whole strategy. But, as the comments on the document by Imperial General Headquarters made clear, the previous emphasis on settlement of the 'China Incident' had now given way to the southern advance as first priority.[90] So even if it proved impossible to end the war in China, armed strength was contemplated in the southern advance, 'depending upon the situation'. In such an event, efforts would be made to restrict Japan's adversaries to Great Britain alone. 'However,' it was acknowledged, 'thorough preparations for the commencement of hostilities against the United States will be made as it may prove impossible to avoid war with that country.' Indeed, even as the Liaison Conference was taking the decision for the southern advance, the United States government was contemplating moves to restrict Japanese access to the vital oil of the Dutch East Indies.[91] Japan and the United States were now set on a collision course.

In July, in the deliberation over the 'Main Principles for Coping with the Changing World Situation', Japanese navy officials had sought to prevent the army going ahead with plans to invade the Dutch East Indies. A compromise formulation was reached, stipulating that armed force would be used only if favourable circumstances arose, and that 'for the present diplomatic means' would be used. But once the United States tightened the noose by threatening Japan's access to crucial resources, the navy's stance became more belligerent. On 1 August the Operations Section of the navy General Staff made plain its support for the stationing of troops in French Indochina. It saw this as a step towards control over Thailand, Burma and Malaya in the southern advance. It would secure necessary raw materials – coal, rubber, iron ore and phosphorus – for Japan's military effort, and it would be strategically advantageous in a war against the United States and Great Britain. The navy envisaged America responding to a Japanese occupation of French Indochina with an embargo on scrap iron and oil. But an American embargo, the General Staff's analysis pointed out, 'would be a matter of life or death to the empire. In that event the empire will be obliged to attack the Dutch East Indies to secure oil.' The navy concluded that military operations against French Indochina should proceed by November, if not earlier; and that 'Japan must be resolved to wage war against other powers'. All preparations were to be undertaken for the mobilization of the fleet. An attack on the Dutch East Indies was only foreseen if the United States imposed tougher economic sanctions. But in its decision for 'preparatory mobilization' of the fleet, which for naval planners meant a state of readiness close to full mobilization for war, the navy General Staff had not only shown that it was ready to contemplate war with America; it had taken the first step in that direction.[92]

The stance adopted by the navy General Staff was not universally accepted even within the navy. Cassandra voices were raised. The head of the Ship Procurement Headquarters stated categorically that if the United States cut off all oil and supplies of essential minerals, 'the navy could barely fight for one year'. The Navy Minister Yoshida, whose health was becoming seriously affected by the anxiety, concurred. 'I trust that the navy General Staff will seriously investigate the relationship between the extent of our naval armaments and our prospects in a protracted war,' he stated.

He added that he did not favour military operations if they were to result in a total United States embargo against Japan. Admiral Nomura Kichisaburo, who in 1941 would be sent to Washington as Japanese ambassador, also warned that a war against the United States 'would, of necessity, be a long one, and this would be very disadvantageous to Japan'. Even the planners in the navy General Staff accepted this logic. 'We are not very confident of our capacity for endurance' in a protracted war with the United States, they acknowledged. Yet, basing all their hopes on a decisive blow in a short conflict, they continued to reckon with and plan for war, 'for the survival of the empire, whether we like it or not'.[93]

The fatalism built into the navy plans for the southern advance nevertheless served the interests of naval leaders. The shift from a northern, land policy, to a southern advance likely to lead to confrontation with the United States in the Pacific meant a sizeable shift in allocation of war resources from the army to the navy. The question of whether Japan could win a war against America became subordinated to the short-term benefits to the navy through a major expansion in its resources.[94]

V

While the navy was making its fateful choice for likely conflict with an adversary whom it was doubtful it could defeat, the politicians were embarking upon the steps that would lead to a full-blown military alliance with the Axis powers. On 30 July 1940 the Foreign Ministry prepared a statement bearing Matsuoka's hallmark, 'On Strengthening Cooperation between Japan, Germany and Italy'. The Konoe government adopted the statement as its guideline, hardening the position adopted at the Ogikubo Conference earlier in the month. It was now expressly stated that Japan was prepared to enter into military alliance with Germany and Italy against Britain, reserving Japan's right of independent decision on the use of force. The document envisaged a military alliance explicitly directed at Great Britain. However, cooperation was to extend to the event of Japan or Germany and Italy becoming involved in war with the United States, though the commitment in such a case only went as far as an agreement to 'confer on measures to be taken'.[95]

The new tone of Japanese policy was rapidly recognized. The American ambassador noted already on 1 August that the Konoe government 'gives every indication of going hell-bent towards the Axis and the establishment of the New Order in East Asia'. 'The German military machine and system and their brilliant successes have gone to the Japanese head like strong wine,' he added.[96]

Immediately, Matsuoka began to put out feelers about Germany's attitude towards a prospective military alliance. The German response was initially cool. By mid-August, however, the Germans had changed their mind. The revised stance was most likely triggered by Churchill's announcement on 20 August that the Americans were supplying fifty American destroyers to help the British war effort. It was not much more than a symbolic contribution, but it was taken as a clear signal that the United States was not holding to strict neutrality, and was prepared to provide significant aid to the beleaguered Great Britain, which might even lead eventually to her entering the war against the Axis powers.[97] Closer relations with Japan suddenly took on a new importance to the Germans. On 23 August the Japanese ambassador in Berlin was informed by Joachim von Ribbentrop, the German Foreign Minister, that he would be sending an envoy, Heinrich Stahmer, to Tokyo as minister plenipotentiary. His brief was to discover Japanese intentions and, if there was willingness, to open negotiations towards an agreement.[98]

Matsuoka's draft of 30 July had meanwhile been favourably received by the army. Indeed, the army began to press Matsuoka hard to conclude negotiations quickly.[99] Within the navy, however, serious differences of opinion remained. The top navy leaders still feared that closer relations with the Axis powers would serve to provoke the United States. Yoshida, the Navy Minister, as noted earlier, was particularly opposed to a pact. But, as some navy leaders wavered – under pressure, it seems, not only from the army but also from middle-echelon naval officers – he became increasingly isolated. Inwardly tormented, he succumbed to a nervous collapse, was taken to hospital on 3 September and resigned next day.[100]

Matsuoka helped influence the choice of Yoshida's replacement – the reticent, softly spoken, more accommodating Oikawa Koshiro, who soon showed himself in agreement with the demands for closer relations with Germany and Italy. Oikawa, in any case, was pushed in that direction by his deputy, Vice-Minister Toyoda Teijiro, a more assertive, politically astute and opportunistic individual, who emerged as the dominant figure in the ministry.[101] Even now, however, fear of war against the United States and Great Britain appears to have held Oikawa back from endorsing the move to a full military alliance with Germany and Italy. He was particularly concerned to avoid an obligation to go to war automatically should the Axis powers become involved in war with the United States. This seemed to be what Matsuoka now had in mind. By early September, the Foreign

Minister had hardened the position he had taken in his draft of 30 July, aimed at Britain, by including new wording in a revised draft. It was now explicitly stated that 'in the event of a danger of either contracting party entering into a state of war with the United States, the other contracting party will assist that party by all possible means'. It amounted to a proposal for a military alliance directed now squarely against the United States as well as Britain. And, from a duty to 'confer on measures to be taken', as stated in the draft of 30 July, the obligation would now be to provide assistance 'by all possible means'. Probably, Matsuoka's more pronounced anti-American line was a response to the American government's moves towards the imposition of the much feared embargo on oil. He believed in diplomacy through strength. He most likely felt that Japanese firmness would serve as a deterrent. Instead, it increased the chances of Japan becoming involved in war with the United States.[102]

Reservations about the implications of such an alliance, particularly fears that Japan could be drawn through German actions into a war with America as well as Britain, persisted on the Japanese side and were specifically voiced by the new Navy Minister, Oikawa. Matsuoka was forced to bow to such views, and he accordingly toned down his draft, omitting the automatic obligation to provide assistance.[103] But despite Oikawa's reluctance to embrace a military alliance which was now favoured by the government, the army and more radical factions within the navy itself, he had not opposed giving Matsuoka the authorization to negotiate closer ties with Germany and Italy. The Foreign Minister was left, therefore, with a fairly free hand to conduct discussions with Stahmer, once the German pleni-potentiary (an amateur diplomat who had formerly headed the Far East section of Ribbentrop's Dienststelle, his agency for foreign affairs[104]) had arrived in Tokyo on 7 September 1940 after a fortnight's wearisome jour-ney, first by air from Berlin to Moscow, then by the trans-Siberian railway to the Japanese capital.[105]

The Germans were keen to have an outright military alliance to deter the United States from entering the war. They were, therefore, less than enamoured by the weaker draft proposed by Matsuoka. But having paved the way, the Japanese Foreign Minister was himself most keen to press ahead with the alliance. 'I'll do it even if it costs me my job,' he re-marked, 'and I'll finish it up in one or two weeks.'[106] The breakthrough came when he showed himself willing to accept the stipulation that Japan would retain her independence in deciding whether to join in such a war. With this concession, the Navy Ministry's hesitancy gave way. At the Liaison Conference on 14 September, Oikawa resignedly accepted the need for the alliance. 'There is no other way,' he remarked.[107] Looking back after the war, Oikawa indicated that he had been persuaded by Matsuoka's firm undertakings about retaining autonomy to avoid being dragged into a conflict, and on the German as well as Japanese intention to keep the Americans out of the war. He remarked, too, that the navy could not sustain its opposition when the alliance was so widely favoured. 'The navy no longer had any grounds for opposing the proposal,' he commented. 'Not only that, but it seemed to me that for the navy to insist stubbornly on its own views (regardless of public opinion, which at that time was turning in favour of the Axis) would lead to a violent internal confrontation. So I told the Cabinet that the navy had no alternative to tide us over the current critical situation.'[108] That evening Tojo was able to report confidentially to the Lord Privy Seal, Kido, that the army and navy had reached agreement on the question of Japan's relations with Germany and Italy.[109] The die was cast.

Oikawa must have been acutely aware that the Navy Ministry's hesitations had not been shared even within the navy itself. An insight into the thinking of the navy General Staff, on far bolder, and far riskier, lines than that of Oikawa himself, was provided by the comments of its vice-chief, Kondo Nobutake, at the Liaison Conference on 14 September, recorded in a memorandum of the Prime Minister, Prince Konoe:

The navy is not yet prepared for war against the United States, but preparations will be completed by April of next year [1941]. By that time we shall have equipped the vessels already in operation and shall have armed 2.5 million tons of merchant ships. After we have completed this, we will be able to defeat the United States, provided we carry on blitz warfare. If we do not carry on blitz warfare and the United States chooses a protracted war, we will be in great trouble. Furthermore, the United States is rapidly building more vessels, which means that the difference between the American fleet potential and ours will become greater, and Japan will never be able to catch up with it. From that point of view, now is the most advantageous time for Japan to start a war.[110]

The crucial intervention at the Liaison Conference was that of Matsuoka himself. The Foreign Minister saw Japan at a crossroads. She needed to decide which way to turn. Should she go with Britain and the United States, or with Germany and Italy? He posed the alternatives. He first envisaged Japan rejecting the German proposal for an alliance. Germany, he stated categorically, would conquer Britain. Germany might even establish a European federation, come to an agreement with the United States and 'not let Japan lay even one finger on the colonies of Britain, Holland, and other powers in the federation'. On the other hand, if concluding an alliance were to lead to war with the United States, then the Japanese economy would suffer severely. He then, however, posed the costs to Japan of an alliance with Britain and the United States. The conditions for this, he stated, would be 'that we should have to settle the China Incident as the United States tells us, give up our hope for a New Order in East Asia, and obey Anglo-American dictates for at least half a century to come'. Would this be acceptable to the people of Japan? he asked. 'Would the hundred thousand spirits of our dead soldiers be satisfied with this?' he added, in a rhetorical flourish. In any case, he argued, the material difficulties would only be avoided in the short term. He reminded his colleagues of the disadvantages that Japan had faced after the settlement following the First World War. 'Who knows what bitter pills we should have to swallow this time?' he asked. His conclusion was obvious: 'an alliance with the United States is unthinkable. The only way left is to ally with Germany and Italy.'[111] He was, following the lobbying, pressing and cajoling of the previous weeks, speaking largely to the converted. Even so, this, effectively, was the moment that defined the new course of Japanese foreign policy.

The decision to proceed with the alliance was rubber-stamped at the Imperial Conference, in the presence of the Emperor, on 19 September.[112] Even now, apprehension was voiced that a pact with Germany might incite the United States to intensify the economic pressure upon Japan and increase her aid to Chiang Kai-shek. However, the worries about Japan's oil supplies only reinforced the views, as voiced by Tojo, the Army Minister, that 'the question of oil can be equated with the question of the Dutch East Indies', and that the decision had already been taken to secure essential resources from that region, if possible by diplomacy, but if not by force.[113] Southern expansion was, in other words, the premiss of Japanese action. This was accepted by all sections of the power-elite. Starting from that premiss, it was difficult, if not impossible, to argue convincingly against a treaty with Germany that, by deterring the United States, was seen as a vehicle to safeguard that expansion. After the conventional rituals of questioning Matsuoka on the pact, therefore, the Imperial Conference duly ended by giving the formal alliance with Germany the seal of the Emperor's approval.

Hirohito was himself full of foreboding. But he accepted the need for the pact. 'Under the present circumstances, this military agreement with Germany can't be helped,' he remarked privately to Konoe on 16 September. 'If there is no other way to handle America, then it can't be helped.' With some pathos, he then asked Konoe: 'What will happen if

Japan should be defeated? Will you, Prime Minister, bear the burden with me?'[114] Konoe, equally pathetic, was reduced to tears.[115]

There were still complex negotiations, with difficult moments, to be conducted.[116] Japan's insistence upon retaining her freedom of action was a sticking point. The Germans wanted a firmer commitment to involvement in a potential German–American war. But the pressures on Matsuoka to resist such a commitment were heavy. In the end, the Germans gave way, even if an element of ambiguity was retained in the final wording of the treaty. As late as 26 September, the very eve of the signing, Japanese leaders, meeting in the Privy Council, were still expressing their worries about the implications of the pact. There were deep concerns about deteriorating relations with America, and about supplies of oil and steel if the worst came to the worst and Japan and the United States went to war. Some reassurance was given about the stockpiling of essential resources. But there was more wishful thinking than hard calculation. Tojo remarked that military equipment was being obtained from Germany, passing through Siberia with Soviet consent. He pointed out, too, the necessity of improving relations with the Soviet Union so that Japan was not faced with conflict in the north as well as in the south. Konoe emphasized that the underlying thought behind the treaty was avoidance of conflict between Japan and the United States – the idea of deterrence – adding, however, that 'a humble attitude will only prompt the United States to become domineering', so 'a demonstration of strength is necessary'. This was the view of Matsuoka, the prime mover of the treaty. The Foreign Minister, pointing to the threat posed by the increasingly anti-Japanese stance of the United States, claimed there was 'no alternative but to take a resolute attitude'.[117]

The 'debate' had been largely formulaic. It was part of the elaborate process of confirming a decision that had already been taken at the Liaison Conference, then ratified at the Imperial Conference. It was nonetheless revealing. Japan's leaders sensed that their country was at a turning point. They faced a fateful choice. It seemed to them that they had to yield to long-term American domination, or take irrevocable and dangerous steps, with unforeseen and incalculable consequences, to resist it.[118] They chose the latter course. At midnight the Privy Council, in the Emperor's presence, unanimously approved the treaty. The following day, 27 September, the Tripartite Pact was finally signed in Berlin. Its key clause pledged the signatories 'to assist one another with all political, economic, and military means when one of the three Contracting Parties is attacked by a power at present not involved in the European war or in the Sino-Japanese conflict'.[119] It was plainly aimed at America. How would the United States react?

VI

It was soon plain that Japan's calculation had backfired. The American response quickly revealed the folly of Matsuoka's claim – a presumption, too, of the German Foreign Ministry, and accepted in varying degrees within Japan's power-elite – that the Tripartite Pact would serve as a deterrent. Instead, it merely confirmed American views that Japan was a belligerent, bullying, imperialist force in the Far East, an Asian equivalent of Nazi Germany, and had to be stopped.[120] Such views seemed confirmed by the entry of Japanese troops into French Indochina on 23 September. This followed intensified pressure on the French to allow right of transit by Japanese forces and use of Indochinese airfields, and took place even as negotiations were continuing. After two days of skirmishes between French and Japanese forces, the French surrendered. Northern Indochina was now occupied by Japan.[121]

Some in the Roosevelt administration had for some time been pressing for a tough line against Japan. The most prominent 'hawks' were the Secretary of War, Henry L. Stimson, the Secretary of the Navy, Frank Knox, Secretary of the Treasury, Henry Morgenthau, and Secretary of the Interior, Harold Ickes. They favoured a total embargo on oil supplies to Japan. This hard line was resisted by the Secretary of State, Cordell Hull, and Under-Secretary Sumner Welles. Backed by Admiral Harold R. Stark, head of Naval Operations, and Admiral James O. Richardson, Commander-in-Chief of the United States fleet, they argued that all-out oil sanctions would simply incite a Japanese attack which the American navy would be powerless to prevent. The authorities of the Dutch East Indies had already made the State Department aware that they did not want American action that would expose them to the threat of Japanese invasion. For the time being, Roosevelt sided with the 'doves', at least in part. An oil embargo was not imposed. However, news that the Japanese and Germans were negotiating a pact was answered by the imposition on 19 September (to take effect from 16 October) of a complete embargo on the export of iron and scrap metal.[122] Even though the dominant forces in the United States administration were still not ready to push Japan over the brink and into war, the scrap metal embargo was a plain signal that America was not going to bow to the pressure that Japan was seeking to exert through the Tripartite Alliance. Washington agreed to warn the Japanese of the continuing American commitment to the status quo in the Far East.[123] This meant further, and increased, support for Chiang Kai-shek, an advantage which the Chinese nationalist leader rapidly recognized. For Japan, it meant that the disastrous imbroglio in China was set to continue indefinitely. Tokyo's recognition in November of the Nanking puppet administration of Wang Ching-wei, when Chiang had predictably refused the terms Japan dangled before him, was met by Roosevelt's announcement that he was considering a huge loan of $100 million to the Chinese nationalist government.[124] By autumn 1940, therefore, relations between Japan and the United States had deteriorated still further. Since neither could back down, it was becoming increasingly evident that only a trial of strength would decide control over south-east Asia.[125]

The essential purpose of the Tripartite Pact, from the Japanese perspective, was to deter the United States from intervening to prevent the southern advance seen as necessary to ensure Japan's control of raw materials and, therefore, her future economic and political security. The gamble in the pact was self-evident. What if the United States did not regard the pact as a deterrent, but as a provocation? What if the effect was to reinforce the determination to prevent Japanese expansion by threatening the lifeline of oil supplies? But from a Japanese perspective at the time, the gamble had to be taken. To take it held great dangers, but also the potential of enormous rewards. Not to take it meant long-term servitude to the Anglo-American powers. It meant, too, that the China War had been in vain. The need for boldness, not caution, carried the day in such a mentality. Profound fears for the future had not been overcome. But they were met with fatalistic resignation. Characteristic in his expression of such an attitude, Admiral Yamamoto Isoroku, former Navy Vice-Minister and soon to become the planning mastermind behind Pearl Harbor, remarked in October 1940: 'It's out of the question! To fight the United States is like fighting the whole world. But it has been decided. So I will fight my best. Doubtless I will die on board the *Nagato* [his flagship].'[126]

Those voicing deep apprehensions, however, were sidelined. In Matsuoka's summary of the issues at the Liaison Conference, the risk was less damaging for Japan's long-term future than not taking it. It was a recipe for disaster. But Matsuoka's penchant for high-flown rhetoric, his belief in diplomatic force and his underlying brinkmanship came into the political equation at a moment when the Japanese military and also the civilian government had become committed to southern expansion, and when American threats to Japan's economy were real, and growing.

The Tripartite Pact was less formidable in reality than in appearance.[127] Its symbolic importance was, nevertheless, great. It confirmed that Japan saw her future shaped by the struggle against the Anglo-American supremacy in the Far East. Though the beginning of open hostilities would take place more than a year later, Japanese strategy and diplomacy were now framed by that imperative.[128] The path to collision with the United States was opening up.

The collision was not inevitable. There had been no invisible hand of destiny guiding Japan on the course to a war against the might of the United States which even her own military were not confident of winning. That disastrous course was the consequence of the fateful choices made by Japan's leaders in the summer and autumn of 1940. Those choices were, however, in good measure shaped by mentalities forged over the previous twenty years or so, and by the way those mentalities interpreted economic realities.

The obvious economic reality was that Japan depended upon the vagaries of world trade for her future prosperity. As a group of islands off the east Asian mainland, Japan could be no more self-sufficient from her natural resources than could Great Britain. But Britain ruled a world Empire. This was seen to provide the classic model for a world power. The leading political philosophies of the time, as Japan was modernizing and beginning to flex her muscles, assumed that acquiring an empire provided the basis of prosperity and future national security. A modern version of mercantilism preached that control over raw materials, and the territory that provided them, offered the route to power and prosperity. Subordination of weaker forces, in order to establish the imperial dominance which was the hallmark of a great power, was inevitable, and justified. Japan came to see herself, much as did Italy and Germany in the European context, as a 'have-not' nation, with a right to expand to safeguard her own survival and security. The western great powers, America most of all, stood in the way of this through their control of resources in south-east Asia, most notably in China itself, and through American naval might in the Pacific. Japanese dependence upon America for essential supplies of oil and metal exposed her Achilles heel as a would-be great power. It highlighted the underlying weakness of her position.[129] Hence, the liberal, democratic principles of the postwar settlement could increasingly come to be interpreted as self-serving for the west, but directly harmful for the 'have-not' nation of Japan.

With Japan in the throes of internal crisis during the 1920s, the bitter wrangles and deep divides in domestic politics seemed to mirror the country's external subservience to the western powers, sealed by the postwar Washington Conference. This provided the backcloth to the upsurge in nationalist-imperialist assertiveness during the 1930s, fired by the success in Manchuria and then the prospect of the much bigger prize in China.

Economic imperatives drove the new ideology, resting upon the 'imperial way' embodied by the deified Emperor, eventually pulling politics into their slipstream. The new, shrill and aggressive nationalism rapidly caught hold among younger officers in the army and the navy, penetrating via military training to the more plebeian recruits to the rank and file. Older officers, and an older generation of civilian politicians, still held to less abrasive ideas of international cooperation. But they gradually but inexorably lost ground to the forces representing the new ideology. By the time the war in China began in 1937, politicians favouring the expansionism that the mentality of the 'imperial way' had spawned were in high offices of state. Konoe epitomized them. But by now politics were in any case being ever more determined by the demands of the army.

China held the key. The longer the war dragged on, the less Japan was capable of cutting her losses and reaching some sort of peace deal that was the basic premiss of improved relations with the United States. The more Japan became mired in an expanding war, at enormous human and material cost, the more hardliners in the army ruled out any retreat. Following the massacres in Shanghai and the 'rape of Nanking', Japan's international standing had fallen drastically. As the United States toughened her stance, the chances of any settlement of the 'China Incident' dwindled. In 1905, President Theodore Roosevelt had used American pressure to broker an end to the war between Japan and Russia. Thirty-five years later there was no prospect of his namesake, the second President Roosevelt, intervening to engineer a settlement of the war between Japan and China. With the lessons of appeasement in Europe fresh in the mind, there was no appetite in America for attempting to appease Japan. But without such a settlement, American-Japanese relations could only worsen. And with that, Japanese oil supplies would inexorably become more endangered. Unwilling to yield to such a threat, the response of Japan's leaders was the turn to a policy of imminent southern expansion. As night follows day, this increased the prospect of war with the United States, a war which even Japanese 'hawks' thought Japan could only win if she could land a swift knockout blow.

By the time the fateful decision for the southern advance was taken, in July 1940, therefore, it was impossible to put forward a convincing alternative strategy. Variants of emphasis certainly existed, often related to the differing levels of fear of war with America. But the fundamental imperative of southern expansion was by now generally accepted throughout Japan's power-elite. Simply to contemplate an alternative was to dismiss it. The very premiss could not be entertained. Better relations with the United States – that is, the avoidance of risk of war – meant effectively to capitulate over China. In the eyes of Japan's leaders, that would have entailed a colossal loss of prestige, with incalculable internal consequences. It would have been portrayed as an insult to the memories of those who had fought, suffered and died for Japan in the war in China, and it would have left Japan, her international strength undermined, even more dependent on America for the long-term future than she had been before embarking on the war in China.

After the Pacific War had run its catastrophic course for Japan, the country was able to rebuild and establish unprecedented prosperity on the basis, precisely, of dependence on the United States and successful incorporation into world trade resting upon capitalist competition and market economies. But the mentalities of 1940 were light years away from those which, in conditions of total defeat, helped Japan rise from the ashes. These earlier mentalities saw no alternative to imperialist expansion to secure the raw materials that the United States, in progressively more belligerent tones, increasingly threatened.

With the very premiss of possible rapprochement with the United States ruled out (short of an utterly improbable American volte-face on China), the expansionist policy – replete with dangers – had to be adopted. The stunning victories of the German army in Europe in spring 1940 appeared to offer the chance Japan had been waiting for to obtain her 'place in the sun'. The opportunity could not be passed over. With the decision for expansion taken in July, the platform was set for Japan to break out of her self-inflicted international isolation and to redirect her foreign allegiances towards the victorious Axis powers. As we saw, those among the Japanese elites who opposed such a shift in policy swiftly lost all influence. Once the navy's opposition evaporated, in early September, the way to the Tripartite Pact signed later in the month was clear.

Japan had made her fateful choices. They did not of necessity mean war in the Pacific. There was still far to go before the decision was taken to attack Pearl Harbor. But the fateful choices of 1941 had been prefigured by those of the previous summer and autumn, which had manoeuvred Japan into a cul-de-sac.[130] Blocked by her refusal to contemplate any concessions over China, Japan's only way out ran the high risk of war in the Pacific. Now that Japan had opted to expand to the south, and to forge a military alliance with Germany and Italy, Pearl Harbor had moved much closer.

4

Rome, Summer and Autumn 1940

Mussolini Decides to Grab His Share

Hitler always faces me with a fait accompli. This time I am going to pay him back in his own coin. He will find out from the papers that I have occupied Greece. In this way the equilibrium will be re-established.   Mussolini, 12 October 1940

At 6 o'clock in the early evening of 10 June, Mussolini spoke from the balcony of the Palazzo Venezia, his headquarters in the heart of Rome, to a large crowd of mainly Fascist enthusiasts, mobilized at short notice. With typical bombast he announced that destiny had determined Italy's entry into the war. Honour, self-interest and the future of the country demanded that Italy must fight. It was to be a fight 'against the plutocratic and reactionary democracies of the West, which have repeatedly blocked the march and even threatened the existence of the Italian people'. Breaking the stranglehold of the western democracies which throttled Italy's scope for expansion and severely limited her power even within the narrow confines of the Mediterranean was vital for the country's freedom, he claimed. He portrayed Italy's war as 'the struggle of a poor people against those who wish to starve us with their retention of all the riches and gold of the earth'.[1]

It had seemed like a good idea at the time. It looked a safe bet that Italy would profit hugely and cheaply from the astonishing victories of the Wehrmacht in western Europe. In fact, as would rapidly become clear, it was an enormous gamble that would soon backfire in catastrophic fashion. Mussolini felt acutely that Fascist Italy had been dragged along at Germany's heels for several years. Italy had once been the senior partner in dealings with Hitler, but the roles had been decisively reversed in the second half of the 1930s in the wake of German foreign-policy successes and territorial expansion. Mussolini smarted under his relegation to the status of a second-rank dictator. And now, more plainly than ever before, Italy had to stand in the shadow of events determined by German military might. Asserting Italy's independent claim to power within the Axis was a key motive in joining the war. But within months any such claim lay in ruins. Far from being an autonomous power waging her own parallel war, Italy would soon become reduced to no more than an adjunct to Germany's quest for hegemony in Europe.

The key staging post en route to that degrading position was Mussolini's second fateful choice within five months: the decision, taken in October 1940, to invade Greece. At 6.00 a.m. on 28 October, Italian troops crossed the borders from occupied Albania into northern Greece. The Greek army was not seen to pose any serious obstacle. Victory would be swift. Mussolini saw himself standing in triumph in Athens after only a brief campaign, something akin to the German crushing of Poland in autumn 1939. The destruction of Greece would be a major step towards the empire in the Balkans and Mediterranean that he craved. Instead, the campaign rapidly proved a fiasco. The Greek forces fought valiantly, helped by good organization, knowledge of difficult terrain and the superior morale of troops repelling an invader of their country. Within a fortnight, it was obvious that the supposed easy triumph was already turning into a humiliation for Mussolini's regime.

The decision to invade Greece had been revealed as a calamitous folly. It was the first defeat for the seemingly invincible Axis forces. And, crucially, through neglecting north Africa for Greece, Mussolini had both exposed Italian troops to military disaster and gravely weakened the Axis position in the desert campaign, the most vital theatre of the war at the time. Had the weak British forces been driven out of Egypt and the Suez Canal region, the war would have taken a different course. Instead, sorely needed Italian troops were diverted to the mounting debacle in Greece. Italy would never recover from the double humiliation in Greece and north Africa. By the spring of 1941, Germany would be forced to intervene militarily to quell the turmoil in the Balkans that Mussolini's intervention had unleashed. The Italian dictator had fervently wanted to avoid German domination of the Balkans. Now his own actions had brought about just that. The repercussions of Mussolini's ill-fated Balkan adventure were massive, not just in their military outcome, but also in the undermining of the authority of the Fascist regime within Italy. It was the beginning of the end for the Italian dictator, as his support – not just at the grass roots, but within the political elite – waned rapidly.

Looking for easy gains, Italy had joined a war which was to bring enormous hardship, heavy destruction and acute suffering to the country, leading to the overthrow of the Fascist regime in 1943, a switch of allegiance to the Allied side in the autumn of that year and bitter months of brutal German occupation in the northern regions before the total defeat of the Third Reich ended the misery. For Mussolini himself, the decisions to enter the war in June 1940 and, within only a few months, to invade Greece would eventually lead to his deposition from power, then his spectacular rescue from imprisonment and restoration as a German puppet-leader. He would finally pay the price in late April 1945 when he and his mistress, Claretta Petacci, were caught and executed by partisans on the banks of Lake Como. Their bodies were subsequently strung up on a girder in a Milan petrol station, the once glorified leader reviled in death by a jeering crowd.

Mussolini himself took the fateful decisions that saw Italy enter the war then embark upon the disastrous invasion of Greece. That much is clear. But how were the decisions arrived at? How far were they his decisions alone? To what extent did arbitrary dictatorial will override the wishes and interests of others within the power-elite of the Fascist state, notably the military? Or did Mussolini's 'decisionism' merely reflect the prevalent attitude within the regime as a whole? Were the decisions pragmatic or ideological in essence, the result of short-term opportunism or longer-term goals, a break with long-standing continuities in Italian expectations, or their presumed fulfilment? Not least, were Mussolini's decisions taken in such circumscribed conditions that, in effect, he had no choice but to take Italy into war and expansionism? Or did he and his regime, whatever their favoured choices, have real options in the summer and autumn of 1940, options they chose to reject in favour of the illusion of easy and rich pickings on the coat-tails of the German conquerors in western Europe?

I

War and expansion had been implicit in Mussolini's ideas from the start of his 'career' as an arch-Fascist. In time, they became explicit. Rambling and discursive though these ideas were, a core element was plain enough. Even before his expulsion from the Socialist Party in November 1914 and his strident advocacy of Italy's intervention in the First World War the following year, Mussolini had welcomed the revolutionary, cleansing agency of war, and its necessity if Italy were to shake off her past and take her place among the great nations. In March 1919, at the foundation meeting in Milan of the *Fasci di Combattimento*, he announced that Italy needed and deserved more territory to accommodate her growing population. Soon afterwards, he held out the prospect of Italy joining Germany, should she not be given her due by the Allies, and eventually destroying Britain's naval strength in the Mediterranean. By the mid-1920s he was presenting his vision of a new warrior class, 'always ready to die', the creation of 'methodical selection', and the basis of the 'great elites that in turn establish empires'. War and revolution would mould the 'new man'. The goal was 'empire'.[2]

The goal remained without practical consequences of note during the years when Fascism was consolidating its hold on the Italian state, and on society. A diplomatic incident involving Greece led to a brief Italian military excursion and occupation of Corfu in summer 1923, before being settled by Greek compensation. A few months later Yugoslavia ceded the disputed city of Fiume to Italy, giving Mussolini a further (and easy) success in foreign policy. And by the end of 1926 Albania had effectively become an economic satellite of Italy, again no more than the most minor of triumphs. But Italy was extremely ill-prepared for foreign adventurism on any serious scale. The country was burdened with huge debts as a legacy of the war. Most regions, particularly in the south, were extremely poor. National income was less than a quarter of that of Great Britain. The industrial base was small, mainly confined to the northern triangle of Milan, Genoa and Turin. As late as 1938–9 Italy produced only a million tons of coal and 2.4 million tons of steel. Britain's output, in comparison, was 230 million tons of coal and 13.4 million tons of steel, Germany's 186 million tons of coal and 22.4 million tons of steel.[3] Rearmament made little headway before the mid-1930s. And among the public, so soon after the terrible losses of the First World War, there was generally little appetite for risking new armed combat. Italy, as its leaders (Mussolini, too) recognized, was as yet by far the weakest of the 'great powers'; in reality, she was merely a would-be 'great power'.

Mussolini remained for the time being sensibly cautious. The position of Austria, on Italy's northern frontier, posed as yet no serious problem. Mussolini still had hopes in the later 1920s of gaining support in Hungary and Austria in order to create an Italian sphere of influence in the Danube region, and was anxious to prevent Austria falling under German influence and control. But the hopes of *Anschluss* with the German Reich that had initially been widespread in Austria after the war had meanwhile died down, and the revisionist Right within Germany which harboured aims of expansion was in the later 1920s still on the political fringes. The other potential difficulty in relations with Germany, the issue of the South Tyrol – part of Italy, but with a majority German-speaking population – had also not materialized into dangerous confrontation. The shrill voices on the radical Right in Germany clamouring for the return of the South Tyrol were only to be heard outside the political mainstream. The most vocal figure on the extreme Right, Adolf Hitler, already looking to good relations with Italy, had in fact risked splitting his still small Nazi Party by indicating a willingness to renounce claims to the South Tyrol.[4] He had wider horizons in mind. And despite feeling much resentment towards the superiority of British and French power, especially in the Mediterranean, Mussolini risked nothing in his dealings with the western democracies (whom he had joined in the Locarno Pact of 1925, aimed at stabilizing Germany's west-European borders).

Mussolini was, then, forced for years to tread warily in foreign policy. But this altered nothing of his underlying interest in territorial aggrandizement, or his belief in war as an agent of national regeneration, the route to the prestige and status befitting a great power.

The disturbance to the international scene that followed Hitler's takeover of power in Germany in 1933 offered Mussolini new opportunities and opened up a more active role in European affairs for Fascist Italy. Mussolini's early concern was to shore up Austrian independence against Nazi pretensions. Relations between Italy and Germany were tense for a time after the assassination by Nazis of the Austrian Chancellor, Engelbert Dollfuss, in July 1934. And when, the following April, at Stresa, Mussolini aligned Fascist Italy with the western democracies against German expansionism, he had Austria primarily in mind. But by then his attention had begun to focus on Abyssinia (Ethiopia), a distant and impoverished country, but with its attractions for Fascist Italy. Mussolini wanted an external triumph, a show of Italian might, a demonstration to the world, and to Italy's own population, of Fascism's power and of national virility. The eastern Mediterranean and north Africa (where Libya had been a colony since 1912) had long been part of the dream of expansion by Italian imperialists. Mussolini's own interest in these regions as the core of a new Fascist empire was, therefore, in essence nothing new. Ideally, Mussolini wanted dominion closer to home, in the Mediterranean region, most notably in the Balkans. Italy's armed forces were, however, still weak in comparison with those of the major European powers. Any notion of expansion into the Balkans, however attractive the proposition sounded, had to be ruled out for the foreseeable future at least. It was still too risky, particularly given the strong French interests in south-eastern Europe.[5] Abyssinia, seen as a primitive, tribal kingdom incapable of offering much resistance to Italian arms, served as a substitute.

The humiliating defeat at Adowa in 1896, after Italian troops had advanced into Abyssinia from their Eritrean colony, still rankled deeply among nationalists. The blooding of the nation in a short, one-sided war of revenge, and a triumph for Fascism, were tempting prospects for the Italian dictator. Success at no cost seemed assured. He had to overcome the hesitation and faint-heartedness of the King, army leaders and the more conservative elements in the power-elite, anxious at the risk he was taking. But the western democracies, he thought, would not intervene. This turned out to be a miscalculation – though one which rapidly rebounded to Mussolini's great advantage. Condemnation of Italian aggression by the League of Nations and the imposition of economic sanctions fuelled hatred of Britain and France within Italy and massively bolstered the popularity of Mussolini and his regime. When Addis Ababa fell the following May, after an extremely brutal campaign which included the extensive use of chemical warfare, Mussolini could announce complete victory, the assumption by the King of Italy of the title of Emperor of Abyssinia, and the existence of a new Roman Empire.

The Duce cult now reached its height.[6] The regime was greatly strengthened, Mussolini's position within it unassailable. The grandiosity of his own self-image knew no bounds. He eagerly anticipated confrontation with the 'decadent' western democracies, divided and weakened by their response to the Abyssinian war. The path to Italy's great future lay, it seemed evident (and not just to Mussolini), only in closer ties with Hitler's Germany – already flexing her muscles, certain to become the dominant power in central Europe and posing a major challenge to France and Britain. Accordingly, Mussolini gave the green light to German remilitarization of the Rhineland in March 1936, accepted that Austria should now fall into the German orbit as she did following an agreement signed in July, and in November that year formed the Axis with Germany as the symbolic seal on the close relationship – one viewed with little relish by most Italians.

In fact, for all the propaganda razzmatazz, the relationship between Italy and Germany was in reality far from close, and became increasingly lopsided. Mussolini had at one time thought of himself as the master and Hitler as the pupil. But his sense of inferiority towards Hitler deepened as his co-dictator chalked up one diplomatic triumph after another. And he could not conceal his awe of German military might. Italian military muscle was, by contrast to that of the Wehrmacht, anything but daunting. A humiliating defeat at Guadalajara in March 1937, after Mussolini had defied the warnings of his army leaders to involve Italy in support for Franco during the Spanish Civil War, was a plain reminder of this. Mussolini's state visit to Germany in September that year merely rubbed in the massive gulf in military strength between the two dictatorships and left him still more awestruck at the power of the Third Reich.

When Hitler annexed Austria in March 1938, he profusely thanked Mussolini for his support. Whatever the position had been four years earlier, however, Mussolini now had little choice in the matter but to acquiesce. He had tied his country to the high-risk expansionism of Nazi Germany. Accordingly, he fully backed the belligerent German stance on the Sudetenland that summer. And he professed his readiness to fight on Germany's side, should – as seemed likely – general European war be the outcome. But this contained more than a small element of bluff. He was well aware of how unprepared Italy was for a major war. When Hitler momentarily wavered, Mussolini snatched at the chance, offered him by Göring, to mediate the settlement at Munich, made possible by the readiness of the western democracies to carve up Czechoslovakia in the interests of the German bully. His euphoric reception on return to Italy as a saviour of Europe's peace did not please him in the slightest. Rather, it confirmed to him that the Italian people were too peace-loving, far from ready for war. Such a verdict was indeed presented by a whole array of reports by Fascist Party functionaries on the state of popular opinion, emphasizing hostility towards the German Axis partners and dread of being dragged into another war.[7]

Mussolini held these fears in contempt. He was aiming at war, not peace. In a far-reaching speech – an updated version of a long-held vision – to the Fascist Grand Council on 4 February 1939, he envisaged a war with the western powers to attain the Italian version of *Lebensraum*. Italy, he said, was effectively landlocked by British domination of the Mediterranean, blocking access to the oceans (and prosperity) through control of the Strait of Gibraltar in the west and the Suez Canal in the east. Encircled by hostile countries and deprived of scope for expansion, Italy was 'a prisoner of the Mediterranean'. The task of Italian policy was, therefore, to 'break the bars of the prison' and 'march to the Ocean'. But whether this 'march' was to the Indian or the Atlantic Ocean, 'we will find ourselves confronted with Anglo-French opposition'.[8]

He was soon enough given another reminder that he could only march to Germany's tune. The German occupation on 15 March of what was left of Czechoslovakia, as usual without prior notice to her Axis partner, showed where the power lay. The Munich settlement brokered by Mussolini had simply been ripped up by Hitler. When Hitler's emissary presented a verbal message of explanation and gratitude to Mussolini, a despondent

Duce wanted to withhold the news from the press. 'The Italians would laugh at me,' he lamented. 'Every time Hitler occupies a country he sends me a message.'[9] However, he saw nothing for it but to accept the German fait accompli with good grace. He even initially resisted the suggestion of Count Galeazzo Ciano, his Foreign Minister since 1936 and married to his daughter, Edda, to annex Albania to give the Italian people some 'compensation' for their humiliation. The annexation of this corrupt and backward little kingdom, already heavily under Italian influence, was, however, only deferred. It took place three weeks later, on 7 April 1939. Albania now became little more than Ciano's 'grand duchy', as the Foreign Minister – young, dashing, but vain, corrupt and lightweight, preferring golf and womanizing to hard work at the diplomatic desk – called it.[10] Compared with Hitler's spectacular coups, it was small beer indeed. But Mussolini saw it merely as a staging post. Already by May he was contemplating using Albania for an attack on Greece to 'drive the British from the Mediterranean basin'.[11] As Ciano told Hitler (who allegedly listened with enthusiasm and managed to keep a straight face), the Italian programme was to make 'Albania a stronghold which will inexorably dominate the Balkans'.[12]

But, immediately, the British guarantee for Greece and Romania that had followed the Italian takeover in Albania had the effect of driving Italy even closer to Germany through a military alliance, the 'Pact of Steel', signed on 22 May 1939.[13] The two countries pledged mutual military assistance and support in the event of one or other power becoming involved in war. It was a case of 'Fascist diplomacy at its sloppiest':[14] Italy had committed herself to unconditional backing of Germany even in a war entirely of German making.

The Italian understanding, as Mussolini soon reminded Hitler, was that war should not be unleashed before 1943 at the earliest, when Italian preparations would be complete.[15] But the very day after the signing of the 'Pact of Steel', Hitler was telling his generals to prepare for war at the first opportunity against Poland.[16] By mid-July, rumours about German intentions towards Poland had hardened into alarming reports from the Italian ambassador in Berlin, Bernardo Attolico, that Germany was preparing to strike at Danzig the following month.[17] Ciano started to worry that Italy would be drawn into the war 'in the most unfavourable conditions', with gold reserves and metal stocks almost at zero-level and military preparations woefully incomplete. He was adamant that war must be avoided.[18] Mussolini wavered between the idea of another 'Munich' – an international peace conference with the aim of postponing war for another three years or so – and the desire to fight alongside Germany, for honour, and to grab 'his part of the booty in Croatia and Dalmatia', as Hitler was tempting him to do. When Ciano met Hitler and Ribbentrop at the German dictator's Alpine residence, the Berghof, in the mountains above Berchtesgaden, on 11–13 August 1939, he was left in no doubt that Germany was set on military action. Italy had been kept in the dark once again about German intentions, and Hitler had 'decided to strike, and strike he will'. Ciano returned to Rome 'disgusted with the Germans', who had 'betrayed us and lied to us' and were now 'dragging us into an adventure which we do not want'. He felt Italy's hands were free, and fervently recommended keeping out of the war.[19] Mussolini's nervousness continued. But his strong instincts were to fight alongside the Germans if it came to armed conflict. There was still a chance, he imagined, that the western democracies would not march. In that case, he wanted to profit from the cheap gains that would be on offer. But should it come to war, as seemed likely, he thought Italy would look cowardly in the eyes of the world if she backed away. Another point weighed with him, according to Ciano: his fear that Hitler, in rage at Italian non-compliance with the 'Pact of Steel', might 'abandon the Polish question in order to square accounts with Italy'.[20]

The stunning news late in the evening of 22 August of Germany's imminent Non-Aggression Pact with the Soviet Union – another surprise for Italy – was a blow for the western democracies that gave Mussolini a fillip. His belligerent mood was encouraged by the sycophantic (and wholly misleading) report of Alberto Pariani, the Under-Secretary for War, of the good state of readiness of the army. This was utterly contradicted by the forthright opinion of King Victor Emmanuel III himself, when Ciano conferred with him on 24 August, that 'we are absolutely in no condition to wage war', and that 'the Army is in a "pitiful" state'. The officers were not qualified, the equipment was old and obsolete, and public opinion was hostile to the Germans. The King was adamant that Italy had to stay out of the war, at least for the time being, and await events. Most importantly, he insisted upon being involved in taking any 'supreme decisions'.[21] It was tantamount to a veto on Mussolini taking Italy into the war.

Next day, Ciano relayed the King's views to a 'furiously warlike' Mussolini, who felt duly deterred from taking the country to war and compelled to accept non-intervention. On receipt of a letter from Hitler asking for 'Italian understanding' for imminent action, Mussolini was forced to admit that 'it will be opportune for me not to take the initiative in military operations in view of the present state of Italian war preparations', adding that intervention was dependent upon immediate delivery of military supplies and raw materials to withstand an attack by Britain and France.[22] A list, extraordinarily exorbitant in its demands, was eventually put together on 26 August. It was embellished still further by Attolico, acting on his own initiative in order to discourage any possible German compliance with the requests by asking for immediate delivery of all supplies requested before Italy could enter the war. That did the trick. The requests were totally impossible for Hitler to fulfil. He let Mussolini know he understood Italy's position and asked only for a continued friendly stance. He proposed, Ciano noted, 'to annihilate Poland and beat France and England without help'. It was a blow to Mussolini's prestige. Hitler had taken his country to war within six years of attaining power, while he, the Duce, was in no position to take Italy to war after almost seventeen years in power. That rankled. He told Hitler on 26 August: 'I leave it to you to imagine my state of mind in finding myself compelled by forces beyond my control not to afford you real solidarity at the moment of action.'[23] His own wishes had been plain. But he had been forced to bow to pressure from within his own regime not to embroil the country in war. For now, he had to swallow the bitter pill and accept the novel status, unknown to international law, of 'non-belligerence' – less demeaning, certainly, than 'neutrality', but falling far short of what Fascist martial values demanded.[24]

It would be ten months before the opportunity arose to make good the climbdown of late August 1939. This time the opportunity would be too good to miss.

II

That in August 1939 Mussolini's wish to take Italy into the war had to yield to pressure to stay out of it, not least because of the King's hostility to intervention, demonstrates real limits to the dictator's power. Mussolini's German counterpart was in a much stronger position. After Hitler became head of state on the death of President Hindenburg at the beginning of August 1934, at which point the army swore an oath of allegiance to his person, his power was absolute in the sense that no individual and no body or institution could pose any constitutional challenge and there was no base of alternative loyalties. He tightened his hold over the armed forces in February 1938 in a reorganization of the central control structure under his own direct leadership. In Italy, by contrast, almost seventeen years after Mussolini had taken power following the 'March on Rome' in October 1922, that power, if not to be underestimated, remained far from total.

Though the diminutive King cut an unimpressive figure and seemed a puny makeweight to Mussolini's domineering presence, he remained the head of state, and with more than merely titular powers. Ultimately, as the events of July 1943 would show, just as he had appointed Mussolini to head the government in 1922, he retained the prerogative of removing him from office. And he offered an alternative focus of loyalty. This was particularly important in the case of the armed forces. Most notably, the officer corps of the army and navy retained a strong sense of allegiance to the monarchy. Their prime loyalty, as they for the most part saw it, was to the King, the head of the armed forces. Whatever combination of bribery and browbeating Mussolini deployed in his dealings with the leaders of the armed forces, it was never sufficient to win their unreserved allegiance. This would prove a fatal weakness in the palace coup of July 1943.

Although there were no overt signs during the uneasy period of non-belligerence in 1939–40 of the later rupture between Mussolini and his military leaders, the dictator could not simply ride roughshod over his senior generals and admirals.[25] He would on more than one occasion bemoan the shortcomings he saw in the military and his inability to purge the officer corps, just as he expressed his intention to eliminate the monarchy as soon as he had the opportunity to do so.[26] As it was, for the time being he had to put up with what he took to be the undue caution, pusillanimity, pessimistic outlook and lack of Fascist 'fighting spirit' of the King and of his military advisers.

The officer corps remained, to Mussolini's chagrin, irredeemably conservative in personnel and structure. Italy lacked the strong militaristic culture that had developed in Germany (especially in Prussia). There was, for the most part, no great enthusiasm for the military in Italian society. The army did not enjoy a high level of prestige, as it did not just in Germany but also in the western democracies, Great Britain and France. It was much the same with the navy, while the air force, as in other countries, was only just beginning to establish itself. What military tradition there was in Italy featured humiliating defeats, notably Adowa in 1896 and Caporetto in 1917, rather than glorious victories. A career in the armed services was, accordingly, not greatly sought after by most well-educated and technically skilled Italians, who in any case were not high in numbers in a poorly educated, industrially underdeveloped society. The outcome was the low calibre and shortage of talent in what amounted practically to a rigid military caste, especially in the army. Had Mussolini been powerful enough to purge the army leadership, he would have had difficulty in replacing those dismissed by men of much better qualities. In practice, he could make little dent in the closed ranks of the senior generals, who, despite their personal and inter-service rivalries, were backed by their close ties to the monarchy.

From 1926 onwards Mussolini had been the minister at the head of each of the three branches of the armed services. But for years he remained diffident in his dealings with the top brass, keen to avoid provoking antagonism, and aware of his own technical deficiencies in military matters as well as the need to protect his own image by keeping out of issues he did not fully comprehend. Little was done to bring about a genuine coordination of the armed forces' leadership. This was to remain the case, seriously damaging strategic planning, throughout the war.[27] The powers of Marshal Pietro Badoglio, chief of General Staff since 1925, to intervene in the internal direction of each of the branches of the armed services, and even to coordinate strategic thinking, were more nominal than real. He served largely as no more than Mussolini's liaison with the leaders of the army, navy and air force and as his chief adviser on military planning. Badoglio's role in masterminding the victory in Abyssinia had bolstered his position and meant that Mussolini could not easily override his advice. But, in its defensive tone, this was seldom what the dictator wanted to hear.

Nor did Mussolini like to face up to the obvious inadequacies of his armed forces and their lack of readiness for major combat.[28] Victory in Abyssinia with the aid of heavy artillery, bombers and mustard gas against a hopelessly inferior enemy (which nonetheless provided surprisingly tenacious resistance for some months) offered little preparation for the engagement in the European war that Mussolini had in mind to gain Italy's place in the sun – though it did give the dictator increased ambition to direct military affairs. Since he saw air and naval power as the key to future dominance in the Mediterranean following a struggle with Britain and France, the air force, above all, and the navy to some extent were given priority over the army in the allocation of resources. But despite substantial rearmament in the navy in the second half of the 1930s, the fleet at the end of the decade was still far from ready for full-scale combat, while its leadership was poor in its operational planning and strategic thinking, defensive-minded and largely rooted in the naval warfare of the past. The air force, too, had flattered to deceive in Abyssinia and then during the Spanish Civil War. Despite notable expansion in the later 1930s, it remained technically and organizationally weak in comparison with its British and German equivalents. The army was disadvantaged by the priority in resource-allocation accorded to the navy and air force, and suffered equally from Italy's small industrial base. Beyond this, it had a leadership locked into the military thinking of yesteryear, unwilling, as well as unable, to break the chains of the past. By the end of the 1930s, as a result, the army was woefully far from the levels of modernization required by new, more mobile forms of warfare. One experienced officer, General Ettore Bastico, warned against idolizing the tank and wanted to 'reserve our reverence for the infantryman and the mule', while as late as 1940 the deputy chief of the army staff, General Mario Roatta, let it be known that he opposed the abolition of horse cavalry.[29]

At the height of his power, then, Mussolini still faced a military caste – particularly strong in the officer corps of the army – that was far from his Fascist ideal, and in some respects obstructionist with regard to his far-reaching plans for war and expansion. And he presided over armed forces that were badly led, ill-coordinated, insufficiently modernized (especially, again, in the army) and inadequately prepared for seriously testing combat.

The leadership of the armed forces amounted to only one – though arguably the most important – of a number of partially autonomous bases of power in the Fascist regime that were far from simply vehicles of Mussolini's supposed 'total' control and domination. It could be claimed with some justice that Fascism in Italy, more than was the case with Hitler's regime in Germany, rested upon a 'power cartel'.[30]

Mussolini's 'seizure of power' in the 'March on Rome' in 1922 was a Fascist myth. In reality, he had been handed power in a deal with the national-conservative power-elites. What transpired 'was not a revolution but an authoritarian compromise' establishing 'a primarily political dictatorship that presided over a semipluralist institutional system'.[31] Big business, the Church and the state bureaucracy retained some independence from Fascist control. In the economic sphere, Mussolini had to work with, rather than dominate over, the leaders of industry, business and finance. In a country where Catholicism was so influential – and there was no plainer reminder of this than the residence of the papacy within Italy's capital city – Mussolini had little choice but to reach a modus vivendi with the Church, as he did in the significant concessions granted through the Lateran Pacts of 1929 in return for the ending of papal hostility to the Italian state. And despite the rhetoric of Fascism's totalitarian ambitions, the party made few inroads into the domination of the apparatus of state government. On the contrary, it found itself shorn of much real power and turned largely into an agency of mass mobilization, propaganda, attempted political indoctrination and acclamation of the leader. Unlike in the Soviet Union, the state, not the party, remained pre-eminent. Mussolini recognized this by taking charge for a time in the latter half of the 1920s of no fewer than eight ministries of state. Although this, of course, significantly helped establish his unassailable leadership position, in reality, since he could not possibly oversee and direct everything in person, it also boosted the role of the state bureaucracy.[32] Even within the Fascist Party itself, Mussolini's position had initially been effectively first among equals, the acknowledged party leader, certainly, but compelled to recognize the independent power-bases of the local chieftains, the *ras* (an Ethiopian term) upon whose control of the local party organization his own power ultimately drew.[33] Nevertheless, by the later 1920s this initial mutual dependency had been transformed into the Duce's outright supremacy over the party.

Mussolini's initial struggle, once in power, had been to subordinate the Fascist Party itself to his complete control. One vehicle for attaining this was the institution of the Fascist Grand Council, which he initially set up in 1922, then, six years later, supposedly turned into 'the supreme organ that coordinates all activities of the regime'. In practice, it rarely met, had no legislative powers and indeed became little more than an agency of Mussolini's personal rule.[34] When Mussolini made his big decisions in 1940, to enter the war, then to attack Greece, he did not even consult the Fascist Grand Council. Nevertheless, as the events of 1943 were to show, even this apparently tame animal could still kick, for it was the Fascist Grand Council which led the revolt against Mussolini that ended with his deposition. Institutionally, then, even the Fascist Grand Council, however emasculated in practice, posed a potential check on Mussolini's power. In Germany, by contrast, Hitler consistently rejected overtures to establish a senate of the Nazi Party, alert as ever to the existence of any collective body that might in certain circumstances be in a position to challenge his personal authority.[35]

Though Mussolini's power was not absolute, it nonetheless expanded massively between 1925 and 1940, to the point where it approached that of an 'absolutist prince' whose decisions were subject to no effective control.[36] Crucial to this development were the gradually increased centralization of control over the party, the growth and elaboration of the extravagant Duce cult, and the impact of the Abyssinian war on Mussolini's standing.

From 1925 onwards, the residual independence of the provincial Fascist bosses, the *ras*, was undermined by the relentless bureaucratic centralization of the party's organization. By the early 1930s, even the most autonomous regional chieftains, such as Roberto Farinacci, the hardline boss of Cremona and party secretary for a brief time in the mid-1920s, had seen their wings clipped. Two general secretaries, ultra-loyal to Mussolini, Augusto Turati and Achille Starace, successfully purged the most unruly elements in the early Fascist movement then converted the party into a huge, enormously bloated organization largely devoted to the attempt to mobilize the masses behind the regime, and especially its leader, and to indoctrinate them in the aims and tenets of Fascism. In these years, the aesthetics of power were carefully honed and orchestrated. By the end of the 1930s the party was vast in size. On the eve of the European war, almost half of the population had formal membership of the party or one of its sub-organizations.[37] But doctrinally, the impact of Fascism was shallow. Ideological commitment to the regime and the 'fighting spirit' of Fascism that Mussolini was anxious to inculcate into the population remained limited – certainly far less profound than the impact of Nazism on the German population.[38]

The Fascist Party had been turned by the 1930s largely into an enormous vehicle of Duce adulation. The full-blown excrescence of the Duce cult accompanied this development. The pseudo-religious strains in the belief that the Duce 'was always right', as Fascist propaganda repeatedly told the population, need no emphasis. And such belief could easily coexist – as did the quasi-deification of Hitler in Germany – with limited allegiance either to the Fascist Party, or its doctrines.[39] But, plainly, the manufacture of the Duce cult produced a level of popular acclamation that enormously strengthened Mussolini's position of power. By the early 1930s he felt strong enough to remove from major office almost all of the earlier prominent figures in the Fascist movement who might have posed some check to his mounting domination. Some bore grudges which would become apparent when Mussolini was later at his most vulnerable, at the Fascist Grand Council's fateful meeting in July 1943. But, for the foreseeable future, the former Fascist potentates, divided and without collective voice, saw their power reduced to personal dependence upon Mussolini.[40] The Duce had bolstered his own position at the expense of his once mighty Fascist comrades. Their replacements were largely mediocrities, outright Mussolini acolytes.

Mussolini himself took back in hand some of the most important ministries, including, in 1933, foreign affairs (seen as too emollient in the hands of the former Foreign Minister and Fascist boss of Bologna, Dino Grandi) and the military ministries.[41] It was a sign that foreign policy was soon to become more assertive. In relation to the other 'big battalions' in the regime – such as big business, the state bureaucracy, the military leadership and, not least, the King himself – Mussolini's popular standing now meant that he was less easy to challenge, that the scope of his domination had increased. The 'power cartel', in other words, though continuing to exist, saw the actual balance of power tip sharply in Mussolini's favour as the 1930s wore on. This meant that the aggressive expansionism to which Mussolini was wedded, especially once he had himself fallen victim to the Duce cult and swallowed the myth of his own infallibility, became a more prominent part of Fascist politics, and was less easy to block by those fearful of its consequences for the country.

A major boost to the inflated domination of the Duce was provided by the Abyssinian war. This was in a real sense Mussolini's war. He had planned for it since 1932. He had pressed resolutely for it and engineered the way to it, despite the attempts by the League of Nations to find a diplomatic solution that would favour Italy. He pushed through the decision for war against alarmist warnings by Badoglio that it would result in war with Britain; against the caution of the conservative establishment that hated risk and also feared embroilment in a wider conflagration; and, not least, against the anxieties of the King, who, Mussolini later claimed, had to be forced to go to war.[42] Once victory was attained the following spring, Mussolini's triumph, trumpeted ceaselessly in a huge outpouring of adulatory propaganda, was complete. His own position had received another massive boost. His 'heroic' image had been burnished still more brightly. The Duce cult reached its apogee. In matters of war and peace, especially, Mussolini towered above all other figures in the regime. His dominance of foreign affairs was not diminished when Ciano, before the war ultra-loyal to Mussolini, took over the Foreign Ministry in 1936. The Abyssinian war had another important consequence for the power-structure in Italy. The old elites, including the King, had not wanted to go to war. But they rejoiced in the glory it brought (even if Mussolini later complained that the King deserved none).[43] More than that, they had favoured the expansionist goals, which had their roots in the pre-1914 imperialist dreams of the conservative establishment and the Liberal governments,[44] even while fearing the repercussions of conflict with the western democracies. And they had become complicit in the savagery of the war in Abyssinia once it had started. The barbarous initiatives in the conduct of the war came as a rule from the military elite rather than from Mussolini himself, though the Duce certainly gave the orders for measures of gross inhumanity.[45]

Following the war in Abyssinia, the commitment to Germany through the formation of the Axis, Italy's involvement in the Spanish Civil War, the part played by Mussolini in brokering the Munich Agreement and the annexation of Albania were all indicators that policy-making in foreign affairs had increasingly become the direct and personal province of the Duce, aided and abetted by Ciano. In matters of war and peace, decision-making was by now highly personalized. Discussion was, it was said, not a part of the 'Fascist style'. Sudden decisions reflected 'Napoleonic' quali-ties.[46] By March 1938 Mussolini was claiming equal status with that of the King as supreme commander of the armed forces.[47] The supposed representative bodies of the Fascist state, the Fascist Grand Council, the Senate (long since confined to Mussolini's appointees) and the Chamber of Fasces and Corporations (the eventual successor, in 1939, to the long moribund remnants of the Chamber of Deputies, the old parliament), had no input into decisions.[48] No institutional gathering or corporate body existed where decisions were collectively reached. The Council of Ministers bore only the most superficial resemblance to the Cabinet of a democratic system of government. It met only when Mussolini summoned it, invariably merely to hear his pronouncements, and was wholly under his dominance; a receptacle for decisions already taken, rather than an agency for helping to shape policy. Mussolini himself decided. In this, the position was directly analogous to that of Hitler's Germany, with the qualification that in the latter case there was no ultimate source of possible constraint on action, whereas Mussolini still had to reckon with the approval of the King, as head of state and focus of army loyalty.

There were only two vehicles within the Fascist state with the potential to influence Mussolini's power of decision on the crucial issues of war and peace. One was the Foreign Ministry, where Ciano's line began in 1939 to veer sharply away from that of his father-in-law in an anxiety to avoid a war that he thought would prove disastrous. However, this was no more than tactical opposition, born out of fear of the consequences of Mussolini's gung-ho wish to embroil Italy in war. Ciano, who harboured private hopes of succeeding Mussolini one day, was equally wedded to notions of expan-sion, quite especially in the Balkans. And the dilettante exercise of his position as Foreign Minister meant that the advice he gave to Mussolini was often personalized, rather than emanating from the expertise of the ministry's professionals. Fascist appointees to higher civil service positions had to some extent radicalized the personnel of a ministry in any case traditionally predisposed to expansion.[49] Beyond that, Ciano had instituted a top tier of the ministry, staffed by favourites and yes-men, which reduced the influence of the traditional apparatus.[50]

The other sphere of possible influence on Mussolini, as we have already noted, was that of his military advisers (and behind them, the King). They had somewhat reluctantly backed Mussolini in the decision to attack Abys-sinia in 1935. But Mussolini had been proved right, which strengthened his own position. A practised servility gradually set in even among his senior military advisers. Generals and admirals, admitted to an audience with the

Duce, would run twenty yards across his enormous room in the Palazzo Venezia before stopping to raise their arms in the Fascist salute.[51] What the military leaders were nonetheless able to convey to Mussolini in 1939 was the lack of readiness of the armed forces for conflict with the western democracies. With extreme reluctance, Mussolini had at the last minute bowed to the pressure from Ciano and his military advisers, and finally conceded when the King had made known his opposition to war.

Mussolini took the decision not to march alongside Germany as a major blow to his (and Italy's) prestige. The next months would see him smarting under the tension between his instinct for war and his acceptance that his armed forces were in no fit state to fight one. He could do no more than hope for opportunities. They would soon present themselves.

III

On 4 September 1939, the day after Great Britain and France had declared war on Germany, Mussolini made plain to Ciano his full solidarity with Hitler's Reich. He was convinced that the French did not want to fight. (He said nothing of Britain, though Ciano's own view was that British involvement ensured that the war would be 'long, uncertain and relentless'.) The Duce went on to indicate, according to Ciano, that 'he is still dreaming of heroic undertakings against Yugoslavia which would bring him to the Romanian oil'. In more sober mood, Ciano implied, the Duce was reconciled to neutrality in order to build up the economic and military strength to intervene 'at the proper moment'. But then he would suddenly revert to the idea, still attractive to him, of joining Germany in the conflict. Ciano felt he had to continue to dissuade Mussolini from this course. 'Otherwise', he prophetically added, 'it will mean the ruin of the country, the ruin of Fascism, and the ruin of the Duce himself.'[52]

German successes in Poland convinced Mussolini that he would soon be able to act as mediator in a new peace settlement. But, despite reminders of Italy's lamentable state of military preparedness – owing in no small measure to the endemic, irremediable inefficiency within the bureaucracy of the armed forces; only ten of the country's sixty-seven divisions were fit for combat in mid-September and the shortage of basic supplies was extraordinary[53] – and the strength of anti-German feeling among the Italian population, his regrets were plainly that he could not fight on Germany's side. A 'great nation', he thought, could not sustain a position of neutrality for long 'without losing face'. It must prepare to intervene.[54] Yet preparing

– and waiting – were all that the frustrated Mussolini could do. He also fluctuated in his confidence of ultimate German victory. He even intimated that a bloody stalemate between Germany and the western powers, leaving Italy to mop up the pieces, would suit him best.[55] As late as spring 1940 he was envisaging any German attack on France as likely to prove both bloody and indecisive.[56] Jealous of Hitler's successes, he would not have been unhappy to see the German dictator 'slowed down'.[57]

But what if the opposite were to happen? Hitler had made plain, when he met Ciano in Berlin on 1 October, that the fates of Germany and Italy were inextricably tied together. Defeat for Germany would mean the end of Italy's dreams of becoming masters of the Mediterranean. And, though showing understanding for the stance of non-belligerence, Hitler intimated that 'at a certain moment, Italy will have to profit from the favourable possibilities which will present themselves in order to join resolutely in the fray'.[58] Mussolini was tormented that a German triumph would come too soon; that Italy would still not be in a position to profit from the opportunity. He knew that Italy could not be ready before 1942 at the earliest.[59] And Italy, as he told Hitler, could not commit herself to a long war.[60] But he 'would like to do something that would get us into the game', Ciano noted that autumn. 'He feels left out, and this pains him.'[61]

Soon after the war had started, Mussolini had spoken of Italy's intervention any time after May 1940. But this optimism soon evaporated. Reports reaching him by the end of the year on the state of military preparations were depressing in the extreme. The army and navy would not be completely ready before 1943–4, the air force earlier, though not before mid-1941. Even such estimates drew on hope more than experience. Mussolini had to abandon hopes of fighting in 1940. He rescheduled the likely date for intervention to the second half of 1941.[62]

Intervention, even if earlier than desirable in terms of military preparations, would still give Italy a unique chance, not to be missed, to attain the goals that Mussolini had held for many years: end British and French dominance in the Mediterranean, turning it into an 'Italian lake'; in so doing, open Italy's access to the oceans, the platform needed for any great power; and bring the Balkans under Italian sway. The concept was of a parallel war – a war within a war. Already in autumn 1939, Mussolini, backed by Ciano, was eyeing up Yugoslavia as a likely target of Italian attack in the foreseeable future, with the aim of turning Croatia into a puppet state. Italy's military planners thought this project one within the capabilities even of the Italian armed forces, and sought to be ready for action in this sphere as early as the following spring. Greece, however, backed by the British guarantee, was another matter. 'Greece is not on our path,' Mussolini had declared.[63] He meant: not for the time being. In the event, no move could be undertaken against Yugoslavia either. Any major disturbance in the Balkans was simply too risky at this stage. It would have to wait until Italy's intervention in a wider conflict offered more propitious circumstances to strike in the Balkans.

By spring 1940 Mussolini was presuming that a German offensive against France would not be long delayed. In mid-March 1940, just prior to meeting Hitler at the Brenner Pass, Mussolini was anticipating that his co-dictator would 'set off the powder keg' before long, and attack in the west. In this event, Italy would retain solidarity with Germany, but still not enter the war until the moment was ripe. He was not thinking of throwing Italian troops into the heat of a front-line battle alongside the Wehrmacht against the seasoned French army. Treading a fine line between non-belligerence and participation in the conflict, he told Ciano that Italian forces would 'tie up an equal number of enemy troops without fighting, but ready, none the less, to go into action at a convenient moment'.[64]

Speaking to Hitler at their Brenner meeting on 18 March, Mussolini declared Italy's entry into the war to be 'inevitable'. This was not on the grounds of military aid for the German war effort – Germany, he said, could manage on her own – but 'because the honour and the interest of Italy demand her intervention in the war'. However, Mussolini was compelled to add that the earliest Italy could intervene would be in around four months' time, when four new battleships would be ready and the air force also prepared. Nor would Italy's financial situation (the country, as he knew, was almost bankrupt, though he did not of course tell Hitler this) allow her to fight a long war. Hitler pointed out that, with France beaten, Britain would be forced to sue for peace and Italy would be master of the Mediterranean. In the attack on France, he envisaged Italian troops advancing alongside the Wehrmacht into the Rhône valley. The Italian air force, he added, if a decisive breakthrough should be dependent upon Italy's contribution, ought in coordination with the Luftwaffe to attack French aerodromes from the south. Mussolini did not respond directly to the points on military tactics. But Hitler had succeeded in his psychological pressure on Mussolini. He had prodded him in the direction that the Duce was in any case temperamentally inclined to go. Mussolini now effectively confirmed to his fellow dictator that Italy would enter the war on Germany's side. He went on to state that he would intervene 'as soon as Germany had advanced victoriously', and would lose no time, if the Allies had been so shattered by the German attack, in delivering the second knockout blow. Should the advance of the German troops be slow, he would wait, and time Italy's intervention to be of maximum use to Germany.[65]

The meeting can only have reinforced Mussolini's sense of inferiority towards Hitler. He hated having to play second fiddle, keeping quiet most of the time while Hitler did the talking. But at least his fears that Hitler was immediately going to fall on France were assuaged. He returned from the Brenner persuaded that, contrary to what he had assumed before the meeting, the German offensive was not imminent.[66] But whenever it came, he had now committed Italy to intervention outright.

The Brenner meeting had left its mark on Mussolini. A few days later, Ciano noted that the Duce was 'in good humour these days' and 'is growing every day more definitively pro-German'. Mussolini was now speaking openly about entering the war on Germany's side, and he outlined for Ciano what he saw as Italy's course of action. He would not operate along-side the Wehrmacht on the southern French front, but instead maintain a defensive position in the Alpine regions. He would do the same in Libya, but take the offensive from Abyssinia against the important port of Djibouti (in the tiny French Somaliland that abutted it) and the British possession of Kenya, to the south. In the Mediterranean, the crucial theatre from an Italian point of view, he would engage in an air and naval offensive against the British and French. Ciano pointed out that Mussolini's bellicosity was starting to tell in bringing other Fascist leaders into line behind intervention. Some, however, remained opposed to what Ciano called 'the adventure'. This was Ciano's own position, though he himself was starting to weaken. As he noted, the mass of the Italian people still wanted nothing to do with war.[67] For Mussolini, their views were irrelevant.

On 31 March Mussolini presented his thoughts in a written memorandum for the King, Ciano and his military leaders. Though Italy would have an important role in any compromise peace, he thought this outcome could be excluded. The war would continue. Germany, he thought, would not engage in a major land offensive in the west until victory was certain. In the meantime, she would continue the 'phoney war', but with intensified air and naval operations. He turned, in a crucial passage, to the choices facing Italy. The only option for Italy, he stated, was to intervene on Germany's side. It was absurd to imagine that she could keep out of the war. Neutrality, in other words, could not be entertained. Nor was a change of policy and shift to the side of the western Allies viable. This, said Mussolini, would bring immediate conflict with Germany, in which Italy would be left to fight alone. Italy's current position had been built upon the alliance with Germany. Her own objectives could only be attained by maintaining this alliance, by fighting a parallel war to gain supremacy in the Mediterranean. The main issue was, therefore, not whether, but when, to fight. He would delay entry as long as possible, aware as he was of the weakness of the armed forces. A long war could not be waged, on economic grounds. But intervention offered opportunities not to be spurned. He then sketched Italian strategy on intervention, much as he had described it privately to Ciano, though with some elaboration.[68]

Addressing the Council of Ministers three days later, Mussolini kept up his rhetorical barrage in favour of war. He thought a German offensive could begin at any moment. Again, he rehearsed the options. Any change of course towards Britain and France would make Italy 'appear servile to the democracies' and bring her into conflict with Germany. By remaining neutral, Italy would 'lose prestige among the nations of the world for a century as a Great Power and for eternity as a Fascist regime'. So the only choice was to 'move with the Germans to advance our own ends'. He went on, in time-honoured fashion, to outline those ends: a Mediterranean empire and access to the ocean. Mussolini, noted Ciano, believed blindly in German victory, and in Hitler's word as to Italy's share of the booty. He himself doubted both.[69]

The military leaders also still needed convincing. The outcome of the meeting of the service chiefs with Badoglio on 9 April was anything but encouraging. They were pessimistic even about a limited offensive, insisted on avoiding close military cooperation with the Germans even in the event of a French collapse, agreed that no offensive from Libya was possible, were sceptical about the prospects of combined air and naval operations in the Mediterranean and expressed anxieties about Italy's position in Abyssinia. Summarizing for Mussolini, Badoglio adjudged that only in the event of the outright demolition of enemy forces by the Germans could Italian intervention be worthwhile.[70] The division between Mussolini's thirst for action and the passivity of the military leadership of the country still ran deep. But it was at this point that the German invasion of Denmark and Norway began to cause a reconsideration of Italian perspectives, a process that would be completed by the Wehrmacht's astonishing successes in the western offensive in May and June.

Mussolini's immediate response to the news of the German occupation of Denmark and Norway was outright approval. 'This is the way to win wars,' he declared. Alone with Ciano, the talk was of Croatia. 'His hands fairly itch,' commented the Foreign Minister. The Duce was keen to quicken the tempo to take advantage of the current disorder in Europe. He was more warlike and more pro-German than ever, in Ciano's estimation, though he said he would not move before the end of August (and a few days later changed this date to spring 1941). He was irritated, however, by an audience with the King, who was still unenthusiastic about intervention. 'It is humiliating to remain with our hands folded while others write history,' Ciano recorded him saying. 'To make a people great it is necessary to send them to battle even if you have to kick them in the pants. This is what I shall do.' But as late as May not just the King, but the Italian military leadership remained for the most part opposed to Italy joining the war. And, though Hitler's successes in Scandinavia had made an impression on public opinion – Mussolini contemptuously remarked that the Italian people were 'like a whore . . . always on the side of the winner' – there was as yet no marked upswing in pro-German or pro-war feeling among the masses.[71]

On the eve of the German western offensive, which began on 10 May 1940, Italian intervention was still not a certainty. Mussolini, to be sure, had become sharply and unremittingly belligerent, as Ciano's diary entries record. Some Fascist leaders had followed his lead. Massive pro-war propaganda had left its mark and doubtless swayed some faint-hearts to support early intervention. The forces supporting war had, in other words, become stronger, particularly after the successful German operations in Scandinavia. But the forces opposed to war were not without weight. They included Count Ciano, even though his resolve was less firm than it had been, the military leadership and not least the King. The decision for war, despite Mussolini's powerful and insistent advocacy, was still in the balance, and by no means a formality. Had the German victory over France been less conclusive, it is even imaginable that intervention could have been postponed, perhaps even to a point where the impetus to join the war faded and non-belligerence or neutrality became seen as less than a temporary status. Caution might have prevailed. Without that comprehensive and calamitous defeat for the Allies, Mussolini would at any rate have been taking a risk to force into war a country whose military elite as well as the broad masses of the population were so lukewarm if not outrightly hostile to fighting a major war on Germany's side. Ciano had received a hint in March that 'the King feels that it may become necessary for him to intervene at any moment to give things a different direction; he is prepared to do this and to do it quickly'.[72] It is not even beyond contemplation that such a move in circumstances seen as less than outrightly favourable might have prompted resistance within the power-elite, possibly even a military coup, backed if not directly initiated by the royal house.

In the event, however, the German victory in the west was swifter, the

French collapse more dramatic, than anyone had foreseen. The balance of power in Europe was completely refashioned. Whatever the position before Hitler launched his attack on the Low Countries and France, the devastating advance of the Wehrmacht had now totally altered the picture. Just as the Japanese rulers, as we saw, rapidly reshaped their strategy in the wake of the astonishing German triumph, so did the power-elite in Italy. As in Japan, the feeling was that Germany was certain to be victorious. With France laid prostrate within a matter of weeks, and the defeat of Britain surely only a matter of time, few in the Italian leadership now doubted that Hitler would win the war. This radically changed attitudes towards Italy's intervention.

In the light of the altered circumstances following the collapse of France, any notion that Mussolini alone pushed an unwilling nation into war and subsequent disaster would be misplaced. The chance of profiting from the destruction of the western democracies was widely seen as too good to miss. During the second half of May, therefore, the arguments in favour of intervention markedly gained in force. Opposition to participation in the war, conversely, became increasingly difficult to articulate. Impressed by the German advances, Dino Grandi, the Fascist boss of Bologna and until now an opponent of intervention, told Ciano: 'We should admit that we were wrong in everything and prepare ourselves for the new times ahead.'[73] Ultra-caution seemed completely misplaced, a recipe only for missing a unique opportunity to make cheap gains. Waverers and doubters now fell into line. For the first and only time, the Italian population became vociferously pro-war. Buoyed by his enthusiastic reception in some of the poorer districts of Rome, Mussolini had no doubt at the beginning of June that ordinary people had become 'accustomed to the idea that his war needs to happen'.[74] The leadership of the armed forces – and with it, the King himself – was won over by the prospect of gain without pain, glory at little or no cost. Significant parts of the Italian ruling establishment had, as we noted, even before the First World War wanted expansion to establish and cement great-power status. Fear of the consequences, not lack of ambition, had held it back. But the traditional expansionist aspirations easily slotted into the far more aggressive and dynamic Fascist version.[75] Now the opportunity that presented itself was as if godsent. When the moment of decision arrived, therefore, Mussolini found himself far from an isolated figure pressing for intervention against a reluctant people. He was by now surfing the tide, if on the foremost wave.

From the first days of the German offensive, Mussolini was certain that the Allies had lost the war. There was no time to waste, he told Ciano on

13 May. 'Within a month I shall declare war. I shall attack France and Great Britain in the air and on the sea. I am no longer thinking of taking up arms against Yugoslavia because it would be a humiliating expedient.' The prospect of action in the Balkans had, therefore, faded temporarily. A bigger prize was at stake. After all, as Ciano reminded him later in the month, 'after the war is won we can obtain what we want anyway'. Ciano's own opposition was now giving way. He offered no response to Mussolini's belligerence. 'Today, for the first time, I did not answer,' he noted in his diary. 'Unfortunately, I can do nothing now to hold the Duce back. He has decided to act, and act he will. Only a new turn in military events can induce him to revise his decision, but for the time being things are going so badly for the Allies that there is no hope.'[76] The next day Mussolini told the German ambassador in Rome, Hans Georg von Mackensen, that he would enter the struggle soon, no longer within months, but weeks or even days. Ciano was now resigned to intervention, though he hoped it would not be too soon, since Italy was still not ready for war. 'A mistake in timing would be fatal to us,' he added.[77] A week or so later, Ciano was mainly concerned with what Italy would get out of intervention. 'If we really have to leap headlong into war,' he wrote, 'we must make a definite deal.' He envisaged meeting Ribbentrop early the following month with a statement of what Italy's share of the war booty should be.[78]

The King, however, was still distinctly anti-German. And he continued to drag his feet about Italian intervention. It did not endear him to the Duce. Mussolini's hatred of the royal house was palpable. He was ready 'to blow' the monarchy – and the papacy with it – 'up to the skies' at the end of the war.[79] Mussolini's ire was provoked not least by the King's refusal to grant him the sole command of the armed forces in the war. In a nebulous arrangement, Victor Emmanuel conceded the political and military conduct of the war while retaining the supreme command in his own hands, a distinction which would come to matter in July 1943.[80] Nevertheless, the King, too, felt compelled to bow to the new circumstances of the German triumph in the west. By 1 June he was resigned to Italy entering the war. But, despite the propaganda barrage that had helped prompt the first demonstrations in favour of intervention in Rome's streets, he thought the country was going to war without enthusiasm. And he envisaged a long war, whose outcome would perhaps ultimately be determined by the entry of the United States into the arena.[81]

The Italian military leaders, who had imagined that much stiffer French resistance would have been offered to the German attack, were also bowing to the inevitable. By the end of May, according to Ciano, Badoglio 'now seems to accept a bad game with good grace, and prepares for war'. Badoglio was still cautious. The war had to be brief. Italy's supplies of vital raw materials were desperately low.[82] The army's chief of staff, Marshal Rodolfo Graziani, advised in late May that the army was in no fit state for offensive action, even against Yugoslavia. The head of the navy, Admiral Domenico Cavagnari, also envisaged only defensive operations, other than a limited effort by submarines in the Mediterranean. And the air force's suggestion of bombing French bases in Corsica was ruled out by Badoglio, since Mussolini himself did not want an air offensive against France at that time.[83] It was hardly a ringing endorsement of war. Such military effort as Italy would make was intended to be brief and in a minor key. The aim was to make the minimal contribution to attain maximum gains at the peace conference that would surely follow hard on the heels of German victory. But if the stance of the military was characterized by resigned acceptance rather than enthusiasm, there was nonetheless no opposition to the decision to go to war.

The same was true of big business. Here, too, the astounding German advances in May had dissipated an earlier preference for non-intervention. Business leaders naturally wanted what they saw as best for business. The fruits of intervention in a short and successful campaign appeared to provide it. And public opinion, so far as it is possible to judge it with accuracy, had now also largely fallen into line. Relentless state-orchestrated pro-war propaganda, greatly intensified over recent weeks, had not been without effect. Steps were taken to acclimatize the population to the onset of war. The glass in the windows of Milan cathedral was taken out and canvas covers put up. Schools closed at the end of May for the summer. Dance halls were shut. Foreign music was discouraged or Italianized: 'St Louis Blues' was to be sung as 'Tristezze di San Luigi'.[84] As the German offensive swept through Belgium and into France student demonstrators in Rome burned French and British flags. Similar demonstrations took place in Milan, Naples and other big cities.[85] One police report from Florence in early June recorded that 'the doubters have fallen silent, and the anti-Fascists are ultracautious . . . the expectation of a swift, easy and bloodless war against a France bled white and an England disorganized and with a decimated fleet, is rapidly maturing'.[86] Mussolini had no need to fear popular opposition to his decision to intervene.

Desperate appeals in May by Britain and the United States not to go to war were predictably rejected out of hand. Personal letters to Mussolini by Churchill and Roosevelt (who was offering, as we saw in Chapter 1, to act as mediator between Italy and the Allies) met a peremptory rebuff. The time when appeasement stood any chance was long past. In the last days of May Mussolini took the decision. Badoglio, according to his postwar account, learned of it on 26 May. He had been in the ante-room, waiting along with Italo Balbo (one of the most prominent and dynamic early Fascist leaders, former air force chief, strongly anti-German and well aware of his country's unreadiness to enter the war, briefly home from his position as Governor of Libya) for an audience with Mussolini. As soon as he entered the Duce's enormous study, Badoglio realized that the meeting would not be routine. Mussolini was 'standing behind his writing-table, his hands on his hips, looking intensely serious, almost solemn'. When he spoke, it was to announce that he had sent a message to Hitler the previous day, stating that he was ready to declare war on Britain after 5 June. Badoglio's memory was playing tricks on him about the timing of Mussolini's letter to Hitler, and also the precise date. Ciano noted in his diary entry for 26 May that Mussolini was *planning* to write to Hitler announcing Italy's intervention for the latter part of June.[87] The message was, in fact, only sent to the Italian ambassador, Dino Alfieri, on 30 May and delivered to Hitler in his western field headquarters that day.[88] Mussolini had subsequently brought the date of entry forward to 5 June following the capitulation of Belgium.[89] Badoglio went on to recall that he and Balbo were dumbfounded at the news, and Mussolini taken aback at the cold reception. Badoglio, so he said, pointed out in forceful terms that Italy was absolutely unprepared for war. 'It is suicide,' he claimed he remarked.[90]

Whether Badoglio really expressed such vehement opposition might be doubted. His memoirs were self-serving, meant to highlight Mussolini's sole responsibility for an act of lunacy. Badoglio stated that he stayed at his post out of a sense of duty, aware that his resignation would have changed nothing and would have been unpopular among the population, and also out of a conviction that he would be able to prevent mistakes which Mussolini was certain to make out of his ignorance of military affairs.[91] But the record of Mussolini's meeting with his military leaders on 29 May, when he formally announced that Italy would enter the war any time after 5 June, contains no reference to any protest from Badoglio or the others present. Even the King now reluctantly acquiesced.[92] Mussolini told his military chiefs – partially recouching what he had said at the end of March – that war was impossible to avoid, and that Italy could only fight on the side of Germany, not of the Allies. He had advanced the date of entry in accordance with the rapidly changing circumstances. He was certain of German victory, and postponing entry would run greater risks than premature intervention. It was important to be in the war before the

Germans had won so that Italy would have a bargaining position at the peace negotiations.[93]

The following day Ciano noted: 'The die is cast. Today Mussolini gave me the communication he has sent to Hitler about our entry into the war. The date chosen is June 5th, unless Hitler himself considers it convenient to postpone it for some days.'[94] In fact, the date did not suit Hitler. It might, he thought, by prompting the removal of some aircraft to the south of France, interfere with German plans for an all-out assault on French airfields. Mussolini grumbled, but rescheduled Italy's big day to 11 June.[95] The previous evening, 10 June, he addressed the crowd from the balcony of the Palazzo Venezia. An American journalist present painted the scene, as Mussolini 'bounced up like a jack-in-the-box on the balcony' to bellow his war declaration to the hundred thousand or so crammed into the square: 'He was greeted with probably the greatest applause he had ever received since he announced the end of the Abyssinian War . . . It looked as though Mussolini was making a "smart move" to realise his revindications upon France with a minimum spilling of blood. They thought France was already beaten and England left in a hopeless position. It was money for jam.'[96] The speech was, of course, no more than an organized propaganda show. Giuseppe Bottai, the Minister of Education, recorded the difficulty organized Fascist cheer-leaders had in rousing the crowd from its 'almost stupefied discipline'.[97] 'It was a pitiable spectacle,' Badoglio later recalled. 'Herded like sheep between the officials and the riff-raff of the Fascist Party, the crowd had orders to applaud every word of the speech. But when it was over, the people dispersed of their own accord in complete silence.'[98] Ciano's contemporary account was less expressive, though also pointed to a lukewarm reception by those other than Fascist diehards. 'The news of the war does not surprise anyone,' remarked Ciano, 'and does not arouse very much enthusiasm.'[99]

Obviously, from Mussolini's point of view Italy had no choice in the matter. The only question for him was not whether, but when, Italy would enter the war. Mussolini has often been portrayed as merely an opportunist, a dictator without driving ideological motivation and with simply an eye on the main chance, an exclusive focus on prestige, personal grandeur and power for its own sake. But this is to underestimate him. Entry into the war did not amount for Mussolini just to seizing the opportunity, important though the precise timing of intervention was. It was an inevitable step if his grandiose aims of an Italian *imperium* centred on the Mediterranean, erected on the ashes of the British and French Empires and the basis for making Italy a world power in deed and not just in presumption, were ever

to be realized. It was the logical outcome of the pretensions he had harboured since coming to power almost two decades earlier. In that time, as
we have seen, Mussolini's hold over Italy had strengthened inordinately.
By 1940 the political system had been fragmented and eroded to the extent
that no constitutional checks, apart from the King himself, could constrain
Mussolini's internal freedom of action. And no corporate body, such as a
Cabinet, helped to form decisions. Personal rule, when it came to questions
of war and peace, had come to mean precisely that. When he took the
decision for war at the end of May 1940, it was not after lengthy, indeed
after any, consultation with a variety of advisers. No one, it is true, among
Italy's political establishment was by then in the slightest doubt about the
Duce's wishes. But equally, no one influenced the implementation of those
wishes. The decision for war was his alone.

Until the heady days of May, alternatives did exist for other important
sections of the Italian political elite, as well as for the mass of the population.
Fascist *prominenti* like Ciano and Grandi, big-business magnates such as
Giovanni Agnelli and Alberto Pirelli, military leaders including Badoglio
and Cavagnari, and not least the King himself, had before May preferred
to stay out of the conflict. Two possibilities beyond Mussolini's favoured
interventionism were at least theoretically available.

The first of these was to switch allegiance from Germany to the Allies.
This, of course, eventually happened in September 1943, but under very
different circumstances. Despite the widespread dislike of Nazi Germany,
stretching from most ordinary Italians to Count Ciano and the King himself,
no one in spring 1940 seriously considered breaking the Axis alliance and
swapping sides. That could only have taken place following a coup to
topple Mussolini – something scarcely feasible in 1940 (even if the King,
as we have seen, appears momentarily and vaguely to have flirted with the
notion in March). And it would have involved Italy in the war anyway, but
against Germany. This would unquestionably have invited Hitler's wrath.
Mussolini himself, as we noted, more than once voiced his fear that crossing
Hitler would mean the might of the Wehrmacht being turned against Italy.
Whether, in such circumstances, Hitler could have held down Italy as well
as the Balkans in turmoil and still turned on the Soviet Union with Britain
unconquered might be questioned. But the question remains purely in the
realm of counter-factual speculation. In reality, the option to ditch Hitler
in favour of the Allies never existed in 1940.

The second alternative was more plausible. This was simply to retain
the status of non-belligerence, or neutrality. Those in Italy favouring
non-intervention had, either explicitly or by default, this option in mind.

Mussolini's rejection of it was, as we have seen, dictated by his ideological aims and his assumption that national 'virility' demanded that a would-be great power should fight and not remain neutral. Apart from Mussolini's psychological disposition and the aspirations to great-power status (which he shared with traditional imperialists in the national-conservative elite), could neutrality have been sustained? Franco managed it for Spain (even if neutrality had effectively been forced upon him when Hitler had proved unwilling to provide massive aid for a Spanish economy in ruins after three years of civil war). But Italy's geographical position, and her alliance with Germany, put her in a different position. One later assessment, though in a work sympathetic to Mussolini and arguing that Italy had no choice but to throw in her lot with Germany, stated that in the event of continued neutrality, she 'would sooner or later have been subjected to ever-increasing pressure by both sides'. In the end, her geographical situation would have brought an ultimatum from one side or the other to permit armed forces to be deployed in Italy. On refusal, Italy 'would have been invaded and devastated by the victors, whoever they were'.[100] This was, however, no more than apologetics. At the time that Mussolini opted for war, his choice was not shaped by any sense that Italy would otherwise be at the mercy of Germany, let alone of Great Britain.

A quite different, far more optimistic scenario was later painted by Churchill. 'It was certainly only common prudence for Mussolini to see how the war would go before committing himself and his country irrevocably,' Churchill wrote:

The process of waiting was by no means unprofitable. Italy was courted by both sides, and gained much consideration for her interests, many profitable contracts, and time to improve her armaments. Thus the twilight months had passed. It is an interesting speculation what the Italian fortunes would have been if this policy had been maintained . . . Peace, prosperity, and growing power would have been the prize of a persistent neutrality. Once Hitler was embroiled with Russia this happy state might have been almost indefinitely prolonged, with ever-growing benefits, and Mussolini might have stood forth in the peace or in the closing year of the war as the wisest statesman the sunny peninsula and its industrious and prolific people had known. This was a more agreeable situation than that which in fact awaited him.[101]

No one can, of course, know how a decision to defer entry to a date that could have become ever more distant would have played out in practice. But Ciano and others thought the prospect had a chance of success. That Italy would have come under pressure from both sides is obvious. This was already happening well before her entry into the war. As early as December 1939 Britain had tried to bribe Italy by an offer of most of the large supplies of coal that were so desperately needed. Italy would pay for the coal largely through the sale of arms. Ciano was well disposed towards the idea. But Mussolini would not sell arms to the British. He repeated his veto when a further attempt to buy Italian goodwill was tried some weeks later. That deal, too, foundered.[102] Hitler lost little time in offering his own economic inducements. The vital coal, which the British blockade ensured could not reach Italy from Germany by sea, would be sent by rail across the Brenner.[103] There is no doubt that such pressure and blandishments would have continued, and intensified, had Italy stayed out of the war. But, with clever diplomacy, Italy could have continued to play off each side against the other, retaining the advantages of neutrality, one-sided as it was, and avoiding being sucked into the maelstrom. By May 1940 Mussolini was being pressed for action from various sides in Germany.[104] Even then he was not *forced* to enter the conflict; he did so willingly. Had Italy not entered the war, it is extremely unlikely that the Germans would have taken any punitive action. A benevolent neutrality in the summer and autumn of 1940 would probably have suited German purposes at least as well as Italian involvement – in some senses better, as things turned out.[105] And from an Italian point of view, there was – apart from Mussolini's sense of urgency – a lot to be said for playing for time. In the climate of May 1940, however, such arguments were lost. All factions of the ruling elite fell in behind Mussolini's dogmatic belligerency. The fateful decision to take Italy into a war against Britain and France for which she was so ill prepared was taken. A heavy price would be paid.

IV

Italian forces had barely stuttered into action by the time the new French premier, Marshal Pétain, sought an armistice from Hitler on 17 June. By then a few air raids, to little effect, on Corsica (in which Ciano took part as leader of a bomber squadron[106]), southern France and Malta and a minor, inconsequential Alpine offensive had constituted practically the sum total of the initial Italian war effort. The armistice plea had come too early, and the Italian engagement had been too puny, for Mussolini to be happy. 'The Duce is an extremist,' Ciano noted on 17 June. 'He would like to go so far as the total occupation of French territory and demands the surrender of the French fleet. But he is aware that his opinion has only a consultative

value. The war has been won by Hitler without any active military participation on the part of Italy, and it is Hitler who will have the last word.
This, naturally, disturbs and saddens him. His reflections on the Italian
people and, above all, on our armed forces are extremely bitter this
evening.'[107]

Mussolini's embarrassment at the minimal Italian contribution to
France's humiliation did not prevent him, en route with Ciano to meet
Hitler in Munich to discuss armistice terms, from concocting a formidable
list of demands to be made of the French. These included occupation of
France as far as the Rhône, together with French cession of Nice, Corsica,
Tunisia and Djibouti. The French fleet and air force would also come into
Italian possession. Hitler voiced no opposition to the occupation zone that
Mussolini demanded. However, he wanted to treat the French leniently in
order to prevent the French fleet going over to the British and the French
government from transferring to north Africa, and also in the hope that it
would persuade Britain to come to the negotiating table. And he was not
prepared to include the Italians in the particular spectacle he had in mind
for agreeing on an armistice. He insisted on Italy conducting a separate
armistice, once the German terms had been settled. Mussolini was 'very
much embarrassed', feeling 'that his role is secondary'.[108]

When he saw the relatively moderate German armistice terms, Mussolini
felt compelled to content himself with the more modest demand of a
thirty-mile demilitarized strip within the French frontier and the hope of
advancing his more extensive demands at the final peace settlement. His
limited armistice demands had been influenced by further military humiliation. While the French were already prostrate and seeking an armistice of
the Germans, Mussolini had decided to launch an Alpine offensive. Badoglio opposed it. Ciano thought it 'rather inglorious to fall upon a defeated
army'. But Mussolini insisted. In dreadful weather conditions the Italian
attack ground to an ignominious halt at the first show of French resistance.
To add to the humiliation, Libyan colonial troops had been overrun by a
British force in north Africa, and an Italian general had been captured.[109]
It was little wonder that, in contrast to the great symbolic significance that
Hitler attached to the signing of the armistice at Compiègne, in the very
same railway coach that had been the scene of Germany's humiliating
capitulation of 1918, Mussolini ordered no publicity for the Italian armistice negotiations, which were conducted 'almost secretly'. The separate
Italian armistice with the French, concluded in Rome, was signed on
24 June.[110] Mussolini was 'bitter because he had wanted to reach the
armistice after a victory by our own armed forces'. Ciano was sure that

the Italian people would be greatly disillusioned by the limited gains war had brought.[111] Bottai indeed registered the popular criticism and sense of disappointment.[112]

Mussolini's thinking, and the war strategy that proceeded from such thoughts, in the weeks following the armistice with France was less than clear. On the one hand, he wanted a quick war together with the booty – and glory – that would follow on a triumphant peace settlement. The prospect of peace negotiations between Britain and Germany without Italy having seriously engaged in battle was not an attractive one for him. So when Britain made it clear that she was going to fight on, following Hitler's tepid encouragement to sue for peace in his Reichstag speech of 19 July 1940, Mussolini was, in a perverse way, not displeased. He had feared that the British would find even such a pallid invitation a pretext to open negotiations. 'That would be sad for Mussolini,' commented Ciano, 'because now more than ever he wants war.'[113]

On the other hand, Mussolini was well aware that Italy was in no fit state to fight a long war. So victory had to come quickly. With Britain determined to continue the war, despite unofficial peace-feelers through neutral channels that continued to give him cause for worry, Mussolini pinned his hopes on the German invasion that he had been told was imminent. He wanted Italian troops to take part alongside the Wehrmacht, but was politely though firmly rebuffed by Hitler. At this, while wanting the invasion to succeed, he hoped that the Germans would get a bloody nose in tough fighting and suffer perhaps a million casualties.[114] With Britain and Germany both weakened, Italy would be in a prime position to maximize its booty. And this was to be considerable. Apart from the extensive gains from France, the territorial aims put together by Ciano included the acquisition of Malta and British Somaliland from Britain together with effective control over former British-controlled countries in the Middle East and north Africa (including Egypt), which would retain only nominal independence.[115]

The best way Italy could have inflicted her own serious damage upon Britain was, in fact, in north Africa, where the British military presence was still weak and the Italians were equal in armoury and superior in numbers. Badoglio still hoped that big gains could be made for little or no military effort. But Mussolini was anxious to accelerate the drive across 350 miles of desert from Libya to Alexandria, to force the British out of Egypt and take over Suez, before a peace settlement could be reached. With characteristic bravado, he told Hitler in July that he would be in Egypt before the end of the month.[116] The enterprise was not helped when Marshal

Balbo, who would have launched the attack from Libya, was shot down and killed when his own side opened fire on his plane near Tobruk at the end of June. His replacement, Graziani, then spent the rest of the summer finding excuses for not pressing home what turned out to be a short-lived advantage. In September, he advanced sixty miles into Egypt and took the fortified base at Sidi Barrani. But he showed no inclination to press on to Alexandria. Whatever Mussolini's urgings, Graziani would find a reason for inaction. Mussolini could do nothing about it. And, from a misplaced sense of pride and sensitivity to prestige, anxious to demonstrate that Italian troops could handle one front on their own, and at the same time equally anxious to keep the Germans out of his own sphere of activity, he declined Hitler's offer of troops to assist in the push for Egypt. Unwilling as on other occasions to affront his co-dictator, Hitler did not insist. The Axis war effort remained two uncoordinated strategies. Meanwhile, the British built up sizeable forces to face the Italians. The chance, possible with German aid, had been missed.[117]

Mussolini's other hope lay in the Balkans. He had temporarily seen prospective military action in this region as a mere sideshow while the main event was taking place in France. But now, egged on by Ciano, he again cast his eyes on what looked to be rich pickings across the Adriatic. And not just Yugoslavia, but now – for the first time in earnest – Greece entered the frame as a concrete object of Italian expansionism. By the autumn, the decision to attack Greece would become the most calamitous mistake Mussolini had made; calamitous for the Greeks, of course, but also calamitous for himself, for the Fascist regime and, in the futile loss of life it caused, for his country.

Ever since the Italian takeover in Albania in April 1939 the Greeks had looked towards Italy with a wary eye, and not without cause. Ciano had noted in his diary on 12 May that year that the new programme of public works in Albania had started well. 'The roads are all planned in such a way as to lead to the Greek border. This plan was ordered by the Duce, who is thinking more and more of attacking Greece at the first opportunity.'[118] As the crisis mounted before the German invasion of Poland relations between Greece and Italy became tense. Italian troops were moved for a while to the border between Albania and Greece, while aircraft violated Greek airspace. On 16 August 1939 Badoglio had been given orders to prepare a plan to invade Greece. But nothing came of it. The tension subsided. On 11 September Mussolini told his representative in Athens, Emanuele Grazzi, that 'Greece does not lie on our path, and we want nothing from her'. Nine days later he was equally plain in speaking to General Alfredo Guzzoni, the military commander in Albania derided by Ciano for being 'small, with such a big belly, and dyed hair'. Mussolini informed him that 'war with Greece is off. Greece is a bare bone, and is not worth the loss of a single Sardinian grenadier.' Italian troops were pulled back to about twelve miles from the Greek border. The General Staff's invasion 'study' was consigned to the bottom drawer.[119] All went quiet until Italy joined in the war in June 1940.

Within days of Italy's entry the temperature rose again amid rumours – denied outright by Ioannis Metaxas, Greece's dull dictator, who looked more like a small-town mayor than a head of state, and who was ironically an admirer of Italy, where he had lived for some years – that the British were abusing Greek neutrality and basing warships in Greece's waters. Ciano stirred the pot. He had outlined to Bottai some weeks earlier his vision of Italian dominance in the Balkans. It included the establishment of protectorates in Croatia and Greece (also taking in Crete), as well as a north African protectorate embracing Egypt, Tunisia, Algeria and Morocco and possession of Corsica.[120] But Mussolini recognized that the realization of these grandiose plans would have to wait. The Germans, he knew, wanted no expansion of the war at this juncture.[121] He had Grazzi tell Metaxas that Italian policy towards Greece was unchanged. Military contingency planning nevertheless continued to include action against Greece *and* Yugoslavia, as well as possible moves to secure the Ticino, the Italian-speaking enclave of Switzerland, if, as was rumoured, the Germans were soon to invade that country. It was little wonder that a frustrated Badoglio was heard to say: 'The enemy changes every day. I expect the order to attack Iraq!'[122]

As regards the Balkans, however, Yugoslavia rather than Greece remained the priority. Mussolini contemplated taking action in August. Hitler, when he met Ciano on 7 July, seemed to encourage Italy's aggressive intentions in that direction. But whatever Hitler had meant to imply, it was not an Italian invasion of Yugoslavia in the immediate future, which he judged likely to set the whole of the Balkans ablaze at a highly delicate moment, provoking Russian intervention. While Hitler conceded that the fate of Yugoslavia was Italy's to determine when the time was ripe, now was expressly not that time. But he repeated that 'everything concerning the Mediterranean, including the Adriatic, is a purely Italian matter, in which he does not intend to interfere' and also indicated his approval for Italian action to prevent the British gaining a foothold in the Greek islands.[123]

Italian military plans for an assault on Yugoslavia continued throughout

July despite Hitler's warning against precipitate action (which had not been passed on by Ciano to Mussolini in its full vigour).[124] In early August Mussolini was still talking about an attack in the second half of September.[125] A few days later, on 11 August, he ordered the foot-dragging Badoglio, who only a short time earlier had issued a directive stipulating that it was not the intention to take military action in the Balkans, to be ready to move by 20 September.[126] That same day, Mussolini set his sights on Greece.

Ciano was the main instigator. He knew how angry Mussolini was about Graziani's tardiness in starting the offensive in north Africa. Graziani had just been in Rome and given Mussolini the impression that the attack on Egypt would start within a few days. He had told Ciano, however, that preparations were far from complete. Ciano's own impression was that the attack would not start for two or three months, if at all. He reported this to Mussolini, who was predictably livid.[127] Adeptly spotting the moment, and shrewdly manipulating the Duce's psychology, Ciano seized the chance to press for an attack on Greece. Mussolini, as we have noted, already favoured moving against Yugoslavia. Ciano now persuaded him without difficulty that Greece, too, should be included in the plans for expansion in the Balkans. Deprived of the chance of glory in France, and now facing the prospect of delays in north Africa, Mussolini saw the attractions of an easy triumph over the Greeks, a nation he held in contempt.

Ciano, for his part, saw in the enterprise the potential to magnify his own power-base. Albania already served effectively as a personal fiefdom for him, run by his minion, Francesco Jacomoni. The prospect of enlargement of his domain, and of easy glory, beckoned. On 10 August Ciano stirred Mussolini's easily aroused antagonism towards Greece. Jacomoni had fed Ciano the story of the treacherous assassination by Greek agents of an Albanian freedom fighter, Daut Hodja, which was now relayed to Mussolini as an indication of Greek untrustworthiness. Hodja was in fact no more than a local bandit and cattle-thief, with a long history of extreme violence and criminality, who had been caught and beheaded by rival criminals – Albanians, not Greeks – two months earlier. But Mussolini needed no persuading. 'The Duce is considering an "act of force, because since 1923 [the short-lived Corfu incident] he has some accounts to settle, and the Greeks deceive themselves if they think that he has forgotten",' noted Ciano, following their meeting.[128] Immediately, the Italian propaganda machine surged into action, eulogizing Hodja's patriotic virtues and castigating the treatment of Albanians by the Greek minority of the border area of Epirus, abutting Albania in northern Greece.[129]

On 11 August, the day after he had set Mussolini on the path to aggression against Greece, Ciano noted that the Duce wanted information on 'Ciamuria' (the contemporary Italian name for Epirus, derived from the Albanian word for the region). He had started agitation on the issue, and had called Jacomoni and General Count Sebastiano Visconti Prasca – Guzzoni's incompetent successor as military commander of Albania, proud of his manly physique, though actually, with his monocle and dyed eyebrows, slightly eccentric in appearance[130] – to Rome for discussions. Mussolini 'speaks of a surprise attack against Greece towards the end of September', Ciano recorded.[131] Ciano was party to the discussions the next day. Mussolini laid down the guidelines for action against Greece. 'If Ciamuria and Corfu are yielded without striking a blow, we shall not ask for anything more. If, on the other hand, any resistance is attempted, we shall go to the limit,' the Duce declared. Jacomoni and Visconti Prasca thought the operation would be easy, and pressed for it to be undertaken immediately. Mussolini preferred to wait until the end of September.[132]

The German Foreign Ministry was, meanwhile, hearing from its representative in Athens, Prince Viktor zu Erbach-Schönberg, that Greece would resist all aggression and refuse to be humiliated by Italy, 'even if that involves the risk of being destroyed'. Popular feeling was running high against Italy.[133] There would be strong support for resistance to Italian intervention. The conclusion was that 'if Italy believes that this is the right moment to realise its territorial claims in relation to Greece, it is mistaken'.[134]

For the Germans, keeping the lid on the simmering tensions in the Balkans was a high priority. Hitler had told Ciano on 20 July that he attached 'the greatest importance to the maintenance of peace in the Danube and Balkan regions'.[135] Soviet interest in the Danube region had been pointedly indicated at the end of June with the annexation of Bessarabia and northern Bukovina – the former a region of Romania which had at one time been part of Tsarist Russia. Hungary, too, had acute border disputes with Romania. These were settled only in late August by German and Italian forced 'arbitration' which truncated large parts of Transylvania, awarding the lion's share to Hungary. The Germans were anxious to prevent disturbance in the region, both to retain their hold on oil from the Romanian oil wells in Ploesti, and to prevent further Soviet encroachment. Keeping the Russians (whose traditional sphere of defensive interests stretched as far as the Bosporus) and the British (guarantors of Greek independence since April 1939, seen as ready to exploit any upheaval in Greece and the Aegean) out of the Balkans was vital to the Germans. Impulsive Italian action against

Yugoslavia could lead to Soviet intervention. Action against Greece could let in the British by the back door. By mid-August, therefore, the message was being diplomatically imparted from Berlin to Rome that Italian action in the Balkans was undesirable at this stage. 'Peace in the Balkans', as Hitler had told Ciano on 20 July in unmistakable terms, remained the outright priority. As he had made plain to the Italian Foreign Minister a few days earlier, the key Italian military aim had to remain Egypt and the Suez Canal.[136]

Ribbentrop repeated the need to keep the Balkans quiet when he met the Italian ambassador, Alfieri, on 16 August. It was crucial, the German Foreign Minister stated, to avoid action that would disturb the status quo there. The Russians should be given no pretext for intervention. The defeat of Britain was the absolute priority.[137] Ciano noted the outcome of Ribbentrop's talks with Alfieri in his diary the following day. It was 'necessary to abandon any plan to attack Yugoslavia', and 'an eventual action against Greece is not at all welcome in Berlin'. He summed up: 'It is a complete order to halt all along the line.'[138]

Mussolini bowed to the pressure, though Ciano ensured that anti-Greek propaganda continued in the Italian press and three army divisions were put on stand-by for dispatch to Albania.[139] Following a reassertion of German anxiety to avoid trouble in the region, stated in plain terms by Ribbentrop to Alfieri at a further meeting on 19 August, Mussolini gave orders three days later to slow down preparations for Yugoslavia and Greece. North Africa again had military priority – though Mussolini continued to give out directives, quite incompatible with Italy's limited resources, for preparations in different possible theatres of war.[140] Ciano recorded that 'the actions against Yugoslavia and Greece are indefinitely postponed'.[141] In the case of Yugoslavia, this was accurate. The operation was effectively abandoned. Hopes had to rest on what Italy could gain in the eventual peace settlement, once Britain had been defeated. Greece, however, was a somewhat different matter. Ciano duly passed on to Jacomoni in Albania the orders from 'higher authorities' to 'slow down the pace of our moves against Greece'. He instructed him, nonetheless, to take the necessary steps to maintain 'in a state of potential efficiency all the dispositions made', avoiding crisis but 'keeping the question alive'.[142] Military plans for an attack on Greece were also continued and refined.[143]

Badoglio evidently thought, even so, that the planners were going through the motions. Word was passed from Supreme Command headquarters to the air force chief of staff, Francesco Pricolo, on 10 September that 'Greece is off'.[144] Mussolini did not, however, see it like that. Though he had given up on Yugoslavia (which could only have been attacked with help from the north from Germany, if serious losses were to be avoided), he was not ready to discard the option to attack Greece as soon as it was feasible. This would be an Italian triumph without hanging on to German coat-tails. More than that: it would ensure that the Balkans did remain Italy's sphere of influence, heading off the possibility, starting to be rumoured, that despite all assurances the Germans intended to stamp their own imprint on the region.[145] However, Mussolini's views changed with his moods. Consistency was not his strong point. On the last day of August, Quirino Armellini, Badoglio's deputy at Supreme Command headquarters, commented in his diary: 'Ciano wants war on Greece to enlarge the boundaries of his grand duchy; Badoglio sees how great a mistake it would be to set the Balkans alight (that is the German position) and wishes to avoid it; and the Duce agrees now with one and now with the other.'[146] There, for an uneasy month of September, the matter rested.

By the time Ribbentrop visited Rome between 19 and 22 September, bringing a new 'surprise'[147] – a military alliance with Japan which he wanted Italy to sign alongside Germany within the next few days – the prospects of an imminent German invasion of England were fading.[148] A long-drawn-out war seemed increasingly likely. Mussolini was not displeased. He still thought a rapid end would be 'catastrophic', as he told Badoglio on the day of Ribbentrop's departure.[149] He was in a buoyant mood. He thought that, with the Germans bogged down in the conflict with Britain, Italy had a chance over the winter to advance through Egypt to Suez, without German aid, and destroy the basis of British strength in the Middle East. Badoglio was just as anxious to prevent the Germans from becoming involved in Italy's 'parallel war'. Ribbentrop had again indicated that Germany wanted no disturbance in the Balkans in the foreseeable future, though he once more acknowledged that Greece and Yugoslavia were a matter of exclusively Italian interest.[150] Mussolini said he would not move against either for the time being, though he took the opportunity to remind Ribbentrop that in the Mediterranean Greece played much the same role in support for Britain as Norway had earlier done in the north.[151]

Ciano did his best to ensure that the question of Greece should not drop from sight. He was still impatient for action.[152] He doctored the Italian version of the minutes of his meeting with Ribbentrop to ensure that they mentioned the necessity of proceeding to 'the liquidation of Greece' – a phrase which did not appear in the German version.[153] And he mentioned to the papal nuncio shortly afterwards that Italy soon, though not immediately, intended to occupy all of Greece because of the untrustworthiness of the Greeks.[154] He seems to have had in mind a rapid military conquest at little cost to acquire Greece as a bargaining counter in a compromise peace settlement, the most likely outcome, he envisaged, of a deteriorating war situation.[155]

Meanwhile, army contingency planning continued. But Badoglio reminded army staff in early October that there was no early likelihood of action.[156] With priority given to north Africa, and more than half of the army in Italy demobilized to help with the harvest, the resources of manpower, limited in any case, were already stretched to the limit and would remain so over the winter.[157] Plans for an attack on Greece were shelved.

They remained dormant during the first days of October. While Ciano had been in Berlin for the signing of the Tripartite Pact on 27 September, Hitler had suggested a meeting with Mussolini at the Brenner Pass. He wanted to review the overall situation in the war, and in particular the position in the Mediterranean, notably the question of Spanish intervention in the war and relations with France. The meeting took place on 4 October. Mussolini was in fine form. He had been in good humour for some days. He was anticipating 'that Italy could score in Egypt a success which affords her the glory she has sought in vain for three centuries' (though he was irritated with Badoglio, whom he blamed for holding back the offensive).[158] The meeting went well. Mussolini received renewed German backing for Italy's territorial claims against France: Nice, Corsica, Tunis and Djibouti.[159] He expressed his confidence in Italian success in Egypt. He had no need, he said, to avail himself of Hitler's offer of specialist forces for the attack.[160] Mussolini returned to Rome in a sunny mood, irritated only by the sluggishness of Badoglio and Graziani over north Africa and voicing his detestation of the King, 'the only defeatist in the country'.[161]

Within days, however, an issue was to arise which would cast a dark shadow over Mussolini's sunny demeanour, and over relations between the Axis partners: the stationing of German troops in Romania. The Germans had engineered an 'invitation' from the new Romanian dictator, General Ion Antonescu, in early September to send a 'military mission' to his country. Crucial from the German point of view was the safeguarding of the Ploesti oilfields. By mid-September, before Ribbentrop visited Rome, the Italians had known of the plans to send German troops to the Ploesti area. Ribbentrop had expressly referred to them when he met Ciano on 19 September, but Ciano had evidently not passed on this important fact to Mussolini.[162] The Ploesti oil was also vital to Italy. Moreover, Mussolini had always regarded the Danube as an area of specific Italian interests. So there was particular sensitivity on the issue; and also on the way Italy was handled by her Axis partner. The sensitivity exploded when Mussolini heard from press reports (which actually anticipated the event) that 15,000 German troops had arrived in Romania. For Mussolini this was a highly unwelcome reminder of the way Hitler had repeatedly informed him of significant German actions only after they had taken place.[163] He was absolutely incensed. He immediately sought, in vain, to attain a similar 'invitation' to have Italian troops sent to the area. 'He is very angry,' Ciano remarked, 'because only German forces are present in the Romanian oil regions.'[164] Ciano told Bottai that it was necessary 'for us to counterbalance their occupation of Romania by invading Greece'.[165] Ribbentrop tried to placate Ciano by telephone on 10 October, and reminded him that he had spoken about the issue in Rome on 19 September. Ciano made no comment. The damage was done.[166]

Within two days Mussolini had taken the decision to attack Greece as soon as preparations could be made. On 12 October, on return to Rome from a few days in the north of the country inspecting Fascist organizations, he was angered by news of further delay before Graziani would begin the long-awaited offensive in north Africa. What he heard from Romania was guaranteed to make him even more irascible. German troops had begun arriving in Bucharest. Not only that: officials in Ribbentrop's ministry had high-handedly wanted to block any reportage of this in the Italian press; and Antonescu would probably only permit the stationing of Italian troops in Romania if the Germans agreed.[167] Mussolini's fury boiled over. Incensed at the slight on his and his country's prestige, he was anxious to retaliate. 'Hitler always faces me with a fait accompli,' he fumed to Ciano. 'This time I am going to pay him back in his own coin. He will find out from the papers that I have occupied Greece. In this way the equilibrium will be re-established.' Mussolini admitted that he had not yet reached agreement with Badoglio about military operations against Greece. 'But I shall send in my resignation as an Italian if anyone objects to our fighting the Greeks,' he added. 'The Duce seems determined to act now,' noted Ciano, delighted that what he had long advocated would at long last happen. The Foreign Minister thought the military operation would be 'useful and easy'.[168]

In this extreme fit of pique and wounded pride, the fateful decision to attack Greece was taken. Not just a sense of personal humiliation, but his standing among the Italian population propelled Mussolini to action. Up to now he had little more than the insignificant conquest in August of the barren outpost of British Somaliland to preen himself about to the Italian people as the spoils of war.[169] He was concerned about the impact on public opinion in Italy of yet another German unilateral move. It would be seen as a further, and wounding, example of the inexorable subordination of Italy to the German juggernaut. A quick victory in Greece would restore the balance, boost his own prestige and bring, at last, a share of the spoils for Italy.[170]

The decision was taken, then, in an impulsive and arbitrary manner – characteristic of Mussolini's personality and of his style of rule. But his fury over the stationing of German troops in Romania constituted the occasion, not the underlying reason, for invading Greece. It affected when, rather than whether, an assault would be launched. An attack on Greece had, as we have seen, long been part of Mussolini's longer-term plans for establishing Italian dominion in the Mediterranean and Balkan regions. Germany had repeatedly conceded that Greece was Italy's to determine. Equally, repeated warnings had been given that turmoil in the Balkans was to be avoided. The Italian military gleaned the impression that at the Brenner meeting Hitler had given Italy carte blanche in Greece.[171] This was undoubtedly a misunderstanding. There is no reference to Greece in the official minutes, Italian or German, so if a hint to this effect was given, it must have been in private discussion between the dictators. Given the consistent German wish to maintain the uneasy status quo in the Balkans, it is inconceivable that Hitler was actually encouraging Mussolini to launch an attack on Greece. The cryptic reference can only denote some generalized concession, compatible with earlier similar statements, that Greece was seen on the German side as belonging to a future Italian dominium, not a target for immediate conquest.

Mussolini himself had until now not seen Greece as an urgent priority. North Africa had seemed the more important and strategically worthwhile theatre. In fact, for some days after reaching his decision to launch an attack on Greece without delay he had envisaged this taking place in tandem with the offensive in Egypt. Only on 16 October did he learn that the latter could not take place for another two months or so.[172] Greece at this point, but only now, assumed outright priority.

On 13 October Mussolini informed Badoglio of the decision to attack Greece that he had unilaterally taken the previous day. He set the date for 26 October. Badoglio appears to have lodged no objection. The following day Mussolini told Badoglio and Roatta, the deputy chief of the army staff, that 'the operation against Greece will not limit itself to Ciamuria, but will take in the whole country, which in the long run may prove a nuisance'. He would give Hitler notice of the attack only at the last moment.[173] The army's earlier contingency plans had only foreseen a limited conquest of Epirus, that is, of the northern parts of Greece. It was the first indication

Roatta had been given that the earlier planning had been superseded.[174] He pointed out that an offensive reaching to Salonika and Athens would require a far larger force than initially contemplated. Three months would be needed to have twenty divisions, the requisite number of troops, in place.[175] The military chiefs were privately doubtful about the feasibility of the Greek operation before Graziani's advance into Egypt had been undertaken. But if Mussolini noted their doubts, he was not listening. Greece would not now wait.

Mussolini summoned a meeting of his military chiefs to take place next day, 15 October, at 11 o'clock in his study at the Palazzo Venezia 'to lay down – in broad outline – the course of action that I have decided to undertake against Greece'. Ciano, Badoglio, his deputy head of Supreme Command Ubaldo Soddu and Roatta, together with Jacomoni and Visconti Prasca, who had been ordered over from Albania, were present. Roatta arrived late. He had been informed of the meeting only a short while earlier by the Duce's private secretary. Remarkably, the chiefs of the naval and air staffs, Cavagnari and Pricolo, were not asked to attend.[176] The meeting lasted only one and a half hours. It was one of the most superficial and dilettantish discussions of high-risk military strategy ever recorded.

Mussolini began by outlining the objectives of the operation: occupying the whole of the southern coast of Albania and the Ionian islands of Zante, Cephalonia and Corfu in a first phase, then the total occupation of Greece in a second phase to put her 'out of action'. This, he reckoned, would strengthen Italy's position in the Mediterranean in relation to Britain, and ensure that Greece remained 'within our politico-economic sphere'. He said he had decided the date, 26 October, which 'must not be postponed even by an hour'. This appears to have been the first time that Roatta heard the date.[177] Yet only the previous day he had insisted that three months would be necessary to prepare for such a full-scale action.

Mussolini saw no complications arising from Yugoslavia or Turkey, and planned to make Bulgaria 'a pawn in our game' by offering her gains in Macedonia. He then turned to Jacomoni. The Governor of Albania asserted that the operation was impatiently awaited in his province. He pointed to possible supply difficulties if the port of Durazzo, the key unloading point, were to be bombed. The state of the roads, though much improved, could also cause problems. He relayed information that the Greeks would resist the action. The scale of resistance would depend upon the swiftness and decisiveness of Italian action. He raised the question of aid for Greece from Britain. A partial occupation might allow British air raids on southern Italy and Albania. Greek aircraft, however, posed no problems. Asked about the morale of the Greek population, he assessed their state of mind as 'profoundly depressed'.

Visconti Prasca then commented on the military situation in Albania. He was highly optimistic. The first phase of the operation had been prepared 'down to the most minute details and is as perfect as is humanly possible'. He judged it would take only ten to fifteen days to occupy Epirus, well before the rainy season could set in to cause serious difficulties. The starting-date of the operation could be advanced, but not put back, the Duce interjected. Visconti Prasca was asked to comment on the morale of his troops. This was excellent, he stated. Around 70,000 men were ready, a superiority of two to one in the front line. As far as he was concerned, 'the Greek air force does not exist'. The only worry from the skies was from the possibility of aid from Britain. He did, however, allude to reservations about extending the advance to Salonika, given the time of year. This would take time. A couple of months would be required. The Duce insisted on the importance of preventing Salonika from becoming a British base. He asked Visconti Prasca about the morale of the Greek troops. 'They are not people who like fighting,' was the lapidary reply. He arranged to simulate an incident to serve as a provocation for the Greek attack. Mussolini advised him not to worry excessively about possible losses. Visconti Prasca replied that he had always ordered the battalions to attack, even against a division.

At this point, Badoglio took up the discussion. He thought the British would be preoccupied with Egypt and highly unlikely to attempt naval landings in Greece. The only possibility of British aid was from the air. Consequently, he favoured an operation against Greece to coincide with the advance on Mersa Matruh in Egypt, thus making it difficult for the British to spare aircraft to help the Greeks. Mussolini, still unaware that Graziani was about to postpone his advance, favoured the taking of Mersa Matruh even before the start of the Greek operation. Pushing on from there would make it even more difficult for the British to provide aid for Greece. And 'after the loss of the Egyptian key point, even if London were still able to carry on, the British Empire would be in a state of defeat', he added, with serene optimism. Badoglio approved of Visconti Prasca's operational plan for Epirus, but stopping there would not be enough. Crete and Morea would also need to be occupied, along with the whole of Greece. This, however, would require about twenty divisions (the figure Roatta had come up with the day before) and take three months.

Mussolini reckoned that the completion of the occupation of Epirus by 10–15 November would allow for a further month to bring in fresh forces needed for the remainder of the operation. He enquired how the march on

Athens was envisaged, once Epirus was occupied. Visconti Prasca foresaw no great difficulties. Five or six divisions would suffice, he thought. Badoglio suggested the march on Athens should precede the taking of Salonika. Roatta agreed with Mussolini's suggestion that two divisions might be enough for that. Mussolini was satisfied that 'things are getting clearer'. Visconti Prasca enjoined that Greece would be cut in two from Athens, and Salonika could be attacked from the Greek capital. He did, however, in a response to a question from Mussolini, point out the difficulty of the terrain between Epirus and Athens: some 170 miles of poor roads over steep hills and a mountain chain where communications were reduced to passage over mule tracks. He thought three mountain divisions would be required. He imagined they could be dispatched to the port of Arta, a good distance down the Greek coast, in a single night.

The final part of the meeting was devoted to the question of using Albanian troops in the attack, and the deployment of anti-aircraft defence in Albania. By this stage, Mussolini adjudged that 'we have now examined all the aspects of the problem'. He summed up: 'Offensive in Epirus; observation and pressure on Salonika; and, as a second phase, the march on Athens.'[178]

What passed for dictatorial decisiveness was in reality the merest veneer of half-baked assumptions, superficial observations, amateurish judgement and wholly uncritical assessment, all based upon the best-case scenario. After years of self-indoctrination, Mussolini was a firm believer in his own infallibility. Jacomoni and Visconti Prasca were prototypical creatures of the regime, capable only of pandering to Mussolini's assessments, wanting to profit from the opportunity of self-aggrandizement, anxious only to please by saying what the Duce wanted to hear. Ciano was largely silent. His preferences were plain. He was content to let his minions do the talking, assured that Mussolini was now pressing for what he himself had wanted all along. Soddu's silence amounted to his own backing for the operation. Badoglio and Roatta raised objections only in the most oblique fashion, pointing to the size and scale of the operation necessary to undertake the complete conquest of Greece, but otherwise providing no opposition even to the most speculative assumptions.[179] Their own underestimation of the Greeks, as well as their lengthy attritional struggles over previous months with Mussolini's impulses in military matters whose complexity he did not remotely grasp, made them the more ready to bow to his imperative. So Mussolini got his way at the meeting without dissent. The decision that he alone had taken had now become an operational directive, with the full collaboration of his military chiefs.

As soon as the military leaders left the meeting, however, and started to give detailed consideration to the planning for an operation whose objectives had been rushed through so carelessly, serious doubts arose – and rapidly multiplied. The landing at Arta, for example, was quite impossible, the naval chief, Cavagnari, asserted. The attack on Mersa Matruh that had been presumed to coincide with, or even precede, the Greek operation was now, they learned, to be postponed for at least two months. And the British, it was feared, would immediately establish bases in southern Greece, and be in a position to attack the Italian fleet at Taranto, on the heel of southern Italy. Badoglio raised these objections when he spoke to Ciano on 17 October. Badoglio's pessimism was evident. Equally gloomy were the views of the chiefs of staff who had 'unanimously pronounced themselves against' the operation.[180] But – deprived of his main logistical argument, the inaccessibility of the harbour at Arta, when it transpired that the Greeks had just dredged a deep-water channel enabling big ships to dock there – Badoglio was pliant at his audience next day with an enraged Mussolini, who had learned of the reservations voiced. Mussolini had told Ciano he would be prepared to accept Badoglio's resignation. But Badoglio never offered it. He came away having achieved nothing, except a delay of two days for the start of the operation, rescheduled to begin on 28 October.[181]

Military preparations now went ahead – over-hastily and incoherently.[182] Even the troop demobilization within Italy was not halted.[183] The auguries for the campaign were not good. Transporting motorized troops to Albania could not be completed in time, it turned out, since the harbour at Durazzo was too cramped. The weather was also poor, and deteriorating, further hampering troop transports and turning Albania's roads into quagmires. King Boris of Bulgaria then, to Mussolini's disgust, refused to join in the attack. Finally, it had become clear that the balance of forces was much less favourable to Italy than Visconti Prasca had implied. Far from outnumbering the Greeks by two to one, the forces were fairly even, even before the Greek mobilization, with extensive reserves in hand, was complete. The commanders on the ground in Albania wanted discretion over the starting-date of the offensive, but Mussolini insisted that 28 October was immovable. Worry that Hitler, currently tied up in his talks with Franco and Pétain, might intervene to put a halt to the operation once he got wind of it was decisive in the timing.[184]

Whatever their logistical concerns, neither the military leadership in Rome nor the commanders on the ground in Albania had any doubts that victory would be easy. The underestimation of the Greeks was general. Ciano talked of a 'walkover',[185] Soddu later wrote of the commonplace expectation of a 'military parade'. The King himself thought the Greeks would crumble at the first assault.[186] This type of presumption reinforced compliance with Mussolini's hurriedly devised imperative to destroy Greece. A rapid victory was vital. The Duce was anxious to avoid the British, perhaps the Turks too, becoming involved in any protracted struggle. He wanted, therefore, and expected, a devastating assault which would 'bring about a complete collapse within a few hours'.[187] He was in excellent spirits as the attack began on 28 October.[188]

His co-dictator was, by contrast, less than delighted when he was given the news, en route back from his talks with Franco and Pétain, that Italy was about to attack Greece. Hitler was said to have been fuming, and greatly worried that the Italian action could set the whole of the Balkans alight and give the British the opportunity to install airbases in the region. He thought it was Mussolini's revenge for Norway and France.[189] In fact, the Germans had received plenty of indirect warning from good sources in the previous days that action against Greece was imminent.[190] Equally, they had been given outright denials by Italian military leaders that anything was afoot. They preferred to believe the denials. Hitler does not appear to have been alarmed before 25 October. Only on that day did a letter, composed six days earlier by Mussolini, reach him, cleverly couched but indicating that the Duce proposed to act on Greece very soon. Even then, the intelligence gleaned from Italy remained contradictory. A meeting with Mussolini, already instigated to discuss the dealings with the Spanish and French leaders just conducted by Hitler, was now brought forward. The dictators would meet in Florence on 28 October. When Hitler arrived for the meeting it was to be given the news, by a beaming Mussolini, that Italian troops had crossed the Greek border from Albania at dawn that morning.[191]

So Mussolini had achieved his own fait accompli. Later, reproaching Mussolini for his rashness when it was already plain that the Italian assault had misfired badly, Hitler said he had hoped in Florence to restrain the Duce from premature action in Greece, and certainly not from undertaking the operation without a prior occupation of Crete, for which he was prepared to provide military assistance.[192] But when they had met in Florence, there were no reproaches. Hitler restrained himself. Whatever his private feelings, he could scarcely have anticipated the scale of the military disaster that Mussolini had invited. He offered German support for the operation and parachute divisions to occupy Crete (to head off British intervention).[193] The rest of the meeting confined itself to a report on his meetings with Pétain, Laval and Franco. He was keen to assuage Mussolini about his dealings with Vichy France, which were not at all to the Italian dictator's liking.[194] Greece was not again mentioned. But it soon would be.

Far from being the expected military stroll in the park, the ill-planned and ill-coordinated attack on Greece rapidly proved an unmitigated military disaster. The advance took place in atrocious weather. Ceaseless, torrential rain and knee-deep mud bogged down the Italian tanks and heavy artillery. Streams were swollen by the autumn rains. Mountain tracks often proved impassable. Planes were grounded by thick mists. Heavy seas hampered naval operations. Shortages of equipment, fuel, ammunition and manpower soon became apparent. Poor training and leadership of the Italian troops also contributed significantly to the mounting debacle. But beyond this, the Greeks defended their country with bravery and tenacity, offering stiff resistance from the onset. Their knowledge of the local terrain was a great advantage, and they were better organized defensively than the Italians were in attack. Within little over a week the Italians were forced to halt their offensive in Epirus. By the time another week had passed they were being pushed back over the Albanian border by a Greek counter-attack. When the front stabilized, as any further advance ground to a halt in abysmal weather conditions, it was about thirty miles within Albania. Mussolini's casually brutal order that all Greek towns with more than 10,000 inhabitants be razed to the ground could not be implemented.[195] Within six weeks, the would-be world power, Italy, had shown herself to be militarily weaker than the flyweight force of Greece. The Achilles heel of the Axis could not have been more plainly revealed.

To make matters worse, the Italian fleet, at anchor at Taranto in southern Italy, was severely damaged by a British torpedo attack in mid-November. Half of the Italian warships were put out of action. Fascist dreams of empire sank along with them. With this one stroke, the balance of naval power in the Mediterranean was decisively altered.[196] And by early December Graziani, his offensive in Libya still stalled and told by Mussolini that Greece now had priority, suffered the first of a number of devastating assaults in the beginning of a British offensive in north Africa. Italian forces were driven out of Egypt by mid-December. In the new year the retreat turned into a full-scale rout. By the end of January 1941 the British had advanced over 200 miles of desert, capturing 113,000 Italian prisoners and over 700 pieces of artillery. Following this, as Churchill later wrote, 'the great Italian army which had invaded and hoped to conquer Egypt scarcely existed as a military force'.[197] Here was a major consequence of the decision to invade Greece. What should have been the vital military effort, the push through Egypt to Suez against still weak British forces, had been completely undermined by the unnecessary Greek adventure, a blunder of the first order, with calamitous costs.

In December Badoglio, made the scapegoat for the debacle in Greece, had been sacked. The military leaders, not just Badoglio, were resentful of the blame passed to them by Mussolini for a catastrophe that he had personally instigated. Mussolini's own prestige was now affected, too, as his popularity fell with the sinking morale at home, worsening living standards and military setbacks. Ciano, well known to have been a leading promoter of the attack on Greece, became the target of much opprobrium, some, no doubt, really directed at his father-in-law. The first cracks – though as yet they posed no direct danger to Mussolini – were also beginning to show in the Fascist leadership, as old party potentates sought to distance themselves from the disasters and jockey for position.

The decision to invade Greece swiftly proved a massive self-inflicted wound. The military situation could, as events rapidly showed, only be remedied by German help, precisely what Mussolini had wanted to avoid. From Hitler's point of view, Greece was a sideshow. He had far bigger fish to fry. Molotov's visit to Berlin in mid-November had concentrated his mind on the need to go ahead with the attack on the Soviet Union the following spring. By mid-December, what came to be known as 'Operation Barbarossa' was enshrined as a military directive. Greece was an unwelcome diversion. Hitler had wanted the Balkans to remain quiet, but he could not ignore the threat now posed, thanks to Mussolini's inopportune adventure, of a threatening British military presence at a vulnerable point. Continued Italian gross incompetence and intensified British involvement compelled German military planners to pay close attention to operations in Greece.[198] By the end of that November contingency plans had been worked out for the occupation of Greece, though Hitler had informed Ciano that Germany could not intervene before spring.[199] When Hitler eventually decided, in March 1941, that a major operation would be necessary to evict the British from the whole of the Greek mainland, the German manpower involved was greater than initially imagined and could only be provided at the expense of the force intended to take care of the southern flank of 'Barbarossa'.[200] The Germans had not envisaged such costly involvement in Greece. The Italians had not wanted them there in the first place. But this was what Mussolini's Balkan adventure had produced: a calamity for Italy, but wider consequences that had a bearing on the course of the war.

V

Looking back near the end of the war, as Germany's inevitable and impending defeat loomed ever closer, Hitler attributed great blame to Mussolini's Greek fiasco as the cause of his own subsequent catastrophe. 'But for the difficulties created for us by the Italians and their idiotic campaign in Greece,' he reportedly commented in mid-February 1945, 'I should have attacked Russia a few weeks earlier.' He believed that the delay in launching 'Barbarossa' had cost him victory in the Soviet Union. A few days later, along similar lines, he lamented that the 'pointless campaign in Greece', launched without warning to Germany of Italian intentions, 'compelled us, contrary to all our plans, to intervene in the Balkans, and that in its turn led to a catastrophic delay in the launching of our attack on Russia. We were compelled to expend some of our best divisions there. And as a net result we were then forced to occupy vast territories in which, but for this stupid show, the presence of any of our troops would have been quite unnecessary.' 'We have no luck with the Latin races,' he bemoaned shortly afterwards. The one friend among the Latins, Mussolini, took advantage of his preoccupation with Spain and France 'to set in motion his disastrous campaign against Greece'.[201]

As an explanation of Germany's calamitous defeat in the Soviet Union this had little to commend it.[202] The five-week delay in launching 'Barbarossa' was not in itself decisive. Probably, given the unusually wet weather conditions, a launch before mid-June would not have been feasible anyway. The reasons for the failure of 'Barbarossa' lay in the hubristic nature of the German war plans – as megalomaniac as they were barbaric – and in the planning flaws and resource limitations that bedevilled the operation from the start. The German descent on Greece in spring 1941, necessitated by the Italian shambles, did cause heavy wear and tear on tanks and other vehicles needed for 'Barbarossa', and also, as we have noted, reduced the forces on the southern flank of the assault. But, although the diversion of German resources into Greece just prior to the attack on the Soviet Union scarcely helped the latter enterprise, Mussolini's foolishness did not undermine 'Barbarossa' before the operation started. It nevertheless had the most serious consequences for the Axis war effort in north Africa.

In the autumn of 1940 this should have been the pivotal theatre. Italy's position prior to launching a north African offensive would indeed have been far stronger had Tunis and above all Malta been taken after she had entered the war.[203] The preparations for such steps had never been taken.

Even so, the Italians still had numerical superiority over the British in the region, though this was rapidly to alter. Graziani deferred his advance repeatedly, aware that Italian strength was insufficient to mount the major offensive through Egypt that Mussolini was constantly urging and expecting. The Germans saw the importance of the sector and offered troops and equipment. The Italian military Supreme Command wanted to take advantage of the offer. It could have made the difference. But Mussolini refused.[204] He was keen to keep the Germans at bay in what he saw as an Italian war theatre. Beyond that, from October onwards vital manpower and resources were directed, not at north Africa, but at Greece. Between October 1940 and May 1941, five times as many men, one and a third times as much *matériel*, three and a half times as many merchant ships and more than twice as many escort vessels were deployed on the Greek operation as in north Africa.[205] The consequences of this diversion of resources, once the British offensive began in December, soon became all too evident.

The implications were, in fact, immediately recognized by German strategists. The naval staff's operational planners summed up the position already by 14 November 1940, little over a fortnight into the Greek debacle: 'Conditions for the Italian Libyan offensive against Egypt have deteriorated. The Naval Staff is of the opinion that Italy will never carry out the Egyptian offensive' – even though this of course, far more obviously than an attack on Greece, had the potential to inflict serious damage on the British war effort, particularly if the Axis could have taken possession of the Suez area. The assessment continued:

The Italian offensive against Greece is decidedly a serious strategic blunder; in view of the anticipated British counteractions it may have an adverse effect on further developments in the Eastern Mediterranean and in the African area, and thus on all future warfare ... The Naval Staff is convinced that the result of the offensive against the Alexandria–Suez area and the development of the situation in the Mediterranean, with their effects on the African and Middle Eastern areas, is of decisive importance for the outcome of the war ... The Italian armed forces have neither the leadership nor the military efficiency to carry the required operations in the Mediterranean area to a successful conclusion with the necessary speed and decision. A successful attack against Egypt by the Italians alone can also scarcely be expected now.[206]

By mid-December it was a case not of the long-awaited offensive against Egypt, but of repairing the fall-out from the disastrous Italian collapse. Despite Rommel's subsequent heroics in the desert campaign, with limited resources, the Italian failure and the alternative priorities for the deployment of German manpower and *matériel* meant that the crucial north African theatre was increasingly exposed to Allied might. To this unhappy state of affairs (from an Axis viewpoint), Mussolini's decision to invade Greece at the end of October 1940 had made a major contribution.

The most direct consequences of Mussolini's fateful move were felt by Greece and Italy. The immediate casualties of the conflict unleashed by the Fascist dictator on 28 October numbered around 150,000 on the Italian side and 90,000 Greeks.[207] For the Greeks, however, this was only the beginning of the misery. Three and a half years of occupation followed the German invasion of April 1941. Beyond the repression of the conquerors, hyperinflation and malnutrition took a high toll. Around a hundred thousand people died of famine during the winter of 1941–2. Only a small fraction of Greece's Jews survived Nazi round-ups and deportation to the death camps. Even liberation, in October 1944, brought no end to Greece's suffering. The bitter aftermath of deep and intractable internal divisions that emerged during the occupation and surfaced fully after liberation was the country's fierce civil war, which flared up in 1946 and lasted until 1949.[208]

For Italy, the ill-fated invasion of Greece (with the attendant disasters of the sinking of much of the fleet at Taranto and the ignominious collapse in north Africa) signalled the end of great-power pretensions once and for all. The idea of a 'parallel war' to build Italy's own *imperium* had been revealed as a chimera. Mussolini had, of course, been the chief ideologue as well as the political leader driving along this cause, but he had been able to build upon, and exploit, long-standing continuities in Italian ambitions to become a genuine great power. For although they were often anxious about the consequences of expansion and armed conflict, and voiced well-founded strategic and tactical reservations, the Italian establishment right up to the King had no principled objections to war in pursuit of empire and national grandeur. If Mussolini could have delivered a successful war, he would have encountered little opposition.

Since the mid-1930s Italy had increasingly been pulled along in Germany's wake. The impulsively devised attack on Greece, to pay Hitler back in his own coin for Romania and for earlier perceived insults when Italy had been condescendingly treated as a junior partner, was meant to wrest back the pride of independent action. Instead, it dragged Italy far deeper into humiliating subservience to Hitler's Germany. The fact that Hitler, as a sop to Mussolini's prestige, allowed the Italians to be a party to the Greek surrender, on 23 April 1941, that German arms had forced, could not hide the scale of Italy's degradation.[209] The cracks in the edifice of Italian Fascism now rapidly started to widen. The disastrous invasion of Greece had 'put Mussolini at odds with his armed forces, shattered the fragile unity of the fascist hierarchy, disillusioned the Italian public and alienated the Italians from their German allies'.[210] By 1943 the cracks were chasmic. The road to Mussolini's deposition in July that year, instigated by the Fascist Grand Council that he himself had set up, now ran straight. The last, bloody phase of the war, with a restored Mussolini as a German puppet heading the savagely repressive Salò Republic as the Wehrmacht fought ferociously to hold on to the occupied northern part of Italy and fend off the advancing Allied armies pushing up from the south, was a terrible finale to the drama. The overture had been in two parts: the decision to intervene in the war in June 1940; then the decision to attack Greece in October 1940.

Just as intervention in the war had been a foregone conclusion for Mussolini, so was the attack on Greece. He had been long set on making Greece a part of Italy's expanding Mediterranean Roman Empire. If he had not attacked in late October 1940, he would probably have done so at the first opportunity that circumstances provided, possibly in spring 1941.[211] Even so, the decision he took in autumn 1940 amounted to a fateful choice, where options were available. Supine and irresolute though they were, Mussolini's military advisers did express unease at the logistical implications of an invasion at such short notice and at that time of year. The timing was not propitious, even as seen by Italian military leaders. The Germans were, as we have noted, aghast at what Mussolini had done. The attack, even if still intended for a later date, could, therefore, have been postponed. Given what happened in north Africa by the end of the year, had it been postponed it might never have taken place at all. And with Greece still independent and neutral, the British, their hands full in north Africa, might have refrained from an intervention that could only be seen as a threat by the Germans, not least to the Romanian oilfields. Greece might then have escaped German subjugation and occupation. The war in the Mediterranean could, therefore, have taken a completely different turn, had not Mussolini invaded Greece when he did.

Mussolini obviously carries prime responsibility for the attack on Greece. He, after all, took the decision, alone, and without consultation, even of his own Fascist Grand Council. And he overrode the objections of Badoglio and the chiefs of staff. On 10 November, when the magnitude of the disaster was already beginning to unfold, Badoglio confronted Mussolini with his responsibility. He referred to the meeting on 15 October. 'As a result of the statements of Ciano and Visconti Prasca,' he declared, 'you decided to attack on 26 October, a date which was subsequently changed to

28 October. We tried to make all possible preparations during this time. I have reviewed these facts to show that neither the general staff nor the army staff had anything to do with the plans that were adopted, which were entirely contrary to our method of procedure. This method is based on the principle of thorough preparation before action is taken.'[212] It was a bold – but partly disingenuous – statement from a man aware that he would soon be made the scapegoat for the Duce's impetuosity. For Badoglio had been less outspoken when the decision was taken. He had not repeated to Mussolini the stringent objections he had voiced to Ciano.[213] The objections of the military chiefs had, in any case, been logistical rather than fundamental. These did not oppose an attack on Greece. They merely had worries about inadequate preparation. Ciano, and his inept henchmen in Albania, Jacomoni and Visconti Prasca, had not even shared these concerns. They had wholeheartedly backed the invasion. Ciano, as we have noted, had been the main proponent of an attack for months. And the underestimation of the Greeks had been as good as unanimous – even stretching to the King.

While the main responsibility for the Greek debacle fairly lies with Mussolini, therefore, the dictator cannot be seen to carry the sole blame. Churchill's pronouncement in December 1940 that 'one man and one man alone' had brought Italy 'to the horrid verge of ruin' was wartime rhetoric, not reasoned analysis.[214] Other sectors of the power-elite in the Fascist regime were at the very least complicit in the decision. Fascist rule had, after all, over many years developed a system that not only elevated the leader to a cult-figure, but had placed decision-making entirely in his hands, abnegating all responsibility for decisions at any lower level.[215] The politically corrupt system, as in the parallel instance of Nazi Germany, had at the same time rewarded subservience, servility, obsequiousness and sycophancy. Beyond that, all forms of political organization had been reduced to no more than a façade: representative bodies solely in outward appearance, but in reality no more than vehicles of propaganda and acclamation of the leader. Organized opposition, in a system that ran on the basis of divide and rule, career advance and material gratification at the dictator's favour, was, therefore, as good as impossible to construct. The dictator had been told, repeatedly, that he was infallible; and he believed the blandishments. Others accepted, whether fawningly or cynically, the rules of the political game. When things worked out well, as they had done in 1936 with a cheap victory over a feeble enemy, they were happy to rejoice and take their share of the triumph. When things went badly, as they did in 1940 and thereafter, they sought to hide their share of the responsibility.

They could do so only to themselves. The imbecility of Mussolini's decision reflected the dictator's severe personal shortcomings. But it was also the imbecility of a political system.

5

Washington, DC, Summer 1940–
Spring 1941

Roosevelt Decides to Lend a Hand

We will say to England, we will give you the guns and the ships that you need, provided that when the war is over you will return to us in kind the guns and the ships that we have loaned to you . . . What do you think of it?

President Roosevelt, 17 December 1940

Without a lead on his part it was useless to expect the people would voluntarily take the initiative in letting him know whether or not they would follow him if he did take the lead.

Henry Stimson, Secretary of War, 22 April 1941

Speaking in Boston on 30 October 1940, during his campaign for election to an unprecedented third term in office, President Franklin Delano Roosevelt made a pledge to his audience. 'And while I am talking to you mothers and fathers,' the President stated, 'I give you one more assurance. I have said this before, but I shall say it again and again and again: Your boys are not going to be sent into any foreign war.'[1] It was seen as the most explicit commitment to American neutrality; to keeping the United States out of the war that gripped Europe and threatened a German defeat of Great Britain.

Roosevelt was telling those listening what they wanted to hear. At the end of September, 83 per cent of those asked in a public opinion survey had favoured staying out of the war against Germany and Italy.[2] Helping the British, whose backs had certainly been to the wall since the catastrophic defeat of the Allies at the hands of the Wehrmacht in May and June, by taking measures that fell short of entering the war was another matter altogether. But only 34.2 per cent of Americans in August 1940 supported doing more to help Britain fight Germany.[3]

The British war effort, that desperate summer, had gained vital sustenance from the hope that America would soon join the war against Hitler's Germany. Winston Churchill was desperately impatient for the United States to leave neutrality behind and actively back Britain's cause. His entire strategic hopes rested upon the presumption of American entry into the war at some point. Some members of Roosevelt's own Cabinet, too, were pushing the President for a more interventionist approach. At this stage, in autumn 1940, no one was advocating sending an American expeditionary force to fight in Europe, but there were other steps, short of full engagement, that would entail active intervention. With British shipping already threatened by German U-boats, Henry Stimson, the Secretary of War, told the President and the Cabinet in December 1940 that 'we ought to forcibly stop the German submarines by our intervention'. Nothing came of it. The President replied that 'he hadn't quite reached that yet'.[4] Nor would he do so for some months.

To Churchill, across the Atlantic, and for the rest of the British government the President's hesitancy was a deep concern (though this was never expressed publicly). It was a worry, too, for those in his administration – and Stimson was not alone in this – who were coming to favour a more robustly interventionist approach. Roosevelt often sounded encouraging, but then his innate caution would prevail once again, leaving them frustrated. Yet to many within the United States, Roosevelt was going much too far. To these, he appeared to be a warmonger, intent upon dragging the country into a faraway conflict. The isolationist lobby, its chief geographical base of support located in the Midwest, and its political roots mainly but not entirely among Roosevelt's political opponents in the Republican Party, was by this time representing no more than a sizeable minority of opinion. But it was an extremely vocal minority, and usually able to make common cause with a far wider swathe of opinion that was not outrightly isolationist, but was at the same time intensely worried about embarking upon a slippery path that would end up in war.

Roosevelt was acutely aware of the tightrope he was treading. On the one hand he was anxious to ensure that he retained the backing of public opinion, and more directly the support of the United States Congress. This demanded a strategy of caution. But he appeared to those around him too often ready to follow, rather than lead, opinion in the country. Where he did lead, it was usually to cajole more than to direct. Harry Hopkins, Roosevelt's closest adviser, reportedly thought in May 1941 that 'the President is loath to get into this war, and he would rather follow public opinion than lead it'.[5] Stimson had put the same point in characteristically forthright terms to the President the previous month: 'without a lead on his part it was useless to expect the people would voluntarily take the initiative in letting him know whether or not they would follow him if he did take the lead.'[6]

On the other hand, in full recognition of the danger Germany posed to the United States, Roosevelt sought to pursue, with the self-interest of upholding America's national security as a legitimate priority, a policy that supported Britain in increasingly direct fashion. This, however, ran the obvious risk of embroiling an unwilling country in precisely the 'foreign war' he had vowed to keep out of. This was the intense dilemma that faced the President from summer 1940 onwards.

At the start of that summer, Great Britain stood alone in Europe against the Nazi menace, and greatly imperilled, with the danger of imminent invasion. Of course, she had the backing of her world Empire and Dominions. They could, however, have provided little practical help in the event of a German landing. To many Americans, Britain seemed as good as lost.

One option for Roosevelt would have been to side with the isolationist lobby, which contended that, with German dominance over the European continent (including Britain) as good as certain for the indefinite future, American interest lay in upholding the strictest neutrality, refraining from any involvement whatsoever in the conflict engulfing faraway nations, and exclusively looking after the concerns of the United States. Given the reluctance witnessed in opinion polls to see America involved in the war, isolationism, had Roosevelt thrown the formidable weight of his political skills and rhetoric behind it, still retained the potential to become far more popular than it was in reality.

Another option would have been to adopt the advice of some members of his administration to take steps which would have committed the United States to a much greater involvement in the European war, perhaps even to the point of joining it. This would, of course, have been to court serious difficulties with public opinion, and the problems in navigating the necessary legislation through the political rapids of the Congress would have been formidable indeed. In any case, the scale of American military preparedness for a major war in summer 1940 was so limited that any overt form of belligerency, even accepting the political risks, would have been highly restricted in practical terms. But, again, had Roosevelt, a profoundly experienced and skilful politician as well as a highly gifted rhetorician, chosen to do so, it is far from inconceivable that he would not have won over the country to a far more interventionist position. He was not prepared to put it to the test.

Fears were still widespread as late as May 1941 that Germany could soon mount the attack on Britain that had not materialized the previous year. These fears only vanished when Hitler turned eastwards, with the attack on the Soviet Union on 22 June 1941. By that point, Roosevelt was well embarked upon a course of action that precluded any lingering possibility of adopting the option of keeping the United States detached from the war in Europe. By the end of spring 1941, though the United States was still months away from direct participation in the war, the Roosevelt administration had taken important steps both in Europe and, increasingly, in the Far East too, that had made it impossible to extricate the country from the spreading conflict. The options had narrowed.

Roosevelt's choice over the previous months had in fact proved to be an extremely cautious path between neutrality and belligerency, one of assistance to Britain through all 'methods short of war' (a phrase coined in January 1939 by the President himself).[7] In summer 1939, Roosevelt had reportedly laid out his options. He thought there were four: 'A, we can go to war at once, sending an expeditionary force abroad, but that's out, of course. B, we can let ourselves be forced in later. C, we can go to war, now or later, but furnish only war supplies and naval and air aid to our allies. And D, we can stay out, following my policy of methods short of war to aid the democracies. And that' – meaning the last of these – 'is what we shall do.'[8] This policy, which the President stuck to, edged, rather than swept, the United States towards involvement in the war. Even so, the steps he did authorize were irreversible. And of these, the most singular, and most important, was the decision – an initiative of the President himself – to open up America's vast material resources to Britain's struggling war effort at no direct financial cost. With the passing of the Lend-Lease bill in March 1941, after three months of intensive debate, the isolationists had lost their last great fight.[9] To be sure, the United States was not yet in the war, and little aid could flow straight away. But America was now bound up in a most tangible fashion with Great Britain, a belligerent already engaged in the fight against Hitler in Europe, and a main adversary in the intensified threat posed by Japan in the Far East. The decision to commit American resources to the British war effort was for the immediate future of largely symbolic importance, but it would become over time the key to Britain's continuing capacity to fight Hitler. Its significance was, therefore, immense.

And yet, despite his unstinting public praise and gratitude for this 'most unsordid act in the history of any nation',[10] Churchill remained frustrated, anxious and at times bleakly pessimistic at Roosevelt's hesitancy, caution and unwillingness to commit the United States to intervention in the war.[11] When he met the President for the first time since the conflict had begun, in August 1941, the British Prime Minister told him: 'I would rather have an American declaration of war now and no supplies for six months than double the supplies and no declaration.'[12] Some in Roosevelt's Cabinet felt almost equally frustrated. The period preceding the German invasion of the Soviet Union in June 1941 has been labelled 'a year of indecision'.[13] It often indeed seemed in those months that Roosevelt's main decision was to avoid having to decide at all.

I

Roosevelt had taken office, on 4 March 1933, amid a full-blown banking crisis and with around a quarter of the workforce – some thirteen or so million Americans – unemployed. His first term was almost completely taken up with an array of often contentious legislative measures that comprised the 'New Deal', the programme of national recovery to rebuild the shattered economy and restore confidence.[14] Much of his energy was consumed in the ensuing internal political struggles.[15] The President's own popularity remained high. He was re-elected in 1936 in a landslide victory. His hold over Congress, however, weakened, especially after elections in November 1938 had bolstered the opposition.[16] And this was at a time when events abroad had started to dominate his second term in office.

The isolationism that had taken hold in America since the end of the First World War – building on long traditions – had, in fact, become still further engrained during Roosevelt's first term. The impact of involvement in the European war in 1917–18 on American society had been profound. Fifty thousand American soldiers had lost their lives in a conflict which, to many United States citizens, had not been their country's concern at all. Most Americans felt this must on no account ever be allowed to happen again. Experiences of the horror of the trenches mingled with resentment at what was widely perceived as European ingratitude when America insisted upon repayment of war loans.[17] There was also a widespread feeling, encouraged by anti-war literature and some histories of what Americans called 'the European War', then later backed by the report of a Senate committee investigating the munitions industry, that America had been inveigled into involvement by foreign financiers, bankers and arms manufacturers who stood to profit from an Allied victory.[18]

The United States had chosen to keep largely aloof from European affairs, rejecting membership of the League of Nations. Certainly, American initiative was crucial in providing plans in 1924, then again five years later, to try to resolve the gnawing problem of German reparations payments, an issue of the most bitter resentment in Germany. And in 1932, the United States joined the Disarmament Conference in Geneva, belatedly (and vainly) attempting to turn another of President Woodrow Wilson's principles for a peaceful postwar world into reality, though long after any genuine hope of doing so had evaporated. But there was little else. Behind a wall of protective tariffs, and an economic boom symbolized by the explosion of automobile production, most Americans were content to ignore the outer world and keep Europe from their minds.

When, with Hitler in power, German assertiveness again started to manifest itself, and across the world Japanese imperialism sounded shrill, dissonant tones, a widespread American sentiment, whether from noble if illusory pacifistic leanings or from national unilateralist tendencies, was to retreat still further into isolationism. 'Let us turn our eyes inward,' advocated the Governor of Pennsylvania, George Earle, a liberal Democrat, in 1935. 'If the world is to become a wilderness of waste, hatred, and bitterness, let us all the more earnestly protect and preserve our own oasis of liberty.'[19] A reflection of prevailing attitudes was the Johnson Act, named after the progressive Republican Hiram Johnson and passed in 1934 to forbid the granting of credits to countries that had defaulted on their war debts to the United States.[20] Then in 1935, to the backcloth of open and large-scale German remilitarization and bullying Italian threats towards Abyssinia, Roosevelt opened the door to legislation that would ensure American neutrality in any future war. The key feature was an arms embargo on the provision of armaments to all belligerents in a war 'between, or among, two or more foreign states', irrespective of American sympathies. Roosevelt, the State Department even more so, would have preferred powers to impose a discretionary arms embargo, discriminating against aggressors. But the President professed himself satisfied with the Neutrality Act, which he signed on 31 August 1935.[21]

The neutrality legislation – renewals and amendments meant that there were five neutrality laws between 1935 and 1937[22] – was designed to prevent any recurrence of the circumstances that had led to American intervention in the First World War. Together with the Johnson Act, the Neutrality Act would later pose obstacles to Roosevelt's attempts to help Britain while steering clear of involvement in a second European war. Meanwhile, of course, it did nothing to hinder aggression by the European powers. Oil, not among the list of embargoed 'implements of war', was still shipped to Mussolini (in fact, in increased quantities), when the Italian dictator unleashed his bombers against Ethiopian tribesmen in 1935.[23] But then America could point to the Europeans themselves who, divided and inept in their response to the Abyssinian crisis, failed to impose an oil embargo on Italy.

When in March 1936 Hitler took advantage of the disarray among the western democracies to remilitarize the Rhineland, Cordell Hull, the Secretary of State, rejected the French plea for an American condemnation of the action on moral grounds.[24] It was a perverse application of neutrality, an unnecessary endorsement by silence of Hitler's breach of the Versailles and Locarno treaties, the basis of the postwar settlement. But then, the British and the French had themselves simply stood by and let it happen.

And when Italy and Germany provided military support for a rebel army, backed by Fascist sympathizers, aiming to overthrow Spain's struggling democracy, the arms embargo in the Neutrality Acts was extended to both sides of the conflict, though in a civil, not an international war. Again, in parallel to the supine non-interventionism of the European democracies, what this did was effectively to deny arms to the Republican defenders of democracy while allowing the assailants to be supported by Fascist arms from Italy and Germany. However, the Spanish Civil War was far away, without much resonance at home. True, a minority in the United States – mainly Catholics and the Left – were activated (along different lines in the conflict) by the crisis in Spain.[25] But two-thirds of Americans, in January 1937, had no opinion about events in Spain that were sounding the death knell of a sister democracy.[26]

Until the later 1930s, Roosevelt had shown little inclination to demur from the prevalent isolationist and pacifist tendencies in the United States. He had witnessed the horrors of the western front at first hand during a visit in 1918, and the experience had left a lasting revulsion.[27] 'I hate war,' he had said in a celebrated phrase of an election address in 1936.[28] It struck a popular chord. 'We are not isolationist,' he stated, 'except insofar as we attempt to isolate ourselves completely from war.' He told the American people that preserving peace would depend upon the day-to-day decisions of the President and the Secretary of State. 'We can keep out of war,' he declared, 'if those who watch and desire have a sufficiently detailed understanding of international affairs to make certain that the small decisions of today do not lead toward war and if at the same time they possess the courage to say no to those who selfishly or unwisely would lead us to war.'[29] Campaign advisers told the President that his opposition to a possible war was the most effective issue in his return to the White House that year.[30]

The rhetoric was easy. Events in Europe seemed far away and of little direct relevance to most Americans, preoccupied with making ends meet and coping with the travails of daily life as the country struggled along the path of economic recovery. The Atlantic appeared to pose a large enough cushion to protect Americans from the dangers again threatening the incorrigibly warlike continent of Europe. But they wanted to take no chances. Seven out of ten Americans believed in autumn 1937 that Congress should have the approval of the population in a referendum before issuing a declaration of war. A constitutional amendment to that effect, tying the President down, not just to a decision of Congress, but to the result of a popular referendum, was only narrowly defeated in the House of Representatives.[31]

While talking peace, Roosevelt, engrossed by domestic issues, did little to prepare America either psychologically or materially for the unpleasant prospect of engagement in troubles ahead, in Europe or in east Asia, which might in reality, whatever the good intentions, prove impossible to avoid. A minimal amount was done over the next years to rearm the American navy and as good as nothing to build up the army. In fact, one of Roosevelt's first measures to cut the budget after his inauguration in 1933 had been to reduce the size of the army, already minuscule at only 140,000 men.[32] The President cherished ideals of peace, harmony, cooperation and free trade throughout the world. It was a noble dream, shared by millions less able than the President to do anything to bring it about. But for the first years of his presidency, apart from reducing US involvement in Latin America, in keeping with his 'good neighbour' policy, and offering future independence to the Philippines, Roosevelt was content to leave it as a distant aspiration.

Down to 1938, he placed foreign policy largely in the hands of his Secretary of State, Cordell Hull.[33] Born in a Tennessee mountain cabin, tall, distinguished looking with silver hair and dark eyes, clever if somewhat unimaginative, highly experienced but often conservative to the point of being doggedly obstinate, moralistic and self-contained but 'plain and approachable as an old shoe',[34] Hull was deeply committed to the principles that President Woodrow Wilson, chief architect of the postwar European settlement, had espoused. He firmly believed that world peace could be brought about on the basis of disarmament, self-determination, non-violent change and diminished commercial rivalry.[35] Hull was watchful but not unduly concerned at this stage about Japan and saw no reason to press for a more interventionist approach to Europe's growing problems. Europe seemed indeed to pose the greater potential danger. But the inaction of the western democracies, France and Great Britain, that led to the policies of appeasement had its counterpart across the Atlantic in the detachment of the Roosevelt administration from the growing menace in Germany.

It was little different in east Asia. When Roosevelt, in response to Japan's attack on China, gave a major speech in Chicago, in the heartland of isolationism, on 5 October 1937, it seemed to herald a change in American policy. In reality, it merely offered a foretaste of the frustration that would afflict his friends and allies over the subsequent four years. Roosevelt used the analogy of the community cooperating in the quarantine of patients in an epidemic to imply that the same must happen in international relations in dealing with those now threatening world peace. But when Britain asked for clarification of what Roosevelt's words meant in terms of practical action, and went on shortly afterwards to suggest a joint naval show of force at Singapore to deter the Japanese, the United States backed away. 'There is such a thing as public opinion in the United States,' the message went out, and the President could not be seen to be tagging along behind the British.[36] 'It is always best and safest', commented the British Prime Minister, Neville Chamberlain, 'to count on *nothing* from the Americans but words.'[37]

Chamberlain did not change his view. When Roosevelt, in January 1938, proposed an initiative aimed at mobilizing countries in Europe and Latin America to agree to principles of international relations, in the hope that a revived sense of collective security, backed by the United States, would persuade the Axis powers to pull back from their course of aggression, the British Prime Minister was dismissive. Churchill later regarded the President's initiative as 'the last frail chance to save the world from tyranny otherwise than by war'.[38] In reality, the chances of such a move deflecting Hitler were nil. But Chamberlain's conclusion went beyond this particular initiative. He was adamant that, should she 'get into trouble', Britain could expect no help from the United States.[39] He preferred to continue down the road to appeasement.

The United States viewed Hitler's expansionist moves in 1938 from afar, with disquiet, certainly, but merely from the sidelines. The takeover of Austria was registered with an air of resignation but no demur. Roosevelt appealed for peace as the Sudeten crisis unfolded during the summer of 1938. After the western democracies had carved up Czechoslovakia during the Munich Conference at the end of September, in a vain bid to satisfy Hitler's insatiable demands, Roosevelt likened their action to the betrayal by Judas Iscariot. But on hearing that Chamberlain would be attending the Conference, where the capitulation to Hitler was an inevitable outcome,

Roosevelt had cabled to the British Prime Minister: 'Good man.'[40] With some justification, the American President has been described at this point as 'a powerless spectator at Munich, a weak and resourceless leader of an unarmed, economically wounded, and diplomatically isolated country'.[41]

Moral indignation in the United States at the German treatment of the Jews was certainly mounting during 1938. It boiled over following the notorious pogroms of 9–10 November, the 'Crystal Night' Nazi outrages against Germany's Jews. But Roosevelt was not prepared to waive the quota system on immigrants to accommodate the desperate Jewish refugees. And a large majority supported their President in this.[42]

Despite his passivity throughout 1938, as Hitler's expansionist drive brought Europe to the brink of war, Munich had caused Roosevelt to recognize the illusion in believing that the United States could remain aloof and detached from what was happening across the Atlantic. His anxieties about Hitler, whom he saw as a 'wild man' and a 'nut', had sharpened.[43] The President was by now much more actively involved in foreign policy, regularly reading the cables from abroad, and frequently discussing the issues that arose with Cordell Hull and others from the State Department. He would often receive Hull and the sharp-minded, urbane and polished, but pompous and formal Under-Secretary of State, Sumner Welles – who had attended the same upper-class preparatory school as the President, had worn white gloves while playing in the country as a child and still had an 'air of suspecting lurking contamination in his surroundings', his demeanour at best 'on the chilly side'[44] – while lying in bed at the White House, propped up against his pillows. They were clear that everything had to be done to prevent war and, should it nevertheless break out, to ensure victory for the western democracies. How to attain these goals was less clear.[45]

By the time of Munich American public opinion was shifting already to see war in Europe as likely. But there was as yet no readiness to welcome the repeal of the neutrality legislation, an issue the President raised in January 1939. And the following months would show how little American diplomacy was able to restrain Hitler. One tangible and new development did arise, however, from the changed emphasis in autumn 1938. This was the commitment to large-scale rearmament, especially in the air (though, of course, this could not be achieved overnight).[46] Alongside this went Roosevelt's personal commitment to production of arms to be procured by the western democracies for their own defence – though this was far from universally shared, and even met with the strong disapproval of his isolationist Secretary of War at the time, Harry H. Woodring.[47] Despite the opposition, it marked the beginning of the policy of help for the European democracies short of war, a policy which Roosevelt would uphold until December 1941.

By the time Hitler had overrun what had remained of Czechoslovakia in March 1939, soon to be followed by Britain's guarantee for Poland, war in Europe within the near future seemed practically a certainty. Many more Americans were starting to see that helping Britain and France to arm against Hitler's Germany could also be regarded as self-help. The administration, with Cordell Hull in the vanguard, now began to exert pressure on Congress to repeal the arms embargo.[48] It was to no avail. The House of Representatives in June, then the Senate the following month, voted to retain it. Six months of intense effort by the administration had met with resounding failure. By leaving Hull to lead the fight for repeal and staying in the background rather than risk his prestige, Roosevelt had badly miscalculated.[49]

As for diplomacy, a speech by Roosevelt in April 1939, offering Hitler and Mussolini talks to settle disarmament and trade if they would guarantee not to attack thirty specified countries during the subsequent ten years, met with a withering reply by the German dictator.[50] America did not figure prominently in Hitler's thinking at this time. He had not reckoned with any serious intervention by the United States in planning his aggression. He felt no need to consider any concessions to the American President's diplomacy of desperation in the spring of 1939.

Nor did Roosevelt's attempt in mid-August 1939 to persuade the Soviet leadership that its best interests lay in reaching a 'satisfactory agreement against aggression' with Great Britain and France meet with any greater success. He asked the Soviet ambassador in Washington, Konstantin Oumansky, about to leave for Moscow, 'to tell Stalin that if his Government joined up with Hitler, it was as certain as that night followed day that as soon as Hitler had conquered France, he would turn on Russia and that it would be the Soviets' turn next'.[51] If these prophetic words were actually delivered to him, Stalin ignored them. Within a fortnight, he had agreed the infamous Non-Aggression Pact with Ribbentrop. War in Europe was now both certain and imminent. As the last rites of peace were being read, Roosevelt appealed to Hitler, the President of Poland and the King of Italy.[52] He knew it was a hopeless cause. He could now only wait for the inevitable.

II

The beginning of the European war nevertheless did have obvious consequences for the United States. Americans could not bury their heads in the
sand and pretend that they were unaffected by a conflict thousands of miles
away, though many doubtless wished to do so. Roosevelt pointed this out
to his fellow countrymen in a 'fireside chat' (as his radio addresses to the
nation were known) on the evening of 3 September, the day of the British
and French declarations of war. 'When peace has been broken anywhere,
the peace of all countries everywhere is in danger,' he told them. 'Passionately though we may desire detachment,' he added, 'we are forced to realize
that every word that comes through the air, every ship that sails the sea,
every battle that is fought, does affect the American future.' But he hoped
and believed, he said, that 'the United States will keep out of this war'.
There should be no false talk 'of America sending its armies to European
fields'. The United States would remain neutral, he emphasized. But he
could not ask, he added, 'that every American remain neutral in thought
as well ... Even a neutral cannot be asked to close his mind or close his
conscience.'[53]

It amounted to a public restatement of the already established doctrine
of support for the European democracies through measures 'short of war'.
Roosevelt could be confident of public backing for this approach. He was
aware that opinion was almost entirely behind Britain and France in the
conflict with Hitler's Germany. But he knew also that this attitude had its
strict limits. Support for the democracies did not equate to participation in
the war on their side. Objections to any direct involvement were as vehement as ever. The only fighting most Americans would contemplate was to
defend the western hemisphere against unprovoked attack.

The President's own preferences actually accorded in good measure with
public opinion. Before the conflict began, he had on a number of occasions
made his own position clear to leading figures in his administration. 'While
I am in the White House I never expect to see American troops sent abroad,'
he had declared.[54] And on the afternoon of 1 September (the day of the
German invasion of Poland), speaking to his Cabinet, some of whom had
hurriedly flown back from their holidays, in front of the portraits of past
presidents and overlooking the garden of the White House, he repeated:
'We aren't going into this war.' He told his army planners that 'whatever
happens, we won't send troops abroad'. The War Department's officials
had put one plan in front of him envisaging sufficient reserves to equip a

possible expeditionary force to Europe, but the President was adamant. 'We need only think of defending this hemisphere,' he declared.[55] He recognized, however, that the attempt to preserve neutrality yet offer the support that Britain and France would need to withstand Hitler's Germany meant the tightrope he was walking would become frayed if the conflict dragged on.

Some measures could now be taken which only a short time earlier would have been highly sensitive. Roosevelt authorized the War Department to build an army of 750,000 men – more than four times its current size (though compared with the vast legions under arms in Europe, still tiny).[56] He had Sumner Welles prepare the arrangements to introduce a security cordon around the shores of the American continent (except Canada) as protection for Allied shipping against naval warfare and the predicted German submarine campaign and personally widened the zone from the proposed 100 to 300 miles.[57] Together with Hull, he thought that, in the altered circumstances, repeal of the embargo legislation, vital if help were to be provided for Britain and France, would now be a straightforward matter, and he resolved to call a special session of Congress to legislate for the change.[58] In the interim, however, there was no avoiding the fact that the existing Neutrality Act had to be invoked, imposing an immediate embargo on the sale of arms and munitions to all belligerents – something both depressing and worrying to the western allies, who were now legally prevented from buying any armaments at all from the United States.[59]

In fact, the repeal of the arms embargo was even now highly contentious, evoking huge hostility from the vocal isolationist lobby. Roosevelt made the repeal his own cause. Where in the spring he had still been reticent, he now personally took the issue to Congress. He said he regretted that Congress had passed the Neutrality Act, and that he had signed it.[60] The repeal of the arms embargo, he argued, would mean true neutrality, an end to even-handed treatment of aggressors and victims, and thereby a better safeguard to peace than retention of the original Act. With the repeal, he declared, 'this Government clearly and definitely will insist that American citizens and American ships keep away from the immediate perils of the actual zones of conflict'.[61] The necessary legislation eventually passed through both houses of Congress by wide majorities in early November, after six weeks of intense debate.[62]

There was, however, a price for the high level of consensus eventually attained. Isolationists succeeded in restoring the cash-and-carry provisions of the 1937 legislation that had expired in May 1939. The provisions had been introduced to enable the United States to continue to profit from foreign trade while remaining neutral. Goods, apart from weaponry and other forbidden items, could be sold to belligerents as long as they were paid for on receipt and transported in foreign ships.[63] There was an absolute ban on credit to belligerents, whether from the US Treasury or from private bankers.[64] The cash-and-carry provisions were advantageous to countries with large cash reserves and strong naval power. Britain and France, rather than Germany, would benefit in Europe. But in the Far East, the perverse effect would be to help Japan at the expense of China. Despite the repeal of the arms embargo, the questions were whether the western democracies could pay for the weapons they needed, and whether, even if the finance could be found, the Americans were willing to supply them in the quantities necessary. Both issues would remain unresolved for more than a year.

As the 'phoney war' – the sarcastic term invented by the isolationist Republican Senator William E. Borah somehow stuck – dragged on into 1940, Roosevelt sent Sumner Welles to Rome, Berlin, Paris and London unofficially to test the waters for a possible negotiated peace. Welles returned at the beginning of April suitably chastened about any chance of a diplomatic initiative to end the conflict. Mussolini had, indeed, said he thought a negotiated peace between Germany and the Allies possible, given settlement of all German and Italian territorial demands. But Welles had become aware that any influence Mussolini might once have possessed had vanished, and he was certain that the Duce would take Italy into the war, when the moment was opportune. Welles had been depressed by the belligerence in Berlin and the low morale of the French. Only in London, in the resilience shown by Winston Churchill, restored to the Cabinet as First Lord of the Treasury, had he encountered anything to impress him.[65]

There were no immediate consequences in Washington from Welles's bleak report. In fact, within days of the Under-Secretary returning, the 'phoney war' came to an abrupt end with the German attack on Denmark and Norway. A month later, the war spectacularly erupted into a new and highly dangerous phase as Hitler launched his devastating western offensive. The President's offer to Mussolini to act as an intermediary in any peace settlement, if Italy would agree to stay out of the war, was, as we saw, peremptorily rejected.[66] For the central players in American foreign policy, as Sumner Welles later put it, May and June 1940 amounted to 'a nightmare of frustration. For the United States government had no means whatever, short of going to war, to which American public opinion was in any case overwhelmingly opposed, of diverting or checking the world cataclysm' and, with that, the threat to the United States itself.[67] He might have added that even a declaration of war by the United States, however unthinkable at the time, would have presented not the slightest hindrance to Hitler nor caused him to hesitate. In spring 1940 the United States possessed neither the military nor the logistical capability to enter the war and block German military ambitions. Little had been done about rearmament. When the French Prime Minister, Paul Reynaud, pleaded for aeroplanes to be sent from the United States, William Bullitt, the American ambassador in Paris, had to tell him that there were none to be had.[68] Indeed, the United States itself only had 1,350 planes available at the time for its own defence.[69] It was the same in response to Reynaud's desperate request for old warships. None could be spared.[70] Roosevelt could only propose sending over 2,000 guns, French in fact, that had been standard issue in the First World War.[71] The American regular army comprised 245,000 men at this time, twentieth in world rankings, one place behind the Dutch. It had only five fully equipped divisions (the Germans deployed 141 divisions in the western campaign alone), equipped with weapons often still of First World War vintage.[72] Even transporting this puny army across the Atlantic could not have been achieved before Hitler had already overrun the Low Countries and France.

As spring drew to a close and the French sued for peace on 17 June then five days later signed a humiliating capitulation, there were few grounds for optimism in Washington about Britain's capacity to stay in the fight. The new British Prime Minister certainly symbolized the new determination in Britain that had impressed Sumner Welles a few weeks earlier. At the most despairing moment towards the end of May, with the British army stranded at Dunkirk, Churchill had indeed persuaded his colleagues in the War Cabinet that the only rational strategy open to Britain was to hold out, dismiss any prospect of negotiation and wait for American help. Whether, and if so when, such help of any meaningful kind would come was at this juncture an open question. Churchill could only hope, not reckon with it. But at least the government now showed defiance. And the British Expeditionary Force had been rescued from Dunkirk. On the last day of the evacuation from Dunkirk, 4 June, Churchill had produced an oratorical masterpiece in a speech to the House of Commons, expressing the new spirit. 'We shall defend our Island, whatever the cost may be,' Churchill told his American listeners to the transatlantic broadcast. 'We shall never surrender.' Even were Britain to be subjugated, the Empire and the British Fleet would fight on from beyond the seas 'until in God's good time, the New World, with all its power and might, steps forth to the rescue and the liberation of the Old'.[73]

It was powerful rhetoric, without a doubt, and not without impact across the Atlantic. Yet it could not dispel the prevailing pessimism about Britain's fate. The American ambassador in London, Joseph Kennedy, had long been a prophet of doom. He thought that in the wake of Dunkirk Hitler would make the British an offer they could not refuse.[74] Others saw no grounds to disagree that Britain would be incapable of holding out. Roosevelt was told that Britain's chances of survival were one in three.[75] The President had his own profound doubts, not least about the fate of the British fleet in the event of a surrender.[76]

The administration had reckoned before May 1940 on one of three scenarios: that the democracies would win the war without active American aid; that the war would turn into a protracted stalemate, in which the United States might eventually be in a position to broker a negotiated peace; or that the dictatorships would seriously threaten to defeat the democracies, though over the course of a long war. What had not been anticipated was a fourth scenario: an astonishingly rapid and sweeping German victory in the west, *before* any meaningful aid could be supplied by the United States.[77] Yet this is precisely what happened. The gloomy prospects of British survival meant that the whole issue of material assistance to Britain now became acute. Aid to Britain was crucial if she was not to go under, yet if Britain were forced to surrender, such aid would be merely a gift to Hitler. As the magnitude of the defeat of France sank in across the Atlantic, the whole critical and contentious issue of aid for Britain was about to enter a new, decisive phase.

III

As he began to confront the momentous issues raised by the fall of France, Franklin D. Roosevelt, now 58 years old, was well into his eighth – and by long-standing convention final – year as President of the United States. Both wealth and high political office had moulded his background. Hailing from a patrician family, he was raised at Hyde Park, a large mansion in the state of New York; his fifth cousin, Theodore Roosevelt, had been President from 1901 to 1909. He had even married a Roosevelt – Eleanor, a distant cousin and niece of Theodore. She was to be the mother of his six children (of whom one died in infancy). Unlike Theodore, Franklin had made his way in politics as a Democrat. He had been appointed Assistant Secretary of the Navy under Woodrow Wilson and ran as the Democratic vice-presidential candidate in the unsuccessful campaign of 1920. Personal tragedy struck the following year, when he contracted polio and was left paralysed in his legs. As elected Governor of New York from

1928, Roosevelt had proved a shrewd and capable politician. He had already made a mark in combating the worst of the Depression in New York when he gained the Democratic presidential nomination in 1932.

His personal charm, seemingly relaxed style, good humour and affable manner helped him persuade his friends and assuage his opponents on many occasions, as he wove his way through the political thickets. Some of his political enemies accused him of deviousness and duplicity. His supporters, on the other hand, admired his cleverness and skilful manoeuvring. He remained, for all his years in power, something of an enigma. 'His bewildering complexity', it has been said, 'had become his most visible trait. He could be bold or cautious, informal or dignified, cruel or kind, intolerant or long-suffering, urbane or almost rustic, impetuous or temporizing, Machiavellian or moralistic.'[78] Whichever way he was viewed, it could scarcely be doubted that by the time he faced the daunting questions of war and peace in the critical months of 1940–41, Roosevelt was the supreme master of the political scene in the United States.

The White House in Roosevelt's time has been described as 'a home inside a mansion inside an executive office'.[79] It was a power-centre, certainly, but an unostentatious one, even in its representative rooms. Roosevelt began the day by reading the newspapers over breakfast in bed, his blue cape with red F.D.R. monogram draped over his pyjamas. His personal aides would then come in to discuss the day's schedule with him. Thereafter he worked as a rule behind his big desk, littered with papers, in the Oval Study, full of books, prints and family photos, each day from 10 o'clock in the morning, looking out through the tall windows into the garden outside. He would usually have a number of visitors to see in the late morning and afternoon, where access to the inner sanctum was controlled by his amiable military aide, Major General Edwin W. Watson, known to all as 'Pa', a big, good-natured Virginian with a distinctive taste in aftershave that was the butt of many a repetitive presidential joke. Then he would dictate letters and memos to his secretaries, the longtime loyal devotee Marguerite 'Missy' LeHand and her assistant, Grace Tully. Congressional representatives would have their audiences with the President on Mondays or Tuesdays. Roosevelt met the press on Tuesday afternoons and Friday mornings. And on Friday afternoon he presided over the Cabinet meeting. In the evenings there was often formal entertainment in the state dining room. Otherwise, Roosevelt liked to spend the evening sorting out his stamp collection (when he was not distracted by phone calls and other business). But this seemingly ordered routine could be, and often was, interrupted by any kind of crisis that had blown up. Roosevelt's way of operating often gave the somewhat misleading impression of a lack of any systematic application. In fact, it spoke of a high personal level of involvement based upon accessibility. The 'air of small-town friendliness' that characterized the White House superficially belied the fact that Roosevelt kept the reins of power very tightly in his own hands.[80]

The US Constitution endows the President with wide powers, though it also imposes checks and balances on his executive authority. Most notably, the powers invested in the legislature and the judiciary were intended to limit presidential power and curb any abuse of it. The doctrine of the separation of powers foresaw the friction which was built into the relations between the President and the Congress.[81]

The duopoly between President and Congress, the complex balance between the powers of each, inevitably produced a need for compromise, often arrived at through wearisome, time-consuming processes and intense lobbying. The absence of swift, perhaps impulsive, decision-making and apparent lack of governmental efficiency were generally regarded as the necessary price of freedom from overweening power. On the other hand, at times of international crisis – and the implications for the United States of the war in Europe and the increasing threat in the Far East certainly amounted to such – the need to negotiate crucial measures through an obstructionist Congress could prove not simply laborious, but weakening when urgent action was called for. Yet precisely at such times it was imperative that the President have national, not partisan backing. Roosevelt's caution, his reluctance to embrace the bold moves that his advisers sometimes advocated, reflected his pronounced sensitivity to the need to carry the country with him. And he was all too aware that the nation was divided on the decisive issue of American involvement in the European war – in favour of giving Britain more material support, certainly, but opposed by four to one to entry into the conflict.[82] Roosevelt often showed consummate political skill in his dealings with Congress. He became, however, increasingly prepared to bypass Congress through use of his prerogative powers, sometimes ingeniously justified, in order to take action which might otherwise have been stymied or held up by protracted debate.[83]

Each President brings his own inimitable style to the exercise of power. Roosevelt was a man of bold ideas, though without a coherent ideology. He was prepared to experiment, then pull back if his initiatives proved unworkable.[84] He exuded confidence, and his genial affability helped to convey his sense of pushing at the limits of the possible to those around him. He focused on ends, not means. The detail of how to get something done he could leave to others.[85] He was impatient with formal bureaucracies, often seeing them as a challenge that he had to circumnavigate. And his interests varied widely across the political spectrum. In many policy areas he did not become personally involved. While he could pore over matters relating to the navy, a passionate interest since his First World War days, he might pay only superficial attention to issues that did not capture his imagination.[86] His discursive approach to problems could prove an irritation to those in his entourage who favoured more direct, forensic analysis. Stimson's impatience for action and Roosevelt's caution and ad hoc improvisations led the Secretary of War to note with a tone of frustration that 'it literally is government on the jump' and that conversation with the President was 'like chasing a vagrant beam of sunshine around a vacant room'.[87] Stimson, like others, did, however, come to appreciate Roosevelt's ingrained shrewdness in engineering, at times through patience, wariness and roundabout means, the passage of the measures he wanted to take. And no one mistook Roosevelt's caution for weakness. In the formulation of policy and in the taking of the key decisions, there was no doubt in anyone's mind of Roosevelt's outright primacy.

The Cabinet, the President's advisory council, played little role as a collective body in the making of decisions. Unlike the government in the British parliamentary system, where members of the Cabinet are elected to Parliament and share collective responsibility for policy, the United States system, drawing upon specific expertise of individuals drawn directly into government and with its clear divorce between the legislature and executive, encourages the President to deal bilaterally with individual departments of his administration. Roosevelt intensified this inbuilt tendency by competition and by often fluid and unclear lines of demarcation among his officials.[88] The Cabinet served little function as an instrument for coordinating the defence programme and tackling critical issues of foreign policy. Decisions, when they could not be postponed, were reached between the President and individual members of the Cabinet or following discussion involving those most directly involved.[89]

The growing crisis from spring 1940 required more flexible and dynamic government. In the wake of the German triumph in western Europe in May and June 1940, there was an urgent need to convert the nation to a defence footing. A belated, massive effort had to be undertaken to mobilize the economy for defence, and to rearm with all haste. And, since national security was bound up with the fate of Britain and France, the attempt had to be made to prevent the destruction of the western democracies.[90] Roosevelt now started to function more as commander-in-chief than as president of a civil administration, centralizing the orchestration of defence in his own hands. He was careful to bypass Congress, without alienating it, using statutes dating from the First World War to create new defence agencies and avoid legislation, strengthening his own position in the process. He began 'to improvise a new government within a government'.[91]

In May 1940 he established the Office for Emergency Management, intended to coordinate the work of all government agencies dealing with defence. Shortly afterwards, towards the end of the month, he revived the Council of National Defense, a body of six Cabinet officers that had lain dormant since the First World War, and created alongside it a seven-man National Defense Advisory Commission, comprised of business leaders and experienced administrators.[92] But these organizations looked impressive only on paper. The Office for Emergency Management was merely an umbrella framework enabling Roosevelt to set up and control agencies for production without resort to Congress.[93] The Council of National Defense, in theory the hub of the defence effort and consisting of Cabinet officers with defence functions, was no more than 'an administrative fiction' and never met at all.[94] And the Advisory Commission was left without a chairman as an 'administrative anomaly', a group of experts without leadership or power, each responsible to the President alone. Defining its responsibilities, it has been said, 'represented a problem in metaphysics'. Confusion and jurisdictional friction between the Commission and the relevant government bureaucracies in the War, Navy and Treasury Departments was the inevitable consequence. Meanwhile, the President's power was enhanced.[95] Temperament matched his sense of constitutional responsibility. He was unwilling to delegate authority to any organization that could have undermined his own direct and personal control; he thought it would have been constitutionally irresponsible to have done so.[96]

In June 1940 Roosevelt made two important personnel changes that affected the shaping of defence policy. He brought in Frank Knox as Secretary of the Navy and Henry L. Stimson as Secretary of War. They were shrewd political appointments in an election year. Both Knox and Stimson had been senior members of previous Republican administrations. Knox, indeed, had been the Republican candidate for Vice-President in 1936, while Stimson had long-standing prior experience under Republican presidents both as Secretary of War and, in the early 1930s, Secretary of State. But apart from widening the political representation of his administration and giving it a bipartisan image at a time of national crisis, Roosevelt also greatly strengthened his own hand in dealing with defence.[97] The previous Secretary of the Navy, Charles Edison, had been ineffectual, while Harry H. Woodring, whom the President now removed from his office as

Secretary of War, had been singularly ill suited to the position, his isolationist tendencies wholly out of tune with the urgency of the situation.[98] In Knox and Stimson, Roosevelt now had in position two men who favoured a more forceful defence policy – indeed were considerably more hawkish than the President himself and ready to push him in a direction he often seemed reluctant to take.

Knox, whose affable demeanour went hand in hand with firm political views, had become the publisher of the Chicago *Daily News* in 1931 and provided a voice for moderate, internationalist Republicanism in a region dominated by the shrill isolationism of the *Chicago Tribune*.[99] Stimson, by now into his seventies, a lawyer by profession though with many years spent in public service, soon became the strong man of the administration. He was a man of firm principles based upon moral rectitude and commitment to the law. He looked the part: silver-grey hair parted in the middle, a brisk moustache, an air of dogged respectability. His subordinates called him Colonel Stimson, his rank in the First World War. The President called him Harry. Stimson detested Nazism to the core, and had scant tolerance for the weak politicians of Britain and France who had failed to stand up to Hitler. He was a good, no-nonsense administrator, given to speaking his mind, with a tendency towards impatience, even brusqueness – also towards the President himself – when frustrated by anything he perceived as a lack of direction or drive.[100] Stimson now brought a much needed dynamism and, despite his advancing years, great vitality to the urgent rearmament programme.

In Knox and Stimson, Roosevelt now had in place two men whose positions were crucial to the military aspects of foreign policy, prepared to back, privately and publicly, both American preparedness and aid to Britain.[101] Stimson, especially, became the most ardent advocate of intervention in the European war. Roosevelt's keen interest in naval affairs led to his active involvement in the operational planning for the navy. He rarely saw Knox alone, and frequently dealt directly both with Admiral Harold 'Betty' Stark, chief of Naval Operations, invariably amenable to the President's proposals, and with the dour Commander-in-Chief of the Atlantic Fleet, Admiral Ernest J. King. With the army, Roosevelt acted differently. He regularly saw Stimson alone, and not just on army matters. And, probably so as not to offend his Secretary of War's proprieties in the way he liked to run his Department, he seldom saw the head of the army, the chief of staff, General George C. Marshall, except in Stimson's presence.[102] The exceptionally able and impressive, eminently austere Marshall, tall, with greying hair and intensely blue eyes, struck up an excellent working relationship with Stimson.[103] Marshall had a reputation for speaking bluntly to his superiors. He had announced his presence in autumn 1938 by disagreeing outright with Roosevelt at an important meeting. Most thought at the time that his promising career was at an end. But Roosevelt made one of his most outstanding appointments several months later when he gave Marshall the position of chief of staff. Stiff formalities were, however, upheld. Marshall always called Roosevelt 'Mr President'. He determined to remain aloof from Roosevelt's charm and never to laugh at his jokes. And after his first rebuff, Roosevelt never again called Marshall 'George'.[104]

In May 1940, after Roosevelt had flatly rejected the army's proposal for a $657 million appropriation, Marshall approached the President and expounded all the arguments in favour of the funding, ending: 'If you don't do something . . . and do it right away, I don't know what is going to happen to this country.' Roosevelt reversed his decision. Marshall later spoke of this as the action that broke the logjam.[105] Marshall continued, however, along with army planners, to oppose armed intervention until effective military strength was built up. Not before early autumn 1941 did the chief of staff come to favour war. In the summer of the previous year, the army's stance was plain. Entry into the war would result in attacks on the United States by Germany, Italy and possibly Japan. 'Our unreadiness to meet such aggression on its own scale is so great that, so long as the choice is left to us, we should avoid the contest until we can be adequately prepared.'[106]

This did not prevent Stimson and Knox from emerging as the most hawkish influences on Roosevelt, pressing upon him an unyielding stance towards both the Axis powers and Japan, while supporting every move to maximize rearmament. They found eager support from the long-standing Secretary to the Treasury and personal friend of the President, Henry Morgenthau, who believed, like Stimson, that Nazism could only be defeated if the United States were to muster its full material power at the earliest possible juncture. Morgenthau, burdened with the major task of organizing war production (which had traditionally fallen to the War Department), came to form a good working relationship with the Secretary of War, based upon mutual respect and close cooperation.[107] Further backing for 'hawks' came from the abrasive and outspoken Secretary of the Interior, Harold L. Ickes, a former Republican who had been a member of the Cabinet since 1933 and shared Morgenthau's sense of impending crisis requiring decisive action.[108]

The State Department, on the other hand, formed something of a counterweight to the hawkish tendencies of those responsible for military and defence matters. It was not that Cordell Hull, Secretary of State since 1933, favoured a soft line towards the aggressors in Europe or in the Far East. A pillar of rectitude in foreign affairs, he detested fascism and took an equally strong line in his moral condemnation of the Japanese. But his ingrained caution made him uneasy about any action that could serve as an unnecessary provocation.[109] The prospect of Japan taking advantage in the Pacific from any American involvement in Europe was indeed worrying, for the President, too. Roosevelt was content to let the wary and experienced Hull deal with the Far East with minimal interference and to keep a fragile peace in the Pacific by avoiding provocation to the Japanese while refraining from action that might condone their aggression in China. The Atlantic was another matter altogether, and here Roosevelt played a more direct and overt role. But even in the Far East, authority was divided. Hull did not preside over the spheres of military deterrence and trade restrictions.[110] Moreover, Hull could find that important issues were delegated to his Under-Secretary, Sumner Welles, a friend and confidant of the President, and a rival he viewed with some animosity and bitter resentment.[111]

The range of views on offer among the President's closest advisers, from the wily caution of Hull to the forthright interventionism of Stimson, enabled Roosevelt to oscillate between options as he chose. Hull was one of the select few able to see the President more or less at will. Given his position, this was essential. But there was little personal empathy. Immediate access did not extend a great deal further. Only Stimson, Welles and, especially, Roosevelt's long-standing most trusted adviser, Harry Hopkins – his New Dealer 'Mr Fixit', who had been in his close entourage since the beginning, had his ear on most matters, even had an apartment in the White House, and was decried by opponents as a combination of Machiavelli, Svengali and Rasputin – had near-automatic access to the President and were most directly exposed to his thinking. Hopkins, chain-smoking, gaunt and in frail health after a life-threatening illness, but with an undiminished liking for horse racing and nightclubs, indefatigable, straight-talking with a knack of cutting to the heart of any issue, and utterly loyal to Roosevelt with 'an extrasensory perception' of his moods, became an indispensable conduit for those in the inner circle who urgently sought to gain the President's ear.[112]

This group – Stimson and Knox, their uniformed heads of the services, Stark and Marshall, Hull and Hopkins – now started to be brought together increasingly at the White House. Stimson dubbed the group the 'War Council'. It was the closest approximation to the Defence Committee of the British War Cabinet, and the nearest Roosevelt came to an institutionalized framework for taking decisions in matters of national security. However, Roosevelt made sure the group did not ossify into a formal bureaucracy. He retained the flexibility to intervene or oversee wherever he wanted, depending on the issue. 'All the threads of policy', it has been said with justification, 'led ultimately to the White House.'[113]

Roosevelt's difficulties were not in ensuring that his chosen line would be adopted by his advisers. Whether they were hardliners or more 'dovish', they acceded, if sometimes in frustration, to Roosevelt's often hesitant policy choices. The President's difficulties lay, as always, with the reception of his actions in Congress and, beyond Capitol Hill, among wider public opinion and its organized lobbies. And here, Roosevelt remained ultra-cautious. Congress still had Democratic majorities in both chambers. But the mid-term elections of 1938 had substantially strengthened the basis of opposition to Roosevelt. Alignment on key committees of conservative Democrats, mainly from the southern states, with Republicans could make life difficult for the President. In particular, the vocal isolationist minority, backed by important press outlets (most notably the influential daily, the *Chicago Tribune*) and lobbies, was able to tap far wider sentiment, sympathetic to the plight of the west European democracies, but opposed to American involvement in the war. Lobby groups, for and against intervention, exploited the mood and gained a good deal of backing – and financial support.

As the presidential election campaign gathered momentum across the summer and autumn, an isolationist organization, America First, founded at the beginning of September, heavily weighted towards the Republicans and highly critical of Roosevelt's foreign policy, saw local groups spring up across the Midwest (where Chicago was the headquarters) and in the north-east. The main theme of their extensive propaganda, pumped home in huge mass meetings, was that Hitler did not endanger the United States and that aid to Britain could only end in American entry into the war in Europe.[114] America First had been established as a counter-lobby to the Committee to Defend America by Aiding the Allies, which was launched in May 1940 and was a presence in every state except North Dakota, advertising widely in the press and on national radio, raising a quarter of a million dollars by July and not stinting in its petitions to the President and Congress. The propaganda from both sides left its mark on opinion. There was a greater readiness to give Britain more material support, but the majority still held to neutrality and isolation.[115] The German sweep through the Low Countries and the increasingly precarious position of France and Britain in May 1940 profoundly worried Americans. Polls showed that only about 30 per cent still believed in an Allied victory, while 78 per cent feared that a triumphant Germany would exert influence in South America and 63 per cent thought Hitler would even seize territory on the American continent.[116] Worried for their own safety, people were greatly alarmed at the state of American preparedness, but divided on how much the United States should be doing to help the Allies, and massively opposed to any direct involvement in the European conflict.

This was the climate of opinion that Roosevelt had to face in the summer and autumn of 1940. It coincided with a key domestic issue: should Roosevelt stand for re-election for an unprecedented third term in office? And it formed the backcloth to the most critical and contentious issue of defence policy that had so far arisen: should the United States comply with Churchill's request and support Great Britain's desperate attempt to hold out against the prospect of German invasion in a tangible way by the sale of fifty destroyers? It was the first of two vital decisions that Roosevelt would make over the coming months. Together, these decisions would reshape the alliance between the United States and Great Britain and pave the way for ever closer cooperation in the struggle against Hitler's Germany.

IV

On 15 May 1940 Winston Churchill sent his first letter as Prime Minister of what would prove to be a voluminous and vitally important correspondence with Roosevelt. The two had met briefly in 1918. The meeting left more of a mark on Roosevelt than on Churchill (who did not remember it): the future American President recalled the future British Prime Minister as being a 'stinker'.[117] He continued into the Second World War to see Churchill as a social reactionary with old-fashioned 'Victorian' views. And he criticized his notorious capacity for alcohol. On hearing of Churchill's appointment as Prime Minister, he said he presumed he was the best man available, even if he was drunk half the time. Churchill, for his part, expressed concern about Roosevelt's own drinking habits, though in this case it was the President's taste for mixed dry and sweet vermouth that the British Prime Minister abhorred. More seriously, he had before the war been critical of the prolonged economic recession in the United States, which he attributed to Roosevelt's clashes with big business. He had been pleased to see the beginnings of American rearmament, limited though they were, but he still harboured doubts about Roosevelt's commitment to British interests during the spring and summer of 1940.[118]

The two had exchanged a series of personal letters since the beginning of the European war, when Churchill had been appointed First Lord of the Admiralty. Roosevelt had initiated the correspondence on 11 September 1939, with the first of what would amount to almost two thousand letters and memoranda exchanged during the next five and a half years.[119] Probably, Roosevelt viewed this early correspondence as a way of keeping a personal conduit, alongside official channels, open to the British government once war had begun in Europe.[120] Churchill's interest was simple and unvarnished: 'it was a good thing to feed [Roosevelt] at intervals,' he told the Foreign Secretary, Lord Halifax.[121] From unpropitious beginnings, the correspondence would help to build a personal rapport between Roosevelt and Churchill which would prove to be of inestimable value in forging the bonds between the United States and Great Britain in 1940–41, eventually turning into a fully fledged war alliance. But there was still a very long way to go when Churchill dispatched his letter to the American President on 15 May 1940.

Churchill began by painting the dismal scene in western Europe where, in the wake of the German advance, 'the small countries are simply smashed up, one by one, like matchwood'. He expected Mussolini to join in 'to share the loot of civilisation'. And he envisaged an attack on Britain in the near future. Britain, he said, would fight on alone, if necessary. 'But I trust you realise, Mr. President,' he continued, 'that the voice and force of the United States may count for nothing if they are withheld too long. You may have a completely subjugated, Nazified Europe established with astonishing swiftness, and the weight may be more than we can bear.' He then came to the point of his letter: his shopping list. 'All I ask now is that you should proclaim non-belligerency, which would mean that you would help us with everything short of actually engaging armed forces. Immediate needs are, first of all, the loan of forty or fifty of your older destroyers to bridge the gap between what we have now and the large new construction we put in hand at the beginning of the war.' He added, for good measure, that Britain also wanted 'several hundred of the latest types of aircraft', along with anti-aircraft equipment and ammunition, steel and other materials. Britain would continue to pay in dollars as long as possible, he wrote, but 'I should like to feel reasonably sure that when we can pay no more you will give us the stuff all the same'.[122]

The letter lost nothing in forthrightness. It reflected the hope, rather than certainty, running through the leadership of the British government that the United States would not let Britain sink, and that 'when our dollars and gold run out there will be no difficulty about credits or gifts'.[123] There were no illusions in Whitehall about the significance of such aid. On 25 May, outlining their contingency planning in the event of a collapse of France, the British chiefs of staff stated their assumption that the United States 'is willing to give us full economic and financial support, *without which we do not think we could continue the war with any chance of success*'.[124] There were already hopes that America would go still further. By mid-June there was wide agreement that what Britain needed was an immediate declaration of war by the United States. A minority view, however, was that the supply of surplus materials by the United States, including destroyers, would probably make her entry into the war and the sending of an American Expeditionary Force to Europe unnecessary.[125]

Aid in order to keep America out of the European war, not draw her in, was increasingly the presumption of the Roosevelt administration. But even that stance ran ahead of public opinion at the time. In May 1940 only 35 per cent of those questioned in opinion polls favoured aid to Britain and France at the risk of American involvement.[126] For Roosevelt, Churchill's request of 15 May was asking too much too soon. To comply with it was to take a gamble, first with public opinion and, secondly, with those in the administration who advocated waiting to see how the battle for France would turn out. Could American aid, even if it were to be given, be provided in time? Was there not the grave danger that it would simply be swallowed up in the defeat about to envelop not just France but, it seemed, most likely Britain as well? The American ambassador in London, Joseph Kennedy, pessimistic to the point of being defeatist, advised caution. On 15 May he reported the impression he had gleaned from Churchill that Britain would be attacked within a month. He thought the United States was in danger of 'holding the bag for a war in which the Allies expect to be beaten', and advised 'that if we had to fight to protect our lives, we would do better fighting in our own back yard'.[127] George Marshall, the chief of staff, argued that accommodating the British would severely weaken American hemispheric defence. Only limited armaments could in any case be made available.[128] And Roosevelt himself had it on what he took to be good authority that Hitler was likely to make Britain an offer of settlement based upon the surrender of British colonies, and – even more importantly – the fleet.[129]

The President's immediate reply to Churchill's request, received in Whitehall on 18 May, was, accordingly, kind in tone but non-committal in content. While he would do what he could to facilitate the provision of equipment (and indeed he had hastily taken the decision to scrape together every available warplane to send to France, little though it amounted to[130]), the request for the loan or gift of the forty or fifty destroyers was turned down flat. There were legal as well as political obstacles. And the Navy Department opposed the release of any ships when national security was of such paramount importance.[131] The President's reply was couched in these terms. The loan or gift of the destroyers, he wrote, would require the authorization of Congress. He indicated that this was unlikely to be forthcoming at the time. Moreover, the destroyers were needed to patrol American waters. In any case, they could not be transferred in time to make a difference in the battle for Europe. The plea for a declaration of non-belligerence was blithely ignored.[132]

There the matter of the destroyers rested for the time being. But not for long. Events in western Europe, unfolding at such a frightening pace, were concentrating American minds, in the White House as well as outside. Strong and widespread opposition to American intervention in the war was still the most profound feature of public opinion at the end of May 1940. According to an opinion poll published on 29 May, only 7.7 per cent of the population favoured entering the war immediately. The figure rose to 19 per cent in favour of intervention if the defeat of the Allies seemed inevitable. But 40 per cent opposed American participation under any circumstances.[133] A despairing plea by the French Prime Minister, Paul Reynaud, that the United States immediately declare war and act by sending its Atlantic fleet to European waters, could in this climate only fall upon deaf ears, even had the President been more temperamentally disposed towards direct American intervention than was the case.[134] It would be many months before American opinion became attuned to the prospect of the country at war once again. Even so, opinion was soon shifting. With Americans glued to their radio sets, listening to the news of daily disaster from Europe, the fall of France and the imminent threat to Great Britain sharpened awareness of the menace to the United States from German domination of the Atlantic. Isolationist feeling was weakening, even in the Midwest heartlands. A sign of this was the rapidly increasing backing for the Committee to Defend America by Aiding the Allies, the pressure group recently founded by William Allen White, a publisher and former supporter of the neutrality legislation, aimed at mobilizing opinion in favour of an interventionist stance.[135] When, on 10 June 1940, the day that Italy joined the war, Roosevelt announced that the United States would 'extend to the opponents of force the material resources of this nation' as well as mobilizing American defence, he was doing no more than articulating the public mood.[136] Four out of five Americans polled in June were in favour of giving more material support to Britain, and two-thirds, recognizing where this might lead, thought the United States would enter the war at some stage.[137]

There was also now massive support, reaching even into previously hardcore isolationist circles, for rapid and wholesale rearmament. Congress backed the President's requests that amounted to a fivefold increase in defence spending in 1940, granting a total of $10.5 billion, a figure unthinkable only a year earlier.[138] But productive capacity was still low. The big dividends from rearmament would only show by 1942. And the question of how much and what to send to Britain, isolated and imperilled after the fall of France, was one that tended to divide, rather than unite, policy-makers. The question of the destroyers, of which the public was still ignorant, had been shelved. But it would not go away.

Churchill had responded to Roosevelt, immediately on receipt of his letter, expressing his understanding of, though regret at, the decision not to provide the destroyers. The battle for France was still raging, and Churchill, in a previous note, had already stated that if American assistance was to play any part in the struggle, it had to come soon. Now he pointed out in bleak terms the 'nightmare' that would arise from the defeat of Britain. 'If members of the present Administration were finished,' he wrote, 'and others came in to parley amid the ruins, you must not be blind to the fact that the sole remaining bargaining counter with Germany would be the Fleet, and if this country was left by the United States to its fate no one would have the right to blame those then responsible if they made the best terms they could for the surviving inhabitants.'[139] Roosevelt sent no immediate reply. But the point struck home. Speaking shortly afterwards to business leaders, the President pointed out that if the British fleet and the French army were removed, 'there is nothing between the Americas and those new forces in Europe'.[140] Soon, the French army was indeed removed from the equation. Under the terms of the armistice with Germany, the French navy was left intact and based in north Africa, to be 'demobilised and disarmed under German or Italian control'.[141] The danger that the Germans would expropriate it was obvious. That left the British navy. Everything possible had to be done to prevent that falling into German hands. Thought was already being given to spiriting it across the Atlantic, to Canada, should Britain fall. But, more immediately, the navy was vital to Britain's chances of surviving a German invasion. In the confines of British coastal waters, the most crucial warship was the destroyer. And of a hundred or so destroyers available in home waters at the beginning of the war, almost half had been lost or damaged.[142] If American destroyers could help keep Britain in the war, the value to the United States would be incalculable. If, however, they were loaned to Britain and then lost to the Germans, they would simply be an unnecessary gift to the enemy, increasing the menace to America.[143] This was the dilemma of the Roosevelt administration when the issue of the loan of destroyers to Britain surfaced again in July 1940.

By then, Roosevelt had been heartened by the firm show of British resolve in the ruthless action taken on 3 July to destroy the French fleet, anchored at Mers-el-Kebir in Algeria, with the loss of life of 1,297 sailors of Britain's former ally. The President had been notified in advance of the action by the British ambassador in Washington, Lord Lothian, and had signalled his approval.[144] But he still showed no readiness to comply with the British destroyer request. When Harold Ickes, the Secretary of the Interior, argued with him that the defence of Britain might depend upon acceding to the request, Roosevelt was adamant. 'We could not send these destroyers unless the Navy could certify that they were useless to us for defense purposes,' the President countered. And 'it would be difficult to do this in view of the fact that we were reconditioning more than one hundred of them to use for our own defense purposes'.[145] As he told Ickes a few days later, he also had to consider the fate of the destroyers should Britain be forced to capitulate to the Germans.[146]

Critical though the situation was, the war in Europe tended for much of July to be superseded by domestic concerns as Roosevelt was preoccupied with the presidential nomination, to be decided at the Democratic Convention in Chicago in the middle of the month. The Republicans, a few weeks earlier, had chosen as their presidential candidate Wendell Willkie, a former Democrat, a striking personality, and, like Roosevelt, strongly in favour of giving all possible aid to Britain. Willkie posed a serious threat to the Democrats, especially since involvement in the European war was the central issue in 1940. The question of who should run against Willkie was, therefore, acute. One name that kept recurring in the list of hopefuls was that of Roosevelt himself. No one else was likely to defeat Willkie.[147] The President had remained coy down to the Convention itself about whether he would be prepared to run for a third term, though his earlier assurances that he would not stand again had given way to equivocation. He diplomatically stayed away from the Convention. But the Roosevelt camp had stage-managed their hero's nomination.

On the second night, 16 July, a prepared statement was read to delegates, announcing that Roosevelt 'has never had and has not today any desire or purpose to continue in the office of the President'. All at once the loudspeakers in the hall started to boom out: 'Pennsylvania Wants Roosevelt! Virginia Wants Roosevelt!', and so on across the states. The delegates started to take up the cry. Standards from the states were brought in and paraded around the hall. It transpired that the disembodied voice that began the clamour had come from Chicago's Commissioner of Sewers, located beneath the hall. The organization of the 'Voice from the Sewers' had been provided by the Democratic Mayor of Chicago, Edward J. Kelly.[148] And Kelly had discussed arrangements for the Convention with Harry Hopkins, Roosevelt's right-hand man.[149] It was a charade, and, in fact, little short of a scandal. But it served its purpose. Roosevelt was duly nominated next day with a massive majority over all other candidates.

With the Convention over, Lord Lothian advised Churchill that it might be a good time to return to the destroyer issue.[150] Churchill had repeated his request on 11 June, the day after Italy had entered the conflict, and he raised this issue once more three days later.[151] On seeing the letter, Morgenthau had asked Grace Tully, one of Roosevelt's personal secretaries, to inform the President of his belief 'that unless we help out the British with some destroyers it is hopeless to expect them to keep going'.[152] But again, the request had fallen on stony ground. And for almost two months since the fall of France, correspondence between Roosevelt and Churchill had lain dormant. The President had been taken up with his nomination for re-election. The Prime Minister and his colleagues might have felt it could be counterproductive to press Roosevelt too hard.[153] But on 31 July Churchill took up the matter of the destroyers once again. German invasion could, it seemed, come at any time. Air raids and U-boat attacks on shipping could now be launched from the whole of the French coastline. A large construction programme of destroyers was under way in Britain, but the ships would not become available until 1941. Meanwhile, the rate of attrition was too high, and the next three or four months would be critical. Churchill felt, therefore, that he had to renew his request for 'fifty or sixty of your oldest destroyers', to be sent at once. 'Mr. President,' he declared, 'with great respect I must tell you that in the long history of the world this is a thing to do *now*.'[154]

The issue had already been taken up earlier in the month by the Century Group, a sub-organization of the Committee to Defend America, comprising a number of influential citizens of New York, and meeting periodically at the Century Association in that city. Since mid-June the Century Group had been engaged in a campaign to send all possible disposable military resources, including naval, to the Allies, seeing their fight as synonymous with America's own, and advocating the abolition of neutrality and recognition of a state of war existing with Germany.[155] On 11 July, at a meeting in New York, the Century Group proposed, as part of a strategy to meet the dangers threatening from Europe, supplying destroyers to Britain in exchange for a number of bases in British possessions close to American shores. This turned out to be a key proposal, and it came from a private initiative, not from within the administration.

It was not in essence a new idea. In fact, the isolationist *Chicago Tribune* had long urged that such bases should be offered by the Allies in return for the cancellation of war debts. But the linkage now to the provision of the needed destroyers was a shrewd move. It offered in embryo the possibility of a deal that would suit America. And it held some appeal even to isolationists. One of the leading figures in the Century Group, Joseph Alsop, a well-known newspaper columnist with good connections to figures in the administration, now persuaded one of the President's assistants, Benjamin Cohen, to compose a memorandum for Roosevelt, arguing that there was no obstacle to selling the destroyers. Cohen showed the memorandum to his boss, Harold Ickes, who brought it to the President's attention (and subsequently wrote in strong support of supplying the destroyers).[156]

Roosevelt, however, remained unconvinced. The United States had 172 over-age warships, many of First World War vintage. Supplying Britain with fifty or so of them would not have crippled the navy. But on 28 June 1940, Congress, showing its distrust of the President, had passed an amendment to the Naval Appropriations bill stipulating that no item of military material could be turned over to a foreign government unless either the chief of staff (Marshall) or the chief of Naval Operations (Stark) had certified that it was useless for the defence of the United States. Precisely that was difficult for Stark to do since he had recently upheld the potential value of the warships before congressional committees.[157] Roosevelt referred to the barrier of the new legislation when he sent Cohen's memorandum on to the Secretary of the Navy, Frank Knox, on 22 July. 'I frankly doubt if Cohen's memorandum would stand up,' the President wrote. 'Also I fear Congress is in no mood at the present time to allow any form of sale.' All he could suggest was that sometime later Congress might be prevailed upon to allow the sale of the destroyers to Canada, but only on condition that their use be confined to defence of the American hemisphere.[158]

The Century Group, however, continued to press. Alsop talked to civilian and military officials in Washington and found an encouraging response. The British ambassador, Lord Lothian, was unsurprisingly supportive. On 25 July, in the light of Alsop's soundings, the Century Group compiled a further memorandum, ending in the proposal that the destroyers be offered immediately in return for naval and air concessions in British possessions in the western hemisphere. A further point of significance now added was to tie the deal to a guarantee that the British fleet would, in the event of a successful German invasion, be neither scuttled nor surrendered but removed to Canadian or American bases from where it would continue to operate. Since the issue was so urgent, members of the group would lobby Roosevelt and urge him to act jointly with Willkie, the Republican challenger, to expedite the matter. Meanwhile, a further publicity campaign would aim to sustain the pressure. Roosevelt met three delegates from the group on 1 August, listened to what they had to say, but remained non-committal. The delegates left disappointed, feeling that the President was apathetic about the issue.[159]

They were wrong in this. On 2 August Roosevelt raised the issue at an unusually important meeting of his Cabinet. Frank Knox, the Secretary of the Navy, had spoken at length to Lothian the previous evening, heard a desperate plea from the ambassador for immediate assistance in sending the destroyers and had met a positive response to the suggestion that Britain transfer land for naval bases on the Atlantic coast to the United States. Before the Cabinet met, Knox had talked over the proposition with Stimson, gained his backing, and that, too, of Harold Ickes.[160] A powerful phalanx of support for the idea existed, therefore, when the Cabinet assembled.

It soon proved, in fact, that there was unanimous support for making the destroyers available to Britain. But the necessary legislation was a stumbling block. It was recognized that if Roosevelt were to seek it without thoroughly preparing the ground, Congress would reject the proposal or subject it to 'interminable delay'. A possible way round the problem was the transfer of British possessions. Discussion at Cabinet had indeed begun with Knox's report of his lengthy telephone conversation with Lothian. Hull, just back from the Pan-American Conference in Havana, thought the transfer of British possessions might fall foul of the agreement reached with the other American republics upholding the policy of retention of existing territorial status in the western hemisphere. Roosevelt himself, agreeing with Hull's objection, then suggested that leasing part of the territory (as was currently the case with a naval base in Trinidad) might provide a solution, an idea that met with general agreement. In addition, the Cabinet agreed to seek assurances from Britain that the fleet would not fall into German hands in the event of defeat. This, it was thought, would also help to assuage opposition within Congress. Hull pointed out that the transfer of the destroyers could only be accomplished through the repeal of the law prohibiting such sales. The best way of approaching this, he suggested, would be for the President and the Republican candidate, Wendell Willkie (already known to be sympathetic), jointly to back the proposal, thereby defusing Republican opposition within Congress. The President was left to contact William Allen White, the leading figure in the Committee to Defend America, to ask his help in brokering agreement with Willkie.[161]

Belatedly, it was a start. But there now followed a protracted period of consultation and legal wrangling about the details of the embryonic deal. Churchill was unwilling, for reasons of morale at home, to give a public assurance about the fleet in the event of a British defeat.[162] The British 'shopping-list', when it was supplied on 8 August, had been substantially enhanced and now stretched to 96 destroyers, 20 motor torpedo-boats, flying-boats, dive-bombers and 250,000 rifles. Above all, it was still an open question whether, even with Willkie's support (and he proved cagy about giving explicit approval), the necessary legislation to permit the provision of the destroyers, accepting British willingness to transfer bases, could be pushed through Congress.[163]

Two developments gave impetus to a process that threatened to become becalmed in legal technicalities. The first was the enormous campaign of agitation unleashed by the Committee to Defend America. The Committee managed to enlist in its cause the support of the revered military leader of the First World War, General John J. Pershing, whose broadcast stirred widespread public backing for the supply of the destroyers, mixed with some incredulity that it was proving so difficult to organize. Once the quid pro quo – the transfer of bases – became public knowledge, the demands for prompt action grew even louder. But so, too, did the voices of the isolationist opposition, warning that 'the sale of the Navy's ships to a nation at war would be an act of war', and that 'if we want to get into the war, the destroyers offer as good a way as any of accomplishing the purpose'. The second factor in the breakthrough was a letter to the *New York Times* by four prominent lawyers, arguing persuasively that the supply of the destroyers could be accommodated within the existing legal framework and urging the President to act on his own authority without delay.[164]

Roosevelt still awaited legal clarification from his Attorney General, Robert H. Jackson. But, finally, on 13 August, after consulting Stimson, Knox, Morgenthau and Welles (standing in for Hull, who was taking a brief and well-earned recuperative break), and with England already facing mounting air attacks, Roosevelt decided to push ahead with the negotiations. Probably at this point, before hearing from the Attorney General, he still contemplated putting the case before Congress rather than taking executive action. But in any case, a lengthy message to Churchill drafted that evening, offering at least fifty destroyers, the motor torpedo-boats and a small number of planes, made plain that the President would accept his private assurances about the fate of the fleet, and outlined the possessions, to be acquired through purchase or a ninety-nine-year lease, in New-foundland, Bermuda, the Bahamas, Jamaica, Trinidad, St Lucia and British Guiana where the Americans wanted to establish naval and air bases. Churchill replied straight away, accepting all the stipulations.[165]

The way seemed finally clear. Or was it? The President still fretted about the isolationist opposition. He feared that acting without the backing of Congress could lose him the forthcoming election. His worries probably lay behind the deliberately misleading impression he unnecessarily conveyed to a press conference on 16 August when he insisted that the acquisition of British possessions was not related to the transfer of destroyers to Britain.[166] Given the feeling in the country, it reflected undue sensitivity.

His confidence grew on hearing the legal opinion of the Attorney General, who had concluded that the destroyers could be certified as not essential to national security – patently a piece of sophistry. Roosevelt told the Canadian Prime Minister, Mackenzie King, on 17 August that he did not need to submit the matter to Congress, and that Britain would have the destroyers within a week. That proved optimistic. Further fine-tuning of the draft agreement was only finalized at the end of the month. It was Churchill in these latter stages who delayed completion by insisting on redrafting the terms of the lease of the bases in order to obfuscate the reality of the deal to the British public: that the United States had come out of it inordinately well.[167] Eventually, the minor but awkward difficulties were resolved. The President gave his approval on 30 August. On the evening of 2 September Cordell Hull for the United States and Lord Lothian for Great Britain signed the agreement. Admiral Stark certified next day that the destroyers were not essential to national security in the light of the acquired bases. The ships finally made their way to Halifax, Nova Scotia, and into British possession.[168]

After the months of hesitation, delay, foot-dragging, legal wrangling and drafting complications, the destroyers proved of little practical value. Only nine were put into service by the Royal Navy before the end of the year, to meet the invasion that never came. And even these were less seaworthy than had been expected. As late as May 1941 no more than thirty were put to use. There were delays, too, in releasing the motor torpedo-boats and the rifles (which, amazingly, had been completely forgotten about in the final draft of the agreement).[169] Nor, despite the flurry of activity in the summer crisis, did the bases pass rapidly into American possession. The precise arrangements for the base leases were not concluded until March 1941.[170]

But the symbolism of the destroyer deal far outweighed any tangible benefit for either side. The reaction in Rome, Berlin and Tokyo was sufficient to demonstrate this. Mussolini purported to be indifferent to the deal. But he interpreted it as bringing the likelihood of American intervention in the war closer.[171] The German reaction was stronger. The delivery of the destroyers was seen as 'an openly hostile act against Germany', marking closer cooperation between Britain and the United States. America, it was now taken for granted, would do everything possible to support Britain and damage Germany. Part of the response was contemplation of a move to occupy the Azores and the Canaries. Hitler himself, however, shrugged off the deal. He thought American rearmament would peak only in 1945. Even so, from the summer of 1940 onwards America was a factor that had to be given the utmost consideration in German strategy.[172] Such consideration, we might recall, played its part in the decision to attack and, it was presumed, rapidly destroy the Soviet Union the following spring. And the destroyer-bases deal helped to hasten the negotiations between Germany and Japan that culminated in the Tripartite Pact of mid-September, aimed at deterring the United States from participation in the war.[173]

In the United States, Roosevelt was above all able to emphasize the huge advantages to American defences from the acquisition of the Atlantic bases. The popular reception was very positive. Isolationists were outflanked by the President's move to tie in the bases with the supply of the destroyers. Traditional isolationism was now starting to run out of steam, even if fear of intervention was still strong. More importantly, as was widely recognized, the Americans had now effectively abandoned neutrality.[174]

For the British, this was the key point. The United States was no longer neutral in any conventional understanding of the term. The totemic aspect of the destroyer deal, privately as well as publicly emphasized by British leaders, was the outward display of American military support for Britain. During the niggly negotiations in late August, the British Foreign Secretary, Lord Halifax, had remarked that 'the idea of the English-United States tie-up on anything is of more value than either bases or destroyers'.[175] Churchill himself had implied the same at the climax of his speech in the House of Commons on 20 August. He spoke of the destroyer deal, at that point still not completed, as meaning 'that these two great organizations of the English-speaking democracies, the British Empire and the United States, will have to be somewhat mixed up together in some of their affairs for mutual and general advantage'. It was a process, he added, in a rhetorical flourish, that he could not stop even if he wanted to do so. 'No one can stop it. Like the Mississippi, it just keeps rolling along. Let it roll. Let it roll on full flood, inexorable, irresistible, benignant, to broader lands and better days.'[176] Rhetoric apart, it was a decisive moment, as Churchill hinted, in demonstrating American solidarity with Britain's war effort. He later described it as 'a decidedly unneutral act by the United States', an event which 'brought the United States definitely nearer to us and to the war'.[177] And so it was, and so it did.

Not that this had been Roosevelt's intention. What seems in retrospect to have been part of an inexorable process did not look like that at the time. That it had taken fully three and a half months since Churchill's first overture to bring the deal to fruition was first and foremost a reflection of Roosevelt's uncertainty in handling public opinion at home and his reluctance to commit himself too far. In an election year, he was cautious of offering any propaganda hostages to fortune to his opponent. And his fear of upsetting Congress made him all the more ready to hide behind legalism when decisive action was called for. In the event, the Germans did not invade, and the destroyers were not needed. But an invasion certainly *seemed* imminent in summer 1940, and still Roosevelt hesitated over the destroyers. In the end, he did take action in authorizing something which he had probably inwardly favoured all along. But by then he was taking no risk with public opinion. Sensitive as ever to anything that might affect his popularity, he had even suggested that the destroyer deal might lose him the forthcoming election.[178] In fact, he had been pushed by public opinion, stirred by the agitation of the lobbies favouring the deal. 'The destroyer deal', it has been aptly noted, 'was at least as much the achievement of private effort as of official action.'[179] With the United States now effectively a non-neutral non-belligerent, it remained to be seen whether the President would take a more active role than he had done in the summer of 1940 in driving ahead the support for Great Britain.

V

The underlying issue remained. The United States was committed, and with a great deal of popular backing, to providing support for Britain short of war. The idea that this was crucial to hemispheric defence – in America's own direct interest, that is – was widely accepted. But the practicalities of supplying aid to Britain raised contentious issues. The destroyer deal had been pushed through on the President's executive authority on what many regarded as legal sleight of hand by the Attorney General that allowed the bypassing of congressional legislation. However, if aid on a major scale were to be provided for Britain, the imprimatur of Congress as the seal of the nation's backing could not be indefinitely avoided.

There were at least two major obstacles to attaining congressional support for massively increased aid. One was the view, vociferously expressed by the isolationist lobby though not confined to them, that arms should not be shipped to Britain when they were directly and obviously needed to build up American military defences. A related concern was that increased arms would necessitate increased support for the ships carrying the *matériel* – inexorably, therefore, drawing the United States closer to involvement in the war. The second obstacle, and certainly a daunting one, was legal and financial. Britain was fast reaching the point where she would be unable to pay for the arms she desperately needed. But under the Johnson Act of 1934, still valid, the United States could not give loans to nations in default on their debts from the First World War. And under the cash-and-carry provisions of the Neutrality Act, introduced in 1937 and renewed in 1939, goods could only be sold to belligerent countries if the money was provided upfront.[180] On the other hand, a drop in British arms orders was out of the question, and not just for the pressing reason that, without the resources of the United States at her disposal, Britain's war effort would before long be exhausted. For domestic reasons, too, the Roosevelt administration wanted to increase, not curtail, supplies to Britain. By the time of his re-election – with a comfortable, if reduced majority – on 5 November 1940, Roosevelt had seen unemployment fall by 3.5 million since the recession of 1937–8. At the end of the year, unemployment stood at its lowest level for a decade. And this was thanks, in the main, to British weapons purchases, worth some $5 billion in orders by the end of 1940.[181]

The matter of aid to Britain was coming to a head by the end of 1940. The presidential election was past, but it had not brought the discernible shift in American policy that the British government had been hoping for. Vague illusions in Whitehall that the United States might even enter the war once Roosevelt was re-elected were rapidly dashed. In fact, there was some sense of anti-climax also in Washington. For some weeks, policy seemed becalmed. The exertions of the election campaign had probably left more of a mark on the President than was immediately visible. At any rate, as has been pointed out, Roosevelt 'again deemed it more advantageous to stay in step with public opinion' than to risk 'a gamble with his powers of leadership'.[182]

In London, Churchill said at the beginning of December that he had been 'rather chilled' by the American attitude since the election. But one keen observer of the Washington scene who was unsurprised at the lack of dynamic action of the Roosevelt administration was the British ambassador, Lord Lothian. On a brief return to England in November, Lothian pointed out to Churchill the belief, still widespread in the United States, that Britain was asking for more than she needed and was less hard-up than she claimed. He advised Churchill to lay out the case for the greatly increased aid, necessary if Britain were not to be forced into a compromise peace during 1941, in a personal letter to the President.[183] On his return to the United States, landing at New York, Lothian had spoken in uncharacteristically blunt and non-diplomatic language to reporters at an impromptu press conference. 'Well boys, Britain's broke; it's your money we want,' the ambassador told the waiting reporters. He repeated the remark, showing it was no off-the-cuff slip of the tongue, for the newsreels shortly afterwards. It was quite unlike Lothian. He claimed to have spoken on his own authority. But the suspicion remains that Churchill himself had prompted a calculated indiscretion.[184]

At any rate, it had the effect desired: putting the matter of the parlous British dollar resources squarely in the public eye. But the immediate response in the Roosevelt administration was far from positive. Cordell Hull was sceptical about the claim that Britain could afford to buy no more. So was Morgenthau, in charge of the Treasury, who pointed out to Lothian that opponents of aid could make political capital out of allowing a bankrupt country to place more orders. Morgenthau was aware that Lothian's remark was not quite what it seemed. Britain was not bankrupt. But dollar resources were running low, if not, Morgenthau surmised, as low as Lothian was claiming. Morgenthau, even so, was struck by Lothian's pessimism about Britain's future, unless large supplies of aid were forthcoming. In fact, the Secretary to the Treasury had been mulling over throughout November ways to meet British needs not just for armaments, but for merchant ships – victims already to U-boats at an alarming rate – to carry the food on which Britain depended.[185] Roosevelt himself, at a Cabinet meeting on 8 November, had hinted at a possible solution. He thought the British still had enough in credit and property in the United States – about $2.5 billion – that they could liquidate to pay for war supplies. But he recognized that the money would run out. 'The time would surely come', the President remarked, 'when Great Britain would need loans or credits.' According to Ickes, 'he suggested that one way to meet that situation would be for us to supply whatever we could under leasing arrangements with England. For instance, he thought that we could lease ships or any other property that was loanable, returnable, and insurable.'[186] In fact, it was not the first time that something like it had occurred to the President. Two years earlier, in

November 1938, following the disastrous Munich Agreement, Roosevelt had mused over the difference it might have made had he been able to sell or lend large numbers of warplanes to the embattled European democracies.[187] Thus did the idea that blossomed into the lend-lease programme begin to germinate.

The idea gained its first airing in public by an indirect route on 26 November 1940, when William Allen White's Committee to Defend America by Aiding the Allies issued a strong statement urging greater assistance to Britain. The statement called upon Congress to revise statutes hampering this assistance, and advocated the building with all speed of the maximum number of merchant ships for rent or lease to Britain. Behind the scenes, the press release had probably been initiated by the President himself, as a trial balloon, a device sometimes used by the White House to test opinion. In this instance, the statement elicited neither an outburst of public support nor sizeable opposition. Opinion, as usual, generally favoured helping Britain short of war, but was still cautious about the risk of American involvement in hostilities. Whatever Roosevelt deduced from the trial balloon, if that is what it was, no action followed from the White House. All the public learned was that the President was about to take a holiday.[188]

The President was about to set sail on the USS *Tuscaloosa* for a ten-day cruise in the Caribbean. Officially, he was visiting the new base sites in the West Indies. He took plenty of state papers with him, and said he would work on a major speech to the nation about the international situation while he was away. But he took no experts on foreign affairs with him. Looking worn out, he needed the trip to recharge his batteries, and mainly spent the time fishing, playing poker, watching films and relaxing with Harry Hopkins, his sole guest, and his aides, his only other accompaniment.[189]

The day before he left Washington, Roosevelt had authorized a complex deal for orders from London worth $2 billion to equip ten British army divisions. The question was how the British were going to fund the deal. Though Roosevelt was still insisting that 'they aren't bust – there's lots of money there', he recognized that most of it was tied up in foreign assets in the Empire and not readily available in dollars. All the available resources in dollars, and more besides, would be used up in the munitions deal and over the coming months. The idea of loaning cargo ships to Britain recurred during the discussion, though there was no suggestion at the time of loaning or leasing aircraft or armaments. Pressed by Morgenthau, Roosevelt agreed that the orders should be placed and the capital investment to build new plants and extend existing ones should come from American funds, with the British paying on delivery for the material produced, adding a surcharge to contribute to the capital costs. But the President told Stimson, 'we have just got to decide what we are going to do for England', adding, 'doing it this way is not doing anything'.[190]

Unless new ways could be found, the end of the road for the current ways of fulfilling the aim of maximum aid for Britain short of war was clearly approaching. That much was recognized by Roosevelt's key advisers, meeting in the President's absence just after he had left for his Caribbean cruise. Frank Knox came to the point and posed the key question, a rhetorical one. 'We are going to pay for the war from now on, are we?' When Morgenthau raised the issue of whether the United States should allow Britain to place the orders, Knox was adamant: 'Got to. No question about it.' But how was this to be done? Discussion still circled around the issue of whether Britain would have to pay cash for the goods produced. There was no resolution to this issue. Those present were agreed that the proposal for any kind of gift or loan, such as Britain would soon request, would have to go to Congress, and was likely to be rejected unless it was obvious that there was no other option. Until British assets were liquidated, this was unlikely.[191] Loans were, given the bad feeling stirred up by Britain's non-payment of her debts from the First World War, not seen as the solution. It was felt better for the United States to place the orders, then turn over the products to Britain, though not as an outright gift, since it was hoped that something might be had in return, or at least unused or undamaged material eventually returned.[192] The idea of a loan in kind, first mooted by Roosevelt, was now tentatively being extended in his absence to cover not just freight ships, but potentially the whole gamut of British armaments demands.

Within days, Churchill's long letter, which Lothian had suggested he write, was on its way to Roosevelt and eventually reached the President in the middle of the Caribbean on 9 December, sent on by the State Department and delivered by a naval seaplane. It had been difficult to compose and went through numerous drafts over a period of longer than a fortnight before it was ready. Churchill later commented, with justification, that it was one of the most important he ever wrote.[193]

Most of the letter presented a *tour d'horizon* of the state of the war, from a British perspective. Churchill stressed the losses of merchant shipping in the Atlantic, the urgent need for ships, planes and munitions, and the tough struggle looming in 1941. He laid strong emphasis on Britain's dependency on help from the United States. The prime need to reduce the loss of tonnage in the Atlantic could be achieved, he tactfully suggested, if the United States were to provide warship escorts to the merchant convoys, a move, he said, which 'would constitute a decisive act of constructive non-belligerency'. Churchill was aware of the magnitude of what he was asking. It would be months before the American public would be ready for such a move. He expressed another hope: 'the gift, loan, or supply of a large number of American vessels of war' to maintain the Atlantic route, and the extension of control by American forces in the western part of the ocean.

Only at the end of his lengthy missive did he reach the crucial issue of finance. He pointed out the drain on dollar credits. 'The moment approaches', he wrote, 'when we shall no longer be able to pay cash for shipping and other supplies.' He combined moral pressure with economic logic: 'I believe you will agree that it would be wrong in principle and mutually disadvantageous in effect if at the height of this struggle Britain were to be divested of all saleable assets, so that after the victory was won with our blood, civilisation saved, and the time gained for the United States to be fully armed against all eventualities, we should stand stripped to the bone.'

He went on to outline the postwar economic problems this would cause for the United States. American exports to Britain would slump. Widespread unemployment would result. He offered no solution, but he ended by placing Britain's future in America's hands. 'Moreover,' he concluded,

I do not believe that the Government and people of the United States would find it in accordance with the principles which guide them to confine the help which they have so generously promised only to such munitions of war and commodities as could be immediately paid for. You may be certain that we shall prove ourselves ready to suffer and sacrifice to the utmost for the Cause, and that we glory in being its champions. The rest we leave with confidence to you and to your people, being sure that ways and means will be found which future generations on both sides of the Atlantic will approve and admire.[194]

Indirectly, with these closing remarks, Churchill was underlining the shift in power-relations between Great Britain and the United States which the first year of the war had laid bare. Morgenthau put it succinctly: 'It gets down to a question of Mr. Churchill putting himself in Mr. Roosevelt's hands with complete confidence. Then it is up to Mr. Roosevelt to say what he will do.'[195] It sounded like the obsequies for the British Empire.

While Morgenthau and other administration leaders continued in Washington to wrestle with the problem of Britain's payments for the material she needed,[196] Roosevelt was sitting in his deckchair on board the *Tuscaloosa* in the balmy sunshine of the Caribbean, pondering Churchill's letter. He read it time and again and for two days seemed deep in thought, profoundly affected by its contents. Hopkins, the President's only confidant on board, left Roosevelt to his ruminations. 'Then one evening,' Hopkins later recounted, 'he suddenly came out with it – the whole programme. He didn't seem to have any clear idea how it could be done legally. But there wasn't a doubt in his mind that he'd find a way to do it.'[197] Perhaps Hopkins was being modest about his own role; perhaps he and Roosevelt had, in fact, examined the possibilities before the President resolved the matter in his own mind; perhaps the decision was less a bolt out of the blue than it was made to seem. However, this is of minor significance. For there is no question that the way round Britain's dollar crisis, the momentous decision that would open up unlimited resources for the British war effort, was found by Roosevelt himself.[198]

Characteristically, Roosevelt was in no hurry to tell the members of his Cabinet about his decision. He told them to avoid action until he returned and could discuss the matter in detail.[199] Before then, the key figures in the administration responsible for foreign and defence policy had met in Hull's office in the State Department to review the situation in the light of Churchill's letter, and notably his call for 'a decisive act of constructive non-belligerency', to have a position worked out for the President on his return. Alongside the Secretary of State himself were Stimson, Knox, General Marshall, Admiral Stark, Sumner Welles and a number of other leading officials. Stark was adamant that at the current rate of shipping losses Britain could not survive longer than six months. Stimson, to the point as ever, drew the conclusion that American defence production could not be raised to the levels necessary for the security of the United States and to prevent Britain's defeat 'until we got into war ourselves'. When he asked Stark what measures were necessary to relieve Britain's plight in the Atlantic, the Admiral replied that the Neutrality Act would have to be repealed to allow US merchant ships to carry supplies to British ports, and that such a move would undoubtedly lead to naval escorts of convoys and, ultimately, in all probability, to American entry into the war. It was a daunting prospect. Unsurprisingly, no clear path forward emerged from the meeting.[200]

By the time the President returned to Washington on the evening of 16 December, tanned, in good spirits, thoroughly 'refuelled' (as Hopkins put it) from his sojourn on board the *Tuscaloosa*, there was an air of some expectancy in the American capital.[201] Next day he told Morgenthau that he had been 'thinking very hard on this trip about what we should do for England', and had come to the conclusion 'that the thing to do is to get away from the dollar sign'. He wanted neither sales nor money loans. Instead, he suggested that 'we will say to England, we will give you the guns and the ships that you need, provided that when the war is over you will return to us in kind the guns and the ships that we have loaned to you'. 'What do you think of it?' the President asked. Morgenthau was instantly enthusiastic.[202] He put it down to one of Roosevelt's 'brilliant flashes'.[203] As we have seen, however, the idea had been forming in the President's mind for some while. It certainly reached back to the time of the destroyer deal, when Roosevelt mused about leasing merchant ships to Britain. The original notion, it has been suggested, arose when the Treasury Department found that old statutes sanctioned the leasing of army property for up to five years if the goods were not necessary for public use.[204] But if that was the case, the Treasury made nothing of the discovery. It took the President to recognize the full potential of the leasing idea. And on 17 December, he put it into the public domain in a way which was novel, clear and compelling.

That afternoon, Roosevelt held a press conference. He began disarmingly by saying there was no particular news. But he thought there might be one thing worth mentioning. He gradually moved into his theme. No major war had been lost for lack of money, he stated. Giving the impression that he was thinking on his feet, he went on to put the case for increased aid to Britain. It was, he said, 'important from a selfish point of view of American defense, that we should do everything to help the British Empire to defend itself'. He pointed out that British orders were 'a tremendous asset to American defense'. He ruled out the need for any repeal of the Johnson or Neutrality Acts. But he thought it necessary to think beyond traditional terms about war finances. He claimed, with some exaggeration, that the administration had been working on the problem for some weeks. Then he advanced what he suggested was only one of a number of possible methods. The United States could take over British orders and 'lease or sell' to Great Britain part of munitions production. What he was trying to do, Roosevelt continued, was to 'get rid of the silly, foolish old dollar sign'. He produced a folksy analogy to explain what he meant. A man would not say to a neighbour whose house was on fire: 'Neighbor, my garden hose cost me fifteen dollars; you have to pay me fifteen dollars for it.' He would lend the neighbour his hose, and get it back later. This was how the munitions problem had to be handled. The details were still to be clarified, the President said, but what he was going to do was to substitute for the dollar sign a 'gentleman's obligation to repay in kind'. 'I think you all get it,' he added. When reporters present asked him whether his scheme would take the country closer to war, Roosevelt was dismissive. But he accepted that Congress would have to give its approval, and that proposals for legislation would be forthcoming in the New Year.[205]

It was a masterly performance; Roosevelt at his very best. The garden-hose parable was not, in fact, Roosevelt's brainwave, as it appeared on the day. It had first been used by Harold Ickes four months earlier, but had evidently stuck in the President's head and been stored away for future use.[206] He had now deployed it, and to brilliant effect. 'It may accurately be said that with that neighbourly analogy Roosevelt won the fight for Lend Lease,' Robert Sherwood, one of the President's speech-writing team, believed.[207] It was still far from a programme. Roosevelt had provided no details; those would, however, all come out one way or the other in the passage of legislation through Congress. He batted away questions about the increased production necessary to provide the material for the British. The implications of ensuring safe delivery of the goods produced to the British armed forces were equally unclear. And there was an obvious flaw in the analogy, not lost on some who heard it. The 'garden hose', in this case, was unlikely to be returned, certainly not intact. But what the President had done with his parable, above all, was to reduce a highly complex, and controversial, issue to utter simplicity – to a story of good neighbourliness which anyone could understand and most would have sympathy with. The issue of aid to Britain was now fully in the public domain, open to rigorous scrutiny and debate on all sides.

Roosevelt backed up his opening gambit with immediate and energetic executive action, approving as a matter of great urgency Stimson's initiative to shake up the reorganization of defence production. The leaderless and hopelessly ineffectual Advisory Commission, set up in the spring, was now replaced by a smaller and more dynamic Office of Production Management with only four members: Stimson, Knox, the director and experienced business leader William Knudsen (head of General Motors), and, as co-director, ensuring the involvement of organized labour, Sidney Hillmann (president of the Amalgamated Clothing Workers). The operational weaknesses of this new organization, too, would be fairly quickly exposed. For now, however, its institution was a clear indication that Roosevelt was anxious to drive ahead with the armaments aid programme, though on the linked question of convoy escorts he remained evasive and non-committal.[208]

Twelve days after his pivotal press conference, on 29 December, Roosevelt was wheeled into the diplomatic reception room at the White House to deliver his first 'fireside chat' to the nation since his re-election. Many at the time, and since, have reckoned it to be among his best and most effective. It may at least in part have been prompted by the hostile response to the lend-lease idea in German foreign propaganda – a response aimed at shoring up the isolationists in the United States, but in fact having the opposite effect of prompting unexpected backing for the President's initiative.[209] However, the main impulse was Roosevelt's wish to explain to the American people 'the plain truth about the gravity of the situation' in which the war had placed the United States,[210] and to drive home the need to provide all-out aid to Britain – an induction into lend-lease.

Roosevelt pulled no punches in elaborating the danger to the security of America. Referring to the Tripartite Pact signed the previous September between Germany, Italy and Japan and directed against the United States, he painted a stark dualistic picture of free, democratic peoples in mortal combat against 'the evil forces' of totalitarian tyranny, set on dominating and enslaving the human race. In an age of air power, the oceans, he went on, were no longer a protection for the United States. It was vital that they did not fall to hostile powers. In this, upholding the fighting potential of Britain (the struggle of the Greeks and the Chinese was also mentioned) was vital. For, 'if Great Britain goes down, the Axis powers will control the continents of Europe, Asia, Africa, Australasia, and the high seas – and they will be in a position to bring enormous military and naval resources against this hemisphere'. There was, therefore, great danger ahead, which had to be faced. Indirectly rounding on his isolationist opponents, the President dismissed the illusion 'that we can save our own skins by shutting our eyes to the fate of other nations'. Appeasement, experience had shown, offered no solution. A 'negotiated peace' was 'nonsense'; it would be no peace at all.

The President turned to his second theme: the need to help Britain. The British were holding out against an 'unholy alliance'. America's future security depended upon the outcome of this struggle. Roosevelt stated categorically: 'there is far less chance of the United States getting into war if we do all we can now to support the nations defending themselves against attack by the Axis than if we acquiesce in their defeat.' He openly accepted that there was risk involved in any course adopted. But the course he was advocating carried, he said, the least risk. There was no demand for an American Expeditionary Force to be sent abroad, and no intention of sending one. 'You can, therefore, nail any talk about sending armies to Europe as deliberate untruth.' But those engaged in the fighting were asking for 'the implements of war', and 'emphatically we must get these weapons to them'. He repeated that his policy was not directed at war, but at keeping war away from America. He appealed to workers and to leaders of industry to redouble their efforts. 'We must have more ships, more guns, more planes – more of everything.' How much would be sent abroad would rest on the judgement of the government's defence experts. The United States had furnished the British with great material support, and would provide more in future. The President concluded his powerful speech with words that had a lasting echo: 'We must be the great arsenal of democracy.'[211]

There was an overwhelming response to the 'fireside chat'. Three-quarters of Americans had heard it, and of those over 60 per cent were in agreement. The White House was inundated with letters and telegrams on the speech – 100 to 1 in favour. Roosevelt was delighted. It was far beyond his expectations. The disapproval, as to be expected, came from the dwindling force of isolationists, but even they were in part disarmed by the speech. Some of the most perceptive published reactions welcomed the clear and firm leadership at last displayed by the President, applauding the end of the uncertainty that had hung like a cloud over American policy during the previous months, and that Roosevelt had finally 'clarified and crystallized America's choice, a choice really made long ago'. The regret was only that 'this approach was delayed at the expense of six months of vital preparation'.[212]

December 1940 was the month in which the key decision – one of the most important of the war – was taken. It was a decision for a programme that amounted to 'nothing short of a declaration of economic warfare on the Axis'.[213] For the first time since well before his re-election, Roosevelt had led, rather than followed, opinion in the country. And opinion was shifting in line with his lead. Now, as many as 70 per cent of those questioned were ready to help Britain win, even at the risk of American involvement in the war. But a huge majority still opposed entering the war there and then. The American people, as one commentator put it, continued to prefer 'their footing on the rim' to being pushed into war.[214]

Roosevelt's 'fireside chat' was swiftly followed by his annual address to Congress on the State of the Union, delivered on 6 January 1941. In another forceful speech, the President outlined the 'four essential human freedoms' for which he was striving. They amounted to a declaration of American aims for a postwar world: freedom of speech, freedom of religion, freedom from want and freedom from fear. Soon afterwards, the President stipulated his budget demands for 1942: of the 17.5 billion dollars requested, 60 per cent was allocated to national defence.[215] The 'arsenal of democracy' had been commissioned.

Even before his speech to Congress, on 2 January, the President's new sense of urgency had led him to commission the Treasury to draft the Lend-Lease bill to take to Congress.[216] From now on, the main responsibility lay with Morgenthau and his team. The bill was given the symbolic number of House Resolution 1776 – the date of the American Revolution. On 10 January it was brought to the House of Representatives. The debates that followed, over a period of two months, were intensive, and were widely reported. There was huge national interest. Almost all Americans knew of the bill, and most of them consistently supported it, even though more than a third of those questioned thought that, if passed, it would bring the United States closer to 'getting into the war'.[217] For the isolationists, the campaign against the bill amounted to a last hurrah. The America First Committee launched a massive campaign of opposition. The young John F. Kennedy was one of those who contributed to its funds.[218] Extensive publicity for the campaign was assured in the pages of the *Chicago Tribune*, published by the larger than life character, and outspoken isolationist, Colonel Robert R. McCormick.[219]

The complex legislative process took its course. In Congress, the opposition was not powerful enough to defeat the bill, but was able to force through a number of amendments. Eventually, the bill was passed by a majority of 260 to 165 in the House of Representatives, 60 to 31 in the Senate. In both chambers, those opposed were mainly Republicans. Roosevelt signed the Lend-Lease law on 11 March 1941. It now gave him the authority to order the production or procurement of 'any defense article for the government of any country whose defense the President deems vital to the defense of the United States'.[220]

Speaking at the annual dinner of the White House Correspondents' Association four days later, the President omitted all the recriminations about his opponents that he had originally thought of including.[221] Instead, he focused on the national unity that the debate on lend-lease had brought to face the tasks ahead. 'Let not the dictators of Europe or Asia doubt our unanimity now,' he proclaimed. The entire country had engaged in a great debate. 'Yes, the decisions of our democracy may be slowly arrived at,' he conceded. 'But when that decision is made, it is proclaimed not with the voice of any one man but with the voice of one hundred and thirty millions. It is binding on us all. And the world is no longer left in doubt.' A sideswipe at his opponents followed: 'This decision is the end of any attempts at appeasement in our land; the end of urging us to get along with dictators; the end of compromise with tyranny and the forces of oppression. And the urgency is *now*.' He underlined the significance of the decision taken: 'We believe firmly that when our production output is in full swing, the democracies of the world will be able to prove that dictatorships cannot win.'[222]

VI

Lend-lease was one of the most important political decisions of the war, and had some of the most far-reaching consequences. For Churchill, it was 'a wonderful decision', bringing new hope and conviction through the knowledge that 'the United States are very closely bound up with us now'.[223] He spoke of it as a 'climacteric' – an 'intense turning-point' – in Britain's war effort.[224] It meant an 'irrevocable commitment' to the alliance of the United States with Great Britain, a 'point of no return' in American policy against Nazi Germany, a 'major step towards war'.[225] The German reaction also spoke volumes for the significance of what had happened. The Wehrmacht leadership interpreted it as 'a declaration of war'. Goebbels described it in the same way. And Hitler immediately decided to extend the combat zone in the north Atlantic as far west as the territorial waters of Greenland.[226]

For Roosevelt's critics, that was precisely what it was intended to do. When the arch-isolationist Senator Burton K. Wheeler declared that lend-lease would 'plough under every fourth American boy', Roosevelt reacted allergically. 'I regard it as the most untruthful, as the most dastardly, unpatriotic thing that has ever been said,' he retorted.[227] And when, in the spring, Charles A. Lindbergh became the darling of the isolationists in the America First anti-Roosevelt campaign, the President privately expressed his conviction that the former aviation hero was a Nazi.[228] Among ardent interventionists, within the administration and outside, lend-lease offered precisely what the isolationists were decrying: the expectation that a sense of urgency and dynamism would now drive American policy faster and closer towards the direct involvement in the war that they deemed necessary and inevitable. Over the months that followed the passing of the Lend-Lease Act, the President pleased neither of his sets of critics. For isolationists, he was going much too far. For interventionists, he was doing far too little. He was, in fact, not steering a middle way. His leanings were invariably towards those who wanted to do more, not less, to help the British in what was a dire phase of the war for them. But it was always to be 'short of war', and his political antennae invariably told him that the route of caution was the right one. The result was that over the spring months American policy seemed to recede into drift, uncertainty and hesitation.

The immediate benefits from lend-lease were not huge. Harry Hopkins was put in charge of the lend-lease programme with something approaching a plenipotentiary mandate to make it work.[229] The administration immediately requested $7 billion in appropriations. Among the first supplies, and a neat reflection of Roosevelt's determining 'fireside chat', were 900,000 feet of fire hose. But only a tiny 1 per cent of the munitions actually used by Britain and the Empire during 1941 came from lend-lease. The immediate significance for the British war effort was largely symbolic. What would result from lend-lease over the course of the war, however, was anything but confined to symbolism. More than half of British deficits were covered by lend-lease, and it would come, too, to be vital to the Soviet war machine. The list of potential recipient countries had been deliberately left open when the legislation was drafted. Aware from intelligence reports of growing signs that Hitler might invade the Soviet Union before the year was out, the administration was anxious to prevent anti-Communists in Congress from limiting the countries that might at some point receive lend-lease. It proved a crucial piece of forethought. By the time the war ended, the scheme had provided over $50 billion worldwide.

Within the United States, lend-lease was the trigger to huge increases in armaments spending. Already in 1941, defence expenditure, as a proportion of gross national product, was almost ten times higher than it had been in 1939. Borrowing, not taxation, accounted for most of the increased spending – a new and lasting trend in financing. The mass-production techniques used meant, too, that big business grew even bigger and its dominance of industrial output more swollen. In essence, the military-industrial complex of postwar America had its foundations in lend-lease.[230]

The decision taken in December and finalized through legislation in March had settled the issue of production. The American war economy was set in motion (though production and organizational blockages and shortcomings meant that it still did not function either smoothly or at full pace). How sufficient goods were going to get to Britain, given the mounting losses of merchant ships in the Atlantic, was, however, still far from resolved. Moreover, lend-lease had cast sharp light on the question which no one was yet ready to face. Could America, its neutrality now completely compromised, its non-belligerency a wholly one-sided affair, continue to remain out of a fighting war when she was so committed to one of the participants through the supply of weaponry? Stimson, as usual, had hit the nail on the head the previous December. 'We cannot permanently be in the position of toolmakers for other nations which fight,' he had concluded

– though he accepted that the country was not yet ready to contemplate intervention.[231]

In these same weeks, nevertheless, the fighting war came a step closer, even if only at the level of contingency planning. Already in November 1940, Admiral Stark had devised a global defence strategy, known as Plan D (or, in naval parlance, 'Plan Dog'). Its basic premiss was that, if and when the United States became involved in a war against Germany, Italy and Japan – and Stark believed that it would ultimately prove necessary to send large land and air forces to Europe and Africa[232] – a strong offensive in the Atlantic, allied to Britain, should take precedence over the Pacific, where a defensive posture would be adopted.[233] Though he never formally adopted Plan Dog, it implicitly lay behind the conclusion Roosevelt reached at a meeting with his top defence advisers on 17 January that upholding the supply lines to Britain was the primary objective. He ordered the navy to prepare for the escort of convoys.[234] It sounded promising. But, as so often, caution prevailed. Roosevelt was far from ready to take this step yet.

Stark had recommended to the President that he authorize secret joint staff talks with the British on possible future action in both oceans.[235] In January 1941 these talks began. Within two months top American and British military planners had worked out a basic agreement on strategy – a document named ABC-1 – if the United States should enter the war. Of course, there was still no commitment to do so. But in the event of war, the basic strategy – following Plan Dog – would be 'Germany First', with a containing attritional struggle against Japan in the Pacific until Germany had been defeated. Indeed, ABC-1 informed strategic thinking in both countries in the months that followed, and actual strategy after December 1941.[236] As Robert Sherwood, who helped Roosevelt write his speeches, later put it, a 'common-law alliance' had developed between the United States and Great Britain six months before the United States would finally enter the war. It had been 'publicly entered into through lend-lease', then 'privately consummated through the Anglo-American staff conversations in Washington'.[237]

Roosevelt had moved far during the winter. The hesitation that had accompanied the destroyer deal, when he had cautiously complied with the pressure from his advisers, had given way to boldness in December and January, when he instigated the lend-lease breakthrough. But the President was not yet prepared to accelerate. In the troubled spring of 1941, his boldness again deserted him. To the immense frustration of the more 'hawkish' elements in his Cabinet, caution once more took over.

Britain was by now facing severe difficulties, and long before the promised

American aid might start to make a difference. The advances made through lend-lease and the ABC-1 military agreement with the Americans threatened to be in vain. By May, British troops had been forced out of Greece and had lost Crete. The diversion to Greece, a vain attempt to prevent a German occupation, had weakened Britain's tenuous hold in north Africa, and, under the new and daring General Erwin Rommel, Axis forces were now threatening to break through, and would soon do so. Worst of all, shipping losses in the Atlantic had soared to almost double their level over the winter. And now the feared new German battleship, the *Bismarck*, was on the loose and set to wreak further havoc among British convoys. It was a bleak outlook. Britain seemed likely to lose the 'battle of the Atlantic'. Churchill, privately irritated and frustrated at Roosevelt's caution, remarked that 'quite unconsciously we are being left very much to our fate'.[238]

Though Roosevelt's isolationist opponents had been strongly in retreat over the Lend-Lease bill, it has been claimed that the President still seemed at times to suffer 'less a fear that Hitler might suddenly attack than that isolationists in the Senate would best him'.[239] Quite specifically, he could not bring himself to take a clear decision on the convoy question. In April he seemed at first in favour of the navy's plan to provide escorts, then against. Despite pressure from the Cabinet 'hawks' – Stimson, Knox, Ickes and Morgenthau – he continued to resist. His view, according to Morgenthau, was 'that public opinion was not yet ready for the United States to convoy ships'. He preferred to wait and was 'not ready to go ahead on "all out aid for England"'.[240] The indications are that he could have carried public opinion on this issue if he had tried.[241] He preferred not to put it to the test. For now, he agreed on 15 April only to a significant extension of the 'security zone' for navy patrols in the Atlantic, now widened to west of a line roughly halfway between Africa and Brazil, including Greenland and the Azores. In this broad tract of the Atlantic, they would report on the location of German submarines, but otherwise do nothing either to attack them (unless themselves threatened) or directly to defend convoys. Soon, this would lead to an American presence on Greenland and Iceland, astride the vital Atlantic route. Roosevelt also allowed around this time the transfer of a small number of warships – smaller than the navy had wanted – from the Pacific to the Atlantic. And plans were mooted (that came to nothing) to occupy the Azores.[242] But Roosevelt was unwilling to go farther. Escorting was still rejected. He remained adamant that in the battle to control the seas, he was not willing to fire the first shot.[243]

Throughout April and May, one of the most anxious phases of the war and among the most worrying of his presidency, Roosevelt seemed hesitant to his entourage – cautious to the point almost of immobilization.[244] When William Bullitt, former ambassador to France, saw him on 23 April, the President said 'that the problem which was troubling him most was that of public opinion. He had just had an argument with Stimson on the subject. Stimson thought that we ought to go to war now. He, the President, felt that we must await an incident and was confident that the Germans would give us an incident.'[245]

Across the Atlantic, Churchill, too, was privately depressed at the President's inactivity and procrastination. His letter to Roosevelt at the beginning of May, written in some irritation, had to be toned down by his advisers.[246] He wanted bolder action. He suggested that what would make the decisive difference in tipping the balance in the war Britain's way 'would be if the United States were immediately to range herself with us as a belligerent power'.[247] The President ignored the plea.

In Washington, in a state of despondency, Stimson, Knox and the Attorney General, Robert Jackson, met Ickes in mid-May to consider sending 'some written representation to the President that we are experiencing a failure of leadership that bodes ill for the country'. They were unanimous that 'the country was tired of words and wanted deeds'. Even the words had not been forthcoming, since Roosevelt had postponed a major speech he intended to deliver on the state of the war. He had retired to his bed, ill – though he seemed well enough to the few allowed to see him in those days. 'Missy' LeHand thought he was suffering from 'a case of sheer exasperation', torn constantly between the isolationists and the interventionists. In the event, there was little enthusiasm for the protest letter. But 'none of us could account for the President's failure of leadership and all of us felt disturbed by the fact that he is surrounded by a very small group and is, in effect, inaccessible to most people, including even members of the Cabinet'.[248]

Given the malaise which all those at the heart of defence policy felt to have descended over the administration, expectations of the President's forthcoming speech – his first since the enactment of lend-lease – were high. Morgenthau, musing on what he might say, 'felt the next move was to get us into the war'. He told Harry Hopkins that he had arrived at the conclusion during the previous ten days 'that if we were going to save England, we would have to get into this war, and that we needed England, if for no other reason, as a stepping stone to bomb Germany'.[249]

Roosevelt finally gave his big speech on the evening of 27 May – the day the news arrived of the sinking of the Bismarck. Several hands had been hard at work on the six drafts of the 'fireside chat', which the President wanted to end, dramatically, by proclaiming a state of emergency. He cabled Churchill, a few hours before his address, to inform the British Prime Minister that his text 'went further than I had thought possible even two weeks ago'.[250]

The speech was, however, not one of Roosevelt's best. For the invited audience in the unbearably hot East Room of the White House, it was a disappointing let-down, though the telegrams that afterwards poured in were overwhelmingly positive, a better response than the President claimed to have expected.[251] Much of it went over similar ground to that of his 'fireside chat' the previous December. In his strongest passage, he promised to 'give every possible assistance to Britain and to all who, with Britain, are resisting Hitlerism or its equivalent with force of arms. Our patrols', he added, 'are helping now to ensure delivery of the needed supplies to Britain. All additional measures necessary to deliver the goods will be taken.' He brought the speech to a climax by declaring: 'I have tonight issued a proclamation that an unlimited national emergency exists and requires the strengthening of our defense to the extreme limit of our national power and authority.'[252]

It sounded dramatic. Perhaps, some of those in his entourage thought, the President was finally halting the drift of previous weeks. Perhaps the urgency that had shaped the decisions at the turn of the year would now return. But what exactly did the declaration of 'unlimited national emergency' mean in practice? When reporters at a press conference next morning asked Roosevelt for details, he promptly undid the good work of the previous evening. He had no plans to request Congress to repeal the neutrality legislation, he said. Nor was he going to order naval escort of shipping. He waved away as 'iffy' a question about the difficulty in reconciling the differences between labour and management in the big armaments drive. Finally, he admitted that his proclamation of unlimited national emergency needed executive orders based upon a revival of emergency laws stretching back over fifty years to become effective. And he had no plans to issue such orders.[253]

The President's inner group were baffled and irritated. Stimson, who along with Knox had been calling in May for immediate introduction of convoy protection, was appalled. Ickes thought that 'to declare a total emergency without acts to follow it up means little', though he added in fairness that it provided at least the framework for significant action. Hopkins was unable to account for the President's 'sudden reversal from a position of strength to one of apparent insouciant weakness'. The 'unaccountability' of his character was all that occurred to Sherwood as an explanation.[254]

But more profound reasons than Roosevelt's impenetrable personality dictated his caution. One was the continuing problem the President saw in trying to mould opinion while not outpacing it. The slight majority in opinion polls in favour of escorting convoys suggested that Roosevelt might be able to push the issue through Congress if he wanted to apply the pressure. But escorting convoys would inevitably lead to armed clashes with German vessels – one step away from war. Would a bare majority in Congress offer the national unity needed in war? And was the country yet ready for war? Opinion polls in the run-up to his speech showed the usual contradictory traits. While 68 per cent thought it more important to help Britain than stay out of the war, a slightly higher percentage thought the President had gone either too far or far enough in his support for the British. And four-fifths of the population were still opposed outright to entry into the war.[255] It was more than sufficient to persuade the President to hold back from bold initiatives. As one of those who saw him at the time in the White House later put it, he felt that as head of the nation he would be more effective if he did not cross the Rubicon.[256]

Another factor was probably crucial. Roosevelt had been aware since the beginning of the year of Hitler's directive to attack the Soviet Union in the spring. At the beginning of March, Sumner Welles had been instructed to pass on the information to the Kremlin.[257] Now, the intelligence signals were pointing to an imminent invasion.[258] Most likely for that reason, Roosevelt wanted to avoid any escalation of aggression in the Atlantic when news came through on 12 June that for the first time a German U-boat had sunk an American ship, the freighter *Robin Moor*. The American reaction was mild.[259] For Roosevelt knew that an attack by Germany on the Soviet Union would put an entirely different complexion on the war in the Atlantic. Providing the Soviet Union could hold out, new prospects would open up in the west.

On 22 June 1941, the President was awakened with the news that a massive German attack on the Soviet Union had begun.

VII

Roosevelt and American policy had travelled an immense distance since the bleak months between May and September had threatened the total eclipse of democracy in Europe. By the time Hitler's forces invaded the Soviet

Union, the United States was still nowhere near ready for war – not ready militarily, psychologically or politically. But the decisions taken by Roosevelt, in particular over the destroyer deal, then especially over lend-lease, had been of the utmost importance to cementing transatlantic bonds, which within months would turn into a fully fledged military alliance against Hitler and would in time prove instrumental in his destruction. From now on, as the German dictator was only too well aware, time and resources were not on his side. He had to risk more to gain more. But the odds were – though the fortunes of war did not show it at the time – beginning to stack up against him. For Britain, it was the reverse. Militarily, she was still weak, and facing reverses in the Balkans, north Africa and, not least, the Atlantic. But for the first time there was more than a glimmer of hope on the horizon. Provided the Atlantic sea routes could be protected, the American 'arsenal of democracy' would soon be at her disposal. And the prospects of the United States actually joining the fighting war had increased sharply. Little wonder that Churchill ended his world broadcast on 27 April 1941 with a rhetorical flourish by citing a nineteenth-century poem to illustrate the new hope: 'In front the sun climbs slow, how slowly! But westward, look, the land is bright.'[260]

With the destroyer deal, lend-lease and the subsequent cautious steps, the President had been faced with difficult choices. He was not short of advice on all sides: go faster; go slower; don't go at all. He had wavered, he had hesitated, he had been pressed by his advisers and by the opinion polls. But, though he had felt his way forward tentatively, his boldness over lend-lease stands out and was vital. Without that decision, even though the immediate flow of aid from it was still small-scale compared with what was later to come, Britain's position would have rapidly and immeasurably deteriorated. As dollar reserves dwindled and losses in the Atlantic mounted, the plight would soon have begun to approach desperation. That Britain would have been forced, as some proponents of lend-lease had claimed at the time, to look for a negotiated peace with Hitler within six months is unlikely. The British government were as aware as the Roosevelt administration of German plans to fall upon the Soviet Union and of the great build-up of armed forces on the eastern front. The German–Soviet war, provided it lasted, would have brought relief for beleaguered Great Britain even in the absence of lend-lease. But how long, without lend-lease, Britain's resources would have held out, even under the new conditions of war raging in the east, is still a moot point.

More important than this unanswerable question is that lend-lease began a commitment with consequences. Though the path to war for the United

States was anything but decided, Roosevelt's advisers had correctly judged that, following lend-lease, it would ultimately become impossible to stay out of the conflict. Ensuring that the goods produced would not simply find their way to the bottom of the Atlantic implied that convoys would have to be escorted across the ocean. That would unquestionably lead to 'incidents' – sinkings and shootings. As Roosevelt himself had pointed out, that sounded like war, and was certainly not far from it.[261] This made him reluctant to order escorting, and he would only come to that point in the autumn. Some in his 'war cabinet', his inner circle on defence matters, were under no illusions about the need not simply to engage in defensive protection of convoys, but actively to participate in the battle of the Atlantic. Nor would it stop there. There were those who had thought that, should America have to become involved eventually, it would be at sea and in the air, but without the need to send ground troops, as in the First World War. But Roosevelt's military advisers did not deceive themselves. They were increasingly certain that the war would only be won through the dispatch of American troops to fight in Europe.

We have followed the reasons why the President acted as he did. Could and should he have acted differently?[262] Had he followed the path the isolationists wanted him to tread, the chances that Britain would have been forced to a negotiated peace, leaving her and the Empire greatly weakened, would have been hugely magnified. But such a path was never at any juncture likely. Nor was it feasible. Since Munich at the latest, the administration, and not just its more 'hawkish' elements, had taken the view that Hitler posed a direct threat to the United States, and to the whole of the western hemisphere. The looming threat across the Pacific, from Japan, added markedly to the urgency of building up defence capacity. Once the war in Europe had begun, and especially once Hitler's troops had overrun Scandinavia, the Low Countries and France, the American people rapidly began to grasp the enormity of the threat facing them. Few were ready to join in the war. But support for help to Britain (and, until her defeat, France) was strong. The purely isolationist line was supported by no more than around a third of the population, and fading. Apart from opinion polls, the overwhelmingly positive reaction to Roosevelt's 'fireside chats' in December 1940 and then in May 1941 indicates that there was widespread backing for a policy of maximum aid to Britain short of war, in America's own interest. Any attempt, in this climate of opinion (admittedly influenced by the administration, not simply responded to), to press ahead with an isolationist policy would have been folly and doomed to failure.

Could intervention, as Stimson, Knox, Stark, Morgenthau and others were urging by May 1941, have been a wiser option than the course Roosevelt steered? With an army smaller than that of Holland and no warplanes or ships available, intervention in the spring and summer of 1940 could have been only of symbolic value. The navy was less weak than the army. But it was needed in the Pacific, to deter the Japanese, as well as in the Atlantic, and this was stretching resources. Removal of the fleet, or most of it, to the Atlantic would have sent a clear signal to Tokyo. Earlier expansion in south-east Asia than actually occurred would have been likely, with serious consequences for British defence in the region. Meanwhile, American as well as British shipping would have been prey to U-boat attacks in the Atlantic. It would have done little to help the supply of material resources to Britain. And none of this would have made any difference to the situation in Europe. Nothing the United States could have done would have hindered in the slightest Hitler's conquest of western Europe.

By spring 1941 the situation had changed. American military strength was growing rapidly as the armaments drive gathered pace. The active help of American naval forces would have significantly reduced British losses in the Atlantic (though the chance capture of a German Enigma coding machine in May and the rapid breaking of U-boat ciphers itself produced a sharp drop in lost shipping over the next six months).[263] A naval war with America in the Atlantic was something that at this juncture Hitler was keen to avoid. American belligerency would have sharply increased the apprehension in Berlin about the opening of a second front in the east. But the prospect of Hitler being sucked into what, with luck, would turn into a prolonged, bloody conflict in the east was precisely what the Americans – and the British – hoped would happen. In any case, nothing suggests that Hitler would have been deterred from his intention to destroy the Soviet Union in a swift and devastating surprise attack. In fact, since he reckoned with having two or three years before having to confront the full economic and military might of the United States, he would probably only have felt confirmed in his diagnosis that a quick knockout blow to the Soviet Union, forcing Britain to the negotiating table, was correct.

Intervention, then, would have been of little practical gain in the months between the defeat of France and the opening of 'Operation Barbarossa' in altering the course or ferocity of German aggression. What might its consequences have been within the United States? Any attempt to take the country into war would have met with extensive and heated opposition. As opinion polls demonstrated, four-fifths of the population rejected intervention, even in May 1941. So had Roosevelt driven America into war, the result would have been intense disunity and disharmony, the opposite of what took place after December 1941.

However, the question is otiose. At no point did Roosevelt consider taking America into war. Had he attempted it, he would have been reminded swiftly and in the most forceful terms (and not just by isolationists) of his explicit commitment in his Boston speech of October 1940, during his re-election campaign, that he would send no American troops to fight in a foreign war. In any case, quite apart from the state of opinion in the country, he knew full well that he had not the slightest chance of persuading Congress to issue a declaration of war.

The interventionists at home, even among Roosevelt's closest advisers, and of course many in Britain, were impatient and critical of the American reluctance to enter the war. But the President's caution, however maddening, was wise. He was successful, above all, in carrying the country with him in his careful steps across the tightrope. When war eventually came – the result of aggression by hostile forces, not any direct action of the President – that would prove vital.

6

Moscow, Spring–Summer 1941

Stalin Decides He Knows Best

*You must understand that Germany will never on its own move
to attack Russia ... If you provoke the Germans on the border,
if you move forces without our permission, then bear in mind that
heads will roll.*

Reported comment of Stalin to his military leaders,
mid-May 1941

'Lenin left us a great legacy, but we, his heirs, have f——d it up.'[1] Stalin
uttered his angry expletive in a bleak moment as he and the small group of
his closest associates were leaving a fraught visit to the Defence Commissariat, six days after the German invasion on 22 June had caught the Soviet
Union astonishingly unawares. It was as close as Stalin came to accepting
responsibility for a calamitous error of judgement that saw the German
army advancing at breakneck speed over 300 miles into Soviet territory
within days, capturing or killing huge numbers of Soviet soldiers, and
destroying thousands of tanks and aircraft in the first wave of attack.
Whether Stalin's chief henchmen accompanying him that day – Vyacheslav
Molotov (the dour, unbending Commissar for Foreign Affairs, who ped-
antically corrected comrades referring to him as 'Stone-Arse' by saying that
Lenin had actually dubbed him 'Iron-Arse'[2]), Georgi Malenkov (manager
of the Communist Party's labyrinthine bureaucracy), Lavrenti Beria (the
ruthless head of State Security) and Anastas Mikoyan (the foreign trade
expert)[3] – were happy to be included in the collective blame for the disaster
that Stalin's earthy outburst implied is unclear. Molotov, doggedly loyal,
was certainly ready to accept collective responsibility, as he continued to
do long after the dictator's death.[4] If the others took a different stance, they
were wise to keep quiet and not point out what all of them knew only too
well: that the crucial decisions that had brought catastrophe to his country
had been taken by Stalin and no one else.

Though so many, and from different sides, were warning him in unmistakable terms of the imminence of German attack, even naming the date of the invasion, Stalin had insisted that he knew best. Only five days before the attack a Soviet agent's report was passed to Stalin by the Commissar for State Security, Vsevolod Merkulov. It warned that military action was imminent. Stalin's response was: 'Comrade Merkulov. You can tell your "source" from Ger[man] air force headquarters to go f—— his mother. This is not a "source" – it's someone spreading *disinformation*. J.St.'[5] It was a characteristically abrasive expression of Stalin's certainty that his own intuition and judgement were right, whatever anyone was telling him. His shock and astonishment on the early morning of 22 June were, then, all the greater, given his earlier self-assurance. But his spontaneous and unique admission six days later of grievous mistakes (if attributed collectively and couched in a crude vernacular) amounted to a tacit acceptance that other policy options had been available that could have avoided the disaster – choices that were not taken.

In retrospect, Stalin's decision that he knew best – a decision for inaction – in the face of all the warnings of impending grave danger for his country seems one of the least comprehensible of the entire war. That this of all men, the most paranoidly suspicious of individuals, should have allowed himself to be deluded about Hitler's intentions appears particularly hard to understand. History would surely have taken a different course had Stalin made other choices. But what might those choices have been? On closer inspection, perhaps those choices were less obvious and more curtailed than they seem in hindsight. The story of Stalin's fateful choice is more complicated than an easy attribution to his arbitrary whim, scarcely credible blindness or stubborn stupidity would permit. This is the story that we now need to unravel. A starting point is how the Soviet Union was ruled, and how decisions were taken in the Stalinist system.

I

By the time Hitler's invasion of Poland on 1 September 1939 unleashed what would turn into the Second World War, Joseph Stalin, soon to celebrate his sixtieth birthday,[6] had been dictator of the Soviet Union for some ten years. In contrast to the precise dating of Hitler's dictatorship to his accession to power in the dramatic events of late January 1933, Stalin's autocracy is not attributable to a specific moment or event. It had emerged gradually, though relentlessly, from his membership of a group of leading

Bolsheviks subordinate to Lenin to the point where his personal hold on power was unchallengeable, unconstrained and utterly decisive in the way the Soviet Union was ruled.

Unlike Hitler's dictatorship in Germany, which rested on the premiss of obedience to the will of an untouchable and infallible 'great Leader', Stalin's essentially ran counter to the theory of collective government on which Soviet rule had been founded. Lenin, though his primacy had been uncontested, had nonetheless operated a form of collective leadership. Heated disputes over policy within the party leadership were not uncommon, and were accepted by Lenin, in the first years after the Bolshevik Revolution. After Lenin's death in 1924, Stalin's own supremacy had arisen out of a bitter internal power-struggle, in which his own mastery of the party's secretariat and administrative apparatus had proved crucial. For some years, during the first Five-Year Plan to force the pace of collectivization of agriculture and industrial development, introduced in late 1928 and formally adopted in spring the following year, his own position remained one of first among equals in the Soviet leadership. And collective leadership was still upheld as the proper way to govern. Three leading members of the Politburo strongly criticized Stalin in early 1929 for appropriating powers to make decisions that by Bolshevik tradition should have been made collectively by the Central Committee of the party. 'We are against the replacement of control by a collective with control by a person,' they declared.[7] They were too late. Stalin already controlled decisions, and how they were made. And he did not forget those who opposed him.

Five years later, the assassination of Sergei Kirov, the popular Leningrad party boss, was a further, vital, staging post on the way to absolute power. That Stalin was behind the murder has never been proved. Probably, it seems, he was not involved.[8] But he was certainly the main beneficiary from the elimination of a leading figure in the party seen by some as a potential rival. The Kirov murder appears to have fuelled still further Stalin's already pronounced paranoid distrust of all around him and morbid fear of attempts to remove him. The assassination marked the beginning of what would eventually develop into an all-out assault on those suspected of being his opponents. Perhaps it worked. For, remarkably, in contrast to a number of known attempts on Hitler's life, Stalin was never the victim of an assassination plot. Soon, the extraordinary waves of terror unleashed against Soviet citizens would come to know no bounds. Stalin's usually groundless but uncontrollable suspicions prompted massive and brutal purges that ravaged the ranks of party functionaries, not halting at some of the foremost Bolshevik leaders and former close comrades of Lenin, and decimating, with lasting and fateful consequences, the leadership of the Red Army. Stalin's own power was enormously strengthened in the process.

The purges – 'the Great Terror' as they have appropriately come to be known – were unleashed from the top. During 1937–8 Stalin personally approved 383 lists, containing the names of 44,000 victims from the party, government, military, intelligence services and other agencies of the regime.[9] This figure was only a fraction of those who were to suffer in the astounding onslaught on his own people. Prominent and long-standing Bolsheviks from the top echelons of the party were among the first victims as Stalin sought to wipe the slate clean of those whose experiences of the 'glory days' under Lenin might have stood in the way of his own claim to be his sole and legitimate heir.[10] Stalin was reported as saying that it was time 'to finish with our enemies because they are in the army, in the staff, even in the Kremlin'.[11] But the purges were also meant to produce a complete renewal of the party's cadres at all levels and throughout the Soviet Union. There was no shortage of willing helpers, as rank-and-file party members, whether from careerist opportunism or ideological conviction or both, rushed to denounce old comrades, and even friends and family, handing them over to the tender mercies of the secret police, the NKVD (People's Commissariat for Internal Affairs).

This body was a vital prop in Stalin's control of the Soviet regime, and was given special status. Its head was personally responsible to Stalin alone, and its functionaries were very well paid and encouraged in their loyalty by numerous material inducements, as well as threatened themselves with draconian punishment when the corruption and criminality endemic in the organization came to light.[12] In July 1937 the NKVD laid before the Politburo its action plan, backed by a huge budget, for the purges. It presented target figures of 75,000 people to be shot and 225,000 to be sent to camps. The plan, approved by the Politburo, turned out to provide only the minimum framework of intended victims. Once unleashed, the purges took on their own momentum as grass-roots activists in the party relished the open licence to wipe out all supposed 'enemies' they could lay their hands on and NKVD agents rushed to fill their 'quotas'. Close to 700,000 people were shot in 1937–8, and more than a million and a half arrested.[13]

The party cadres were soon able to replenish themselves, and now with out-and-out Stalin loyalists. But for the Red Army, the catastrophe was more lastingly damaging. The purges of the army were driven by the same underlying aim of rooting out all real or imaginary opponents and turning the military, too, into an unquestioning, ultra-loyal vehicle of the political leadership. But whereas new party functionaries could easily be trained, lost military leadership skills and technical abilities could not be replaced overnight. And the losses in such areas were massive. In all, 34,301 officers were arrested or expelled from the armed forces in 1937–8. Some 30 per cent were reinstated by the beginning of 1940. But 22,705 were either shot or their fate remains unknown.[14] Higher ranks suffered disproportionately in the 'decapitation' of the Red Army.[15] Of the 101 members of the supreme military leadership, 91 were arrested, and of these 80 shot. Among them were three out of five of the Marshals of the Soviet Union (the highest military rank), three out of the four army commanders, all heads of military districts, nearly all divisional commanders, all commanders of the air force and two admirals of the fleet.[16] Most were victims of absurd, trumped-up charges of anti-Soviet activity.

The most prominent victim, and the most classic demonstration of the bizarrely self-destructive nature of the military purges, was Marshal Mikhail Tukhachevsky, the most brilliant military strategist in the Soviet Union and the chief advocate and planner of a modernized, well-trained, enlarged, technologically developed military organization. Stalin's elephantine memory doubtless recalled that, as Political Commissar to the southwestern front in 1920 after the Polish capture of Kiev, he had failed to supply cavalry troops demanded by Tukhachevsky, with disastrous consequences.[17] The outspoken Tukhachevsky clashed further with Stalin during the 1930s about the level of political controls on a professionalized military machine. And his relationship with the incompetent Defence Commissar, Marshal Kliment Voroshilov, a Stalin devotee and close associate, was fraught – more than ever during his brief time as Deputy Commissar of Defence in 1936–7.[18] In May 1937 Tukhachevsky was arrested, tortured into a confession of involvement in a conspiracy to overthrow the Soviet state and executed. Stalin dubbed him a spy, who 'gave our operational plan . . . – our holy of holies – to the German Reichswehr'. His wife, daughter and other members of his family were killed on Stalin's orders, or sent to camps.[19]

Recovery from such a consciously directed bloodletting of the leadership of the armed forces could not be speedy. Stalin was overheard asking Voroshilov, in charge of defence, in autumn 1938 – as Europe was anticipating another war in the near future – whether there were any officers left capable of commanding a division.[20] A plan for the reorganization of the armed forces drawn up the previous autumn calculated that they would not be ready for war before the end of 1942.[21] The inadequacy of the army was indeed to be revealed in the humiliating campaign of the 'Winter War' with Finland in 1939–40. By the summer of 1941, as 'Barbarossa' was launched, 75 per cent of field officers and 70 per cent of political commissars had held their posts for less than a year.[22] The lack of experience in vital areas of military command was a direct consequence of the purges.

Countless numbers of Soviet citizens, inside and outside the party, supported the purges (and became complicit in them), believing they were a legitimate witchhunt to eradicate the 'enemy within'. Far from undermining Stalin's support, they enhanced it, though mainly out of awe and fear of their Leader rather than from warm adulation.[23] For if mass acclamation was a key prop of Hitler's power in Germany, terror that potentially posed a threat to each individual, however elevated the status, and the universal fear that ran in its wake, was the basis of Stalin's. It now provided the platform for the full unfolding of the Stalinist dictatorship – not the fabled 'dictatorship of the proletariat', but the dictatorship of one man.

Remembering the contested route to his later supremacy, and conscious of the theories of collective leadership which his personal rule was negating, Stalin in fact continued in the 1930s to deny that he was a dictator, put his name to decrees alongside co-signatories (and not in first place) and insisted that 'decisions are made by the party and acted upon by its chosen organs, the Central Committee and the Politburo'.[24] But by the time the Second World War began, this had long been the most blatant of fictions.

The Central Committee, the party's sovereign body, had for years been no more than a sham. Its membership had swollen since Lenin's day (when it had comprised forty-six voting and non-voting members), and the frequency of its meetings had declined. It had become, in fact, a vehicle entirely controlled by Stalin and serving merely to implement his will and legitimate his power. In the fevered atmosphere of 1937, the purge year, members were even prepared to denounce each other in full session of the Central Committee in order to curry favour with Stalin.[25]

The Politburo, technically a subcommittee of the Central Committee, and in theory the decision-making body of the party, had some fifteen members and in the 1920s had met weekly. This, though retaining a constant size, was meeting less frequently by the later 1930s. There were 153 meetings between 1930 and 1934, only 69 between 1934 and 1939, and a halving of the latter figure in the following three years.[26] Some of its business was by then hived off to commissions or subcommittees.[27] And even before the purges of 1937, Stalin was systematically diluting the power of significant figures in the Politburo, dispersing some of them to posts outside Moscow, and concentrating control still further in his own hands. The Politburo fragmented and atrophied in function. Stalin increasingly operated with small groups drawn ad hoc and at his whim from within the membership of the Politburo. Formal sessions of the Politburo declined sharply in the later 1930s. Only six took place in 1938, two in 1939 and two in 1940.[28] By this time, informal meetings with varying personnel were often taking place at Stalin's dacha over dinner and copious amounts of vodka. By the beginning of the war, 'operational matters' – meaning all crucial issues that Stalin wished to discuss with his closest associates – and in particular the concerns, by now greatly magnified, of foreign policy, were dealt with by a quintet – the 'Big Five' – of Stalin, Molotov, Malenkov, Beria and Mikoyan.[29] But within the 'Big Five', there was no doubt in anyone's mind whose opinion really counted.

Far more than had been the case under Lenin during the early years following the Revolution, the state government was dominated in the immediate prewar years by the party's increasingly elaborate organizational apparatus. Lenin's most important power-base had derived from his position as chairman of the Council of People's Commissars – effectively Prime Minister of the state government. Stalin, though from 1929 at the latest the pre-eminent Soviet leader, took this position only in 1941 (after which, in wartime conditions, the role of the state greatly expanded). Until then, from 1930 onwards, Molotov had been Prime Minister. That he was, and saw himself as, wholly subordinate to Stalin indicated where power really resided. Intertwined though they were at all levels, the party apparatus controlled the state. And Stalin, holding all threads of the highly centralized organization in his own hands, controlled the party.

As Stalin's power expanded, and as the position of his subordinates, even their survival, depended on his grace and favour, obsequiousness and fawning even at the highest level of the regime reflected the growth of a strong personality cult that would have its apogee during the wartime and postwar years. By the beginning of the war, the process of constructing the image of Stalin as superman was already well under way. The bloated army of bureaucrats and apparatchiks – the 'little Stalins' and party drones in the provinces – could be guaranteed, encouraged by fear of the consequences of denunciation if they did not do so, to implement what they took to be the wishes of 'our Leader, Teacher and Friend, Comrade Stalin'.[30] It was no different at the top of the regime. Fear and dependence brought compliance and subservience. Stalin, shrewd and calculating, invariably testing the weakness and resilience of those around him as he did external enemies, was adept at playing individuals off against each other and exploiting vulnerable points of their personality or political misjudgements. The mass purges of 1937 ensured that Stalin would not be threatened, that his despotism would not be challenged, whatever his own paranoia told him.

The purges also greatly weakened the position of the army's General Staff in its dealings with the political leadership, most especially with Stalin himself. Beyond that, a huge purge of the staff of the Foreign Ministry when Molotov replaced Maxim Litvinov at the head of the Foreign Commissariat at the beginning of May 1939[31] meant not only a loss of experience, but that in this crucial conduit of policy formation, and at such a vital time, subservience dominated over professional judgement. But fear and servility, the reverse of the coin to the cult of the Leader's infallibility, were scarcely recipes for good governance. Stalin – cautious, distrustful and cold-bloodedly ruthless – was increasingly told what his sycophantic and anxious subordinates thought he wanted to hear. This would play its part in the disaster of June 1941.

In the vital months prior to the launch of 'Barbarossa', therefore, decisions on all matters of importance within the Soviet Union were taken by Stalin personally. There was discussion, sometimes lengthy and usually informal, with fluctuating groups from within the 'inner circle'. But those who met Stalin on a regular basis saw each other as rivals, and were, consequently, divided among themselves. They were also acutely aware that their tenure was insecure. Their dependence on Stalin was total. So, therefore, was their loyalty to him. This did not make for an open exchange of views. Even Stalin's most long-standing and trusted associates, insofar as the dictator trusted anyone, were extremely cautious at expressing views which he might take to be critical. He himself often held back during meetings from voicing his opinion until others had spoken. This only enhanced the wariness of those asked to commit themselves. The reinforcement of Stalin's own views was, therefore, almost guaranteed. This would prove a major weakness, rather than a strength, as invasion loomed.

During most of the 1930s the leadership of the Soviet Union had largely been preoccupied with the Stalinist revolution and its internal consequences. Foreign affairs, however, never sank far below the surface, particularly once Hitler had become Chancellor of the German Reich in January 1933. They exerted a continuing, if indirect, influence on domestic reconstruction. Preparing a socialist society for a war which Stalin and all his associates assumed to be coming in the foreseeable future was an underlying tenet of policy. And by 1938, just as Stalin was in the process of annihilating the leadership of his own army, that war suddenly began to appear very close. The Soviet Union, as Stalin more than anyone knew, was quite unready for it, the depleted armed forces especially unprepared. But foreign affairs now became a priority.

II

That the Soviet Union should have been caught so unawares by the German assault in June 1941 is not only staggering when we take Stalin's intensely distrustful personality into account. It is also hard to explain in the light of the twin concerns – conventional, despite their ideological colouring – that had driven Soviet foreign policy since the 1920s: national self-interest and national security. Whatever cynical tactical manoeuvring or opportunistic twisting and turning had taken place found justification in those terms. That protection of Soviet security failed so catastrophically in 1941 seems, therefore, astonishing.

The initial notion of 'exporting' the Bolshevik revolution to bring about the imminent overthrow of world capitalism had been abandoned following the end of the Russian Civil War in 1921. Thereafter the revolutionary foreign policy advocated by Leon Trotsky (whose influence now began to decline) came to be replaced by more conventional diplomacy. Two central tenets shaped the approach to Soviet foreign relations by the mid-1920s. The first was that war was inevitable as the imperialist powers competed to control the world's material resources. War would be waged between rival imperialist countries (as in the First World War), and would benefit the Soviet Union and the cause of socialist revolution. But the Soviet Union would also find itself the target of imperialist ambitions, and directly threatened by war. So – the second tenet – socialism had to be constructed in the foreseeable future not through world revolution but within the Soviet Union itself (as the state became officially designated in 1924), which would thereby over time become strong and impregnable in the face of a great and mounting threat from hostile and rapacious imperialist forces.

Of course, the idea of Communist revolution spreading to other countries was not given up. The work of the Comintern – the Third Communist International, established in 1919 – was to exploit the crises seen as intrinsic to the capitalist system, and to prepare the ground for eventual revolution. But this would be an organic process over an indeterminate period of time (though it is true that as early as 1925 Stalin envisaged major and prolonged war in Europe at some juncture as an engine of general revolutionary change).[32] Meanwhile, Comintern operations in other countries were always subordinated to the paramount aim of protecting the interests of the Soviet Union, the one country where socialist revolution had already created a new framework for society. And for the foreseeable future, it was obvious that the Soviet Union would remain militarily and economically weak, compared with the great imperialist powers. Recognition of this demanded policies of rapid and forced strengthening of Soviet economic and military resources while at the same time operating pragmatically in international relations. It was assumed that the Soviet Union and capitalist countries, whatever their fundamental ideological differences, would for a lengthy period of time have to cooperate on a basis of 'peaceful coexistence'. This would allow for the development and maximization of good trading and economic relations with capitalist countries even where conditions of mutual political antipathy prevailed.

The corollary, in external affairs, was that the Soviet Union sought to break down the international isolation that had followed the Bolshevik Revolution of 1917. In this, the Soviet state was highly successful. Diplomatic relations were established with thirteen countries during 1924–5 alone. With many other countries, including Russia's neighbours, a modus vivendi was found. By the end of the 1920s only the United States, among major powers, still refused recognition of the Soviet Union. Nowhere was there a sign of capitalist states forming an aggressive alliance against the Soviet Union. In the meantime, numerous commercial agreements had been reached with major European countries.[33]

A special place in Soviet foreign relations in the postwar world fell to Germany. This was established by the Treaty of Rapallo in 1922, which repaired the breakdown that had followed the Revolution and created the basis of flourishing economic and, beneath the surface, military cooperation that lasted until Hitler's arrival in power eleven years later. The Bolshevik state emerging from a ferocious and barbaric civil war and the new German liberal democracy struggling through severe initial crisis were hardly natural bedfellows. But circumstances threw them together and underpinned a treaty of mutual self-interest. Russia wanted to emerge from her international isolation, Germany to show the victorious western powers, France and Great Britain, which were pressing hard on reparations, that she had the option of a new ally in the east. From the Soviet side, it was a hedge against western powers intervening militarily again in Russia as they had done in the Civil War, however unlikely this had become in practice. From the German perspective, it headed off any possible renewal of the alliance that they had fought against during the First World War, though such a revival was now even more improbable.[34] Politically, Rapallo was of more symbolic than real importance. In economic and military terms, the treaty had greater significance. Both countries saw the advantages of closer trading arrangements. By the end of the 1920s, Germany had developed into the Soviet Union's most important commercial partner.[35]

And in the military arena, secret agreements following Rapallo offered both countries a way round the restrictions of the postwar order arising from Soviet isolation on the one hand and severe constraints imposed upon Germany by the Versailles Treaty on the other. Some parts of the agreements – a Junkers contract to build an aircraft factory in the Soviet Union, and an agreement for joint production of poison gas – never came to fruition. But cooperation of personnel on military exercises, experiments with chemical warfare and exchange of intelligence took place.[36]

By the end of the 1920s the political aspect of the Rapallo Treaty had lost its edge. Though Germany had signed a treaty of neutrality with the Soviet Union in Berlin in April 1926, her signing of the Treaty of Locarno five months earlier had signalled the improvement in relations with the western democracies, France and Great Britain. The end of Germany's international isolation, further and clearly marked by her entry into the League of Nations in 1926, had drained the significance that had been attached to the links with the Soviet Union, established four years earlier. But military cooperation continued. Economically, as the Soviet Union entered its big push for collectivization and Germany the terminal crisis of democracy that would let Hitler into power, the commercial links between the two countries even intensified. By 1932 almost half of Soviet imports came from Germany.[37]

By then, however, the storm winds were starting to gather force. On both sides of the Soviet Union new threats were emerging. In the Far East, following the 'Manchurian Incident' in 1931, the shrill tones of militaristic nationalism could increasingly be heard from the old enemy, Japan. In Germany, meanwhile, Hitler, the most extreme voice of militant anti-Bolshevism, was on the verge of power.

The Nazi takeover in Germany completely altered the framework of Soviet foreign relations. Fear of war now became a prevailing theme. By the end of 1933, the anti-Soviet thrust of the new regime was reflected in diplomatic coolness, directly promoted by Hitler. Rapallo was dead. Germany's non-aggression treaty with Poland, signed in January 1934, was the most overt demonstration of a significant shift in German foreign policy and a new course towards the Soviet Union. Many in Germany, from Conservatives to Communists, had dismissed Hitler as nothing more than a loudmouth who would either quickly pass from the scene or moderate his rantings. Official Comintern dogma continued to preach that the German leader represented the last, desperate fling of failing capitalism. But the Soviet leadership viewed the threat of Hitler with deadly seriousness. Already in March 1933, *Izvestiya*, the central government organ, commented that 'the National Socialists [had] developed a foreign policy programme against the existence of the USSR'.[38] A month later, Sergei Alexandrovsky, a political counsellor in the Berlin embassy, reported that Hitler's future foreign policy meant 'military adventurism and, ultimately, war and intervention against the USSR'.[39] Soviet leaders were aware of what Hitler had written in *Mein Kampf* in the mid-1920s and were far from ready to dismiss his outpourings as merely the radical rhetoric of a political hothead. At the 17th Party Congress of the Communist Party of the Soviet Union on 31 January 1934, Nikolai Bukharin, later to be one of Stalin's purge victims, spoke of the possibility of a 'counterrevolutionary invasion' of his country either from 'fascist Germany' or from Imperial Japan. He went on to cite extensively from the passages in *Mein Kampf* in which Hitler spoke of Germany's mission to acquire land in the east by force, at the cost of the Soviet Union. Bukharin concluded: 'Hitler therefore calls quite frankly for the destruction of our state. He says openly that the German people must reach for the sword to expropriate the properties of the Soviet Union that it allegedly needs.' Bukharin saw in this the enemy which 'will oppose us in all the mighty battles that History inflicts on us'.[40]

A realignment of Soviet foreign policy was obviously necessary. The Commissar for Foreign Affairs, Maxim Litvinov (who would be replaced by Molotov in 1939), was the chief proponent of the need to work with the western democracies, France and Great Britain, to construct a system of collective security in Europe. In 1934 the Soviet Union – by now also recognized, since November of the previous year, by the United States of America – joined the League of Nations and became the most prominent advocate of an 'international peace front' to combat the threat of aggression posed by Germany, Italy and Japan.[41] In May 1935 the Soviet Union signed a treaty of mutual assistance with France and followed it up with a similar treaty with Czechoslovakia (though coming into operation only if France, which already had a mutual defence alliance with the Czechs, acted first). The Soviet Union was the strongest supporter of sanctions against Mussolini later that year, in 1936 supplied arms to Republican forces in Spain at the outbreak of the civil war there, and in 1937, when Japan invaded China, provided aid for Chiang Kai-shek's nationalists.

In Soviet thinking, a new imperialist war could only be postponed, not prevented, by collective security. A major conflagration would obviously involve the Soviet Union, directly or indirectly. In fact, another war, it was thought, would be a world war, most likely involving an attack on the Soviet Union by a coalition of imperialist countries, threatening her from west and east.[42] And never far from the surface was the suspicion that there were forces in the west anxious to appease Hitler by deflecting his attention to the Soviet Union, or even considering joining forces with Nazi Germany in an anti-Bolshevik crusade. Support for collective security aimed, therefore, at buying precious time. But the more the League of Nations and hopes of collective security fell apart amid the western powers' endeavours to come to an arrangement with Hitler, the more the suspicions grew. The Soviet Union's international isolation, never surmounted, was highlighted more plainly than ever as the west caved in to Hitler's expansionism in 1938. 'The League of Nations and collective security are dead,' Litvinov himself acknowledged in October that year. 'International relations are entering an era of the most violent upsurge of savagery and brute force and policy of the mailed fist.'[43]

With the weakness of the western democracies laid bare, Soviet fears of becoming dragged into an inevitable conflict – and of being unprepared for it – were hugely magnified. As the Sudeten crisis unfolded across the summer of 1938, the Soviet Union partially mobilized and proclaimed its readiness to fight to defend Czechoslovakia against aggression.[44] The offer of assistance could be made in the near certainty that it would not have to be put into practice. Military involvement necessitated passage of troops through Poland (which would not permit it) and Romania (where limited permission was only belatedly given, and with severe restrictions). In any case, and far from the least consideration, the Red Army, its leadership drastically weakened by the purges of the previous year, was in 1938, as we have already noted, nowhere near ready for engagement in a major conflict. Its own planning foresaw full readiness for war as attainable only by the turn of the year 1942–3.[45] Moreover, as Stalin knew only too well, Soviet armed intervention in Czechoslovakia was in any case only possible if the French moved first to fulfil their treaty obligations. And over the summer, with the French tied to the British and Chamberlain showing every endeavour to reach agreement with Hitler, it was never likely – quite apart from continuing western distaste for the Soviet Union – that Red Army troops would be called upon. As it was, the readiness of Britain and France to yield to Hitler's bullying and collude in the carve-up of Czechoslovakia in the Munich Conference of 29–30 September 1938 had obvious meaning in Soviet eyes: war was coming, and the Soviet Union could reckon on no help from the west.

The underlying thinking, on the Soviet side, behind the notorious Hitler–Stalin Pact that so astonished the world in August 1939 rested on such considerations. In his speech to the 18th Party Congress on 10 March 1939,

Stalin had outlined the growing danger from 'the new imperialist war' as the system of collective security had collapsed in the wake of British and French refusal to take a common and direct stand against Hitler. He ended by declaring that the Soviet Union would not 'be drawn into conflict by warmongers who are accustomed to have others pull their chestnuts out of the fire for them'.[46] As Stalin's remarks indicated, loss of hope in the readiness of the western democracies to combat Hitler went hand in hand with deepened distrust of their motives. That the west would favour a German–Soviet war, and might even lend support to Germany's fight, was a constant component of thinking in the Kremlin.

Five days after Stalin's speech, Hitler occupied what was left of the Czech lands. This finally triggered the British and French to act. The guarantee for Poland resulted, followed by similar guarantees to Greece and Romania. But the Soviet Union refused Anglo-French proposals for a pact that offered the prospect of assistance to the USSR only *after* she had herself provided armed support on being dragged into a war against Germany launched solely on the initiative of Britain and France.[47] Instead, the Soviet Union proposed a full-scale military alliance – a triple pact between the USSR, France and Great Britain to provide mutual security against German aggression towards any one of them.[48] But Britain and France were unenthusiastic. Anti-Soviet feeling, and underestimation of Soviet military potential, still prevailed.[49] On the other side, the dilatory western response could be seen as confirmation of the 'unswerving line of policy – of setting Germany on to the USSR'.[50] So nothing materialized in the last hope of containing Hitler short of all-out war. Foot-dragging by the western democracies continued to the point at which the sensational Hitler–Stalin Pact on 23 August 1939 abruptly turned international diplomacy on its head.

Behind the scenes, the pact had, in fact, been brewing for some months.[51] Economic contacts provided the opening. German-Soviet economic relations had, in fact, continued – though trade declined – after Hitler had come to power, despite the severe worsening of the diplomatic climate and the shrill anti-Soviet rhetoric of Nazi leaders. The Soviet Union had made overtures in 1935–6 to improve economic links with Germany, and to use these as a vehicle to promote some degree of political détente. But nothing came of them. Soviet attempts to obtain armaments through new credit arrangements were predictably rebuffed. And hopes that Hitler's vehement anti-Soviet policy might be diluted by those in the regime's elite presumed to be less hostile were soon dashed.[52] By early 1937 relations between the Soviet Union and Germany had ebbed to a low point. That is how they remained until spring 1939, when economic contacts were once again the starting point for an attempt to produce a new basis for political relations, and this time with startling results.

For this time not just the Soviets but the Germans, especially, were interested in a rapprochement. And from tentative beginnings, Germany's interest became all the more urgent as the summer progressed and the likelihood grew that plans to attack Poland might result in war with the western democracies. A deal with the Soviet Union would at one and the same time head off any possibility of the mooted 'grand coalition' against Germany (a repeat of the constellation of 1914), deter Britain from intervention in the Polish conflict and leave Poland hopelessly exposed to the might of German arms. Ribbentrop, the German Foreign Minister, for long made the running, with Hitler at first hesitant. From the Soviet point of view, improved political relations with Germany would at the very least ensure economic benefits, which were desperately needed for industrialization plans, and in particular for the build-up of the armed forces. Imports of industrial goods from Germany had fallen from 46 per cent of all Soviet imports in 1932 to a mere 4.7 per cent by 1938. Stalin himself took a direct and detailed interest in the advantages for Soviet armaments to be obtained from improved trade with Germany.[53] But the Soviet interest in a rapprochement with Nazi Germany went much further than the economic advantages this would bring. The Soviet leadership (and not just Stalin) fully recognized that collective security was dead, was intensely suspicious of the intentions of the western powers, remained wary of the danger from Japan to the east and was desperate to buy time against a German threat presumed certain to be directed against the USSR at some point. For all these reasons, a political understanding with Nazi Germany was increasingly seen to make sense. Stalin, like Hitler for long cautious, finally committed himself only that August.

By then, the soundings which had been made during trade negotiations in the spring and had been accompanied by mutual suspicions had evolved into tentative steps towards a political agreement, and one involving the mutual territorial interests of both countries. The dilatoriness of the British and French during the spring and summer in agreeing to the trilateral pact of mutual assistance sought by the Soviet Union encouraged Molotov in his view that he was dealing with 'crooks and cheats'[54] and merely pandered to Stalin's already capacious suspicions. That London and Paris had dispatched a low-level delegation, which appeared evasive and was in any case unable to give binding commitments, rather than a high-ranking minister, equipped with plenipotentiary powers, was also regarded as demeaning and lacking in seriousness.[55] By mid-August, with the Polish crisis at fever-pitch and in the awareness of Hitler's imminent aim to attack Poland,[56] it was obvious to the Soviet leadership that nothing could be expected from the west. The alternative had now to be taken.

By the time the talks with British representatives were formally broken off, Stalin had already let Hitler know that he was ready to sign a non-aggression pact with Germany as soon as possible.[57] Within four days, on 23 August, Ribbentrop was in Moscow and the most infamous diplomatic move in history was rapidly concluded. It suited both sides. At his Alpine retreat near Berchtesgaden, Hitler slapped his thigh in delight at the news of his diplomatic coup.[58] At his dacha on the outskirts of Moscow, Stalin was equally pleased. But he was under no illusions about the Germans. 'Of course it's all a game to see who can fool whom,' Nikita Khrushchev, at that time party boss in Kiev and a member of the Politburo, recalled Stalin saying. 'I know what Hitler's up to. He thinks he's outsmarted me, but actually it's I who have tricked him.' He told his dinner companions from the Politburo that night that 'because of this treaty the war would pass us by for a while longer. We would be able to stay neutral and save our strength.'[59]

The Soviet Union and Germany, ideological polar opposites whose governments (as Stalin elegantly put it) had spent years 'pouring buckets of shit over each other's heads',[60] were now bound together through a non-aggression pact. A secret added protocol assigned the Baltic to the Soviet sphere of influence and drew a line halfway through Poland, with the western part earmarked for Germany. Soviet interests and security were, as they always had been, the only concerns at stake for the Kremlin. Cynical though the deal had been, these now seemed safeguarded for the foreseeable future. Stalin knew he had attained more secure borders in the Baltic. More than all else, he had staved off any imminent threat to the Soviet Union from Hitler's Germany, and had gained vital time. This had to be utilized to prepare the Red Army for war. Stalin had read parts of *Mein Kampf* as he was on the threshold of the devil's pact with Hitler. He had underlined the passages dealing with Germany's need to acquire new lands in the east at the expense of Russia.[61] He knew what was coming. But he thought the Soviet Union would have three years to be ready for the onslaught. And by the end of 1942 the Red Army would be fit for the showdown. In the meantime, the Soviet Union could benefit materially, and territorially, from its new friendship with the former arch-enemy.

III

Soviet leaders had grounds to feel satisfied with the fruits of the first months of their country's new relationship with Nazi Germany. Under agreements of 19 August 1939 (just before the pact), widened in February 1940 and renegotiated to lay down new delivery schedules in January 1941, trade between the Soviet Union and Germany rapidly recovered from the nadir of the later 1930s to reach a level roughly in line with that when Hitler took power. Germany was the recipient of millions of tons of grain, timber and petroleum products as well as tens of thousands of tons of precious manganese and chromium. The Soviet Union received in return machinery, construction equipment, chemical products and other manufactured goods. The Germans came out better from the economic arrangements. The Soviet Union delivered its raw materials more or less on schedule whereas there were often delays in reciprocal deliveries of manufactured goods. And Germany still provided as good as nothing in response to Soviet demands for armaments.[62] But from the Soviet perspective, the trading arrangements were secondary to the main aim of the pact: security. And in this respect, the balance sheet from the first period of German-Soviet cooperation was encouraging. 'As regards safeguarding the security of our country, we have achieved no mean success,' was Molotov's verdict before the Supreme Soviet at the end of March 1940.[63]

Apart from keeping the Soviet Union out of the European war, the pact (and in particular its secret protocol) had opened the door to territorial aggrandizement, whose chief objective – in contrast to that of Nazi Germany, even if the effect of occupation was almost as dire for the subjected peoples – was to bolster security. The eastern part of Poland had been occupied in mid-September 1939 – a cynical piece of realpolitik that marked the first step in constructing a cordon sanitaire around Soviet western borders. Before the end of the month, Ribbentrop was back in Moscow to sign the German-Soviet Boundary and Friendship Treaty, agreeing to transfer Lithuania into the Soviet sphere of influence in return for extended parts of central Poland, which passed to Germany. Alongside Lithuania, the other Baltic republics of Latvia and Estonia were also forced during the following weeks into subservience to the USSR, and compelled to allow Soviet troops to be based on their territory. Finland proved, however, a step too far. Pressure on the Finns in the autumn to make territorial concessions aimed at strengthening Soviet northern defences produced not compliance but defiance and, by the end of November, full-scale war. The bitter conflict through the depths of the winter saved Finland's independence. By the time the Finns sued for peace the following March, 200,000 Soviet soldiers lay dead. The Red Army, which had sent over a million troops to fight in Finland, had been humiliated by the tiny Finnish forces. The Germans were not alone in the gross underestimation of Soviet fighting potential that was a legacy of the 'Winter War'.

Stalin's hopes in this first phase of the European war were that the western democracies and Nazi Germany would wear each other down and fight to a standstill. His worry was that they would at some point come to a deal – and together turn on the Soviet Union.[64] The hopes were dashed by the speed of the German victory in the west in May and June 1940. The worry, on the other hand, was magnified.

The rapidity of France's collapse took the Soviet leadership completely by surprise. All calculations now had to be revised. With western Europe prostrate at Hitler's feet, apart from Great Britain (and how long would she hold out before being conquered, or, more likely, capitulating and joining Germany's side, as long predicted?), the Soviet Union was more exposed than ever. Stalin immediately recognized this. Khrushchev was with Stalin as the news came through of France's defeat. He later recalled Stalin's reaction. 'He'd obviously lost all confidence in the ability of our army to put up a fight. It was as though he'd thrown up his hands in despair and given up after Hitler crushed the French army and occupied Paris . . . He let fly with some choice Russian curses and said that now Hitler was sure to beat our brains in.'[65]

The Red Army, as Finland had exposed only too cruelly, was far from ready to counter the threat. In the wake of the disastrous showing in the Winter War, steps were taken to adjust as far as possible to the new situation. The pace of rearmament was sharply stepped up. Workers were subjected to even more draconian labour discipline than had previously existed in order to increase arms production. The armed forces were reorganized as some purged officers returned and the next generation of commanders (some to gain fame during the coming years) took up key posts.[66] Without delay, too, the fragile remaining independence of the Baltic republics was ended. In June, Latvia, Estonia and Lithuania were annexed under the flimsy pretext of alleged anti-Soviet activity and fully incorporated into the USSR in order to shore up the Soviet defensive position in the north. There were even contingency plans, laid down in September 1940 but never put into operation, for a new war against Finland.[67]

In southern Europe, as well, there was a new urgency to Soviet diplomatic moves. Here, the Balkans held the key. After France's defeat, the Soviet

leadership reckoned that Britain would before long be forced to the conference table. The Soviet Union needed to be strong enough to defend its
interests in the face of German dominance in western and central Europe.
Soviet influence over the Balkans, the Black Sea and the Turkish Straits,
areas where Russia had traditionally sought to exert her power way back
in Tsarist times, was seen as crucial to fending off likely German designs
also on this vital region and protecting against any threat of invasion from
the south. There was also the question of British strategic interests in this
region, and the danger this would pose to the Soviet Union should Britain
and Germany come to some 'arrangement' in a peace settlement. The
perceived need to extend Soviet control of the Danube basin and the Balkans
lay behind the annexation in July of Bessarabia, transferred to Romania
in 1919 but prior to that falling within the Russian Empire, and northern
Bukovina, historically a Romanian territory which had never previously
belonged to Russia. For a time, in the summer of 1940, the Soviet Union
even hoped to use the Italians to broker a deal to divide the Balkans into
separate spheres of influence between the USSR and the Axis powers. This,
predictably, held no attractions for Germany, keen to keep the Soviets out
of such a strategically important region and especially anxious to gain a
dominant hold over Romania, where the Ploesti oil wells were indispensable
to the German armed forces.

German and Italian arbitration at the end of August – with the Soviet
Union excluded – of the disputed Romanian-Hungarian borders then
drew Romania directly into Germany's orbit. The Soviets claimed that the
arbitration – from their perspective a direct anti-Soviet move – violated
the requirement to consult on matters of common interest laid down in the
pact of the previous year. The Germans, naturally, ignored the complaint,
and Soviet hopes of a sphere of influence in the Danube basin and Balkans
were, with this, effectively ended. When, in September, German military
'missions', on 'invitation', entered Romania – and a little later in the month,
Finland – the threat to Soviet interests was obvious.[68]

These territorial issues, where Soviet and German interests conflicted,
unavoidably prompted a rise in tension between the two countries during
the summer and autumn. The Tripartite Pact on 27 September, linking
Germany (and Italy) with Japan, the USSR's dangerous eastern enemy, did
little to improve matters, even though its thrust was anti-American, not
anti-Soviet. Then, at the end of October, Mussolini's disastrous invasion
of Greece lit the touchpaper to the Balkan powder keg, prompting British
intervention and opening up the certain prospect of German military
involvement in the region – something scarcely guaranteed to reverse the

serious deterioration in relations between the Soviet Union and Germany that had set in during recent weeks. This was the climate in which Molotov, on Ribbentrop's invitation, arrived in Berlin on 12 November for talks with the Reich Foreign Minister and with Hitler.

The talks went badly.[69] Ribbentrop was mainly concerned with persuading the Soviet Union to join the Tripartite Pact and become part of what he saw as a Euro-Asiatic bloc which would divide the world into German, Italian, Japanese and Soviet spheres of influence. He encouraged Molotov to look to the Soviet Union expanding in the direction of the Persian Gulf, the Middle East and India. Hitler wanted above all to discover more about Soviet intentions. But Molotov's dogged persistence on matters of detail reminded him of a pedantic schoolmaster. He became increasingly irritated. The talks simply confirmed his negative views on the Soviet Union – probably what he had implicitly been looking for, anyway.

Molotov's agenda, laid out in careful consultation with Stalin, was more specific and mainly directed at the issues which had led to the deterioration in relations between the Soviet Union and Germany in recent months.[70] Finland, Romania and the Balkans were particularly sensitive areas, where the Soviet Union felt cause for grievance. But no headway was made. Mutual suspicion and underlying antagonism pervaded the talks, which led nowhere. Hitler felt wholly vindicated in his view that the conflicting interests of Germany and the Soviet Union could never be peacefully reconciled. A clash was inevitable. Hitler saw Molotov's visit as confirmation that the attack envisaged since July could not be delayed. By mid-December, as we saw, a military directive had been devised, scheduling the invasion for the coming spring.

From the Soviet perspective, the talks, inconclusive as they were, altered nothing. They had no dramatic consequences. Certainly, Molotov returned to Moscow with a sense of having achieved little. And the Soviet leadership remained particularly sour at what they saw as grave breaches of the pact in German action in Romania and Finland.[71] They had been largely outmanoeuvred in the Balkans, and in Romania especially. And from July onwards, even before Hitler had announced to his generals the intention to invade the Soviet Union the following year, reports had been filtering through from the well-informed intelligence network of German preparations for war against the USSR and of the transfer and concentration of troops in East Prussia, close to the Russian border.[72] But, whatever their suspicions about German intentions in the long run, Stalin and Molotov, the two key figures in shaping Soviet foreign affairs, expected no military conflict in the near future. Now as before anxious above all to gain time, maintaining the pact of 1939 remained their priority. In this, they had few options. The straitjacket of choice was in part a consequence of the speed with which Germany had established mastery over much of Europe since the spring. But it was also partly self-inflicted. Soviet options were mainly circumscribed by the poor state of the Red Army, which would not be fully prepared for war for another two years. And for this, Stalin himself, through the lethal purges he had launched against his experienced and talented military leaders three years earlier, bore the main responsibility.

IV

On 1 January 1938 the Soviet armed forces comprised 1,605,520 men, just under three-quarters of them in the army. This was not far removed from the planned size when Stalin expected to be ready for war, at the end of 1942.[73] The plan was, however, rapidly overtaken by events once the European war began. The Soviet occupation of eastern Poland, and especially the war against Finland, saw the mobilization of large numbers of reservists, increasing the army size by little short of two million soldiers. Remarkably, however, almost 700,000 reservists were then demobilized following the end of the Finnish war as the Politburo ordered a return to peacetime status for many units. It took the shock of the German victory in France to reverse this trend and instigate the all-out drive for drastic and rapid expansion.[74]

However, serious weaknesses in leadership and experience in the military command left by the purges could not be rapidly repaired. Around 4,000 officers arrested during the purges were released to take up command posts. But the thousand or so newly promoted senior officers had little time to gain the requisite experience before the German onslaught began.[75] There were also organizational flaws (which the campaign in Finland had revealed). And the armed forces were seriously under-equipped in modern weaponry. Despite the intensification of war production that had followed the jolt caused by Hitler's victory in the west that summer, industry was unable to meet the urgent need for armaments. Grave shortages still existed when Hitler struck. Part of the problem lay with Stalin's leadership and the nature of the regime.

Like Hitler, Stalin had a sharp mind (however warped), and his excellent memory gave him a good grasp on detail. His understanding of military affairs was, nevertheless, in essence that of an informed amateur. He lacked the training and expertise of the professional. This led to seemingly contradictory tendencies, both harmful. On the one hand, he was inclined to interfere in matters of detail, such as on specific artillery types, often on a whim.[76] On the other hand, he was forced to rely heavily upon the judgement of those whom he trusted – and they were few in number – in the top echelons of military command. Once the big drive for expansion and reconstruction of the Red Army had begun in summer 1940, he had frequent briefings, usually late at night in his dacha, from his military leaders. They also sent in regular written reports on the state of the army.[77] And Stalin checked up on the army leadership through reports from Beria, head of the secret police, and others.[78] But since he seldom left the Kremlin or his nearby dacha to inspect the genuine condition of the armed forces, he was all the more dependent upon what he was told.

Until he was sacked as Defence Commissar, in May 1940, following the poor performance of the Red Army in the Finnish war, Marshal Voroshilov had had Stalin's ear on important military matters. But Stalin's confidence had been misplaced. Voroshilov had been negligent, idle and incompetent when it came to addressing the urgent need of building up the armed forces. Matters improved greatly once Marshal S. K. Timoshenko replaced Voroshilov. But even now, Stalin was prepared to take military advice from such individuals as the odious L. Z. Mekhlis, former editor of the Party newspaper, *Pravda*, and by 1940 head of the Political Directorate of the Red Army. Khrushchev considered Mekhlis 'a nitwit' and was appalled that he enjoyed such influence over Stalin on military matters.[79]

If Stalin had harboured any illusions about the quality of the Red Army following the debacle in Finland, they could only have been dashed by the devastating top-secret report presented in December 1940 by Timoshenko, outlining the grave deficiencies of the nation's armed forces. The lengthy report, compiled on the basis of thorough assessments after Timoshenko had taken over from Voroshilov the previous May, cannot have made pleasurable reading for Stalin. The whole organizational support structure for administration and provisioning was inadequate, the report ran, and, in many aspects, out of date. So lacking had the central administration been, that not even exact figures for the strength of the Red Army at the point of Timoshenko's takeover existed. Equally extraordinary was the fact that, under the heading 'Operative Planning', the first item stated: 'At the time of the hand-over and takeover of the People's Commissariat for Defence, no operational war plan is available; an operational total plan or partial plans do not exist.' Nor had any training programmes for senior commanders and their staffs been conducted either by Voroshilov or by the General Staff, and no checks on operational training in military districts were in place. There were not enough airfields in key districts. There was even a shortage of maps. In addition, there were serious weaknesses in transport and communications. There was no updated mobilization plan, and no training programme for the three million ill-prepared reservists.

Timoshenko also criticized the inability of the officer academies to produce an adequate military leadership, a shortage especially marked in the infantry. There were serious deficiencies in the training of the troops for battlefield action. And the weaponry was old-fashioned, not up to the needs of modern warfare. Aircraft lagged notably behind those of other states, and for the air force, too, the drastic shortage of trained personnel was highlighted. Similar weaknesses in modern weaponry were noted for motorized units and in artillery. One of the greatest deficiencies emphasized was the absence of organized and systematic intelligence on the state of the armies of other countries. Air-defences could not provide protection from attack from the skies. And ground defence preparations behind the front lines were poor.[80] All in all, the picture was scarcely that of an army close to readiness for a major war, or capable of defending the Soviet Union from invasion, let alone itself launching any offensive operations.

Timoshenko may well have exaggerated the shortcomings to save himself from future criticism by attaching blame to his predecessor for the magnitude of the task he was facing. Even so, it was a shocking indictment of the state of the armed forces. The failings could not be put right immediately. It would take a considerable time to make the Red Army ready for major combat. This in itself imposed the most decisive limitation on Stalin's operative choices over the coming months. The only option, Stalin and Molotov agreed, was to do everything possible and with the utmost speed to prepare the armed forces for the inevitable showdown. But in the meantime, it was crucial to avoid any provocation that might give Hitler a pretext for attack.

These twin considerations effectively framed Soviet policy in the months before the launch of 'Barbarossa'. And, indeed, a huge amount was achieved in rearmament. Production of armaments was a third higher in 1940 than in the previous year. And the armed forces grew massively in size to 5.4 million soldiers in 1941, compared with 1.6 million at the beginning of 1938.[81] They were mostly deployed on the Soviet Union's western borders, and became vastly better equipped. But morale and discipline were often poor.[82] Relatively few of the tanks and planes were the latest models, and there were numerous obstacles to a smooth flow of production.[83] Too much ground had been lost, gravely abetted by the purges, to make good the backwardness in technology and organizational deficits.[84] More time was needed. Stalin thought he would gain it. He was convinced that Hitler would not attack in the east before the war in the west was conclusively won. The likelihood was in Stalin's mind – and his judgement was shared by Molotov and the rest of the Soviet political and military leadership – that the invasion would come only when the Red Army was ready to meet it. Until then, ultimate caution and, where necessary, appeasement of Nazi Germany were the requirement. Winning time was of the essence: the overriding imperative.

Under this extreme pressure, Soviet military strategy had to be reassessed. Soviet strategic theory had rested upon the ideas developed by Tukhachevsky in the 1920s and 1930s. These envisaged a modernized, technologically developed army capable of transforming defence into attack by absorbing the first enemy assault then swiftly transferring the war onto the enemy's territory in what were dubbed 'deep operations'. A lengthy defensive war was not envisaged. The emphasis was on the ability, having weathered the initial storm, to provide an immediate, decisive blow in an all-out strike of airborne and ground forces, supported by massed armoured and mechanized units.[85] The theory was predicated upon a notion of how war would begin: with an ultimatum, a formal declaration, then full-scale mobilization lasting days, or even weeks (as in 1914), and with frontier battles allowing the 'deep operations' to come into play.[86] The surprise attack, tactical brilliance and devastating speed of the German blitzkrieg in the west then cast serious doubt on such premises. Nevertheless, the planning of the Soviet General Staff in 1940 and 1941 amounted to a modification, rather than radical revision, of Tukhachevsky's 'deep operations' theories. Even when the later war hero General Georgi Zhukov took over as chief of the General Staff at the end of January 1941, the expectation remained that the Red Army would be able to contain the enemy during the initial attack, then turn defence into attack in a devastating counter-blow.[87] The strategic plans of the General Staff proceeded on the basis of such thinking.

Timoshenko, as we have noted, had been scathing in his criticism of the absence of an operational war plan when he took over from Voroshilov in May 1940. Indeed, the previous plan, designed in 1938 by Marshal V. M. Shaposhnikov, at that time chief of the General Staff, had been rendered mainly redundant by the changed circumstances that the European war had brought about. Despite Timoshenko's dismissive remarks, however, there were strong elements of continuity with Shaposhnikov's concept in subsequent plans.

Shaposhnikov had seen a threat to the Soviet Union from Japan in the east, and a greater one from Germany and Poland, together with Italy and the Baltic countries, in the west. Working on the theory of strategic defence in depth to contain the enemy before conversion into an offensive, Shaposhnikov posited two variants for an attack against the Soviet western front. Soviet defences had to be ready for an attack, either to the north of the Pripet marshes in Poland towards Vilnius in Lithuania and on to Minsk, or to the south of the marshes, through southern Poland in the direction of Kiev. Shaposhnikov still held to notions of mobilization soon to be exposed as wholly obsolete. He thought the northern variant somewhat more likely since the enemy attack could take place on the twentieth day of mobilization, whereas 28–30 days would be needed for the southern variant. And he envisaged a Soviet decision on whether to place the weight of defence on the northern or southern variant being taken only around the tenth day of mobilization, when it was plain which direction the enemy offensive was taking.[88]

By August 1940, when he was replaced as chief of staff by General K. A. Meretskov, Shaposhnikov's plan was in need of stringent revision. Poland no longer existed, the Baltic states of Latvia, Estonia and Lithuania were now part of the Soviet Union, Finland had fallen within the German orbit and Germany had extended her grip on the Danube basin so that Romania and Hungary could be regarded as her allies in any future conflict. Moreover, Italy had entered the war, and Axis influence in the Mediterranean and Balkans was substantially strengthened. Timoshenko and Meretskov now reversed Shaposhnikov's precedence attached to the northern variant. In their reassessment, presented to Stalin on 5 October, they envisaged the main strike coming from the south. Stalin agreed. 'I think the most important thing for the Germans is the grain in the Ukraine and the coal of the Donbas,' he remarked.[89] By the middle of the month, the revised plan, predicated on the main German attack coming south of the Pripet marshes, was adopted. The Balkans, in this scenario, played a central role in Soviet strategic thinking. Under the revised plan, the Red Army would engage 'to the south of Brest-Litovsk in order, by means of powerful blows in the directions of Lublin and Cracow and further to Breslau, to cut Germany off from the Balkan countries in the very first stage of the war, to deprive her of its most important economic bases, and decisively to influence the Balkan countries on the question of their participation in the war'. This reassessment remained essentially intact as the basis of Soviet operational war planning until the eve of 'Barbarossa'.[90]

At the end of December 1940, bringing to a close a conference of top military leaders convened by Stalin following the depressing report on the state of the armed forces presented earlier in the month, Timoshenko summed up the proceedings by saying that 'although the war with Germany might be difficult and long, the country had all it needed for a struggle to full victory'. Probably the optimistic assessment was what Timoshenko thought Stalin wanted to hear. Instead, it gave the Soviet dictator a sleepless night.[91] His unease could not have been quelled by the results of two war games conducted in early January.

They were concerned purely with defence strategy. Both games assumed aggression from the west: an invasion of the Soviet Union. And both, remarkably, omitted the vital initial stage of defence, starting their assessment only at the phase, presumed to be several weeks after the war had begun, when the 'enemy' had already penetrated into Soviet territory. The first of the games posited an attack in the north, with Zhukov leading the 'enemy' forces and General D. G. Pavlov commanding the Soviet army. Pavlov failed to repel the 'enemy', which ended well inside Soviet territory. In the second game, Zhukov and Pavlov swapped sides. Here, the southern variant was tested. Zhukov worked on 'deep operations' theory, contained the attack in the south, then destroyed twenty enemy divisions and was able to advance on one flank about a hundred miles into Poland. Even then, the German offensive could not be wholly contained. The results were not viewed as satisfactory. At a meeting soon afterwards in the Kremlin, with the Politburo present, Stalin severely berated the chief of staff, Meretskov, then sacked him on the spot. Zhukov, who had proved such an effective commander in the war games, was promoted to the new chief of the General Staff.[92]

By March, influenced by the war games and by a recently completed blueprint for mobilization (which, again, in attempting to please Stalin had provided wildly optimistic and unrealistic figures on manpower and armaments), a revised operational plan was ready. It reaffirmed the decision taken the previous autumn and seemingly justified in the war games, that the main weight of Soviet defence would be directed towards the expected southern, not northern, variant of German attack. The assumption was that the key German thrust would be towards the Ukraine.[93] It would prove a serious miscalculation.

The frenetic months of planning revision and feverish expansion since the previous summer – and the tempo was to accelerate even more sharply – had produced ambivalent results. On the one hand, a massive amount had unquestionably been accomplished in a remarkably short time. On the other hand, there was still far to go before defences would be ready for the predicted onslaught. The outcome of the war games had highlighted major deficiencies remaining in defence strategy. And projected estimates of manpower and armaments tended to inflate current strength and put the most positive gloss on future capability. The mobilization plan of February had outlined a staggering wartime strength of 8,700,000 soldiers in over 300 fully equipped divisions, 60 of them tank and a further 30 motorized divisions, and an air-strength of some 14,000 aircraft. The aims of the plan were meant to be fulfilled by the end of 1941. But the figures concealed much of the truth. Not enough vehicles could be produced to equip fully the tank and motorized divisions even by 1943. Even with optimal production, there would be a 75 per cent shortfall on the vital medium-sized tanks (mainly the later renowned T-34s) as late as 1 January 1942. The figures for aircraft were also wholly unrealistic in the short term. And when the war actually began in June 1941, a quarter of the divisions stipulated in the plan existed only on paper.[94]

Stalin and his 'inner circle', who were fully briefed on the plans and their practical limitations, knew that any German attack during 1941 would pose extreme danger for the Soviet Union. The Red Army would still be ill-equipped to counter the threat. The country's defences would be at the very least severely stretched. In so many vital spheres – tank and aircraft production, border fortifications, manpower – completion targets were scheduled for no earlier than the beginning of 1942.[95] The problems had been compounded by Stalin's decision, overriding opposition from his military advisers, to abandon the system of fortifications, known as the 'Stalin Line', begun in the 1920s and stretching across the Soviet Union's former frontier, in favour of new fortifications to be constructed in forward positions on the new frontier. This would prove a serious error in June 1941. On the eve of the German attack, crucial defence areas were still unprovided with minefields, camouflage or effective fields of fire, and most of the strongpoints belatedly set up on Zhukov's orders had no artillery. Meanwhile, when Stalin at last agreed that the old line of fortifications should at least be partly manned, the troops found them 'overgrown with grass and tall weeds', concrete shells with empty gun emplacements.[96]

Stalin drew one conclusion from all this. There was no option: conflict with Germany must at all costs be delayed until 1942 at the earliest. 'We all, Stalin included, knew that conflict was inevitable,' Mikoyan recalled, 'but we were also aware of our lack of preparations for it.'[97] Stalin later told Churchill that he knew the war was coming, but thought he might gain another six months or so.[98] This meant a policy of mollifying Germany and avoiding confrontation, offering not the slightest provocation for German aggression. None of Stalin's closest associates differed from this analysis. They held to it even as the indications mounted that Hitler was preparing to attack in 1941. Stalin viewed such signs with equanimity. He thought he could read Hitler's mind. Hitler was not stupid, he thought. He would not risk a war on two fronts. He would first want to cover his rear in the west. The British were proving tenacious, and German victory on the western front did not seem imminent. If the Germans did not attack in the summer of 1941, the ferocious Russian winter would see to it that they could not do so before the following spring. So Stalin was confident he could fend off Hitler until 1942. By then, the Red Army would be ready for him.

V

Meanwhile, with military options foreclosed, everything possible had to be done on the diplomatic front. Here, the first months of 1941 brought only partial success. On the gains side was a joint declaration of neutrality signed with Turkey in March. This headed off the danger of Turkey joining the Tripartite Pact and reduced the threat to the Soviet Union on her southern flank, where the Turkish Straits had traditionally proved a vulnerable point of Russian defences.[99] More important still was the neutrality pact signed with Japan in April which left Stalin euphoric at this major improvement to the security of the Soviet eastern front, eliminating – or at least greatly reducing – the prospect of the USSR being attacked from the east as well as the west. On the debit side, hopes of keeping Bulgaria – traditionally well disposed towards Russia and of strategic importance to Soviet security in the Balkans – out of the clutches of the Germans had failed by the end of February, when Sofia agreed to join the Tripartite Pact and allow German troops to be stationed on Bulgarian soil. By early April, rapid moves to forge a treaty of alliance with Yugoslavia, where a popular coup had overthrown the government which had decided to join the Axis, had been immediately vitiated by the German invasion and subsequent rapid conquest of the country. The capitulation of Greece, too, to Hitler's forces meant that by the end of April, aside from Turkish neutrality, the Balkans were now squarely in the German domain and the southern frontier of the Soviet Union exposed to Germany and her allies. At every point in the diplomatic game of chess, Stalin had found himself outmanoeuvred by Hitler. Military weakness was compounded by diplomatic isolation.

Stalin remained greatly worried, too, that Britain would seek a deal with Hitler, ending the bogey of the two-front war and allowing Germany to turn eastwards unthreatened from the west. Britain's military weakness, exposed by the withdrawal of 100,000 men from Greece when the Germans invaded, and in north Africa through Rommel's startling successes, made the prospect seem a real one. None other than the British ambassador in Moscow, Sir Stafford Cripps, now alerted Stalin and Molotov to precisely such a scenario. 'It was not outside the bounds of possibility, if the war were protracted for a long period,' stated Cripps on 18 April, 'that there might be a temptation for Great Britain (and especially for certain circles in Great Britain) to come to some arrangement to end the war on the sort of basis which has recently been suggested in certain German quarters.'[100] The British government was at the time trying to induce the Soviet Union to throw her military might behind the defence of Yugoslavia and Greece to form a 'Balkan front' against Hitler. Stressing the mounting threat posed by Germany to the USSR itself was part of this diplomatic offensive. Instead, however, what Cripps succeeded in doing was to alarm the Soviet leadership about the likelihood of an 'arrangement' between Germany and Great Britain. When Winston Churchill then sent a message via Cripps to Stalin, delivered in the Kremlin on 21 April, warning the Soviet leader of the danger of a German attack, the impact was wholly counterproductive. All the message did was to set the alarm bells ringing even more loudly and intensify Stalin's paranoia. He presumed that Churchill was trying to entice him into a war with Germany in a move aimed at serving only British interests. 'Look at that,' he told Zhukov, 'we are being threatened with the Germans, and the Germans with the Soviet Union, and they are playing us off against one another. It is a subtle political game.'[101]

Churchill later described Stalin and his associates in the Kremlin as 'simpletons' and 'the most completely outwitted bunglers of the Second World War', and thought that, through direct contact with the Soviet chief, he might have prevented the disaster that befell his country on 22 June 1941.[102] Even belatedly, Churchill did not see how his well-intended message would inevitably be construed in Moscow. In the context, Stalin's reaction was not wholly irrational. In any case, by the time Churchill sent his warning Stalin was inundated with intelligence reports informing him of the growing threat from Germany.

With so many Communist sympathizers abroad, Stalin's regime had no shortage of informers willing, often at considerable risk to their own safety, to provide the state security organs with a flow of intelligence – varied in quality, often contradictory, but sometimes significant.[103] Digests of reports were forwarded at frequent intervals by Vsevolod Merkulov, head of the NKGB (responsible for external affairs, and hived off in early February 1941 from Beria's NKVD, left in charge of internal security).[104]

Despite approving Merkulov's appointment, Stalin had no high opinion of him, regarding him as weak and over-anxious to please. The flaw was, of course, built into the system. But perhaps the fact that Merkulov wrote plays and fiction in his spare time did not help.[105] At any rate, Stalin distrusted his reports. Nor did he think he could rely upon the military intelligence reports, again sometimes summarizing important information, sent to him by the head of the GRU (the Soviet military intelligence), General Filip Golikov. Still further intelligence reports reached Stalin via the Foreign Ministry's sources.[106] Once more, they were treated with scepticism. Vital intelligence, for which agents had often risked their lives, was consequently dismissed as a matter of course by Stalin as 'disinformation'. In fact, there *was* a good deal of disinformation deliberately put in circulation. Much of it was successfully placed by the Germans themselves (such as the story that the build-up of troops in the east was a deception aimed at British intelligence, a cover for the planned invasion of Britain).[107] So there was certainly room for distrust and scepticism of uncorroborated intelligence. But Stalin's own profound cynicism went much further than healthy scepticism. It led him to disbelieve all information, however compelling and however well placed the source, which contradicted his own analysis of German intentions. And this, perversely, came to rest upon the successful German deception that any attack would be preceded by an ultimatum, which would give him time to concede, mobilize or even pre-empt.[108] The complete mistrust of all intelligence coupled with the certainty that his own analysis was right amounted ultimately to the reason why Stalin was caught so totally by surprise on 22 June 1941.

As early as 5 December 1940, the newly appointed Soviet ambassador to Germany, Vladimir Dekanozov, a former senior officer in the NKVD, received an anonymous letter warning that Hitler would attack the Soviet Union the following spring.[109] This was indeed at precisely the point that Hitler was confirming to his military leaders the decision to prepare to invade the USSR in May 1941, embodied in the directive for what was now called 'Operation Barbarossa' on 18 December. Within eleven days, Soviet military intelligence in Berlin was forwarding to Moscow the information it had received from 'most well-informed high military circles that Hitler has given the order to prepare for war with the USSR. War will be declared in March 1941.' Verification of the information was sent to Stalin personally in early January 1941.[110]

Two of the best-placed agents, supplying a flow of excellent information, were the German Communist sympathizers Harro Schulze-Boysen (whose codename was 'Starshina', or 'the Elder') and Arvid Harnack (known as

'Korsicanets', or the 'Corsican'). Through family connections (his father was a nephew of Admiral Alfred von Tirpitz, the former head of the German navy, and his mother was related to Hermann Göring), Schulze-Boysen was able to join Luftwaffe headquarters in 1941 as an officer. There he gained access to top-secret material. Harnack, a lawyer who had studied for some time in the United States, was a nephew of Adolf von Harnack, an eminent theologian, and since 1935 had worked in the Economics Ministry in Berlin. Like Schulze-Boysen (with whom he came into contact after the outbreak of war), he had access to privileged information. Both were won over in 1940 to work secretly for Soviet intelligence. They were eventually uncovered and executed in 1942. But in 1941, as German preparations to attack the USSR were under way, they were able to tap sources close to the heart of Nazi military and economic planning.

At the beginning of March 1941, 'Corsican' reported serious discussions within the German leadership about attacking the USSR. His report was passed to Stalin, Molotov, Timoshenko and Beria. Contingency plans for occupation of the western parts of the Soviet Union were being drawn up, he indicated. And he relayed reports that General Franz Halder, chief of the German army's General Staff, thought the occupation of the Ukraine and the Caucasus would be easy, and pay rich dividends, information which fitted the Soviet presumption that any strike would have its main thrust in the south.[111] A further report, sent on to the Soviet leadership two days later, pointed out that the build-up of troops on the Soviet border was now so large that it was quite evidently an invasion force. However, this report suggested that the USSR would be attacked only following an assault on Turkey; moreover, that Ribbentrop and even Hitler thought Germany would gain more economically by retaining trade links with the Soviet Union than by invasion and occupation. Notions in the Soviet leadership that there might be a split in the upper echelons of the Nazi regime, and even that Hitler might not belong to the most aggressive faction in the matter of designs on the Soviet Union, were thereby given some support.[112]

A few days later, yet another report from 'Corsican' found its way to Stalin's desk. This mentioned German spy planes photographing Soviet territory, particularly around the naval base of Kronstadt, near Leningrad. It also relayed second-hand information from two German generals that an attack on the USSR was planned for the spring. German High Command, it was said, thought Soviet forces would be defeated after little more than a week. The occupation of the Ukraine – again the focus on the Soviet 'granary' – would deprive the USSR of its main source of food. The Wehrmacht would rapidly advance eastwards, and within twenty-five days would be beyond the Urals.[113] Towards the end of March, 'Corsican' passed on information from the German Ministry of Air, detailing planning for the bombing of communications in the USSR, aerial reconnaissance of Soviet towns and the expectation among Luftwaffe officers that operations would begin in late April or early May. An important consideration, it was said, was the German aim of taking the crops before retreating Soviet forces had time to destroy them.[114]

In April the volume of reports intensified. Precise details were given of the build-up of German forces along the border, troop movements and construction of fortifications and aerodromes.[115] 'The Elder' ('Starshina') reported remarks of an officer who had contact with Göring that Hitler considered it necessary to launch a preventive war against the USSR. A point followed which was lodged in the minds of Stalin and other Soviet leaders. Before war was declared, Germany would issue an ultimatum that the Soviet Union join the Tripartite Pact and submit to German demands – predominantly ruthless economic exploitation and political subordination, it was presumed. The attack would follow if the USSR refused to comply with the ultimatum.[116] A few days later, 'Starshina' was relaying information that most German officers were opposed to Hitler and did not support the idea of attacking the USSR. He thought the opportunity for a decisive blow by the Wehrmacht was fading.[117]

By the end of the month, 'Corsican', following a secret meeting of leading German officials in the Economics Ministry, again laid the emphasis on the demands for supplies of raw materials from the Soviet Union, to be achieved either by peace or by war.[118] And on 6 May a communication from another extremely well-informed source, Richard Sorge (known as 'Ramzai'), a Soviet spy located in the German embassy in Tokyo, noted that, according to the German ambassador, General Eugen Ott, Hitler was determined to defeat the USSR and gain the economic resources of the western parts of the Soviet Union. Once the grain had been sown, Germany could attack at any time to reap the harvest. German generals, in Ott's view, believed that an eastern campaign would prove no hindrance to the war against Britain. The Soviet forces, they thought, were unprepared, defences weak, and the Red Army could be routed within a matter of weeks.[119] These, and countless other agents' reports, were routinely summarized by Merkulov, head of external security, and the digests sent on to the Soviet leadership.[120]

In retrospect, ignoring such information seems sheer folly. Leaving aside the hearsay nature of much of it, that it was not always consistent and that it did not match the actual pattern of the invasion, it did point unequivocally to a German attack on the Soviet Union – and in the near future. From

Stalin's perspective, however, it was less obvious. The reports just cited were only part of an increasing flow of information, starting to turn into a torrent. But a good deal of it actually came through British, American or other foreign channels.[121] This was instinctively distrusted by Stalin, as we have seen, and his distrust was encouraged by his own intelligence chiefs. On 20 March 1941 General Golikov, head of military intelligence, presented a report to the Defence and Foreign Commissariats and the Central Committee which outlined a long list of various views from an array of sources on German intentions towards the USSR. He preceded this by stating that much of the agent information about a spring attack on the Soviet Union came from Anglo-American sources, whose main aim was to worsen the relationship between Germany and the USSR. His own view was that the Germans would attack the Soviet Union only once they had defeated Britain. Persistent rumours that the attack would occur in the spring of 1941, he suggested, ought to be viewed as disinformation spread by the British, and also the German, intelligence services.[122] This was no more than pandering to Stalin's preformed judgement.

Stalin and his associates were not alone, however, in misreading the signals. Foreign intelligence services were also for the most part misled.[123] German deception strategy – that the build-up of troops in the east was a front for 'Operation Sealion' (the invasion of England), or was to culminate in an ultimatum to Stalin to demand territory and raw materials from the Soviet Union – played a notable part in this.[124] British intelligence, sometimes swallowing the false messages deliberately put into circulation by the Germans, was late in coming to the realization that an invasion was indeed being planned. Early reports on Hitler's intended aggression were dismissed as unreliable rumour, wishful thinking or defensive moves against possible Soviet attack. Then it was seen as a 'war of nerves' by the Germans to prevent intervention in the Balkans or to extricate more material resources from the Soviet Union.[125]

Reading the intelligence runes was, therefore, anything but straightforward. Molotov was still unrepentant many years later on the allegation that Stalin's cardinal error was to ignore the intelligence he was receiving. 'We are blamed because we ignored our intelligence,' said Molotov. 'Yes, they warned us. But if we had heeded them, had given Hitler the slightest excuse, he would have attacked us earlier.' (When that might have been, Molotov did not indicate. Since, as was obvious, the Germans had been in no position to attack during the summer months of 1940, and the Russian winter ruled out any such move during subsequent months, the earliest date of any invasion had to be spring 1941 – when, indeed, Hitler initially intended to launch it.) 'We knew the war was coming soon, that we were weaker than Germany, that we would have to retreat,' Molotov continued. 'We did everything to postpone the war . . . Stalin reckoned before the war that only in 1943 would we be able to meet the Germans as equals.' His interrogator brought Molotov back to the stream of intelligence reports. 'We could not have relied on our intelligence,' Molotov replied. 'You have to listen to them, but you also have to verify their information. Intelligence agents could push you into such a dangerous position that you would never get out of it. Provocateurs everywhere are innumerable . . . You couldn't trust such reports.'[126] Molotov's views were an echo of Stalin's own.

By the beginning of May, nevertheless, the flood of worrying information could no longer be simply ignored. Even Stalin saw that some action was necessary. It was primarily aimed at sending a message to Germany, providing public reassurance and bolstering troop morale. At the same time Timoshenko and Zhukov were viewing the warnings with more anxious eyes than Stalin's. They were by now favouring a different sort of action. They were at work on a drastically revised military plan – one which placed the emphasis on a Soviet offensive.

VI

On 5 May Stalin replaced Molotov as chairman of the Council of People's Commissars – the equivalent of Prime Minister. He was now for the first time officially head of the state government, as well as the party (as its General Secretary). In reality, the move, made public the next day, was in many ways cosmetic. Though Molotov had previously headed the state government, Stalin's supremacy had never been in doubt. But by officially taking over, Stalin was now offering reassurance to the Soviet public. He was in total control. The well-being of the country was in the best hands. He knew what to do.

But the move went beyond morale-boosting. Converting Politburo decisions into government decrees, a process necessary to ensure party dominance, had entailed cumbersome formalities. At such a critical time, these were now greatly streamlined.[127] At least as important was the impression to be conveyed abroad, most crucially to Germany. At the formal level of diplomacy, Stalin's lack of responsibility for state government had been something of a complication. Formal negotiations had to pass through Molotov, even though it was obvious that Stalin was really in charge. This complication was now bypassed. It was meant to show the Germans that in negotiations to stabilize relations they could deal with Stalin himself. The German ambassador in Moscow, Count Friedrich Werner von der Schulenburg, who secretly opposed the looming invasion, correspondingly reported to Berlin his conviction 'that Stalin will use his new position in order to take part personally in the maintenance and development of good relations between the Soviets and Germany'.[128] The Germans soon had reason to be satisfied with Stalin the Prime Minister. He denied rumours of military concentrations on the frontier, resumed diplomatic relations with the pro-German government of Iraq and closed the Norwegian, Belgian and Yugoslav embassies in Moscow – all to appease Hitler.[129]

On the day that he became the Soviet premier, Stalin gave a major speech in Moscow before hundreds of graduates of the Military Academy, along with the elite of the Red Army, representatives of the Defence Commissariat and General Staff, and important government figures. Unlike Hitler, Stalin seldom gave speeches, even behind closed doors. His previous major speech had been in March 1939, at the 18th Party Congress.[130] And, again unlike Hitler, Stalin's style of speech was calm and measured (even to the point of dullness), the content structured and ordered. But the rarity of his speeches and the gravity of the situation increased the interest, at home and also in Berlin, in what Stalin had said. Little could be known for certain. The newspapers next day carried only a lapidary note of his address.[131]

In all, an audience of around 1,500 heard Stalin speak for around forty minutes about the great advances achieved in modernizing and building up the Red Army to its current position of strength. He provided an array of impressive figures on the huge improvements in the size and fighting capability of the armed forces and their modern weaponry. Turning to the German army, he attributed the great victories in the west to the ability to learn from earlier failures and the weakness of the French. He was insistent that the German army was not invincible, and, drawing an analogy with Napoleon, that its aim of conquest (which had replaced the earlier one of freedom from the Versailles Treaty) would not be achieved. In the reception that followed, Stalin gave three short toasts. In the third, he corrected an officer who wanted to toast his peace policy. The peace policy had served the country's defences well, Stalin said. It had been pursued until the army had been rebuilt and given modern weaponry. But now, he declared, the Soviet Union had to move from defensive to offensive operations. 'The Red Army is a modern army,' he ended, 'but a modern army is an attacking army.'[132] Some interpreters have seen in these words the aim of launching a preventive attack on Germany, precisely what Nazi propaganda claimed to justify the invasion of the USSR.[133] But the brief remarks offered no more than a terse restatement of the long-standing military strategy of converting defence into devastating attack, though it is certainly true that they presented, and were seen to present, a new emphasis upon offence. And they were, as was the main speech preceding the toasts, explicitly aimed at effect. The outright purpose was to instil belief in the Red Army's fighting capacity, to bolster morale through the confidence exuded at the very top of the Soviet Union. That the speech set the tone for the new propaganda directives for the army and civilian population which were prepared in its aftermath also suggests that the building of morale was its key purpose.[134]

The speech has been seen as aimed primarily at spreading disinformation abroad. Had that been the case, Soviet intelligence would have been adept at leaking its content. As it was, even the Germans, whose interest in what Stalin had to say was obvious, had to be content with a completely bowdlerized version passed on only a month later by the ambassador in Moscow. Schulenburg, who, at the time it was delivered, had been unable to discover the content of the speech, now provided a wholly misleading version, suggesting that Stalin had emphasized that the Red Army was still weak compared to the Wehrmacht, and had wanted to prepare his audience for a 'new compromise' with Germany.[135] No accurate version of the speech, it seems, found its way to Berlin, or anywhere else.[136] And a deliberate leak stressing the feeble state of the Red Army was scarcely in the Soviet interest. So, for all the speculation, the objective of the speech is best viewed as domestic, rather than external – to shore up the morale and self-belief of the leaders of the Red Army.

It had, however, immediate consequences for the military leadership's operational planning, which was also most likely affected by the latest comprehensive assessment by military intelligence of the number of German divisions massing on the western borders of the Soviet Union.[137] The earlier plans, from September 1940 and March 1941, were now rapidly revised. By 15 May Timoshenko and Zhukov were ready to present the new plan to Stalin.[138] Though building directly on the earlier plans, it differed in one striking respect. It now envisaged a major pre-emptive strike, as Zhukov later acknowledged, to forestall the enemy by attacking the German army before it was ready to launch its own offensive. As before, the main directional thrust was towards southern Poland, where the enemy would be destroyed by a 'sudden blow' on land and from the air. The advance included the conquest of Warsaw, and subsequently the destruction of German forces in northern Poland and the overrunning of East Prussia.[139]

The plan has given succour to those anxious to assert that Hitler, as he claimed, launched 'Barbarossa' to head off a Soviet pre-emptive strike which was under preparation. But nothing supports such a far-fetched interpretation. The Nazi leadership knew, of course, that they were not invading the Soviet Union to head off a pre-emptive strike. 'Barbarossa' had been instigated months earlier, and for aggressive, not defensive, reasons. And the Soviet plan of 15 May provides no 'smoking gun'.

Certainly, it proposed a pre-emptive strike. In this, it converted the traditional emphasis on the rapid transition from 'deep defence' to offence into a stress on attack as a form of defence. Unlike the German fiction of a Soviet threat, the menace from Hitler's forces was evident to the Soviet military leadership as daily reports of the build-up of troops and violations of the borders for aerial reconnaissance poured in. The idea of the pre-emptive strike contained in the 15 May plan arose directly from the need to *protect* the Soviet Union, and was inspired by Stalin's speech ten days earlier. That is, it was an offensive plan born out of defensive necessity.[140]

Worried as they were by the incessant flow of intelligence reports on troop movements together with indications (if not always consistent) of hostile German intent towards the Soviet Union, Timoshenko and Zhukov nevertheless most probably thought, like Stalin, that the German attack was not imminent. Red Army estimates indicated that the German build-up in the east had not been great in recent weeks, and that a far larger concentration of strength would have to occur before any attack took place.[141] And, as the Soviet military leaders were only too well aware, the forces available to the Red Army nowhere approached those required under the 15 May plan, and major deficiencies were still obvious in transport and supplies. The plan also encompassed the construction of huge defensive fortifications, which were nowhere near completion. As a blueprint for action in the near future, therefore, the plan was utterly unrealistic.[142] Most probably, Timoshenko and Zhukov had in mind an offensive at some stage in the more distant future, probably at the earliest during the summer of 1942.

In any case, speculation on the possible timing of any pre-emptive strike is fruitless. When Timoshenko and Zhukov presented the plan – still in draft form – to Stalin, he rejected it outright. 'He immediately exploded when he heard about the pre-emptive blow against the German forces,' Zhukov reputedly commented at a later date. '"Have you gone mad? Do you want to provoke the Germans?", he barked out irritably.' Timoshenko and Zhukov reminded Stalin of what he had said on 5 May. '"I said that in order to encourage the people there, so that they would think about victory and not about the invincibility of the German army, which is what the world's press is blaring on about'', growled Stalin. And thus was buried our idea for a pre-emptive blow,' Zhukov concluded.[143]

An account of the postwar testimony of Timoshenko was equally explicit about Stalin's reaction. Stalin, in this version, accused both Zhukov and Timoshenko of being warmongers. When Timoshenko referred to his speech of 5 May, Stalin retorted: 'Look everyone . . . Timoshenko is healthy and has a large head, but his brain is evidently tiny . . . What I said [on 5 May] was for the people. Their vigilance had to be raised. And you must understand that Germany will never on its own move to attack Russia . . . If you provoke the Germans on the border, if you move forces without our permission, then bear in mind that heads will roll.' Stalin then stormed out, slamming the door.[144]

Stalin stuck to his policy of non-provocation and playing for time. So keen was he to avoid provoking the Germans that deliveries of raw materials to Germany in line with earlier trade agreements were still being met in full only six days before the Wehrmacht attacked. Even down to the morning of the invasion itself, Soviet goods were being unloaded at stations on the Polish borders.[145] About the same time, Lieutenant-General Kirponos, the Red Army commander in Kiev, who had written to Stalin informing him that a German offensive in the near future was more than likely and had moved some units into more favourable defensive positions on the frontier, had his orders countermanded.[146] Stalin remained unshaken in his conviction that the Germans would not invade until they had attained victory or a compromise settlement in the west. 'Hitler and his generals are not so stupid as to fight at the same time on two fronts,' Zhukov remembered Stalin saying during his angry riposte to the plan. 'That broke the neck of the Germans in the First World War.' Again Stalin insisted that Hitler was not strong enough to fight on two fronts and – here wholly misjudging his foe – 'he won't go in for adventures'.[147]

Did Stalin miss an opportunity in turning his back on the military plan of 15 May offered to him by Timoshenko and Zhukov? That was not what Zhukov himself later thought. Recalling his own inexperience at the time as chief of the General Staff (a position he had not wanted, aware that his real strength was as a field commander), he admitted that he had been wrong, and that Stalin's judgement on the plan was correct. Had a pre-emptive strike been attempted, Zhukov adjudged, the consequences for the Soviet Union would have been even more catastrophic. In all probability, he concluded, the Soviet Union would have been quickly defeated, Moscow and Leningrad would have fallen in 1941, and Hitler's forces would have been in a position to conclude the war successfully.[148]

While Timoshenko and Zhukov were unsuccessfully trying to persuade Stalin to adopt their modified operational plan, and while frenzied work to build up the Red Army was under way, urgent diplomatic efforts to avoid or at least postpone war continued. Most of these revolved around the German ambassador in Moscow, Schulenburg, who would be executed by the Nazi regime just over three years later for his association with the conspiracy to assassinate Hitler. Schulenburg still believed in May 1941 that war could be prevented if the Soviet Union complied with German material and territorial demands. He reported to Berlin his conviction that Stalin had taken over the office of Prime Minister because he had set himself the goal of 'preserving the Soviet Union from a conflict with Germany'.[149] And he backed up the conviction by transmitting the Soviet offer of five million tons of grain to be delivered to Germany the following year.[150] Naturally, such reports, if ever they reached him, cut no ice with Hitler. But Schulenburg in turn was deliberately fed misleading information from Berlin. He was directed, for instance, to quell rumours, deliberately spread, it was claimed, by the British to stir up conflict between the Soviet Union and Germany. He was told that the rumours of German troop concentrations and impending war were 'very detrimental to the further peaceful development of German-Russian relations'.[151] And during an audience with Hitler himself in Berlin at the end of April, the German dictator had explicitly told him: 'I do not intend a war against Russia.'[152] Schulenburg was sure that Hitler had lied to him. Even so, in the weeks that followed, he conveyed his own belief to Stalin and Molotov that war was not inevitable, reinforcing in their minds the notion that a diplomatic solution might still be possible, and sowing still further distrust of British intentions.[153]

The distrust was significantly hardened in the wake of Rudolf Hess's flight into British captivity on 10 May. The British government, itself led by intelligence into believing until early June that German troop movements were designed to force the Soviet leadership into negotiations,[154] tried to use Hess's mysterious arrival to stiffen resistance by instilling fear in Stalin at 'being left alone to face the music' and encouraging him to forge an alliance between the USSR and Britain.[155] The attempt misfired totally. Instead, it simply shored up Stalin's paranoia. His immediate reaction on hearing the news of Hess's flight and capture was, according to Khrushchev, to presume that he was on a secret mission, at Hitler's behest, to negotiate with the British about ending the war to free Germany for the push to the east.[156] But he soon became less certain. Other possibilities implanted themselves in his mind. Soviet intelligence reported rumours offering different interpretations. Ivan Maisky, the long-standing and perceptive Soviet ambassador in London, added to the uncertainty through his reports, since he himself had difficulty in reaching a clear conclusion on the purpose of Hess's mission. All this contributed to Stalin's own unease. Unsure whether Churchill's government was trying to inveigle him into a war against Germany, whether the British and the Germans were about to do a deal to join forces against Bolshevism (as he had always anticipated), or whether Hess represented a faction opposed to a Hitler thought to prefer negotiations with the Soviet Union, Stalin was confirmed only in his belief in the utter untrustworthiness of the British and took all warnings emanating from London to be outright disinformation.[157]

The rumour and counter-rumour feeding the innumerable intelligence reports were open to different interpretations, some of them playing directly to Stalin's prejudices. Dekanozov, the Soviet ambassador in Berlin, for instance, reported as follows to Moscow in early June: 'Parallel to the rumours circulating about the imminent war between Germany and the Soviet Union, rumours were spread in Germany of a rapprochement between Germany and the Soviet Union, either on the basis of far-reaching "concessions" on the part of the Soviet Union' – a long-term lease of the Ukraine was frequently mentioned – 'or on the basis of "division of spheres of influence" and undertakings on the part of the Soviet Union not to interfere in European affairs.'[158] The Soviet ambassador was, in fact, unwittingly relaying a piece of deliberate German misinformation.

Making sense of the mountain of conflicting intelligence reports and countervailing rumours was far from straightforward. Timoshenko and Zhukov, certainly, became increasingly anxious as quite specific reports of German troop concentrations poured in. But when, on the night of 11–12 June, they advocated putting the troops on a war footing and moving forces to forward positions to strengthen defensive capacity, Stalin was dismissive: 'I am certain that Hitler will not risk creating a second front by attacking the Soviet Union,' he declared. 'Hitler is not such an idiot and understands that the Soviet Union is not Poland, not France, and not even England.' His anger mounted. He rejected the mobilization and movement of troops to the western borders, fuming: 'That means war.' Concealed reinforcements of the western borders were, in fact, now carried out, though within constraints ordered by Stalin to ensure that there could be no sign of provocation.[159] The last-minute, improvised mobilization was, in fact, both limited in scope and flawed in execution.[160] On 13 June Timoshenko and Zhukov gave orders to the Kiev military district to transfer command headquarters and a number of divisions at night and in total secrecy closer to the Soviet border. This was to be carried out by the beginning of July.

In mid-June, according to information given to Stalin by the General Staff, a total of 186 divisions were deployed on the western front, more than half of them to the south-west. Most had been secretly moved there from the interior of the country in preceding weeks.[161] But only on 19 June were orders given to start to camouflage aerodromes and other vital installations, and to disperse the aircraft around the airfields. Even now, Stalin was keen to retain secrecy, to avoid any provocation.[162]

It is hard to imagine that Stalin himself did not by now harbour hidden doubts about his own convictions. He must, in solitary moments, have wondered whether he had not for months been outbluffed by Hitler. During the last weeks before the invasion, he seemed restless and worried, took to drinking more heavily, seeking out company as a diversion, replacing working stints at the Kremlin by lengthy dinners at his dacha.[163] However sure he was of his own judgement – and he betrayed no uncertainty to those who saw him regularly at this time – it would have been extraordinary if he had not found cause to worry in the information now showering in from all sides.

On 2 June Beria provided him with a digest of intelligence stipulating the exact location of German troops and their headquarters, although, characteristically, he diluted the impact of his report by concluding that if Germany were to begin a war against the Soviet Union, it would not be before an agreement had been reached between Germany and Great Britain.[164] Other reports were less ambivalent and were now, by any measure, becoming distinctly disconcerting.

The day before Beria delivered his digest, Richard Sorge ('Ramzai') had dispatched two reports from Tokyo based upon information emanating from Berlin. Ambassador Ott had learned that the German attack on the USSR would begin in the second half of June, Sorge indicated, and was 95 per cent certain that war would begin.[165] In a second report, also on 1 June, 'Ramzai' passed on information he had received from an acquaintance, Lieutenant-Colonel Erwin Scholl, who was passing through Tokyo en route to a new posting at the German embassy in Bangkok. Scholl told him that war would begin on 15 June. Scholl also mentioned that the limited Soviet defensive lines (concentrated, as we have seen, in the south) were a weakness, since the main German attack would be launched on its left flank (that is, in the north).[166] When Sorge's telegram was decoded and translated into Russian, his superiors added the disparaging comment: 'Suspicious. To be listed with telegrams intended as provocations.'[167] Stalin had long been disparaging about Sorge, dismissing the man risking his life for Soviet intelligence as 'a little shit'.[168] The Stalinist system was at all levels preprogrammed to supply the Soviet dictator with confirmation of his own prejudice.

On 12 June Stalin, Molotov and Beria received information provided by 'Starshina' (Schulze-Boysen) of talk within the upper echelons of the Luftwaffe and Air Ministry indicating that a decision had been made to attack the USSR. Whether demands would be made of the Soviet Union beforehand or whether there would be a surprise attack was unknown.[169] The same day, a report reached the Foreign Ministry and Central Committee noting a total of 2,080 violations of the Soviet border by German aeroplanes between 1 January and 10 June, some penetrating as far as sixty miles or so into districts with defence fortifications and large troop concentrations. Ninety-one planes had violated the borders during the first ten days of June. One military plane, which had flown a hundred and twenty miles into Soviet territory and been forced to land, had on board maps and aerial photographs of a region in the Ukraine.[170] On 17 June, another report from 'Starshina', based within Luftwaffe headquarters, told Stalin, Molotov and Beria that all German military measures for an attack on the USSR were complete, and that the blow could come at any time. The report gave a list of immediate bombing targets and the designated German heads of the future occupied territories.[171] Two days later a Soviet agent in Rome passed on information, said to be derived from the Italian ambassador in Moscow, Augusto Rosso, that Germany would attack the USSR sometime between 20 and 25 June.[172] In mid-June information came in from 'Lucy' (an émigré German anti-Fascist publisher, named Rudolf Rössler), a Soviet agent based in Lucerne, in Switzerland, stipulating the date of the attack (22 June) and providing details of the German operational plan.[173] 'Ramzai' (Sorge) in Tokyo reported on 20 June the view of Ambassador Ott that war was inevitable, and that the German military believed Soviet defences to be weaker than those of Poland.[174] On the same day the Soviet agent in Sofia informed Moscow that the attack would come on either 21 or 22 June.[175] Nor were the danger signs to be derived only from intelligence reports. By now, most of the German embassy staff, in a state of great nervousness, had left Moscow. Italian, Romanian and Hungarian embassy staff swiftly followed.[176]

However, Soviet distrust of reports from agents and from foreign intelligence services continued unabated. The distrust was, as before, especially pronounced towards Britain – perhaps in part a veiled reflection of Stalin's belief that the British would act with equal duplicity to his own double-dealing in 1939. On 14 June the official Soviet news organ, *Tass*, published a communiqué denouncing British press rumours of imminent war between

Germany and the USSR. Molotov later claimed the *Tass* communiqué had been 'a last resort. If we had managed to delay the war for the summer, it would have been very difficult to start it in the fall.'[177] Reports of the rumours had been passed to Moscow by the Soviet ambassador in London, Ivan Maisky, who continued to believe that German troop movements on the Soviet border were just a part of Hitler's 'war of nerves'.[178] Stalin hoped, by publishing the communiqué, to elicit an equivalent denunciation from the German side of the rumours. None was forthcoming.[179]

In fact, British intelligence, long convinced that German troop movements were to exert pressure on the Soviet Union, had by now changed its tune and become – belatedly – convinced that an invasion of the USSR was imminent.[180] The head of the Foreign Office, Sir Alexander Cadogan, barely able to believe that Hitler might invade the Soviet Union in preference to exploiting his conquests in the Balkans to attack the British in north Africa and the Middle East, nevertheless summoned Maisky to his office on 16 June and passed on precise and detailed evidence of the imminent threat. Maisky, himself greatly disturbed by the reports, relayed the information to Moscow, though with the usual caveats to meet the expectations of his leaders.[181]

The information, like other British warnings, was taken with a large pinch of salt in Moscow. But one of the last warnings received before the German onslaught was from a recognized friend, the Chinese Communist leader Mao Zedong. On 21 June, Georgi Dimitrov, the General Secretary of the Comintern Executive Committee, noted in his diary that he had received a telegram from Mao. It stated that Germany would attack that very day. Dimitrov noted that rumours of such an attack were mounting on all sides. He telephoned Molotov to ask about the position to be adopted by Communist parties. Molotov's reply was that 'it was all a game'.[182] He said he would speak with Comrade Stalin about it.[183]

He knew what response to expect. Stalin remained in complete denial. His position throughout had been: he knew best. Given the structure of leadership and decision-making in the Soviet Union, together with the fear of recrimination that underpinned any perceived opposition, it was difficult even to put a countervailing argument, let alone to persuade Stalin that he was wrong. So the other Soviet leaders, from conviction or convenience, were compliant. Even on the day before the German invasion, Beria wrote to Stalin criticizing the increasingly urgent warnings from one of his own acolytes, the Soviet ambassador in Berlin, Dekanozov. He told Stalin of his view that Dekanozov should be dismissed and punished 'because he is bombarding me incessantly with disinformation. Hitler is allegedly preparing an invasion of the USSR. Now, he [Dekanozov] has told me that this invasion is to begin tomorrow.'[184] Stalin's own obscenity about what he took to be disinformation was cited near the beginning of this chapter. The vehemence of his outburst was, nevertheless, in all probability a sign of his own inner doubts that he had been right all along. The problem was that his stance had dictated policy at every stage. And now Stalin, paralysed by his own analysis into inaction, had no alternative to offer. When a German deserter, a former Communist, appeared at a border post in the Ukraine at 8 p.m. on the evening of 21 June, saying that Hitler's forces would invade next morning, Stalin was at least anxious enough to agree to Zhukov's directive to warn all military districts of a possible surprise attack at dawn and ordered all units to be made ready for combat. But it was far too little, and far too late. And even now Stalin still thought that 'perhaps the question can be settled peacefully'.[185]

Whatever his inner doubts, his unwavering conviction for so long that he was right, in the face of mounting evidence to the contrary, had left Stalin with no choice but to believe – or perhaps just to hope – that he was not wrong.

He was. His illusions were shattered by a telephone call from Zhukov at 3.40 a.m. on the morning of 22 June. A massive German attack had started on all parts of the western front. The war had begun.

VII

Stalin was speechless when he heard the news. All Zhukov could hear was his heavy breathing on the telephone. Stalin gave no immediate orders for countermeasures. He told Zhukov and Timoshenko to go straight away to the Kremlin. Members of the Politburo were also summoned. The meeting, under the direst circumstances imaginable, finally began at 5.45 a.m., Moscow time, just over an hour after the attack had started. Astonishingly, Stalin thought the attack might have been unleashed as a provocation by German officers acting on their own initiative. 'Hitler simply does not know about it,' he stated. He poured out his bile on Ribbentrop instead. For some time, Stalin did not rule out the possibility that the attack was to intimidate the Soviet Union into political submission. He would not order action by the Red Army until he had heard from Berlin.

Schulenburg was contacted and told to come immediately. He had, in fact, been trying to arrange a meeting with Molotov. When he arrived, Schulenburg read out a telegram that had arrived at 3 a.m., Berlin time, stating that Germany had been forced to take 'countermeasures' against the concentration of Soviet forces. Schulenburg spoke of his own 'despondency, caused by the inexcusable and unexpected action of his own government'. Shocked and angry, Molotov retorted that it was 'a breach of confidence unprecedented in history'. He returned to Stalin's office to announce that Germany had declared war on the Soviet Union.[186]

Stalin received the news in silence. He seemed shocked, tired and depressed. But he soon pulled himself together. 'The enemy will be beaten all along the line,' he declared.[187] At this stage, he was unaware of the full scale of the disaster that was unfolding. He still thought the Red Army could swiftly turn the tables on the enemy and inflict a crushing defeat on the German invaders. The directive that Timoshenko composed (though it bore Stalin's imprint) and dispatched to all military districts at 7.15 a.m. ordered Red Army units to 'use all their strength and means to come down on the enemy's forces and destroy them where they have violated the Soviet border'. But a Soviet offensive was still held back. 'Until further orders, ground troops are not to cross the border,' ran the directive. Meanwhile, the enemy's aircraft would be destroyed on the ground and bombing raids carried out up to a hundred miles into German territory.[188] In fact, by now much of the Soviet air force had already been put out of action. The unreality of the directive was compounded by another, fourteen hours later, that still spoke of taking the area of Lublin – fifty-five miles inside German-occupied Poland.[189]

Nevertheless, during the course of the day consciousness of the scale of the calamity began to become clear. At midday, Molotov – not Stalin (subdued, and unable to announce the beginning of the war)[190] – spoke to the Soviet people. With a slight nervous stammer, he told them of 'an unparalleled act of perfidy in the history of civilised nations'. He referred to losses of two hundred.[191] The address, heard by fearful and incredulous citizens, listening in border areas as bombs rained down from the skies, ended with words drafted by Stalin: 'Our cause is just, the enemy will be smashed, victory will be ours.'[192] Stalin himself was meanwhile immersed in non-stop meetings, issuing decrees and directives and trying to ascertain the seriousness of the invasion. Only that afternoon, when the Politburo met at 4.00 p.m., did the full gravity of what had happened become apparent. Timoshenko reported that the severity of the German attack had exceeded all expectations. The Soviet air force and border forces had experienced heavy losses. Some 1,200 planes had been lost, 800 of them destroyed on the ground. German forces were advancing rapidly into the heart of the country. Almost unbelievably, Minsk, the capital of Belorussia, was under threat. Stalin thought that 'inconceivable', branded the invasion a 'monstrous crime' and angrily declared that heads would roll.[193] Among the first was to be that of General Pavlov, the Commander-in-Chief of the western front, who would be executed within a month along with three other front commanders. Even Stalin thought the charges of 'anti-Soviet military conspiracy' were absurd. But he confirmed the sentences, and wanted the fronts to be informed 'so they know that defeatists will be punished without mercy'. Eight generals in all were shot – scapegoats for the debacle.[194]

The news from the front worsened by the day. By 28 June that which Stalin had described as 'inconceivable' – the fall of Minsk, laying open the way to Smolensk and Moscow itself – had happened. As many as 400,000 Soviet troops had been trapped in the German encirclement. In no more than a week the Wehrmacht had advanced some 300 miles into Soviet territory. The psychological shock of what had happened now hit Stalin. For two days he did not appear in the Kremlin. He could not be contacted. In self-confinement at his dacha, he appears to have been briefly in a state of near nervous collapse. Finally, the members of his inner circle plucked up courage to drive out to his dacha. They found him looking haggard and depressed, seemingly nervous at the arrival of his leading henchmen. If, as was later claimed (probably with some exaggeration), he thought they might have come to hold him to account for his failings, and to depose him, he had nothing to fear. They persuaded him to return to the Kremlin, now as chairman of a newly formed State Defence Committee, an all-powerful small War Cabinet, with wide-ranging powers. Next day, 1 July, he was back in the Kremlin, and in full control. Two days later, he gave a powerful address to the nation, combining patriotic rhetoric with threats of merciless reprisals 'against cowards, panic-mongers and deserters'.[195] The low point of Stalin's personal adjustment to the disaster that had befallen the Soviet Union had passed.

At this very time, even so, Stalin, together with Molotov and Beria, seems to have been secretly contemplating putting out feelers to Hitler to see what his conditions would be for halting the attack. The idea was to win more time for the USSR to regather military strength. The cession to Germany of substantial territory, including the Baltic republics, the Ukraine and Bessarabia, was mooted. Molotov apparently spoke of a second Brest-Litovsk treaty, referring to the amputation of Russian territory that ended Russian participation in the First World War. If Lenin could do it, such was the implication, it could be done again – a lesser evil, to cut losses, and prepare militarily for a time when the lost lands could be recovered. According to the postwar testimony of General Pavel Sudoplatov, then deputy head of the NKVD's intelligence section, he was assigned to put the proposals, under conditions of the highest secrecy, to a trusted intermediary, the Bulgarian ambassador to Moscow, Ivan Stamenov, in a Moscow restaurant. The meeting took place. But Stamenov appears to have thought his interlocutor was eliciting his own impressions of whether it was worthwhile passing the information to Berlin. His view, perhaps tailored to what he thought his dinner companion wanted to hear, was that Soviet superiority would ultimately prevail. Germany would be defeated in the war. Whether or not he had misinterpreted what was expected of him, Stamenov passed on no message. Sudoplatov himself reported back to Beria and the issue was quietly dropped.[196]

According to Zhukov, Stalin considered putting out peace-feelers on a second occasion.[197] This was in October 1941, soon after the advancing German army had smashed the Soviet front line in the great encirclements at Brjansk and Viaz'ma, where as many as 673,000 Red Army soldiers were captured. If there were such thoughts, they could only have arisen out of desperation. But the second story of possible peace overtures sounds implausible. The chances of Hitler stopping with Moscow apparently at his mercy would have been remote. In any case, no overtures were made.

Moscow was, however, indeed by now within the sights of the Wehrmacht. The deepest crisis in that crisis-ridden year was mounting for the the increasingly panic-stricken population of the Soviet capital. When the Germans broke through the capital's main strategic defence on the night of 14–15 October, the survival not only of Moscow, but of the Soviet state itself, was in question. The State Defence Committee ordered the evacuation of most of the government to Kuibyshev, on the Volga 400 miles to the south-east. Factories and industrial installations were made ready for detonation. So was the Moscow underground. The moves reflected a belief among the top Soviet leadership that Moscow could soon fall to the Germans.[198] Among ordinary Muscovites, what came to be known as 'the big skedaddle' began, as hundreds of thousands voted with their feet and rushed to leave the city.[199] Possibly a fifth of the city's population took flight as the panic spread.[200] Lenin's embalmed body was removed from its Kremlin mausoleum and shipped east, to be secretly housed in a former Tsarist school.[201] Preparations were made for Stalin, too, to leave Moscow. His dacha near the city was mined. Offices and a bomb shelter had been made ready for him at Kuibyshev. A plane waited to transport him out of Moscow. So did a special train.[202] Beria was encouraging the complete relocation of the government to Kuibyshev. Stalin faced another vital decision. According to testimony, if at a much later date, from Nikolai Vasilievich Ponomariov, in 1941 a military liaison communications officer in Stalin's entourage, he was told on the evening of 16 October to prepare for immediate evacuation and driven to the railway station. Stalin's bodyguards were on the platform. The train was ready for departure, but Stalin never appeared. Zhukov, it seems, had persuaded him that Moscow could be held.[203] Stalin stayed. When asked at a later date what would have resulted from a different decision by Stalin, to leave the city and move to Kuibyshev, Molotov replied: 'Moscow would have burned.' He went on to say that the Germans would have taken the city, the Soviet Union would have collapsed and this would have led to the break-up of the coalition against Hitler.[204] This was, perhaps, an over-dramatic surmise. But Stalin's decision to stay was unquestionably an important boost to morale for the city of Moscow, and for the Soviet Union generally. Word rapidly circulated. The strong Leader was still at the helm, and would stay with his people in the capital. The immediate crisis subsided. The panic dissipated as quickly as it had arisen. But the danger was still not at an end.

The tide of the German onslaught would only be stemmed in the first successful counter-offensive of the Red Army, in December 1941, with the spearhead of the Wehrmacht on the outskirts of Moscow. It was a turning point. Never again would the threat be so grave. For the hitherto all-conquering Wehrmacht, the winter crisis before Moscow was a key moment. In retrospect, it is not too fanciful to see in it the beginning of the end for the Third Reich. For the Soviet Union, there were still many dark days ahead before victory was achieved. By that date, 8 May 1945, huge tracts of the country were in ruins and some twenty-five million Soviet citizens lay dead. The cost of Stalin's decision that he knew best had been colossal.

VIII

The scale of the catastrophe was unprecedented in history. And it followed what still stands out as one of the most extraordinary miscalculations of all time. Stalin had, as we have detailed, repeatedly drawn the wrong conclusion about German intentions, even down to the eve of the invasion. Attempts to satisfy German economic demands continued to the last. Warnings from all sides were ignored. Those who tried to press arguments to the contrary were treated with contempt. Stalin was insistent: he understood how Hitler thought. The German dictator would attack; but not yet. Hitler's first priority, he was sure, was the economic exploitation of the USSR.

The insistence upon economic appeasement rested upon this disastrous misconception.[205] With unfinished business in the west, Hitler's early priority had to be Soviet submission, not all-out war. This would win Germany benefits for an economy in trouble, and it would put further pressure on the west. Meanwhile, furious Soviet rearmament would continue. If peace negotiations should take place, the Soviet Union needed to be involved, and from a position of strength. Even as the danger signs mounted, Stalin was confident that he could defer conflict with Germany throughout the spring and summer of 1941. By then it would be too late to invade that year. And by 1942, the Soviet Union would be ready for Hitler. Stalin's thinking ran roughly along such lines. His conviction that he was right, and that all warnings to the contrary were disinformation or were hopelessly wrong misreadings of the situation, became ever more entrenched. The combination of fear, subservience and admiration that underpinned the Soviet dictator's autocracy meant that serious alternatives could scarcely be proposed, let alone adopted. But what might the alternatives have been? What options existed to avoid the calamity?

Molotov, at Stalin's right hand the entire time, persistently took the view that whatever mistakes were made were unavoidable.[206] Khrushchev, by contrast, castigated Stalin's miscalculations and errors of leadership in his denunciation of the dead dictator, in 1956, blaming them on the arbitrary actions of one man who had accumulated total power.[207] This heavy personalization of responsibility conveniently exonerated those, not excluding Khrushchev himself, who had applauded Stalin and supported his policies. It also largely whitewashed the military leadership – though their own shortcomings cannot be entirely laid at Stalin's door. More recent research has qualified this assessment. Even so, Khrushchev's withering verdict still has wide currency. The realistic choices confronting Stalin are seldom posed. And yet, one leading authority, who has subjected the evidence to meticulous scrutiny, concluded that 'Stalin's failure to prepare for the German onslaught primarily reflected the unappealing political choices which the Soviet Union faced before the outbreak of the Second World War', adding that 'even with hindsight, it is hard to devise alternatives which Stalin could have safely pursued'.[208]

What does seem obvious is that whatever options Stalin might have had narrowed sharply over time. Earlier decisions, and the thinking that lay behind them, had necessarily meant that by the eve of the German invasion his room for manoeuvre had become greatly constrained. But some years before this, his hands had been less tied. It was then that he made a catastrophic error that limited his later options.

With no external pressure, he instigated in 1937, as we noted earlier, the decimation of his army leadership, with immeasurably harmful consequences for the rebuilding of a professionalized military force capable of countering the rapidly growing danger from Hitler's Germany. Apart from the phantoms in the minds of Stalin and his acolytes, the purges lacked all rationale. They were wholly unnecessary. Stalin was not compelled to have the purges carried out; he chose this option. But not only did they do incalculable damage to the future construction of Soviet military strength; they also instilled in Hitler and his advisers an indelible notion of the weakness of the Red Army. To Hitler, this very weakness was an invitation to strike before a powerful military machine could be constructed. In Hitler's eyes, then, Stalin's purges gave him the chance. He thought Stalin must be mad. As early as 1937 he had remarked: 'Russia knows nothing other than Bolshevism. That is the danger which we will have to knock down sometime.'[209] In choosing to destroy his army leadership, Stalin removed his most important backbone of strength at a later date, when the crisis unfolded. An immense effort was put into a crash programme of rearmament and militarization in 1940 and 1941. But too much ground had been lost. It could not be completed before the German threat became overwhelming. That Stalin had left himself with too little military room for manoeuvre in 1940–41 is in good measure attributable, therefore, to the choice he made in 1937–8 to undermine his own military capacity. And this was just as Europe was being thrown into upheaval by the German incorporation of Austria and much of Czechoslovakia, with the complicity of the hapless western democracies.

By 1939, with war looming in Europe, Stalin now faced a second, highly unenviable choice. Should he ally himself with the western democracies, whom he intensely distrusted, or with Nazi Germany, the ideological arch-enemy? This, indeed, turned into a fateful choice. We have noted the plausible reasoning that made Stalin, in August 1939, opt for a pact with Hitler. Britain and France had shown little appetite for an alliance with the Soviet Union. Stalin, along with other Soviet leaders, thought western motives were scarcely less cynical than Hitler's. At least a pact with Germany would provide some breathing space. And it held out the prospect of Germany and the western powers fighting each other to a standstill, to the ultimate benefit of the Soviet Union.

What the consequences might have been in the unlikely event of Stalin joining forces with the west can only be a matter of counter-factual speculation. Hitler's attack on Poland would have been riskier in such an eventuality. And those in high places within Germany, fearful of the consequences of involvement in a general European war against powerful enemies, would have had their hand strengthened. Hitler postponed the mobilization against Poland once, at the last minute, and might have been further deterred had he faced a triple alliance of the USSR and the western powers, a reconstitution of the anti-German coalition of 1914. But he might have gone ahead and invaded Poland anyway.[210] The western democracies would probably still have done nothing militarily to help Poland.[211] In such circumstances, the Soviet Union would also have most likely refrained from direct conflict, but would have found Germany after victory in Poland not as an ally but, instead, as an enemy on her doorstep. Perhaps, then, a German attack on the Soviet Union would have come earlier than it did. On the other hand, Hitler's big western offensive in spring 1940 (which greatly upset Stalin's calculations) would have been far more hazardous with a hostile Soviet Union poised in the east. Who knows how it might have turned out? The guessing-game is pointless. The variables in the equation are simply too many to make speculation fruitful.

What does seem apparent, however, is that Stalin was too blinkered by his ideological preconceptions to allow the Soviet Union to play other than a passive role in dealings with the west in the summer of 1939.[212] It was certainly the case that Britain and France did little during those months to expedite the 'grand alliance' that might have been the last hope of blocking Hitler. They had scant interest in joining forces with the detested and distrusted Soviet Union. The negotiations as European war grew close were predictably sluggish. But the Soviet Union was also locked into passivity. More urgent and determined diplomacy on Stalin's part could conceivably have paved the way, despite British and French hesitations, for a new triple alliance with the west. It would at the very least have given Hitler and the German ruling elites pause for thought. However, Stalin was content to let the negotiations with the western democracies drift on while the war clouds gathered ominously. The result was that inaction from the Soviet, not just the western, side eventually pushed the choice towards that which made most sense in terms of the USSR's security at the time, the pact with Hitler's Germany.

Stalin saw the pact as a great Soviet diplomatic coup. But in practice it worked more in favour of Germany than of the Soviet Union. Certainly, the USSR was able to extend its defensive frontiers westwards through territorial aggrandizement. And the removal of the imminent threat from Germany allowed time to rebuild the Red Army and prepare defences. Obviously, however, the time was insufficient. The rebuilding was flawed and inadequate. And the Germans, too, were given time to make themselves ready, not just militarily, but also in the spread of diplomatic sway. During 1940, after the German victory over France had completely upturned the balance of power in Europe, Hitler was able to exert increasing influence over the countries of the Danube basin. German dominance in Romania, especially, and the vain attempts by Stalin and Molotov to prevent the Balkans and, in the north, Finland falling within the German orbit led to the growing tension that was so manifest in the visit of Molotov to Berlin in November 1940. Mussolini's Balkan adventure had meanwhile destabilized the region even further. And by the following spring, German intervention in Yugoslavia and Greece squeezed out any last hope of Soviet influence in south-eastern Europe (as well as contributing to the concealment of 'Barbarossa', since Stalin could see little sense in Hitler striking to the east that year immediately following his conquests in the Balkans).[213] The Soviet Union was now fully isolated. Turkey, the gateway to the Black Sea, remained neutral, though relatively well disposed towards Great Britain. Otherwise, the USSR was more or less ringed in the west by countries under German influence. The pact had brought short-term advantage to the Soviet Union, but over its duration the danger from Germany had become greatly magnified. Whether Stalin made the right choice in 1939 might, therefore, be justifiably questioned.

Between August 1939 and June 1941, Stalin's policy, as we have seen, was consistently to rearm with all speed, but to mollify Germany as far as possible. He was not naive enough to believe that conflict with Germany could be avoided. He had read and digested the parts of *Mein Kampf* that advocated the winning of 'living space' in the east. But he thought he could head off trouble until 1942, and he believed he could 'read' Hitler's intentions: to force the Soviet Union into political submission before reaching a settlement with Britain and only then to turn his aggression eastwards. Stalin thought Hitler would act with the same cold, brutal rationality that he himself would have deployed. Sure that Hitler would pose an ultimatum before any attack (a German deception that Stalin swallowed), he felt confident that he could win time. Meanwhile, the least provocation had to be avoided. This was doubly important, from Stalin's point of view, since the Soviet Union continued to face the additional, if lesser, threat from the east, from Japan. But it made him excessively cautious.[214] Was there an alternative to this policy?

Stalin's policy of avoiding war at all costs was strongly criticized, many years later, by Marshal Alexander Mikhailovich Vasilevsky, deputy head of the operational administration of the General Staff in 1941 and from

1942 to 1945 chief of the General Staff and Deputy Commissar for Defence.[215] Vasilevsky claimed that

> Stalin did not grasp the limit beyond which such a line became not only unnecessary, but dangerous. Such a limit should have been correctly determined, the armed forces brought to full combat readiness at the maximum possible speed, accelerated mobilisation carried out, and the country converted into a single armed camp. While trying to put off armed conflict, whatever hidden work was possible should have been carried out and completed earlier. There was more than enough evidence that Germany planned a military attack on our country . . . We had come, due to circumstances beyond our control, to the Rubicon of war, and it was necessary determinedly to take a step forward.[216]

Rearmament and militarization were, in fact, as we noted, under way at a frantic pace during 1940 and 1941. But Vasilevsky was emphatic that much more should have been done: early and full mobilization of the armed forces for combat readiness. The implication is that the policy of non-provocation had reached a point where it had become highly dangerous. Full mobilization should have been undertaken at this point. The risk of an earlier German attack would have had to be borne. But it would have been a risk worth taking. As Stalin's military advisers knew, the earliest the Germans could have invaded was, in fact, when they did attack, in spring 1941. The worst that 'provocation' could have achieved, in other words, was what took place anyway (though Stalin had wanted to avoid what he probably for long envisaged as limited German action, not necessarily all-out war, to seize border territory and compel greater economic dependence).[217]

They also knew that in summer 1940 the Japanese leadership had opted for the advance to the south. A prior attack by Japan from the east could, therefore, be as good as ruled out.[218] A show of deterrence, rather than allowing the German build-up to take place unchallenged over so many months, might, then, have proved successful in staving off the attack for the few precious months of the summer of 1941. Moreover, advertising Soviet strength would have countered the overriding image of the Red Army's weakness that prevailed within the German leadership. Instead, Stalin, petrified about offering any provocation, allowed repeated German reconnaissance flights to take photographs recording precise details of Soviet military installations and troop placements, evidence which confirmed the impression that the Wehrmacht would sweep through the Red Army's ranks.[219] Stalin was unquestionably in an unenviable position. But the preference for non-provocation over deterrence was another fateful choice.

By June 1941 the options had drastically diminished. As we noted, Zhukov later acknowledged that Stalin's rejection of the pre-emptive strike plan of 15 May 1941 had been correct. To pursue the plan would have courted even greater disaster. As it was, the frontier defences were hopelessly stretched, divisions badly deployed, fortifications incomplete.[220] To compound the problem, Soviet military planning in 1940 and 1941 had anticipated the main German thrust in any attack coming through southern Poland, south of the Pripet marshes. And this is where the bulk of the Soviet forces were arrayed in June 1941. But, completely unanticipated by the Red Army command, the crushing German advance, when it came, was through the central area of the front, north of the Pripet marshes, in the direction of Minsk, Smolensk and Moscow.[221] Collectively, then endorsed by Stalin, the Soviet military leadership had disastrously chosen the wrong option.

Ultimately, the failings were those of a system of highly personalized rule. 'Stalin was the greatest authority for all of us, and it never occurred to anybody to question his opinion and assessment of the situation,' Zhukov later commented.[222] In a climate of fear and sycophancy, where one individual's paranoid phobias, sense of his own infallible judgement, limitations in military strategy and ruthless unpredictability had become decisive structural components of the Soviet system, there could be no correctives to Stalin's preferred options. Toadying, at all levels, was endemic. The Politburo kowtowed. The military were generally no different and, when voicing reservations, were browbeaten into submission. The refusal of the Soviet dictator to accede to requests from his commanders, only a week or so before the invasion, to have troops at battle readiness in better defensive positions was symptomatic of a system where reason had lost its way.

Stalin's despairing obscenity, days after the invasion, with which this chapter began, is easy to understand. It reflected his own sense that the Soviet leadership collectively, and he personally, had made a calamitous miscalculation. In the end, for all the self-deception and delusions, his options could be narrowed down to a straightforward choice: was he to do everything imaginable to prepare the Soviet Union for war with Germany in 1941 (which could not objectively be ruled out), or persist in his belief (with attendant risks) that conflict could be postponed until 1942? Did he, putting it another way, prefer to work on the basis of a best-case or worst-case scenario? The answer is obvious. It was indeed a fateful choice. And yet, the path to that choice had been anything but a straight one. Even at this distance, it is impossible to be certain about what would have been the most advantageous turning at the crucial junctions. What can be plainly seen is that the choices Stalin made courted disaster. The astonishing recovery from that disaster is another story.

7

Washington, DC,
Summer–Autumn 1941

Roosevelt Decides to Wage Undeclared War

*If he were to put the issue of peace and war to Congress, they
would debate it for three months. The President had said he would
wage war, but not declare it, and that he would become more and
more provocative ... He would look for an 'incident' which
would justify him in opening hostilities.*

Churchill's report of President Roosevelt's remarks,
19 August 1941

The German invasion of the Soviet Union on 22 June 1941 took the
emerging global conflict onto a new plane. Fresh hope for the western allies,
Great Britain and the United States, but also fresh uncertainties, entered
the picture. The administration of President Franklin D. Roosevelt needed
to reconsider the strategic options.

Germany was now involved in a war on two fronts. When Britain and
the United States were most fearing a major thrust to north Africa and the
Middle East following the German dominance of the Balkans in spring
1941, Hitler had chosen to attack the Soviet Union. The defeat of Great
Britain by armed invasion, which had seemed such a danger – to the defence
of the United States, too – in the summer of 1940, and had appeared to
remain a distinct possibility as late as spring 1941, had now receded (though
not completely vanished). And a new, potentially powerful, if for the
western partners uncomfortable, ally had been forced to enter the arena in
the defence against Hitler's Germany. All this posed grounds for optimism
at a point when the fortunes of war had seemed bleak.

But there were also great uncertainties. First and foremost, would the
Soviet Union hold out against Hitler's onslaught? The United States War
Department advised President Roosevelt that Hitler's forces would conquer
the Soviet Union within a period of one to three months. British military
authorities took a similar view. They thought Hitler's eastern campaign

would be over in six to eight weeks. After that, Hitler would transfer his forces to the west. The invasion of the United Kingdom could only be seen as temporarily postponed.[1] With Germany, after defeating the Soviet Union, master of effectively the entire European continent, an invasion might not even be necessary to force Britain to the negotiating table. At any rate, the question of how the United States should react in the changed circumstances allowed more than one answer.

In Britain, Churchill, exultant at the new development, did not hesitate for an instant and immediately committed Britain to aid for the Soviet Union, a step on the way to full-scale military alliance. Ideological differences were completely subordinated to practical necessity (even if Churchill, behind the public gestures, had in mind only limited measures of support, aimed at keeping the Soviet Union in the war).[2] Britain had nothing to lose and everything to gain from such an alliance in the fight against Hitler. For the United States it was less straightforward. Hostility to Communism was both widespread and deep-seated. Many, not just among isolationists, thought it to be no bad thing if the Nazis and Bolsheviks fought themselves to a standstill, imposing maximum destruction on each other and avoiding in the process any American commitment to the conflict. Since neither posed an imminent threat, nothing like the same urgency as in Britain was felt about the need to jump into bed with Stalin. In any case, if victory in the east were to go Hitler's way, and within a matter of weeks, there was little to be said for dispatching arms and equipment much needed for American defences to the Soviet Union. They would not arrive in time to make any difference in the conflict, and at the expected Soviet defeat would merely fall into the hands of the Nazis. A more sensible strategy would surely be to bolster Britain's chances in the subsequent struggle when Hitler once more turned westwards, as part of the United States' own defence.[3] One option was, therefore, simply to wait and see how the war in the Soviet Union would turn out before taking any action.

Another uncertainty was how Japan would react to the dramatic new turn of events. Thanks to the ability (through the appropriately codenamed MAGIC intelligence intercepts) to read dispatches from Tokyo to the embassy in Washington, the Roosevelt administration knew what was in the minds of Japan's leaders, an inestimable advantage.[4] The President's advisers were aware of the sharp division of opinion in Tokyo about moving swiftly to take advantage of the German invasion by attacking the Soviet Union from the east (a policy fervently advocated by the Foreign Minister, Matsuoka Yosuke), or adhering to the previously agreed strategy of the southern advance. Fending off an attack from the east as well as trying to cope with the inroads Hitler's troops were making in the west would plainly have weakened the Soviet Union's chances of holding out. That in turn would have enhanced a policy of extreme caution in offering aid to Stalin. By early July, however, policy-makers in Washington had learned, through MAGIC, that Japan's leaders had confirmed the southern advance and would make no strike against the Soviet Union, at least until they were sure that Hitler was conclusively winning. This was clearly a boost to Stalin's chances of survival.

On the other hand, the imminent expansionist course in south-east Asia pushed Japan inexorably towards a clash with the United States. Though President Roosevelt still hoped to keep Japan quiet in order to deal with what was still regarded as the greater threat of Hitler across the Atlantic, the question of what to do in the Pacific had become an urgent one. On 1 July, still unsure what course the Japanese would adopt, Roosevelt told Harold Ickes, his Secretary of the Interior, that it was 'terribly important for the control of the Atlantic for us to help to keep peace in the Pacific'. He added: 'I simply have not got enough Navy to go round – and every little episode in the Pacific means fewer ships in the Atlantic.'[5]

A day later the Japanese decision not to reverse policy in favour of the northern option and to go south after all was made. Aware through MAGIC of Tokyo's plans, the President now came under increasing pressure from the hawks in his administration to curb Japanese belligerency. On 10 July he let the British know that he 'would immediately impose various embargoes, both economic and financial', in the event of Japan taking 'any overt step' in south-east Asia.[6] The Japanese invasion of southern Indochina which began on 24 July soon emerged as that 'overt step'. Before the end of the month all Japanese assets in the United States were frozen and supplies of oil to Japan, essential for the construction of the 'Greater East Asia Co-Prosperity Sphere', were embargoed. With those steps, the showdown in the Pacific loomed.

For now, however, we turn away from Japan to examine the ways in which the Roosevelt administration faced the greater threat, as it saw it, of the war in Europe in the changed circumstances following the German invasion of the Soviet Union. And here, though the circumstances had altered, Roosevelt's basic dilemma had not. The issue that still faced him was how to provide maximum aid for Britain (and now, he thought an imperative, to the Soviet Union too), a policy supported by the majority of the population, without involving the United States directly in the war, which the American people overwhelmingly opposed.

An immediate issue, already mentioned, was the question of providing material aid to the Soviet Union through extending lend-lease. Though no immediate decision was taken to do so, early measures were taken to meet Soviet orders for goods, and by November the Soviet Union had indeed become eligible for lend-lease.[7] A second, and far more hazardous, question was how to approach, from the standpoint of neutrality, the battle raging in the Atlantic. Here, Roosevelt's dilemma posed itself in increasingly sharp contours. It made little sense to provide goods for Britain if they were merely to find their way to the bottom of the Atlantic. But helping to protect the transit of the vital material against the raids of U-boats ran the obvious and increasing risk of dragging the United States into the war. Given the continuing voluble isolationist lobby, the high-decibel publicity campaign against intervention by the America First organization, and the strength of opposition (from a variety of motives) certain to be encountered in Congress to moves seen as likely to lead towards involvement in the European war, Roosevelt felt justified in continuing his difficult balancing-act of placating public opinion while running ever greater risks of armed confrontation in an 'undeclared war'.

On more than one occasion, the President would imply that he was seeking an incident to remove his dilemma. Yet when incidents did arise in the autumn months, he fought shy of exploiting them fully to take the United States directly into the war. Despite the convictions of many of his detractors, at the time and since, that the President was actively seeking to take his country to war, his actions suggest that he did want to avoid it as long as possible while simultaneously recognizing that America's involvement at some point had become inevitable. He knew in any case that his chances, even as tensions rose across the autumn, of obtaining a declaration of war from Congress were as good as nil. But although only Congress could declare war, the Constitution of the United States, as Roosevelt was well aware, accords the President wide powers as Commander-in-Chief to *make* war, even without a formal declaration. Former Presidents had availed themselves of such powers. Later ones would also do so. Roosevelt sought legal confirmation of his constitutional powers to deploy the navy 'in any manner that to him seems proper' in the national interest – that is, in pursuing the 'undeclared war' with Hitler's U-boats in the Atlantic.[8]

As the war had widened over the previous twelve months or so, Roosevelt's own options had, in fact, narrowed. In the aftermath of the German invasion of the Soviet Union, the President faced the inexorable logic of the decisions he had taken earlier to assist Great Britain. True, he could have resisted the extension of lend-lease to the Soviet Union. He was under no pressure from public opinion to assist Stalin. And, certainly in the first weeks after the German invasion, there were differing views among his advisers on the merits of providing aid. Here, the President himself took the lead. He pushed for aid to Russia. It proved not only a logical step, but a vitally important one, which over time would make a significant contribution to securing victory for the Allies. On the issue of aid to Britain, the President, even had he wanted to do so (which he did not), could not easily have extricated himself from the consequences of the lend-lease decision taken at the start of the year. Only had Britain been overrun by Hitler's troops and forced into capitulation following a rapid German victory in the east could Roosevelt have terminated lend-lease and pulled back from the commitment to the British war effort. But since more optimistic signs of protracted Soviet defence soon became evident, there was everything to gain from increased aid to Britain (as well as the start of supplies to the Soviet Union).

The inevitable consequence of this was, as already noted, the increase of tension between the United States and Germany in the Atlantic, and the acute problem at home for the President of deciding what to do about the issue of armed escorts for convoys. Since, whatever steps he took, Roosevelt was determined to avoid asking Congress for a declaration of war and running the risk of near-certain political defeat that would completely divide the population and destroy any hope of national unity, this left him only with the option of continuing the policy he had begun the previous year: taking all measures in the fight against Hitler 'short of war'. But 'short of war' had now come to mean 'undeclared war', even to the extent of armed clashes in the Atlantic which, despite the state of non-belligerency that technically prevailed in American-German relations, threatened to explode into all-out conflict. Roosevelt's choice in the summer and autumn of 1941 had narrowed, therefore, to one effectively forced upon him by the decisions he had made earlier, and by the strategic constellation that had emerged. This was to push ever closer to the brink, without going over the edge.

I

In his powerful speech on the evening of 22 June 1941 – heard by millions of Americans as they tuned in to their radios that afternoon across the Atlantic – Winston Churchill had specifically linked the fates of the Soviet Union, Great Britain and the United States in the fight against Hitler's Germany. Hitler's invasion of the Soviet Union, he had stated, 'is no more than a prelude to an attempted invasion of the British Isles'. Doubtless Hitler hoped, he added, 'that all this may be accomplished before the fleet and air power of the United States may intervene'. Should this invasion of Britain take place, he warned, the scene would be set for the final act, 'the subjugation of the Western Hemisphere to his will and to his system'. The conclusion was evident: 'The Russian danger is therefore our danger, and the danger of the United States, just as the cause of any Russian fighting for his hearth and home is the cause of free men and free peoples in every quarter of the globe.'[9]

President Roosevelt was of similar mind, though less decisive in action. A careful (though non-committal) statement put out on 23 June by Sumner Welles (Acting Secretary of State in the temporary absence through illness of Cordell Hull), which the President had approved, indicated that 'any rallying of the forces opposing Hitlerism, from whatever source', would benefit the United States' own defence and security, and ended by re-asserting the administration's long-held view that 'Hitler's armies are today the chief dangers of the Americas'.[10] But the statement offered nothing concrete. Next day, commenting on Welles's statement in a press conference, Roosevelt was more forthright. 'Of course we are going to give all the aid we possibly can to Russia,' he stated.[11] He now released Soviet funds in the United States – amounting to around $40 million – that had previously been frozen, and indicated his readiness to provide aid, noting, however, his ignorance of what was needed. Most significantly, the White House announced on 26 June that the President would not invoke the Neutrality Law against the Soviet Union. This meant that the port of Vladivostok, on the far-eastern rim of the Soviet Union, would, crucially, remain a lifeline for American ships to deliver supplies.[12]

It all pointed in the right direction. But it was no more than a modest start. The President's military advisers favoured a bolder course. Henry Stimson, Secretary of War, had sent Roosevelt a memorandum on 23 June, only a day after the German invasion of the Soviet Union, outlining the thoughts of the leading military strategists in the War Department, including those of the chief of staff, George Marshall. Stimson described Germany's attack as 'an almost providential occurrence', allowing the United States a brief respite in which 'to push with the utmost vigour our movements in the Atlantic theatre of operations' as the best way 'to help Britain, to discourage Germany, and to strengthen our own position of defence against our most imminent danger'. The respite, argued Stimson, would last from one to three months. That time allowed for no hesitation in seizing the initiative.[13] Frank Knox, Secretary of the Navy, agreed. Writing to the President the same day, he saw an opportunity, not to be missed, to 'strike effectively at Germany' – 'the sooner the better'. The President, he asserted, should lose no time in seizing the psychological opportunity to start the escorting of ships. Admiral Harold Stark, chief of Naval Operations, joined in the chorus. With Knox's approval, he proposed that escorting of convoys in the Atlantic should begin immediately, aware that this 'would almost certainly involve us in war', and considering 'every day of delay in our getting into the war as dangerous'.[14]

But the President continued in his policy of 'making haste slowly'.[15] Stimson, frustrated as so often by what he saw as Roosevelt's unwillingness to grasp the nettle, thought that, while Hitler's forces were making spectacular gains in their eastern assault, America had lost her way. He was uncharacteristically pessimistic in his diary entry of 2 July: 'Altogether, tonight I feel more up against it than ever before. It is a problem whether this country has it in itself to meet such an emergency. Whether we are really powerful enough and sincere enough and devoted enough to meet the Germans is getting to be more and more of a real problem.'[16]

Equally hawkish, as usual, was Harold Ickes, Secretary of the Interior. In a letter to the President on 23 June, he wrote: 'It may be difficult to get into this war the right way, but if we do not do it now, we will be, when our turn comes, without an ally anywhere in the world.'[17] Ickes suggested that an embargo on oil to Japan, certain to be popular, would make it possible 'to get into this war in an effective way. And if we should thus indirectly be brought in, we would avoid the criticism that we had gone in as an ally of communistic Russia.'[18] But the likely opposition in the United States even to providing aid for 'communistic Russia' made Roosevelt cautious. Before committing himself, he wanted to test opinion.

It turned out to be predictably split. Isolationists momentarily had a field day. One isolationist Senator expressed the views of many when he said: 'It's a case of dog eat dog. Stalin is as bloody-handed as Hitler. I don't think we should help either one. We should tend to our own business, as we should have been doing all along. The whole business shows the absolute instability of European alliances and points to the necessity of our staying out of all of them.'[19] Vehement anti-Communist Catholics also railed against any support for Stalin's atheistic regime. According to opinion polls, even so, very few Americans favoured a Nazi victory in the bitter struggle raging in eastern Europe. And important news organs recognized that, despite the dislike of Communism, practical realities necessitated as much support as possible for the Soviet Union.[20]

Roosevelt also needed to know what the Soviet Union wanted, whether it could be delivered and that it was not going to be squandered in a rapid defeat by Hitler's forces.[21] On the last consideration, the President had been from the outset among the optimists – far more so than his military advisers – about the prospects of the Red Army holding out. One of those encouraging such optimism, which in the face of the devastating German inroads initially seemed to rest upon little more than unfounded hope, was the former American ambassador in Moscow, Joseph E. Davies, now based at the State Department as Cordell Hull's Special Assistant for War Emergency Problems and Policies. Davies had from the start been a forceful advocate of aid to the Soviet Union. 'This Hitler attack', he had written in his diary on 7 July, 'was a God-given break in the situation for nonaggressor nations and Soviet resistance should be stimulated in every way possible.'[22] In a memorandum compiled a few days later, Davies argued, on the basis of his extensive experience of the Soviet Union, that even should Hitler occupy White Russia and the Ukraine, the likelihood was that Stalin could retreat behind the Urals and continue to fight 'for a considerable time'. It made sense, therefore, also in heading off any possibility of Stalin feeling forced to accept a negotiated settlement with Hitler, to let him know 'that our attitude is "all out" to beat Hitler and that our historic policy of friendliness to Russia still exists'.[23]

On the question of Soviet needs, initial soundings were taken in Moscow within a week of the German invasion. In Washington, a special committee was then immediately set up to deal with Soviet orders. Lend-lease was not contemplated at this stage. It was presumed that supplies would be purchased, not donated, though consideration was given to extending credit over five years or exchanging American equipment for Soviet raw materials. In fact, when the Soviet 'shopping-list' was put before the Cabinet on 18 July it turned out to be enormous. Included were requests for 6,000 planes, 20,000 anti-aircraft guns and industrial plant and equipment to the value of around $50 million. Not only was it a formidable list; the administrative machinery to dispatch any of it was nothing like so streamlined as the establishment of the committee to handle Soviet orders had implied. Foot-dragging and lack of coordination in the half-dozen agencies involved meant irritating inefficiency. The President himself intervened in peremptory fashion at the beginning of August, pointing out that in nearly six weeks little had been done to satisfy Soviet requests so that 'the Russians feel that they have been given the run-around in the United States'.[24] According to Ickes, Roosevelt's intervention – mainly targeting the State Department and War Department – amounted to 'one of the most complete dressings down that I have witnessed'. The President was only too well

aware that if any attempt was to be made to help the Red Army to hold
out until the onset of autumn rain and snow from October onwards could
start to provide a much needed respite from the German onslaught, the
hold-ups had to be bypassed and supplies hastened. 'This was a time to
take some risks,' he felt.[25]

On the day after the presidential outburst, 2 August, the State Department put on record 'that the Government of the United States has decided
to give all economic assistance practicable for the purpose of strengthening the Soviet Union in its struggle against armed aggression'.[26] In fact,
however, early supplies were on a very modest scale. Exports worth only
$6.5 million were dispatched to the Soviet Union in July. Estimates to the
beginning of October totalled no more than $29 million. The immediate
reality was that the Soviet fight for survival against the German invader
down to autumn 1941 had to be sustained with little more than marginal
assistance from the United States.[27]

New life was breathed into the question of aid for the Soviet Union
through the visit to Moscow at the end of July 1941 by Roosevelt's lend-
lease administrator, close confidant and personal emissary, Harry Hopkins,
later described as 'one of the most extraordinarily important and valuable
missions of the whole war'.[28] The mission arose from a personal initiative
of Hopkins himself, swiftly backed by Roosevelt (and receiving the approval
of Sumner Welles, at the State Department). Hopkins had, in fact, suggested
such a mission only three days after 'Barbarossa', and the President had
signalled his assent within twenty-four hours. Sending aid to Russia seemed
infinitely preferable to Roosevelt to having to dispatch American troops to
fight in Europe. Nothing had materialized at that point.[29] Just over a month
later, however, the idea was resuscitated. The outcome was crucial not
simply for the necessary spur it gave to material provision for the Soviet
Union, but also for establishing a direct, personal link, bypassing formal
diplomatic channels, between Roosevelt and Stalin. Hopkins's mission
helped to lay the foundations of the eventual 'grand alliance' of the Soviet
Union, Great Britain and the United States.

The idea of Hopkins going to Moscow arose out of his visit in July to
London to discuss the meeting of Churchill and Roosevelt planned to take
place at sea, near Newfoundland, the following month, as well as matters
relating to lend-lease and questions of overall war strategy. The American
military had been critical of the British diversion of ships and equipment
to the campaign in the Middle East, and urged concentration on the Atlantic
and defence of the British Isles. At his meeting with Hopkins and both
British and American military representatives, Churchill resolutely upheld

the need to reinforce the Middle East and warned of the mounting danger in the Far East. Hopkins realized that information on an essential piece of the strategic jigsaw puzzle – how long the Soviet Union could hold out – was missing. Churchill and Roosevelt, at their planned meeting the following month, would be operating in a vacuum if better information than currently available were not gathered before then. Hopkins suggested he should fly straight away to Moscow to try to find some answers directly from Stalin himself. Roosevelt cabled his immediate approval and sent Stalin a personal letter of introduction to Hopkins. Churchill supplied the transport, and Hopkins – tired, frail and wracked with pain from his long battle with cancer – was within twenty-four hours on his long, hazardous and highly uncomfortable flight across the Arctic route to Archangel, and then on to Moscow.[30]

Hopkins arrived in the Soviet capital on the morning of 30 July 1941. Wearing a homburg lent to him by Churchill (bearing the initials W.S.C. inside the rim) – he had lost his own hat in London – he was by early evening on his way to the Kremlin for a meeting with Stalin himself.[31] They were soon discussing Soviet aid – what was immediately needed, and what would be required for a long war. Stalin stressed the immediate need for anti-aircraft and large-scale machine guns to defend Russian cities. He also urgently wanted a million rifles. In the longer term he required high-octane aviation gasoline and aluminium for aircraft construction, beyond the items on the extensive list already presented in Washington. 'Give us anti-aircraft guns and the aluminium and we can fight for three or four years,' he stated.[32] It was one of a number of comments from Stalin which greatly encouraged Hopkins. Contrary to the initial views of the American military experts, it seemed that there were distinct prospects of the Soviet Union holding out in the face of the German onslaught and sustaining the struggle in a long war.

Hopkins's second lengthy interview with Stalin the following evening was even more instructive. The Soviet leader acknowledged that the Red Army had been caught off guard in a surprise attack, and that he had believed Hitler would not strike.[33] But, without underestimating the German army – capable, he thought, of engaging in a winter campaign in Russia – he was confident that Soviet troops would hold out. (In fact, his predictions of where the German advance would be halted turned out to be highly optimistic. The territorial losses soon became far more severe than he had anticipated.) And once the autumn rains began, he was sure the Germans would have to go on the defensive. He provided Hopkins with details of Soviet armaments and production rates in a display of frankness that Laurence Steinhardt, the American ambassador in Moscow, found astonishing. Asked about the location of munitions plants, Stalin told Hopkins that many of the larger factories had already been dispersed eastwards. He jotted down on a piece of paper a repeated urgent request for guns – anti-aircraft, machine and rifles – and aluminium. And he immediately welcomed Hopkins's suggestion of a tripartite conference of the emerging allies – the Soviet Union, Great Britain and the United States – in Moscow once the front had stabilized, which he presumed would be by October, to explore the relative strategic interests of the three countries and how best to satisfy Soviet requirements.[34]

Finally, after surveying the military situation, Stalin asked Hopkins to pass a personal message to Roosevelt, urging the United States to enter the war against Hitler. He thought Britain and the Soviet Union, without the help of the United States, would find it difficult to crush the German military machine. It was inevitable, in his view, that the United States and Germany would eventually fight each other. Remarkably, he was even prepared – no doubt a sign of his desperation – to welcome American troops on any part of the Russian front and entirely under American control. He ended by stating his confidence that the Red Army could hold out, but added that 'the problem of supply by next spring would be a serious one and that he needed our help'. This part of Hopkins's report was marked 'For the President Only', and kept in a single copy.[35]

Hopkins left Moscow on 1 August, greatly impressed by Stalin and what he had heard of the Soviet determination to withstand the German attack. In the haste of his departure from the Soviet capital, he managed to leave behind his bag of essential medicines, and was ill, exhausted and in great discomfort on what seemed an endless, turbulent return flight in strong headwinds from Archangel to Scapa Flow, in the Orkney Islands, north of Scotland. Looking at the end of his tether, more dead than alive, Hopkins was given two days to recover before joining Churchill on board the *Prince of Wales* for the battleship's journey across the Atlantic for the meeting with President Roosevelt off Newfoundland.[36]

Hopkins's Moscow trip was a crucial juncture on the road to providing aid – in time to prove indispensable – for the Soviet war effort. A more positive image of Stalin and the Soviet Union began to circulate in influential American newspapers. Opinion polls showed that most Americans were in favour of aid to the Soviet Union. One reason was the belief that if the Russians were helped, Hitler could be defeated in Europe without American intervention.[37] The positive public opinion helped Roosevelt ignore the opposition of isolationists to Soviet aid, which was now being planned on a larger basis. Most importantly, Hopkins's optimism about the Soviet capacity to withstand the invasion seemed ever more realistic as the weeks passed. Certainly, the Germans had made massive advances, greater than Stalin had predicted in his talks with Hopkins. But the presumption among military experts in both America and Britain of a rapid German triumph had proved false. And as the calendar dragged slowly towards the time when the severe Russian weather would set in, it began to appear possible, even likely, that Hitler had bitten off more than he could chew.

By September, despite further major Soviet setbacks, including the devastating loss of Kiev during that month, there was no doubt that the German advance had slowed. Roosevelt and Churchill felt able to embark on the planning of long-term substantial and coordinated aid.[38] The meeting of British, American and Soviet representatives, initiated by Hopkins's visit, took place in Moscow at the end of the month, and the United States and Britain (with her Empire) agreed to meet as many as possible of Stalin's requests, offering aircraft (1,800 over the next nine months), tanks, aluminium, 90,000 jeeps and lorries and much else besides.[39] The first agreement for deliveries was signed on 1 October.[40]

Transport and payment were still problems. Roosevelt, conscious of public opinion which, though mainly (other than loud opposition from the isolationist lobby) keen to supply aid, was equally keen that the Soviets should pay for it, and without extended credit, was still seeking to extract payment from Russian gold reserves. When the unpalatable Soviet ambassador, Konstantin Oumansky, proved stubborn, unaccommodating and unwilling to acknowledge that gold reserves could be used to cover payments, an angry and frustrated Roosevelt described him in a Cabinet meeting as 'a dirty little liar'.[41] But the President was already preparing to provide aid by extending lend-lease to Stalin. Spurred by the positive public response, despite the vociferous isolationists, to reports brought back from the recent Moscow conference of tough Soviet resistance, he was now ready to test the issue in Congress. To ensure that his proposal would not be blocked, he included it in a bill for large-scale appropriations for the armed forces, something hard for patriotic congressmen to reject.[42]

On 10 October an amendment by isolationists to prevent the Soviet Union from benefiting from lend-lease was defeated in the House of Representatives then, almost a fortnight later, in the Senate. With that, the President knew he was home and dry. Near the end of the month, he let Stalin know that the Soviet Union would receive up to $1 billion of lend-lease aid, to be repaid without interest over a ten-year period, beginning five years after the end of the war. By 1 November Roosevelt had congressional sanction. The American offer was made public five days later and on 7 November the Soviet Union was deemed eligible for aid under lend-lease. By then, the Germans were no more than thirty miles from Moscow. But American opinion was now overwhelmingly behind the Soviet Union, urging on the Red Army, keen to support its heroic fight, and feeling that, even in this dark hour, and even if Moscow itself were to fall, Soviet resilience might ultimately prevail.[43]

Meanwhile, the longer the Red Army held out, the more chance there was that the mighty arsenal of the United States would start to have an effect. Equipment to the value of only $65 million had reached the Soviet Union by the time of the Japanese attack on Pearl Harbor. The Soviet repulse of the German incursion in December almost at the gates of Moscow owed as good as nothing to western aid. That the Americans would eventually provide more than $10 billion through lend-lease was foreseen by no one at this juncture.[44] But, over time, this aid would make an indispensable contribution to the Soviet war effort.

In the immediate term, the extension of aid to the Soviet Union, a move in which Roosevelt's personal hand had been both visible and decisive, drew the United States yet one step closer towards direct involvement in the European war. Roosevelt had faced a choice. His military advisers had been dubious about the wisdom of committing aid in what they thought was likely to be a lost cause. Isolationists and Catholics had formed a voluble body of oppositional opinion at home. Others in his entourage, however, had pressed for a commitment. Though initially cautious, as usual, Roosevelt had been more optimistic from the start than most of his advisers about the Soviet capacity to hold out. And he had immediately grasped that Hitler's opening of an eastern front held a potential key to the entire war. In a letter to his ambassador in Vichy France on 26 June, he had written: 'Now comes this Russian diversion. If it is more than just that, it will mean the liberation of Europe from Nazi domination.'[45] It followed that the United States should provide as much support as possible for the Soviet defence. He had given, therefore, prompt backing to Hopkins's mission, and had then been ready to take the extension of lend-lease to Congress, despite known continuing opposition.

Retreating from a commitment to aid for the Soviet Union in the teeth of such opposition was never likely. It would have been to back minority opinion against the majority that favoured aid. And it would have reversed the course of action 'short of war' that Roosevelt had, whatever the tactical hesitancy at times, consistently followed. Moreover, unlike the isolationists, Roosevelt had never viewed Hitler's Russian war through the narrow lens of letting two bloodthirsty dictators slug it out in the hope of preventing the United States from having to fight. He was well aware that it was only a matter of time before America would have to enter the war. And this would mean, despite his election promise the previous year, eventually having to send large numbers of American troops to fight in Europe if the objective of defeating Nazism were to be attained.

In the personal message he had sent via Hopkins, Stalin had openly stated that Hitler's army would finally be crushed only once the United States had entered the fray. This was no more than what Roosevelt's own military advisers were telling him. In July the army's War Plans Division started work on preparing an extensive Victory Program (which would eventually be delivered to the President in September) surveying projected needs on all likely military fronts. It came up with the conclusion that the complete military defeat of Germany could only be accomplished through the United States entering the war and sending a large force – probably some five million men – to fight in Europe. It envisaged an army totalling almost nine million men to be equipped, trained and mobilized for operations by 1 July 1943, a requirement demanding a doubling of production plans.[46]

Roosevelt had always seen Hitler, not Stalin, as the threat to American security. 'I do not think we need worry about any possibility of Russian domination,' he had written just after the German invasion had begun.[47] Domination by a victorious Germany, on the other hand, could not be ruled out. Support for Stalin was, then, the logical and necessary policy. Still, it fell short of the actual participation for which neither the President nor his people were ready. And the bitter fighting in the Soviet Union was far away. If anything was going to prompt the United States to enter the shooting match, it would have to arise much closer to home. It seemed highly likely to be the intensified conflict in the Atlantic.

II

In a letter to Mackenzie King, Prime Minister of Canada, on 1 July, Roosevelt had expressed his view 'that if the Russians should fail to hold out through the summer, there may be an intensified effort against Britain itself, and especially for control of the Atlantic. We may be able to help a good deal more than seems apparent today,' he added.[48] It was a cryptic allusion to the issue of providing escorts for convoys. To Stimson, Knox and others, the diversion of Hitler's attack on the Soviet Union had provided the ideal moment to take the initiative in the Atlantic. They wanted Roosevelt to seize the opportunity while it lasted to introduce the escorting of convoys by American warships. The President seemed for a while to accept the arguments and agreed to the compiling of plans for escorting ships of any nationality in the western Atlantic, to take effect from 11 July 1941. It looked as if he had taken a crucial step, involving the protection of British convoys by American armed vessels. It was a step his military advisers had long advocated. But within days, most probably concerned about public anxieties about escorting and how this might play into the hands of his congressional opponents, he changed his mind. The uncertainties about Japan meant that he would not permit Knox to transfer more warships from the Pacific to the Atlantic. And Knox had his work cut out to persuade the President to approve plans to escort even American ships as far as Iceland.[49] Once more, he appeared to the 'hawks' in his Cabinet to be backtracking when boldness was called for.[50]

In early July, nevertheless, Roosevelt did take another step towards the brink – and in this case unquestionably a bold one. On 7 July a brigade of 4,400 American marines landed to begin the occupation of Iceland. This was Roosevelt indeed taking advantage of Hitler's 'diversion' to the east to enhance the security of the western hemisphere.[51]

The move had a prehistory stretching back to May 1940, when Churchill, anxious to avoid a sudden German occupation of such a vital strategic location astride the Atlantic shipping lanes, had sent a British infantry brigade to the island. Reinforcements of British and Canadian troops had followed in June and July. But Churchill had been anxious to redeploy the troops elsewhere, and also keen to involve the United States more directly in the war. He wanted American troops to replace the British force at the earliest opportunity. The British and American military had then agreed, early in 1941, that defence of the island in the event of war would fall to the United States. By mid-June, Admiral Stark had designed instructions to put in the American troops, at this point envisaged as being under British command. 'I realize that this is practically an act of war,' he jotted on his cover note to Harry Hopkins who, Stark hoped, would smooth the passage of his operational instructions with the President.[52] He gained Roosevelt's approval. But the President would not act without a formal invitation from the government of Iceland, which was not forthcoming until 1 July.[53] Six days later Roosevelt announced the move into Iceland, 'to supplement and perhaps eventually replace the British force', as he put it, though the relief of an equivalent number of British troops began straight away.[54] The dispatch of marines rather than soldiers from the army enabled the President to bypass the restrictions – highly sensitive to public opinion – under the

Selective Service Act, which prevented draftees from serving outside the western hemisphere. The marines were volunteers, professional fighting men, as they saw themselves, and not the 'boys' whom Roosevelt had promised only months earlier would not be sent to fight in foreign wars.[55]

It was a distinctly unneutral act. An elated Churchill told the House of Commons it was 'an event of first-rate political and strategic importance; in fact, it is one of the most important things that has happened since the war began'.[56] Privately, he took the view (shared by the British ambassador in Washington, Lord Halifax) that its significance was in accelerating American intervention in the war alongside Britain.[57] Indeed, it did take the United States closer to hostilities in the Atlantic. Perhaps, as has been claimed, 'if ever there was a point when Roosevelt knowingly crossed some threshold between aiding Britain in order to stay out of war and aiding Britain by joining in the war, July 1941 was probably the time'.[58]

Eight days after the American troops had landed, the western hemisphere was designated as including Iceland, even though 'everyone concedes [it] is in the eastern hemisphere and therefore logically attached to the continent of Europe'.[59] At Iceland, the American defence zone and the German combat zone intersected. The prospects of 'incidents' involving German submarines and the US navy, now engaged in the defence of Iceland as well as escort duties for American convoys as far as the island, were now far greater than they had been. But the occupation of Iceland was approved by 61 per cent of Americans questioned in an opinion survey, with only 20 per cent opposed.[60] Despite his fears of a 'vitriolic outburst' against the move,[61] the President was carrying the population step by step with him to the brink. But still he remained cautious of pushing opinion too far, too quickly. Though the opportunity appeared to present itself to introduce the escort of non-American convoys, Roosevelt did not seize it.

The President's sensitivity towards public opinion was shown to be justified in the heated debates that flared up in July and August over the issue of amending the Selective Service Act of 1940. At stake was nothing less than what General Marshall described as the 'disintegration of the army'.[62] Had the administration failed to carry through Congress the amendments it was proposing, the large army envisaged under the Victory Program (still being prepared) for future engagement in Europe would have been impossible. The strength of public feeling in the country, alongside the intense battle in Congress, was a sharp reminder to Roosevelt that, whatever the level of readiness to support Britain, and now the Soviet Union too, the opposition to any notion of American soldiers being sent to fight abroad was as vehement as ever.

The Selective Service Act of August 1940 had allowed the army to draft up to 900,000 men, but only for a period of one year, unless Congress (not the President) should declare that national security was imperilled. A second stipulation had been that men drafted could not serve outside the western hemisphere (a condition which Roosevelt circumvented in the occupation of Iceland by using marines). The President's declaration in May of a state of unlimited national emergency had no bearing on the Act; Congress leaders told Roosevelt that they could not muster the votes to amend it; and the expiry date was looming for the first men conscripted the previous autumn. Moreover, around the country families wanted their 'boys' back home, while in the army itself morale among the draftees was so poor that it seemed many were on the point of deserting if they were not to gain their promised release. It was by any assessment an awkward, indeed critical, situation for the President. His first inclination, as so often, was towards caution. He wanted to avoid the struggle in Congress. Stimson, Knox and especially Marshall worked for days to persuade Roosevelt to confront Congress. The issue plainly could not be ducked for long. Eventually, he agreed to brave the inevitable and extensive opposition.

Three resolutions of amendment to the original Act were introduced on 10 July: to retain draftees in service as long as the national emergency lasted; to allow them to be sent beyond the western hemisphere; and to remove the upper limit of 900,000 men on the size of the army. The opposition was bitter and mostly along party-political lines. The most heated attacks, predictably, came from Republicans. But many Democrats who had backed earlier measures were also deeply concerned at the implications of giving the President powers to send troops abroad. The usual isolationist core of opposition could on this occasion, therefore, reckon with a wider base of anxious support – with Congressmen anxious not least at the reaction of their constituents if they voted to keep 'their boys' in military service. Eventually, the bill passed through the Senate on 7 August by the reasonably comfortable margin of 45 to 30. The main drama, however, was reserved for the debate in the House of Representatives. When that ended, on 12 August, the bill secured its passage by a single vote: 203 to 202.[63]

It was later described, with pardonable hyperbole, as 'one of the decisive battles of the war'.[64] Doubtless, if the vote had gone the other way the administration would have been compelled to bring in new measures to ensure its military planning was not vitiated. But valuable time would have been lost. The attack on Pearl Harbor, four months later, would have struck a country with its army in a process of dissolution.[65] Most significantly, as the prospect of global conflict loomed ever larger, the vote carried the warning to Roosevelt, as expressed by the high priest of isolationism, Senator Burton K. Wheeler, 'that the Administration could not get a resolution through the Congress for a declaration of war'.[66]

While the torrid debates were preoccupying Congress and much of the country, Roosevelt and Churchill were meeting for the first time since either of them had taken office. The meeting gave tangible expression to Churchill's words a year earlier, that Britain, with its Empire, and the United States were becoming 'somewhat mixed up together'.[67] For Churchill, a personal meeting with Roosevelt was of immense importance. 'Nothing must stand in the way of his friendship for the President on which so much depended,' one of the Prime Minister's aides had noted. That Roosevelt had sought the meeting was significant, Churchill thought. He would not have done so 'unless he contemplated some further step'.[68] But nothing significant was on Roosevelt's agenda. He wanted as far as possible to coordinate policy on a number of vital issues, to iron out any differences and to get to know Churchill. But he did not have in mind what Churchill was hoping for: a decision to take America into the war.[69]

Plans for a meeting had been laid as early as the spring. Eventually, the crucial talks took place in secret between 9 and 12 August aboard the American heavy cruiser *Augusta* and the British battleship *Prince of Wales*, which had borne Harry Hopkins alongside Churchill across the Atlantic to Placentia Bay, just off the disused Newfoundland silver-mining settlement of Argentia. Roosevelt and Churchill were accompanied by military top brass and important diplomatic officials in the discussions on the two warships, anchored alongside each other.[70]

The talks ranged widely, embracing aid to the Soviet Union, convoys in the Atlantic, the Japanese menace in south-east Asia and the postwar order. Oddly, perhaps, the Atlantic Conference was devoted less to the Atlantic than the Pacific. With Hitler preoccupied by the Wehrmacht's progress in Russia, the danger in the west had at least temporarily subsided. The American occupation of Iceland had gone smoothly. A sort of uneasy stalemate had settled over the Atlantic. In the Far East, by contrast, the tension had mounted sharply since the Japanese invasion of southern Indochina and the American imposition of an oil embargo. The more immediate menace seemed to come from that direction. Little by way of concrete action emerged from the talks. Churchill urged a strong American line on any further Japanese expansion, amounting effectively to an ultimatum. Roosevelt agreed to use 'hard language' when warning the Japanese ambassador in Washington on his return, though in the event, on the intervention of the State Department, he toned this down. Despite the oil embargo, deterrence, not provocation, remained the policy. The aim was to keep the Pacific quiet as long as possible.[71]

As regards the Atlantic, though it figured less prominently in the talks, there was encouragement for the British. Roosevelt, disappointing Churchill's hopes, had swiftly ruled out expectations of immediate American involvement in the war. But two steps were agreed that seemed to have the potential to bring the moment of intervention closer.

Roosevelt was seriously worried about Nazi agents penetrating the bulge of Africa and opening the way for Hitler to make a quick strike through the Iberian peninsula into north Africa.[72] The relatively short distance across the southern Atlantic from the bulge of Africa to Brazil had long been a concern of American strategic planners, envisaging this as the simplest way for German troops to establish a footing on the American continent. To head off any danger, Roosevelt was willing to promise Churchill (who had outlined the danger of a German thrust to take Gibraltar, the gateway to the south Atlantic routes as well as controlling entry to the Mediterranean) that he would send occupying forces to the Azores once Britain could arrange for an invitation from Portugal (analogous to that from Iceland).[73] Nothing came of it. In the event, there was no German takeover in Gibraltar, no need (at least, not at this stage) for an invitation from Portugal and no occupation by American troops of the Azores.

A second point of agreement gave Churchill some satisfaction. Roosevelt finally consented to provide armed escorts for all shipping, not just American or Icelandic, across the western Atlantic as far as Iceland. British ships could at last reckon with American protection. It was what the 'hawks' in his Cabinet had been exhorting the President to do for months. Admiral Stark sent out instructions from Placentia Bay, to take effect from 16 September.[74] The President had taken an important (and in British eyes long overdue) step, amounting to 'the beginning of undeclared hostilities with Germany'.[75] At least, that was Churchill's understanding. In fact, only the contingency plans for escorting had actually been decided, while the implementation still rested on the President's order. When he returned to Washington, he did nothing at first to expedite the implementation.[76] Technical and logistical problems – organizing the communications links with British naval intelligence, and making sure the ships were in the right place at the right time, for instance – posed their own obstacle to any immediate start.[77] But the President's real difficulty was political. How he was going to tell the American public, and broach the matter to Congress, he still did not know.[78] According to Churchill's report on the talks to the

British Cabinet, the President had told him 'he was skating on pretty thin ice in his relations with Congress'. Asking Congress for a declaration of war, Roosevelt went on, would produce a three-month debate. (His real belief, in fact, was that a request to Congress for a declaration of war would be defeated by two or three to one.[79]) Instead, he said, 'he would wage war, but not declare it, and that he would become more and more provocative ... He would look for an "incident" which would justify him in opening hostilities'.[80]

In practical terms, the Conference ended by achieving little. It was of importance, nevertheless. Out of it came the Atlantic Charter, a statement of principles, largely an American inspiration, for a postwar world envisaged by the United States and Great Britain. Though not all of the eight points of the Charter, amounting in effect to a declaration of democratic war aims, had an easy birth, final agreement on the wording was reached by 12 August and the text was made public two days later. The Charter proclaimed that the United States and United Kingdom sought no territorial or other aggrandizement, wished no territorial changes beyond the wishes of the peoples concerned, respected the right of all peoples to choose their form of government, would endeavour to promote equal access to trade and raw materials, would work for economic advancement and social security for all and would strive for world peace and disarmament.[81]

The Charter, whose initial purpose had been mainly as propaganda, came to have historic significance as a list of democratic rights and principles that would later become enshrined in the aims of the United Nations. But the real value of the Atlantic Conference at the time lay less in its statement of abstract war aims – noble though they were, they were widely viewed on both sides of the ocean as no substitute for firm joint policy declarations – than in the personal relations that were cemented between Roosevelt and Churchill.[82] An understanding of profound importance was established, and on a direct, personal basis, between the two leaders. The sense of trust created at the Conference would last throughout the vagaries of the war.

The meeting left its mark on both. For Churchill, it evoked the common purpose of the two countries, symbolized movingly for him in the joint church service on the Sunday morning of 10 August, on the quarterdeck of the *Prince of Wales*, as British and American sailors together sang hymns he had chosen beneath the ship's big guns while the flags of the two nations draped the pulpit side by side. He later described 'the fact alone of the United States, still technically neutral, joining with a belligerent power' in drawing up the Atlantic Charter as 'astonishing'.[83] For Roosevelt, too, the meeting had been significant, and not simply for the joint declaration of war aims embodied in the Charter. Like Churchill, he had been greatly moved by the symbolism of the joint church service on the *Prince of Wales*, the 'keynote' of the entire Conference, as he recorded. 'If nothing else had happened while we were here, that would have cemented us,' his son Elliott, present on board, reported him saying.[84] He had established a personal rapport with Churchill. But he was also pleased at the tone of the Conference, which implicitly acknowledged American leadership in the informal alliance with Britain and her Empire.[85] And though he had formally agreed little of substance during the Conference, he had gained sharper insight into British strategic thinking and how, with American help, the war against Hitler could be won.[86] He was starting more clearly to see the eastern front as the key to the outcome of the war, and his determination to provide aid to the Soviet Union found expression in the warmly couched message to Stalin that he and Churchill sent on 12 August, the last day of the Conference, proposing a meeting in Moscow (as Hopkins had suggested during his visit) to work out arrangements for long-term aid.[87] He was also now prepared to move away from neutrality to adopt a more actively belligerent role in the 'battle of the Atlantic' amounting to a limited, undeclared war against Germany, one which ran an increased risk of the United States being fully drawn into hostilities.[88]

The crucial question of when the United States would enter the war had, however, come no closer to finding an answer. Certainly, Roosevelt's comment about provoking an incident seemed to suggest that it was merely a matter of time. But when might that be? From a British perspective, the issue could not be stretched out indefinitely. Yet there was little expectation that American entry was imminent. News of the alarmingly close vote on the renewal of the Selective Service Act, which had reached Placentia Bay on the last day of the Conference, offered scant encouragement.[89] And Churchill's initial high spirits on his return from the meeting had been dissipated by the reaction at home.[90] Not only was the public response to the meeting muted (as it had been in the United States); the Cabinet seemed far from encouraged by the talks to believe that the United States would soon be in the war alongside Britain. Lord Beaverbrook, Churchill's Minister of Supply, had travelled on to Washington from Placentia Bay and had reported back that there was no chance of the United States entering the war until a direct attack on its own territory forced it to do so. This was thought to be highly unlikely until both Britain and Russia had been defeated.[91] Roosevelt's rejoinder to criticism by alarmed isolationists that the Atlantic Conference had taken the United States no closer to war gave further sustenance to the deflated mood in Britain.[92]

Towards the end of August, a depressed Churchill sent Harry Hopkins 'one of the gloomiest messages that ever came to the White House from the normally confident, ebullient Prime Minister'. Churchill pointed out the heavy British shipping losses to U-boats in the Atlantic – 50,000 tons in the previous two days. 'I don't know what will happen if England is fighting alone when 1942 comes,' he added. He noted that Hitler's submarines were keeping clear of the zone defined as belonging to the western hemisphere, so that 'there was little prospect of an "incident" serious enough to bring the United States into the war'.[93]

Less than a week after Churchill's dispirited message to Hopkins, however, an incident did take place which gave Roosevelt the opportunity to make public his escort policy, and edged the United States closer to the brink.

III

In the early morning of 4 September, a German submarine, the U-652, was spotted by a British bomber patrolling about 165 miles south of Iceland, at a point within the overlap between the German combat area and the American security zone. The submarine dived to avoid the immediate danger. But her location was signalled to an American destroyer in the immediate vicinity, the USS *Greer*, carrying mail and a few military passengers to Iceland. Since she was not escorting American shipping, the *Greer* had no authority to attack, and was officially bound only to report the submarine's position. Nevertheless, the *Greer* closed in and trailed the submerged U-boat for over an hour, taking sonar readings of her position and flashing these to the British bomber, which dropped four depth charges. These easily missed their target, and the bomber returned to base. But the pursuit continued, and an hour and a half later, following the *Greer*'s radio signal, another British plane arrived to search for the U-boat. The pursuit had gone on for around four hours when the U-boat's commander, presumably fearing that the batteries would fail and force him to the surface, decided to turn the tables. He fired two torpedoes at the *Greer*, though each of them passed harmlessly by. The *Greer* now retaliated by dropping eight depth charges, but inflicted only minor damage on the U-652. A British destroyer arrived on the scene an hour or so later and also dropped a depth charge, to no effect. The *Greer* made a last attempt to destroy the U-boat in mid-afternoon, dropping eleven more depth charges, though now missing by a long distance. Only in the early evening, about ten hours after taking up the chase, did the *Greer* give up and sail on to Iceland.[94]

A radio report of the incident was swiftly transmitted to Washington and made available to the President. Without delay, the Navy Department put out a press release about a submarine attack on the *Greer*.[95] At his press conference next day, 5 September, Roosevelt emphasized the deliberate nature of the U-boat's attack, in daylight, on a ship with an identification number, flying the American flag and within the US security zone. He also stated that he had given orders to 'eliminate' the submarine if it could be found.[96]

At this point, the President may not have been in full cognizance of the facts. No mention, of course, was made of the harassing role of the *Greer*. In the circumstances, the U-652 could be said to have fired its torpedoes in self-defence. Nor was it certain that she had recognized the destroyer as American. She had been under attack by British warplanes, within the German combat zone, and had merely chanced to gain a periscope glimpse of a four-funnel destroyer similar to those transferred to Britain the previous autumn.[97] But no such considerations were likely to deter Roosevelt, now given an opportunity of the kind he had awaited.

At lunch that day, 5 September, the President sketched for Harry Hopkins and Cordell Hull the outlines of a speech to the nation, long planned, which, in the light of the *Greer* incident, he now intended to deliver the following week. He intended to pull no punches. Hull, apparently no less outraged by what had happened, also spoke assertively. But when the Secretary of State summarized his views on paper to send them to the White House, doubts set in and he made no recommendation for action. In the absence of the President (who had travelled to Hyde Park to attend his mother's funeral), Hopkins and Judge Samuel Rosenman, Roosevelt's other main speech-writer, worked on the address with no input from the State Department. They incorporated some passages composed by the President himself (they were in touch with him by telephone during the drafting) and by the time he travelled back to Washington, the speech was as good as ready. He tried it out that evening, 10 September, on Stimson, Knox and Hull, who gave their warm approval. A few minor adjustments were made to the wording. Then, the following morning, Roosevelt read it out to a group of congressional leaders. Only one, a Republican isolationist, did not like it. The Secretary of State, however, despite his expression of agreement the previous evening, was again having second thoughts. He told Hopkins that 'the speech was too strong', and wanted 'all reference to shooting first, or shooting of any kind', to be removed. He spoke to Roosevelt along the same lines. But there was to be no weakening of the tenor of the speech.[98] It was among the most hard-hitting the President had ever made.

Roosevelt began in similar vein to that of his press conference six days earlier. The attack on the *Greer* had been in the American self-defence zone, in broad daylight, and with the ship's identity unmistakable. 'I tell you the blunt fact,' he declared, 'that the German submarine fired first upon this American destroyer without warning, and with deliberate design to sink her.' He described it as 'piracy legally and morally', and referred to several incidents – including that of the sinking of the merchant ship, the *Robin Moor*, in July, which had prompted no retaliatory action – to show that the *Greer* was no isolated case, but 'part of a general plan'. The Nazi design, he continued, was to acquire absolute control of the seas as a prelude to domination of the western hemisphere by force of arms. A sideswipe at isolationists followed. Americans could not continue deluding themselves, the President stated, by the 'romantic notion' that they could 'go on living happily and peacefully in a Nazi-dominated world'. No appeasement was possible. A line had to be drawn. Supply routes to the enemies of Hitler had to be kept open, and the freedom of the seas upheld. He used a telling metaphor (adapting a remark by a luncheon guest a little while earlier[99]) to drive home the need for preventive attack in the Atlantic. 'When you see a rattlesnake poised to strike, you do not wait until he has struck before you crush him. These Nazi submarines and raiders are the rattlesnakes of the Atlantic.' It was a powerful image. He came to its policy implications, and the crucial – much belated in some eyes – introduction of escorting of convoys. 'Upon our naval and air patrol – now operating in large number over a vast expanse of the Atlantic Ocean – falls the duty of maintaining the American policy of freedom of the seas – now. That means, very simply, very clearly, that our patrolling vessels and planes will protect all merchant ships – not only American ships but ships of any flag – engaged in commerce in our defensive waters.' The aim, he emphasized, was solely defensive. But then came the explicit warning to the Axis: 'From now on, if German or Italian vessels of war enter the waters, the protection of which is necessary for American defence, they do so at their own peril.'[100]

As the President finished speaking, the playing of the national anthem brought the audience – family, friends, advisers and a large press contingent – assembled in the Diplomatic Reception Room of the White House to hear the address (carried worldwide by radio) to their feet in an emotional finale.[101] The President had outmanoeuvred his opponents. The isolationists were isolated. The escorting of convoys had been introduced. The official orders went out two days later. The escorting began on 16 September.[102]

'Thus was the long-standing issue of American naval escort resolved by the declaration of the shooting war' is an apposite description of what had occurred.[103]

Though he had not used the phrase, what he had unmistakably initiated was a policy of 'shoot on sight'. The banner headline of the *New York Times* next day ran: 'Roosevelt Orders Navy to Shoot First'.[104] Isolationists predictably and vigorously protested.[105] But public opinion favoured 'shoot on sight', 62 per cent approving with only 28 per cent against. This showed the impact of the *Greer* incident, and the President's exploitation of it. Two days before it happened, only a bare majority of 52 per cent had favoured the US navy 'convoying' war materials to Britain.[106] The American people had been brought behind a policy practically guaranteed to draw the United States into future armed clashes with German vessels in the Atlantic. Open warfare was round the corner. As Admiral Stark, chief of Naval Operations, put it on 22 September: 'So far as the Atlantic is concerned, we are all but, if not actually in it.'[107]

Roosevelt's detractors, at the time and since, accused him of deceiving the American people 'in a gigantic conspiracy to drive them into war' (as alleged in the rabidly isolationist *Chicago Tribune*).[108] His *Greer* speech had certainly been economical with the truth about the incident. He had made no mention of the circumstances of lengthy pursuit and harassment of the U-652 before she had fired her torpedo salvo. Though it was true that the submarine had fired first, it had not been without provocation. The American people learned nothing of this. Roosevelt's claim that the *Greer* was part of a systematic Nazi attack on American shipping was also a distortion. It was, in a sense, surprising that there had been so few, not so many, incidents. The President and his military advisers were, however, aware that Hitler was not likely to be seeking outright conflict in the Atlantic before he had crushed the Soviet Union. (In fact, although Roosevelt could not know it, Hitler had given express orders forbidding provocation in the Atlantic while he had his hands full in the east.[109]) Apologists for the President claimed he was not fully informed of the facts of the incident. But if, in his press conference on 5 September, the President was still not in full knowledge of what had taken place, this is unlikely to have been the case six days later. (Hull's reticence about the statement may, indeed, have been precisely because, legally, right in the incident was by no means unequivocally on the American side.) There is little doubt, therefore, that Roosevelt used some sleight of hand in his speech. Was this justified?

He himself justified his action in terms of national defence interest and saw it as his clear, inescapable obligation as President.[110] It is not easy to claim that he was wrong in this, given the long-term threat posed by Hitler's regime.[111] Did he have a choice? His options were, in fact, by now severely constrained. If he had used a degree of hyperbole to make the introduction of escorting more palatable to the American people, the policy itself was quite in accord with the cautious but consistent steps taken over previous months. Stimson was only one of those pointing out from the outset the logic of lend-lease – approved by Congress – necessitating the protection of the *matériel* to be shipped across the Atlantic. So the only effective choice Roosevelt faced in September 1941 was whether to take the executive action he did, whether to risk further protracted, bitter debate and possible defeat in Congress, or whether to ignore the *Greer* incident and delay the introduction of escorting yet further.

Either alternative course would have pandered to minority isolationist feeling. But this offered no real option. The strategic problem in contending with the German threat (exacerbated by the growing tension in the Pacific) would not as a consequence have disappeared or lessened. And to pass up the chance of introducing escorting would have been to fly in the face of the advice he was receiving from his military experts. It would also have meant reneging on the promise he gave Churchill at Placentia Bay, and would therefore have been potentially damaging to the Atlantic alliance on which Hitler's ultimate defeat was seen to rest. This in turn would have been to take a huge risk with Britain's future capacity to continue fighting. As Roosevelt's military experts put it on the very day of his speech, 11 September, 'the immediate and strong reinforcement of British forces in the Atlantic by United States naval and air contingents, supplemented by a large additional shipping tonnage, will be required if the United Kingdom is to remain in the war'.[112] And, as Roosevelt had seen all along, the defence interests of the United States would be irreparably damaged if Britain were to be forced to capitulate or to negotiate an unfavourable settlement, leaving Hitler in charge of the European continent and dominating the Atlantic. Isolationist notions that America could bury her head in the sand and Hitler would leave her alone were, as Roosevelt had incessantly pointed out, dangerous illusions. By 1941, the United States could, in her own interest, not afford to stand on the sidelines in the 'battle of the Atlantic'.

Roosevelt followed the only course of action possible. His exploitation of the *Greer* incident was clever politics, not an abuse of power. It had brought the majority of the public behind the escorting policy in a way which would probably not earlier have been possible. Lord Halifax, the British ambassador in Washington, described to Churchill the President's dilemma, as he himself saw it: to steer a course between '(1) the wish of

70% of Americans to keep out of war; [and] (2) the wish of 70% of Americans to do everything to break Hitler, even it if means war.'[113] Again, the President's way of 'making haste slowly' had proved both successful and justified. But there was no mistake about it: he had indeed now taken the United States to the brink of all-out conflict with Nazi Germany. Could sporadic skirmishing continue indefinitely? Or might little now be needed to transform the 'undeclared war' into the all-out conflagration which would demand American boys being sent to fight – something the President had ruled out during his electoral campaign less than a year earlier?

The latter seemed the more likely eventuality as the inevitable further incidents in the Atlantic occurred in the autumn. Pushing in the same direction was the news emerging soon after Roosevelt's 'fireside chat' of 11 September that the President had discussed measures to bring about the repeal of the 1939 Neutrality Act with congressional leaders.[114] But as autumn dragged on, and the clashes in the Atlantic led to no great flare-up, the first possibility, that of indefinite undeclared war, began to seem a possibility. By now, in any case, the danger of war in the Pacific was at least as great as all-out conflict with Germany. And that was something the President had to bear carefully in mind when deciding how to react to incidents in the Atlantic.

IV

These incidents did not take long to materialize. When on 19 September the *Pink Star*, a Danish freighter registered in Panama but requisitioned by the US Maritime Commission, was torpedoed, questions arose about the necessity of arming merchant ships, something not permissible under the 1939 Neutrality Act.[115] The sinking of a number of other freight ships flying the Panamanian flag though American-owned – a ruse to avoid falling foul of the neutrality legislation – raised the same issue.[116]

It was a torpedo attack on another American destroyer, the USS *Kearny*, south of Iceland on 17 October, that gave Roosevelt his best opportunity to highlight the deficiencies of the Neutrality Act in the changed circumstances. The *Kearny* was one of four American destroyers responding to a call for assistance from a Canadian-escorted convoy under assault from a U-boat 'wolfpack'. Several ships went down in a night-long battle with the marauders. The destroyers launched a hail of depth charges, but in the mêlée the *Kearny* was hit by a torpedo. She was damaged, though not sunk, and was able to limp on to Iceland. But eleven of her crew had died, and twenty-four were injured.[117] It was a poignant moment for a nation not officially at war. Roosevelt did not let the chance slip. The 'Navy and Total Defense Day' on 27 October provided the occasion for a notably fiery address by the President, his most outspoken before Pearl Harbor.

'We have wished to avoid shooting. But the shooting has started. And history has recorded who fired the first shot,' he began. 'America has been attacked.' Continuing in this vein, he claimed: 'Hitler's torpedo was directed at every American.' It was an attempt 'to frighten the American people off the high seas – to force us to make a trembling retreat'. He referred to secret maps in his possession of German plans to dominate South America, and a Nazi design for the eradication of religion – British forgeries swallowed by a gullible President[118] – using 'these grim truths' to discredit isolationists (though he did not directly refer to them) who were presenting a gift to the Nazis through exposing apparent American disunity. He posited, as in earlier speeches, the absolute choice in a future world between American freedom and Nazi tyranny, and pledged once more the complete destruction of Hitlerism. The United States, he continued, was producing ever more arms for those involved in the actual fighting, 'and it is the Nation's will that these vital arms and supplies of all kinds shall neither be locked up in American harbors nor sent to the bottom of the sea'. It was in defiance of that will that American ships had been sunk and sailors killed. 'I say that we do not propose to take this lying down,' he declared. 'That determination of ours not to take it lying down has been expressed in the orders to the American Navy to shoot on sight. Those orders stand.' He came to the relevance of this to the neutrality legislation: 'Our American merchant ships must be armed to defend themselves against the rattlesnakes of the sea. Our American merchant ships must be free to carry our American goods into the harbors of our friends. Our American merchant ships must be protected by our American Navy.' It meant 'total national defense'. He concluded his peroration on an emotive note: 'Today in the face of this newest and greatest challenge of them all, we Americans have cleared our decks and taken our battle stations. We stand ready in the defense of our Nation and in the faith of our fathers to do what God has given us the power to see as our full duty.'[119] It sounded like the preface to a declaration of war. But no request to Congress was forthcoming.

According to a later comment by Roosevelt's speech-writer, Samuel Rosenman, the President had believed when the European war started in September 1939 that the United States could stay out, and that remained his view during 1940. But, though there had been no definitive incident that had changed his mind, during 1941 he had gradually come to the conclusion that American involvement was as good as inevitable.[120] This conviction collided, however, with political realities at home. Speaking to Lord Halifax after the *Greer* affair, Roosevelt had reportedly said that 'if he asked for a declaration of war he wouldn't get it, and opinion would swing against him'.[121] That remained his position. It meant a policy of waiting for things to happen.

As autumn deepened, Roosevelt felt his hands were tied by three considerations. At home, isolationist clamour had been stirred again by the neutrality legislation revisions which had been proposed to Congress, and by the escalation of conflict in the Atlantic. In terms of production and rearmament, the United States was still not ready for war. And, with the pot starting to boil in the Far East, it was a question of how long Roosevelt could keep the lid on. As he had said earlier in the year, he did not have 'enough Navy to go round', and war in the Pacific would mean diversions from the Atlantic.[122] Perhaps a combination of these considerations led Roosevelt to take a surprisingly soft line, compared with his response to the *Greer* and *Kearny* incidents, when another American destroyer, the USS *Reuben James*, was attacked by a U-boat 600 miles west of Ireland on 31 October. In this incident, the worst of the three clashes involving American warships, a torpedo struck the ammunition magazine of the destroyer, which sank within five minutes, with the loss of a hundred and fifteen men. Given the inflammatory way Roosevelt had spoken following earlier attacks, where there had been less damage caused and fewer casualties, his restraint on this occasion was striking. It signalled that, despite his previous belligerent statements, he was still far from ready to use a clash in the 'undeclared war' of the Atlantic to take the United States into full-scale hostilities.

If he had been contemplating seeking a declaration of war – and there is not the slightest evidence that this was in his mind during these months – the question of revisions to the Neutrality Act would have dissuaded him.

The logic of repealing at least some sections of the 1939 legislation followed from the enactment of lend-lease. If weapons and merchandise were to be transported across the Atlantic, it made sense if the merchant ships were armed, and if American vessels could carry their cargoes all the way to Britain. The question of asking Congress to repeal the relevant sections of the Act was aired in spring 1941. But Cordell Hull had advised against it, on the grounds of the strength of isolationist opposition.[123] He seems to have changed his mind by the end of June, when he urged the President to discuss amending the Act with congressional leaders as a matter of urgency. Roosevelt carried out the discussions, but did not feel confident

1. French soldiers surrender in May 1940 as the Wehrmacht sweeps through the Low Countries and northern France. The rapidity of the German victory had a dramatic effect upon war plans, not just in Europe, but also in the Far East.

2. Allied troops at Dunkirk waiting and hoping to be rescued from the beaches at the end of May 1940. The success of the evacuation surpassed all expectations in the government and armed forces' leadership.

3. Grim faces in Downing Street, 1940: Winston Churchill and Lord Halifax, whose disagreement dominated the War Cabinet's critical discussions between 25 and 28 May about whether to seek a negotiated end to the war. The decision to continue the fight vitally affected German strategy.

4. Grand Admiral Erich Raeder, Commander-in-Chief of the German navy, whose strategic preferences differed from those of the German dictator, Adolf Hitler.

5. Hitler and the Spanish dictator, General Francisco Franco, inspect a guard of honour during their meeting at Hendaye in October 1940, which revealed the insuperable obstacles of a 'peripheral strategy' involving Spain.

6. The Soviet Commissar for Foreign Affairs, Vyacheslav Molotov (with the German Foreign Minister, Joachim von Ribbentrop, to his right), during his visit to Berlin in November 1940, which convinced Hitler that an attack on the Soviet Union had to be carried out without delay.

7. Japanese tanks roll through part of southern China during the bitter and brutal war that began in summer 1937 and proved an insuperable barrier to any prospect of a peaceful settlement in the Far East.

8. Prince Konoe Fumimaro, three times Prime Minister of Japan, who supported the war in China and the southern expansion but resigned in October 1941 when his attempts to find a diplomatic way out of the escalating crisis with the United States failed.

9. The Japanese ambassador in Berlin, Kurusu Saburo, speaks at the signing of the Tripartite Pact between Japan, Germany and Italy on 27 September 1940. On his left are the Italian Foreign Minister, Count Galeazzo Ciano, and Hitler.

10. Mixed expressions on Italian faces as Italy enters the war on 10 June 1940.

11. (*From left to right*) Benito Mussolini, Hitler, Ciano and Ribbentrop meet in the Palazzo Vecchio in Florence on 28 October 1940, the day that Italy launched the attack on Greece.

12. Italian artillery fire on Greek positions at the Albanian border after the ill-fated invasion of Greece had stalled.

13. President Franklin Delano Roosevelt discusses foreign policy in 1940 with his long-standing Secretary of State, Cordell Hull, a voice of caution in the administration though ultimately unbending in the face of the mounting threat from Japan.

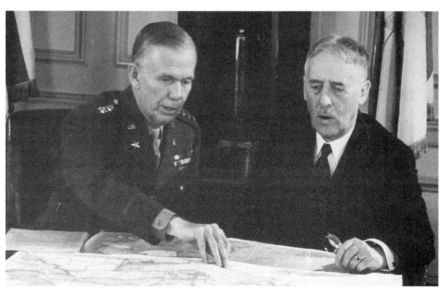

14. General George C. Marshall, an outstandingly able chief of staff, assesses strategy with the experienced and determined Secretary of War, Henry L. Stimson, one of the 'hawkish' influences on the President.

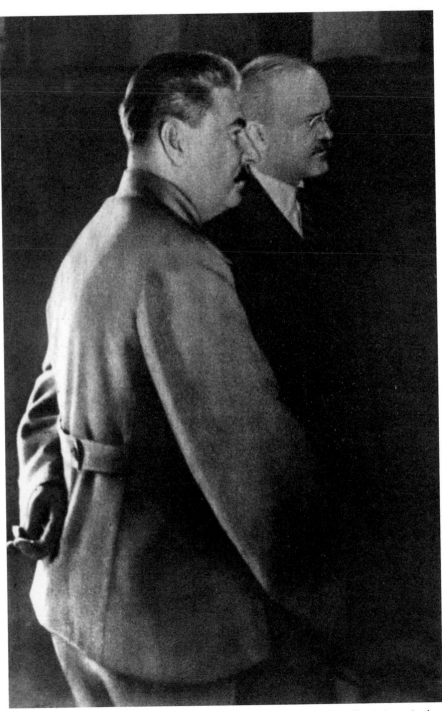

15. Joseph Stalin with Molotov, who subserviently swallowed his leader's dismissive attitude to all warnings of a German invasion in 1941.

16. Young Soviet soldiers among the hundreds of thousands captured by Germans within the first few weeks of the invasion in June 1941. More than three million Soviet prisoners of war would die in German captivity.

17. Soviet tanks bogged down in marshy terrain in summer 1941 during the devastating German advance.

18. Roosevelt and Churchill on board HMS *Prince of Wales* at the meeting in Placentia Bay in August 1941 which gave rise to the Atlantic Charter.

19. General Tojo Hideki, the 'hawkish' Army Minister who became Prime Minister in October 1941, pictured here the following month, around the time that he was leading ministerial discussions in favour of an attack on the United States.

20. Emperor Hirohito conducts a military review in Tokyo on 6 December 1941, the day before the attack on Pearl Harbor.

21. American defences are caught unawares as bombs rain down during the attack on Pearl Harbor, 7 December 1941.

22. German troops under attack as the advance towards Moscow slows during autumn 1941.

23. A German tank of the 2nd SS Panzer Division, not far from Moscow, where German forces encountered their first major crisis of the war during the Soviet counter-offensive that began on 5 December 1941.

24. Hitler announces the German declaration of war on the United States to the Reichstag on 11 December 1941.

25. Heinrich Himmler, head of the SS, responsible to Hitler for carrying out the 'final solution'.

26. Reinhard Heydrich, head of the Security Police, mandated to prepare 'a complete solution to the Jewish question', and in charge of its organizational planning.

27. The infamous Babi Yar massacre near Kiev, where Security Police units murdered 33,771 Jews, including women and children, within two days at the end of September 1941. The victims here are waiting to be killed, on the edge of a mass grave containing the bodies of some who have already been shot dead.

28. Distraught reactions to the slaughter of Jews in Lemberg in July 1941, as local inhabitants look upon the victims and search for relatives among the dead.

enough to go ahead until the *Greer* incident in early September gave him his opportunity.[124] In the last week of the month Hull proposed modifications rather than the outright repeal of the entire Act (certain parts of which, such as the collection of funds for belligerents, the administration had an interest in continuing to control).[125]

The President received a great deal of conflicting advice from leading members of his administration on running the risk of an unfavourable verdict from Congress.[126] Opinion in the country, influenced by some leading newspapers, supported the amendments. A Gallup poll on 5 October indicated that 70 per cent of those asked thought the defeat of Hitler was more important than keeping the country out of the war.[127] But opinion in Congress was another matter altogether. Isolationist feeling was once more whipped up. The passing of the amendments in Congress could not be taken for granted.

Informal soundings in the Senate in early October suggested that the President was wise to progress cautiously. Roosevelt decided to test the waters, with the repeal initially only of the section of the Act prohibiting the arming of merchant ships (Section VI), on which the highest degree of consensus could be expected. He put the proposal to Congress on 9 October. It was the beginning of a further bitter debate. As it was approaching its conclusion, news of the attack on the *Kearny* came through. This probably had an impact. The repeal of Section VI was approved by the House of Representatives on 17 October, with a sizeable majority (259 to 138). Even so, 113 Republicans had rejected even this measure.[128]

A good deal more rancour followed when the resolution to repeal Sections II and III (excluding American shipping from designated combat zones) came before the Senate. Roosevelt's belligerent speech following the attack on the *Kearny*, then the sinking of the *Reuben James*, inflamed isolationist opposition.[129] One arch-isolationist publicly proposed that Roosevelt should seek a vote from Congress on whether or not the United States should enter the war. There was no danger of the President falling into such an obvious trap. The very suggestion was enough to show Roosevelt that his caution was justified; were he to follow such a course, 'he would meet with certain and disastrous defeat'.[130] Eventually, on 7 November the resolution was passed by the Senate, but only by the uncomfortable margin of 50 to 37 votes. Again, most Republicans were in opposition. It was the smallest majority on any foreign-policy issue in the Senate since war had started in Europe.[131] In the House of Representatives it was even worse. The amendments were approved there by a slim majority of only 18 votes, 212 in favour, 194 against.[132] Roosevelt had got what he wanted. But the struggle on such logical consequences of what had already been agreed months earlier when the Lend-Lease bill was enacted showed once more in clear terms that any attempt to seek a declaration of war from Congress would have resulted in resounding failure.

V

The narrow passage of the amendments to the neutrality legislation showed that clashes in the Atlantic such as those involving the *Greer*, the *Kearny* and the *Reuben James* were far from sufficient to persuade Congress that the United States should formally enter the war.[133] But without the likelihood of obtaining a declaration of war, Roosevelt was left with no option. His only choice was to continue the 'undeclared war'.

This was, in any case, Roosevelt's preference. 'We don't want a declared war with Germany,' he told a press conference in early November, 'because we are acting in defense – self-defense – every action.'[134] His entire policy for more than a year had been directed at providing maximum help to Britain (and, more recently, the Soviet Union) as part of American defence, in the – diminishing – hope that the United States would be able to keep out of the direct fighting. Despite the accusations of his detractors, that he was working by devious means to take the country into war, the evidence suggests that the President had been genuine in his earlier expressions of his abhorrence of war, but that he had gradually and reluctantly come to the conclusion that American involvement was both inevitable and necessary if Hitler were to be defeated.[135]

There were, however, good reasons to defer the moment of entry as long as possible.[136] The longer America could remain out of the formal combat, the more advanced her military build-up and the mobilization of an arms economy would be. Moreover, a declaration of war would doubtless have resulted in domestic clamour to utilize the arms and equipment now being sent to Great Britain and the Soviet Union for the United States' armed forces, leading to a weakening, not strengthening, of the resistance to Hitler on the European fighting front in the short term – perhaps with disastrous consequences. American shipping losses to preying U-boats in the Atlantic would, as an immediate consequence, probably have mounted sharply. There was also the real concern that a declaration of war against Germany would immediately bring Japan – Hitler's ally under the Tripartite Pact – into the war. Having to fight in the Pacific would certainly complicate dealing with Hitler, which was consistently seen as the main event.[137] By the autumn the signs were mounting strongly that Japan's entry was simply a matter of time. But American policy was nevertheless to delay that moment as long as possible.

Beyond these considerations, there was, as always, the question of public opinion – not just congressional opposition – to ponder. Public opinion was, to go from the results of surveys, more favourably disposed towards Roosevelt and his policy on the war than Congress, where hardbitten isolationists could always reckon with the additional backing of those with their own varied reasons for wanting to give the President a bloody nose. But the large percentage of the public consistently opposed to entry into the war could not be ignored. Perhaps some of that opinion could be won over. However, Roosevelt's powerful speeches had not dented it to any great extent. The fact had to be faced: unless the United States were to be attacked, a declaration of war – even in the unlikely event that it could be pushed through Congress – would undoubtedly produce a bitterly divided country.

It seems as if Roosevelt had settled in autumn 1941 for as long a period as possible of partial, undeclared hostilities with Germany. Perhaps as justification for avoiding what Churchill had long been pressing for, the President told Lord Halifax that, in any case, 'declarations of war were going out of fashion'.[138] The limited and unprovocative way that he introduced convoying all the way across the Atlantic directly to Britain (and also to Russia) in late November and early December does not suggest he was in any haste to move beyond the current stalemate in relations with Germany. In Roosevelt's ideal scenario, this would have continued for some months.[139] This strategy nevertheless had a limited time-span. The Victory Program, eventually laid before the President in September (and giving rise to an enormous furore when a damaging leak enabled the leading isolationist organ, the *Chicago Tribune*, to publish its details in the first week of December[140]), had after all concluded that Hitler could only be defeated by sending millions of men to fight in Europe by 1943.[141] The prognosis in the plan had envisaged the defeat of the Soviet Union before that date. But even with the Red Army providing far stiffer resistance than American military strategists had forecast, destroying Hitler meant American soldiers fighting a land war in Europe. The document was explicit: 'if our European enemies are to be defeated, it will be necessary for the United States to enter the war.'[142] That day, Roosevelt was hoping, could be delayed. But it could not be postponed indefinitely if Nazism were to be crushed.[143]

The Victory Program recommended 'holding Japan in check pending future developments'.[144] By late November 1941 future developments were

329

certainly pending. Intercepts of Japanese diplomatic intelligence were telling the White House that aggression by Japan was imminent. Roosevelt had hoped to take the United States to the brink but not beyond in the Atlantic, and to keep Japan at bay. But those hopes exploded with the bombs that fell on American ships at anchor far away in the south Pacific on that clear sunny morning of 7 December 1941.

The events of that morning were dire indeed from an American perspective. But Roosevelt, who had striven to hold off direct participation in the growing global conflagration while preparing for it, finally had an incident capable of bringing a united people into the war.

8

Tokyo, Autumn 1941

Japan Decides to Go to War

If we miss the present opportunity to go to war, we will have to submit to American dictation. Therefore, I recognize that it is inevitable that we must decide to start a war against the United States.   Hara Yoshimichi, President of the Privy Council,
5 November 1941

Two years from now we will have no petroleum for military use. Ships will stop moving. When I think about the strengthening of American defences in the south-west Pacific, the expansion of the American fleet, the unfinished China Incident, and so on, I see no end to difficulties. We can talk about austerity and suffering, but can our people endure such a life for a long time?
Tojo Hideki, Japanese Prime Minister, 5 November 1941

In the summer of 1941, Japan's leaders suddenly faced new options. These were framed, as they had been the previous year, by the immediate global consequences of events far away. As earlier, Hitler had made the decisive move. The German invasion of the Soviet Union on 22 June 1941, like the victory over France almost exactly a year earlier, caught Japan's power-elite unawares, in spite of the clear warnings they had been given. Hitler's attack destroyed at one stroke Japanese hopes of building a coalition of forces together with Germany, Italy and the Soviet Union aimed at deterring the western powers from hostilities in the Far East against Japan while she was establishing her dominance of a 'Greater East Asia Co-Prosperity Sphere'. The driving force behind such a strategy had been the Foreign Minister, Matsuoka Yosuke, who in April, following visits to Berlin and Rome, had engineered a spectacular diplomatic success with the signing of the Japanese-Soviet Neutrality Pact in Moscow. That strategy was now in ruins. Instead, the prospect loomed of the Soviet Union compelled, despite ideological differences, to turn towards Britain and America for support in the clash with Nazi Germany. Japan was set to become more diplomatically isolated than ever. And she still had found no exit route from the China quagmire.

Japan's leaders differed sharply in how they judged the opportunities and the dangers that had emerged. But overnight, it was clear, the question of an alternative strategy had arisen. Should Japan postpone, at least temporarily, the policy of expansion to the south, determined the previous summer, in favour of a northern advance to strike at the Soviet Union from the east while the Stalinist regime was reeling from the devastating German assault from the west? Much seemed to speak in favour of grasping the chance that had presented itself. There were powerful advocates of such a drastic reordering of priorities, the most outspoken of them Matsuoka himself. In typically ebullient fashion, he simply cast off the strategy that he had been urging for months. 'Great men will change their minds,' he declared. 'Previously I advocated going south, but now I favour the north.'[1]

Some in the army leadership, too, relished the prospect of landing a fatal blow on the traditional enemy to the north. Army leaders were, however, more cautious than Matsuoka. Japan had, after all, lost around 17,000 men killed or injured in bitter clashes with Soviet troops in the summer of 1939 – the 'Nomonhan Incident' – over a stretch of disputed territory on the Manchurian-Mongolian border. They were less sure than Matsuoka that Germany would prove victorious in the Soviet Union. And, as they were well aware, Soviet forces greatly outnumbered Japan's troop contingent in the north. A military build-up necessary for a northern offensive could not be accomplished overnight. They preferred, therefore, to see how the German-Soviet war developed before committing themselves to an attack in the north, which at this juncture would be a hazardous enterprise. The navy, of course, remained in any case wedded to the southern advance.[2]

Matsuoka became, therefore, an increasingly isolated figure. He soon encountered the combined opposition of the army and navy representatives. In a series of meetings at the end of June, his plans suffered a complete rebuff. The northern option was ruled out – or at least postponed until Germany had proved utterly victorious in the war against the Soviet Union. Defeated and lacking all support in high quarters, Matsuoka was forced to resign as Foreign Minister in mid-July, to be replaced by the more emollient Admiral Toyoda Teijiro.

Shortly afterwards Japan took a crucial step in the planned southern advance. Following pressure on Vichy France, 40,000 Japanese troops (later swelling to 185,000) moved into French Indochina on 28 July.[3] Japan was now in a position to close off the supplies to Chiang Kai-shek passing through the Burma Road. And the way to the oil of the Dutch East Indies now lay open. Aware in advance of the move through intelligence intercepts, the American administration had already started to take retaliatory steps. On 23 July the American Secretary of State, Cordell Hull, informed the Japanese ambassador in Washington, Nomura Kichisaburo, that he was terminating diplomatic deliberations that had been proceeding, for the most part unofficially, for months in the hope of improving the worsening relations between Japan and the United States. Three days later, all Japanese assets in the United States were frozen (followed over the next days by identical measures in Britain, Canada, the Philippines, New Zealand and the Netherlands).[4] Japan would no longer be able to buy oil from America. Keen to avoid provoking a Japanese invasion of the Dutch East Indies, President Roosevelt fought shy of imposing a total oil embargo. Small quantities of low-grade oil, not fit for usage in aircraft, could still be exported. The President appears to have had in mind at this stage temporary restrictions to serve as a deterrent, rather than a total and complete stoppage. But he was in effect bypassed by the administration's hawks in the Treasury and on the newly formed Economic Defense Board, which would not permit the release of funds even to obtain inferior grades of oil. Roosevelt did not discover until early September that Japan had received no oil after 25 July.[5] Effectively, therefore, a total embargo on oil to Japan had been imposed.[6] The Japanese military had seriously miscalculated. They had continued to believe that America would not impose a total oil embargo.[7] Konoe's government was thrown into near panic.[8] Without oil, Japan's quest for power and prosperity was doomed. But Japan had less than two years of oil reserves left, and was rapidly consuming remaining supplies.[9] The clock was ticking.[10]

The southern advance could not wait. The oil of the Dutch East Indies had to be secured for Japan. But that meant, with certainty, a clash not only with the Dutch authorities, but also with Great Britain, and, most threatening to Japan, with the United States. Not only were America, Britain and the Dutch in effective alliance. Their interests were also bound up in the fate of China, where Chiang Kai-shek's nationalists had been engaged (with western support) in the most bitter and brutal of conflicts with the Japanese for over four years – a conflict with no end in sight, and one that had already cost hundreds of thousands of lives. Japan was preparing, therefore, for a possible gigantic showdown with what had come to be labelled the ABCD (American, British, Chinese and Dutch) powers. America's own position (with Britain egging her on) had hardened sharply over the summer. This had pushed Japan still further into the corner where her own policies had driven her. By August 1941, therefore, the outlook was bleak. Intransigence had set in on both sides. War was beginning to appear inevitable. The only question seemed to be: when? The die was cast. Or was it?

In retrospect, the path to the Pacific War appears undeviating. But at the time, even in autumn, Japan's leaders still thought there were possibilities of avoiding the conflict; that options, if narrowed, remained open. Indeed, that was the case. In autumn 1941 there were still significant figures – including the Prime Minister, Konoe, the Foreign Minister, Toyoda, and Emperor Hirohito himself – opposed to war. Even within the army and navy leadership there was hesitation; and much anxiety about the consequences of war. Opinion in the elites was split. Some, especially in the military (backed by the chauvinism of a general public whose belligerence had been whipped up for years by manipulated mass media), were gung-ho. Others were fearful. A protracted war (which was likely), they were sure, could not be won. Its consequences for Japan would be incalculably calamitous. Many more entertained a samurai-like fatalism. War would come. It might mean even Japan's destruction. But that would have to be endured. There could be no retreat. Destruction with honour was better than survival with shame.

These, broadly sketched, were the mentalities that helped shape the way Japan's options were viewed in autumn 1941. By the end of November, the fateful choice had been made. It was to be war. The fleet had already set out for Pearl Harbor. How was this momentous decision arrived at?

I

In August 1941, following the American imposition of the oil embargo, the storm clouds over the Pacific started to gather rapidly. Some among Japan's leaders, previous advocates of the assertiveness that had led to the current predicament, were now gripped by anxiety and foreboding.

The new Foreign Minister, Toyoda Teijiro, tried to bridge the increasingly yawning gulf between American and Japanese interests with proposals drawn up on 5 August and put to Washington the following day. He stipulated that Japan had no intention of stationing troops in the south-west Pacific beyond French Indochina. And she was prepared to guarantee the neutrality of the Philippines (an American possession). These minimal concessions were all the Japanese had to offer. In return, the United States would have to cease military measures against Japan in the south-west

Pacific, urging Britain and the Netherlands to do the same. The United States would also cooperate in Japan's acquisition of natural resources in the Dutch East Indies, restore normal commercial relations, act as a mediator to end the war in China, and accept Japan's special position in French Indochina even once troops were withdrawn.[11] It was scarcely an endearing package from an American perspective. It remained a dead letter.

Another initiative came from an even higher level. Though he had fully supported Japan's expansionist programme and backed the continuing war in China, the Prime Minister, Prince Konoe Fumimaro, was now so disturbed by developments that he contemplated a last, desperate attempt to head off what seemed increasingly like an inexorable collision course with America. He proposed a personal meeting with President Roosevelt, at Honolulu or at sea in the mid-Pacific.[12] Such a proposal had no precedent in Japanese history. And it carried dangers, physical as well as political, for the Prime Minister. Speaking to military leaders, he justified the initiative, not through a wish to bridge the differences with the United States at whatever cost, but by showing the world that Japan had done everything possible to avoid war. 'If it comes to war after we have done all that can be done, that can't be helped,' he declared. 'In that case we will have come to a resolution and the people will also be fully prepared. Moreover, it will be clearly understood by the world in general that we have shown good faith in going to such lengths.'[13] Privately, he appears to have been ready to offer a number of limited concessions, such as the withdrawal of troops from Indochina. According to later testimony of those close to him, Konoe would, if necessary, have sought the Emperor's approval by telegram and agreed to the concessions in order to outflank the army and to save the peace.[14] Given Konoe's usual weakness and indeterminacy, whether he would have taken such a bold step might justifiably be doubted. And had he made any concessions likely to have swayed the Americans, these would almost certainly have been opposed by the military – and by violently anti-American public opinion – back home. At least two plots by fanaticized radical nationalists to murder Konoe were uncovered.[15] Change of government by assassination had only a few years earlier been effected more than once. Konoe, as friendly voices had warned him, would probably not have lived to tell the tale. If he was serious in thinking that he could outmanoeuvre the army by his ploy, he was greatly underestimating the hold which by now the military leadership in both army and navy had gained over the levers of power in Japan.

The Emperor endorsed the idea of a summit with President Roosevelt at an audience with Konoe on 4 August and urged him to proceed without delay.[16] The Foreign Minister, Toyoda, also backed the scheme as a last hope of avoiding disaster. Oikawa Koshiro, the Navy Minister – often hesitant, ambivalent and wavering in his views – was prepared to go along with the suggestion. Possibly he thought its chances of success were slight. He certainly knew that the navy's preparations were well advanced, and that its expeditionary force would be virtually ready for action by the beginning of September.[17] The more forthright Army Minister, Tojo Hideki, gave only conditional approval on behalf of the army. He would not oppose the move; but only as long as Konoe was prepared to uphold the basic, non-negotiable principles of Japanese policy and ready to commit Japan to war against the United States should Roosevelt prove unyielding.[18]

Below ministerial level, others in the military were even less well disposed towards Konoe's initiative. The chief of the navy General Staff, Nagano Osami, remained dogmatically of the view that diplomatic negotiations with the United States should be broken off, and that Japan should go to war. Among naval planners, the view was that the planned summit meeting was 'an odd artifice'. There was scarcely greater endearment in the army. The chief of the army General Staff, Sugiyama Gen, and the Operations Division chief, the hawkish Tanaka Shin'ichi, were willing to acknowledge Konoe's move as 'one last effort', since 'if Roosevelt misinterprets our Empire's true intentions and persists in pursuing the same old policies, no objections can possibly be raised to prevent our confronting this with resolute determination to join battle with the United States'. Likely failure, in other words, would legitimate war. And there was another advantage: 'We can't say that Konoe can't go to the United States. We figure it's 80 percent certain that his trip will end up a failure, but even if he does fail we'll have pinned the Prime Minister down about not resigning.' The manoeuvre was likely to bring about, then, the change in political leadership in Japan that many in the military were already thinking was long overdue. Sugiyama and Tanaka nevertheless struck a note of caution. Pinning the slippery Konoe down 'might be like trying to nail jelly to a wall'.[19]

The Japanese ambassador in Washington, Nomura Kichisaburo – a tall, good-natured, one-eyed, retired admiral with limited command of English, much given to bowing, and relatively pro-American in his views – was instructed on 7 August to seek the summit between Konoe and Roosevelt.[20] The American Secretary of State, Cordell Hull, however, fed by MAGIC digests of Japanese intelligence intercepts, reacted coolly. The move into southern Indochina had confirmed his assumptions. 'Nothing will stop them except force,' he had said on 2 August.[21] He told Nomura bluntly six days later: 'We can begin consultations only when Japan stops using force.' He showed scant interest in the idea of a summit meeting, remarking that he had little confidence in putting it to Roosevelt without evidence of a change in Japanese policy.[22]

Meanwhile, Roosevelt was preoccupied with another summit meeting – one that *was* taking place. Between 9 and 12 August 1941 he was engaged in his high-level talks with Winston Churchill, at Placentia Bay, Newfoundland. To the western powers, the reaffirmation of the commitment to freedom, peace, economic liberalism and rejection of force in international affairs enunciated in the Atlantic Charter signed at the end of their historic conference was a powerful declaration of noble principles. But from a Japanese perspective, the joint statement of Roosevelt and Churchill looked quite different. Its very principles seemed threatening. As Tokyo's leading newspaper, *Asahi*, reported, they seemed simply to restate the determination of the western powers to maintain 'a system of world domination on the basis of Anglo-American world views'.[23] Only submission by Japan to this aim, the conclusion was drawn, would avoid war. The augurs, both in Tokyo and in Washington, for the sort of concessions capable of heading off war that might be made in a Konoe–Roosevelt summit were not promising.

On the American cruiser *Augusta*, during their talks in Placentia Bay, Churchill had urged Roosevelt to take a tough line with the Japanese. Roosevelt was, however, keener to play for time. He had no illusions about Japanese intentions, since the Americans had been reading their intelligence signals for months. But deferring the outbreak of hostilities even for a few weeks would help American military preparations, and would assist the British, so he argued, to build up defences around Singapore. 'I think I can baby them along for three months,' he told Churchill.[24]

When he met Nomura on 17 August, on his return from Placentia Bay, Roosevelt handed him a warning (drawn up during his meeting with Churchill, and based on the latter's draft) that further Japanese advances in the south-west Pacific would prompt American countermeasures, perhaps leading to war. But, retreating from the hard line he appeared to have offered Churchill, the President then gave the Japanese ambassador a second, more conciliatory note. If Japan were to suspend her expansionism and 'embark upon a peaceful program for the Pacific', he would be ready to reopen conversations with Japan. He suggested a meeting in mid-October in Juneau, Alaska. Nomura was sure that Roosevelt was in earnest. 'A reply should be made before this opportunity is lost,' he cabled Tokyo. His government should 'decide on this matter urgently'.[25]

The American ambassador in Tokyo, Joseph C. Grew, highly experienced in Japanese affairs and attuned to their ways of thinking, still firmly believed that skilful diplomacy could find a way out of the impasse. When told of the proposed summit between Roosevelt and Konoe by the Japanese Foreign Minister, Toyoda, on 18 August, he immediately sent a message to Washington, urging 'with all the force at his command, for the sake of avoiding the obviously growing possibility of an utterly futile war between Japan and the United States, that this Japanese proposal not be turned aside without very prayerful consideration'. He was sure, he added in subsequent dispatches, that the Japanese government was ready to make far-reaching concessions. He advised not an immediate attempt to produce a general plan for the reconstruction of the Far East, but a step-by-step relaxation of American sanctions to match actions on Japan's side to implement its proposed commitments.[26]

The Japanese response to Roosevelt's warning and accompanying note – a cordial message from Konoe and formal reply – was agreed by the Liaison Conference on 26 August.[27] Nomura handed them both to the American President two days later.[28] In a personal message, couched in terms of goodwill and regret for past misunderstandings, Konoe urged a meeting as soon as possible, preferably in Hawaii, to 'explore whether it is possible to save the situation'. Discussion of the problems in the Pacific should be broadly framed. Detail could be worked out later by officials. The formal note stressed that Japanese actions had been necessary for national self-defence and underlined the threat posed by American countermeasures. But it was also conciliatory in tone. Japan was prepared, it went on, to remove her troops from Indochina as soon as a just peace could be established in east Asia. There was no intention to advance into neighbouring countries, nor to attack the Soviet Union. 'In a word,' it declared, 'the Japanese Government has no intention of using, without provocation, military force against any neighbouring nation.'[29]

Roosevelt was suitably cordial, even affable, when he received Nomura. He looked forward, he said, to three or four days with Prince Konoe. He was pleased to learn that the Prime Minister spoke good English. He again suggested Juneau as the venue. But he proposed no date. In truth, he was still 'babying' Japan along. Secretary of State Hull in any case poured cold water on hopes of a summit when he met Nomura later that evening. Influenced less by Ambassador Grew than by the head of the State Department's Division of Far Eastern Affairs, the hawkish Stanley K. Hornbeck, and even more so by MAGIC intercepts, Hull was duly mistrustful of a summit without a precise, preformed agenda. 'It seemed to us that Japan was striving to push us into a conference from which general statements would issue,' he wrote later, 'and Japan could then interpret and apply these statements to suit her own purposes,' even citing the President's endorsement. 'It was difficult to believe that the Konoye [Konoe] Government would dare to agree to proposals we could accept,' he added. 'A substantial opposition existed in Japan to any efforts to improve relations with the United States.'[30]

This opposition had meanwhile been active in preparing its own ground. It comprised, in the main, differing factions, each with its own agenda, in both the army and navy, especially among middle-echelon officers. Since the opposition, whatever its factional differences, could always fall back upon the immutability of Japanese expansionist aims and the need to ensure that the sacrifices in the 'China Incident' had not been in vain, it always had good chances of blocking any initiative that posited meaningful concessions. In the first week of September, the counter-position to Konoe's proposals for a summit with Roosevelt was finalized, then confirmed as national policy in the presence of the Emperor. It amounted to a decision that Japan would go to war if agreement could not be reached with the United States within an extremely tight time frame – less than six weeks.

II

Already by 16 August, the day before Roosevelt and Nomura spoke in Washington of a possible summit between the President and Prince Konoe, the bureau and division chiefs of the army's and navy's planning staff were meeting in Tokyo to discuss a proposed 'Plan for Carrying out the Empire's Policies'. The essence of the 'Plan', put forward by the navy, was that Japan should both prepare for war and at the same time conduct diplomacy. This amounted to a compromise. The navy believed a decision for war could follow mobilization; the army wanted it the other way round. But in the compromise, diplomacy was only given the briefest of chances. The countdown to hostilities was already stipulated. The navy had told the army the previous day that it would like an agreement between the two services on operations to be reached by 20 September, and war preparations to be concluded by 15 October. Mid-October was the envisaged diplomacy deadline. If agreement could not be reached by then, Japan would exercise force. Drafts of the 'Plan' were fine-tuned in almost daily meetings between army and navy staff over the next two weeks. Lengthy deliberations over minor wording amendments reflected the nuances of different factions and interests. But nothing of substance was altered. The fundamentals were not in dispute. By 30 August, the document was finalized and agreed as 'Essentials for Carrying out the Empire's Policies'.[31] The critical stipulation was: 'In the event that by early October there is still no prospect of obtaining our demands through diplomatic negotiations, we shall immediately resolve to go to war with the United States (Britain, Holland).'[32]

The demands offered little prospect of diplomatic success. The United States and Great Britain should cease giving military and economic aid to Chiang Kai-shek; they should not extend their military presence in the Far East; and they should provide Japan with necessary economic resources. In return, Japan would agree not to advance from Indochina into neighbouring areas, apart from China, would withdraw from Indochina once a just peace in the Far East had been established, and was prepared to guarantee the neutrality of the Philippines.[33] In fact, on the day before the Liaison Conference on 3 September, called to discuss the 'Essentials', Sugiyama, the army's chief of staff, sent Konoe a warning shot across the bow, in case he showed any sign of weakening. There could be no wavering, Sugiyama emphasized, on the three fundamental principles: the alliance with the Axis powers, the attainment of the Greater East Asia Co-Prosperity Sphere and the stationing of troops in China.[34] These formed the basis of army–navy understanding. Without support from the military, no civilian government could survive. But with such inflexible fundamentals of policy upheld by the military (and with much broader acceptance both among the elites and in public opinion), no diplomatic move stood much chance of success. Konoe was now in a bind partly of his own making. He could not back down from a commitment to the basic principles which he himself had been instrumental in establishing since the beginning of the war in China. But without a weakening of those principles, he had little or nothing to offer Roosevelt in the summit that he was still intent on promoting.

Konoe's heavily compromised position was probably the main reason – alongside his ingrained weakness and supine nature – why he raised no objections at the seven-hour-long Liaison Conference on 3 September, when the 'Essentials for Carrying Out the Empire's Policies' were deliberated, then adopted. The other main proponent of a diplomatic settlement present at the meeting, the Foreign Minister, Toyoda, was equally compliant. The tone of the meeting was set by the bellicose chiefs of staff, Nagano and Sugiyama. It was plain that, while both were prepared to tolerate a short period of diplomatic soundings, their main concern was urgent preparation for the war that was judged to be highly likely. Neither was prepared to contemplate any loss of time in mobilization. War, if it were to come – and both thought it well-nigh inevitable – had to come soon. 'Although I am confident that at the present time we have a chance to win a war,' stated Nagano, 'I fear this opportunity will disappear with the passage of time.' His prognosis was one that should have given rise to the gravest doubts about the wisdom of his proposed course of action. He hoped for a quick showdown in a decisive battle with the enemy in Japanese waters. That would not in itself end the war. But it might give Japan the resources to fight a long war. 'If, on the contrary,' Nagano frankly pointed out, 'we get into a long war without a decisive battle, we will be in difficulty, especially since our supply of resources will become depleted. If we cannot obtain these resources, it will not be possible to carry on a long war.' His conclusion was that the armed forces had no alternative 'but to push forward'. Sugiyama concurred. The target date for war preparations could be no later than the last ten days of October. Diplomatic objectives must be attained within the first ten days of the month. 'Failing this,' he said, 'we must push forward. We cannot let things be dragged out.' The main reason he gave for this was the ability to be able to act in the north the following spring – an army, though not a navy, priority.

The remainder of the Conference was largely spent in discussion of wording amendments to the proposed 'Essentials'. Strikingly, however, there was no rooted objection. Though long, the meeting was smooth. The crucial document, setting a timetable for a decision on war, was accepted without serious demur. Even more remarkable was that Nagano's prognosis – imprecise, highly speculative and not altogether encouraging as it was – did not encounter serious questioning, let alone criticism. Even the navy's own planners thought the odds would run strongly against Japan if the war were protracted, which was likely to be the case. Nagano was aware of this thinking. But his own inability to offer more than a determination to go to war resting upon lack of a perceived alternative and reliance on good luck drew no resistance from Konoe, Toyoda or the rest of the Liaison Conference.[35]

The vital document, advocating a policy committing Japan to war, was rubber-stamped by the Cabinet late the next day. The last, and most formal, stage of adoption was to present it to the Imperial Conference, sitting in the Emperor's presence, on 6 September. Once that had taken place, it would be enshrined as national policy and, sealed with the Emperor's imprimatur, as good as impossible to change.

The evening before, Konoe went to the palace to brief the Emperor formally on the 'Essentials for Carrying out the Empire's Policies' (though Hirohito was, as usual, well abreast of developments and recognized that he would probably soon be called upon to make 'a truly grave decision').[36] The Emperor was alarmed at what the document endorsed by the Liaison Conference implied. He thought it gave precedence to war over diplomacy, and wanted Konoe to alter the highly dangerous October deadline imposed on negotiations. The Prime Minister could offer only the consolation that he would do his utmost to succeed in the negotiations, but said it was difficult to amend a decision taken by the Liaison Conference. He suggested the Emperor question the chiefs of staff.[37]

A little later, Nagano and Sugiyama appeared at the palace, with Konoe in attendance. Hirohito asked about the probability of victory in the event of war with the United States. When Sugiyama replied that victory was probable within three months, the Emperor became angry – a most rare occurrence. 'At the time of the China Incident, the army told me that we could achieve peace immediately after dealing them one blow with three divisions,' Hirohito objected, adding: 'Sugiyama, you were Army Minister at that time.' Sugiyama answered lamely that China was a vast area, and Japan had encountered unexpected difficulties. 'Isn't the Pacific Ocean even more vast?' the Emperor retorted. He reminded his chief of staff of his warnings at the time, then asked directly: 'Sugiyama, are you lying to me?' Nagano intervened to save his colleague's embarrassment. He agreed that victory could not be totally guaranteed. This was the case in all conflicts. He then presented a medical analogy. If a doctor says there is a 70 per cent chance of saving a sick patient by an operation, but that not operating would mean certain death, then surgery would surely be chosen. 'And if, after the surgery, the patient dies, one must say that was meant to be. This indeed', he claimed, with dubious logic, 'is the situation we face today . . . If we waste time, let the days pass, and are forced to fight after it is too late to fight, then we won't be able to do a thing about it.' It was a strange argument. But it seemed to calm the Emperor. Konoe asked whether he should change the agenda for the next day's Imperial Conference. The Emperor replied: 'There is no need to change anything.'[38]

Could the Emperor at this crucial juncture have done other than resignedly accept that which he had just fundamentally questioned? Did he have a choice? Could he have opted to give his complete backing to diplomacy and rejected the countdown to a decision for war? One counsellor at least thought other options were available to him. He was advised by Shigemitsu Mamoru, former ambassador to Great Britain, that Japan could best retain her status as a great power and influence postwar politics by staying out of the European conflict and re-examining her own current policies.[39] In plain terms, this implied backing away from an alliance with the Axis powers and making concessions on China and south-east Asia sufficient to impress the Americans in negotiations. But substantial concessions were opposed by most of the power-elite, while without them the oil-clock would continue running down. In any case, the Emperor's power was more limited in practice than it was in theory. Constitutionally, the Emperor still held executive power. In theory, the armed forces acted in accordance with his will. And it was certainly true that the leaders of government as well as the armed forces felt a bond of honour through obedience to the Emperor. But, quite apart from Hirohito's less than forceful personality, to try to exercise executive power by overriding a decision reached in a Liaison Conference by the army and navy High Command in combination with the leadership of the civil government would have been to take a great risk with the standing of the imperial throne. In practice, it was unthinkable. Hirohito certainly preferred peace to the dangers of war with America. But he had inwardly as well as externally favoured the steps in the quest for Japan's power and glory that had placed the country in its present plight. He could not order an unwilling military to retreat from a stance which had become associated in the eyes of most of the general public, as well as major sections of the elites, with Japan's national honour. To have attempted conflict with the military leadership in those circumstances would conceivably have been to put the position of the monarchy itself in jeopardy.

Twenty minutes before the beginning of the Imperial Conference, scheduled for 10 o'clock on the morning of 6 September, Hirohito sent for his chief counsellor, the Lord Keeper of the Privy Seal, Kido Koichi, and told him that he wanted to raise some questions at the meeting. This was quite contrary to convention. The Emperor's traditional role was to sit silently, while his Privy Council President, Hara Yoshimichi, posed questions on his behalf to ministers and armed forces' leaders. Kido advised him that the tradition should be upheld on this occasion, too, but that it would be fitting for the Emperor to give a warning at the end of the meeting to encourage active cooperation in the pursuit of success in the forthcoming negotiations.[40]

A momentous Imperial Conference began with a statement by the Prime Minister, Prince Konoe, on the increasingly strained international situation.[41] A united front of the United States, Great Britain and the Netherlands stood opposed to the Empire. The Soviet Union might well join them. If this situation continued, over time Japan would be unable to sustain her national power. Konoe laid the stress on diplomatic measures to prevent the disaster of war. But should they fail within a specified time, he said, 'I believe we cannot help but take the ultimate step in order to defend ourselves'. It was scarcely a ringing endorsement of the overriding need (which Konoe had privately expressed) to make significant sacrifices for the greater good of peace.

Nagano, the navy's chief of staff, followed. He rehearsed the same arguments he had advanced at the Liaison Conference three days earlier. The key factor was time. Delay would reduce Japan 'to a crippled condition'. He pointed out that oil supplies 'are dwindling day by day. This will cause a gradual weakening of our national defence, and lead to a situation in which, if we maintain the status quo, the capacity of our Empire to act will be reduced in the days to come,' while American and British military preparedness was being strengthened. As at the Liaison Conference, his prognosis in the event of war was based upon a best-case scenario. *If* Japan could swiftly defeat American and British naval forces 'in the areas of the ocean we have in mind' (meaning in the Far East), and *if*, in a likely prolonged war, strategic areas and raw materials could be obtained to make Japan's position impregnable, then there was a good *chance* of victory. Even then the outcome would depend upon overall national power and unforeseeable developments in the world situation. But – this was the gist of his statement – Japan's best opportunity lay in the immediate future. She could not afford to wait. Diplomacy must be given its chance. However, stringent time limits had to be set. And results must be obtained which would mean that Japan was not to be compelled to fight at a later date – and in more disadvantageous circumstances. It was a worrying assessment, an irrational one for a nation likely to embark upon a major war against a country with overwhelming advantages in strength and resources. The line of argument contained obvious flaws, weaknesses and untested assumptions. But no serious scrutiny followed.

Nor was there any rigorous interrogation of Sugiyama, the army chief of staff, who began by expressing his complete agreement with Nagano's statement. Sugiyama outlined the pressure of time which had determined late October as the completion date of war preparations. He accepted, of course, the need to exhaust all diplomatic measures, but it was obvious that they were for him of secondary importance. The main concern was to be ready for war in the near future. He added – his own optimistic prognosis – that 'if we could take advantage of the winter season and quickly finish our military operations in the South, I believe we would be in a position to deal with any changes in the Northern situation that might take place next spring or thereafter'. (This rested on the army's highly optimistic estimation, prepared for the Imperial Conference: 'It is virtually certain that Germany will sweep through the greater part of Soviet Europe within the year and that the Stalin regime will flee east of the Urals . . . It is clear that the Stalin regime, having lost Soviet Europe, will weaken with the passage of time and lose its capacity to prosecute the war.'[42])

After Toyoda had provided a lengthy description of diplomatic dealings with the United States since the spring, the director of the Planning Board, General Suzuki Teiichi, addressed the issue of material resources. As a result of the economic embargo by the western powers, 'our Empire's national power is declining day by day', he reported. 'Our liquid fuel stockpile, which is the most important, will reach bottom by June or July of next year, even if we impose strict wartime controls on the civilian demand.' His conclusion was obvious: 'it is vitally important for the survival of our Empire that we make up our minds to establish and stabilise a firm economic base.' That meant military action.

The President of the Privy Council, Hara, now took the opportunity to pose questions on behalf of the Emperor. In contrast to the military leaders, he placed the emphasis squarely upon diplomacy. Conventional efforts would not suffice. Every possible means had to be tried. He supported Konoe's initiative to meet President Roosevelt. He accepted that military preparations had to be made for the eventuality that diplomacy ultimately failed. But he was troubled by the draft of the 'Essentials for Carrying out the Empire's Policies' presented to the Conference. It implied a primacy given to war, not diplomacy. The Navy Minister, Oikawa, tried to assuage him. There was no priority for war. This would be a last resort only when and if the most serious diplomatic effort had failed. Hara seemed contented. A decision for war, should Konoe's efforts fail, would, he took it, be subject to careful deliberation. As long as diplomatic negotiations were carried out and taken as far as possible, he was satisfied. But before the proposal facing the Conference received the Imperial Assent, Hara asked for full support to be placed behind Konoe's forthcoming visit to the United States and in avoiding 'the worst possible situation between Japan and the United States'. At this point, there was an embarrassing silence. Then something extraordinary occurred. The Emperor himself, in his squeaky high-pitched voice, asked: 'Why don't you answer?' After a moment or two, Oikawa took it upon himself to utter that, although war preparations would be started, every effort to negotiate would be undertaken. There was a further awkward silence. Neither Nagano nor Sugiyama commented. Then the Emperor spoke again. 'Why doesn't the High Command answer?' At this point Hirohito took out of his pocket a piece of paper and read out a short – and delphic – reflection composed by his grandfather, Emperor Meiji, at the beginning of the war with Russia in 1904:

Across the four seas
All are brothers.
In such a world,
Why do the waves rage,
The winds roar?

He said he frequently read the composition to remind him of Emperor Meiji's 'peace-loving spirit'.[43] Nagano and Sugiyama, taken aback, rose apologetically in turn to underline their agreement with Hara's emphasis on the vital importance of peace negotiations as a priority. With that, the unusual and tense Imperial Conference drew to a close.

The Emperor's extraordinary intervention, and the evident disagreements over the relative weighting of diplomatic negotiations and military preparations, could not conceal the enormous significance of what had just received the Imperial Assent and, therefore, become national policy: that Japan was now virtually committed to war. If, within a matter of a mere few weeks, diplomatic negotiations – not yet even scheduled, and foreseen as having only scant chances of success – turned out to be predictably unfavourable, a decision for war would be confirmed. For all its drama, at the Imperial Conference, as at the Liaison Conference that had preceded it, the lack of fundamental opposition to this most probable, and highly fateful, development was striking. The compromise reached between those favouring early military action, mainly the armed services leaders, and those stressing the urgency of diplomacy was in essence a hollow one. While the military leaders forcefully advanced their case, paying little more than lip-service to diplomacy, the supporters of negotiations were weak, defensive and willing to accept the ultimate rationale of war before the winter against the United States. Moreover, no voice was raised to challenge the military logic, the limitations of Japanese *matériel* and manpower in a long war, or the very inflexibility of the negotiating position as regards China or the southern advance to build the 'Greater East Asia Co-Prosperity Sphere'. Though unease at the worrying prospect of war was manifest, and though there were plainly disagreements within Japan's ruling elites, there was no division between 'doves' and 'hawks'. The dividing line fell rather between those with cold feet and the fatalists.

The latter, prominent among the military, took the view that war, whatever its outcome, was inevitable. The thinking was reflected in an answer prepared by the army General Staff for possible use at the Imperial Conference. To the question whether war with Britain and the United States was unavoidable, the prepared answer stated:

The construction of a New Order in East Asia, centring on the Empire's disposition of the China Incident, is unshakeable national policy. However, United States policy towards Japan rests on a status quo world view that would obstruct the Empire's rise and expansion in East Asia in order to dominate the world and defend democracy. The policy of Japan is in fundamental contradiction to this. Collisions between the two will finally develop into war after periods of tension and relaxation. This may be said to have the nature of historical inevitability. So long as the United States does not alter its policies towards Japan, the realities of the situation will reduce the Empire to the point of no return where it cannot help but resort to war as the final means of self-preservation and self-defence. If for the sake of a temporary peace we were now to yield one step to the United States by a partial retreat from state policy, the strengthening of America's military position will lead to its demanding further retreats of ten steps then a hundred. Ultimately, the Empire will wind up having to do whatever the United States wants it to do.[44]

This, rather than the lukewarm underwriting of Konoe's peace manoeuvres, represented the true face of thinking, not just of the army, but of the navy as well. It amounted to a fatalistic acceptance that Japan could only break free of dependence upon America by a military gamble that might well end in disaster. Given the dominance of such thinking in the Japanese elite, the chances of avoiding war were now slim indeed.

III

Losing no time once the Imperial Conference was over, Konoe left for an unofficial – and highly secret – meeting with the American ambassador, Joseph Grew, at the residence of Count Bunkichi Ito, head of one of Japan's great noble families. The only other persons present were the Prime Minister's private secretary, Ushiba Tomohiko, the United States embassy counsellor, Eugene H. Dooman (who had been born in Japan and had a deep knowledge of the country he had lived in for twenty-three years), and Konoe's mistress. Konoe had managed to reach her by telephone while she was at the hairdressers and told her to be ready. A car would soon pick her up to take her to the secret rendezvous. With the servants dismissed for the evening to maintain absolute secrecy, her job was to look after the catering arrangements. She was introduced as the 'daughter of the house'. With Ushiba and Dooman translating, Konoe and Grew talked frankly for three hours. Konoe stressed how anxious he was to have the meeting with

Roosevelt, and that time was of the essence. He thought that, in direct talks with the President, he could resolve the immediate problems and prevent war. This was the absolute priority. A detailed agreement could be worked out later by officials. He acknowledged his own responsibility for the 'China Incident', the Tripartite Pact and the deterioration of relations with the United States. He was even prepared, he suggested, to accept in principle the 'Four Principles', of the inviolability of territorial sovereignty, non-interference in the internal affairs of other countries, equality of commercial opportunity and preservation of the status quo in the pacific, laid down in April by Cordell Hull as the non-negotiable basis of American policy. Konoe thought he could carry the Japanese people with him. He was aware of the risk to his life – an assassination attempt by four armed nationalist fanatics only a few days later was foiled by security guards[45] – but regarded this as unimportant in the greater purpose of saving the peace. Grew and Dooman returned convinced of Konoe's sincerity. Grew, in what he told Konoe would be 'the most important cable' of his career, exhorted Washington to approve the meeting with the President. But Cordell Hull remained deeply suspicious. And Stanley Hornbeck, his chief adviser, was as hostile as ever.[46]

Roosevelt himself had already indicated a changed, hardened tone to Nomura on receiving the Japanese ambassador again, in Hull's presence, on 3 September, on the same date that the important Liaison Conference was taking place in Tokyo. The President this time gave Nomura no encouragement. He, like Prince Konoe, had public opinion to take into account, he said. And opinion was vehement in its demands 'that there be no changes in our policy in order to accommodate Japan'. He professed still to want a meeting with Konoe. But a summit, he pointed out, could not be undertaken without preliminary talks. There were still major differences which would have to be cleared up beforehand. Hull's 'Four Principles' were once more emphasized. Essentially, Roosevelt was stating once more that agreement was only possible if Japan bowed in advance to American demands on China and the Tripartite Pact, renouncing her claim to dominance of the 'new order' in the Far East and ending discrimination in international trade. The limited concessions, intended to pave the way for the summit, offered by Toyoda in a dispatch transmitted on 4 September before hearing the report of Nomura's meeting with Roosevelt, were scarcely sufficient to alter this basic American position.[47]

Even so, Nomura cabled his view to Tokyo on 11 September that a significant Japanese move on China would pave the way for Konoe to meet

Roosevelt. His cable smacked of increasing desperation. He proposed, by now more in hope than belief, to let the Americans know that Japan would agree to withdraw all its troops from China within two years of an end of hostilities. He thought this might provide at least the basis for discussions at a summit. Negotiations for a ceasefire and a subsequent peace conference would then take longer, he somewhat cynically calculated, so that any actual withdrawal would still be some years down the line, by which time much might have happened to alter circumstances. He asked for a firm decision on troop withdrawal.[48]

This was provided by the Liaison Conference on 13 September, and adopted as policy a week later. But the terms were unlikely to prove endearing to the Americans as a basis for peace negotiations. The army, angered at even the moderate watering down of Japanese demands by Toyoda on 4 September, now stiffened them again. The 'Basic Terms of Peace between Japan and China', presented to the Liaison Conference, insisted on the continued stationing of Japanese forces in northern China and Inner Mongolia for defence against Communism. Other troops would be withdrawn as soon as the 'China Incident' was settled. But this was to be brought about by merging the Chungking government of Chiang Kai-shek with the Japanese puppet regime under Wang Ching-wei in Nanking – something which it was obvious the Chinese nationalists would never freely accept. China and Japan would cooperate economically. Manchukuo was, of course, to be recognized.[49] The army's position was that, should these terms be rejected, Japan must be ready to go to war.[50]

Toyoda, the Foreign Minister, was reluctant to present this tougher set of demands to the Americans, certain that it would meet outright rejection. Ambassador Nomura confirmed this on 27 September when he eventually received the new 'Draft Understanding'. By this point, the armed forces were rapidly losing confidence in Toyoda, and in Konoe. The fragile compromise that had temporarily held together those factions in the elite pressing for war without delay and those hoping to stave off war through negotiations was now breaking apart. On 25 September Sugiyama and Nagano, the chiefs of staff of the army and navy, had successfully pressed for a deadline of 15 October to be set for the successful completion of negotiations with the United States. By that date, the decision for war or peace had to be taken. Konoe was shocked. He threatened to resign. But Kido reminded him that he himself had been present at the Imperial Conference on 6 September when 'early October' was accepted as the last date a decision could be taken.[51] Konoe backed down. Unable to abdicate responsibility for, or change the course of, unfolding events which he thought disastrous, the Prime Minister left Tokyo and retired, wearied and depressed, to his home in the seaside resort of Kamakura.[52]

The predictable American reply to the Japanese terms was not long in coming. Behind the language of diplomacy, when Hull met Nomura on 2 October, stood the blunt rejection of the Japanese proposals and an unyielding restatement of American demands, which in turn were by now inflexible and completely unacceptable to Japan. Hull also indicated his doubts about the value of a meeting between Konoe and Roosevelt until Japan was prepared to alter its stance.[53] China, as had been the case throughout, was the crux. War, it now seemed plain, could only be avoided if Konoe could persuade his army leadership to commit itself to troop withdrawals from China. Of that, there was not the slightest chance. Toyoda was overruled by the military representatives in the Liaison Conference on 4 October when he wanted to reply to Hull's uncompromising note. The army and navy chiefs of staff had lost patience with American delaying tactics. They wanted an end to further attempts at negotiation.[54]

Even so, the navy was not altogether united in its stance. The Navy Minister, Oikawa – a born waverer, in contrast to the Army Minister, Tojo – visited Konoe at Kamakura and told him that 'we must be prepared to do nothing less than swallow whole the United States proposal', promising the navy's support and presuming that the army would also comply.[55] It was wishful thinking. The hopes of Konoe and Oikawa, aligned to those of Toyoda, of overthrowing the Imperial Conference's decision of 6 September were doomed to failure. Oikawa could not even rely upon the united backing of the navy, let alone of the army. The chief of staff, Nagano, was the most forthright of those who insisted on an early decision, and a commitment to the policy that war would follow if negotiations had not been brought to a successful conclusion – meaning acceptance of Japanese demands – by mid-October. Between Oikawa and Nagano, other voices could be heard from navy leaders, worrying about the consequences of a war with the United States, advising caution, implying that the army would have to soften its stance if the navy opted for continued negotiation, but ultimately ambiguous and refusing to speak forcefully and plainly for peace rather than war. The head of the navy's Operations Division, Fukudome Shigeru, summed up the concerns of those whose feet were turning cold when he said on 6 October, at a meeting of army and navy planning chiefs: 'I have no confidence in South Seas operations. As far as losses of ships are concerned, 1.4 million tons will be sunk in the first year of the war. The results of the new war games conducted by the Combined Fleet are that there will be no ships for civilian requirements in the third year of the war. I have no confidence.'⁵⁶ But such serious doubts stemming from the centre of naval planning operations remained without practical consequences. The divisions remained. And it was Oikawa rather than Nagano who found himself increasingly isolated within the navy leadership.

The army, meanwhile, was far more united. Its stance was more un-equivocal than that of the navy. Negotiations, it was adjudged, stood no chance of success (though they could be continued until 15 October). Most pointedly, it was stated that no changes, even minor ones in wording, were to be made on the issue of the stationing of troops in China. Nevertheless, Fukudome's statement had worried army leaders. If it were true, they agreed that the Army and Navy Ministers and chiefs of staff would have to resign for having misled the Imperial Conference into sanctioning a war which Japan had no chance of winning. The claim would have to be clarified. But when Tojo and Oikawa met on the morning of 7 October, incisiveness clashed with ambiguity. Tojo was emphatic that to accept Hull's 'Four Principles' was to return to the position of the 1920s, under the Nine Power Treaty, and to Japan's state of powerlessness before the 'Manchurian Incident'. This would upturn the whole of Japanese policy since 1931, and totally undermine the aim of the 'Greater East Asia Co-Prosperity Sphere'. His other point of no compromise was the stationing of troops. This was the 'absolute minimum demand'. To withdraw troops from northern China and Mongolia would threaten the existence of Man-chukuo. Once again, it would mean a return to the country's weakness and exposure to American dominance. All Oikawa could offer as a parry to such a clear and unbending position was that negotiations should continue, but that he did not want to alter the Imperial Conference decision, nor to object to a resolution for war.⁵⁷

With the clock ticking towards the deadline of 15 October, and with unity and clarity on the question of peace or war still missing, Konoe summoned a meeting of the crucial five government ministers (the Foreign, Army and Navy Ministers, and General Suzuki of the Cabinet Planning Board, besides himself) to take place at his Ogikubo residence on the outskirts of Tokyo on Sunday, 12 October. The meeting gave Konoe few grounds for celebrations on his fiftieth birthday. Tojo declared at the outset in his usual blunt manner that negotiations held out no promise. Oikawa could have taken the opportunity to declare the navy's unwilling-ness to risk a war that, as Fukudome had stated some days earlier, some of its leading planners feared could not be won. A clear stance from the navy might, even at this juncture, have shifted the odds in favour of peace, not war. Instead, Oikawa simply restated the dilemma of negotiations or military action. He added, however, that if the route of negotiations were chosen, this would mean a decision 'not to resort to war for perhaps several years', a line that ran counter to the policy adopted at the Imperial Conference on 6 September. Oikawa then baulked at advancing any recommendation, leaving the decision to the Prime Minister. Konoe asked how the Foreign Minister, Toyoda, estimated the prospects of negotiations. Put on the spot, Toyoda equivocated. He could not say with confidence that they would prove successful. It would depend upon what the other side had to say. Tojo pounced on the truthful, but in the context utterly feeble, answer. 'Such a wobbly position will put me in a bind. I won't be able to persuade the High Command to go along,' the Army Minister exclaimed. 'There must be much greater grounds for confidence.' Oikawa agreed that Japan might find herself 'strung along', then ultimately sucked into war anyway. Konoe said that, of the two options, he chose diplomatic negotiations. But Tojo countered that this was simply a subjective view. He could not convince the High Command on that basis alone. The meeting ended inconclusively. But the army's stance was now dominant. It had not been supported outright at the meeting. But nor had any of the other four present directly rejected Tojo's position.[58] The crisis of Konoe's government was deepening.

It plunged to the point of no return on 14 October. Konoe had arranged to meet Tojo for a private discussion just prior to the Cabinet meeting that day. All this meeting did was to reveal how wide the gulf between the two men had become. Konoe said he was sure that to open negotiations with a chance of rescuing peace hinged upon the issue of Japanese troops in China. He suggested to Tojo that Japan 'ought to give in for a time', accede to 'the formality of withdrawing troops and save ourselves from the crisis of a Japanese-American war'. It was necessary, he stated, 'to end the China Incident'. The Army Minister was appalled at what he saw as a breach of trust by Konoe, now retreating from a formal agreement at the Imperial Conference. He rejected the suggestion out of hand. 'If at this time we yield to the United States,' Konoe recalled Tojo saying, 'she will take steps that are more and more high-handed, and will probably find no place to stop. The problem of withdrawing troops is one, you say, of forgetting the honour and of seizing the fruits, but, to this, I find it difficult to agree from the point of view of maintaining the fighting spirit of the Army.' Konoe replied that American superiority in material resources meant Japan had to proceed with great caution. Tojo's disdain for Konoe now meant reason momentarily deserted him. 'There are times when we must have the courage to do extraordinary things – like jumping, with eyes closed, off the veranda of the Kiyomizu Temple' (a Buddhist shrine in Kyoto, on the edge of a cliff), he snapped. The difference between the Prime Minister and him, Tojo stated, ending his extraordinary outburst, could be put down to personality. The implication was clear. Bolder leadership than that which Konoe could provide was necessary at this critical juncture.[59]

Tojo also spoke with great passion at the Cabinet meeting that followed. 'To submit to the contentions of the United States in their entirety', he thundered, 'will annihilate the gains from the China Incident and by extension threaten the existence of Manchukuo, even affecting Japanese rule over Korea and Taiwan.' The obvious intimation was that Japan would be cast back to powerlessness such as she had not experienced since before the time of the great Emperor Meiji. Tojo pointed to the millions of Japanese troops who had fought against hardship, the hundreds of thousands of war casualties, the billions spent on the struggle for the future of the nation. 'Of course, if we want to go back to the little Japan of pre-Manchurian Incident days, there's nothing else to be said, is there?' he asked, rhetorically. There was nothing for it. Japan simply had to insist upon the stationing of troops in China, the heart of her demands. To concede now to the United States would be to endanger that future. It would mean a foreign policy amounting merely to submission.[60] The Cabinet listened in silence, cowed by the Army Minister's fervour, as he reminded them that they remained committed to the policy agreed by the Imperial Conference of 6 September: if no diplomatic settlement had been agreed by early October, then it would be war. Military preparations had been proceeding in accordance with that decision. They could now only be stopped by agreement with the United States on the issue of troops in China.[61] The logic was plain. Only a new Cabinet, not bound by the decision of 6 September, could reverse the momentum for war.

Konoe understood the logic. He arrived for dinner with two colleagues that evening dressed in a traditional Japanese gown to say that he was there only to enjoy their hospitality. Their planned discussion was no longer necessary. His Cabinet was about to fall.[62] In the early evening of 16 October, Konoe went to the palace and presented his resignation.

In his letter to the Emperor, Konoe expressed his continued belief that 'given time, the possibility of reaching an agreement with the United States is not hopeless'. The crux remained the withdrawal of troops from China. As he had done in speaking to Tojo, Konoe now advised the Emperor that the issue could 'be settled if we are willing to sacrifice our honour to some extent and agree to the formula suggested by America'. He could at any rate not agree to plunging into a great war with the China Incident still unsettled, especially since he felt his grave responsibility for the unfolding of events since 1937. 'Now is the time', he wrote, 'for us to sacrifice the present for the future.' He admitted, however, that he had failed to persuade Tojo of this, and that the War Minister was adamantly of the view that Japan should 'grasp the present opportunity and get ready for war at once'. He realized, therefore, Konoe concluded, that his ideas could not prevail, and that he could not carry out his governmental responsibilities.[63]

Despite his unyielding stance over the previous days, Tojo himself had belatedly, and somewhat surprisingly, come to see, even before Konoe had resigned, that, in the face of the navy's hesitation and uncertainty, the decision by the Imperial Conference of 6 September needed to be re-examined. Only a new government, unbound by that decision, could undertake the task. When sounded out on a possible replacement for Konoe, Tojo suggested Prince Higashikuni, an army officer and close relative of the Emperor, as the only person capable of holding together the army and navy and sustaining national unity while abandoning the time limit set for a war decision and conducting a thorough policy review. Konoe agreed, following a sleepless night, that Higashikuni would be the best choice. But, under the express advice of Kido, anxious not to risk the prestige of the imperial house in an attempt to master the crisis, Hirohito rejected the proposal. Decisive was Kido's point that a Cabinet led by a royal prince might eventually 'cause the Imperial House to become an object of public hatred'. An astonished Tojo found himself summoned to the palace and asked by the Emperor to serve as Prime Minister. Tojo's belated doubts about the course set for war, his unquestioning loyalty to the Emperor, his lack of political ambition and his ability to hold the army in check had persuaded Kido to favour him over the only other individual considered at this point, the irresolute Navy Minister, Oikawa.[64] But this could not disguise the fact: the most fundamental opponent of troop withdrawals from China, the man who had taken the hardest line on negotiations and, more than any other, had shaped the current crisis on the decision for war or peace, General Tojo Hideki, was now running the Japanese government.

IV

Tojo was a military man through and through, a career officer who had worked his way up through army officialdom. It had been his second nature to look no further than army interests. His refusal to budge on the issue of the stationing of troops in China, the potential lifeline to peace negotiations that had brought down Konoe's administration, was testimony to the rigidity of his stance in upholding the priority of army concerns. He was a man of limited vision, with an unquestioning sense of obedience and service to the Emperor. 'We're still only human, but the Emperor is divine,' he remarked. 'I shall always bow my head to His Excellency's divinity and greatness.'[65] Now, called to take an office he had never in his wildest dreams imagined occupying, he was at once, and for the first time in his career, compelled to look beyond the army, to the wider interests of the nation at a time of great crisis.

Ironically, his appointment as Prime Minister offered a last glimmer of hope that war might be avoided. In pressing the appointment, Kido had overcome opposition in the gathering of senior statesmen – the seven former heads of government, on whose judgement Hirohito relied in selecting a new Prime Minister – by arguing that Tojo would not start a war if the Emperor spoke to him, and would be capable of handling negotiations with the United States.[66] Tojo had left the audience with the Emperor asking for time to reflect upon the burden of responsibility now thrust upon him. The Emperor had asked him to bring about closer cooperation between the army and the navy – meaning, if cryptically expressed, that the armed services should be persuaded to unite behind the push for a negotiated settlement – and summoned Oikawa to tell him the same. Tojo and Oikawa were, shortly afterwards, joined by Kido, who explained the Emperor's wishes in more explicit terms. The new Cabinet, Kido indicated, should on the Emperor's orders re-examine state policy 'without being obsessed with the Imperial Conference decision of 6 September'. This was a remarkable step. Never before had the Emperor been known to order the bypassing of a decision taken in his own presence at an Imperial Conference. Tojo was being asked to 'go back to blank paper' – to start, that is, with a clean sheet.[67]

Tojo assembled his Cabinet with great speed. In this, he quickly showed that he knew his own mind; he would not brook interference. He rejected Oikawa's suggestion that he be replaced as Navy Minister by Toyoda Soemu. Tojo thought this would cause trouble with the army, well aware of Toyoda's antipathy towards their leadership. Oikawa gave way, and agreed to Shimada Shigetaro, Commander-in-Chief of the Yokosuka naval station, as his replacement. Tojo also brusquely dismissed attempts by the army to influence his selection of ministers.[68] Of particular importance was the position of Foreign Minister. Here, Tojo's rejection of suggestions that he bring back the stridently anti-American and pro-Axis Matsuoka was a sign of his readiness to follow the Emperor's instructions to find a way to prevent war, even at this late hour. Instead, he made Togo Shigenori, former ambassador in Berlin and Moscow, a highly experienced diplomat, his Foreign Minister. Togo accepted the nomination as long as there was a serious intention to work for successful negotiations with America. He was assured that this would be the case, and that the army would have to agree to concessions to make that possible. Tojo himself retained the Army Ministry as a lever to attempt to bend the army to his policy. He also took over home affairs, with a view to quelling possible internal unrest if a deal should be struck with the United States.[69]

In fact, the prospects on the American side for such a deal, at least some sort of pieced-together arrangement to prevent the headlong rush to war and buy time for some months, were not wholly extinguished. Tojo's appointment had sounded alarm bells in London and in Chungking. The British Foreign Office and Chinese nationalists alike feared an immediate move by Japan to cut off supplies to China, bringing Chiang Kai-shek's struggle to its knees. They pressed the Americans for support.[70] Washington, too, viewed Tojo's appointment with foreboding. War seemed all at once much closer. At the State Department, Cordell Hull adjudged Tojo to be a 'typical Japanese officer, with a small-bore, straight-laced, one-track mind' and 'rather stupid'. He feared the worst.[71] President Roosevelt was, however, also listening to advice from the Joint Army-Navy Board, reminding him that the United States navy was still not ready to take on Japan in the Pacific without seriously, perhaps fatally, undermining the support it was giving to Britain in the Atlantic, still seen as the priority.[72] So all chances of staving off war were not yet fully foreclosed on either the American or the Japanese side.

However, Tojo had been ultra-hawkish in policy direction for too long to change course convincingly at the eleventh hour. And though, in contrast to the weak and vacillating Konoe, he had the appearance of being Japan's strong man, he was no match for the military forces that he himself had helped to unleash. Despite his military background, and the retention of the position of Army Minister, he had no direct control over the operational staff of the army, let alone of the navy. Here, the personnel was unchanged. And both branches of the armed forces had gone too far down the line, wedded themselves too deeply to war preparations, to be prepared to back off now. The pressure they had exerted on Konoe, which had brought about the deadline of mid-October for the decision for war and, eventually, the fall of the Cabinet, had been predicated upon the assertion that Japan could not wait, militarily, without becoming weaker and losing advantage in the Pacific. Even though the Emperor had instructed Tojo to ignore the decision confirmed at the Imperial Conference of 6 September that had set that deadline, the premiss on which it rested could not be simply swept aside. Moreover, the Emperor's instruction had not been formally conveyed to the High Command. The chiefs of the army and navy General Staffs, Sugiyama and Nagano, and their subordinates, therefore felt no compulsion to comply with it.[73] Tojo was, in other words, still in the bind that had broken Konoe. His room for manoeuvre was limited in the extreme. Either he had to bring off at breakneck speed successful negotiations to prevent war, at least temporarily, or go to war.

But negotiations meant substantial concessions. These had not been forthcoming under Konoe, and it was hard to see how they could become attainable under Tojo. Indeed, the first declaration of his Cabinet was to avow adherence to 'the unshakable national policy of the Empire'. This, the declaration went on, was 'to bring the China Incident to a successful conclusion, firmly establish the Greater East Asia Co-Prosperity Sphere, and contribute to world peace'.[74] But, as previous months had shown, precisely this policy had brought Japan to the brink of war. It did not offer a promising recipe for the major concessions on which peace depended.

The alternative was to follow the military logic. This meant war before the year was out. The decision, having been put back from mid-October, could not be put off indefinitely. In fact, it would have to be taken within the following couple of weeks. This was the setting for the feverish activity that took place in the first fortnight of Tojo's premiership.

Tojo's difficulties in dealing with the High Command began immediately. His first Cabinet meeting, on 18 October, the day of his government's formation, had before it a number of hypothetical questions about the further course of the war and the prospects of Japan attaining in the immediate future even its minimum demands through negotiations with the United States. The questions were meant to serve as the basis for a re-examination of the decision of 6 September.[75] The response of the High Command when it received a copy of the questions, however, was that 'there really is no room for re-examination'. Nagano, the navy's chief of staff, put it bluntly: 'The decision of the Imperial Conference is not open to change.'[76] His subordinates argued forcefully that a diplomatic solution at this stage could only come about through a complete volte-face, amounting 'to throwing in our lot with the Anglo-American camp' and incurring 'the contempt of the Chinese and a great loss of national prestige'.[77] The army's General Staff also adopted a truculent stance. There was outright refusal to contemplate withdrawal of troops from China, in full recognition that this undermined any hope of successful negotiations. Resistance to the notion of re-examination of state policy even led to talk of overthrowing the new Cabinet no sooner than it had been formed. The unchanged stance of the High Command caused Tojo insuperable difficulties from the outset. He was unsure how to act. He told his new Navy Minister, Shimada, that he was 'truly in the dark about what to do'.[78]

The Liaison Conference, meeting every day (apart from 26 October) for over a week between 23 October and 1 November in almost permanent crisis session, faced the same quandary. The hypothetical questions on the likely course of the war and prospects for negotiations provided the framework for discussions which, despite pressure from Nagano and Sugi-yama for a quick decision, were protracted and often contorted. A central issue was Japan's ability to wage war if hostilities should drag on. This revolved largely around availability of raw materials, especially oil and steel, and her shipping capacity and shipbuilding capability. Strikingly, even at this stage the head of the Planning Board, General Suzuki Teiichi, and the newly appointed Finance Minister, Kaya Okinori, had only limited information at their disposal. Kaya complained at the inability to arrive at a 'precise judgement, rather than a statement of generalities'.[79] The new Foreign Minister, Togo, later recounted his astonishment at the lack of precise statistical data necessary for informed estimates, since the High Command was unwilling to divulge operational details or troop numbers.[80] Even so, such information as was available left no room for doubt: Japan presided over insufficient raw materials, shipping and shipbuilding capacity to fight for more than two years, before the overwhelmingly superior resources of the United States would inexorably begin to tell. 'We can manage somehow in 1942 and 1943,' Tojo himself remarked in relation to army allocations. 'We do not know what will happen after 1944.'[81] Oil – even taking into account that which could be extracted from the Dutch East Indies – would only last for two and a half years. Synthetic oil pro-duction would not be in a position for three years to make good the shortfall, and even that would depend upon the availability of a million tons of steel and other large amounts of precious resources to construct the manufacturing plant. As it was, because of shortage of steel, shipbuilding capacity would fall drastically, rather than rise, by the third year of the war. The demands on state finances, meanwhile, were colossal.[82] It was by any stretch of the imagination a gloomy prognosis. The military chiefs could counter the undeniable deficiencies in the long run only by pointing to the uncertainties of war, the need for clever strategy and good luck, and the necessity to maximize early advantages to prepare the ground for a

358

longer struggle. It was planning for the best-case scenario, not preparing for the worst.

The deliberations, given the pressure of time, were painstakingly slow, much to the irritation of the chiefs of staff. At one point, it was noted that 'the Prime Minister took about thirty minutes to explain why every minute counted'.[83] The question of the prospects in negotiations with the Americans was only reached on 30 October. It was recognized that there was no hope of immediate success. When possible Japanese concessions were broached, no changes of substance to what had been stipulated in early September proved acceptable, other than agreeing, with regard to commerce in China, that 'the principle of equal opportunity throughout the world' could be granted – something which Nagano said would show Japan's generosity.[84] A heated debate arose over the question of stationing troops in China. It had been decided that 'as a diplomatic gesture' this could be for about twenty-five years. Even that met with vehement army objections. Togo, the Foreign Minister, on the other hand, 'forgetting reality' (as the Conference notes had it), favoured withdrawing troops straight away. Eventually, Tojo – who as Army Minister under Konoe had been the most adamant opponent of any concession on the stationing of troops – proposed 'that a certain number of years "close to being forever" be mentioned'. The feeling was, however, that whatever the number of years indicated, the proposal would be rejected by the United States. When it came to assessing the impact of the American conditions, were they to be accepted, all except Togo ('who gave everyone a strange feeling' by suggesting that everything could turn out for the better) were agreed that Japan 'would become a third-rate country'.

The Prime Minister drew proceedings to a close by declaring that a decision had to be reached on 1 November, even if the meeting should continue all night. He offered three possibilities for consideration. The first was that Japan should avoid war and undergo great hardships. The second was an immediate decision for war. The third was to decide on war but carry on military preparations and diplomacy side by side.[85] Though there was still some hope, expressed at the Conference, that in the last case some compromise agreement could be stitched together even at this stage, this was neither the wish nor the expectation of the military representatives.

The Liaison Conference that took place in the imperial palace on 1 November 1941 – the sixty-sixth since such meetings had been established in 1937 – was a historic one.[86] It lasted for seventeen hours, amid great tension and some heated exchanges. By its conclusion, war was as good as certain.

V

Tojo's efforts prior to the meeting to establish a consensus behind the proposal – the third of the options he had put forward on 30 October – to continue negotiations while completing preparations for military operations had not been successful. While the Army Ministry backed the proposal, the General Staff (directly responsible to the Emperor for matters relating to strategic planning) did not. Sugiyama was insistent: negotiations were at an end; the morale of the troops was at stake; there could be no pulling back; the only solution was war. His position was, therefore, clear – and different to that of the Prime Minister. In his view, the Liaison Conference had to adopt the second of the three propositions: to determine to go to war immediately. In a late-night meeting the previous day, Tojo had managed to persuade Kaya, the Finance Minister, and Suzuki, the director of the Planning Board, to support his third option. But the Foreign Minister, Togo, stood out alone for the first proposal: avoidance of war even at the cost of lasting privation. Shimada, the new Navy Minister and also present at the late-night discussion, had his own agenda. On the eve of a momentous decision, he made his approval of war dependent upon a major increase in allocation of steel for the navy, at the expense of the army and civilian use. This issue, in fact, was to take up the first half of the Liaison Conference, lasting several hours before being resolved in favour of Shimada's demand. With that, the navy was, like the army, committed to war.[87]

With the steel allocation issue decided, the Conference turned to discuss the three options proposed by Tojo. The divisions left unresolved in the prior discussions now resurfaced. Deliberations first focused upon the first proposition: not to engage in war. Kaya tried several times to press the navy on the long-term chances of success. 'If we go along, as at present, without war, and three years hence the American fleet comes to attack us, will the Navy have a chance of winning or won't it?' he asked. 'Nobody knows,' was Nagano's reply. Kaya asked again whether Japan could win a war on the seas. Nagano simply reasserted his view that 'it would be easier to engage in a war now', when the foundations had been laid, than in three years' time. Kaya was not satisfied. 'If there were chances of victory in the third year of the war, it would be all right to go to war,' he stated. 'But according to Nagano's explanation, this is not certain. Moreover, I would judge that the chances of the United States making war on us are slight, so my conclusion must be that it would not be a good idea to declare war now.'

Togo backed the Finance Minister. Nagano pointed to the uncertainty of the future. America would be stronger in three years' time. 'Well, then, when can we go to war and win?' retorted Kaya. It was the question Nagano had been waiting for. 'Now!' he declared, with vehemence. '[A better] time for war will not come later!' He was backed in this judgement by Suzuki. Kaya remained unconvinced, but no longer pursued the first option. With that, the proposal to pull back from war at all costs was dead. Since this proposal had been tied to the assumption that its acceptance would condemn Japan to many years of hardship and privation it was hardly an attractive recommendation. Its dismissal out of hand was more or less a formality. Kaya's stance had been largely rhetorical, since he had already committed himself at the meeting with Tojo the previous evening to the third proposition.

The Conference then turned to the second proposition, to go to war immediately. Sugiyama produced a statement of the army's position: abandonment of hope in successful negotiations; determination to begin war against the United States, Britain and the Netherlands at the beginning of December; negotiations with the United States to continue until then but only as a pretext to give Japan an early advantage in war; and, finally, strengthening of ties with Germany and Italy. Kaya and Togo objected straight away. It was a great turning point in Japan's long history. The fate of the nation was at stake. 'It's outrageous to ask us to resort to diplomatic trickery,' they said. 'We can't do it.' They pressed for a last attempt at negotiations. The blunt and forthright Tsukada Osamu, the army vice-chief of staff, a man not given to nuance and intellectual refinement, could hold back no longer. He was impatient with the calls for further negotiations. He wanted a decision on going to war immediately, which he specified as 1 December, and only then to consider the question of diplomacy. Nagano's deputy, the navy vice-chief of staff Ito Seiichi, suddenly threw a new date into the discussion. 'As far as the Navy is concerned,' he interjected, 'you can negotiate until 20 November.' Tsukada immediately rejoined: 'As for the Army, negotiations will be all right until 13 November, but no later.' The military leaders were, therefore, now introducing dates not previously discussed, and imposing an even tighter deadline on negotiations than had been envisaged up to now. Togo was appalled. 'I cannot accept deadlines or conditions if they make it unlikely that diplomacy will succeed,' he objected. 'You must obviously give up the idea of going to war.'

It was by now impossible to separate discussion of the second proposal (an immediate decision for war) from the third (simultaneous negotiations and war preparations). Tojo and his Foreign Minister both sought guarantees from the army that 'if diplomacy is successful we will give up going to war'. 'That's impossible,' Tsukada shot back. The chiefs of staff agreed that this would throw military preparations into confusion. When, in an aside to his deputy, Shimada suggested negotiations could be continued until two days before the outbreak of war, Tsukada brusquely told him: 'Please keep quiet. What you've just said won't do.' Tempers were fraying. Tojo suggested a twenty-minute break. During that time, the army and navy chiefs of operational planning, Tanaka and Fukudome, were called in. It was eventually agreed that negotiations could continue until five days prior to the outbreak of war. This was stipulated as 30 November. Under further pressure, Tsukada accepted that this meant midnight on that date. The final time for decision was now fixed. If diplomacy were successful by that date, war would be called off. But if diplomacy failed by this tight deadline, Japan would go to war.

By now it was 10 o'clock in the evening and the Conference had been in session for eleven hours. There was still the question of the negotiating terms to discuss. Before the Conference was the plan already agreed in essentials two days earlier. The plan posited a comprehensive settlement of the issues separating Japan and the United States. The only concession on the stationing of troops in China was that this was foreseen as lasting for twenty-five years. On troops in Indochina, it was agreed to evacuate them once the 'China Incident' was solved and a 'just peace' concluded in the Far East. The principle of non-discrimination in trade was accepted, if applied throughout the world (something quite unachievable in practice). On the Tripartite Pact, Japan's own discretion in deciding whether to take action was reiterated. Finally, Japan continued to reject the inclusion of the American 'Four Principles' in any formal agreement.[88] The plan offered only a marginal adjustment to the position effectively already rejected by the United States. It stood, therefore, scant chance of success now. But Togo now surprised the Conference by referring to this as Plan A and introducing a Plan B which had not been the subject of any prior consultation with the military leaders. Sugiyama had, before the Conference began, sought and obtained from Tojo assurances that there would be no reduction in the terms proposed under what was now Plan A. But precisely that was now on the table as Plan B.

What Togo had in mind – and he had run the document past both the American and British ambassadors in Tokyo – was simply a device to prevent war in the short term, an indication of the absolutely minimum conditions acceptable to Japan. Togo thought there was no hope for Plan A, and that to try to negotiate on that basis would put him in an impossible position. Plan B, a brief document, left China out of consideration and concentrated on the south. It aimed not at a final or comprehensive agreement – impossible in the time-span – but to avoid further deterioration in relations with the United States. It agreed to withdraw Japanese troops immediately to northern French Indochina and, following settlement of the 'China Incident', eventually from Indochina altogether. Meanwhile, Japan and the United States would promise not to make military advances in south-east Asia, other than in Indochina. They would cooperate in guaranteeing necessary resources from the Dutch East Indies and the United States would supply Japan with the oil she needed in the restoration of trading relations to what they had been before the freezing of assets. Finally, the United States would not hinder efforts towards peace between Japan and China.[89]

The military representatives were appalled at the extent of the concessions. Sugiyama and Tsukada rejected outright the withdrawal of troops from Indochina. Both were adamant: Togo should proceed only with Plan A. Nagano agreed. Tsukada, summarizing the positions adopted on the respective merits of war and negotiations by those who had expressed their views, then established his own stance, lest anyone still be in doubt of it, and in inimitable style: 'In general, the prospects if we go to war are not bright,' he began. 'We all wonder if there isn't some way to proceed peacefully.' However, he went on, 'it is not possible to maintain the status quo'. With doubtful logic he then added: 'Hence, one unavoidably reaches the conclusion that we must go to war.' At this point, Tsukada was only just slipping into gear. Having begun by accepting that Japan's chances in a war against the United States were not good, he resorted to national fatalism. 'I, Tsukada,' he declared, 'believe that war cannot be avoided. Now is the time. Even if we don't go to war now, we must do so next year, or the year after that. Now is the time. The moral spirit of Japan, the Land of the Gods, will shine on this occasion.' He moved from fatalism to best-case-scenario military optimism. 'The probability of Japan's push southward enabling Germany and Italy to defeat Britain is high, and the probability of forcing China to capitulate is even higher than it is now. Then we could even force Russia to capitulate. If we take the South, we will be able to strike a strong blow against American resources of national defence. That is, we will build an iron wall, and within it we will destroy, one by one, the enemy states in Asia; and in addition, we will defeat America and Britain.' This was the thinking of one of the highest representatives of the military elite. It was pure lunacy.

Togo held his ground in the face of such irrationality. Again the debate became heated. Togo's resignation seemed possible. But this would have brought down the government. A new Cabinet might have opposed the war. This was the consideration put to the army chiefs in another brief recess. It concentrated their minds. They made minor wording amendments, particularly on restoration of trade relations, supplies of oil and non-interference in the settlement of the war with China. All were designed to toughen up the terms as far as possible without triggering a change of government. With these limited changes, they had to accept Togo's proposal, whatever their distaste. When the Conference adjourned at 1.30 a.m. on 2 November, it had determined 'in order to resolve the present critical situation, to assure [Japan's] self-preservation and self-defence, and to establish a New Order in Greater East Asia ... to go to war against the United States, Britain, and Holland', with a deadline for initiating military action in early December. Only if negotiations proved successful by 'zero hour on 1 December' would military action be suspended.[90]

Togo and Kaya had asked for a few hours to think over the implications before giving their consent. By early next afternoon they had complied. The decision of the Liaison Conference was now unanimous. The Emperor, when Tojo reported to him on the outcome of the Conference, exhorted the Prime Minister 'to do everything you possibly can to seek a negotiated settlement'. The deferential Tojo was indeed anxious to fulfil the Emperor's wishes. He put the chances of successful negotiations at fifty-fifty. His Foreign Minister, Togo, put them, more realistically, at no better than one in ten.[91]

On 5 November at 10.30 a.m. Japan's leaders assembled at the palace in the presence of the Emperor for the Imperial Conference – which on this occasion went unreported in the press[92] – to ratify the decision taken three days earlier. Unlike the heated atmosphere of the Liaison Conference on that occasion, this time there was no dissension. But there was a dejected and anxious mood among the participants, shared also by the Emperor.[93]

Tojo began by reminding those present of the background to the revision of the 'Essentials for Carrying out the Empire's Policies' that had been agreed on 6 September. As a result of the intervening deliberations, he said, 'we have come to the conclusion that we must now decide to go to war, set the time for military action at the beginning of December, concentrate all of our efforts on completing preparations for war, and at the same time try to break the impasse by means of diplomacy'. Togo pointed out that there was little room left for diplomatic manoeuvring. Suzuki and Kaya gave lengthy summaries of the raw materials and financial situation. Suzuki's argument was that, as regards material resources, war was preferable to 'just sitting tight and waiting for the enemy to put pressure on us'. Kaya noted that 'it will not be possible for some time for us to give much consideration to the living conditions of the people' of the occupied territories, 'and for a while we will have to pursue a so-called policy of exploitation'. The chiefs of staff then commented on war preparations. Sugiyama emphasized once more that time would work against Japan if war should be delayed.

Hara, the President of the Privy Council, posed questions at this point, as convention demanded, on behalf of the Emperor. Tojo responded on the issue of stationing troops in China. He again emphasized Japan's sacrifices since the war there had begun. Withdrawal of troops would leave Japan worse off than she had been prior to the war. China would be more powerful than before and 'would even attempt to rule Manchuria, Korea, and Formosa [Taiwan]', he added. 'We can expect an expansion of our country only by stationing troops. This the United States does not welcome.' Hara turned to the detail of Togo's Plans A and B. Togo admitted that he could expect no settlement from Plan A. Even Plan B would mèet serious obstacles. There were only two weeks left for negotiations. 'To my regret,' Togo said, 'there is little hope for success.' Hara, too, greatly regretted this, stressing again the importance of a negotiated settlement, though he concluded that 'it is impossible, from the standpoint of our domestic political situation and of our self-preservation, to accept all of the American demands. We must hold fast to our position.' He correctly viewed the war in China as the root of the problem. But he saw no immediate way out of it. Japan could not let the current situation continue. 'If we miss the present opportunity to go to war, we will have to submit to American dictation. Therefore, I recognize that it is inevitable that we must decide to start a war against the United States.' The Emperor on this occasion remained silent. There can be no doubt that Hara was echoing Hirohito's sentiments.

Tojo brought the Conference to a close. He acknowledged the grave difficulties the war would bring. Again, he painted a picture of an even less attractive alternative. 'Two years from now we will have no petroleum for military use. Ships will stop moving. When I think about the strengthening of American defences in the south-west Pacific, the expansion of the American fleet, the unfinished China Incident, and so on, I see no end to difficulties. We can talk about austerity and suffering, but can our people endure such a life for a long time?' He feared Japan would become 'a third-class nation after two or three years if we just sat tight'.[94]

This was the ultimate reasoning for war. Peace but austerity in a world dominated by America, or war with probable defeat but upholding national honour were the alternatives.[95] War was seen as preferable. As the American ambassador in Tokyo, Joseph Grew, put it, Japan would risk 'national hara-kiri' rather than 'yield to foreign pressure', adding cryptically that 'Japanese sanity cannot be measured by American standards of logic'.[96] The fateful Imperial Conference ended. The decision was that, short of a diplomatic miracle, Japan would go to war. No objections were raised. The Emperor's seal of approval was given.

VI

Everything now hung by a frayed thread of diplomacy. As a last-ditch effort, and to help the struggling Nomura, Togo sent a highly experienced diplomat, Kurusu Saburo, to Washington as his special emissary with the mission of brokering a holding peace if at all possible. Kurusu, a tiny, dapper man, had served as ambassador to Germany and indeed signed the Tripartite Pact, but was also well acquainted with the United States through his American wife of British descent.[97] The auguries were not good; Hull 'felt from the start that he was deceitful'.[98] In Tokyo, Tojo now put the chances of success at 30 per cent – down from 50 per cent a few days earlier. He asked Kurusu to do his best.[99]

Preparations for war were meanwhile well advanced. An attack on Pearl Harbor had been proposed by Admiral Yamamoto Isoroku (who would eventually lead the assault) in May 1941, tested in war games in September, and adopted by Nagano on 20 October.[100] This would be one prong of the overall offensive. In tandem with this daring move would proceed a widespread assault on Malaya and the Philippines, leading to an attack on the Dutch East Indies. Within four to eight months, Japan would have attained the dominance in south-east Asia and the western Pacific needed to combat the United States over a lengthier period or to force a negotiated peace to her advantage. This was the strategic aim. At the same time, it was presumed, the severance of aid to China as a consequence of the expansion would cut off the lifeblood of Chiang Kai-shek's struggle. Finally, though this was outside Japan's direct control, it was hoped that German military successes against Britain and the Soviet Union would be accompanied by the Axis powers declaring war on the United States, which would then become enfeebled through prolonged embroilment in the European conflict.[101] By the beginning of November, the Japanese strategic plan had then taken something approaching its final shape. On 3 November, Yamamoto, as Commander-in-Chief of the Combined Fleet, approved the secret operations order, which began by stating that 'The Japanese Empire is expecting war to break out with the United States, Great Britain, and the Netherlands'.[102]

The Emperor, briefed daily by his chiefs of staff, was fully apprised of developments and showed an acute awareness of tactical detail. On 4 November, he attended – exceptionally – a lengthy meeting of the Supreme War Council at which the chiefs of staff and the Prime Minister were questioned.[103] Hirohito was still wracked with doubts and worries. He feared the consequences of war. And he had concerns about important details of the military operations. These were justified. For whatever the precise military planning for the offensive, the overall strategy was flawed. Too much was left to factors which Japan could not determine. And too much was predicated upon the best-case scenario. But, whatever his inner anxieties, the Emperor confirmed the strategic war plan in the middle of the month.[104]

The task facing Nomura and Kurusu was daunting in the extreme. It was not helped by the fact that the secret instructions from Togo to Nomura accompanying the transmitted text of Plans A and B – like all other secret traffic from Tokyo, immediately intercepted by American intelligence and decoded before being sent on to Hull – were distorted through inaccurate translation in a way that enhanced suspicions of Japanese duplicity.[105] Distortions or not, there was no mistaking the implication of the intercepted traffic: Japan was preparing for war in the very near future.[106] In the State Department, Stanley Hornbeck was advising Hull to ignore the appeals by Ambassador Grew in Tokyo to take seriously the Japanese desire to avoid war. Knowing from the intelligence intercepts that Japan was talking peace but preparing for war did nothing to win over the hard-nosed Hornbeck, who thought Grew too ready to trust Japanese intentions. And Hornbeck, rather than Grew, had the ear of the American Secretary of State.[107]

Even so, at first it seemed that the faint hope of those still working for a compromise settlement might be justified. By 15 November Plan A was predictably rejected.[108] But the American government was still playing for time. And the administration was not speaking with one clear voice. While Hull and the State Department dampened prospects of an accommodation, the President himself appeared still open to the possibility of one. Urged by his military advisers to practise caution towards Japan and concentrate on defeating Germany, Roosevelt told Hull and a distinctly unimpressed Henry Stimson, the Secretary of War, that he was contemplating proposing a six-month truce during which there would be no troop movements. The President, receiving the Japanese ambassador on 10 November, hinted at the possibility of what he called a 'modus vivendi'. When they met again a week later, this time with Kurusu (who had arrived on 10 November) in attendance, Roosevelt seemed to open up the prospect of a breakthrough in the critical issue of China. He indicated that the United States did not want to intervene or mediate in the Sino-Japanese dispute. According to Nomura's dispatch, the President coined the word 'introducer' to describe what he saw as America's role in prompting a settlement. Kurusu reported back to Tokyo that Roosevelt had 'considerable enthusiasm for a Japanese-American accord'. Nomura was so encouraged that, on his own initiative, he suggested that the United States rescind the freeze on Japanese assets in return for Japan's withdrawal of troops. This was going much too far for Tokyo. Nomura was called to order by Togo, and told to resubmit Plan B (which, Kurusu had already told Tokyo, would in its entirety probably be unacceptable).[109] Nomura duly presented Plan B to Hull on 20 November. It triggered the last episode in the diplomatic drama.

Hull's cold reception dismayed Nomura and Kurusu. He declared that the American public saw Japan and Nazi Germany in partnership to divide up the world. The Tripartite Pact, he stated, had strengthened such feeling. Privately, Hull was utterly negative about the current proposal. He viewed it as an ultimatum, later saying its stipulations were 'of so preposterous a character that no American official could ever have dreamed of accepting them'.[110]

Whatever his private views, Hull did not, however, dismiss Plan B outright. In fact, the American reply, in its final draft of 25 November, was surprisingly conciliatory.[111] It had taken account of a pencilled note sent over a week earlier by Roosevelt to Hull, proposing a 'modus vivendi' – the term he had used at the beginning of November when talking to Nomura – for a six-month period. In the President's brief formulation, Japan would stop troop movements and agree not to invoke the Tripartite Pact even if America became involved in the war in Europe. The United States, for her part, would resume economic relations with Japan and broker the beginning of talks between Japan and China.[112] The idea had the backing of military top brass, keen to win time to bolster defences in the Philippines. At this point it seemed as if perhaps some common ground could even now be found between the Japanese Plan B and the State Department's incorporation of the President's idea of a temporary modus vivendi.[113] But by late that evening, Hull had abandoned the possibility. The Chinese had been predictably vehemently hostile to any concessions to Japan. The British, Dutch and Australian governments were only lukewarm.[114] In any case, the Secretary of State's reluctance to reach an accommodation with the

Japanese on anything but unyielding American terms had never been significantly diluted. It had, in fact, been reinforced by the intercept of a message from Tokyo to Nomura on 22 November, extending the deadline for negotiations from 25 to 29 November, but emphasizing that this 'deadline absolutely cannot be changed. After that things are automatically going to happen.' Any residual hope in the State Department of finding a modus vivendi was largely dispelled by the anger at this message.[115]

What had specifically changed Hull's mind, however, had been the abrasive reaction to the 'modus vivendi' proposal by Chiang Kai-shek, fearful that American appeasement was about to take place at the expense of China.[116] A message from Churchill to Roosevelt, backing Chiang and expressing British anxiety about a collapse of China, confirmed Hull's rejection of the 'modus vivendi'.[117] 'The slight prospect of Japan's agreeing to the modus vivendi', the Secretary of State concluded, 'did not warrant assuming the risks involved in proceeding with it, especially the risk of collapse of Chinese morale and resistance, and even of disintegration in China.'[118] Roosevelt, on the other hand, seemed even early next morning, 26 November, to imply that the 'modus vivendi' could be rescued, saying he could assuage the Chinese. The President's mood darkened measurably only a little later, however, when he was given reports of a Japanese convoy carrying about 50,000 troops, sighted south of Taiwan. Roosevelt was incandescent at what he saw as evidence of bad faith on the part of the Japanese. He said it 'changed the whole situation'. Soon afterwards, Hull arrived at the White House, proposing that the 'modus vivendi' be abandoned. Instead, he suggested offering the Japanese a new and 'comprehensive basic proposal for a general peaceful settlement'. Roosevelt agreed.[119]

Hull's proposal, compiled without consulting either military chiefs or the representatives of Britain or other unofficial allies, was presented to Kurusu and Nomura late that same afternoon. Its ten points were an uncompromising restatement of American basic principles on which all previous attempts at negotiation had foundered. They made new demands, and were much sharper in tone than any previous American proposals.[120] They summarily required Japan to withdraw her troops from China as well as Indochina, to renounce her extraterritorial rights and concessions dating back to the turn of the century, following the Boxer Rebellion, to recognize no other Chinese government but that of Chiang Kai-shek, and effectively to abrogate the Tripartite Pact. The United States in return would unfreeze Japanese assets and work towards a new trade agreement as a basis for restabilizing economic relations. Hull suggested the proposal might open the path to long-term discussions towards peace in the Pacific. This was simply disingenuous. Hull was clear in his own mind that negotiations had run into the buffers.[121] 'It's as far as we can go,' he told the dismayed Japanese envoys, who, recognizing the certain peremptory rejection of the proposal in Tokyo, wanted to discuss it informally with a view to tempering its demands before sending it on.[122] Hull later acknowledged that 'we had no serious thought that Japan would accept our proposal'.[123]

Predictably, the 'Ten Points' were seen, when the cable arrived in Tokyo on 27 November, as an ultimatum – practically an insult.[124] There was anger as well as consternation among Japan's leaders. More than all else, the demand to withdraw from the whole of China infuriated them. They took this to apply to Manchuria, too, which would indeed have meant a return to the situation before 1931, and a serious undermining of Japan's economy. Hull had, in fact, not intended this specific reading. Manchuria, for him, was not an immediate concern.[125] The misunderstanding had arisen from poor, overhasty drafting. It was a significant irritant. But it probably made no appreciable difference to Japan's response.

Those who had pressed for continued negotiations in the hope of avoiding war now felt the rug pulled from beneath them. For those, mainly in the army and navy General Staffs, who had urged war, the 'Hull Note' (as it later came to be called) was a heaven-sent opportunity. The army, in particular, had feared all along that Plan B might pave the way for an accommodation. They had wanted tough new conditions on oil supplies inserted into Japanese demands, which would effectively have sabotaged any possibility of the plan being accepted.[126] Now the General Staff reacted with relief, even elation: 'This must be divine grace; this makes it easy for the Empire to cross the Rubicon and determine on going to war. That's great, just great!' was one response.[127]

Among the last pleas, based on dread at the consequences of military conflict, to continue negotiations and avoid war, even if it meant prolonged poverty and hardship for Japan, were those of a number of the 'senior statesmen', the former Prime Ministers who met Tojo and four members of his Cabinet on the morning of 29 November. But by this point even Togo conceded that negotiations had reached the end of the road. Tojo himself now spoke forcefully in favour of military action. Whatever their doubts, none of those present voiced fundamental opposition.[128] Tojo recalled after the war the tenor of opinion expressed at the meeting, that 'if this war was for self-existence, then we must be prepared to wage war, even if we foresaw eventual defeat'.[129]

The Emperor still had his own anxieties. His brother, Prince Takamatsu, tried on 30 November to persuade him not to take the empire to war. But when Hirohito summoned his navy leaders later that day to ascertain the readiness for war, the Navy Minister, Shimada, expressed confidence in victory. Nagano told him that the navy's large task force, including six aircraft carriers, was already at sea and steaming towards Pearl Harbor. Under sealed orders, it had set sail from Hitokappu Bay in the remote southern Kurile islands at 6.00 a.m. on 26 November, and was by now part-way across the Pacific, some 1,800 nautical miles from Hawaii.[130] Nagano had already revealed, with some reluctance and in a low voice, to the Liaison Conference the previous evening that 'zero hour is 8 December'. Even the Prime Minister learned this now for the first time. Surprise was of the essence. Negotiations would have to continue, but only as a cloak to conceal the impending strike.[131]

Only the Emperor's sanction for war remained still to be granted. Kido had told Hirohito that 'the decision this time will be enormously important. Once you grant the imperial sanction, there can be no going back. If you have even the slightest doubt, make absolutely sure until you are convinced.'[132]

The Imperial Conference met in the afternoon of 1 December. Nineteen leaders of the government and the military assembled before the Emperor, seated as usual on a dais in front of a gold screen at the end of the room.[133] First Tojo, then – at great length – the Foreign Minister, Togo, rehearsed the tale of the breakdown of diplomatic negotiations with the United States. Other ministers described the readiness for war in their respective spheres. The most important statement was that of Nagano, speaking for both the navy and the army General Staffs. Preparations for military operations were complete, he said. 'We are now in a position to begin these operations, according to predetermined plans, as soon as we receive the Imperial Command to resort to force.'[134] Hara began his usual questioning by remarking that, although they were dealing with a very grave subject, 'every step that could be taken has been taken', so that he had 'nothing in particular to add'.[135] He ended – speaking, as always, on behalf of the Emperor – by stating that Japan could not tolerate the 'utterly conceited, obstinate, and disrespectful' attitude of the United States:

If we were to give in, we would give up in one stroke not only our gains in the Sino-Japanese and Russo-Japanese wars, but also the benefits of the Manchurian Incident. This we cannot do. We are loath to compel our people to suffer even greater hardships, on top of what they have endured during the four years since the China Incident. But it is clear that the existence of our country is being threatened, that the great achievements of the Emperor Meiji would all come to nought, and that there is nothing else we can do. Therefore, [he concluded] I believe that if negotiations with the United States are hopeless, then the commencement of war, in accordance with the decision of the previous Imperial Conference, is inevitable.

His final comment was to exhort the government to look for an early settlement of what promised to be a long war, and to do everything to prevent internal unrest.[136] Tojo assured him that this would be done and adjourned the meeting with expressions of loyalty to the Emperor. Sugiyama noted that 'His Majesty nodded in agreement with the statements being made, and displayed no signs of uneasiness. He seemed to be in an excellent mood, and we were filled with awe.'[137] All those present bowed as the Emperor, expressionless, withdrew. The proposal for war, signed by all those present, was delivered shortly afterwards to Hirohito. After briefly reflecting on the gravity of his decision, and remarking that to accept Hull's demands would have been humiliating, the Emperor put his seal to the documents. With that, he gave his approval to war.[138]

VII

The next day, he was fully initiated into the military plans by Sugiyama and Nagano. They explained the details of the attack on Pearl Harbor on 8 December (Japanese time, 7 December in Hawaii). Nagano explained that the day, a Sunday, was ideal since the American warships would be at anchor. He asked for the Emperor's approval. It was swiftly given. Yamamoto, in command of the Combined Fleet, was immediately informed. He telegraphed the task force at 5.30 p.m. that day: 'Commencement of hostilities set for 8 December. Carry out attack as planned.'[139]

The pretence of maintaining diplomatic negotiations until the very last moment, to maintain the element of military surprise, required delicate timing. A lengthy document, comprising fourteen points, was drawn up. It ended by stating that hope of cooperation with the United States had finally been lost, and that no accord could be reached even if negotiations were to continue.[140] It was meant to be presented to the American government at 1.00 p.m. in Washington (7.30 a.m. in Hawaii) half an hour before the attack on Pearl Harbor began.[141] This was cutting it fine – in fact, too fine. Incompetence by the Japanese embassy in Washington meant the decoding of the vital message was inexcusably delayed. And the fourteenth and last point was deliberately held back as long as possible in Tokyo. This part of the text was eventually decoded only by 12.30 p.m., and a clean copy of the entire text was not ready until 1.50 p.m.[142]

The American administration had itself, however, been able to intercept the Japanese cable. Roosevelt received the first thirteen parts at 9.30 p.m. on 6 December, remarking: 'This means war.'[143] (The President had sent a personal message to Hirohito earlier that evening, seeking the withdrawal of Japanese troops from Indochina to preserve peace in the region. But he was aware how futile the attempt was. It was duly dismissed out of hand by Tojo, without bothering to put it before the Emperor, who was said to have been annoyed by it.[144]) Hull, Stimson and Knox had sight of the decoded text an hour earlier. They arranged to meet next morning. They had not thought it necessary to meet earlier, or to issue special warnings to military bases to add to the earlier warnings already dispatched to American commanders across the Pacific, including Hawaii and the Philippines, that war with Japan was imminent.[145] A Japanese attack was by now expected any day – though no one imagined this would be on Pearl Harbor.[146] The sighting on 5 December (Washington time) of three Japanese convoys off the southern tip of Indochina and heading into the Gulf of Siam suggested that the attack was likely, and in the very near future, against Malaya or Siam – at any rate somewhere in south-east Asia and the south Pacific. A direct attack on American possessions was thought less likely (though when the first news of Pearl Harbor came through, one immediate response was that it was a mistake, and that the Philippines had been attacked).[147]

But incompetence was not confined to the Japanese embassy. The office of Admiral Stark, chief of US Naval Operations, had possession of the last part of the decoded text no later than 11.30 a.m. (Washington time; 6.00 a.m. in Hawaii) on 7 December. George Marshall, the army chief of staff, also had the decoded message by that time. He and Stark spoke twice on the telephone. They eventually decided to send out a warning. It reached the commanders in San Francisco, the Panama Canal and the Philippines by noon, Washington time. But atmospheric conditions blocked communication with Hawaii. Neither the direct scramble telephone nor naval radio communications were used. Remarkably, the message was sent instead by Western Union's commercial telegram service, which had no direct line to Honolulu. It still had not arrived in Hawaii when the Japanese attack began.[148]

Out of a clear blue sky, the first wave of Japanese dive-bombers began their attack on the American fleet at anchor in Pearl Harbor at 7.50 a.m., Hawaiian time (1.20 p.m. in Washington).[149] When the attack subsided at

9.45 a.m. and the pall of smoke over the big naval base finally cleared, the mighty battleships *Arizona*, *Oklahoma* and *California* had been sunk, the *West Virginia* was going down in flames, the *Nevada* was aground and a further three battleships were damaged. In all, eighteen ships were sunk or damaged; 188 planes had been destroyed and a further 159 damaged. The death toll of American servicemen reached 2,403; another 1,178 were wounded.[150] But, crucially, the aircraft carriers were at sea. The submarine pens also escaped the bombing. And, in fact, most of the damaged ships turned out to be repairable and later returned to action. So it was a mighty – though not a knockout – blow to the American war machine.

Nor was there any follow-up to Pearl Harbor, an indication of the barren strategic armoury of the Japanese in their attempt to inflict a decisive defeat upon the United States. Yamamoto had, in fact, foreseen this crippling limitation in a private letter written the previous January. 'Should hostilities once break out between Japan and the United States,' he had written, 'it is not enough that we take Guam and the Philippines, nor even Hawaii and San Francisco. We should have to march into Washington and sign the treaty (i.e. dictate the terms of peace) in the White House'.[151]

Even so, Pearl Harbor had been a massive shock.[152] The wider Japanese offensive had also begun. By an error in timing, the assault on the Malay peninsula had started even before the bombing of Pearl Harbor. Landings were soon under way as well in the Philippines. In the early hours, Singapore was bombed. Hong Kong was attacked some hours later. As news of the Japanese military successes was broadcast early in the morning of 8 December in Tokyo, bystanders in the streets applauded.[153] Japan was still not officially at war. At 11 o'clock that morning, seven and a half hours since the news of the successful onslaught on Pearl Harbor had reached the imperial palace, Emperor Hirohito put his seal on the declaration of war. He was said to have been 'in a splendid mood' that day.[154]

In Washington, Cordell Hull received the news of Pearl Harbor from the President just after two o'clock. He was about to receive Nomura and Kurusu. A quarter of an hour later, the Japanese envoys entered the room. The Secretary of State refused to shake hands, and left them standing. He looked at the final Japanese note. 'In all my fifty years of public service,' he then witheringly declared, 'I have never seen a document that was more crowded with infamous falsehoods and distortions – infamous falsehoods and distortions on a scale so huge that I never imagined until today that any Government on this planet was capable of uttering them.' He nodded curtly towards the door. Nomura and Kurusu were peremptorily dismissed.[155]

At one o'clock the next day, President Roosevelt addressed Congress. He told the packed chamber of the House of Representatives: 'Yesterday, December 7, 1941 – a date which will live in infamy – the United States of America was suddenly and deliberately attacked by naval and air forces of the Empire of Japan.' Applause repeatedly broke into his speech, which ended by asking Congress to declare 'that since the unprovoked and dastardly attack by Japan on Sunday, December 7, 1941, a state of war has existed between the United States and the Japanese Empire'. A roar of approval greeted the words. When the formal vote was taken, a single Representative, Jeannette Rankin of Montana, was opposed to war, as she had been in 1917. All other 388 members of the House of Representatives, and all members of the Senate, were in favour.[156] The Japanese attack on Pearl Harbor had ensured that the United States had never been more united. Without the Japanese attack, it is doubtful that Roosevelt could have attained a declaration of war in the Pacific from Congress. Pearl Harbor had removed the need to put that to the test. The President signed the declaration of war at 4.10 p.m. Great Britain and the governments of the British Commonwealth followed immediately with their own declarations. The Pacific War had begun.[157]

VIII

Less than four years later, Japan lay prostrate, two of her cities obliterated by the only nuclear bombs so far to be dropped in war, her population defeated and demoralized, her economy wasted, the country under enemy occupation. These were the dire consequences of the fateful choices made by Japan's leaders. How open and unconstrained had those choices been? And when, if at all, did they narrow down to the point where options had in effect disappeared, where no real choice remained? What by then, if not earlier, were the genuine limitations on Japan's freedom of choice? And is it possible to distinguish between objective constraints on decisions, and psychological, subjective determinants?

The questions are easier to pose than to answer. But it seems possible to highlight a number of crucial steps taken by Japan's civilian and military leadership, backed by a manipulated public opinion, which had the effect of significantly and consistently narrowing the range of choice available, until options all but disappeared in the autumn of 1941.

The first narrowing of options had begun way back in 1931, with the 'Mukden Incident' that led to the effective annexation of Manchuria.

Increasing unrest within Japan had accompanied mounting animosity towards western industrial competitors, especially the United States and Great Britain, in part because of high tariffs on imported Japanese goods. Hostility towards the perceived disadvantages of the postwar 'Washington system' shaped a climate which fostered nationalism and militaristic tendencies. Neo-mercantilist tendencies, looking to the benefits of autarky to be derived from a colonial system, or at least territories dependent upon Japan, gained ground.[158] This was the backcloth to the support given by the Japanese government to the independent action taken by the Kwantung Army in Manchuria. Japan had had a stake in Manchuria since the war with China in 1894–5. Control of the region would strengthen Japan economically. And it would bolster Japanese defences against the Soviet Union, seen as a growing threat. So the reasons – economic, military and in terms of domestic politics – for supporting the independently initiated aggression by the Kwantung Army are evident. But they did not *compel* that support. The Japanese government had a choice. In deciding to back aggression, it gave a substantial boost to the military in Japan, which was now in the process of regaining much of the influence in domestic politics that it had lost in the 1920s, and was beginning to flex its muscles. And it also promoted the populist nationalist rhetoric which was starting to sound ever more shrill. In years to come Manchuria became almost totemic: a return to the 'Washington system' that had existed before 1931, with its implied exploitation of Japan by the western powers, was invariably put forward as a prospect that could not be contemplated. Manchuria in this way helped to shape later decisions.

The Japanese takeover in Manchuria was a watershed. There was no intrinsic connection with the 'China Incident' six years later. But the forces it helped unleash had become strengthened in the interim. And Japan had become internationally more isolated. Populist clamour and militarist expansionism in the army combined in 1937 to turn the 'China Incident' into an unending war which sucked in manpower and resources for diminishing returns, and at the same time became the single most important stumbling block to any accommodation with the United States. But the idea of a 'holy war' against China stretched beyond military factions of the Japanese government. There was practically no voice among leading civilian politicians which opposed the war. Prince Konoe, Prime Minister for the first time and four years later a desperate advocate of a last-minute deal to avoid a Pacific War, was only one of its ardent advocates. Again, the government in Tokyo had a choice. It could have decided not to expand the initial minor incident into a major conflict. It chose, instead, to try to destroy China. This, with the attendant atrocities that shocked the west, backed Japan much further into a corner from which it became ever more difficult to extricate herself.

We have followed the making of crucial decisions in 1940 and 1941 in close detail. Though the factional nature of Japanese government meant that nuances of policy were frequently proposed, and decision-making was a complex and often laborious business, by 1940 no significant individual or faction, the military least of all, stood against the imperative of expansion in the near future into south-east Asia to create a Japanese economic *imperium*. Expansionism had by now become a universally accepted ideology among the ruling elites. It was most fervently held among the strongest sections of those elites: among the leadership and middle-ranking echelons of the army and the navy. In the summer of 1940, again the following summer and, finally, in autumn 1941, policy options were available. But they were narrowing.

Once the decision was taken in summer 1940 (exploiting the disarray of Great Britain following Hitler's western offensive) to advance to the south, this became a further non-negotiable element in the pursuit of any diplomatic settlement. Japan tied herself even further into an anti-American, as well as anti-British, stance with the consequential decision, later that summer, to form a military alliance with the Axis powers. By now, the collision course with the United States was becoming ever clearer. The Japanese government had been aware that it was taking this course, and of the dangers that entailed. It nevertheless chose to embark upon it. The option, still available, of backing down from expansion, with the growing prospect of military conflict with a mighty enemy, in favour of re-entry into international trade, with its inbuilt competition (seen to disfavour Japan), was rejected outright.

In the summer of 1941, the gods had appeared to favour Japan once more. Germany's sudden attack on the Soviet Union and rapid inroads into the country, accompanied by devastating blows against the Red Army, offered the potential to attack the beleaguered traditional enemy from the east. For six weeks or so this was actively deliberated. But the choice was made to continue the preparations for the southern advance. By now Japan was completely locked in to her own economic and ideological imperatives. These, intertwined, became even more apparent once the Americans turned off the oil-tap following the Japanese dispatch of troops into French Indochina in July. From now on, war was inevitable unless a conscious decision were made to avoid it.

Important voices from within the Japanese leadership were indeed raised in the autumn of 1941 in favour of a decision for war. But by now, there was great apprehension blending into outright fear at the consequences for Japan of a war with America. The Emperor himself wanted to avoid war. So did Prince Konoe, now serving his third term of office as Prime Minister and desperately seeking a personal meeting with President Roosevelt to head off conflict – a course of action which eventually brought down his government. When Konoe's Cabinet fell, even Tojo, the new Prime Minister and previously an ultra-hawk, became an earnest advocate of a negotiated accommodation with the United States. His Foreign Minister, Togo, was chosen with a view to engineering such an arrangement. The dispatch of Kurusu as special envoy to assist the beleaguered ambassador in Washington, Nomura, was a further sign of the seriousness of Japan's attempt, at the eleventh hour, to find a way out of the impasse. As late as 29 November 1941, the day before the Imperial Conference confirmed the decision to go to war, most of the *jushin* – the group of senior statesmen, former Prime Ministers – still wanted to prevent the conflagration they feared so much.

If such weighty figures were speaking out in favour of peace, why was the ultimate decision one for war? Part of the answer lies, of course, in the hardening position of the United States, which pushed Japan ever further into a tight cul-de-sac. There has been much subsequent speculation about the likely or possible course of events had the American administration, above all the Secretary of State, Cordell Hull, been less intransigent, more open to negotiation, especially in autumn 1941. Could it not have been in America's own interests, at least short-term, to weaken her commitment to China in favour of a settlement with Japan instead of rigid insistence on Japanese withdrawal from a country in which the United States had no prime stake?[159] Might not peace in the Pacific have been saved had Roosevelt indeed consented to meet Konoe?[160] Could not even a last-minute prevention of war have been attained if the United States, instead of bringing down the shutters at the end of November through Hull's peremptory Ten Points, had been prepared to continue with the President's suggested 'modus vivendi'? Some who had participated in the tortured process in Tokyo that ended in the decision for war later claimed that had Roosevelt's 'modus vivendi' been received by the Japanese government, or even had Hull's 'Note' excluded Manchukuo from the demand for troop withdrawals from China instead of mistakenly allowing the presumption that it was included, then new proposals and new compromises would have been forthcoming. Possibly, so the counter-factual argument ran, Tojo's government might have fallen and been replaced by a pro-peace Cabinet. Possibly, the further debate in the Liaison Conference, prompted by the 'modus vivendi', would in any case have necessitated a postponement of the mobilization for war.[161] And once the war machine had been halted, even if only temporarily, it could not have been restarted until the spring. A respite would have been gained, perhaps leading to a permanent new basis of power-relations in the Far East.

It seems wishful thinking. Certainly, the Roosevelt administration had become more intransigent. But the American stance had hardened precisely in response to Japan's refusal at any point since 1937 to halt her relentless pursuit of expansion and dominance in the Far East. And, as war approached, intelligence intercepts provided confirmation that expansion with a view to establishing a 'new order' in the region was non-negotiable. The issue of withdrawal from the Chinese mainland was equally intractable. China had become such a breaking point in all attempts at negotiation not just for idealistic reasons, although China had indeed become a moral cause in America, and the anti-Japanese backlash in the United States stirred by accounts of atrocities by Japan's army against Chinese civilians had certainly made American public opinion a factor which the Roosevelt administration could not ignore in its treatment of the Far East.[162] Nor were economic concerns the prime determinant in the American adherence to the cause of the Chinese nationalists. The Pacific, rather than the Asian continent, was central to American interests in the region. The chief consideration, becoming more rather than less important, was the need to hold together what had come to be known as the ABCD coalition – the loose alliance of America, Britain, China and the Dutch East Indies authorities. To have abandoned China would have had the most serious consequences for Britain's position in the Far East. This would have put relations between the United States and Britain under intense strain at a crucial juncture in the Atlantic War, and in the wider struggle against Nazi Germany – still seen in America, too, as the priority – particularly since Japan was in formal alliance with the Axis powers. For this reason above all, China remained the pivot. The United States could not contemplate undermining Chiang Kai-shek for short-term gain in preventing an immediate war in the Pacific, not least since it was all but certain that Japanese designs on power in the region would most likely have meant that war was simply being postponed, not avoided.[163]

The main reasons for the narrowing of Japan's options to the point where she was left with war as the only remaining course of action are to be found not in Washington, but in Tokyo. Certainly, the wish to avoid war was voiced in prominent quarters in the autumn of 1941. But the same individuals who now wanted peace had at every stage up to then supported the steps which had led to the point where Japan was peering into the abyss of war. Konoe is a prime, but far from isolated, example of those who had avidly backed aggressive expansionism until it had left no exit route from impending disaster. But *fear* of war did not equate with *opposition* to the policy decisions that had taken Japan to the brink. At no point was there a concerted and forthright rejection of policy choices that were seen to bristle with danger. For no faction of the elites could there be a retreat from the goals of a victorious settlement in China and successful expansion to establish the 'Greater East Asia Co-Prosperity Sphere' – or, in other words, Japanese domination of the Far East. These aims had not just become an economic imperative. They reflected honour and national pride, the prestige and standing of a great power. The alternatives were seen as not just poverty, but defeat, humiliation, ignominy and an end to great-power status in permanent subordination to the United States.

Such thinking had become all-embracing in Japan over the previous decade, as the Depression had destabilized politics and society, discrediting belief in the virtues of an Anglo-American-dominated international economy. It permeated both the power-elite and the mass of the population, whose shrill chauvinism had been deliberately encouraged, where not directly manufactured, by government-inspired mass media ever since the 'Manchurian Incident'. Most important of all, it allowed the influence of the most powerful faction, the military, to become completely decisive. Although the army and the navy had differing interests and agendas, the combination of the quest for dominance in China (along with bolstering defences in the north against the Soviet Union) and the prospect of expansion to the south was more than enough to hold them together. Moreover, the military always held the trump cards in the political debate: withdrawal from China would mean accepting that the huge sacrifices since 1937 had been in vain; abandoning the southern advance would mean that prosperity and security would be surrendered in favour of poverty and deprivation; pulling back from the Axis would mean lasting submission to the United States; and refusal to go to war in the autumn of 1941 would mean postponing inevitable conflict to a time when the balance of power would be less favourable to Japan. At every stage, as the political options narrowed, the chiefs of the General Staffs of both armed services, urged on by gung-ho middle-echelon officers in their planning and operational sections, were the most forceful and outspoken advocates of war. By the late summer of 1941, they had pushed through, against no serious opposition, a commitment to military action before the end of the year. The last serious political choice made by the Japanese leadership was to agree to a military timetable which meant that diplomacy, however faint its prospect of success, was forced to compete against the clock. The weakness of the other factions of Japan's elite had allowed the army and navy General Staffs increasingly to dictate policy options, down to the point where those options gave way to the military imperative: war.

Ironically, when that terrible war was finally over, Japan found herself more dependent economically upon the United States than had been foreseeable before the conflict, deprived of any great-power status, shorn of all military capability, but, over time, enjoying a prosperity unimaginable to the citizens of the country in the troubled and turbulent interwar era.

9

Berlin, Autumn 1941

Hitler Decides to Declare War on the United States

He emphasizes the extraordinary significance of the Japanese entry into the war, above all with regard to our U-boat war ... The Führer is convinced that even if Japan had not joined the war, he would have had to declare war on the Americans sooner or later. Now the east Asian conflict drops like a present into our lap.

Reported comments of Hitler to his party leaders,
12 December 1941

It has been described as the 'most puzzling' of Hitler's decisions during the Second World War.[1] At the climax of his long speech in the Reichstag on the afternoon of 11 December 1941, Hitler announced that the attempt by Germany and Italy to prevent the war widening, and to maintain relations with the United States of America, despite years of 'intolerable provocation by President Roosevelt', had failed. Consequently, in accordance with the terms of the Tripartite Pact of 27 September 1940, Germany and Italy saw themselves compelled, alongside Japan, 'together to carry out the struggle for defence, and thereby for the upholding of freedom and independence of their peoples and empires against the United States of America and England'.[2] The formal declaration of war had been starchily read out earlier that afternoon to the American chargé d'affaires in Berlin by Joachim von Ribbentrop, the Reich Foreign Minister, whose curt bow at the end of the audience had terminated relations between Germany and the United States.[3]

Four days later, the regular digest of opinion soundings among the German people, compiled by the Security Service (*Sicherheitsdienst*, SD), which had begun life as the Nazi Party's own surveillance organ and had later become part of the regime's huge and expanding SS-police network, claimed that 'the declaration of war on the United States did not come at all as a surprise and was widely interpreted as official confirmation of what already existed in reality'. How accurate this lapidary description of opinion was can only be surmised. Even the same report went on to record 'very occasional remarks of surprise and a certain concern about the addition of a new enemy' to be heard in the countryside. And there was evidently, so the report indicated, speculation about what this implied, with expectations of a long-drawn-out war at sea lasting for years.[4] Even before the declaration of war on America, pessimistic voices could be heard out of earshot of police informers prophesying that the war would last five years, that American aid had saved Britain, that perhaps Germany would not win and that in the end a compromise settlement would be reached.[5] One ordinary soldier, confident that Germany would eventually prove victorious, nevertheless confided to his diary on the day of Hitler's Reichstag speech, that it meant 'war for our lifetime'. 'Poor parents,' he added.[6]

Those worried and horrified at the war now stretching out way into the future, and extending to a mighty new belligerent with access to unimaginable resources, were well advised not to broadcast their views. But privately such anxieties were widespread. Memories of the First World War were still painfully strong. According to reports filtering out of underground socialist sources, many Germans had 'not forgotten that it was America's participation in the last world war which decided its outcome and sealed the fate of Germany'.[7] A German officer based in Warsaw, in a letter to his wife on the day after the declaration of war, wrote that the news had struck him 'with horror'. 'What probably every German feared', he added, 'has become true.'[8] Such fears came on top of immense worries about loved ones in an army bogged down in Russia's icy wastes and facing Germany's first serious military crisis since the war had begun over two years earlier.

Even Joseph Goebbels, Hitler's Propaganda Minister and one of his closest and most trusted associates, obliquely hinted at his apprehension about bringing a powerful new enemy directly into the conflict. Jotting down the gist of a telephone conversation with Hitler, soon after the news broke in Berlin of the Japanese attack on Pearl Harbor, Goebbels noted that Germany 'on the basis of the Tripartite Pact' would 'probably not avoid a declaration of war on the United States'. Then came a telling phrase in his diary. 'But that's now not so bad', since, he presumed, American supplies to Britain would have to be diverted to the war in the Pacific.[9] It was the merest unwitting intimation that Goebbels, too, saw war against the United States as a worrying development. And the subconscious doubt rapidly disappeared, of course, beneath the usual effusions of confidence.

The military leadership, already only too well aware of the magnitude of the crisis on the eastern front, were less sanguine, at least if we can rely upon their postwar recollections. Hitler's Luftwaffe adjutant, Nicolaus von

Below, just back from a month's leave, was told that Pearl Harbor provided a signal for Germany to declare war on America. He was shocked, he later wrote, at Hitler's 'cluelessness' about the American 'potential', the economic and military power which had been decisive once before, in the First World War. He saw it as an expression of Hitler's 'dilettante' approach and his limited knowledge of foreign countries.[10]

Rear Admiral (as he then was) Karl Dönitz, Commander-in-Chief of the German U-boat fleet and a firm Hitler loyalist in the ranks of the higher officer corps, was equally taken aback by the news that Germany was at war with America. He had told Hitler in September that, should the United States be drawn into the war, he wished to be given due warning so that his U-boats would be properly placed to take full advantage of the element of surprise to strike a major blow while anti-submarine defences were still weak. 'In the event,' he later wrote, 'things turned out differently. German High Command was itself taken by surprise by the Japanese attack on Pearl Harbor on December 7, 1941; and at that time there was not a single German U-boat in American waters.'[11]

General Walter Warlimont, second in charge to General Alfred Jodl, Hitler's chief adviser on operational planning, underlined the charge of amateurish, ill-conceived strategy imposed through spontaneous decisions taken without consultation or reflection. He himself had just heard the news of the declaration of war in Hitler's field headquarters in East Prussia, where he was just discussing the implications with some staff officers, when Jodl telephoned him from Berlin on the afternoon of 11 December. 'You have heard that the Führer has just declared war on America?' Jodl asked. 'Yes and we couldn't be more surprised,' Warlimont replied. Jodl pointed out that it was urgently necessary now to consider where the United States might deploy her forces. Warlimont agreed, adding that 'so far we have never even considered a war against the United States and so have no data on which to base this examination'.[12]

The decision to declare war on the United States, Warlimont recalled, 'was another entirely independent decision on which no advice from the Wehrmacht had either been asked or given; as a result we were now faced with a war on two fronts in the most serious conceivable form. Hitler's war plan had hitherto aimed at the rapid elimination of Russia as "a factor of military importance" in order subsequently to use the concentrated power of the Wehrmacht to bring the war in the west to an end. Now the best that could be hoped for was to escape being crushed between two enemies in east and west whose combined war potential was vastly superior to our own.'[13] Warlimont took the view that Hitler was 'literally mesmerized by his own concept of the political situation and did not take the military implications adequately into account'.[14]

Hitler, then, had declared war on such a powerful nation as the United States abruptly, without consultation with his military strategists (except, presumably, the ultra-loyalist Jodl and the head of the High Command of the Wehrmacht, the toadying Field Marshal Wilhelm Keitel), without anything approaching proper preparation for such a conflict, and, as Dönitz recalled, without taking cognizance of immediate logistical considerations. Nor had a declaration of war been formally necessary or in any way binding on Germany. Hitler had stated in his Reichstag speech that the declaration had been in accordance with the terms of the Tripartite Pact. But this was not the case. Ribbentrop (according to his later, self-serving account) had reminded Hitler that Germany was bound under the pact only to aid Japan if she were to be attacked by a third party.[15] Since Japan had attacked America, not the other way round, Germany was not committed to intervene. The leading official in the German Foreign Ministry, State Secretary Ernst von Weizsäcker, later pointed out the great surprise at Hitler's claim in his speech that Germany had been obliged under the Tripartite Pact to declare war on the United States. He saw this as 'legally an error and politically a mistake'.[16]

The surprise and foreboding, not just among ordinary Germans but among those in Hitler's entourage and in the highest circles of government and the military, at the declaration of war on the United States provide a clear indication that the opening of hostilities with America was seen as neither a foregone conclusion nor an outright necessity. Even in the eyes of Germany's military and diplomatic leaders there had been a choice. Hitler had faced options, and chosen war with the United States. As he himself viewed it, of course, a state of war had already existed in practice in the Atlantic, and in the fact of direct American support for Britain, then also for the Soviet Union. But we have seen reason to suppose that the 'undeclared war' in the Atlantic could, from Roosevelt's perspective, have continued into the indefinite future, even after the Japanese attack on Pearl Harbor. Hitler was well aware of Roosevelt's difficulties with American public opinion, and even more so of his problems with Congress. He knew that the American President had only by the narrowest of margins attained support for an extension of the Selective Service Act in August 1941, and how he had not dared risk asking Congress for a declaration of war until the blatant Japanese act of aggression in the bombing of Pearl Harbor on 7 December. Even after the declaration of war on Japan, there was absolutely no guarantee that Roosevelt would have secured a congressional mandate for war against Germany. Hitler took that difficult, even unenviable, question away from Roosevelt on 11 December.

Yet Hitler had the Pacific diversion he wanted even without a declaration of war on America. And he knew no way at this point of defeating the United States. His U-boats could certainly attack American shipping in the Atlantic. But he had no means of attacking the American mainland, bombing cities in the United States or disrupting the build-up of her military might. Now, with the declaration of war, the pressure of time – the urgency of attaining complete victory in Europe and acquiring economic strength and military muscle to be able to defeat, or at least fend off, the United States – had become even more acute. Time was less than ever on Germany's side. As Hitler knew, within two years or so the Americans expected to have a huge land army ready to fight on the European continent. It took in reality somewhat longer than expected for this 'second front', so eagerly awaited by Stalin, to materialize (though the landing in north Africa, then the push up through southern Italy, did commence in 1943), and the invasion of Nazi-occupied western Europe, which Britain could never have carried out without American help, began only in June 1944. But with his decision on 11 December 1941 Hitler had gone a long way towards sealing Germany's eventual fate. It seems exactly the move which he should have avoided at all costs. It looks like madness, even from a distant vantage point in time. Why, independently of advice, and at a critical juncture of the bitter contest for supremacy on the eastern front, did he opt for war against a new and extremely powerful enemy in the west, and one he did not know how to defeat? Just how puzzling was this decision?

I

In terms of the politics of international power, the United States had figured only on the fringes of Hitler's thoughts before the late 1930s. He was concentrated squarely upon Europe. America, in another hemisphere and determined, it seemed, to follow the political path of isolationism, was largely irrelevant to Hitler's conception of future German foreign policy.

The economic potential and racial composition of the United States nevertheless had implications for his ideological construct – how he saw Germany's current problems and future hopes. Characteristically, his central ideas of 'living space' and race held the key to his image of America. In America's vast country, with a dominant white 'Nordic' racial core, to which he attributed her economic success and high standard of living, he saw a model for his vision of German 'living space' in Europe.[17] America's economic advancement had been made possible in his view not simply (as was generally presumed) by technological innovation and modern rationalization of management and production, but by territorial expansion to fit the growing population: by colonizing the west 'after the white man had shot down the millions of redskins to a few hundred thousand'.[18] This matched his view of how German prosperity and dominance of Europe could only be attained by expansion – and this, 'by the sword'. By the beginning of the 1930s Hitler regarded America in economic terms as 'the toughest rival possible'.[19] He did not spell out the wider implications of this in public, though by now he had contemplated them in private. At some dim and distant future date, a German-dominated Europe would have to face a contest for supremacy with the United States. This implication was reinforced – though the reinforcement was unspoken – by another unwavering strand of his image of America: that it was a country, though with a good racial stock in its white population, dominated by Jewish capital, and by Jewish control of politics and culture.[20]

During the 1920s Hitler's image of America (apart from its peculiarly vehement antisemitic content and additional heavy focus on Freemasonry) had largely matched widespread stereotypes in right-wing circles in Germany. Unsurprisingly, in the early years of his political 'career', America's role in the First World War – which he saw as dictated by the interests of Jewish finance capital and Freemasonry – was the point of reference. Alongside this went expressions of hatred for President Woodrow Wilson, widely condemned on the German Right for what was seen as his part in bringing about the 'November Revolution' in 1918, then the national humiliation of the Versailles Treaty the following June.[21] In one of his very earliest speeches, in December 1919, Hitler ranked America alongside Britain as Germany's 'absolute enemies', a conventional view such a short time after the First World War. For America, he reckoned, money, even drenched with blood, was all that mattered. His association of America with the power of the Jews followed promptly: 'For the Jew, the money-purse is the most sacred object.' America, he concluded, was bound to have joined in the war, and left it with the lion's share of the spoils.[22] Similar sentiments recurred in a number of his speeches in the years before the putsch at the end of 1923, without ever becoming a dominant theme.

Nor did America occupy any place of prominence in Hitler's assessment of future German foreign policy in the second part of his tract, *Mein Kampf*, which he began in 1924 while interned following the failed putsch and completed in the summer of 1926, more than a year after his release. Only a brief passage towards the end touched on America's position in world affairs, as a country controlled by Jews, the coming rival and eventual inheritor of the doomed British Empire. 'It is Jews who govern the stock exchange forces of the American Union,' Hitler wrote. 'Every year makes them more and more the controlling masters of the producers in a nation of one hundred and twenty millions.' The looming threat was to Great Britain. 'No ties of kinship can prevent a certain feeling of envious concern in England towards the growth of the American Union in all fields of international, economic and power politics,' he averred. 'The former colonial country, child of the great mother, seems to be growing into a new master of the world.'[23] The threat to Germany, in Hitler's warped worldview, of an emerging great power run by Jews, was implicit, but far off in the distant future. He did not embroider upon it.

By 1928, when he composed his 'Second Book' – mainly a tract related to the question of the South Tyrol, a sensitive issue at the time and probably the reason why this treatise remained unpublished until its discovery long after the war – the prospect of a showdown with the United States at some point in the long-term future had adopted at least shadowy form in Hitler's mind. Notions of a threat to Europe from the growing economic might of America were as commonplace in Germany at the end of the 1920s as general anti-American prejudice.[24] Even so, Hitler's racist world-view, linked to his assumptions about geopolitics, gave them a different twist.

In the second half of the 1920s, he had become far more preoccupied with geopolitical issues, with the 'space question' as he usually called it, than in the years before the putsch. Mainly, this meant providing justification for his view that Germany had to expand to survive, and that the expansion had to come at the cost of the Soviet Union. It meant, too, elaborating upon his view, already expressed in *Mein Kampf*, that Germany should turn her back on earlier alignments in foreign policy and seek an alliance with Great Britain and Italy. In this thinking, the position of far-off, isolationist America played no part. However, the image we have already cursorily summarized of an emerging economic colossus with the potential to become a great power in the world – and one with a 'healthy racial core', but controlled by Jews and Freemasons – now did have a bearing. He came to incorporate that image in his vision of the future status of Germany as a world power, and to envisage its consequences.

He saw these, typically, in racial terms. Impressed (as many were at the time[25]) by American racially restrictive immigration legislation and propagated ideas on public health and eugenics, Hitler portrayed a young, racially virile white population, representing a selection of the 'best' migrants from Europe, in competition with a decadent and declining racial stock of the old continent. 'The danger arises', he wrote, 'that the signifi- cance of racially inferior Europe will gradually lead to a new determination of the fate of the world by the people of the North American continent.' The only way to block this threat was through a racial renaissance in Europe.[26] 'In the future,' therefore, 'the only state that will be able to stand up to North America will be the state that has understood how – through the character of its internal life as well as through the substance of its external policy – to raise the racial value of its people and bring it into the most practical national form for this purpose.' This was the duty laid down for the Nazi movement. The implication was clear. 'It is thoughtless to believe that the conflict between Europe' – dominated, of course, by a racially purified Germany – 'and America would always be of a peaceful economic nature.' Eventually, America would turn outwards. The clash with Europe to determine ultimate hegemony could not be avoided.[27]

Hitler had less to say about the United States during the early 1930s.[28] In line with many contemporaries and with the approach taken in the Nazi press, he regarded America as being significantly weakened by the economic crisis set in motion by the Wall Street Crash at the end of October 1929. According to his associate Ernst Hanfstaengl, himself of part-American descent, Hitler remarked that a country beset with its own domestic prob- lems could not hope to play a part in foreign affairs.[29] The crisis presumably also shored up his view that free markets and liberal capitalism could not offer the security that national long-term survival required. But, in fact, he said little in public about the Depression in the United States, reserving his rhetorical fire-power for assaults on the failing democratic system at home. And temporary weakness through economic crisis was still compatible with Hitler's long-term vision of an eventual clash between the United States and Europe, a view he continued to hold into the 1940s.[30]

No straight line, however, leads from these vague musings about the distant future to later policy decisions about America. Consonant with the scant attention Hitler had paid to the United States during his rise to power, America was little more than a sideshow for him and his government once he had taken office as Reich Chancellor. He displayed no overt interest in the United States during his first years in power, and America scarcely figured in the formulation of foreign policy. Nevertheless, with Hitler's tacit approval, there was an inexorable decline in relations between Ger- many and the United States down to the beginning of the European war. Certainly, he did nothing to try to stem this deterioration. Nor could he have done so without reversing the racism and militarism upon which his regime was founded.

Germany's relations with the United States had been good, and improving, before 1933. This soon changed under the new Nazi regime. Disputes about trade tariffs and Germany's readiness to renege on repayment of credits owing to the United States formed part of the rapid downturn in goodwill between the two countries. But other issues were more important still. The persecution of the Jews, the first serious outrages already all too evident in the spring of 1933, brought revulsion in the United States and spurred the growth of anti-German feeling. So did the attacks on the Christian Churches, the burning of the books of racially or politically 'undesirable' authors and the brutal police terror against political opponents. Beyond the mounting disgust at Nazi barbarism, the strident militarism of Hitler's regime and the obvious signs, soon apparent, that Germany was starting to rearm (with all the implications that held for the future peace of Europe) were viewed across the Atlantic with increasing foreboding.[31]

Unsurprisingly, the deterioration in relations also found its echo in German images of the United States. Concerns about foreign trade with the United States, then the staging of the Olympic Games in 1936, meant that German propaganda in the early years of the Nazi regime remained relatively muted in its anti-Americanism, certainly in contrast with its shrill tone in the late 1930s. Even so, criticism of the alleged role of the Jews in the United States was frequent, and gathered in intensity. So, from the mid-1930s onwards, did negative comment about the 'New Deal', about American cultural and racial decline and about President Roosevelt himself.[32]

The growth of antagonism across the Atlantic towards Germany caused Hitler no sleepless nights. If the antipathy was inevitable from a German viewpoint, given the ideological priorities of the Nazi regime, which could not accommodate American liberal sentiment, then it gave few grounds for worry. The United States, after all, was still in the throes of prolonged economic depression; she remained in the grip of isolationism; and her military capability was very low. Hitler could feel confident, therefore, that the United States' own interests would keep her aloof from European affairs for the foreseeable future. This interpretation was underscored at the very outset of his rule by his Foreign Minister, Konstantin von Neurath. Though Washington could not be expected to support German demands and wishes, suggested Neurath, 'the lack of interest of the United States in European affairs would probably not alter under President Roosevelt'.[33] The reshaping of Europe, Hitler must have been convinced, would remain a matter of little direct American concern. From the perspective of Hitler and the Nazi leadership, the United States, it seemed, could be more or less ignored as a factor in German foreign policy.

Little suggests that Hitler changed his mind in the last years before the war. When, on 5 November 1937, Hitler expounded to his military leaders his ideas about expansion into Austria and Czechoslovakia, and posited a number of differing scenarios about Germany's involvement in war for 'living space' by 1943–5 at the latest, he did not even mention the United States.[34] America remained an irrelevance to Hitler the following year as German ambitions became reality, with Austria then the Sudetenland swallowed up by the Reich.

Even so, there was by now more than the occasional straw in the wind to indicate that things were changing. Roosevelt's 'quarantine speech' of 5 October 1937, in which the American President advocated the international isolation of those countries threatening world peace – plainly, Germany, Italy and Japan – was interpreted by the German ambassador in Washington, Hans Heinrich Dieckhoff, as an indication that the United States might be moving out of isolationism. Dieckhoff reported in early December that, although for the time being the United States was likely to continue a passive foreign policy, this would cease, despite internal opposition, if her own interests were at stake or she was intolerably provoked, and 'in a conflict in which the existence of Great Britain is at stake America will put her weight into the scales on the side of the British'.[35] The mutual antagonism of the United States and Germany now became ever more apparent. The volume of anti-American propaganda in Germany was turned up sharply, while across the Atlantic mounting detestation for Nazism mingled with growing alarm as Hitler's aggression took Europe to the verge of war. Revulsion at Nazi barbarism reached a peak in reactions to the horrific nationwide pogroms against the Jews on 9–10 November 1938, the so-called *Reichskristallnacht* (Reich Crystal Night).[36] A tidal wave of outrage swept across America. The American ambassador to Berlin was recalled 'for report and consultation' (though, in fact, never to return). Shortly afterwards, in retaliation, the German ambassador in Washington was summoned back to Berlin.[37] There was no move to a full breach of diplomatic relations, but the German Foreign Ministry was concerned about the possibility of economic sanctions.[38] The concern was justified. The American Treasury backed off at the last minute, on the intervention of Cordell Hull, the Secretary of State, from imposing punitive tariffs on German imports.[39]

Speaking to representatives of the German press the day following

Reichskristallnacht (though not mentioning the pogrom by a single word), Hitler, in contrast to his views a decade earlier, was contemptuous of the inferior racial quality that he saw in the mixed ethnic population of the United States.[40] But he and other Nazi leaders were now beginning to take seriously the prospect of America as a potential future enemy. Hitler spoke in January 1939 of the United States as 'agitating' against Germany. Plainly, she ranked by now among 'the enemies of the Reich'.[41] His anger at the reactions to *Reichskristallnacht* in the United States and paranoia about the power of the Jews in America combined in ever shriller attacks on Roosevelt and the Jewish warmongers allegedly calling the tune.

This formed part of the background to the important speech that Hitler delivered to the Reichstag on 30 January 1939, the sixth anniversary of his 'seizure of power'. At its centre lay the presumed power of the Jews, which Hitler had consistently seen as the dominant force in American government and economic might. The tenor of the speech was an attack on the threat which he saw posed by Jewish finance in Britain and the United States to Germany's economy and national security. He depicted the Jews as warmongers forcing Germany into a conflict she did not want. Germany was, however, ready to meet the challenge and was prepared for a struggle to the death. And should it come to war – here Hitler offered his own terrible threat – then those who had caused it, the Jews, would perish. The result would be 'the annihilation of the Jewish race in Europe'.[42]

When, the day after Hitler's baleful speech, Roosevelt implied that the threat of Hitler meant America's frontiers now lay on the Rhine (a figure of speech he had used to justify the delivery of planes to France), it produced a veritable barrage of assaults in the German press.[43] This was a prelude to Hitler's frontal attack on Roosevelt in his Reichstag speech at the end of April.

Roosevelt, though, as we have seen, handicapped in his scope for action by domestic opinion and isolationist clamour against any move that hinted at dragging America into Europe's travails, had since Munich the previous autumn become ever more concerned about the likelihood of war and about the damaging failure of British and French appeasement policy. The horrors of *Reichskristallnacht* had then revealed the full barbarity of the Nazi regime. And in mid-March had come the occupation by Hitler's Wehrmacht of what remained of Czechoslovakia, followed, in early April, by the invasion of Albania by the troops of the other 'mad dog', Mussolini. In the days that followed, Roosevelt contemplated a public message that amounted in effect to a personal appeal to Hitler and Mussolini to back away from the path of aggression and war and to demonstrate their sincere commitment to peaceful development in Europe. The message, after numerous redraftings, was published on 15 April 1939. The centrepoint was Roosevelt's proposal that the Axis dictators should give an assurance that for a period of at least ten years they would attack none of a list of thirty named independent nations, mainly European but also including some in the Middle East. For his part, Roosevelt committed the United States to participation in discussions aimed at reducing armaments and opening up international trade on equal terms to all countries.[44]

Hitler was infuriated and insulted by what he saw as Roosevelt's arrogance in a message published before it had even been officially received in Berlin.[45] He at first deemed it beneath his dignity to reply to 'so contemptible a creature', but, probably because Roosevelt's speech had evidently made a generally favourable impression upon international opinion, eventually felt that he had to respond.[46] When he did so, in a speech to the Reichstag on 28 April, his riposte was withering.[47] He had enquired of the thirty named countries, he claimed, and none felt threatened by Germany. Some countries (he mentioned Syria as one), however, had been unable to give a reply because their own freedom of action had been curtailed by the democratic states. And was not Palestine occupied by British, not German troops? The Republic of Ireland, too, feared aggression from Britain, not from Germany. Roosevelt's appeal to disarmament equally played into Hitler's hands, since the German dictator had no difficulty in making great capital of the way in which the victorious powers had denuded Germany of armed defences after the First World War while finding no shortage of reasons to avoid disarming themselves.

Hitler's sarcastic sallies had the assembled tame Nazi Reichstag deputies in fits of laughter. It was one of his most effective speeches. Goebbels was ecstatic. 'A terrible flogging of Roosevelt. That really smacks him around the ears. The house is bent double with laughing. It's a pleasure to hear it. The success among the public is immense. Anybody publicly attacking the Führer certainly gets his comeuppance . . . He's a genius of political tactics and strategy. Nobody can do it like him. What a pygmy a man like Roosevelt is in comparison.'[48] Not only Nazis recognized the effectiveness of Hitler's rhetoric. William Shirer, an American journalist in Berlin at the time who heard the speech, thought Hitler's answer to Roosevelt 'rather shrewd' in playing upon the sympathies of appeasers and isolationists in America and Europe.[49]

Beyond such circles, even so, Hitler's 'reckoning' with Roosevelt had little currency. Rather, as it appeared to many, Roosevelt was claiming the moral high ground with an appeal to reason and peace in the face of proven aggressive intent. The impact of the speech, and of Roosevelt's intervention that had provoked it, was in any case of passing importance. What was significant was that the divide between the United States and Germany had been exposed in the most visible fashion. It was clear where the United States stood in the conflict between the democracies and the Axis powers.

From the German perspective, whatever the appearances of neutrality, the United States had to be regarded as essentially a hostile power. This meant that, after years of near irrelevance in German policy formation, the United States had now to be viewed strategically, not just ideologically. The key issue in the event – ever more probable – of European war in the foreseeable future was to ensure that America did not enter the conflict. In German thinking, however, this was not likely; there was no undue cause for concern. A presidential election was due in autumn 1940. No risks would be taken with public opinion before then. In any case, the force of isolationism ruled out intervention. And, beyond that, American military weakness was only too evident, with rearmament and industrial war production merely in their beginnings. German planning was indeed reckoning with a long war, or series of wars. But the early stages, it was presumed, would rapidly prove victorious before the United States was in any position to intervene. Hitler was confident that war with Poland, when it came, would be swiftly decided by German force of arms. He expected the western democracies to stay out of any military action against Poland. But, should they intervene, he again had no doubt that Germany would prevail. The western democracies, Britain as well as France, would be defeated, or would concede in a negotiated settlement in the face of overwhelming German military supremacy. The Americans would stay aloof. The future show-down with 'Jewish-Bolshevism' would follow at some stage with the backing, or at least the quiescence, of the west European powers. And this, too, would be over quickly. Conflict with the United States at some point in the future – not before the mid-1940s at the earliest – would be on the basis of a Germany dominating the whole of the European continent, and by this time with a mighty battle-fleet ready to contest control over the oceans.

This remained mere nebulous musing. But the central assumption, as war loomed ever closer in the summer of 1939, was broadly – and the thinking was still inchoate rather than concisely worked out – that Germany would have established her ascendancy in Europe before the United States became a factor of major strategic significance.

II

Even so, nothing could be taken for granted. As war began in Europe in September 1939, Hitler was acutely aware that he had only a limited period of time to achieve supremacy in Europe before American military and industrial potential would start to make itself felt in the conflict. Increasingly, America now had to be reckoned with. Speed was more than ever of the essence. Germany had to be victorious before American intervention could tip the balance.

Though Hitler was convinced that there was little prospect of an early entry of the United States into the war, he wanted to take no chances. Nothing was to be done to offer undue provocation. Attacks on President Roosevelt in the German press, commonplace and venomous in the months preceding the war, now ceased on orders from Goebbels' Ministry of Propaganda. The press was instructed to apply absolute discretion in reporting on American affairs.[50] Hitler also reined in the gung-ho naval leadership, anxious to unleash their U-boats even at the risk of sinking neutral American ships. More than once in the autumn, Hitler insisted to the Commander-in-Chief of the navy, Grand Admiral Erich Raeder, that everything should be done to avoid naval incidents with the United States. On 23 February 1940 he categorically refused permission to Raeder for two submarines to patrol waters off the Canadian coast, near Halifax, Nova Scotia, a crucial port for British convoys, because of 'the psychological effect that any such step might have in the United States'. In early March, the navy received explicit orders banning the stopping, capturing or sinking of any American ships, wherever they might be.[51]

German military prognoses in autumn 1939 reckoned that there might be a period of grace lasting no longer than a year and a half before the industrial and military potential of America would begin to make itself felt. An analysis by the High Command of the Wehrmacht concluded that, for the time being, the United States could just about manage to meet the demands of her own armed forces and would need about a year to start producing large numbers of planes, tanks and other military vehicles. But after around one to one and a half years, there would be 'a level of productivity in all spheres of armaments which far outstretches all other countries'.[52] This assessment accorded with that of reports from the German military attaché in Washington that the state of military preparation in the United States ruled out any intervention before the late summer of 1940, but that thereafter a full American participation in the war was possible.[53] The German embassy in Washington took the view that Roosevelt's administration was reckoning with a long war, did not expect a rapid defeat of Britain and France and would intervene in the event of the democracies either facing disaster or, alternatively, approaching victory. The necessary popular support for intervention would be created, it was presumed.[54]

Hitler's sense of urgency to complete the military defeat of France and force the British to a negotiated settlement from a position of weakness becomes all the more understandable in the light of such reports. At the beginning of the war, he had expressed his confidence that he would have 'solved all problems in Europe' long before the Americans could intervene. But privately he had added: 'woe betide us if we're not finished by then.'[55] As Poland lay prostrate, only a few weeks later, he urged an immediate attack on France on the grounds that time was running against Germany, militarily and economically.[56] And just before the start of the western offensive in May 1940 he justified his move to his friend Mussolini by pointing to 'the recurring undertone of threats in Mr. Roosevelt's telegrams, notes, and inquiries' as providing 'ample reason for seeing to it that the war is brought to an end as soon as possible'.[57]

On the very day that Italy declared war, 10 June 1940, President Roosevelt had publicly avowed to 'extend to the opponents of force' the material resources of the United States.[58] Just over a month later, an analysis Hitler received of a speech by Roosevelt, delivered (in accepting the Democratic nomination for the forthcoming presidential election) on 19 July, made plain that the American President stood resolutely opposed to Germany and ready to back Britain in a continued struggle.[59] The implications for Germany's war were evident: it had to be won quickly and conclusively before American resources – and possibly direct intervention – could tell. Hitler drew his conclusion. The signals from across the Atlantic influenced the decision which he announced at the end of the month to his generals: to prepare to attack and defeat the Soviet Union in a 'lightning war' of a mere few months. The war he had always been ideologically determined to fight now had a vital strategic purpose: ending British hopes of any Continental ally, thereby forcing Britain to accept the inevitable and come to terms; and, by so doing, removing the threat of American intervention. London and Washington had, as it were, to be defeated via Moscow.

Hitler's strategy had become global in its dimensions. It now reached out to the role of Japan in the Far East. Defeat of the Soviet Union by the Wehrmacht would free Japan from any threat from her old enemy to the north. It would open up the way which Japan was already deliberating: a move to the south, implying an attack on British possessions in the Far East, with the further desired effect of keeping the Americans occupied in the Pacific. Within weeks, the new interest in Japan had led to the moves to that eventually culminated in the Tripartite Pact of 27 September 1940 and underpinned Ribbentrop's short-lived hopes of constructing a new world order aimed at undermining British world power and the international strength of the United States.[60]

Meanwhile, the destroyer deal concluded between Churchill and Roosevelt in early September had given Hitler the most tangible indication of America's increasing support for the undefeated Britain. The hawkish Admiral Raeder now imagined American entry into the war to be a certainty.[61] But the emerging Atlantic alliance which the destroyer deal symbolized, and the visibly anti-German tenor of the American administration, had to be swallowed. Still Hitler wanted no provocation. Firm restrictions were placed upon the press reportage in Germany.[62]

The lifting of the restraint on anti-American propaganda followed in the wake of Roosevelt's press conference on 17 December (where he used the metaphor of lending a neighbour a garden hose to put out a fire to introduce what would soon materialize as the policy of lend-lease), then his 'arsenal of democracy' speech near the end of the month.[63] Taking the gloves off in the propaganda war was a reflection of how seriously the move to introduce lend-lease was viewed by the Nazi regime. Admiral Raeder, keen as ever to exploit the latest development to push for greater naval aggression in the Atlantic, emphasized the implications of lend-lease to Hitler on 27 December. His conclusion, that 'very strong support will be forthcoming [for Britain] only by the end of 1941 or the beginning of 1942',[64] underlined what Hitler himself had told Jodl ten days earlier: that Germany had to establish her Continental dominance by the end of 1941, before America could intervene. A memorandum composed on 9 January by Hans Dieckhoff, the former ambassador to the United States, who had come to be regarded as an expert on America in the German Foreign Ministry, outlined the seriousness of the implications. He pointed out that it would be a mistake to believe that the United States' entry into the war would not change the situation. In such an event, industrial production would increase sharply, allowing greater supplies of arms, munitions and planes to be made available to Britain. Without American intervention, a British collapse offered the prospect of a peace settlement and an end to the war. 'If, however, the United States is also in the war,' Dieckhoff added, 'then, even if England collapses, the war against the United States will continue, and it will be difficult to arrive at a peace.'[65] It was about as far as a senior diplomat could go in implying that American involvement in the war – seen as increasingly likely, now all the more so in the light of lend-lease – would mean a German victory could not be won. The implication was reinforced a month later by a report from the German military attaché in the Washington embassy, General Friedrich von Bötticher, estimating that American production of warplanes would triple in the course of 1941. By that time the rate of production would have overtaken Germany's own.[66]

Publicly, Hitler resorted to threats, a device he frequently used, though now, for the first time perhaps, deployed from a position, at least as far as the United States was concerned, approaching weakness. Speaking in the Reichstag on 30 January 1941, the eighth anniversary of his 'seizure of power', he declared: 'No one should be under any illusion. Anyone who believes he can help England must know one thing above all: every ship, with or without escort, that comes within range of our torpedoes will be torpedoed!'[67] It was a threat he did not dare implement for fear of provoking exactly what he was still wanting at all costs to avoid. More important than this still empty threat was the strategic conclusion that Hitler privately drew from the moves towards lend-lease.

First, it confirmed him in his thinking that Germany's chance of total victory – that is, keeping the Americans out of the war – rested upon the rapid destruction of the Soviet Union. And, secondly, it drew him still further in the direction of an active policy towards Japan, something which had made no progress since the conclusion of the Tripartite Pact the previous September. 'The smashing of Russia would also allow Japan to turn with all her might against the United States,' he told his military leaders on 9 January. And this would prevent the United States from entering the war.[68] The navy's report on the meeting explicitly drew out the strategic thinking, and consequences, in Hitler's exposé. 'If the USA and Russia should enter the war against Germany,' the report of Hitler's comments ran, 'the situation would become very complicated. Hence any possibility for such a threat to develop must be eliminated at the very beginning. If the Russian threat were non-existent, we should wage war on Britain indefinitely. If Russia collapsed, Japan would be greatly relieved; this in turn would mean increased danger to the USA.' Hitler then added a further reflection, indicating the way he was starting to invest hopes in Japan: 'Regarding Japanese interest in Singapore, the Führer feels that the Japanese should be given a free hand even if this may entail the risk that the USA is thus forced to take drastic steps.'[69] Japanese expansion in the Far East, in other words, was now starting to form an intrinsic part of Germany's strategy for final victory in Europe. Rapid defeat of the Soviet Union was the key to both.

With the passing of the Lend-Lease Act on 11 March 1941, the German leadership concluded, as an article in the *Völkischer Beobachter* (the main Nazi daily newspaper) stated, that the United States was now irredeemably committed to support for Germany's enemies. 'We now know what and against whom we are fighting,' the article declared. 'The final struggle has begun.'[70] According to a report on reactions in the High Command of the Wehrmacht to Roosevelt's speech announcing the implementation of the Lend-Lease Act, the general view was that it 'may be regarded as a declaration of war on Germany'.[71] Hitler himself, amid the abuse he showered on President Roosevelt, agreed that the Americans had given him a reason for war. He was not yet ready for it, but 'it will come to war with the United States one way or the other', he remarked. Roosevelt, and the Jewish financiers behind him, worried about their losses if Germany should win the war, would see to that. His only regret, Hitler went on, was that he still had no aircraft capable of bombing American cities. He would happily hand out such a lesson to the American Jews. The Lend-Lease Act had brought additional problems, but these could be mastered 'by a merciless sea war'. It was important to increase the tonnage sunk by U-boats. But the Americans were themselves for the time being still constrained by the limitations of their armaments capacity.[72]

It was 'as a countermeasure to the expected effects of the aid to England law of the United States' that, on 25 March 1941, Hitler extended the German combat zone to the waters around Iceland and the fringes of the American neutrality zone. This followed rumours reaching Berlin that the American administration was contemplating providing naval escorts for convoys as far as Iceland.[73] As we have seen, it would be some months before Roosevelt finally agreed to the escorting of convoys which the more hawkish members of his administration were already urging. But from the German perspective, escorting was one of a number of issues in the spring of 1941 which gave the impression that Roosevelt was deliberately escalating the conflict in the Atlantic, seeking a provocation that would enable him to take America into the war.

The permission in late March granted to the British to have their warships repaired in American docks, then the seizure of Axis vessels in American ports at the end of the month and the agreement with Greenland to establish a military base there were all seen as self-evidently hostile acts towards Germany. They were accompanied by rumours of American plans to occupy the Azores (which the Germans had for a while considered possessing to pre-empt the Americans – a move Hitler still favoured in order to provide a base for long-range bombers to attack the United States).[74] And, though Roosevelt's administration introduced patrolling (to warn British convoys of lurking German submarines) rather than fully fledged escorting, this, too, augured future trouble.

The first apparent clash of an American destroyer, the USS *Niblack*, with what was – wrongly, as it turned out – taken to be a German U-boat in April seemed a sign of things to come, which could only hasten the descent into full-scale conflict. The sinking of the *Robin Moor* on 21 May provided an even more dangerous flashpoint, and was followed, six days later, by Roosevelt's big speech declaring his administration's intention to do everything to prevent German dominance of the Atlantic, and introducing a state of 'unlimited emergency'.[75] The unexpected American soft-pedalling of the *Robin Moor* sinking came as a notable relief to Berlin, as did the fact that no significant action followed the fanfare preceding Roosevelt's major speech. A period of mounting tension over the spring had subsided into an uneasy stalemate. The last thing Hitler had wanted, preoccupied as he was by military action in the Balkans and, especially, the build-up to 'Operation Barbarossa', was the entry of America into the war as a result of some incident in the Atlantic.

He had, in fact, repeatedly given instructions to the trigger-happy Admiral Raeder, heading a bellicose German naval leadership anxious to engage fully with the increasing American threat in the Atlantic, to avoid all incidents that could be seen as a provocation. The *Robin Moor* sinking had been carried out in disregard for Hitler's explicit orders, but remained, until the autumn, a stray incident. The strict prohibition on German submarines taking any action against American shipping was repeated as 'Barbarossa' approached. At the beginning of June, Hitler informed Raeder that 'the question of searching American merchant ships is to be postponed until units of the fleet are sent to operate in the Atlantic', clearly a temporary ban until the war at sea could finally be fought with no holds barred.[76]

On 21 June, the day before the invasion of the Soviet Union, the question of German naval action against American ships in the Atlantic was again raised by Admiral Raeder. He brought up a near-incident the previous day, when a U-boat had encountered an ageing American battleship, the *Texas*, with a destroyer escort, ten miles within the proclaimed German combat area. The submarine had given chase, but the *Texas* had eventually steamed away unscathed and unaware of the danger.[77] Raeder welcomed the incident, as he did that of the *Robin Moor*, and gave Hitler his opinion that 'where the United States is concerned firm measures are always more effective than apparent yielding'. But Hitler was adamant. 'For the present,' the report of his meeting with Raeder ran, 'the Führer wishes to avoid incidents with American warships and merchant ships outside the closed area under all circumstances. For the closed area, clearly defined orders will be necessary which will not involve submarines in confused and dangerous conditions, and which can be carried out.'

Raeder himself, getting the message, proposed a fifty- or hundred-mile strip inside the boundary of the combat zone, within which attacks on American warships should be avoided. Hitler wanted no misunderstandings. 'The Führer declares in detail', the report continued, 'that until operation "Barbarossa" is well under way he wishes to avoid any incident with the United States. After a few weeks the situation will become clearer, and can be expected to have a favourable effect on the United States and Japan; America will have less inclination to enter the war, due to the threat from Japan which will then increase.'[78] With that statement, not only was the temporary nature of the ban on attacking American shipping made plain, but the globally strategic aims of the attack on the Soviet Union were evident. In these aims, the position of Japan was crucial.

Uneasy and uncertain about Japanese intentions since the signing of the Tripartite Pact, the Nazi leadership had actively sought to persuade Japan to attack Singapore. Hitler's war directive of 5 March 1941, on 'Co-operation with Japan', began: 'The aim of the cooperation based on the Tripartite Pact has to be to bring Japan to active operations in the Far East as soon as possible. Strong English forces will be tied up as a result, and the main interest of the United States of America will be diverted to the Pacific.'[79] Some days earlier, Ribbentrop had actively tried to persuade Oshima Hiroshi, the newly re-appointed and overtly pro-Axis Japanese ambassador in Berlin, to strike against Singapore.[80] This, it was recognized, ran the risk of bringing American involvement in the war, something German policy was otherwise striving at all costs to avoid. The apparent contradiction was, however, merely superficial. American involvement in the Pacific, it was thought, would hinder rather than encourage participation in Europe. But, beyond that consideration, it was felt that a rapid strike against Singapore, bastion of British possessions in the Far East, while avoiding aggression towards the American base in the Philippines, could be undertaken without any declaration of war by the United States, and yet still preoccupy the Americans with defence in the Pacific at the expense of the Atlantic. A further worry lay behind the intensified German attempts to persuade the Japanese to act against Singapore. If and when

Germany found herself at war with the United States, she desperately wanted Japan to be alongside her in the conflict. And, still apprehensive about Japanese intentions, there was the lingering fear that some rapprochement might be found with the United States, leaving Germany facing the eventual deployment of American might alone.[81]

This worry continued throughout the spring of 1941, enhanced by German awareness of the Japanese moves to defuse the mounting tension between Japan and the United States, a development which seemed to conflict with the impression given by Oshima, supportive of German policy, and the messages filtering to Berlin via the German embassy in Tokyo about the anti-American, pro-Axis stance of the Japanese Foreign Minister, Matsuoka. When Matsuoka paid a visit to Berlin at the end of March 1941 every effort was made both by Ribbentrop and by Hitler himself to press him to commit to an early strike against Singapore. 'The capture of Singapore', said Ribbentrop, 'would perhaps be most likely to keep America out of the war because the United States could scarcely risk sending its fleet into Japanese waters. If today, in a war against England, Japan were to succeed with one decisive stroke, such as the attack on Singapore, Roosevelt would be in a very difficult position. It would be difficult for him to take any effective action against Japan.'[82] Hitler, in his own audience with the Japanese Foreign Minister, pulled out all the rhetorical stops. Germany had, he said, taken account of the possibility of American aid to Britain. But this could have no worthwhile effect before 1942. And Japan need have no fear of the Soviet Union in the event of a move against Singapore, given the German divisions on the eastern border ready to be deployed if need be (though Hitler divulged nothing of the actual plans to invade). He urged 'joint action' now by the Tripartite Pact powers. No time could be more favourable for the Japanese to act. But, to Hitler's disappointment, Matsuoka stonewalled. An attack on Singapore, he commented, was a matter of time, and in his own opinion the earlier it came the better. But other views, he said, prevailed in Tokyo. He could offer no commitment.[83]

In their further meeting after the Japanese Foreign Minister's brief courtesy call on Mussolini, Hitler again exuded a confidence that belied his underlying anxiety. In the event that America should enter the war, Germany would prove victorious, he claimed. She would wage war with her U-boats and Luftwaffe, and had taken precautions to ensure that there could be no American landing in Europe. In any case, American troops were no match for German soldiers. He went on to make an unprovoked promise of significance. If Japan should come into conflict with the United States, Germany would immediately 'draw the consequences'. America would seek to pick off her enemies one by one. 'Therefore Germany would', declared Hitler, 'promptly take part in the case of a conflict between Japan and America, for the strength of the allies in the Tripartite Pact lay in their acting in common. Their weakness would be in allowing themselves to be defeated separately.'[84] These unprompted remarks give a clue to Hitler's reasons for declaring war on the United States eight months later. But for now he had to accept that Japanese intentions were unclear, and that nothing he could do was able to push Japan into the aggression in the Far East that he desired.

As the date neared for Hitler to launch his all-out offensive against the Soviet Union, Japanese plans remained nebulous. The Germans tried to encourage a more distinctly anti-American stance.[85] But nothing materialized. On 6 June, the German ambassador in Tokyo, General Eugen Ott, reported that Japan was trying to improve relations with the United States to prevent American entry into the war. As a consequence a Japanese attack on Singapore had been shelved for the time being, since it was assumed that this 'would bring America to enter the war at once'. Ott was sure that the Japanese would honour their pledge to fight if the United States took the initiative in entering the war. But if America entered the war as a result of a conflict between Germany and Russia, Japan would feel no obligation to fight under the Tripartite Pact.[86]

When German troops fell on the Soviet Union on 22 June, therefore, the stakes from Hitler's point of view could scarcely have been higher. A speedy triumph in the Soviet Union was absolutely imperative. German total victory depended upon a quick knockout blow against Stalin's forces, aided if at all possible by a Japanese strike in the Far East aimed at Britain and America. Japan's actions, which Hitler could not control, were now a crucial component of German strategy. For behind the whole strategy lay the spectre of American intervention. Once America joined the war, as seemed inevitable if the struggle were to become prolonged, Germany's chances would rapidly diminish. It came back to what Hitler had told Jodl on 17 December 1940: 'We must solve all continental European problems in 1941 since from 1942 onwards the United States would be in a position to intervene.'[87]

III

America was understandably far from the forefront of Hitler's thoughts over the weeks following the onslaught against the Soviet Union. But if the problem of the United States was at the back of Hitler's mind, it was not out of it. It was crucial above all, over this phase, until victory could be achieved, that no incidents involving American shipping should disturb the Atlantic front and serve as a conceivable pretext that Roosevelt might exploit to take America into the war. With Admiral Raeder and his colleagues still champing at the bit, Hitler could do no other than adamantly persist in the policy, already adopted before 'Barbarossa', of holding his U-boats in check, despite Roosevelt's intensified 'undeclared war' in the Atlantic. 'Germany's attitude to America', it was reported by the navy's leadership on 8 July, was 'to remain as before: not to let herself be provoked'.[88]

The previous day American troops had set foot in Iceland. This further departure from the neutrality of the United States unquestionably made the war in the Atlantic more difficult for Germany, with its obvious consequence of easing the passage of British convoys using the same route as American vessels supplying the troops in Iceland. But Hitler was not prepared to countenance any retaliatory measures. U-boat commanders in the north Atlantic had, in fact, promptly requested permission to take action in Icelandic waters. But policy remained the same: avoid any provocation.

Raeder was unhappy. On 9 July, at the 'Wolf's Lair', the 'Führer Headquarters' that had been set up in East Prussia, he sought a decision from Hitler on whether 'the occupation of Iceland by the USA is to be considered as an entry into the war, or as an act of provocation which should be ignored'. The response offers an insight into Hitler's thinking. 'The Führer', Raeder's notes of the meeting ran, 'explains in detail that he is most anxious to postpone the United States' entry into the war for another one or two months. On the one hand the Eastern Campaign must be carried on with the entire Air Force, which is ready for this task and which he does not wish to divert even in part; on the other hand, a victorious campaign on the Eastern Front will have a tremendous effect on the whole situation and probably also on the attitude of the USA. Therefore for the time being he does not wish the existing instructions changed, but rather wants to be sure that incidents will be avoided.'[89]

Whether the postponement of conflict with the United States for some two months was envisaged as leading, after a triumphant end to the eastern campaign, to Germany opening hostilities or to a presumed move by Roose-velt to enter the war was not made clear. But the sense of Hitler's comments implies that in such an eventuality the move would have been made by Germany. This is reinforced by his remarks to Raeder just over a fortnight later, on 25 July. Hitler repeated that he wanted to avoid having the United States declare war while the eastern campaign was still in progress. But 'after the eastern campaign he reserves the right to take severe action against the USA as well'.[90] In the high summer of 1941, then, with the Wehrmacht rampaging eastwards, Hitler was contemplating war with the United States in the near future – but only once the Soviet Union had been crushed.

Victory in the east seemed at this time almost achieved. The chief of the army General Staff, General Franz Halder, had as early as 3 July concluded that it was not going too far to claim that the eastern campaign had been won within the space of two weeks.[91] The arrogant presumption would soon rebound drastically. But it was in this euphoric atmosphere that Hitler ruminated on war against the United States once his hands were free in the east.

In the middle of July he opened up to Oshima, the Japanese ambassador in Berlin, the giddy prospect of a combined effort by Germany and Japan to demolish the threat first of the Soviet Union, then of the United States. 'We won't get round the showdown with America,' Hitler told him. It should not be presumed, because he was not doing anything at present, that he accepted the American occupation of Iceland. He had no fear of America. The European armaments industry was far greater than the American. And he had experienced American soldiers in the First World War: the Germans were far superior. As soon as the eastern campaign was over, he would transfer his efforts from land to building up the navy and air force. (A war directive to this effect had, in fact, been issued the previous day. The extended emphasis upon U-boats, not surface ships, clearly had Britain and America in its sights.[92] And we might recall that Hitler, already in May, was envisaging bases on the Azores for long-range bombers to attack the United States.[93]) He lavished praise upon the Wehrmacht, then told Oshima that the destruction of Russia was in the supreme interest both of Germany and of Japan. Russia would always be the ally of their enemies. Germany was menaced in the east by the Soviet Union and in the west by the United States, he declared. For Japan, it was the other way round. He was therefore of the opinion, he went on, 'that we should jointly destroy them'.

The current conditions for Japanese intervention, he implied to Oshima, were optimal. 'The Russian war was won', he roundly declared. Soviet resistance would soon be broken. He would be finished in the east by September. He did not need any help. He could continue the struggle alone. But, he stated, the smashing of the Soviet Union also brought the moment of fate for Japan. He and Ribbentrop (also present) had already encouraged Japan to push into Siberia. An attack on Vladivostok had temporarily become the substitute for Singapore.[94] Hitler's strategic aim now became apparent. 'What would America then do? How would she then conduct the war?' he asked. 'The destruction of Russia must become the political life's work of Germany and Japan. And we could make it easy for ourselves if we acted at the same time, if we cut off Russia's life-support at the same time.' It offered the chance – and the hope. 'If we were able to keep the United States out of the war at all,' he concluded, 'it would only be through the destruction of Russia and only then, if Japan and Germany act in clinical fashion [*eiskalt*] and definitively.'[95]

Again, Hitler had veered between the idea of the destruction of the Soviet Union to keep America out of the war, and as a platform for aggression against the United States. Either way, the talk with Oshima, with the war in the east presumed won, indicated that the United States figured centrally in Hitler's thoughts on attaining final victory. Mastery in Europe (reverting to his ideas of 1928 in the 'Second Book') had to be viewed in its global implications. It was the premiss for the showdown with the United States that Hitler again here saw as inevitable. And, though he was obviously speaking for effect, hoping to impress the Japanese to act as he wanted, Japan's position in Hitler's strategic vision at this point was plainly pivotal. But he could do nothing except hope that the leaders of Japan would see matters as he did. In reality, he was, and remained, quite in the dark about Japanese intentions. He was still convinced a month later that Japan would attack the Soviet Union.[96] Unknown to him, on 2 July, almost two weeks before Hitler's talk with Oshima, the Japanese leadership had already decided against the 'northern option' of attacking the Soviet Union. The leaders of Japan were less sure than Hitler was that the German war in the east was already won.

Within a month of the rosy vista Hitler was painting for Oshima's benefit, the mood in his East Prussian headquarters had turned distinctly gloomier. Despite continuing German advances, it was now obvious that the quick knockout had not succeeded. Logistical difficulties were mounting alongside the growing numbers of casualties. Above all, Soviet defences were proving more resilient than had been forecast. On 11 August, General Halder acknowledged that 'we have underestimated the Russian colossus'.[97] The war, it was ever more clear, would drag on through the winter. Hitler, suffering from dysentery and high nervous tension, was embroiled by mid-August in the first of many damaging conflicts with his leading military advisers. Should the primary objective be Moscow, as his generals were suggesting, or still, as the 'Barbarossa' plan had laid down and Hitler insisted, the push to secure the key industrial and oil-rich regions of the southern Soviet Union and the dominance of the Baltic through the conquest of Leningrad in the north?[98] As the decision – which only weeks later resolved itself into the desperate big autumn push for Moscow before the winter snows set in – hung in the air and Hitler's generals recoiled beneath his thunderous outbursts, news of the Atlantic Charter, the outcome of Churchill's meeting with Roosevelt in Placentia Bay, Newfoundland, filtered through.

Goebbels immediately, cynically and with some accuracy summed up the Atlantic Charter as 'a typical propaganda product' – something about which he knew a great deal. 'Evidently Churchill had set out to draw America into the war,' he commented. 'In that he did not succeed. Roosevelt can't at the moment bring about the entry of the United States into the war because of American popular opinion. So obviously they've agreed on this gigantic propaganda bluff.' Goebbels instructed the German press to pour out all its vitriol on the eight points of the Charter. He acknowledged that, through the Charter, Roosevelt had allied himself unequivocally with the aims of the British belligerents. But on no account could it be claimed 'that through this Declaration a transformation in the general war situation had taken place'.[99] The line that the Atlantic Charter was 'a great big bluff' was taken up by Ribbentrop in a memorandum he drew up for Hitler on 17 August.[100]

The following day, Goebbels visited a sick and irritable Hitler in his field headquarters. Unsurprisingly, the German dictator was dismissive about the significance of the Atlantic Charter, much as Goebbels himself had predicted. Here, as repeatedly, Hitler's views on the United States were shaped, at least in part, by the dispatches relayed to him from the German military attaché in Washington, Bötticher, who had cabled the message that the Atlantic Conference was of no importance. Bötticher had consistently (and erroneously) believed that the United States was so preoccupied with Japan that the Pacific was her priority. Correspondingly, he minimized the threat to Germany. And he further pandered to Hitler's prejudices through his frequently reported belief that the Jews were running America.[101] Bötticher had now signalled that the meeting between Churchill and Roosevelt would do nothing to alter the course of events or the balance of forces. America could not enter the war as yet, whatever the declarations, since military preparations were incomplete and she feared war on two fronts. He saw the internal differences in the United States as a reflection of 'the conflict between the Jewish conception of the world and true Americanism', the latter opposed to intervention.[102]

Given such background information, it was a foregone conclusion that Hitler would be unimpressed by the Atlantic Charter. Grossly overestimating some recent parliamentary criticism of Churchill, he thought the British Prime Minister's domestic difficulties lay behind his attempt to persuade Roosevelt to enter the war.[103] The American President was unable to oblige, as he actually wanted to do, because he had to be cautious of the domestic situation in the United States. (Hitler was well apprised of the bitter debates in Congress over the extension of the Selective Service Act.) Roosevelt and Churchill had settled on the Declaration of the Atlantic Charter, in his view, because they were in no position to decide on anything of practical value. The Charter, Hitler concluded, 'can do us no harm at all'.[104]

Japanese intentions were still a matter merely of guesswork. 'The Führer is convinced that Japan will carry out the attack on Vladivostok as soon as forces have been assembled,' Raeder noted from his meeting with Hitler on 22 August. 'The present aloofness can be explained by the fact that the assembling of forces is to be accomplished undisturbed, and the attack is to come as a surprise move.'[105] Hitler's optimism was unfounded and misplaced. The German Foreign Ministry, in fact, was far less sanguine than Hitler about Japan's intentions. The replacement of the pro-Axis Japanese Foreign Minister Matsuoka in mid-July by Admiral Toyoda, known to be more conciliatory towards America, was not seen as a positive sign. It stirred worries that Japan, faced with the freezing of Japanese assets in the United States on 26 July as a reaction to the occupation of southern Indochina, might be anxious to reach a rapprochement with the Americans. The unease was heightened by information gleaned at the end of August that an important message from the Japanese premier, Prince Konoe, had been passed to President Roosevelt. This was interpreted as a move to avoid conflict, precisely the opposite of what Germany wanted. The Germans were left guessing. But they could not avoid the suspicion that the Japanese were anything but anxious to rush into action that would invite a clash with the United States.[106]

It was at this stage that the *Greer* incident gave a new twist to events in the Atlantic. Goebbels was initially inclined to play it down. He even thought at first that it had probably been an English submarine deliberately attempting to create a provocation to bring the Americans into the war. He still took the view that Roosevelt's position was not strong enough to risk war. He was surprised at the way the American press was exploiting the affair. For his part, he was prepared to let the German press attack Roosevelt personally, but not to link these attacks to the incident in the Atlantic and offer any provocation. 'Our position is for the time being extraordinarily difficult,' he noted. 'We have to operate with great sensitivity and the utmost tact.'[107] But when Roosevelt delivered his 'shoot-on-sight' speech on 11 September, Goebbels told the press to fire a full-scale broadside at the President. He interpreted the speech as Roosevelt's commencement of an unofficial war. Only American opinion, he presumed, was holding back an officially declared war. And it need not be doubted, he thought, that if there should be a series of armed clashes Roosevelt could whip up opinion without difficulty to back an official declaration. That this would be unwelcome to Germany at this stage, Goebbels made plain. 'The entry of the United States into the war would be not so much materially but psychologically extremely unpleasant,' he commented. 'But that, too, would have to be borne.'[108] A day later, he summed up his own (and without doubt Hitler's) feelings. 'The longer a formal declaration of war can be delayed, the better it is for us. If, what we are all hoping and urgently yearning for, we have brought the eastern campaign to a victorious conclusion, then it can't harm us much more.'[109]

The caution that Goebbels voiced was not shared by Raeder and the naval leadership. As before, they were keen to engage fully in the battle of the Atlantic and did not want to accept the American escalation in the *Greer* affair lying down. On 17 September, Raeder and U-boat chief Admiral Dönitz put a number of proposals to Hitler to amend the combat instructions to submarines in the Atlantic. Apart from their interest in maximizing the sectoral interests of the navy, both felt that Germany's best chance of victory lay in cutting off British supplies from the United States. To do this meant expanding the war at sea to American ships assisting British convoys. Hesitation in such an undertaking, they thought, was a grave mistake. They wanted the freedom to attack convoy escorts without regard to the blockade area, and to attack American vessels if they were helping the enemy or engaged in an assault or a pursuit. They also sought the recognition of only a twenty-mile neutrality zone off the American coast. The proposals amounted to little less than unrestricted licence for U-boats in the Atlantic. But they went much too far for Hitler at this crucial juncture in the eastern campaign. 'On the basis of a detailed discussion of the situation as a whole,' recorded Raeder, 'in which it appears that the end of September will bring the great decision in the Russian campaign, the Führer requests that care should be taken to avoid any incidents in the war on merchant shipping before about the middle of October.'[110] But, of course, the end of September did not bring victory in the Soviet Union. And the middle of October came and went without any change in Hitler's orders to the U-boats in the Atlantic.

Hitler's attention, and that of his leading generals, was meanwhile focused intently upon the unfolding drama on the eastern front. Though the advance on Moscow had commenced at the start of October, the chances of taking the city before the winter were dwindling. The timetable was by now awry. The grand strategic scheme behind 'Barbarossa' lay already on the verge of ruination. But the threat from the United States, rearming fast, had not diminished. To the German leadership, Roosevelt – pushed by Jewish warmongers – was determined to take America into the war.

Action by Japan in the Far East was increasingly imperative from Berlin's perspective. But a subtle difference had taken place in German expectations of Japan. When Hitler had talked to Oshima in July, he had hoped, even presumed, that the Japanese would cooperate in the demolition of the Soviet Union, and then deal with America. Now, the hopes were starting to rise that the simmering tension between Japan and the United States would not cool into some uneasy rapprochement, but would boil over into full-scale war in the Pacific. By this time, Hitler wanted to avoid imposing pressure on Japan. He did not want it to appear that Germany needed the Japanese.[111] Despite this, on 13 September Ribbentrop, warning that Roosevelt's aggression was certain to lead to war between the Axis powers and the United States, sought assurances from Tokyo that Japan would honour her commitments under the Tripartite Pact. He wanted a warning to Washington along those lines.[112]

New hope arose from the change of government in Tokyo on 18 October. The end of Konoe's government and the new Cabinet formed under General Tojo, known to be a militant, were correctly interpreted as a sign that the basis for negotiations with Washington had failed. Hitler remained sceptical. He saw a mismatch between strong words and action from the new Japanese Cabinet. He distrusted Tojo, thought the construction of the new Cabinet was a tactical bluff to force concessions from America, and had as great a difficulty as ever in reading Japanese intentions, which remained completely opaque. Even Oshima was kept ignorant of his government's aims.[113] But Goebbels presumed 'that now at least gradually the Japanese intervention will start to get going'.[114] That, in turn, would preoccupy the Americans, distract them from the Atlantic and the European war, and allow the Germans time to finish off the Soviets. As long as the eastern campaign was unresolved, however, the prohibition of incidents that might be dangerous flashpoints in relations with the United States had to be upheld.

So although such incidents did indeed multiply, they received only passing attention in the German press, and their significance was seen as domestically contrived by Roosevelt. The torpedoing of the *Kearny* on 17 October was thus portrayed as an invention by the American President to help the passage through Congress of the controversial bill to repeal important sections of the Neutrality Act.[115] And when the *Reuben James* went down on 31 October, the German press contented itself with a vehement denunciation of the claims by Roosevelt about the secret documents he alleged to have in his possession illustrating Nazi intentions for South America. On the consequences of the sinking itself, Goebbels summed up, perceptively enough: 'Roosevelt probably has no use for war at present. He has first to see how things go with Japan, and then public opinion in the United States stands in his way. Anyway, I don't think there is need for anxiety at the moment.'[116] In a speech to the Nazi Party 'old guard' on 8 November 1941, the anniversary of the ill-fated putsch of 1923, Hitler underlined his own moderation in the Atlantic, in contrast to the trigger-happy actions of the Americans and the provocations of Roosevelt, and again poured scorn on the President's alleged evidence of Nazi plans in South America.[117] Speaking to Raeder five days later, Hitler confirmed that the orders to the navy would remain unchanged even if Congress repealed the Neutrality Law. He agreed that it remained naval policy 'to lessen the possibilities of incidents with American forces'.[118] Nevertheless, as Hitler must have seen, this policy (which naval leaders had, as we have noted, long been straining to have changed) could not continue indefinitely once the American Neutrality Laws had been amended without conceding the battle of the Atlantic, and, with that, the strengthening of the vital supply-line to Britain that enabled the British war effort to continue.[119] The German toleration policy necessarily, therefore, had time limits – undefined, but real.

During the autumn, Hitler had talked more than once in his usual sweeping, though vague, fashion about the great showdown with the United States as an obligation of the next generation. It was a return to (or a repeat of) what he had envisaged in the 1920s. But how far he believed what he was saying is difficult to judge. As always, it was the effect on those listening that counted for him.[120] For by this time Hitler knew better than most that the showdown would come earlier than that. The truth was that war with America could now not be avoided, or even long delayed.

With neither the Germans nor the Americans prepared, however, to push over the brink and into the cauldron of war in the Atlantic, it would be events in the Pacific, uncontrollable by Hitler's Reich, that would eventually bring the fateful decision that took Germany into outright hostilities against the United States.

IV

Ribbentrop's request of 13 September, seeking assurances from Japan under the terms of the Tripartite Act in the event of war between Germany and the United States, remained unanswered throughout October. The change of Japanese government in the middle of the month, when the hardline General Tojo had replaced Konoe as Prime Minister, had, to external appearances, brought no substantial alteration in policy. Hitler, it was reported in the Foreign Office, expected little of the new Cabinet. He had, it seems, changed his mind since the summer about Japan entering the war against the Soviet Union and now had some anxiety that this might be in Tojo's mind. It was not now what he wanted. Conflict between Japan and the United States in the Pacific was far more desirable from his point of view. He still harboured by now dwindling hopes that he could force Britain to the conference table by defeating the Soviet Union. 'If Russia collapses now and England wants to make peace with us,' he reportedly said, 'Japan could be an obstacle for us.'[121] What impact Tojo's takeover of power had on relations between Tokyo and Washington was unclear to the German leadership. The impression gleaned from the German ambassador in Tokyo, General Ott, was that relations between Japan and the United States had deteriorated. But there was little sign of any obvious action. Towards the end of the month, Goebbels noted a rise in tension, but at no more than the propaganda level. 'It is very questionable', he remarked, 'whether Tojo will proceed to decisive action. Perhaps the Führer is right to be sceptical. At any rate, we should not harbour false hopes.'[122] At the end of the month, Ott reported that the Japanese had still not come to a decision on the warning to the United States which Germany had sought six weeks earlier, on 13 September.[123] It was highly discouraging.

Goebbels, influenced by Hitler, was now an outright sceptic about the Japanese. Tojo 'talks tough, but he doesn't shoot', was the Propaganda Minister's verdict on 6 November. 'The Japanese are evidently not yet inclined to intervene actively in the conflict,' he added. 'Thank goodness that we didn't reckon with the active military support of Japan, so that our calculations are not substantially affected by this fact.'[124] But Goebbels was not fully in the picture.

Things had by this point just started to move. And the overtures had come from Tokyo, not Berlin. The first straw in the wind was a message from Ott on 5 November about a tentative approach from the Japanese navy 'concerning a German assurance not to conclude a separate peace or armistice in case of a Japanese-American war'.[125] More promising still – and the opening to a flurry of exchanges – was a feeler transmitted by General Okamoto Kio Puku, the head of the foreign armies section of the Japanese General Staff, on 18 November. Okamoto reported that a peaceful solution to the problems between Japan and the United States was unlikely, in the view of the Japanese General Staff. Should relations break down, the Japanese would resort to 'self-help', which would be followed by the entry of the United States into the war. What Okamoto wanted, on behalf of the General Staff, was both states, Germany and Japan, to 'obligate themselves not to conclude any armistice or peace separately but only jointly'.[126] Ribbentrop provided a quick response. He had Ott pass on the message on 21 November: it was taken for granted in Berlin that any armistice or peace, in the event of war between Japan or Germany and the United States, could only be concluded jointly, and that this could be made a formal agreement.[127]

The Japanese wasted no time. Within two days, on 23 November, Ott was transmitting Okamoto's reply, which made it evident that Tojo himself had been consulted. The diplomatic ratchet was now turned one notch further. Okamoto had wanted to hear from Ott, the ambassador reported, whether in his view 'Germany would also consider herself at war with the United States if Japan should open hostilities'.[128] The Tripartite Pact, we might recall, had stipulated as its condition for any joint action aggression by a third force. But what if Japan fired the first shot? On that eventuality, nothing had been agreed. Oddly, Hitler's verbal expression of readiness at his meeting the previous April with Matsuoka to offer Germany's immediate support in the event of Japan becoming embroiled in conflict with America, without any qualification about the aggressor, had in the meantime been forgotten or ignored.[129] Whether it had been inaccurately reported at the time in Tokyo, not treated as a serious and binding commitment by Hitler, or simply overlooked, is unclear. In any case, it had been less than a formal agreement. So what Okamoto was now seeking was formal assurance that Germany would offer military support in a war Japan herself had started – something not covered by the pact. Giving such a guarantee would commit the German Reich to war with America – an eventuality which up to this juncture everything had been done to avoid. The initiative for deciding on Germany's war with the United States would have been passed to Japan. In return for such a guarantee, Okamoto was offering precisely nothing. And, though Hitler and Ribbentrop were unaware of this, the Japanese government, as they sought an agreement with Germany to rule out a separate peace with America, were prepared to meet a German request to engage in the war against the Soviet Union with a firm refusal. Should this become a German condition of support for the Japanese war against America, no agreement would be entered into.[130] But that would not halt the Japanese preparations, now entering their final stages.

Of these the Germans knew nothing. Ernst von Weizsäcker, State Secretary in the German Foreign Office, had noted in his diary on 23 November that it would be difficult to close the gap between Japanese and American demands, but that Tokyo provided little information on the progress of the negotiations with Washington.[131] Goebbels continued to bemoan Tojo's perceived lack of aggression. 'There can at present be no talk of Japanese intentions to intervene in the war,' he concluded in mid-November.[132] In fact, the Japanese leaders had already fixed 25 November as their deadline for reaching agreement with the Americans. If none were achieved by that date, there would be war. None was received; and the next day the naval task force set out in secret for Pearl Harbor.

Okamoto's key question, posed on 23 November, received no answer for five days.[133] But once Ribbentrop learned, on 27 November, that the Americans had presented Japan with an ultimatum almost certain to result in an end to negotiations and a breakdown of relations, he moved swiftly, doubtless after consultation with Hitler.[134] Next day he told Oshima, the Japanese ambassador, that in his view Japan could not now avoid a showdown with the United States. The situation, he thought, could never be more favourable than the present. He vehemently urged Japan to declare war straight away, on the United States as well as on Britain. According to Oshima's dispatch to Tokyo, the German Foreign Minister then stated: 'Should Japan become engaged in a war with the United States, Germany of course would join the war immediately. There is absolutely no possibility of Germany's entering into a separate peace with the United States under such circumstances. The Führer is determined on that point.'[135]

On 30 November in Tokyo, Ott assured the Japanese Foreign Minister, Togo, that Germany would stand by Japan.[136] An urgent reply was cabled to Oshima. He was to inform Hitler and Ribbentrop secretly that 'there is extreme danger that war may suddenly break out between the Anglo-Saxon nations and Japan through some clash of arms'. He was to add that 'war may come quicker than anyone dreams'.[137] He was to ensure that Ribbentrop's spoken promise was turned into a written agreement. Late on the evening of 1 December, or in the early hours of 2 December, Oshima signalled Tokyo's agreement to Ribbentrop. But before a formal agreement could be drawn up, Ribbentrop needed Hitler's final approval.[138]

Even in the early 1940s heads of state were rarely out of telephone or radio contact. But for the next three days it indeed appears that Hitler was incommunicado, stranded after a flying visit to the eastern front and unable to return to his East Prussian headquarters until 4 December. Only then could Ribbentrop reach him for a final decision, which led to the rushed drafting of a new agreement effectively superseding the Tripartite Pact of the previous year and presented to Oshima that night.[139] With Hitler's approval, the die was now effectively cast that would take Germany into war against America.

Rome was immediately contacted by an impatient Ribbentrop and fell into line straight away. Mussolini was pleased at the Japanese initiative. 'Thus we arrive at the war between continents, which I have foreseen since September 1939,' he declared.[140] Under the vital first two articles, all the partners committed themselves to involvement if war should break out between any one of them and the United States, and to conclude no armistice or peace with the United States or Britain other than by complete mutual consent.[141] All that remained was for it to be signed. Weizsäcker expected matters to be finalized by 6 December.[142] But that did not happen. Details still had to be ironed out. It took time.

German leaders had for some days sensed that the crisis in relations between Japan and the United States was coming to the boil. With German troops bogged down in the Russian wastes and a major military crisis brewing on the approaches to Moscow, this was extremely welcome news. So was the prospect dangled by Oshima of a Japanese move on Singapore in the near future.[143] The urgency to accommodate Japanese requests for a revised tripartite agreement reflected this feeling that a key turning point in the conflict, to Germany's advantage, was approaching.

Not everyone shared Hitler's (and Ribbentrop's) optimism about the Japanese. In the Foreign Office, Weizsäcker commented that the Japanese had for some days regarded a clash with the United States as inevitable. The military effect of Japan's entry into the war from a German point of view seemed to him fairly evenly balanced. But overall, rational and pessimistic about Germany's long-term chances, he did not welcome Japanese participation.[144] News was by now filtering through from the Foreign Office to army General Staff headquarters that the storm was likely to break soon. General Halder heard on 6 December that conflict between Japan and the United States was 'possibly imminent'.[145] Goebbels, outside the information loop about the diplomatic toings and froings between Tokyo and Berlin, repeatedly registered the mounting tension. On 6 December he noted: 'The row between Washington and Tokyo is still at a critical peak. I no longer have the impression that things can be mended. Sometime the bomb will go off in this conflict.'[146]

He had no idea how close he was to the truth. Early next morning, Hawaii time, the Japanese bombed Pearl Harbor. It was evening in central Europe on 7 December when the stunning news reached Hitler's head-quarters.

V

The German leadership had no prior inkling of a Japanese attack. They seem, in fact, to have been hoping that the first strike would come from the Americans.[147] In the first week of December 'we did not believe there would be a direct attack by Japan on America', Weizsäcker later recalled. When news of Pearl Harbor broke, the Foreign Office at first thought it was a hoax.[148] That was Ribbentrop's first, angry reaction. He thought it was probably a propaganda trick by Germany's enemies, and that his press department had fallen for it. He asked for further enquiries to be made and a report given to him next morning.[149] Confirmation came through faster than that. In Rome, Count Ciano, the Italian Foreign Minister, received a telephone call that night from an excited Ribbentrop. 'He is joyful over the Japanese attack on the United States,' Ciano noted. He offered Ribbentrop his congratulations, but was doubtful about the advantages the new development would bring. 'One thing is now certain,' he thought. 'America will enter the conflict, and the conflict itself will be long enough to permit her to put all her potential strength into action.'[150] Weizsäcker was privately also unsure about the benefits for Germany. Japan, he reflected, had now ranked herself with the 'aggressors'. 'The military effect would have to be a very big one to justify this procedure. Now our relations with the United States will also be legally clarified very quickly,' he adjudged.[151]

Goebbels, though attentively following the growing tension in relations between Japan and the United States, was equally surprised at the news of Pearl Harbor. 'Suddenly, like a bolt from the blue, the news breaks that Japan has attacked the United States,' he wrote in his diary. 'The war has arrived.' It was what he had been hoping for but doubting would happen over the past weeks. He was still unsure where the attack had taken place; 'somewhere in the Pacific' was all he knew. During the night came further news. Roosevelt had summoned Congress and war had been declared on Japan from 6 a.m. that morning. Soon afterwards Hitler was on the line. He was 'extraordinarily happy' about the turn of events. He wanted the Reichstag to be summoned for Wednesday (10 December) – it was now in the early hours of Monday – to clarify the German position. As always, Hitler immediately thought of the propaganda effect. He was wasting no time. Goebbels now reckoned (we noted his comment near the beginning of the chapter), presumably on the basis of his conversation with Hitler, on a German declaration of war against the United States in accordance with the Tripartite Pact. But he saw a notable advantage in the sharp reduction of weaponry provided by the United States for aid to Britain, and also that Germany was now in some ways 'shielded on the flanks', since America would be distracted by events in the Pacific. 'For the Führer and for the whole headquarters there is the purest joy about the development. At least now we have a serious threat removed from round our neck for the time being,' he recorded, his views unquestioningly echoing if not directly quoting Hitler's own. 'Roosevelt will not be able to be as bold over the coming as in the previous weeks and months,' he added. 'This war has become a world war in the truest meaning of the word. From small beginnings, its waves have now enveloped the entire globe.' Now was Germany's great chance, once the present crisis was surmounted. 'If we win this contest, then nothing stands in the way of fulfilling the dream of German world power,' he summed up.[152]

For Hitler, immersed in the deepening crisis on the eastern front, where the Soviet counter-offensive against the frozen and exhausted German troops not far from Moscow had begun two days before Pearl Harbor, the elation at events in the distant Pacific was unalloyed. 'We can't lose the war at all,' was his relieved reassessment of the situation. 'We now have an ally which has never been conquered in 3,000 years.'[153] For him it was no less than 'a deliverance'.[154] When he had burst in, clutching the telegram with the news of war between Japan and America, the astonished Keitel had the feeling that Hitler had been freed from a nightmare.[155] As the word rapidly spread, the entire headquarters was 'caught up in an ecstasy of rejoicing'.[156] Had Hitler realized that, when the dust settled over Pearl Harbor, the damage inflicted by the Japanese raid would prove to be substantially less than the knockout blow needed in Tokyo, his mood might have been less ecstatic. As it was, he was sure that his long-held presumption would turn out to be correct: America would now be tied down by the war in the Pacific; and Britain's position would be undermined both by the dwindling supplies coming across the Atlantic and by Japanese attacks on her possessions in the Far East. The prognosis for Germany's chances had improved at a stroke. Little wonder that Hitler was still beaming with optimism when he arrived in Berlin on 9 December.[157]

There was never the slightest doubt, given these views, that Hitler would use the occasion to take Germany into war with the United States. This was, we have seen, no mere spontaneous, emotional reaction to Pearl Harbor itself. For weeks beforehand, the dealings with the Japanese had been predicated on Germany entering a war against the United States which might be caused by events outside German control. On hearing the news of Pearl Harbor, Hitler did not hesitate for a moment. That Germany would now declare war on the United States was taken for granted by Goebbels from his telephone conversation with Hitler. When Hitler's Luftwaffe adjutant, Nicolaus von Below, returned to Führer Headquarters on the morning of 9 December after a period of leave, he immediately gleaned the impression that Pearl Harbor was seen as a signal to declare war on America.[158] And Wolfgang Brocke, then a young officer attached to Hitler's headquarters, recalled, if long after the events, that Hitler's immediate reaction on hearing the news of Pearl Harbor had been that he could now declare war on the United States.[159]

Unquestionably, the battle of the Atlantic was the imperative behind Hitler's vital decision. Keitel connected Hitler's elation on hearing the news of Pearl Harbor with the feeling that it brought a relief from the consequences of America's 'undeclared war', which had worked to Germany's disadvantage.[160] And without waiting for the declaration of war, on 8–9 December Hitler removed the shackles from his U-boats. From now on, they had free licence to attack American shipping.[161] That was a notable relief for submarine commanders, noted Goebbels. It was impossible to fight a 'torpedo war' when the commander had to study half a dozen instruction manuals to work out whether he had permission to fire. Much of the failure of the war at sea could be attributed to the way the U-boats had been hamstrung. 'That's now over. No more free zones will be acknowledged, and the American flag will no longer be respected. Anyone caught on the way to England must reckon with being torpedoed by our U-boats.'[162] This reflected Hitler's thinking.

When Ribbentrop saw him on the morning of 9 December – before the declaration of war, but after his 'licence to kill' orders had been sent out to the U-boats – Hitler stated that the main reason for Germany now entering the war was 'that the United States is already shooting against our ships. They have been a forceful factor in this war, and they have, through their actions, already created a situation, which is practically, let's say, of war.'[163] For months he had held his naval leaders back while they had chafed at the bit because of the constraints under which they had to operate in the Atlantic. And all the time, the Americans had been gradually intensifying their 'undeclared war'. The provocations had mounted, and still Hitler had felt forced to hold back. But let no one say he bore his grudges lightly. He could not wait for the moment when he was at last free to retaliate. The vehemence with which, in his Reichstag speech on 11 December, he poured out his hitherto unresolved grievances against what he portrayed as an almost endless catalogue of American transgressions in the Atlantic over many months was not purely for propaganda effect.[164] It reflected his inner burning desire to get even with President Roosevelt. Even more importantly, the U-boats were his only method of attacking America. And without forcing the United States onto the retreat, or at least to a readiness for concessions, the war could not now be ended.

The clearest possible indication of Hitler's thinking can be seen in his confidential remarks to his party leaders the following afternoon. They make plain that, in his crucial decision, the war in the Atlantic was uppermost in his mind.

Goebbels recapitulated what Hitler had to say:

He emphasizes the extraordinary significance of the Japanese entry into the war, above all with regard to our U-boat war. Our U-boat commanders had reached the point where they didn't know any longer whether or not they should fire their torpedoes. A U-boat war can't be won in the long run if the U-boats are not free to fire. The Führer is convinced that even if Japan had not joined the war, he would have had to declare war on the Americans sooner or later. Now the east Asian conflict drops like a present into our lap. All German agencies have indeed worked to bring it about, but even so it came so quickly as to be partly unexpected. Psychologically, too, that's of inestimable value to us. A declaration of war by us on the Americans without the counterpart of the east Asian conflict would have been hard to take for the German people. Now everyone accepts this development almost as a matter of course. The Führer has gone through an extraordinarily tough inner struggle in the past weeks and months about this question. He knew that either the U-boat war would be condemned altogether to ineffectiveness or that he would have to take the decisive step to wage war against America. This heavy burden has been taken from him. He views the struggle in the Atlantic now far more positively than previously. He thinks the number of sinkings will rise rapidly. He regards the tonnage problem as altogether decisive in the war effort. The one who solves this problem will probably win the war.[165]

For Hitler, his remarks make clear, the one-sided state of 'undeclared war' was the main reason for his decision. He now had the justification he needed for opening up all-out submarine warfare in the Atlantic and preventing the U-boats being as 'worthless' as they had proved in 1915–16.[166] In the declaration of war on the United States, too, the reverberations of the First World War that had left such an indelible mark on Hitler could still be felt.

Pearl Harbor provided the occasion. Without the Japanese attack on the United States he evidently would not have felt confident about taking such a giant step. The hasty diplomacy since the first Japanese overtures in early November about firmer military commitments than those stipulated in the Tripartite Pact had presumably been undertaken with an eye on the increasing likelihood of Germany, as well as Japan, becoming involved in hostilities with the United States in the near future. Negotiations had reached the stage where Germany was ready to sign a formal agreement binding her to join the war even if Japan, not the United States, launched the attack. More by good luck than good judgement this agreement had still not been signed when the bombs fell on Pearl Harbor. Hitler was not obliged, therefore, by the Tripartite Pact or any other treaty to do anything at all. He had what he wanted: Japan's engagement in war against the United States in the Pacific. He could have been content with the presumption that, through the godsend of Pearl Harbor, America would have her energies diverted into the Pacific. He could simply have maintained the existing fraught relations with the United States. Or he could have altered the orders to his U-boats (which Raeder had been clamouring for over the past months) without declaring war – which, in fact, he did do for the two days before his Reichstag speech. But he chose neither to remain passive, nor just to escalate confrontation in the Atlantic (which would have had the likely effect of putting increased pressure on Roosevelt to risk either a declaration of war or a loss of face). Instead, he decided (unnecessarily, therefore, from the point of view of his existing international commitments) on a full declaration of hostilities against the United States. And this was a decision that he evidently took very swiftly, and without consultation.

Even so, there was a delay, despite pressure from Tokyo, before he made the declaration. Hitler knew his speech was a vital one. It would be heard around the world, not least in Japan and America, and it had to have a big impact at home. He had been promising Goebbels for weeks that he would speak to the German people. But things had hardly gone according to plan in the eastern campaign. Now, at last, he had some substance for a speech, something he could turn to good propaganda effect. Ribbentrop told Oshima on 9 December that Hitler was assessing the best way, from the psychological point of view, of declaring war on the United States.[167] By 10 December, however, the date initially envisaged for the meeting of the Reichstag had to be put back. Hitler had been held up by an endless array of meetings and had not even begun work on his speech.[168] He wanted to prepare it especially carefully. So he postponed the Reichstag meeting by a day.[169] There were banal reasons, therefore, for the delay in reaching the declaration of war. But there was another, less banal reason. This was the draft agreement, still unsigned, with Japan.

When he met Hitler on the morning of 9 December, Ribbentrop passed on Oshima's request for an immediate declaration of war on the United States. Whether he was suffering from a belated bout of cold feet, or was simply reminding Hitler of Germany's strict obligations in such a crucial decision, the Foreign Minister pointed out that there was no commitment to declare war under the Tripartite Pact. That had bound Germany to military aid for Japan only in the event of an attack on her ally. But Japan, not America, had unleashed the conflict. Hitler's response, however, was that 'if we don't stand on the side of Japan, the pact is politically dead'.[170]

Ribbentrop later claimed that he had tried to dissuade Hitler from a declaration of war. 'I never wanted the USA to be drawn into the war,' he claimed, 'but then, as later, the Japanese had their own ideas.'[171] His demeanour at the time lends little credence to this subsequent apologia. He had not demurred from the more binding arrangement with Japan, mooted for over two weeks; he had enthused to Ciano after Pearl Harbor; and, speaking to the Italian ambassador, Dino Alfieri, on 9 December, he had referred to Japan's involvement on the side of the Axis as 'the most important event to develop since the beginning of the war'.[172] On 8 December, the day before meeting Hitler, Ribbentrop had given Oshima a draft of the proposed new agreement with Japan, and sent it that evening to Ott. He asked for it to be accepted without delay because it 'may be announced here in a special form', an evident reference to Hitler's forthcoming Reichstag speech.[173]

There were, it turned out, still some small points on which the Japanese wanted clarification. Final authorization only came through on Wednesday, the 10th, and the important agreement was finally signed by Ribbentrop, Alfieri and Oshima on the Thursday, just before the declaration of war. In his speech that afternoon, 11 December, Hitler read out the whole of the agreement.[174] It was an indication of the value he attached to it. The key clause was the second: the agreement not to conclude an armistice or peace treaty with the United States or England without complete mutual consent.

This now seemed to Hitler watertight. He had a formal agreement with an ally who had historically proved invincible. The agreement prevented Japan from concluding an early peace with America, as she had done with Russia in 1905. In the First World War, American entry had tipped the balance. With Japan and America now locked in conflict in the Pacific, and with no Japanese 'get-out clause' unless Germany agreed, the chances of a repeat seemed, if not altogether eradicated, then at least massively reduced.[175] Without such an agreement, there was always the possibility in Hitler's mind that Japan and the United States could reach some sort of compromise peace that would leave Germany facing the might of America on her own.[176] So with the war in the east likely to drag on into the indefinite future, what became dubbed the 'no-separate-peace treaty'[177] seemed a good basis for the declaration of war on the United States to which Hitler was in any case temperamentally inclined. This would ensure that America would be tied down in the Pacific. More than that, she would be unable to concentrate wholly on that theatre, but would be faced with a two-front war. In this way, the weight of American arms, which Hitler anticipated coming online during 1942, could be fully directed neither at Japan, possibly forcing her to sue for peace, nor at Germany before the war in the east was won and Europe lay at her feet.[178]

One other factor, always important to Hitler, also played a part: prestige. 'A great power doesn't let itself have war declared on it, it declares war itself,' Ribbentrop, doubtless echoing his master's voice, told Weizsäcker.[179] It seemed better to Weizsäcker that the declaration should come from America rather than Germany. He did not see the importance of the gesture towards Japan. But such an argument was pointless.[180] For Hitler, America had ranked herself squarely among Germany's enemies, especially over the past eighteen months, and above all with her pointed escalation of aggression during the autumn. Despite the conflict that had now opened up in the Pacific, there was no doubt in his mind that it was only a matter of time – and he presumed it would happen sooner rather than later – before the United States declared war on Germany. Only three days before Pearl Harbor the sensational publication in the isolationist *Chicago Tribune* of the Victory Program envisaging a mighty army to fight in Europe – a claim not denied by the Roosevelt administration – had come as a revelation of American war aims to Nazi leaders in Berlin.[181] It seemed likely that an American declaration of war on Japan would soon be followed by a similar declaration against her partners in the Tripartite Pact. That would have been harder to 'sell' at home, Hitler must have calculated, than a declaration, on grounds which he could justify, by Germany herself on the United States.

As Goebbels admitted, a stroke of luck had brought Japan into the conflict.[182] That had overnight given a major boost to Germany's prospects, especially in the critical battle of the Atlantic. As usual, Hitler sought immediately to grasp the opportunity and to recover the initiative in the war which he had seemed in danger of losing. Hitler's extraordinarily inflated hopes in his Japanese ally led him on 11 December to his fateful choice: all-out war against an enemy whom, as he conceded to Oshima at the beginning of January 1942, he had no idea how to defeat.[183]

VI

Was Hitler's decision to declare war on the United States on 11 December 1941, then, a puzzle, a grandiose moment of megalomaniac madness? It has often been seen as such. But, in fact, there is no puzzle. From Hitler's perspective it was only anticipating the inevitable. Far from appearing inexplicable or baffling, Hitler's decision was consistent with the views he had held on America since the 1920s, and, especially, with his strategic thinking in 1940–41 about the United States, Japan and the future course of the war. It also accorded with his implicit fear that time was not on Germany's side, that America had to be defeated, or at least held in check, before her economic might could sway the conflict, as it had done in the First World War. Given his underlying premises, his decision was quite rational.

That does not mean it was sensible. But the lunacy of Hitler's project was the gigantic gamble of the bid for world power, not just this precise part of it. Certainly, he felt a rush of blood after Pearl Harbor. Neither he nor anyone else in the Nazi leadership had anticipated an attack of such boldness. The very audacity of the Japanese strike appealed to him. It was *his* sort of move. And, grossly overestimating Japan's war potential, he thought its effect was far greater than it turned out to be. In those days, reeling from setbacks on the eastern front (the first, devastating Soviet counter-offensive of the war had just begun), he could not have wished for better news than a Japanese assault on the American fleet at anchor. Japan and America at war was exactly what he wanted. The decisions that followed were taken in this mood of exhilaration. But they were not driven by spontaneous, irrational emotion. Letting his U-boats loose on American shipping came first. He had no doubt been itching to do this all autumn. Now he need hold back no longer. This in itself, he imagined, would turn the battle of the Atlantic Germany's way (and, indeed, a small number of U-boats at work off the north American coast were able to wreak havoc on Allied shipping in early 1942).[184] It preceded the bigger decision, to declare war on the United States. Prestige and propaganda considerations dictated that this should come from Germany and that he should not passively await a declaration by America. But Hitler's own decision – and, as we have seen, it *was* his, taken without consultation apart from with the subservient Ribbentrop, and presumably also Keitel and Jodl – had been preceded by moves, rational from his point of view, and dating back several weeks, to prevent Japan, once in the war, from leaving it at a time that did not suit Germany. Only when what effectively amounted to a new tripartite pact had been concluded did Hitler declare war.

Were Hitler's options in December 1941, therefore, as wide open as appears to be the case from the suggestion that his decision was puzzling? We need to return for a moment to the place of the United States in his developing war strategy in 1940–41. He was receiving mainly reliable information from General Bötticher, his well-informed military attaché in Washington, about the pace of American rearmament. But Bötticher misled Hitler in two ways. First, he overrated the importance of the Pacific in American overall strategy, downplaying the commitment to the war in Europe. And secondly, though he left no doubt about the rapid progress being made in the United States' rearmament, if from a very low initial base, he was adamant that America would not be ready for war before Germany had won it. This was the message he passed to Berlin.[185] The miscalculation in intelligence matched Hitler's own prognosis. Aware of the impending danger from across the Atlantic, to which he had no early answer in terms of weaponry, Hitler's aim, lasting from his victory over France until the weakening of the Wehrmacht's advance in the Soviet Union, had been to keep the United States out of the war until German hegemony in Europe was finally established. This had been the strategic idea behind 'Operation Barbarossa'. With Britain forced to the negotiating table after Germany had crushed the Soviet Union, America would be forced back on her own hemisphere. Sometime, there would be a final showdown between a German-dominated Europe and the United States – the scenario he had depicted in the 1920s – but that would not happen in his lifetime.

In the whirlwind of early German successes in the Soviet Union in June and July 1941, he had temporarily deviated from this distant grand vista. A joint enterprise with the Japanese to destroy the Soviet Union and then turn together on the United States in the near future seemed for a while an attractive proposition. But the Japanese, their thinking in any case impenetrable to Hitler, did not move against Siberia, just as they had earlier not followed the German invitation to make an early strike at Singapore. Meanwhile, the German advance had started to run into trouble in the Soviet Union. The eastern campaign, against all prognoses, was not going to be won easily – and not that year. It was going to be a long haul. And it seemed to Hitler that, exploiting the circumstances, Roosevelt was now openly provoking him through intensified aggression in the Atlantic, about which in the current circumstances he could do nothing.

Japan's intentions were still not clear. She made aggressive noises, but at the same time, it appeared, was prepared to negotiate with Washington. By autumn, however, the situation had finally become clarified. Relations between Japan and the United States had irredeemably broken down. War was now highly likely. In changed circumstances in the east, Hitler had to consider the role of Japan in a new light with regard to America's place in his own strategy. America, it was by now obvious, could *not* be kept out of the war indefinitely. The question was only when she would join it. He had said more than once that he expected her to be ready for war by 1942. The United States, it was increasingly certain, would have to be faced *before*, not after, the war against the Soviet Union – Hitler's 'real' war – was over. The role of Japan in his thinking was now, therefore, to tie the Americans down as long and as completely as possible in the Pacific, and thoroughly weaken the British in the Far East, taking their possessions, undermining their bastions and eventually destroying the heart of their Empire, India.[186] Germany's role, in supporting Japan by entering a war against America which, to Hitler, was inevitable anyway, was to prevent the Americans defeating the Japanese or forcing them to agree terms, before turning on Germany. The United States, through the German intervention, would be forced into a war across two oceans.[187]

This, Hitler calculated, would give him time to finish off the unexpectedly resilient Soviets or at least reach a satisfactory point where he could conclude the eastern campaign, perhaps by some sort of deal with Stalin, but on his own terms. Japan's entry into the war in December 1941 gave him that chance, as he saw it; hence, his elation at the news of Pearl Harbor. From his perspective, therefore, the declaration of war against the United States at this juncture was no great gamble, let alone a puzzling decision. He felt he had no option. The decision seemed to him to open up the path to victory which was beginning by autumn 1941 to recede. For him, therefore, it was the only decision he could make.

Despite his own construction of possibilities, did he objectively have the option of refraining from a declaration of war, a decision which might have given Germany new chances in the conflict? Objectively, of course, he was not compelled to take Germany into a war with the United States. A German declaration of war did not have to follow the attack on Pearl Harbor. Even Ribbentrop, as we noted, pointed out to him that there was no treaty obligation to do so. But what might have ensued had he chosen not to declare war on the United States? Is it likely, had Hitler not been so rash in declaring war, that the United States would have retreated from the Atlantic theatre, pulled back aid to Britain and the Soviet Union, left Europe alone and concentrated on the Pacific, allowing the Nazi leader to get on with his war against Bolshevism? Might Roosevelt have refrained from pressing for his own declaration of war out of fear of a defeat in Congress? Would the war, in other words, have taken an entirely different turn had Hitler been less ready to rush into Japan's arms when he had no need to do so? In a guessing-game, there are many possibilities. But there are fewer likelihoods. And the actions as well as the reflections of those close to the decisions at the time provide few hints that a completely different scenario might have emerged.

Of course, cooler heads might have chosen other options. Weizsäcker, in the Foreign Office, for one thought it would be better to wait for an American declaration of war. That would surely have been a more sensible ploy. Roosevelt would have been left with the predicament of whether to try to persuade both Congress and the American public, overnight preoccupied with the new war in the Pacific and the desire to take revenge on Japan, that Germany was still the main enemy, and that a declaration of war on the European Axis powers was necessary. Had such a declaration been forthcoming, clever German propaganda could have turned it to advantage: a war that Germany had not wanted and done everything to avoid being forced upon the country by American plutocracy, and now requiring a backs-to-the-wall fight. That type of propaganda was lost because of Hitler's insistence upon the prestige of a German declaration.

But it is worth noting that Weizsäcker was not imagining that Germany's plight would have been drastically altered had Hitler not been so foolhardy in his seizure of the moment to plunge into an unnecessary declaration. Weizsäcker does not appear to have doubted that the war with the United States would now ensue. His difference from Hitler was on preferring to be the object of the declaration, rather than making it, as he thought, as an unnecessary gesture to Japan. But it was not a presumption that, by refraining from declaring war on the United States, Germany would be able to avoid that war. Weizsäcker, every bit as much as Hitler, now expected Germany to be embroiled in conflict with America.

The thinking on the other side of the Atlantic was similar. In fact, on the very evening after the dramatic events at Pearl Harbor, President Roosevelt dined with members of his Cabinet and top military advisers to discuss the action now needed. A declaration of war next morning against Japan had already been decided on, and in the meantime the Japanese had, belatedly and formally, declared war on the United States. Roosevelt and his advisers considered whether they should now declare war on other members of the Axis. 'We assumed, however, that it was inevitable that Germany would declare war on us,' Cordell Hull, the Secretary of State, recalled. 'The intercepted Japanese messages passing back and forth between Berlin and Tokyo' – read by the Americans through their MAGIC codebreaker – 'had given us to understand that there was a definite undertaking on this point between the two Governments. We therefore decided to wait and let Hitler and Mussolini issue their declarations first. Meantime we would take no chances and would act, for example in the Atlantic, on the assumption that we were at war with the European section of the Axis as well.'[188]

In the absence of the rash German move, could the United States have sustained the status quo in the Atlantic, and avoided a declaration of her own? If he had gone to Congress to seek a declaration of war on Germany when Japan had been the aggressor against America, Roosevelt would doubtless have encountered some serious opposition.[189] That in itself was a deterrent to making the attempt. He was duly cautious, and had already resisted pressure from Henry Stimson, the Secretary of War, to include Germany and Italy alongside Japan in the request to Congress immediately after Pearl Harbor.[190] Hitler conveniently eliminated that problem for him.

But even had he not done so, American moves towards full involvement in the war in the near future would have been likely. The Roosevelt administration had consistently linked Germany and Italy together with Japan as a joint threat to the free world. And the Atlantic had always been the first priority. When he returned from delivering his message to Congress inviting the declaration of war on Japan, Roosevelt immediately reminded his advisers that the main target remained Germany.[191] It followed that the war could not be restricted to the Pacific, despite the navy's preference for a concentration on that theatre. Though it can only be speculation, from the tenor of Hull's remarks it even seems at least conceivable that Roosevelt, had he not been aware of what was happening in Berlin, might have exploited the post-Pearl Harbor climate to take America into full-scale war also against Germany and Italy. Again, the logic of the Victory Program, which had been leaked in December, meant that the United States would, before too long, be sending a major land force to fight in Europe. Roosevelt's military advisers had always insisted that this was the only way to be rid of Hitler.

Roosevelt had for his part always been adamant that only the removal of Hitler guaranteed the future safety and freedom of the United States. Backing out of the battle for the Atlantic, retreating from lend-lease supplies to Britain and leaving Hitler a free hand on the European continent in order to concentrate on the Pacific would have contradicted not only Roosevelt's professed aims and ideals in foreign policy, as he had enunciated them since the mid-1930s, but would also have flown in the face of the consistent advice he had received from his military leaders for months, and the concrete, extensive planning that had followed from it. Roosevelt might, it is true, still not have wanted to risk proposing a formal declaration to Congress in December 1941, though the circumstances, after Pearl Harbor, were probably as propitious as could be imagined. However, it is hard to see that the shadow-fighting in the Atlantic could have continued indefinitely at the level of autumn 1941, even if Germany had not declared war.

Hitler's decision, prior to the declaration of war and not dependent upon it, to reverse previous policy and unleash his U-boats on American shipping in itself altered the uneasy stalemate that had existed in the Atlantic. In the months that followed, the German intensification of the U-boat war took hostilities deep into American coastal waters and faced Allied shipping with serious and mounting problems.[192] These were compounded because of the demands of the Pacific – immediately after Pearl Harbor Roosevelt had been forced to transfer some warships from the Atlantic to counter the Japanese threat[193] – and plainly had to be contested with all power and urgency. The American war against Germany, in other words, even if it had stayed 'undeclared', could not have remained at the level of autumn 1941. An American move to full-scale, all-out conflict at some point in the coming months, if not straight away, would have been well-nigh unavoidable.[194] Before much longer, it might be reasonably surmised, Roosevelt would have engaged the United States in all-out hostilities with Germany, whether through a formal declaration or, failing that, by extension of the presidential prerogative to the point where a formal declaration would merely have confirmed existing reality. Either way, Germany and the United States would soon have been at war.

Perversely, therefore, Hitler's decision to declare war on the United States on 11 December 1941, often seen not only as baffling but as a hopelessly foolhardy choice, one which finally condemned Germany to calamity, was probably less fateful than many of the political decisions we have been considering. That is to say, it was not a deciding moment in taking Germany down the path of catastrophe when triumph might have beckoned had a declaration of war been avoided. A different, less headstrong leader might indeed have hesitated, to await developments and, in particular, see how America would react. But, assuming such a leader had taken Germany this far and was not prepared to end the war in some sort of compromise settlement at this point, such an alternative decision would in all probability not have greatly altered history.

Germany did, in fact, recover, remarkably, from the winter crisis before Moscow, and went on to attain new, and in some ways surprising, military success in the first half of 1942. A new big offensive to take the Caucasus oilfields was launched that summer, though with weaker forces than had formed the 'Barbarossa' attack the previous year. Only in the autumn did it become clear, as the terrible battle of Stalingrad ran its course, that Hitler's Reich was in the throes of a cataclysmic defeat which, alongside the massive reverses in north Africa (where the American-led landing, 'Operation Torch', had taken place in early November), proved the unmistakable turning point of the war. Already by then, in the faraway Pacific the decisive battle of Midway in June 1942 had broken Japanese sea-power. This, followed by the hard-earned American victory at Guadalcanal in the Solomon Islands, finally sealed in January 1943, turned the tide of the Pacific War.[195] There was a long, long way to go, in the Far East and in Europe. But there was no way back for either Germany or Japan. Both were now increasingly exposed to the seemingly limitless supplies of men and arms from America.

The entry into the war of the United States at the end of 1941, as it had done in 1917, massively tipped the scales. American might, added to British forces, in the west, together with the relentless steamroller of the Red Army in the east, eventually crushed Germany. But by December 1941 the German gamble for world power was in any case fundamentally lost. Churchill certainly thought so – at least, retrospectively he said he did.[196] And Hitler himself fleetingly appears in autumn 1941 to have contemplated for the first time the possibility of defeat in remarking (a point to which he would return in the face of catastrophe in early 1945) that if in the end the German people should not prove strong enough, then Germany deserved to go under and be destroyed by the stronger power.[197] It was a momentary flickering, but revealing for all that. Beneath the veneer, Hitler seems to have recognized that his chances of total victory had by now all but evaporated. The plan for the eastern campaign had collapsed. And war with the United States was now as good as inevitable.

He anticipated this inevitability by declaring war himself. It was a characteristic attempt to wrest back the initiative through a bold move. But for the first time it was a move doomed from the very outset to failure.

IO

Berlin/East Prussia, Summer–Autumn 1941

Hitler Decides to Kill the Jews

They said to us in Berlin: why are you giving us all this trouble? We can't do anything with them in the Ostland *or in the Reich Commissariat [the Ukraine] either. Liquidate them yourselves! . . . We must destroy the Jews wherever we find them and wherever it is possible to do so.*

Hans Frank, Governor General of Poland, 16 December 1941

On 12 December 1941, the day after he had announced Germany's declaration of war on the United States of America, Hitler addressed his party leaders in the Reich Chancellery in Berlin. After a lengthy survey of the state of the war, he turned to the position of the Jews. His Propaganda Minister, Joseph Goebbels, recorded what he had to say: 'With regard to the Jewish Question, the Führer is determined to make a clean sweep. He prophesied that if they brought about another world war, they would experience their annihilation. This was no empty talk. The world war is here. The annihilation of the Jews must be the necessary consequence. This question is to be viewed without sentimentality. We're not to have sympathy with the Jews, but only sympathy with our German people. If the German people has again now sacrificed around 160,000 dead in the eastern campaign, the instigators of this bloody conflict will have to pay for it with their own lives.'[1]

By this time the Jews had been 'paying with their own lives', as Hitler saw it, for almost six months. Across the whole of the summer, since the invasion of the Soviet Union on 22 June, killing units of the German Security Police had slaughtered Jews in their tens of thousands, starting mainly with the men but before long including women and children. Just one of the four *Einsatzgruppen* or task forces, sent in behind the rapidly advancing Wehrmacht to wipe out 'subversive elements', rampaging through the Baltic, had murdered a precisely calculated 229,052 Jews by the end of the year.[2] That was the first horrific phase of genocide. But by the autumn the genocide had extended beyond the occupied parts of the Soviet Union and was rapidly entering a second, wider and ultimately comprehensive phase. This aimed at nothing less than the physical extermination of the Jews of the whole of German-occupied Europe – what the Nazis would label the 'Final Solution of the Jewish Question'.

The full implementation of the extermination programme would not get under way until the spring and summer of 1942, when the death-mills in the killing centres of occupied Poland commenced their industrial-style gassing operations and the dragnet became gradually stretched across the whole of Europe, east to west, north to south. The last ghastly stage of the mass transports and immense production-line gassings would not take place until the summer of 1944, when, with Germany forced ever closer to inexorable defeat, almost half a million Hungarian Jews were murdered in the gas chambers of Auschwitz-Birkenau. Even then, the torment of the Jews was far from over. Tens of thousands were still to die in the horrors of the 'death marches' from east to west as the death camps in occupied Poland were closed down in the face of the rapid advance of the Red Army and surviving prisoners forced back into already disastrously overfilled labour or concentration camps (such as Bergen-Belsen) inside the Reich.

This untold misery, suffering and death followed from two crucial decisions – or, better, sets of decisions – in 1941. The first of these, in the summer, was to kill the Jews of the Soviet Union. The second, in the autumn, was to extend the killing to the whole of Nazi-occupied Europe. By the time Hitler's Reich collapsed, the death toll lay, by the most reliable accounts, between 5.29 and just over 6 million Jews.[3] The target was, however, close to double this figure. As laid down in January 1942, a total of no fewer than 11 million Jews were envisaged as falling within the 'Final Solution'.[4]

The decision to kill the Jews of Europe had no precedent. It was a decision like no other in history. The nearest parallel had been the killing of between a million and a million and a half Armenians by the Turks in 1915 (some two-thirds of those living in Turkey at that time). There were some similarities. There had been a lengthy prehistory of Turkish hostility towards the Armenians, punctuated with outbreaks of terrible violence and massacres. There were ideological imperatives driving along radicalization. And the emergence of full-scale genocide took place in the context of an immensely brutal war. The murderous programme was then carried out with the backing of the Turkish government.[5] But there were also important differences.[6] Biological racism did not drive this genocide. Possibly as many as

20,000 Armenians avoided slaughter by converting to Islam.[7] Conversion to Christianity could, of course, offer no protection to Jews in Nazi Germany. No existing policy of physical destruction of the Armenian community lay behind this earlier genocide. It had not been bureaucratically planned and was initially disorganized, arising from increasingly vicious, cruel responses to unforeseen crises in 1914–15.[8] The Nazi genocide, though initiated only in 1941, was a logical – indeed, in certain respects inexorable – development from the premises of Nazi power. From 1933 onwards its quasi-intellectual underpinnings in uncompromising biological antisemitism became enshrined in state ideology (given embodiment in the highest authority in the land). This then impelled systematic, increasingly radical persecution, efficiently implemented by modern bureaucratic machinery, culminating in meticulously planned extermination carried out by new, industrial-style technology, and aimed at the eventual total eradication of every Jew in Europe.

It was a decision, too, wholly unlike in its nature those which we have been following in previous chapters. Those, including Hitler's, possessed (in varying degrees) a recognizable rationality – given the starting premises – in terms of the politics behind military strategy. This was certainly the case from the viewpoint of those taking the decisions. And a certain logic behind them – if warped in some cases – can be perceived even today, however disastrous the decisions turned out to be. The decision to kill the Jews was of an entirely different kind. However logical the path to genocide might have been, given the course of Nazi persecution of the Jews, the pathology of demonic antisemitism that lay at its roots defies rationality. And yet this decision, too, was, in a different but most fundamental sense, a war decision. The decision to wage war to the death against the Jews was in Nazi thinking part of and intrinsic to, not separate from, the vast military war in which they were engaged.

I

Hitler's address to his party leaders on 12 December 1941 made this clear. The Jews, he believed, had caused the war. They would now have to pay for it by forfeiting their own lives. He had, he said, prophesied this. It was a reference to the passage in his speech to the Reichstag on 30 January 1939, the sixth anniversary of his 'seizure of power', in which he had declared: 'In the course of my life I have very often been a prophet, and have usually been ridiculed for it . . . Today I will once more be a prophet:

if the international Jewish financiers in and outside Europe should succeed in plunging the nations once more into a world war, then the result will not be the Bolshevizing of the earth, and thus the victory of Jewry, but the annihilation of the Jewish race in Europe!'[9] This was no inauguration of the extermination programme. But it reflected a genocidal mentality, a certainty in Hitler's mind that Jews would carry the blame for another war – as, in his perverted psychology, they had done for the First World War – and that as a consequence they would *somehow* perish.

It was a 'prophecy' that never left him. He referred to it more than a dozen times, both privately and in public, during precisely the years when the 'final solution' was in full swing. And he always deliberately misdated his 'prophecy' to 1 September 1939, the day the European war began with the German invasion of Poland – when, in fact, in his Reichstag speech that day he never mentioned the Jews at all. The connection between the Jews and the war was, then, implanted in his mind from the beginning of the conflict. It was still there at the very end, when, dictating his 'Political Testament' on the eve of his suicide in the Berlin bunker, he once more held the Jews responsible for the war, but stated that this time the 'real culprit' had been forced 'to atone for his guilt'.[10]

This was Hitler's mentality: the war could never be won unless the Jews were to be destroyed. It was a mentality that had lingered with him since the First World War had ended in what for him was untold catastrophe, cowardly capitulation, detested revolution and national humiliation. Like many others on the Right in Germany at the time, he held the Jews responsible. As the misery, suffering and losses had mounted, the spotlight in the search for scapegoats had been turned, in a ceaseless barrage of propaganda by pro-war lobbies, relentlessly – and utterly unjustifiably – on Jews. They were blamed as war-profiteers, as shirkers avoiding military service and as fomenters of internal unrest that undermined the military effort. Hitler's own existing deep-seated antisemitism fed on these base calumnies. The part played by key figures such as Leon Trotsky in the Russian Revolution, and at home the fact that prominent leaders of the hated socialist upheavals – most plainly in the short-lived Bavarian experiment with a Soviet-style government in April 1919 – had been Jewish offered further rich sustenance to the vicious hatred of Jews which was by now rampant on the nationalist Right. Hitler sucked all this in, his own profound prejudices cemented into the pathological fixation that would never leave him: that the Jews were responsible for all Germany's ills.

For Hitler, a second war had to be fought to undo the calamity of the first, to reverse the course of history. And avenging the causes of that catastrophe that had ushered in the 'Jewish' republic of Weimar, a regime produced by the 'criminals' of November 1918 who had ruined Germany, meant the destruction of the Jews. 'The removal of the Jews altogether' had to be the 'final aim' of any national government in Germany, he had written in his first political statement, in September 1919.[11] 'The sacrifice of millions at the front', he had declared in a terrible passage towards the end of *Mein Kampf* a few years later, need not have happened if 'twelve or fifteen thousand of these Hebrew corrupters of the people had been held under poison gas' at the beginning of the war.[12] It was not a blueprint for genocide. But the connection between war and the Jews, an idea that, once embedded in Hitler's mind, never left it, had unmistakable genocidal connotations. And from 1933 the man with this idea ruled Germany.

The idea was not confined only to Hitler's mind. In the direct aftermath of the *Reichskristallnacht* pogrom on 9–10 November 1938, Hermann Göring, Hitler's chief paladin, spoke in inner Nazi circles of 'a great showdown with the Jews' in the event of another war.[13] Two weeks later, on 24 November, the main SS newspaper, *Das Schwarze Korps*, spoke of eradicating Jews as criminals 'with fire and sword', resulting in 'the actual and final end of Jewry in Germany, its complete annihilation'. Such sentiments were by this time shared entirely or in good part by other leading Nazis. And, of crucial importance, they had become institutionalized in the most ideologically dynamic segment of the Nazi regime – the burgeoning empire that had come under the aegis of the SS-run Security Police. Here, careers could be made by developing an expertise on the 'Jewish Question'. Adolf Eichmann, later the orchestrator of the 'final solution', was the paradigmatic example.[14] But careerism and ideology went hand in hand. Those who earned their spurs by working ceaselessly to find ways of 'solving' the 'Jewish problem' were in the main true believers in the cause. They had long since imbibed the doctrine that the Jew was the root of evil, and that a strong, dominant Reich had to be one purged of 'impure elements', most especially of Jews.[15]

As supreme leader of the regime, Hitler embodied the basic belief that Germany's salvation rested on the removal of the Jews. Others strived in different ways to implement this ideological imperative. In the Security Police, the 'mission' had taken institutional form. And it was incorporated in the wider aim of war and conquest. Hitler's explicit linkage of the Jews and war had not only been able to play upon and exploit existing deep antisemitic prejudice. It had also given it a dynamic, messianic, purpose. By the time the war started, the Nazi leadership had been forged into a proto-genocidal elite.

Underpinning the genocidal mentality was a demonization of the Jew which had become the central figment of the Nazi imagination. This transcended practical considerations. Jews were a tiny minority of the German population – a mere 0.76 per cent in 1933 – and self-evidently in no position to challenge for power in the state, make competing claims on territory or scarce resources or pose in any other than phantasmic fashion the sort of perceived threat which served as the pretext for a number of instances of 'ethnic cleansing' in the twentieth century. The Nazi image of the Jew went way beyond conventional hatreds. It presupposed the Jew as nothing less than the supreme *existential* danger. Within Germany, Jews were seen as 'poisoning' German culture. The 'true' essence of what was supposedly German was set against the subversive currents of 'Jewish' materialism and corruption. But the danger was seen to go even further. Dominating, in Nazi imagery, both the capitalism behind the 'plutocratic' enemies, Great Britain and the United States, and the Bolshevism behind the Soviet enemy, the Jew posed the ultimate threat to Germany's very existence. In fact, the Jew stood for a world which was totally anathema to Nazism, a set of moral values which had filtered through both Judaism and Christianity to form the foundations of the civilization that, as he repeatedly made plain, Hitler wanted to eradicate. In this sense, Nazism amounted to an apocalyptic vision of a renewed nation and society which would arise out of the destruction and eradication of the corrosive values epitomized by the Jew. It was no less than a fundamental attempt to change the course of history, to attain national redemption by eliminating not only all Jewish influence, but the Jews themselves.[16]

Resting upon such a premiss, the decision to kill the Jews of Europe, though it arose in quite specific circumstances in 1941, followed an inexorable, awful logic. In examining other fateful decisions made by political leaders in 1940 and 1941, we have considered what, if any, alternative choices were open to them, as they viewed the situation at the time. But in looking at the decision to kill the Jews, no such alternatives posed themselves; or, rather, they posed themselves only as alternative methods of destruction.

In another way, too, the decision to kill the Jews was unique among those we have examined. It was no conventional decision, such as to go to war or not, taken after confidential discussions with a small number of ministers, generals or other associates, but then proclaimed publicly. It was a state secret of the highest order, not to be talked about even by the initiated. The most incriminating orders were given orally. Camouflage language was used in discussions at the highest level. Hitler himself never spoke directly of the killing of the Jews, even in his innermost circle. Heinrich Himmler, head of the SS and responsible to Hitler alone for the implementation of the extermination programme, in contrast, did speak explicitly about the killing of the Jews. But this was at a late stage, in addressing SS men, then, subsequently, party leaders in early October 1943. With the prospect of defeat looming ever larger, it was the openness of a band of sworn conspirators, those who had burned their boats and were in it together. Himmler insisted that they had acted with a moral right and duty 'to destroy this people which wanted to destroy us'. He described the 'extermination of the Jewish people' as a 'glorious page in our history that has never been written and is never to be written'.[17] His comments combined perverted pride in a fulfilment of a historic duty with the implicit sense that a crime of enormous proportions had been committed, one which had been necessary but could never be divulged.

Given such secrecy even within the upper echelons of the regime, a yet further difference from the decisions explored so far is self-evident. The decision to kill the Jews can only be pieced together on the basis of circumstantial evidence. In fact, the question of precisely when and how the decision was taken cannot be answered with certainty. Indeed, to speak of a 'decision' may itself be misleading in its implication of one finite moment when a precise pronouncement was delivered. A series of authorizations, each building cumulatively upon the last, is probably a more appropriate way of imagining what took place. But even if that is what happened, the authorizations, taken together, amounted to a resolve that the Jews of Europe should cease to exist. That is, they added up to a decision – even if it was one made up of parts.

We have, in fact, already noted that there were at least two parts to the decision: first to kill the Jews of the Soviet Union, then to extend the killing – a second phase which might have necessitated more than a single further authorization. Hitler's role in the making of the decision, or decisions, cannot be precisely reconstructed. No written order has been found. Almost certainly, none will be found. But Hitler's fingerprints are all over the 'final solution'. Jews would doubtless have suffered discrimination under any nationalist leader in Germany at the time. The transformation into all-out genocide nevertheless needed Hitler. When, in March 1942, Goebbels described Hitler as 'the unswerving champion and spokesman of a radical solution' to the 'Jewish Question', he was stating the obvious.[18] Without Hitler, the 'final solution' would have been unthinkable.

II

Antisemitism was virulent and endemic throughout most of Europe in the decades preceding the Nazi genocide. As the 'final solution' unfolded, long-standing hatreds ensured that Nazi rulers in the countries they conquered never lacked willing helpers to carry out the deportations, then killing, of Jews. But the 'final solution' itself could not have arisen anywhere other than Germany. It had to be a German creation.[19]

Hatred of Jews had traditionally been at its most vicious in the Russian Empire and eastern Europe, where brutal pogroms – the word itself is Russian – and localized massacres of Jews had long been endemic. In the Habsburg Empire, too, antisemitism was rampant. Hitler himself had in his Vienna days been a youthful admirer of two outspoken antisemites, the Pan-German leader Georg Schönerer and the mayor of the city, Karl Lueger.[20] Nor was deep prejudice about Jews lacking in western Europe. France had been rocked just before the turn of the twentieth century by the 'Dreyfus affair', when the trial and sentence to a penitentiary on cooked-up charges of treason of Alfred Dreyfus, a captain in the French army, gave rise to a frenzy of antisemitic outpourings.[21]

Germany before the First World War was far from being Europe's heartland of antisemitism. The small, mainly well-to-do Jewish community wanted to be assimilated. Archaic legal restrictions preventing this had by now been abolished. But the very fact that Jews were thriving in Imperial Germany caused resentment and animosity. Economic depression in the 1880s spawned an upsurge. A specifically antisemitic party was founded in the 1890s, and, though it lost most of its support within a decade or so, this had now mainly found its way into mainstream politics, most notably in the Conservative Party, and into the shrill nationalism of patriotic associations, pressure groups and student unions. There was certainly plenty of hatred of Jews in evidence. Even in Bismarck's time more than five hundred antisemitic publications appeared.[22] As the nineteenth century reached its close, published anti-Jewish rhetoric increased rather than lessened in quantity and became, if anything, even more vicious. Theodor Fritsch's populist tract *Handbuch der Judenfrage* (Handbook of the Jewish Question), which Hitler later claimed to have 'intensively studied', chalked up its twenty-fifth edition within five years of publication in 1887. And the racist diatribe by the Germanized Englishman Houston Stewart Chamberlain, *Grundlagen des 19. Jahrhunderts* (Foundations of the Nineteeth Century), portraying the Jew as the embodiment of evil and 'proving' that Jesus Christ was an aryan, became a bestseller on its appearance in 1900.[23]

Antisemitism was, then, widespread throughout Germany, but for the most part discriminatory rather than given to major pogrom-like outrages as in eastern Europe (though small-scale, localized violence was no rarity). The rhetoric of the pernicious antisemitic literature in circulation was certainly frightening in its talk of Jews as poison, bacilli, parasites or vermin. The implications were obvious. But politics and rhetoric were far apart. None of this found its way into state-supported action. The Jewish experience in Imperial Germany was ambivalent. Alongside the discrimination ran distinct promise for a better future.[24] An observer of the European scene on the eve of war in 1914 would, even with the greatest foresight, have found it hard to imagine that a generation or so later Germany would unleash a programme of mass extermination to wipe out the Jews of Europe.

Hatred of Jews would, by itself, not have produced the 'final solution'. It was, of course, an indispensable component. But more was needed. Hitler himself saw in 1919 that hot-headed antisemitic outbursts, leading to pogroms, had to be converted into more systematic 'rational' persecution if the ultimate 'removal' of Jews (by which, at the time, he almost certainly meant expulsion from Germany) was to be attained.[25]

To turn commonplace antisemitic prejudice and hatred, however appalling, into a programme for genocide they had first to be harnessed to the more widely appealing goal of national renewal. This had to be popularized through a party which could gain state power. The state power then had to be utilized to make the removal of Jews the central focus of policy within the framework of utopian plans for national salvation. The aim of removal of the Jews had to be institutionalized by organs of the state capable of systematic planning and ruthless implementation. Finally, the immensely brutalized conditions of a total war portrayed as a struggle for national survival were required to produce the accelerated drive to complete eradication of the perceived fundamental enemy. Precisely this, of course, happened under Nazism. It is hard to see how it could have happened anywhere else. There was nothing inevitable about Nazism's triumph, no one-way street from German antisemitism to the death camps. But once Hitler had total power in the state, the odds against a genocidal outcome narrowed sharply – even if no one at the time could conceivably imagine the full scale of the eventual horror.

Without the First World War this would, in any case, have been unthinkable. As the high hopes of 1914 turned to the immense disillusionment and bitterness that accompanied the mounting losses and dreadful material hardships of the later war years, the search for scapegoats did not have to look far. It became easy to stir up animosity towards Jews. Hysterical antisemitism was built into the agitation of the pro-war lobby. Opposition to the war was decried as Jewish-fomented defeatism. Once the Bolshevik Revolution had taken place, Jews were, in addition, seen as the agents of world revolution. And when catastrophic defeat was accompanied by socialist revolution in Germany, subversion by Jews became a centrepiece of explanations of the trauma.

Hitler believed passionately that the Jews had caused Germany's disaster. But he was far from alone in the burning hatred that festered within him from this time. His early successes in the Munich beerhalls came from the way he could tap such sentiments. Most of those who were to become the provincial leaders of his party, the *Gauleiter*, his indispensable regional viceroys, came from the same generation and felt much as he did about the baleful influence of the Jews. The roughnecks in his paramilitary organiz-ation, the SA (*Sturmabteilung*, the stormtrooper section), were also for the most part vicious antisemites – or became such once they had joined. But both paramilitary activity, embracing vitriolic antisemitism, and the radical ethnic-nationalist (*völkisch*) ideas of Hitler and the infant Nazi movement, had a far wider currency.

Many in intellectual circles and in the broader, well-read sectors of the middle classes, far removed from the vicious paramilitary thugs, dreamed of national unity and regeneration to overcome the rancour, divisions and perceived cultural and moral decline of the new socialist-run democ-racy. Removal of what was seen as corrosive Jewish influence fitted into ideas of national resurgence, the rebuilding of the Reich by a future great leader. That Germany's 'redemption' could only come about by 'remov-ing' the Jews had been *one* strand of political culture stretching back to Richard Wagner – though neither the great composer nor practically any-one else imagined this to mean physical extirpation.[26] Amid widespread conservative-reactionary cultural pessimism framed by a lost war, the end of the monarchy, socialist revolution and a hated democratic system, anti-semitism found a fertile breeding-ground. The antidote was a new millen-arianism, a national rebirth. Among the well-educated young Germans attending universities in the early 1920s were those who would qualify with doctorates in law, taking in and digesting ideas about the inner renewal of the German people by removing 'harmful influences', just as detox-ification revitalizes the human body. The most pernicious 'harmful influ-ence' that had to be removed, they learned, was that of the Jew. Some of those swallowing these ideas as students would later join the Security Police, become the planners of genocide and lead the murderous *Einsatzgruppen* in Russia.[27]

Between 1916 and 1923, then, antisemitism had established itself as a central component of right-wing thinking in Germany, and was now taken up in the politics of mass movements, among them of course the still small Nazi Party. The calmer middle years of the Weimar Republic from 1924 to 1929 flattered to deceive. The antisemitic fundamentalists had been temporarily forced out of the limelight. But they had not disappeared. And even in a pluralist democracy Jews, outside their own organizations and some liberal and left-wing circles, found few friends or defenders. Once that democracy crumbled and collapsed from 1930 onwards, opening up the path for Hitler's rise to power, increasing numbers of Germans were exposed to the full antisemitic armoury as they became drawn into the ever-expanding Nazi movement.

Antisemitism was seldom the main attraction of Nazism. But once in the party and its affiliations, there was no escaping it. By the time Hitler became Chancellor of Germany, he had behind him an enormous mass movement of some 850,000 members and around a half a million stormtroopers, all of them wedded to political aims that left no place for Jews in Germany. Beyond the party faithful, more than thirteen million Germans now backed Hitler. They were not all committed antisemites. But they all voted for Hitler in the full knowledge that he and his party favoured measures to ensure the total exclusion of Jews from German society.

The years of the Weimar Republic between 1919 and 1933 were certainly uneasy ones for Jews. They were subjected to unending agitation, frequent discrimination and sporadic violence. Even so, it was possible for a Jew to feel 'at home' in Germany in those years.[28] That altered abruptly on 30 January 1933, when Hitler took power.

Hitler's personal paranoid fixation with the Jews as an omnipresent and omnipotent force within and outside Germany, the paramount threat to the nation, responsible for the lost war and all the ills that had followed from it, was shared in its entire lunacy by relatively few. The arcanum of his own peculiar 'world-view' had not won power for Hitler. But through different refractions – mutated, distorted and adapted – his hatred of the Jews had permeated in some sort of way by the time he was appointed Reich Chancellor the crude notions of millions as part of his broad message of restoring national unity and strength. And now, with the power of the state itself at the beckoning of a leader driven by pathological delusions about the Jews, whose word was a command to an army of apparatchiks, and who was accorded near-deified status by an adoring public, the quest to remove the Jews from Germany could take new political and institutional form. From now on, there was no hiding-place for Jews in Germany. The sensible, far-sighted or plain lucky ones left. Many others moved to the relative anonymity of the big city. But there was no safety; only borrowed time.

Already in spring 1933 the first big discriminatory steps were taken. Jews were ousted from the civil service. Barriers were placed in their way to entering the legal profession, practising as doctors and obtaining school places for their children. A national boycott of Jewish shops and stores lasted only a single day, 1 April, but local and regional attempts to force Jews out of business did not let up. Not only did the antisemitic climate worsen; now the state gave its backing to those who were making the lives of Jews a misery. A second major wave of antisemitic agitation and violence in the spring and summer of 1935 ended with the promulgation of the infamous Nuremberg Laws in September – the overture to a succession of decrees taking away all civil rights from Jews and reducing them to the status of social pariahs. The expansion of the Reich in 1938 saw open antisemitic violence plumb new depths in Vienna, following the *Anschluss*, then in the annexed Sudetenland. But it was the orgy of destruction unleashed on Jews, their property and their synagogues throughout Germany on the night of 9–10 November 1938, cynically dubbed 'Reich Crystal Night' from the amount of broken glass littering the streets of big cities following the pogroms, that opened the eyes of the Jewish community, and the rest of the world, to the full viciousness of Nazi persecution. Wherever they could, Jews fled. To help them on their way, the regime rounded up between 20,000 and 30,000 Jews as pawns until the money for their emigration could be drummed up. Measures were now rapidly taken to force remaining Jews out of the economy. The process of 'aryaniz-ation' – the compulsory sales at giveaway prices of Jewish businesses – moved into its final stages. On the eve of war, a terrified, impoverished, numerically much reduced Jewish community stood at the mercy of Hitler's henchmen. Hitler's own rhetoric in his speech of 30 January 1939, and the actions of his regime, had by now left no Jews in any doubt that they had much to fear from the advent of a new war, a prospect which seemed by the day to become more certain.

Much of the radicalization of persecution between 1933 and 1939 had taken place with little or no specific direction by Hitler himself. Years later, he acknowledged that 'even regarding the Jews' he had been compelled 'for long to remain inactive' – mainly out of foreign policy considerations, not desire, of course.[29] He seldom needed to be active, except where a major decision (such as the passing of the Nuremberg Laws in 1935, or unleashing the pogrom in November 1938) was concerned. It sufficed that he provided the general guidelines for what was required.[30] Characteristically, Hitler would give some 'signal' or 'green light' to his minions to indicate his wishes on measures against the Jews. Radicals would follow the prompt to intensify the persecution. This would either find Hitler's subsequent sanction, or would be channelled into discriminatory legislation. Either way, the momentum of persecution was sustained, its level ever more radical. Hitler's underlings at different levels of the regime were adept at knowing how to 'work towards the Führer' along the lines he would wish.[31] This was not only the case for party apparatchiks and bureaucrats in government offices. It applied in exemplary fashion to the expanding realm of policing, security and surveillance under the control of Reichsführer-SS Heinrich Himmler and his right-hand man, the arch-technocrat of power Reinhard Heydrich.

By 1939, 'removal' of the Jews from Germany had proceeded a long way. But from the point of view of the Nazi leadership, it had not gone nearly far enough. Nazi policy towards Jews had been far from a straightforward route to a prescribed goal. It had encountered blockages, had experienced stops and starts and had followed a 'twisted road'[32] – though never a path that deviated for long from ever-escalating radicalization of persecution. Despite the intensified persecution, by the end of 1938 over two-thirds of the Jewish population of 1933 still lived in Germany. And for most of these, as the Nazi authorities concluded, there was nowhere to go. Emigration was not an option.[33] Since 1937, the Jewish desk of the SD had been looking for ways to speed up their expulsion. A far-reaching idea was a territorial solution: ship the Jews out to some foreign, inhospitable place and dump them there. Some of the more barren regions of South America were among the zany ideas mooted for a while.[34] Nothing, of course, came of such far-flung notions. They were to recur, however, in a different – and even more dangerous – setting in 1940. Pogroms had been another method contemplated to speed up emigration. And, indeed, the terror of *Reichskristallnacht* prompted a flood of refugees, desperate now to leave Germany under any circumstances. Foreign doors to Jewish immigration that had largely been closed were temporarily forced open. Almost as many Jews left in 1938–9 as in the previous four years of Nazi rule.[35] Even so, on the eve of the war Jews in Germany still numbered not much less than half of the figure of 1933. The Nazis were still far from a complete 'solution to the Jewish Question', even within the Reich.

As late as November 1938, immediately following *Reichskristallnacht*,

Heydrich had thought it would take a decade to be rid of all the remaining Jews.[36] He was soon given his chance to take the matter in hand. The wanton destruction of Jewish property by Nazi hordes had been widely criticized – though far less so the aim of forcing Jews out of Germany – and turned out to be the final explosion of large-scale public atrocities within the bounds of the Reich.[37] A more 'rational' policy was needed. On 24 January 1939 Heydrich was appointed head of a Central Office for Jewish Emigration. This drew its inspiration from what the Nazi leadership saw as a highly successful operation, masterminded by Adolf Eichmann, in Vienna the previous year (where the proportion of Jews leaving had been far in excess of the rate for Germany itself).[38] When units of the Security Police moved into Poland behind the invasion force in September 1939, Heydrich now occupied a pivotal position in dealing with the 'Jewish Question' in the newly conquered territories. It was a task that dwarfed any that he had taken on before the war. The job had then been to expedite the forced emigration of what remained of a Jewish community that had numbered around half a million at the time of Hitler's accession to power. And now, with the initial aim still unfulfilled, the conquest of Poland had brought a further two million Jews within the Nazi orbit. The 'Jewish Question' to be solved was no longer confined to Germany. It was a part of the war. And it had become much larger, not smaller, with the outbreak of hostilities.

III

Poland became in many ways an experimental ground for what was to come. Three large regions of the conquered country abutting Germany's eastern borders were incorporated into the Reich. But in contrast to Austria and the Sudetenland the year before, where the population had been overwhelmingly ethnic German, most of those in the newly annexed territories were Poles. Ethnic Germans were a minority. And a further small minority in these provinces were Jews. The aim of the new rulers was clear. The provinces, long contested between Germany and Poland, were to become fully Germanized, and as quickly as possible. Removing the Poles, it was plain, could not be done overnight. But clearing out the Jews, the lowest of the low in a vanquished population treated like dirt by the new overlords, seemed an easily manageable task. One of the most ruthless of these overlords, Arthur Greiser, the boss of what came to be designated Gau Wartheland (usually called the 'Warthegau'), with its headquarters in Posen, presumed in November 1939 that the 'Jewish Question' was no longer a problem and would be solved in the immediate future.[39] But Greiser, and other Nazi leaders, presumed too much. They had not reckoned with the logistical difficulties that stood in the way of their objectives, however ruthless they were prepared to be.

The initial idea was to create a huge reservation in a strip lying between the rivers Vistula and Bug, in the extreme east of the part of Poland occupied by Germany (following the division of the country between the Reich and the Soviet Union). Jews from the newly annexed provinces, and in addition all the Reich's Jews and 30,000 Gypsies, would be rounded up, loaded into cattle wagons and packed off to this dumping-ground. Hitler had approved the deportations. Heydrich expected them to last for about a year.[40]

This was utterly illusory. Before autumn had passed, the idea of the reservation beyond the Vistula had been given up. Instead, Jews were to be deported into all four districts of the largest part of what remained of Poland, the 'General Government' with its headquarters in Cracow and not designated for incorporation into the Reich. A second notion swiftly to be abandoned – or rather, postponed – was the rapid deportation of the Reich Jews. Eichmann had organized the deportation of several thousand Jews from Mährisch-Ostrau in the Protectorate (what remained of Czecho-slovakia, now under German rule), Katowice in Upper Silesia, and Vienna to the Lublin district of eastern Poland in autumn 1939, and had presumed this would be the first stage of the removal of the Jews from Germany and Austria. However, the deportations were no sooner started than they were halted on orders from above, most probably from Himmler.[41] The Reichs-führer-SS had been given broad new powers by Hitler in early October to control resettlement in the occupied eastern territories. His priority was to find space in the newly annexed provinces, beginning with the 'Warthegau', to accommodate ethnic Germans from the Baltic and elsewhere beyond Germany's areas of occupation. This meant the urgent removal not only of Jews but of vast numbers of Poles. In November the figure of a million Poles and Jews to be removed by February was mentioned.[42] Deportation of Jews from the Reich, former Austria and the Protectorate had less urgency.

Staggering brutality was deployed in rounding up and deporting Poles and Jews from the 'Warthegau', but the targets in successive grandiose plans proved utterly impossible to meet. Little headway had been made by the time that Hans Frank, the head of the General Government who had earlier welcomed the plans to send Jews east of the Vistula, commenting that 'the more that die the better',[43] was closing the doors on further deportations into his area. He simply had no possibility of accommodating huge numbers of deported Poles into his already overpopulated and impoverished region, desperately short of food supplies, he lamented. As for Jews, he wanted to make his area 'Jew-free', not to turn it into a dumping-ground for Jews from other, more privileged areas. But he recognized that in the short term, the General Government would have to take in more than half a million additional Jews and that 'only then can we gradually talk about what must happen to them'. He still had in mind a huge Jewish reservation in the eastern extremities of his region, on the border with the Soviet-controlled part of former Poland.[44]

By spring 1940 it was evident to the Nazi leadership that their schemes for immense population transfer and resettlement (of which the Jews were only one part) could not be realized within the existing bounds of the occupied Polish territories. Leaders in the annexed provinces, most of all Greiser in the 'Warthegau', were frantic to be rid of the Jews under their aegis, but no avenue was open for their deportation. Ghettos, initially envisaged as no more than temporary holding places until their inhabitants could be deported, turned into more lasting institutions. The largest of them, Łódź in the 'Warthegau' and later Warsaw in the General Government, offered such opportunities for profit and corruption that their Nazi administrators were loath to contemplate their dissolution. Frank, meanwhile, was becoming even more obdurate. He had, it is true, told Hitler and Himmler that he had no other interest than to serve the Reich's need in making his region 'the receptacle of all elements that stream into the General Government from outside, be they Poles, Jews, Gypsies etc.' But he had then convinced Heydrich that the food situation in the General Government made it impossible to continue the resettlement programme.[45] An impasse had been reached.

A possible way out had, however, been mentioned by Frank himself as early as January, when he had seized upon the old antisemitic idea, first advanced by the German racist writer Paul de Lagarde in the 1880s, of settling millions of Jews in Madagascar, a French colony.[46] This, Frank suggested, would create space in the General Government.[47] At the time, it was no more than a pipe dream. But precisely this prospect opened up with the German military triumph in the western offensive in spring 1940. Five days after the German advance began, Himmler, in a memorandum prepared for Hitler on the treatment of the 'alien population in the east', remarked – seemingly as not much more than an aside – that he hoped to see the term 'Jew' 'completely extinguished through the possibility of a large-scale emigration of all Jews to Africa or to some other colony'.[48]

Perhaps Himmler had put out the idea of deporting the Jews to Africa (Madagascar was not specifically mentioned) as a feeler. If so, he had met with no objection. Hitler approved the memorandum. And it must soon have been obvious in wider sections of the regime's leadership what was in the wind. For, as the defeat of France became a foregone conclusion, a proposal emanating from the Foreign Ministry envisaged Madagascar, not the General Government, as the destination for deported Jews. The idea was rapidly picked up. Madagascar would provide the answer to all the blockages in Poland. When, in July, Himmler halted deportations into his region,[49] Frank felt 'colossal relief'.[50] His difficulties would soon be over. Not only would no more Jews enter his domain; those there, in excess of two million, were to be shipped overseas and would cease to be his problem.

Madagascar, as the mooted new location of a Jewish reservation, was an idea with a short lifespan. But for several months in 1940 it was taken seriously at the highest level of the Reich leadership. And now, for the first time, a solution to the 'Jewish Question' was envisaged that embraced western Europe. Heydrich swiftly moved to acquire control. He spoke of the need to find a 'territorial final solution' to the 'entire problem' of the three and a quarter million Jews under German rule.[51] Eichmann and his associates were put to work to design plans. By mid-August they were ready. Four million Jews – a million per year over the next four years – would be shipped off to the inhospitable island in the Indian Ocean, a faraway place where they would be out of sight and out of mind. The entire operation would be directed by the Security Police. There would be no independent existence there for the Jews. Their new home, a massive reservation or 'super-ghetto', would be run by the SS. The previous autumn, it had been recognized (and welcomed) that deporting the Jews to the Lublin district would decimate the Jewish population.[52] Nothing different could have been expected from the 'Magadascar Project'. The Jews, it was obvious, were being sent there to rot. The genocidal implications were plain. But the idea was stillborn. Not even the basic prerequisites were satisfied. Vanquished France could certainly have been compelled to cede Madagascar as a mandate under German aegis. But with Britain refusing to come to terms, the shipping fleet and security on the seas necessary to freight the Jews to Madagascar were unobtainable. Eichmann's blueprint was left to gather dust in a forgotten corner of Heydrich's desk.[53] By now, a better option was becoming feasible.

Hitler's decision in December 1940 that the attack on the Soviet Union would go ahead the following spring had massive implications for the attainment of racial objectives. On the one hand, millions more Jews would fall into Nazi hands, at a time when no solution had been found to the problem of deporting the existing almost four million (soon to be recalculated at almost six million) in the German sphere. And whichever invasion routes the Wehrmacht might take, large numbers of Jews would lie within their path. On the other hand, the expected rapidly attained victory would open up the possibility of population transfer and resettlement through racial 'cleansing' on a gigantic scale.

By the time the invasion was launched, plans for precisely this were being compiled. The SS anticipated the removal, mainly through deportation to Siberia, of no fewer than thirty-one million people, mainly Slavs, over the next quarter of a century or so. It was taken for granted that five to six million Jews would 'disappear' as the first stage.[54]

Before such plans were conceived, presumed victory in the east conjured up a new potential for solving the 'Jewish Question'. In place of the already obsolete notion of Madagascar, there was now the prospect of deporting Europe's Jews 'to the east', into the icy wastes of former Soviet territory, where the freezing cold, malnutrition, exhaustion and disease could be expected rapidly to take their toll. This is what Hitler had in mind when he cryptically commented at the beginning of February 1941 that, with Madagascar raising insuperable problems, 'he was now thinking about something else, not exactly more friendly'.[55]

By this time, Hitler's unfriendly thoughts had already been transmitted to Himmler and Heydrich, who had been quick to see what an attack on the Soviet Union might mean for their own spheres of power. For Himmler, the planning possibilities for reordering the racial composition of eastern Europe were endless. For Heydrich, huge new tasks loomed for his Security Police. Beyond that lay the attainable prospect of accomplishing a 'final solution' to the 'Jewish Question'. From the beginning of 1941 this term was in frequent use. It referred, however, not, as it later came to do, to the programmed extermination in the gas chambers of the death camps, but to a territorial resettlement – though itself genocidal in implication – in the east as a replacement for the 'Madagascar Project'.

Certainly by January 1941, Himmler and Heydrich knew what was in Hitler's mind. On 21 January, Theo Dannecker, one of Eichmann's closest colleagues, noted: 'In accordance with the will of the Führer, the Jewish question within the part of Europe ruled or controlled by Germany is to be subjected after the war to a final solution.' Through Himmler and Göring, Hitler had commissioned Heydrich with submitting 'a final solution project'. Profiting from his experience, Heydrich had been able to put together the proposal in its essentials very quickly, and it was already in the hands of Hitler and Göring. To implement it, however, would require a huge amount of work and detailed planning of both the wholesale deportations needed and also of the 'settlement action in a territory yet to be determined'.[56]

The phrase had been first used in notes prepared by Eichmann for a speech on 'settlement' to be made by Himmler on 10 December 1940 to party leaders gathered in Berlin. Eichmann had estimated then that the deportations would encompass 5.8 million Jews – 1.8 million more than had been foreseen in the intended deportations to Madagascar, since the figure now covered Jews not just in territories under direct German rule, but within the 'European economic sphere of the German people'. The total comprised the number of Jews in continental Europe west of the German-Soviet demarcation line running through Poland.[57]

Himmler had explicitly referred in his speech to the 'emigration of Jews' from the General Government – an area previously designated to take in Jews (as well as Poles) – in order to make room for Polish workers.[58] But where were the two million Jews in the General Government to be sent to? Madagascar, it was obvious, was no longer a possibility. But only a few days later Hitler would give the military directive for an attack the following spring on the Soviet Union. Himmler would certainly have known what was coming. The 'territory yet to be determined' could only mean some still undesignated region of the vast area expected within the coming year to fall under German control.

Since maximum secrecy surrounded the attack on the Soviet Union, no specification of the intended territory for this 'final solution' could be mentioned outside the circle of initiates. There was, therefore, still official talk of the General Government as the location. But those 'in the know' were aware that this was now mere camouflage. Eichmann acknowledged in March that the General Government was in no position to take in any more Jews.[59] When Göring and Heydrich spoke of the latter's remit having to accommodate the responsibilities of Alfred Rosenberg, earmarked to take over a Ministry for the Eastern Territories, set up to oversee the conquered Soviet lands, it was plain that the territory envisaged for the 'final solution', though not specified, lay farther east than the General Government.[60]

Hitler promised Hans Frank in March, in fact, that his province would be the first to be made free of Jews.[61] Other provincial Nazi leaders, sensing what was afoot, now joined in the pressure to have their areas cleared of Jews. Goebbels gleaned misleading information that Vienna would soon be 'free of Jews', and that Berlin's turn was also imminent. 'Later,' Goebbels noted, 'the Jews will have to get out of Europe altogether.'[62]

Meanwhile, plans had to be made not only for the 'final solution' of the pan-European 'Jewish Question', but for the treatment of the Soviet Jews in the wake of the forthcoming invasion. By spring, such considerations were enmeshed in the wider designs for a war which, Hitler left none of his military leaders in any doubt, would be a far cry from what had taken place in western Europe.[63] This, he declared categorically, would be a 'war of annihilation'. The 'Jewish-Bolshevik intelligentsia' was to be 'eliminated'.[64] The army leadership collaborated closely with Himmler and Heydrich on methods of operation. Orders were worked out by army leaders to liquidate forthwith all political commissars who were to be captured. Göring asked Heydrich to prepare a brief guide for the army about the Soviet secret police, political commissars and Jews 'so that they would know in practice whom they had to put up against the wall'.[65] By May, Heydrich was assembling four *Einsatzgruppen*, each of between 600 and 1,000 men drawn mainly from the Security Police and SD, which would enter the Soviet Union in the rear of the army to deal with all 'subversive elements'. In his briefings, Heydrich was both expansive and imprecise in designating the target groups. Jews, Gypsies, saboteurs and all Communist functionaries were a danger. He emphasized that Jewry was at the root of Bolshevism and, in accordance with the Führer's aims, had to be eradicated.[66]

By the time German troops crossed the Soviet frontiers on 22 June, then, Hitler's regime had already moved a long way in a genocidal direction. The momentum had built up sharply during a period of nearly two years since Poland had been crushed. The numbers of Jews who had fallen under Nazi rule with the conquest of Poland, the barbarous treatment of the subjugated country – in which Jews were its lowest, most despised stratum – and the impossibility of finding a solution to an invented problem, however grandiose the vistas and however brutal the methods, all forced the ever more frantic search for a way out of the impasse. The favourable fortunes of war had momentarily offered the fantasy of a rapid European-wide remedy overseas, in Madagascar. Britain's obstinacy in insisting on fighting on swiftly ruled out that option. But the decision in late 1940 to smash the Soviet Union the following year opened a new possibility, and drove the radicalization still further. Now, the alluring prospect of a final territorial solution, where the Jews of Europe would die out in the arctic wastes of the Soviet Union, interlocked with plans for an annihilatory war in which

Jews, seen as the lifeblood of Bolshevism, lay in the path of the German army and were regarded as open season for the Security Police *Einsatzgruppen* in the rear. The trajectory was genocidal. But the steps into all-out genocide, even in the Soviet Union, had not yet been taken.

Hitler's own role in the development since September 1939 had been decisive and yet shadowy. He had at the outset laid down the ground rules for the barbarity in Poland. Of this there is no doubt.[67] Had he not done so, there would surely still have been atrocities. There was too much pent-up anti-Polish as well as anti-Jewish feeling to have prevented serious outbursts of violence against the civilian population. But if Hitler had issued explicit instructions to prevent and outlaw such actions, in all probability nothing remotely on the scale of the programmed inhumanity that occurred would have taken place.

As it was, having unleashed the ruthless programme of 'ethnic cleansing', Hitler could leave the planning and orchestration to Himmler and Heydrich. He also gave an open licence to his provincial chieftains, the *Gauleiter*, in the east, saying that he would not ask about the methods they used to Germanize their regions, and that he did not care about legal niceties.[68] But where key policy-decisions were necessary, resort had to be made to Hitler.

He alone could decide about the deportation of Reich Jews, for which some of his underlings were pressing. The mounting deportation problems within occupied Poland were also brought to his attention – not that he could solve them – and he was called upon on more than one occasion to placate Hans Frank about the absorption of Jews into the General Government. He certainly approved the lurch into the ill-conceived 'Madagascar Project'. And, as we noted, Heydrich's commission to work out a proposal to dispatch the Jews of Europe to an unspecified destination in the east, a territorial 'final solution', derived from Hitler. Himmler, Heydrich and Göring – nominally in charge of anti-Jewish policy since *Reichskristallnacht*, and up to his neck in planning for the economic exploitation of the east – were all extremely powerful figures. But their power emanated from Hitler. Without his mandate, their writ did not run. Behind the increasingly radical search for a solution to the 'Jewish Question' lay ultimately, therefore, the ideological imperative embodied by Hitler and by now permeating the entire regime: that another war would somehow bring about the destruction of the Jews.

On 30 January 1941, precisely as planning for a 'final solution' moved into a new gear with the possibility of deporting Europe's Jews to a dreadful, if unspecified, fate in the Soviet Union, Hitler for the first time returned, in his speech to the Reichstag commemorating the eighth anniversary of his 'seizure of power', to his 'prophecy' of January 1939.[69] The timing was no accident. Hitler was obliquely signifying what was in his own mind: that the hour of the showdown with the Jews was approaching.

IV

With the crossing of the Soviet frontiers in the early hours of 22 June 1941, the 'war of annihilation' that Hitler had promised began. Nazi barbarism moved on to a new plane. Given the instructions to the army before the campaign began, it is hardly surprising that uncontrolled atrocities by ordinary soldiers began immediately. 'I have observed that senseless shootings of both prisoners of war and civilians have taken place,' commented one troop commander only three days after the attack had started. Five days later he had to repeat his order to desist from 'irresponsible, senseless and criminal' shootings, which he bluntly described as 'murder'. He nevertheless reasserted the need to uphold 'the Führer's calls for ruthless action against Bolshevism (political commissars) and any kind of partisan', and stated that the aim of the war was to restore peace and order to 'this land which has suffered terribly for many years from the oppression of a Jewish and criminal group'.[70]

Even for a troop commander such as this one, who deplored and tried to halt arbitrary atrocities committed by his force, there was the acceptance of the need for ruthlessness towards commissars and partisans, and a belief that Jews – bracketed with criminals – were behind the Bolshevik regime. The mentality was widespread. This was a war like no other. And Jews were seen as central to it.

It was in this ideological climate that the killing of the Jews rapidly escalated as part of an unprecedentedly murderous campaign in which untold butchery was deployed against the civilian population and prisoners of war (who by the autumn would be dying in German camps at the rate of 6,000 per day).[71] Heydrich, as we have noted, had briefed the assembled *Einsatzgruppen* on their tasks when they entered the Soviet Union. But, contrary to what was once widely accepted, he passed on no order at these briefings for wholesale genocide against Soviet Jews. Such a directive, verbally passed on by Himmler, would come some weeks into the campaign, and as the first big leap in an escalatory process of genocide. Even then it would take the shape of an incitement to extreme murderous actions rather than a formal order.

Heydrich's earlier instructions to the *Einsatzgruppen* had been more restrictive than this subsequent amplification, but, typically, imprecise. On 2 July, probably to cover the actions of the *Einsatzgruppen* against possible objections from army leaders, he had provided a written remit that stipulated the execution of Communist functionaries, various 'extremist elements' and 'all Jews in party and state positions'.[72] This probably corresponded broadly with what he had told the commanders of the killing squads in the earlier verbal briefings, except that these were evidently couched in such a way that wide discretion was conceded to the *Einsatzgruppen* about the definition of the target-groups, and they were plainly encouraged to interpret the remit on the Jews liberally and as they thought fit. Rather than an explicit order, Heydrich's directions amounted to a murderous but open mandate, obviously capable of being translated into action in differing degrees since the *Einsatzgruppen* and their sub-units did not behave in uniform fashion during the early stages of 'Barbarossa'.

In fact, shootings by units from the *Einsatzgruppen* were only part of the initial wave of killing in which a centrally directed ideological thrust interacted with 'an incoherent, locally and regionally varied sequence of measures' taken by those on the ground.[73] Already on 24 June the head of the Gestapo office in Tilsit, in East Prussia near the Lithuanian border, gave the orders to shoot 200 local Jews, allegedly 'for crimes against the Wehrmacht' during the bold but futile resistance by Soviet border troops in the early hours of the invasion. The orders were taken on his own initiative, in accordance with the 'fundamental agreement with the cleansing actions' of the newly appointed leader of the *Einsatzgruppe* designated for the Baltic, Franz Walter Stahlecker.[74] Three days later Police Battalion 309 slaughtered two thousand Jews in Białystok. More than a quarter of them, including women and children, had been driven into a synagogue which was then set on fire. The 'action' had been initiated by a few fanaticized Nazis within the battalion's ranks.[75] But such individuals knew that such murderous brutality was now being verbally encouraged by SS leaders. Word soon passed round about what was expected.

Some units, most notably in the Baltic, were within a short time killing male Jews in very large numbers. In Kowno in Lithuania, for instance, 2,514 Jews were shot in a single day on 6 July.[76] Pogroms, deliberately fomented by the German invaders, giving full licence to the vicious and widespread hatred of Jews among the local population, made their own contribution to the unfolding horror.[77] In other regions, the killing was less unconstrained and largely confined to the Jewish 'intelligentsia'.[78] In this early phase after the invasion, then, there was central encouragement for the killing actions, but a good deal of room was left for local initiative. If the actions were already outrightly murderous on a large scale, there had as yet been no explicit and general genocidal order. For Soviet Jews, the stage of total genocide was, however, soon to be reached.

It cannot be traced to a single order on a specific day. This is not how Nazi genocidal policy worked. Exactly how and when the key steps into genocide were taken and authorized rests upon the assembly of difficult evidence.[79] Hitler's utterly unbureaucratic style of rule, his emphasis upon secrecy and his characteristic usage of camouflage language and signals for action rather than unequivocal orders drape a veil over his interventions. At the next level down, whatever files Himmler and Heydrich kept on the 'final solution' were doubtless incinerated as the Reich fell into ruins. At any rate, they have not survived. And the later testimony of Nazi leaders, leaders of the death squads and middle-managers of mass murder has often proved fallible, at times also contradictory, on matters of detail. It was often, of course, also self-servingly mendacious. Even so, surviving documentation and later testimony permit a highly plausible reconstruction of the main stages of the unfolding genocide.

These did not follow explicit orders descending from the apex to the base of a pyramid. Rather, there was a complex interrelationship of 'green lights' for action coming from above and initiatives taken from below, combining to produce a spiral of radicalization. Through their own initiative in interpreting how they imagined they were expected to act, those directly involved in the killing forced the pace of rapid radicalization on the ground, in turn affecting the way the leadership itself reacted and amended policy. But the operations at the 'periphery', though they developed their own dynamic, were not independent of central instigation and control. They had been unleashed, fomented and sanctioned by 'guidelines for action' emanating from the 'centre'. That is, the key steps of the escalation into total genocide followed some form of central directive. This was invariably transmitted through verbal indications of what was required or 'encouragement' for action passed on by Heydrich or, more often, Himmler. These were in the main broadly couched imperatives rather than clearly defined instructions. This mirrored, it seems most likely, the way in which Hitler himself indicated his 'wishes' in confidential meetings 'under four eyes' with Himmler.

Such secret meetings, with no minutes taken and no one else present (except, on occasion, Heydrich), started a dialectical process. The expressed 'wishes of the Führer' would find immediate executive action through Himmler. Through the medium of Himmler, then of lower-level leaders of the Security Police, they would percolate down, at different times and in varied formulations, to those carrying out the killing operations. Given a broad mandate which they could interpret in their own way, as long as this matched the imperative of intensified severity, the local leaders would then act as they saw fit, use their own initiative and deploy the invited extreme measures. These would in turn find sanction on high, and result in yet a further upwards ratchet of radicalization. Just such a process occurred in mid-summer 1941. It converted partial into total genocide in the Soviet Union.

On 15 July Himmler returned to the Führer Headquarters in East Prussia, where he had mainly been based since the start of the Russian campaign, after a brief trip to Berlin. Probably, he was expecting to attend an important meeting which Hitler was holding the following afternoon to lay out the framework of the future control and exploitation of the occupied territories of the Soviet Union after a war which was presumed to be as good as won. In the event, Himmler did not attend the meeting, possibly because he was diverted through the need to deal with the capture of an important prisoner of war taken that day – Stalin's son. Whether he saw or spoke by telephone with Hitler before the meeting cannot be established. But if he was away during the time of the meeting, he was soon back at headquarters, where the following day he had a lengthy lunchtime discussion about the previous day's deliberations. Hans Heinrich Lammers, the head of the Reich Chancellery, was present and explained Hitler's orders about the distribution of powers in the occupied east.[80] The outcome was that Himmler had been given overall responsibility for policing and security in the east.[81]

It was practically an open-ended mandate, only nominally restricted by the exhortation to respect the jurisdiction of the newly appointed Minister for the Occupied Eastern Territories, Alfred Rosenberg. Himmler received the minutes of the meeting shortly afterwards. He would have seen there – and doubtless heard much more about it verbally – that Hitler had spoken of 'exterminating anything opposing us' and pacifying the newly subjugated territory by shooting dead anyone 'who even looked askance'.[82] Such draconian sentiments framed Himmler's new security remit, offering the widest scope for extension of his powers. But to take full advantage of this, he needed far larger police forces in the east than were currently available. And, given the mass shootings of Jews that had already taken place and the equation in the Nazi mindset of Jews with subversion and partisan activity (which Stalin had encouraged in his first speech to the people of the Soviet Union since the German invasion, on 3 July), it was obvious that more police meant more killing – an intensification of the aim to 'cleanse' the newly occupied areas of Jews and thereby, in Nazi thinking, to 'secure' them.

On 18 July, the day after receiving Hitler's decree according him responsibility for security in the east, Himmler cancelled a planned journey to the General Government.[83] Most likely, he was already at work in exploiting his new position. It is plausible to presume that he spoke at least by telephone with Hitler about his new tasks, and the need, if they were to be accomplished, to increase drastically the police forces in the eastern territories. He had in fact already had such ideas in mind even before the invasion took place. Hitler's allocation of responsibilities for the east in the meeting on 16 July now gave him the chance to put the ideas into operation – and thereby substantially to extend his own powers. Between 19 and 22 July, Himmler dispatched two big SS brigades, totalling 11,000 men, to sweep through the Pripet marshes, the huge boggy region stretching over parts of southern Belorussia and northern Ukraine. With this, he had almost quadrupled the numbers of SS men behind the German lines within a week of Hitler's meeting. This was only the start. Further huge expansion in policing followed. By the end of 1941, the numbers in police battalions in the east had reached 33,000 – more than eleven times the size of the original *Einsatzgruppen* that had been sent in the previous June.[84]

Himmler needed no specific orders from Hitler to focus the attention of the newly dispatched units on killing Jews. From the outset of the eastern campaign, Jews had been the prime target of the killing squads. Already the numbers of Jews murdered vastly outstripped those of other victims. Their alleged subversive and oppositional behaviour was used as pseudo-justification for the massacres. The new remit for the most rapid and comprehensive 'pacification' of the eastern territories inevitably, therefore, had the direst consequences for Jews. The Pripet marshes, the location of Himmler's newly dispatched SS brigades, were seen as a particular trouble spot in the occupied territories.[85] On 1 August the SS Cavalry-Regiment 2 circulated an explicit order from Himmler: 'All Jews must be shot. Drive the female Jews into the swamps.'[86] Commanders still managed to interpret the 'explicit' order in varying ways.[87] But within a fortnight, they were reporting the 'de-Jewification' (*Entjudung*) of entire towns and villages in the region. Not just male Jews but women and children were now also being killed. One commander took Himmler literally and reported that the women and children had been driven into the swamps, which, however, were too shallow for drowning.[88] A comment some weeks later by Hitler shows that he was aware of the Pripet action. He had just reminded his evening guests – Himmler and Heydrich – of his 'prophecy', and again blamed the Jews for the dead of the First World War and of the present conflict, when he said: 'Don't anyone tell me we can't send them into the marshes! Who bothers, then, about our people? It's good when the horror precedes us that we are exterminating Jewry.'[89]

In his oblique comments, Hitler had linked together the Pripet action, the extermination of the Jews and his own 'prophecy' from 1939. As the widened assault on Jews in the east was beginning, on 1 August, the head of the Gestapo, Heinrich Müller, pointed out that Hitler wanted reports on the work of the *Einsatzgruppen* to be regularly sent to him.[90] On the same date, Müller had ordered illustrative material on the *Einsatzgruppen* operations to be assembled for Hitler 'as quickly as possible'. A fortnight later, Hitler's cameraman, Walter Frentz, was present at the shooting of Jews in Minsk, attended by Himmler, to film the massacre. Whether Hitler or Himmler actually viewed the film cannot be proven. But, clearly, Hitler was keen to be informed about the progress in exterminating the Jews in the east, and at a crucial juncture.[91] His expressed interest might fairly be taken to indicate an awareness that a new, more overtly and outrightly genocidal phase was beginning in the Soviet Union.

Even now, not all Jews everywhere were immediately slaughtered. Manpower and logistics alone constituted a hindrance. And the way directives were passed down left much scope for differing interpretations and emphases. The rate and timing of escalation in the murder were, therefore, not uniform. One of the units of *Einsatzgruppe* A, for instance, operating with exceptional brutality in Lithuania, registered 4,239 Jews (135 of whom were women) killed in July, but 37,186 in August (most of them in the second half of the month) and 56,459 in September, the majority comprising women and children.[92] On the other hand, it was the second half of September before the already high killing rate of *Einsatzgruppe* B, in Belorussia, sharply increased. Women and children were, even so, often, if not always, included in the shootings. But in this region, too, entire Jewish communities were now being eradicated.[93]

Overall, the numbers massacred assumed dimensions far beyond those of the first weeks of the Soviet campaign. The major escalation followed Himmler's visit to the Minsk area in mid-August, where he experienced a mass shooting of Jews (including some women), discussed gassing methods with two of his commanders and, according to some postwar testimony, spoke of the 'total liquidation of Jews in the east', apparently claiming to have received an order from Hitler stipulating that all Jews, including women and children, were to be exterminated.[94] The testimony is not wholly reliable, and no other evidence exists for the transmission of a clear order from Hitler. Whether or not Himmler himself actually gave direct orders now that women and children were also to be killed is also less than certain.[95] That is, nevertheless, what appears to have been understood. Himmler had conveyed to his leading commanders his widened security remit with its clear implication to wipe out the Jews in the occupied Soviet Union. This was not written down and transmitted in an explicit message. It was far too sensitive for that. The verbal transmission, passing down through briefings at varying levels, meant that different units heard at different times what was required of them.[96] But, by word of mouth, the news still circulated rapidly. By the end of August, the genocidal attempt to wipe out Soviet Jewry was well under way.

The escalation in the slaughter followed from a process of mutually reinforcing radicalization between those carrying out the killing and those at the regime's heart, laying down the guidelines of a policy of annihilation. Himmler was the main carrier of the mandate, the conveyer of guidelines for action to his commanders and police chiefs in the occupied territories, who passed it down the line to their men. But there was a still higher authority.

The huge extension of the police forces in the east arose immediately from Himmler's remit to 'pacify' the occupied territories, decreed by Hitler on 17 July following the crucial meeting on laying down the political jurisdiction of Nazi bosses. And it was scarcely coincidental that Hitler showed marked interest in the killing operations at the beginning of August, precisely at the time that Himmler was about to pass on widely couched instructions about extending the murder to Jewish women and children. Hitler's 'green light' to shoot anyone 'who even looked askance' – and, very probably, other drastic comments that were not minuted – had been sufficient to instigate the genocidal radicalization. Despite the variations in the timing of implementation, the widened remit of Himmler following the meeting in Hitler's headquarters on 16 July, and the inclusion, made known by mid-August, of Jewish women and children in the killing, amounted to a decision to eradicate the Jews of the Soviet Union.

V

The broader decision, to kill all the Jews of Europe, had not yet been taken. It was linked to, if separable from, the prior decision to wipe out Soviet Jewry.

In January 1942 the numbers of Soviet Jews were still estimated at five millions, although by then hundreds of thousands had been slaughtered.[97] But when around the turn of the year 1940–41 Eichmann had worked out the numbers of those from Europe west of the Soviet Union to be deported into a 'territory yet to be determined', he had made no reference to the millions of Jews already on Soviet soil. Excluding Soviet Jews, Eichmann reckoned the number to be deported to total almost six million (to which now several hundred thousand in the former Soviet area of Poland had to be added).[98]

Plainly, by the time German troops crossed the Soviet border in June no clear and conclusive decision had been reached about an overall policy towards Soviet Jews – whether they were to be deported further east or simply killed. But ideology and logistics combined to make the rapid emergence of total genocide in the captured Soviet territories practically inevitable.

Deportation could never have been a feasible option. Even had the eastern campaign swiftly ended in German victory, as had been presumed, the mobilization of transport to ferry millions of Jews from all over Europe to some distant destination in former Soviet territory would have been a colossal undertaking. And if the Soviet Jews were not simply to be massacred where they were, there was the additional problem of transporting these, too, to whatever immense reservations were vaguely envisaged. The difficulties would have been equally enormous. In reality, of course, these issues never arose. As the German advance slowed, a continuation of the war into the coming year became a certainty and the prospect of a territory into which to expel the non-Soviet Jews faded into a lingering fantasy, the fate of the Soviet Jews themselves was sealed. By midsummer it had become plain. The only solution was to kill them wherever they could be found. And in an already genocidal climate, but with the option of deporting the remainder of Europe's Jews *into* the Soviet Union rapidly receding, the question of what should be done with them now gained intense urgency.

At first, it had looked as if early victory over the Red Army would swiftly open up the possibility of a total solution through mass deportation. Soon after the Russian campaign had begun, Hitler had spoken more than once of Jews as a bacillus. He felt like the Robert Koch (the discoverer of the tuberculosis bacillus) of politics, he said, describing the Jews as the 'ferment of all social decomposition'. He had proved, he went on, that a state could live without Jews.[99] He repeated the bacillus analogy when meeting the visiting Croatian minister Marshal Sladko Kvaternik a few days later. 'If there were no more Jews in Europe,' he told Kvaternik, 'the unity of the

European states would be no longer disturbed.' Whether they were sent to Siberia or Madagascar, he added, was a matter of indifference.[100] For his foreign visitor, Hitler was holding to the fiction of overseas deportation. For Nazi leaders, however, every 'special announcement' by the Wehrmacht of further advances in the Soviet Union raised new expectations of the imminent deportation of the Jews to 'the east' or 'Siberia' (taken loosely to mean somewhere in the Soviet Union). Hitler's comments offer clues to his thinking about the Jews at this juncture. At a time when massacres were crystallizing into full-scale genocide in the Soviet Union, such hints about the need for a radical solution throughout Europe would not have been lost on Himmler or Heydrich.

In July, as German victory in the Soviet Union, to be followed by the capitulation of Great Britain and a triumphant end to the war, seemed tantalizingly close, plans were compiled in the Reich Security Headquarters for a grandiose 'final solution of the Jewish Question' which Heydrich had already announced in May as 'doubtless forthcoming'.[101] At the end of the month, Heydrich instructed Eichmann to draft an authorization from Göring (nominally in charge of the 'Jewish Question' since November 1938) to prepare 'a complete solution of the Jewish Question in the German sphere of influence in Europe'. Heydrich, we might recall, had already provided Göring in March 1940 with a draft plan to solve the 'Jewish Question'. What he was now seeking was formal authorization of what he had already verbally been granted – a step he evidently felt necessary at a key juncture in order to deal with heads of the civil administration and other agencies (especially Rosenberg's 'Eastern Ministry') which could interfere with the implementation of his plans. With Europe seemingly at Germany's feet, the time had arrived, it appeared, to carry out the deportation of the Continent's Jews into the Soviet Union – and to their deaths through 'natural wastage' from slave labour, malnutrition and exposure to a raw climate. For Jews incapable of working – children, elderly, infirm – suggestions of liquidation as a solution were already being proposed.[102]

Over the following weeks, however, as the German advance slowed and the magnitude of the misjudgement about the fighting capacity of the Red Army was glaringly revealed, the genocidal solution through deportation to the Soviet Union – the prospect which had been the dominant idea since the start of the year – rapidly became unrealistic. The last hopes of territorial 'resettlement' in 'the east', after the General Government then Madagascar had come to nothing, were postponed indefinitely. But the pressure to deport the Jews had meanwhile intensified, not lessened. There was simply no possibility of reconciling the increased pressure to deport with the insurmountable blockages on doing so. Meanwhile, mass killing of Jews had spread rapidly in the Soviet Union. And in the Reich itself, as news of the bitter fighting in the east filtered through, the public mood against the Jews, fomented by Goebbels' propaganda, was turning extremely ugly.

Jews in German towns and cities, hounded and persecuted at every turn, were depicted by vicious propaganda as subversives, agitators and troublemakers. They were portrayed as idlers who ought to be 'carted off' to Russia or, better still (it was ominously suggested), simply killed.[103] In the middle of August Goebbels put the case for compelling the Jews to wear an identifying badge to a fractious and ailing Hitler, and was given the green light. The wearing of the 'Yellow Star' by all Jews was introduced on 1 September. The Jews in Germany were now a marked minority – clearly visible, openly exposed to their persecutors, totally defenceless. The move was accompanied by the circulation to all Nazi Party offices of Hitler's 'prophecy' of 1939, that another war would result in the destruction of the Jews.[104]

Heydrich had been less successful with a proposal in August to deport Germany's Jews. Hitler had turned down the suggestion of 'evacuations during the war'. But he gave permission for a 'partial evacuation of the larger cities'.[105] Perhaps the old notion that the Jews were 'hostages' or 'pawns' whose presence in German hands might help to fend off an entry into the war by the supposedly Jewish-dominated United States still influenced him. More likely, he held to the view that there was simply nowhere to send the Jews to as long as the war in the east was unfinished. Poland, it had long been accepted, could take in no more Jews. But deporting the Jews into the Soviet Union at this juncture was not practicable. All available transport was needed for the front. This was for the time being a more urgent cause than using trains to ferry German Jews into Russia. Moreover, since Hitler viewed the Jews as a treacherous 'fifth column', deporting them to the Soviet Union while a bitter war against the 'Jewish-Bolshevik' enemy was still raging would in his eyes have been a dangerous move. The areas behind the battle-lines, where Soviet Jews were being slaughtered in their tens of thousands, were in any case scarcely fitted to accommodate a mass import of Jews from the Reich. And if the Jews were simply to be deported there in order to be shot, then the existing killing-units, though expanded since the outset of the eastern campaign, would need to be much enlarged. The 'final solution of the Jewish Question', Hitler presumably told Heydrich, would have to wait a little longer, until the war was over.

Nevertheless, within the upper echelons of the SS and Security Police preparations for the 'coming final solution' continued. And the question was now posed about the fate of the deportees. Were they to be given 'a certain form of existence'; or were they to be 'completely eradicated'?[106] The question gained immediate urgency when, in the middle of September, Hitler changed his mind on the deportation of the Reich Jews. Stalin's brutal deportation of hundreds of thousands of ethnic Germans, for centuries settled along the Volga, appears to have prompted the volte-face. The pressure from within Germany and in some occupied countries, most notably at this time France, to 'evacuate' the Jews to the east had become intense. Vengeance for the fate of the Volga Germans, an argument pressed on Hitler by a number of Nazi leaders, placated his underlings in opening the previously closed door to deportation from the Reich. This was the decision, unquestionably Hitler's, which initiated the emergence over the coming weeks of the culminating phase of the genocidal process.

Within the following three months, what the 'final solution' meant would become clarified for those directly involved in its planning and organization. No longer did it refer to a territorial settlement on former Soviet territory (with the unspoken implication that the Jews would gradually die out). It now meant the physical annihilation of Jews throughout Europe. And since the prospect of deportation into the Soviet Union was rapidly receding, this would have to take place closer to home. Parts of occupied Poland were now starting to come under consideration as the location of the extermination programme. This most closely guarded secret was, in autumn 1941, in its full ramifications still confined to the leadership of the SS and Security Police. The civil authorities were as yet not fully initiated into what was planned. The uncertainties and confusion that prevailed that autumn reflected both the level of secrecy attached to the 'final solution', and the fact that it was still in its planning stage; imminent, rather than fully developed. But, triggered by Hitler's agreement in September to the deportation of the Reich Jews, the steps into total genocide now followed rapidly.

The issue of where the Jews were to go, and what was to happen to them on arrival, now became extremely pressing. On 18 September Himmler informed Arthur Greiser, boss of the 'Warthegau', that he would have to accommodate 60,000 Jews in the Łódź ghetto in his area for the winter, prior to further deportation 'to the east' the following spring. This was to meet Hitler's wish to have the Jews removed from the Reich and the former Czech lands as soon as possible.[107] But the Łódź ghetto was bursting at the seams, protested the local authorities. It could take in no more Jews. Himmler insisted, though the figure was reduced to 20,000 Jews (and 5,000

Gypsies). The suggestion had already been made in July that Jews in the Łódź ghetto incapable of working should be killed on the grounds that the ghetto could not sustain them.[108] And now large additional numbers were being sent precisely there. The quid pro quo, almost certainly, was permission granted from Berlin to exterminate the Jews of Łódź who were unable to work. The search for a suitable extermination site in the region began within weeks of the deportation order reaching Greiser. The gassing of Jews at Chelmno commenced in the first week of December.[109]

The 'Warthegau' was only one of the regions designated for the reception of the deported Jews. Heydrich specifically mentioned Riga and Minsk, alongside the 'Warthegau', in early October.[110] No clear blueprint for systematic mass murder had been devised by the time the first deportation trains started to rumble out of Vienna, Prague, Berlin and other cities, beginning on 15 October.[111] But the message emanating from Himmler and Heydrich – themselves certainly acting in accordance with Hitler's wish, however broadly he had couched it – was that the final hour for the Jews of Europe was about to toll.

In the meantime, those being sent Jews should act as they saw fit and take whatever radical initiative was needed. The invitation was accepted. During October and November, killing of Jews in huge numbers was adopted in differing regions of the Nazi empire as the way out of the self-manufactured problems. German Jews transported to Kowno and Riga in November were shot immediately on arrival. By now, mass shooting had spread beyond the borders of the Soviet Union. Close collaboration between the Wehrmacht, the SS and the Foreign Ministry led to the shooting of 8,000 Jews in Serbia in October as reprisals against partisan activity. In East Galicia, incorporated since the beginning of 'Barbarossa' into the General Government, around 30,000 Jews were shot in the autumn, though mass shooting in this region had been a feature since June.[112]

The use of poison gas was now starting to be recognized as an alternative method of killing – one which Himmler was ready to see adopted as being 'more humane' for the killers than shooting. In October, Heydrich commissioned the extended use of gas-vans. Reconnoitring a site for their deployment was already under way in the 'Warthegau'. A similar method was foreseen for Riga. And a stationary gas chamber, it seems, was planned for Mogilev, to deal with the Jews being sent to Minsk. In the General Government, which was spared the intake of further Jews, the first stages of what would become Belzec extermination camp had begun in September (when the gassing experts from the 'euthanasia action', halted the previous month, had become available). Construction of gas chambers started at the beginning of November, by which date Hans Frank was aware that the Jews of his domain who were incapable of working were to be deported 'over the Bug', to their certain deaths.[113]

These regional killings still fell short of a systematic, coordinated programme. The civilian authorities in the occupied territories were certainly as yet unaware of any comprehensive, central directive for genocide. In Minsk, the local Nazi leader, the General Commissar of Belorussia, Wilhelm Kube, objected to the shooting of Reich Jews – 'human beings from our cultural sphere', whom he distinguished from the 'native brutish hordes' – and sought clarity on the treatment of Jews with war decorations, those married to 'aryans', and part-Jews (*Mischlinge*). Hinrich Lohse, Reich Commissar for the Eastern Territory, pressed by the army to keep skilled Jewish workers, wanted to know whether economic considerations made a difference to the treatment of Jews.[114] Lohse was soon told that economic criteria were irrelevant. Jews were to be eradicated whatever the economic disadvantages might be.

To all appearances, a fundamental decision to exterminate Europe's Jews had by now been taken. Conceivably, it happened the previous month, in November.[115] In this month – and November was so pivotal in the Nazi calendar for its connections both with the 'shameful' German capitulation in 1918 and the 'heroism' of the failed putsch of 1923 – it looks as if the calamity of 1918 and the fate of the Jews were much on Hitler's mind in the context of the current war. At lunchtime on 5 November, with Himmler present, he had said he could not permit 'criminals' to stay alive while 'the best men' were dying at the front. 'We experienced that in 1918,' he said. He made no specific mention of the Jews. It is unlikely, however, that they were far from his mind. That evening, after Himmler had left, he rambled on at length about the Jews. The end of the war would bring their ruin, he declared. He ended his diatribe with the words: 'We can live without the Jews, but they can't live without us. If that is known in Europe, a feeling of solidarity will quickly arise. At present the Jew lives from the fact that he destroys this.'[116] Three days later, in Munich, addressing the party's putsch veterans on the eighteenth anniversary of the event, he castigated the Jews as the instigators of the war. A world coalition inspired by Jews, such was his message, would never triumph over Germany. It was the continuation of the struggle that did not end in 1918, he claimed. Germany had been cheated of victory then. Who the cheats were was unspoken but obvious. 'But that was only the beginning, the first act of this drama,' he stated. 'The second and the finale will now be written. And this time we will make good what we were then cheated of.'[117] It was allusive, not direct.

And so were his comments to his usual entourage in his field headquarters in the early hours of the night of 1–2 December, where he said: 'He who destroys life, exposes himself to death. And nothing other than this is happening to them.' He meant: to the Jews.[118] Within a week the gas-vans at Chelmno, the first of the death installations to begin operations, started their terrible work.

By now, the time was ripe for general clarification. With that in mind, Heydrich had sent out invitations on 29 November to those in the civilian administration most affected by the changing policy towards the Jews – several state secretaries, and a number of SS representatives. Hans Frank, the Governor General of Poland, and the SS chief in his domain, Friedrich-Wilhelm Krüger, were swiftly added to the list, though their initial omission suggests that the General Government – not intended as the recipient for any deported German Jews – was not regarded as central to the discussion. Plainly, therefore, the participants were not about to learn of a detailed programme for gassing millions of Jews in extermination camps located in that region. Nor were precise arrangements for deportations a subject for a meeting that lacked a transport specialist. The recipients of the invitation were, in fact, largely in the dark about the aim of the meeting.

Some divined, correctly, that the treatment of *Mischlinge* would figure on the agenda. But the most important clues were contained in the wording of the invitation. This began by repeating the commission, nominally from Göring, to Heydrich of 31 July, then went on to speak about the necessity 'of achieving a common view among the central agencies involved' in 'the organisational and technical preparations for a comprehensive solution of the Jewish Question', a matter of 'extraordinary significance'.[119] In other words, Heydrich's authority had once more to be established beyond question as the organization of the 'comprehensive solution of the Jewish Question', already laid down in July, entered its crucial phase. Heydrich's meeting had been scheduled to take place on 9 December. But crucial events intervened in the first days of the month, and the meeting had to be postponed.

On the 5th the German advance ground to a halt in intense cold not far from Moscow as a huge and devastating Soviet counter-offensive began. Any thoughts of deporting vast numbers of Jews into the Soviet Union in the foreseeable future were now completely illusory. The deportation plans that had underpinned Nazi hopes of solving the 'Jewish Question' over the past year had to be abandoned. Two days later, on the 7th, the Japanese bombed Pearl Harbor, triggering the German declaration of war on the United States on the 11th, and confirming that the conflict had become truly global. On the 12th Hitler explained to his party leaders, as we saw, what this meant for the Jews. In his 'prophecy' of 30 January 1939, he had promised their destruction in the event of another world war. His terrible conclusion followed: 'The world war is here. The annihilation of the Jews must be the necessary consequence.'[120]

It was no conventional order. Nor was it an explicit decision. But it was an unmistakable signal. Those listening to Hitler were no clearer than they had been before about *how* the Jews were going to be destroyed. But they were left under no illusions: the destruction *would* take place, and now during the war rather than once victory had been won. This was the message to be relayed to subordinates in key positions in the occupied territories.

Among those in Hitler's audience on 12 December had been Hans Frank. He returned to the General Government and, four days later, repeated what he had heard to his own underlings in his domain. He even used some of Hitler's own phrases. Notably, he cited the 'prophecy'. The war would be only a partial success if Europe's Jews were to survive it, he remarked. They had to disappear. He said he had entered negotiations about deporting the Jews to the east, and referred to a large meeting which would take place in Berlin about this – a reference to Heydrich's meeting, postponed because of the events of early December. 'In any event,' Frank went on, 'a great Jewish migration will commence.' He came to the murderous consequences – the aim horribly clear, if the method of attainment was not. 'But what is to happen to the Jews?' he asked. 'Do you believe they'll be accommodated in village settlements in the *Ostland*? They said to us in Berlin: why are you giving us all this trouble? We can't do anything with them in the *Ostland* or in the Reich Commissariat [the Ukraine] either. Liquidate them yourselves! . . . We must destroy the Jews wherever we find them and wherever it is possible to do so.' Though Frank was still anticipating the deportation of the Jews of the General Government to the east, he was being told that it was pointless to send them there and encouraged to resort to mass killing on his own territory. He had as yet no clear notion of how this was to be carried out. He estimated the number of Jews in his region at 3.5 million (including half-Jews). 'We can't shoot these 3.5 million Jews,' he said, 'we can't poison them, but we must be able to take steps that will somehow lead to success in extermination.'[121] At this stage, Frank evidently knew nothing of a programme to carry out the 'final solution of the Jewish Question' on the territory of the General Government itself, instead of further east, and through gas chambers installed in a number of extermination camps. Yet with the exclusion for the indefinite future of Soviet territory as a deportation venue, precisely this new extermination strategy started to take shape in the weeks to come.

Heydrich's meeting was reconvened for 20 January 1942 at a different venue close to the Wannsee, a beautiful large lake on the outskirts of Berlin. The participants differed slightly from those scheduled for the original meeting. But they represented similar interests. Much had happened since the Göring mandate had been signed, back in July. And there had been major developments even since the initial invitations had been sent out. What was now being organizationally and technically prepared was no longer a deportation plan for territorial settlement in the east, however murderous that would have been in practice, but a coherent genocidal programme to kill eleven million European Jews in ways and by means still to be fully established, but in need of Continental coordination. Eichmann later doctored the minutes of the meeting to eliminate 'certain over-plain talk'.[122] But probably Heydrich did not go into detail about the methods of killing. No one doubted what was intended. When Hans Frank's representative at the meeting, Dr Josef Bühler, his State Secretary, asked for the 'final solution' to start by removing the Jews of the General Government (who, he said, were mainly unable to work) since transport and manpower posed no great problem, he plainly grasped the new possibilities of mass killing, and closer to hand than the territory of the Soviet Union.[123] Since Hans Frank had been aware in the autumn of discussions about the construction of Belzec,[124] there was presumably some notion of what those possibilities might entail. There was no need for Heydrich to elaborate.

It would be some weeks after the Wannsee Conference, in March 1942, that the gas chambers of Belzec, then Sobibor and Treblinka started their grisly operations in the General Government. The largest death camp, Auschwitz-Birkenau, in Upper Silesia, would also begin killing Jews in March. And only by the spring would the deportations of Jews from western Europe to the death camps in occupied Poland commence.[125] The Wannsee Conference was still an interim stage in the emergence of the 'final solution'. But if the arrangements in January 1942 were still in an embryonic stage, by this time the decision to kill the Jews of Europe had already been taken.

VI

Heinrich Himmler, the head of the SS, has been described as 'the architect' of the 'final solution'.[126] So has his immediate subordinate, Reinhard Heydrich, head of the Security Police.[127] But ultimate authority rested with neither of them. Nor was the mind behind what was to emerge as the 'final solution' that of either Himmler or Heydrich. Indeed, if the construction metaphor is to be retained, Himmler might be described as the architect of the murderous edifice, and Heydrich as the master-builder. But the person who commissioned the project, the inspiration behind the design, had mandated both of them. This was Hitler.

Of course, the complex 'politics of annihilation' can by no means be reduced simply to an expression of Hitler's will. Many agencies throughout the Nazi regime, not just the top echelons of the SS, were necessary for total genocide to emerge over time as the 'final solution of the Jewish Question'. Complicity was widely shared. Hitler was no 'micro-manager'. That was not his style. In any case, he did not need to be. There was no shortage of those endeavouring to the best of their ability to put into practice what they took to be his wishes. No regular flow of edicts or decrees from Hitler was required to push along the radicalization.

Even so, at all crucial junctures of policy-making even in the 1930s – for example, the boycott of April 1933, the Nuremberg Laws of September 1935, the pogrom of November 1938 and its aftermath – Hitler's authorization had been needed. This continued during the war. The decision to impose on Jews the wearing of the 'Yellow Star' from September 1941 onwards, all subordinate leaders accepted, could only be taken by Hitler. So could the decision later that month to deport the Reich Jews – a decision which practically overnight enormously intensified the genocidal pressures. It is inconceivable that the decision to move to all-out physical extermination did not also require Hitler's authorization.

Himmler, Heydrich and others directly involved in the 'final solution' indicated that they were acting in accordance with Hitler's wishes, or with his approval. With the extermination programme moving towards its climacteric in summer 1942, Himmler declared: 'The occupied eastern territories are being made free of Jews. The Führer has placed the implementation of this very difficult order on my shoulders.'[128] Subordinate SS leaders were repeatedly informed, and were in no doubt, that in implementing the 'final solution' they were fulfilling 'the wish of the Führer'.[129] Unquestionably, they were correct.

Hitler's 'wish' may never have been expressed, even to Himmler, as a precise, unequivocal directive, given on a specific occasion, to kill the European Jews. It would have sufficed to give blanket authorization to the Reichsführer-SS to proceed with the 'final solution'. But both key stages in the autumn directly involved Hitler. The first was the decision in September to deport the Reich Jews at a time when there was nowhere to send them.

Genocidal impulses in a number of different regions followed rapidly, one after the other, from this decision. They did not yet amount to a programme. But the direction was plain, and the momentum building. The second was the new impetus given to finding a comprehensive 'final solution' that followed the declaration of war on the United States and the beginning of a prolonged global conflict in December. Deportation into Soviet territory, it was obvious, could not now be carried out for many months, if at all. But the 'final solution' could not wait. By the time Heydrich was able to convene the previously postponed Wannsee Conference, no further fundamental decision was needed. The task had become one of organization and implementation.

As the most terrible war in history, which Hitler more than any other single individual was responsible for unleashing, drew to its horrific close, the German dictator sought to justify the conflict to his own entourage – and to posterity. Once again, he resorted to his 'prophecy': 'I have fought openly against the Jews,' he stated. 'I gave them a last warning at the outbreak of war' – as always a misdating of his 'prophecy' to the date that war began. 'I never left them in uncertainty', he continued, 'that if they were to plunge the world into war again they would this time not be spared – that the vermin in Europe would be finally eradicated.' He was proud of what he had done. 'I have lanced the Jewish boil,' he declared. 'Posterity will be eternally grateful to us.'[130]

Of all the fateful decisions we have considered in preceding chapters, the decision to kill the Jews, unfolding over the summer and autumn of 1941, is the one where it is least possible to conceive of alternatives. Had the invasion of the Soviet Union proceeded as the German leadership hoped it would, the 'final solution' known to history would not have taken that particular form. The killing fields would, in all probability, then have been mainly in the Soviet Union, not in Poland. But as long as the Nazi regime was in power and engaged in the war, the Jews would have perished in one way or another. Only the method and timing would have differed.

The decision to kill the Jews arose from an earlier aim, absolutely intrinsic to Nazism, to 'remove' them. Hitler had never lost sight of this aim since 1919. It did not initially mean physically annihilate. But such a meaning was potentially, and over the course of time actually, also embraced by it. The aim of 'removal' was in this way proto-genocidal. Only the 'successful' (from the Nazi perspective) expulsion of Germany's Jews before war began could have prevented the logical progression into genocide itself for these Jews. But even then the intended expansion by conquest of the Nazi leadership would inevitably have resulted – as in practice it did – in vast numbers of further Jews falling within the clutches of the Third Reich. 'Removal' of these Jews was impossible without genocide, even if that had largely arisen from the deliberately imposed ravages of slave labour, malnutrition and disease. Only the prevention of war (ruled out by the politics of appeasement), the toppling of Hitler from within (for which the will was lacking among the German elites) or the rapid defeat of Hitler's Germany in the early stages of the war (an utter impossibility in military terms) could have precluded such an outcome. Otherwise, the only other way in which the Jews might have been spared their appalling fate is if better prepared Soviet defences had repelled a German invasion, forcing a compromise peace settlement, perhaps even with Hitler no longer in power. Stalin's obtuseness ruled out this possibility.

Germany's aggression was the main cause of Europe's second descent into war within a generation. It was also the crucial trigger, in the summer of 1940, to the spiral of events that we have followed, transforming conflicts at opposite ends of the globe by December 1941 into world war. Behind that aggression lay an ideological 'mission' embodied by the figure of Adolf Hitler. And inherent in that 'mission' was the 'removal' of the Jews. In this way, the Nazi war on the Jews was a central component of, inextricable from, the Second World War itself – the greatest slaughter the world has ever known.

Afterthoughts

Things *might* have turned out differently. The British government *could* have chosen in May 1940 to seek out a negotiated settlement with Hitler. The German leadership *could* have concentrated its attack on the Mediterranean and north Africa, not the Soviet Union. Japan *could* have decided to extricate herself from the damaging China imbroglio and not embarked upon the risky expansion to the south. Mussolini *might* have awaited events before deciding whether it was worthwhile taking his country into the war and *could* in any case have avoided the disaster in Greece. Roosevelt *might* have sided with the isolationists and not run the political risks of helping Britain and pushing to the brink of direct involvement in the war. Stalin *might* have heeded the numerous warnings and better prepared his country to meet the German onslaught. The Japanese *could* have attacked the Soviet Union from the east while the Germans were still advancing from the west. Hitler *might* have refrained from declaring war on the United States, an enemy he did not know how to defeat.

In theory these were alternative options. Any one of them could have altered the course of history. A rich variety of imaginary 'what if' scenarios might be constructed on such a basis – a harmless but pointless diversion from the real question of what happened and why. For the preceding chapters have shown in each case why these alternatives were ruled out.

Among the more feasible propositions was the possibility of Britain putting out feelers towards a negotiated peace in the spring of 1940. The immediate context of military catastrophe in France, together with the known readiness of some figures in the British establishment – including, at the very heart of government, the Foreign Secretary, Lord Halifax – to consider such an outcome, and the relatively weak position at this point of the new Prime Minister, Winston Churchill, meant it could not be dismissed out of hand. But when three days of debate in the War Cabinet eventually concluded with a firm decision to fight on, it was on the basis of reasoned argument, led by Churchill but accepted by a collective decision of all those involved, including Halifax.

At the other end of the spectrum, Hitler's decision to attack the Soviet Union and the Japanese decision to expand into south-east Asia were choices where alternatives had minimal chance of acceptance – or even of finding a hearing.

Hitler had for nearly twenty years seen war against the Soviet Union at some point as vital for Germany's future. This was *his* war. He had wanted to undertake the crucial showdown with Britain's assistance, or at least tolerance. Had Britain capitulated in 1940, the attack would surely have gone ahead on those terms. As it was, he had to reckon with Britain's continued hostility. But far from reducing the commitment to war in the east, and in the foreseeable future, this intensified it. For in 1940–41 Hitler's ideological fixation merged with military and strategic considerations into the decision for invasion. For years, he had justified the need to expand without delay with the argument that time was running against Germany. Now he could put that argument with force. He was aware that from 1942 onwards American arms and resources would increasingly weigh in the scales on the side of Great Britain. He still had no means of combating this. Meanwhile, in central and eastern Europe he could see a future Soviet threat to German dominance surely emerging (and confirmed in his mind by what he had heard when Molotov visited Berlin in November 1940).

The preferences of those in the German military leadership for a priority to be given to north Africa and the Mediterranean cut no ice with Hitler. Given the nature of the German regime, there was no possibility of any alternative based upon those premises countering the strategy favoured by Hitler himself. From Hitler's point of view, the decision to attack and destroy the Soviet Union – an undertaking he wanted ideologically – was strategically forced upon him. He had to gain victory in the east before Stalin could build up his defences and before the Americans entered the war. Rapid triumph over the Soviet Union was the route to complete victory in the war – compelling capitulation from Britain, keeping the Americans out and destroying any basis for future Soviet challenge for dominance in central Europe and the Balkans.

Japan's choice of southern expansion was equally inflexible, and paired here with similar inflexibility over the war in China. No alternative was feasible from a Japanese perspective. The China quagmire allowed no retreat for Japan without national humiliation. The more the Americans dug their heels in over China, the greater the impasse became. At the same time the commitment to expansion to cement Japan's standing as a great power, with extended dominion to provide the lasting basis for assured supremacy in east Asia, had permeated all sections of the elite, particularly the army and navy, and was backed by a manufactured shrill consensus of public opinion. No retreat from this commitment was possible either. It was a big risk. Expansion into south-east Asia would axiomatically lead to confrontation not only with Great Britain, but, even more importantly, with the United States in the Pacific. The extreme Japanese dependency on America for raw materials, especially oil, greatly increased the risk. But without the oil of the Dutch East Indies to supplant American oil, the economic self-sufficiency seen as essential for great-power status could never be achieved. Japan would always remain precariously dependent upon the United States. So when the upheaval in Europe following the German victory over France provided what was seen as a golden opportunity, no segment of the power-elite opposed it. Collectively, the Japanese government chose imperialist expansion to the south, despite the risks.

When an alternative choice posed itself, for a brief moment, following the German attack on the Soviet Union, it was for expansion to the north, against the old Russian enemy. Even then the southern advance would merely have been postponed for a time. When the northern alternative was rejected, since a strike to the north was adjudged too premature to be certain of benefits, the southern advance – favoured by the dominant elements in both navy and army – was reconfirmed. A clash with the United States then became inevitable. Even though the Japanese leadership was aware that such a clash would most probably result in national disaster if victory were not swiftly attained, prestige allowed no pulling back, either from the southern expansion or from the war in China. Not only Pearl Harbor, but the road to Hiroshima and Nagasaki beckoned.

The colossal risks which both Germany and Japan were prepared to undertake were ultimately rooted in the understanding among the power-elites in both countries of the imperative of expansion to acquire empire and overcome their status as perceived 'have-not' nations. The imperialist dominance of Great Britain and the international power (even without formal empire) of the United States posed the great challenge. The need to counter with the utmost urgency the growing economic disparity, quite especially the increasing material strength of the United States, which could only work over time against the 'have-not' nations, meant that the quest for dominion as the foundation of national power could not be delayed. This was the basis of the rationale, accepted by the power-elites in Germany and Japan, for undertaking such high-level risks that even national survival was put at stake. Economic domination of the Eurasian land mass by

Germany and of south-east Asia by Japan would, as American analysts recognized, have undermined the position of the United States as a world power. This was certainly the presumption in Berlin and Tokyo. From the perspective of the German and Japanese leadership, the gamble had to be taken.

In parallel fashion, if less grandiose in vision, the imperial dream under-pinned Mussolini's ambitions. He, too, was determined to overcome the disadvantages widely regarded within Italy's elite as stemming from her weakness as a 'have-not' nation. The fateful choices of 1940 were framed by this imperative. In the summer of 1940, as Germany's final victory seemed imminent, Italy's ruling elites (including the King), despite some cold feet, were persuaded by Mussolini's belligerency. The advantages of joining a war apparently already won outweighed, it seemed, the risks of becoming involved in a war Italy was ill-equipped to fight.

In the case of the calamitous decision to attack Greece, the elites were divided. The military leadership was cautious, aware of the risks involved. But opposition was at best muted. Mussolini could reckon with their com-pliance, if not their enthusiasm. Egged on by Ciano, his Foreign Minister, the Duce saw the Balkans, and Greece in particular, as the chance to create an Italian *imperium* – at the same time showing Hitler that he was not compelled to be tugged along in the German dictator's slipstream. Here, too, prestige played its part in the courting of disaster. But the decision to invade Greece was waiting to happen. It was ultimately also preformed by long-standing Italian ambitions – embodied in Mussolini – to join the 'have' nations, and become an imperialist 'great power'.

Stalin's options were drastically narrowed by his own staggering mis-judgement of German intentions. And given Stalin's unchallengeable supremacy within the Soviet regime, his miscalculations – as with those of Hitler and Mussolini – were the miscalculations of an entire system. His paranoid suspicions, long since an inherent component of his rule, meant that he distrusted and disbelieved good intelligence while perversely (since it supported his subjective assessment) believing deliberate German disin-formation. In the climate of fear and suspicion that pervaded the regime, he was also fed distorted evaluations by those in charge of sifting the intelligence, themselves victims of the general ideological presupposition that the interests of the western democracies lay in fomenting war between Germany and the Soviet Union, a notion abetted by the successful German disinformation campaign. Stalin's certainty that there would be no German attack before an ultimatum posing severe demands – perhaps a new 'Brest-Litovsk' – and that he could gain the time necessary to complete the rebuilding of the Red Army (which had been severely and unnecessarily weakened by his own brutal purges some years earlier) led him, catastrophically, to ignore all warnings and to berate his increasingly worried military advisers. They in turn were certain, in their own postwar apologias, that Stalin, even at the risk of provoking the Germans and even with the frantic rearmament programme still incomplete, could have mobilized Soviet defences to be ready to meet any invasion. The strategic thinking of the Soviet military leadership, which Stalin relied upon, was, however, also deficient. Deployment of Soviet defences not on the border, but in much deeper-lying formations, would have avoided the rapid demolition of front-line forces in the immediate German attack, and provided the basis for organized counter-offensives. The initial huge breakthrough by the Wehrmacht would thereby have been prevented. But military strategy had long rested upon the principle of offensive action as the best form of defence. This, and Stalin's disastrous certainty in his own judgement, exposed the Soviet Union to the calamity of 22 June 1941.

Roosevelt's choices, too, appear more open in theory than in practice. His early leanings towards isolationism in foreign policy were already fading fast in the later 1930s, as German and Japanese bellicosity increasingly threatened world peace – and American interests. The President had to reckon with isolationist feeling in the country, and even more so in Congress. The isolationist minority sustained a loud, discordant clamour. But it had no following within the administration. Among the President's advisers – some more belligerent, some more cautious – there was unanimity behind the need urgently to rearm and build up American defences. There was soon extensive acknowledgement, too, of the necessity – again in America's own interest – of underwriting the British war effort, and of resolute firmness against Japanese aggression in the Far East. From these premises, the destroyer deal, lend-lease, the Atlantic Charter, the 'undeclared war' in the Atlantic and Cordell Hull's unbending 'Ten Points' – seen as an ultimatum in Japan – were logical developments, in the thrust of their policy more rather than less likely. By the autumn of 1941, the most obvious outcome, whether through formal declaration or not, was war in the near future against both Japan and Germany.

Once Japan had pre-empted the need for any decision by Roosevelt to risk a vote in Congress on a declaration of war, outright confrontation with Germany – still seen in Washington as the greater danger – was never likely to be long delayed. Again, any difficult choice on political tactics was taken from Roosevelt by Hitler's rapid decision to declare war on the United States. But, far from being the arbitrary irrationality that it has often puzzlingly seemed, this decision was inherently logical from Hitler's point of view. America had long been an adversary which Hitler knew Germany would at some point have to confront. By the autumn of 1941 his options were reduced to the question of when to open hostilities. Pearl Harbor gave him what seemed a gilt-edged chance. The conclusion of new, more binding ties to a seemingly indomitable ally provided the opportunity to anticipate the inevitable and declare war in order to turn the tables on America in the Atlantic while her hands were full in the Pacific.

Over the previous months, Hitler had commissioned the 'final solution', aimed at ending Jewish existence in Europe. As the war had widened, with no likelihood of imminent German victory, this 'final solution' had emerged as the inexorable outcome of an escalating Nazi persecution which was increasingly genocidal in character. At the root of the Jewish tragedy was the Nazi ideological obsession, held more fervently by Hitler than any other, of 'removing' the Jews to 'cleanse' the German nation and pave the way for a racially pure 'new order' in Europe which would overthrow the centuries-old dominance of Judaeo-Christian values and beliefs. Here, by 1941, the only choice had turned out to be the methods and location of killing. Alternatives had by this time been reduced to techniques and organization of mass murder.

The fateful choices that were made were not predetermined or axiomatic. But they did reflect the sort of political system that produced them.

The fascist-style authoritarian systems made the most dynamic, but also the most catastrophic, choices. In both Germany and Italy, highly personalized regimes had been established in which the making of decisions was vested in all-powerful leaders. These could rely upon the backing – or at very least obedient acceptance – of all sections of the power-elite. Their supremacy was also upheld by plebiscitary acclamation from the masses, manufactured and manipulated by the toxicity of ceaseless propaganda and the ruthless repression of dissentient views. In these systems, the leaders might or might not choose to listen to advice. But they reserved the right – seen as the prerogative of leadership – to decide alone. In governmental terms, it was an extraordinary level of freedom – but one fraught with equally extraordinary risk, with the inbuilt potential for calamitous error.

Hitler's own freedom of action had been increasingly unshackled from institutional constraints after he took power in 1933. By the time war broke out it was as good as absolute. Not even the remnants of collective government were left. The Reich Cabinet had ceased to meet. The armed forces were directly under Hitler's control. All vital agencies in the regime, most importantly the apparatus of repression, were held by Hitler loyalists.

Even the sections of the German power-elites that did not share the complete Hitlerian world-view supported the parts of it that added up to expansion, conquest and establishment of Germany's Continental dominance at the cost of brutally subjugated peoples, particularly those of eastern Europe. They had shared Hitler's triumphs, most singularly the remarkable victory over France in 1940. Whatever private misgivings they might have harboured, they were in no position to oppose the logical extension of his great gamble: war against the Soviet Union, then against the United States.

Mussolini's internal position was inherently less strong than Hitler's. He was not the head of state, and the army's allegiance (as proved to be critical in 1943) was ultimately to the King, not to the Duce. Even so, his own internal dominance was unchallenged. He controlled all the important ministries of state. The party ensured loyalty and was the main conduit for the Duce cult. This, parallel to the Führer cult in Germany, had helped establish a personal supremacy which meant that arbitrary decision-making had become structurally embedded in the Fascist system. The fateful choices to enter the war, then, utterly ill-prepared, to invade Greece, were, as much as the disastrous decisions by Hitler that invited immense suffering and bloodshed for his own German people, both the free choices of an all-powerful individual, and at the same time systemically pre-programmed disasters in waiting.

The Japanese system shared many affinities with the regimes of Italian Fascism and German National Socialism. But there were also significant differences. Here, no possibility of arbitrary decision-making fell to any individual. In fact, of the six systems examined, this was in many respects the most overtly collective form of government. The Emperor was more than a figurehead, but had no dictatorial, or genuinely regal, powers to force decisions upon his country. Nor did he attempt to do so. Rather, he backed – sometimes hesitantly, even fearfully – the decisions of his government. Imperial majesty was only upheld by posing as the last resort of regime consensus, not by risking confrontation with his government, even less with his military. The Achilles heel of the system was, in fact, the position of the military. Constitutionally subject only to the Emperor, not the civilian government, the armed forces enjoyed a high degree of autonomy to shape national policy. Ministers falling foul of the military were soon ousted – or assassinated. The Prime Minister, therefore, had to act largely at the behest of the dominant forces in the army and navy. These in turn, in a peculiarity of the Japanese system, were heavily influenced by the views percolating upwards from factions based in the middle echelons of the officer corps.

In reality, however, the pressure from below operated within the framework of fixed ideological parameters of the quest for national greatness resting upon expansion, conquest and dominion. The strategy and tactics leading to these goals could give rise to heated debate. The goals themselves were not in dispute. The collective government was, therefore, wedded to the same inflexible ends. And, as with Germany and Italy, national prestige played an inordinate part in the making of crucial decisions. Anything that smacked of loss of face was guaranteed unanimous rejection. Ultimately, therefore, the collective decision-making in Japan worked in similar fashion to the individualistic pattern in Germany and Italy. There was an inherent propensity to take the high-risk gamble rather than withdraw to a perceived humiliating compromise that would undermine the central ideological objectives and advertise national weakness, not strength.

Stalin's gamble, that Hitler would not attack in 1941, was of a different kind. But his grave error of judgement also reflected his system of rule. Here, as in Hitler's Germany, the personality of the ruler had become a determinant of the system itself. Terror and purges had undermined bureaucratic stability and military efficiency. The institutions of collective government, as in Germany, had long since been eroded. The most important of them, the Politburo, had in recent years met less and less frequently. Even when it did meet, it was no more than a vehicle of Stalin's own power. Fear, intimidation, toadying and sycophancy prevailed even at the highest levels of the regime. They meant that there was no counter to Stalin's own assessment. Here too, then, the ruler had an autonomy in the making of decisions that was unusual even in authoritarian systems of rule.

The contrast with the two democratic systems, those of Great Britain and the United States, was stark. Here, given long-established, well-oiled bureaucratic machinery of government that framed the policy-choices for the leaders, allowing for rational assessment of risks and advantages, there was little scope for arbitrary decision-making. Yet there were divergences in the way these systems operated.

The British War Cabinet in May 1940 was a genuine collective, even if its members carried differing weight. Churchill had the dignity of the office of Prime Minister behind his views. But he was new to the post, and at this stage was regarded with scepticism if not outright disapproval by some elements even within his own party (which he did not yet lead). He could not dictate policy, and had to accept the continued importance of the two heavy-weights of the previous administration, Chamberlain and Halifax, while the two Labour members, Attlee and Greenwood, had as yet little standing. Churchill carried the day through sound argument as well as force of personality. Even in the extreme gravity of the situation, the decision had arisen from rational debate. Halifax and Chamberlain, like Churchill, had advanced reasoned calculations. The ideological parameters were as plain as in the case of the authoritarian systems, and were agreed by all. But they were defensive in nature: upholding Britain's independence as a nation, and preserving her Empire. Only the ways to those ends separated Churchill and Halifax. At the end of the debate, Halifax did not demur at the decision arrived at, even though it ran counter to his own suggestion. Churchill's own position, building upon his propagandistic exploitation of the 'miracle of Dunkirk', now went from strength to strength. His dominance within the Cabinet was soon ensured. Since he controlled the Defence Ministry, too, the balance tipped in the direction of prime-ministerial and away from outrightly collective government. Churchill's personality traits prompted frequent intervention (or interference) in military matters, much to the irritation of his chiefs of staff and commanders. But his sense of collective responsibility for government remained. At their meeting at Placentia Bay in August 1941, Roosevelt was surprised at the need felt by Churchill to wire his Cabinet colleagues in London to seek their approval for what he was doing. Some of the President's own Cabinet colleagues were not even aware of where Roosevelt was at the time.

The presidential system of the United States, unlike the British form of government, was not based upon collective responsibility for decisions. Roosevelt's Cabinet was an advisory body. Some of the members of his administration had great experience and their views carried much weight. Hull and Welles at the State Department, Morgenthau at the Treasury, Stimson and Marshall for the army, Knox and Stark for the navy, each backed by expert staff, were prominent among the individuals to whom Roosevelt listened. But the decisions were his alone. The checks here, as provided by the makers of the Constitution, did not come from within the executive, but from the legislature. Roosevelt was, and felt himself to be, confined by Congress to an extent that Churchill never experienced with the British Parliament.

And behind Congress there was public opinion to consider. Of the six systems under review, only in the United States was the opinion of ordinary citizens a factor of the first importance in the making of decisions. In Britain, public opinion was irrelevant to the crucial decision of May 1940. Thereafter, it was heavily steered by the government while continuing to have little or no input into decision-making. Morale was more important than opinion. And Churchill's rousing rhetoric of the summer of 1940, linked to the outward signs of national defiance, the staving off of the

Luftwaffe in the 'Battle of Britain' and the failure of Hitler's forces to invade, ensured that this was high – something not to be underestimated, especially compared with what it had been under his predecessor or what it might have been under an alternative premier. In the four variants of authoritarianism considered, opinion expressed in public was that which propaganda and indoctrination had manufactured and induced. Its role was to provide plebiscitary backing for regime action, to deter the formation of oppositional attitudes and on occasion to stimulate pressure to encourage the leadership to move in the direction that it wanted to anyway. Only in the United States did public opinion have a marked influence upon executive action. From the summer of 1940 down to Pearl Harbor, and even to the German declaration of war four days later, Roosevelt felt obliged to keep public opinion on his side. He could massage it through his 'fireside chats' and other public addresses. But he could not ignore it. His policy in these crucial months was determined in good measure by the need to prepare the public for something it did not want and which he had solemnly promised to avoid: sending American troops to fight in another war in Europe.

Without the individuals whose names have dominated the preceding pages – Hitler, Stalin, Mussolini, Konoe and Tojo, Churchill and Roosevelt – the course of history would have been different. But how different? The role of the individual set against the impersonal, external determinants of change is a perpetual conundrum in the interpretation of history. In a sense, it poses a false dichotomy. Individuals are not detached from the impersonal forces that condition their actions, as previous chapters have clearly shown. Relative economic strength and potential was one such force, in turn imposing constraints on the mobilization of resources and manpower. The conduct of the enemy was another. This could only be anticipated through the gathering and interpretation of intelligence. Yet in each case, the governments under review either had deficient intelligence at its disposal or made lamentable use of good intelligence, or both. And even the best intelligence supply, as in the American ability (through MAGIC) to crack Japanese codes, did not prevent Pearl Harbor. So in all instances governments had to react to unpredictable circumstances. This was particularly the case with those governments (Great Britain, the United States and the Soviet Union) which were reacting defensively to the strategic initiatives of Germany, Italy and Japan.

Yet another impersonal force operated within each governmental system. Bureaucratic planning and evaluation of policy proposals contributed to the 'pre-packaging' of decisions, often as the outcome of in-fighting for influence and resources within organizations. The scope for this was greater, however, in the differently structured democratic systems of Great Britain and the United States, as well as in the strange form of 'collective authoritarianism' in Japan, than it was in Germany, Italy or the Soviet Union, where bureaucracies served as the functioning tools of dictatorship.

Despite the existence of such external and internal determinants, the individuals at the centre of our enquiry were not ciphers or mere 'frontmen'. They had an input that is not simply reducible to a personalized representational function of such forces. Historical change, certainly in the short term, invariably results from the interaction of external determinants and individual agency. The fateful choices reviewed in preceding chapters provide ample evidence of this.

The individuals with the greatest political autonomy were the dictators of Germany, Italy and the Soviet Union. Other leaders in their place might well have taken other decisions, avoiding the disastrous judgements they made. Would a Reich Chancellor Göring have chosen to attack the Soviet Union? Would a Prime Minister Badoglio have decided to invade Greece? Would a General Secretary Malenkov have rejected the flood of warnings about a German strike? Simply to pose the questions offers not only unlikely scenarios, but enters a conjectural realm where no answers are possible. It does, however, serve to underline the indispensability to their actions of the personalities of Hitler, Mussolini and Stalin. Their fateful choices were directly determined by the sort of individuals they happened to be. At the same time, though, they were not made in a vacuum as arbitrary whims of personality. They were choices made under preconditions and under external constraints.

Ideological fixations were an important part of this. So were the actions of others whom they could not control. In Hitler's case, the sense of time running strongly against Germany – a correct appreciation – forced his hand in deciding on 'Operation Barbarossa' and in declaring war on America. Mussolini, too, felt under great pressure, in this instance to forge his own empire in the Mediterranean and Balkans before it was too late and he was completely upstaged by Germany. Stalin's confine was the state of his army and the knowledge that he would not be ready to confront Germany with the necessary forces before 1942, prompting the need he felt to avoid any conceivable provocation to tempt Hitler to invade before then. In each case, these individuals made history – although, to adapt a thought of Karl Marx, not under circumstances of their choosing.

At the opposite end of the scale, the personality of the Japanese Prime Minister was not of the first importance in the making of policy decisions. Konoe and Tojo were certainly very different individuals. By autumn 1941

Konoe would have been prepared to go a long way to appease the United States, while Tojo was inflexible in refusing any concession to American demands. But both had earlier committed themselves to the same policy of expansion in south-east Asia while maintaining the attritional war in China. Konoe became dispensable once he showed himself ready to retreat too far from this commitment. Matsuoka, the most forceful personality in Japanese politics, had already left the scene when his own inimitable attempt to upturn the existing priorities took him outside the mainstream consensus, failed to win support and stirred powerful enemies anxious to bring about his downfall. In the consensual nature of a formation of decisions that had emanated from the most powerful military factions, the scope allowed to the individual was necessarily diminished.

In the differently structured democracies, the role of the individual in the making of the fateful choices was greater than in the case of Japan, though arguably less crucial when compared with the dictatorships. Like the dictators, the democratic leaders operated on the basis of widely accepted ideological belief-systems. In fact, the ideological commitment – in this case, to democratic freedoms and the political and social structures that supported them – was almost certainly both deeper and wider than the fascistic and militaristic values of Germany, Italy and Japan, or the Communist world-view in the Soviet Union.

Without Churchill, the decision in the British Cabinet in May 1940 might conceivably have gone another way – with unforeseen consequences. Both Halifax and Churchill were striving for the same ends: national survival and independence. But Halifax's policy choice could – most probably would – have inaugurated a different course of development, one probably more damaging for Britain. So it was the country's inordinate good fortune to have as its Prime Minister Churchill, not Halifax. Personality mattered. But so did reasoned argument. It had to. Churchill was not yet the national hero he subsequently became, when his personality certainly became a factor of the first importance to the British war effort.

The value of Roosevelt's personal role is similarly hard to overestimate. Yet the quandary he faced would have confronted any President at the time. His opponent in the presidential election campaign of 1940, Wendell Willkie, a dynamic figure and attractive personality, was no isolationist. He was as firm as the President about the need for America to combat the dangers to American interests from Europe and Japan. He favoured the policy of aid for Britain. Some in Britain thought at the time that he might prove better than Roosevelt at mobilizing American industry. Willkie, like Roosevelt, would have had to straddle the line between helping Britain yet not alienating public and congressional opinion. Whether, however, he would have done it as well as Roosevelt; whether he would have had the experience – and political cunning – to pull it off as the President did; whether he could have sufficiently freed himself from the isolationist lobby within his Republican Party (which had persuaded him to denounce the destroyer deal); whether he would have had the lateral thinking needed to create the idea of lend-lease; whether he would have struck the vital rapport with Churchill that was so important to the forging of the alliance: on all of these, a sceptical answer is justified. Roosevelt's personality was as important as Churchill's to the style of governance he adopted, to the fateful choices he made and to the way he made them.

The choices faced by these men between May 1940 and December 1941 were unenviable. In each case the stakes were enormous. What seems to posterity an inevitable course of events did not look like that at the time. The fateful choices made by the leaders of Germany, the Soviet Union, Italy, Japan, Great Britain and the United States in those nineteen months changed the world.

For nearly four years after the events explored here, the global war raged on. The stupendous losses from military combat, and from genocide, mounted drastically. For over two years, between the summer of 1940 and the autumn of 1942, the outcome was far from certain. Both Hitler and the Japanese leadership knew that the odds would tell against them in a long war. So it proved. But it was a close-run thing – closer than is often presumed. Eventually, but only from 1943 onwards, the defeat of the Axis was in sight, at first dimly, then more brightly, and in the end glaringly. The unlikely combination of an indomitable Soviet fighting machine and limitless American resources and resolve finally ensured victory in both Europe and the Far East. The courage and tenacity of the British armed forces and those of the Empire had also made an indispensable contribution to the defeat of Nazism and Japanese militarism. But it was the curtain-call as a world power of a battered and bankrupt Britain. The liquidation of the British Empire followed – if gradually, then nevertheless inexorably. The next decades belonged to the new superpowers, the United States and the Soviet Union, the victors of the war. The foundations of another potential superpower of the future, China, were laid soon after the end of the great conflict in the wake of the turmoil in the Far East. Between them, the leaders of Germany and Japan had produced a world which was the exact opposite of all that they had striven for. Whatever the gigantic cost, it had been worth paying to see that the world they had wanted could never come about.

Notes

ABBREVIATIONS

BA/MA   Bundesarchiv/Militärarchiv (German Military Archive, Freiburg)

DDI   *I documenti diplomatici italiani*, 9th series, 1939–1943, Rome, 1954–60

DGFP   *Documents on German Foreign Policy, 1918–1945. Series D (1937–1945)*, London, 1957–66

DRZW   *Das Deutsche Reich und der Zweite Weltkrieg*, vols. 3–4, ed. Militärgeschichtliches Forschungsamt, Stuttgart, 1983–4

IMT   *Trial of the Major War Criminals before the International Military Tribunal, 14 November 1945–1 October 1946*, 42 vols., Nuremberg, 1947–9

KTB d. OKW   *Kriegstagebuch des Oberkommandos der Wehrmacht (Wehrmachtführungsstab)*, ed. Percy Ernst Schramm, 4 vols., Frankfurt am Main, 1961–5

PRO   Public Record Office, London (now National Archives)

FORETHOUGHTS

1. For the term, an invention of the American Cold War diplomat George Kennan, see Hans-Ulrich Wehler, 'Die Urkatastrophe. Der Erste Weltkrieg als Auftakt und Vorbild für den Zweiten Weltkrieg', *Der Spiegel*, 8 (16 Feb. 2004), reprinted in Stephan Burgdorff and Klaus Wiegrefe (eds.), *Der Erste Weltkrieg. Die Urkatastrophe des 20. Jahrhunderts*, Munich, 2004, pp. 23–35.

2. For the scale of mortalities, see Niall Ferguson, *The War of the World. History's Age of Hatred*, London, 2006, pp. xxxiv–xxxv, 649–50; and Norman Davies, *Europe. A History*, London, 1996, pp. 1328–9, where the losses in the Second World War are probably conservative estimates.

3. For a superb account of the legacy of the war for the European continent, see the magisterial work by Tony Judt, *Postwar. A History of Europe since 1945*, London, 2005.

4. The term was invented by the Polish lawyer Raphael Lemkin in 1944, was used in the indictment of major German war criminals a year later and enshrined in a United Nations convention in 1948 (Leo Kuper, *Genocide. Its Political Use in the Twentieth Century*, Harmondsworth, 1981, pp. 19–23; Michael Mann, *The Dark Side of Democracy. Explaining Ethnic Cleansing*, Cambridge, 2005, p. 17).

5. Gerhard L. Weinberg, *A World at Arms. A Global History of World War II*, Cambridge, 1994, p. 186, expresses similar sentiments in stating that 'the next five years of war [after September 1940] would see the decisions made in the last months of its first year carried out', though this compression of timescale omits some dramatic and fundamental decisions over subsequent months, considered in the later chapters of this book.

6. The case for playing down the role of government leaders as 'rational actors' in the taking of vital decisions in foreign policy and emphasizing the structuring of political choices through the input of governmental bureaucracies and the jockeying for influence of competing groups within a system was articulated by Graham T. Allison, *The Essence of Decision. Explaining the Cuban Missile Crisis*, Boston, 1971.

7. Frank Freidel, *Franklin D. Roosevelt. A Rendezvous with Destiny*, Boston, 1990, pp. 348–9.

8. See David Reynolds, *In Command of History. Churchill Fighting and Writing the Second World War*, London, 2004, pp. 169–73, for the way Churchill concealed the divisions that surfaced in the War Cabinet discussions of late May 1940, and more generally for an excellent analysis of the way his war memoirs were constructed and how they have shaped subsequent views on the great conflict.

9. The balance of economic power only shifted inexorably to the Allies during 1942, to become overwhelming from 1943 onwards. See Mark Harrison (ed.), *The Economics of World War II. Six Great Powers in International Comparison*, Cambridge, 1998, especially the editor's introductory chapter on 'The Economics of World War II. An Overview' (pp. 1–42); and I. C. B. Dear and M. R. D. Foot (eds.), *The Oxford Companion to the Second World War*, Oxford/New York, 1995, pp. 1060–62.

10. Emphatic in his view that ultimate triumph in the Second World War might have gone to the Axis powers is Richard Overy, *Why the Allies Won*, London, 1995, esp. pp. 314–25.

CHAPTER I. LONDON, SPRING 1940

1. Winston S. Churchill, *The Second World War*, vol. 2: *Their Finest Hour*, London, 1949, p. 157 (and similar comments on p. 199). See David Reynolds, *In Command of History. Churchill Fighting and Writing the Second World War*, London, 2004, p. 169.

2. In fact, an oversight led to a tacit acknowledgement that precisely this issue had indeed been mooted. The text of the telegram which Churchill sent to the French premier, M. Paul Reynaud, on 28 May 1940 included the following sentence: 'In the formula prepared last Sunday by Lord Halifax it was suggested that if Signor Mussolini would co-operate with us in securing a settlement of all European questions which would safeguard our independence and form the basis of a just and durable peace for Europe we should be prepared to discuss his claims in the Mediterranean' (Churchill, *The Second World War*, vol. 2, p. 110). See Reynolds, *In Command of History*, pp. 171–2, for the editorial lapse that allowed this trailer to events to be retained when Churchill had expunged reference to it in the text.

3. 'Cato', *Guilty Men*, London, 1940. And see Peter Clarke, *Hope and Glory. Britain 1900–1990*, London, 1996, p. 198.

4. Zara Steiner, *The Lights that Failed. European International History 1919–1933*, Oxford, 2005, pp. 25–7.

5. See Clarke, pp. 128–34.

6. Charles Loch Mowat, *Britain between the Wars, 1918–1940*, London, 1956, pp. 259–62.

7. See A. J. P. Taylor, *English History 1914–1945*, Harmondsworth, 1970, p. 330.

8. Steiner, p. 609.

9. Martin Gilbert, *Winston S. Churchill*, vol. 5: *1922–1939*, London, 1976, p. 76.

10. See the outstanding biography by Jonathan Wright, *Gustav Stresemann, Weimar's Greatest Statesman*, Oxford, 2002, pp. 301–7 and chapter 8.

11. Quoted in R. A. C. Parker, *Chamberlain and Appeasement. British Policy and the Coming of the Second World War*, London, 1993, p. 37.

12. Parker, *Chamberlain and Appeasement*, pp. 38–9.

13. Parker, *Chamberlain and Appeasement*, p. 43.

14. Ian Kershaw, *Making Friends with Hitler. Lord Londonderry and Britain's Road to War*, London, 2004, p. 105.

15. See Parker, *Chamberlain and Appeasement*, pp. 272–93; and, for the priority given to air rearmament and a comparison of spending on the three services, N. H. Gibbs, *Grand Strategy*, vol. 1: *Rearmament Policy*, London, 1976, p. 532.

16. Quoted in Parker, *Chamberlain and Appeasement*, p. 66.

17. Quoted in Parker, *Chamberlain and Appeasement*, p. 65.

18. Parker, *Chamberlain and Appeasement*, p. 69.

19. See John Charmley, *Churchill: The End of Glory. A Political Biography*, London, 1993, p. 344, also for scepticism about the likely deterrent impact of a 'grand alliance'.

20. Quoted in Parker, *Chamberlain and Appeasement*, p. 252.

21. Birmingham University Library, Neville Chamberlain Papers, NC18/1/1158, 25.5.40.

22. Parker, *Chamberlain and Appeasement*, p. 184.

23. Winston S. Churchill, *The Second World War*, vol. 1: *The Gathering Storm*,

London, 1948, p. 292 (where he mentions that his words gave rise to hefty and prolonged protest in the House of Commons); and quoted in R. A. C. Parker, *Churchill and Appeasement*, London, 2000, p. 187.

24. Quoted in David Irving, *Churchill's War*, vol. 1: *The Struggle for Power*, Bullsbrook, Australia, 1987, p. 9.

25. Taylor, *English History, 1914–1945*, p. 321.

26. Thomas Jones, *A Diary with Letters 1931–1950*, London, 1954, p. 204. 'You are the only man who can hold Winston, who is amazingly valuable, but whose judgement is not 100% reliable,' Lord Hankey, Minister without Portfolio in the War Cabinet, told Chamberlain on the day before his resignation (Churchill Archives Centre, HNKY 4/32, 9.5.40).

27. N. J. Crowson, *Facing Fascism. The Conservative Party and the European Dictators 1935–40*, London, 1997, p. 185.

28. Parker, *Churchill and Appeasement*, pp. 143–4, 224–5.

29. Keith Feiling, *The Life of Neville Chamberlain*, London, 1946, p. 424.

30. Kershaw, *Making Friends with Hitler*, pp. 300–301.

31. *The Diaries of Sir Alexander Cadogan 1938–1945*, ed. David Dilks, London, 1971, pp. 221–4 (7–12.10.39); Christopher Hill, *Cabinet Decisions on Foreign Policy. The British Experience, October 1938–June 1941*, Cambridge, 1991, pp. 115–26, 144. The door was far from closed, however, on a negotiated settlement on the basis of acceptable terms. News filtered through to the Germans later in October that R. A. Butler, Under-Secretary at the Foreign Office, had made this plain to both the Soviet and Italian ambassadors in London (Das Politische Archiv des Auswärtigen Amtes, Berlin, R29570, Fiche-Nr. 187, Frames 169830, 169847).

32. Churchill, *The Second World War*, vol. 1, p. 494.

33. Churchill, *The Second World War*, vol. 1, p. 526.

34. See esp. Andrew Roberts, *'The Holy Fox'. The Life of Lord Halifax*, paperback edn., London, 1997, pp. 195 ff.

35. Churchill, *The Second World War*, vol. 1, p. 601.

36. Charmley, pp. 399–400.

37. *Chips. The Diaries of Sir Henry Channon*, ed. Robert Rhodes James, London, 1967, p. 252 (13.5.40). And see Charmley, p. 396. The initial lack of warmth for Churchill on the Conservative benches qualifies the point made by Hill (p. 170), that a new Prime Minister could conventionally call upon support, and that Churchill started with the legitimacy of one who had long advocated rearmament and had opposed the Munich settlement.

38. Churchill himself was not sure that his government would last. See David Dilks, 'The Twilight War and the Fall of France. Chamberlain and Churchill in 1940', *Transactions of the Royal Historical Society*, 5th series, 28 (1978), p. 81.

39. Roberts, p. 208; John Lukacs, *Five Days in London. May 1940*, paperback edn., New Haven/London, 2001, p. 14; Taylor, *English History, 1914–1945*, p. 579.

40. Birmingham University Library, Neville Chamberlain Papers, NC18/1/1155 (11.5.40). Churchill had actually written on 10 May, the day he took office: 'To a very large extent I am in your hands – and I feel no fear of that' (quoted in Feiling, p. 442).

41. Birmingham University Library, Neville Chamberlain Papers, NC2/24A (10.5.40); Lukacs, *Five Days in London*, p. 17.

42. Quoted in Guy Nicholas Esnouf, 'British Government War Aims and Attitudes towards a Negotiated Peace, September 1939 to July 1940', unpublished Ph.D. thesis, King's College, London, 1988, p. 189.

43. Angus Calder, *The People's War*, London, 1969, p. 106.

44. *The Diplomatic Diaries of Oliver Harvey 1937–1940*, ed. John Harvey, London, 1970, p. 362 (19.5.40).

45. Quoted in The Earl of Avon, *The Eden Memoirs. The Reckoning*, London, 1965, p. 107; and see also Lukacs, *Five Days in London*, pp. 18–19.

46. P. M. H. Bell, *A Certain Eventuality . . . Britain and the Fall of France*, London, 1974, p. 19.

47. Paul Reynaud, *In the Thick of the Fight 1930–1945*, London, 1955, p. 320; *The Memoirs of General the Lord Ismay*, London, 1960, pp. 126–9; Bell, pp. 18, 32.

48. Churchill's private pessimism, or rather, perhaps, disappointment, about the United States in these days surfaced in his rejection on 27 May of Lord Lothian's suggestion that Britain should lease landing grounds on British territory for American security and in order to make a deep impression on the American administration. 'The United States had given us practically no help in the war,' Churchill rejoined, 'and now that they saw how great was the danger, their attitude was that they wanted to keep everything which would help us for their own defence' (PRO, Cab 65/7, Frame 00294, fol. 172; and extract printed in *The Churchill War Papers*, vol. 2: *Never Surrender, May 1940–December 1940*, ed. Martin Gilbert, London, 1995, p. 163).

49. Notes of Paul Baudouin, Secretary of the French War Cabinet, quoted by William L. Langer and S. Everett Gleason, *The Challenge to Isolation, 1937–1940*, New York, 1952, p. 453.

50. *The Diaries of Sir Alexander Cadogan*, pp. 285 (17.5.40), 288 (21.5.40).

51. The British public were unaware of the full desperation of the plight, and of the scale of the evacuation from Dunkirk, until 31 May (Juliet Gardiner, *Wartime Britain 1939–1945*, London, 2004, p. 172).

52. Birmingham University Library, Neville Chamberlain Papers, NC18/1/1156. Ismay, too, was struck, on returning to London from Paris, by 'a world in which everyone seemed calm, cheerful and resolute' (*Memoirs*, p. 129).

53. Lukacs, *Five Days in London*, pp. 27–38, for a summary of the varied shades of opinion.

54. General Ismay recalled, however, how fleeting the optimism was before the anxieties resurfaced (*Memoirs*, p. 130).

55. Bell, p. 15; Lukacs, *Five Days in London*, p. 27.

56. Christa Schroeder, *Er war mein Chef. Aus dem Nachlaß der Sekretärin von Adolf Hitler*, ed. Anton Joachimsthaler, Munich/Vienna, 1985, p. 105; *Hitlers politisches Testament. Die Bormann Diktate vom Februar und April 1945*, Hamburg, 1981, p. 113.

57. See Ian Kershaw, *Hitler, 1936-1945. Nemesis*, London, 2000, pp. 295-6 and p. 921 nn. 63 and 66; also Heinz Magenheimer, *Hitler's War. Germany's Key Strategic Decisions 1940-1945*, London, 1998, p. 24.

58. Churchill, *The Second World War*, vol. 2, p. 67.

59. Reynaud, pp. 379 ff. The British Cabinet was no more convinced than Churchill himself of the irreversible defeat of the French until 26 May, when the British Expeditionary Force was already preparing for embarkation (Hill, p. 152).

60. *The Churchill War Papers*, vol. 2, p. 133 (War Cabinet minutes, 24.5.40).

61. *The Ironside Diaries, 1937-1940*, ed. Roderick Macleod and Denis Kelly, London, 1962, p. 331 (23.5.40).

62. *The Ironside Diaries, 1937-1940*, p. 332 (25.5.40); and see Esnouf, p. 195.

63. Quoted in Reynaud, p. 379, from Gort's report to the government of 25.5.40.

64. Lukacs, *Five Days in London*, p. 137.

65. Hill (p. 181) adjudges that 'had the B.E.F. in fact been lost, Britain's military position would have seemed irredeemable' – with likely implications for the way the War Cabinet viewed the situation.

66. David Reynolds, 'Churchill and the British "Decision" to Fight on in 1940. Right Policy, Wrong Reasons', in Richard Langhorne (ed.), *Diplomacy and Intelligence during the Second World War*, Cambridge, 1985, p. 148.

67. Reynaud, pp. 398-400.

68. Reynaud, p. 403; Churchill, *The Second World War*, vol. 2, p. 108. The drafts of Churchill's letter to Mussolini of 16 May are in PRO, Prem 4/19/5.

69. *The Diplomatic Diaries of Oliver Harvey*, p. 367 (25.5.40).

70. *The Diaries of Sir Alexander Cadogan*, p. 289 (24.5.40); Esnouf, p. 204.

71. Birmingham University Library, Neville Chamberlain Papers, NC2/24A, fols. 108-9 (16.5.40).

72. Churchill, *The Second World War*, vol. 2, pp. 23 (15.5.40), 51 (18.5.40).

73. PRO, Cab 65/7, fol. 172 (27.5.40).

74. Lukacs, *Five Days in London*, p. 76.

75. PRO, Cab 65/7, Frame 266, p. 243 (24.5.40).

76. Roberts, pp. 211-12; David Reynolds, *The Creation of the Anglo-American Alliance 1937-1941. A Study in Competitive Co-operation*, Chapel Hill, NC, 1982, pp. 103, 324 n. 39.

77. PRO, Cab 65/7, Frame 300, p. 274 (27.5.40).

78. Reynaud, pp. 406-9; *The Diplomatic Diaries of Oliver Harvey*, p. 368 (26.5.40); Bell, p. 39; Llewellyn Woodward, *British Foreign Policy in the Second World War*, vol. 1, London, 1970, pp. 234-5, 237-8.

79. *The Diaries of Sir Alexander Cadogan* (24.5.40); Roberts, pp. 212-13. The

published edition of the Cadogan diaries says 'Van approached . . . with sugges-tion we should offer to discuss Mediterranean with Italy', omitting the words from the manuscript (Churchill Archives Centre, ACAD 1/9) 'by Paresci'. Unless the name could not be deciphered, it is hard to understand why it was not included. See also John Costello, *Ten Days that Saved the West*, London, 1991, p. 193.

80. PRO, Cab 65/7, Frame 278, p. 255 (25.5.40).

81. *The Diaries of Sir Alexander Cadogan*, p. 289 (25.5.40).

82. PRO, Cab 65/13, fols. 159, 160ᵛ, Halifax dispatch to Sir Percy Loraine (Rome), 25.5.40; Esnouf, pp. 206–9; Roberts, pp. 213–14; Lukacs, pp. 92–4; Hill, p. 156; Woodward, pp. 236–7. Halifax thought the meeting went well. But feedback from Paresci was that the Foreign Secretary had made a poor impression through offering no concrete proposals. Immediate satisfaction of Italian claims in the Mediterranean had seemingly been expected. In Sir Alexander Cadogan's view, Bastianini was 'an ass' and there was 'nothing to be got out of him' (*The Diaries of Sir Alexander Cadogan*, pp. 289–90 (25.5.40, 26.5.40)). Bastianini's own memoirs (Giuseppe Bastianini, *Volevo fermare Mussolini. Memorie di un diplomatico fascista*, Milan, 2005; orig. edn., *Uomini, cose, fatti. Memorie di un ambasciatore*, Milan, 1959) omit all reference to his important meeting with Halifax.

83. PRO, Cab 65/13, fols. 140–41 (26.5.40).

84. PRO, Cab 66/7, fols. 319–26; Bell, pp. 49–51; Lukacs, *Five Days in London*, pp. 106–8. As Hill (pp. 154–5) points out, the conclusions reached may in part have been prompted by the way Churchill had couched the terms of reference, hinting at the sort of answer he wanted.

85. PRO, Cab 65/13, fols. 146–8 (26.5.40).

86. Reynaud, pp. 404–6.

87. Birmingham University Library, Neville Chamberlain Papers, NC2/24A, fols. 114–17 (26.5.40); *The Diaries of Sir Alexander Cadogan*, p. 290 (26.5.40).

88. Harold Nicolson, *Diaries and Letters 1930–1964*, ed. Stanley Olson, New York, 1980, pp. 185–6 (26.5.40).

89. Birmingham University Library, Neville Chamberlain Papers, NC2/24A, fols. 114–17 (26.5.40).

90. Lukacs, p. 113, implies that something more grave was at stake in a meeting under 'conditions of secrecy' which 'had no precedent in the modern history of Britain', but Chamberlain (Birmingham University Library, Neville Chamberlain Papers, NC2/24A, fols. 116–17 (26.5.40)) specifically mentions that, once Reynaud had left, 'Greenwood was sent for and told what had passed'. This would account for a brief, informal gathering of the War Cabinet ministers before formal proceedings recommenced. Greenwood's sole point, according to Chamberlain, was that 'we had a good chance of outlasting Hitler'. Chamberlain had the impression that Greenwood had not 'thought things out'.

91. Borthwick Institute, University of York, Diary of Lord Halifax, A7.8.4, fols. 140–41 (26.5.40).

92. PRO, Cab 65/13, fols. 148–50 (26.5.40); Lukacs, pp. 114–16.

93. PRO, Cab 65/13, fols. 150–52 (26.5.40); Bell, pp. 41–2.

94. PRO, Cab 66/7, fols. 335–7 (26.5.40); Esnouf, pp. 213–16; Bell, p. 40; Lukacs, *Five Days in London*, pp. 118–19. The second part of Halifax's paper outlined the text, agreed with the French, of Roosevelt's approach to Mussolini, put forward that day. Halifax added a postscript, warning his colleagues in the War Cabinet that, according to information received from the British ambassador in Rome, Sir Percy Loraine, Roosevelt's previous intervention had been resented by Mussolini and any further approach 'would only be interpreted as a sign of weakness and would do no good'. Even so, it was thought that the Reynaud approach could not make matters worse, and that it was important to point out the implications for Mussolini of German dominance in Europe. By the time the War Cabinet met next day, Halifax had received a cryptic note from Loraine to say 'that matters had now gone beyond the stage at which his [i.e. Sir Percy's] views counted for anything'. Loraine had reported that 'Herr Hitler thought that he could reach a satisfactory conclusion with the French on his own account', and did not want the Italians to enter the war (PRO, Cab 65/13, fols. 175–6 (27.5.40)).

95. Esnouf, pp. 214–15; Roberts, p. 218.

96. Summarized in Lukacs, *Five Days in London*, pp. 141–5.

97. See Churchill, *The Second World War*, vol. 2, p. 89.

98. Churchill, *The Second World War*, vol. 2, pp. 77, 80,.

99. *The Diaries of Sir Alexander Cadogan*, pp. 290–91 (27.5.40).

100. John Colville, *The Fringes of Power. Downing Street Diaries 1939–1955*, London, 1985, pp. 140–41 (27.5.40).

101. Borthwick Institute, University of York, Diary of Lord Halifax, A7.8.4, fol. 142 (27.5.40).

102. For British perceptions of German economic crisis and social unrest, see Reynolds, 'Churchill and the British "Decision" to Fight on in 1940', pp. 157–9; and R. J. Overy, *War and Economy in the Third Reich*, Oxford, 1994, pp. 208–12.

103. PRO, Cab 65/13, fols. 175–81 (27.5.40); Bell, pp. 42–5; Esnouf, pp. 218–20; Lukacs, pp. 146–53; Roberts, pp. 219–20. Jonathan Knight, 'Churchill and the Approach to Mussolini and Hitler in May 1940. A Note', *British Journal of International Studies*, 3 (1977), pp. 92–6, also discusses this meeting of the War Cabinet, though (p. 93) – after misdating Halifax's meeting with Bastianini to 26 rather than 25 May – he then appears to assume that it comprised the *only* discussion of the peace terms and mistakenly concludes: 'it quickly became apparent that the Cabinet was opposed to making any approach to Mussolini.'

104. Borthwick Institute, University of York, Diary of Lord Halifax, A7.8.4, p. 142 (27.5.40). Halifax voiced his anger and frustration to the Under-Secretary at the Foreign Office, Sir Alexander Cadogan, and also told him of his scarcely veiled resignation threat, saying he could not work with Churchill

any longer. Cadogan's response was: 'Nonsense: his rhodomontades probably bore you as much as they do me, but don't do anything silly under the stress of that.' Before he did anything, Cadogan advised, he should consult Chamberlain. Halifax promised to do this, and added that, as Cadogan knew, he was not one to take hasty decisions (*The Diaries of Sir Alexander Cadogan*, p. 291 (27.5.40)).

105. See Roberts, pp. 220–21.

106. Birmingham University Library, Neville Chamberlain Papers, NC2/24A, fol. 118 (27.5.40).

107. Reynaud, p. 408, citing the account of William Phillips, the American ambassador in Rome.

108. *Ciano's Diary 1939–1943*, ed. Malcolm Muggeridge, London, 1947, p. 255 (27.5.40).

109. *The Diaries of Sir Alexander Cadogan*, p. 291.

110. Churchill, *The Second World War*, vol. 2, pp. 84–6 (quotation p. 84).

111. Reynaud, pp. 411–12; *The Diplomatic Diaries of Oliver Harvey*, p. 371 (27.5.40).

112. Birmingham University Library, Neville Chamberlain Papers, NC2/24A, fol. 119 (28.5.40).

113. The following report of the discussion at the War Cabinet from PRO, Cab 65/13, fols. 184–90 (28.5.40); extracts in Lukacs, pp. 180–83.

114. Hill, pp. 174–5. How far, in fact, Churchill himself believed that an eventual negotiated peace settlement was avoidable has been questioned by David Reynolds, 'Churchill the Appeaser? Between Hitler, Roosevelt and Stalin in World War Two', in Michael Dockrill and Brian McKercher (eds.), *Diplomacy and World Power. Studies in British Foreign Policy, 1890–1950*, Cambridge, 1996, pp. 211–15.

115. Birmingham University Library, Neville Chamberlain Papers, NC2/24A, fol. 119 (28.5.40).

116. Borthwick Institute, University of York, Diary of Lord Halifax, A7.8.4, p. 144 (28.5.40).

117. His own views were outlined in an incomplete, undated and unsigned hand-written draft among Churchill's papers, which was prepared around this time as the basis of his comments either to the War Cabinet or to the wider group of ministers whom he met on 28 May. In the draft, Churchill stated: 'I cannot feel that the offer wh[ich] France is proposing to make to Mussolini will have the slightest influence upon the realities of the case ['situation' crossed out]', continuing: 'I fear that if we entered upon this path we sh[oul]d soon find that it lead [*sic*] to Mussolini being a mediator between us & Germany, & to an armistice & conference under the conditions of our being at Hitler's mercy' (PRO, Prem 3/174/4, fols. 11–13).

118. A point made by Charmley, p. 405.

119. *The Second World War Diary of Hugh Dalton, 1940–1945*, ed. Ben Pimlott,

London, 1988, pp. 26, 28; also printed in *The Churchill War Papers*, vol. 2, pp. 182–4.

120. Churchill, *The Second World War*, vol. 2, pp. 87–8; and see Bell, pp. 46–8; Charmley, pp. 405–7; Lukacs, pp. 2–5, 183–4; Roberts, p. 225; and Roy Jenkins, *Churchill*, London, 2001, pp. 607–8.

121. PRO, Cab 65/13, fols. 189–90 (28.5.40).

122. PRO, Cab 65/13, fol. 189.

123. The concession, which Churchill had made at the War Cabinet, of leaving open the possibility of mediation by Mussolini at some future date was the one worrying aspect of the reply in the eyes of Oliver Harvey, formerly private secretary to Anthony Eden and now at the British embassy in Paris. Harvey had evidently read between the lines of the telegram, or heard something of Halifax's proposal: 'It looks as if Halifax', whom he had also served as private secretary, 'may have evolved some scheme for mediation by Italy on an offer of terms of Hitler,' he wrote. 'Incredible though it sounds, I cannot put it past him. It would be fatal' (*The Diplomatic Diaries of Oliver Harvey*, p. 372 (29.5.40)).

124. PRO, Cab 65/13, fols. 197–8; printed in Churchill, *The Second World War*, vol. 2, pp. 109–11, and Reynaud, pp. 412–13. See also Bell, p. 47; and Esnouf, 220–22.

125. Reynaud, pp. 414–15; Churchill, *The Second World War*, vol. 2, p. 111.

126. *Ciano's Diary*, p. 263 (10.6.40).

127. Churchill, *The Second World War*, vol. 2, p. 102; Bell, p. 17. Gerhard L. Weinberg, *A World at Arms. A Global History of World War II*, Cambridge, 1994, pp. 142–3, suggests that 'only until it became obvious, as it did by May 28 and 29, that substantial numbers of the British Expeditionary Force could be extricated from the disaster on the continent, was there any willingness even to think about the possibility of peace. As evacuation became a reality, and it thus appeared possible to organize some defense of the home islands, all thought of a compromise vanished.' But by 30 May no more than 120,000 men had been brought off the Dunkirk beaches (Churchill, *The Second World War*, vol. 2, p. 95), and even then organized *successful* home defence was far from assured. The decision not to entertain negotiation had been taken *before* there appeared to be any hope of rescuing almost the whole of the trapped army.

128. Churchill, *The Second World War*, vol. 2, pp. 103–4; and quoted in Martin Gilbert, *Winston S. Churchill 1939–1941*, vol. 6: *Finest Hour*, paperback edn., London, 1983, pp. 464, 468.

129. Quoted in Hill, p. 183. This did not, however, stop the speculation in Britain and abroad that a peace settlement would still be sought. The high point of the rumours and suspicions, which continued to circulate in June and July, came on the day of the French capitulation when an indiscretion by R. A. Butler, Under-Secretary for Foreign Affairs, reported by the Swedish chargé d'affaires in London, Bjorn Prytz, created a misleading impression (which soon leaked out) that Britain was ready to entertain a compromise peace. Prytz also passed on

remarks from other Members of Parliament that Lord Halifax would soon replace Churchill as Prime Minister. For a reliable summary of the Butler–Prytz affair, see Ulrich Schlie, *Kein Friede mit Deutschland. Die geheimen Gespräche im Zweiten Weltkrieg 1939–1941*, Munich/Berlin, 1994, pp. 214–16. Lukacs, pp. 203–4, provides a brief account, Costello, pp. 303–20, a longer one – though an interpretation much criticized in an unpublished paper, 'The Political Beliefs of R. A. Butler', by Patrick Higgins (which the author kindly allowed me to see).

130. Hill (pp. 160–62) suggests that Halifax, despite his experience and seniority, was at a disadvantage not just – or even mainly – because of Churchill's dynamism and force of personality, but because he was attempting to feel his way towards an argument in which a deal with Mussolini and a general settlement involving Hitler were not clearly separated, and in a War Cabinet where he was opposed by the leader of the government while his other colleagues were initially undecided. Even so, this is another way of stating that the clearer – and more compelling – argument was on Churchill's side.

131. As Reynolds, 'Churchill the Appeaser?', p. 213, points out, though it was perhaps in part a debating gambit to show Halifax that he was not an unreasonable 'diehard', Churchill meant it.

132. A point also recognized by Jenkins, p. 602.

133. See Dalton's recollection of what Churchill had said at the meeting of those ministers not in the War Cabinet on 28 May 1940, in *The Second World War Diary of Hugh Dalton*, p. 28.

134. Reynolds, *In Command of History*, p. 171.

135. They were first fully examined by Philip Bell, in chapter 3 of *A Certain Eventuality*, thoroughly explored in chapters 7 and 8 of Esnouf's doctoral thesis (which, remarkably, was never published), analysed by Reynolds, 'Churchill and the British "Decision" to Fight on in 1940', and by Hill (ch. 6), vividly described in Costello, chs. 9–10, again outlined, if briefly, in Roberts's fine biography of Halifax (ch. 22), and made into a gripping book-length drama in Lukacs' *Five Days in London*. The debt owed in this chapter to these works will be obvious.

136. According to Costello, pp. 254–5, the evidence suggests that 'Halifax was correct in his argument that Germany was prepared to offer terms that did not threaten British independence'. This is to misread Nazi intentions. Hitler's expressions of his readiness to spare Britain and her Empire did not mean that he would have granted her the independence which Costello implies. Any independence would have been only of the sort accorded the Vichy regime in France, and then merely in the short term. It is an extremely naive view of Hitler's long-term goals to presume that they allowed for the survival of Britain and her Empire as an independent power entity. In reality, satellite status dependent upon Germany would have been inevitable. A more balanced appraisal is provided by Reynolds, 'Churchill the Appeaser?', pp. 200–206.

137. *The Second World War Diary of Hugh Dalton*, p. 28.

138. Lukacs, *Five Days in London*, p. 128; Nicolson, p. 166 (20.8.39).

139. Birmingham University Library, Neville Chamberlain Papers, NC2/24A, fol. 119 (28.5.40). And see Dilks, pp. 82-3. Lukacs, p. 129, writes that 'during the crucial days of late May Lloyd George's name did not come up'. As Chamberlain's diary entry indicates, it did.

140. Reynolds, 'Churchill and the British "Decision" to Fight on in 1940', pp. 150-51.

141. Schlie, p. 217.

142. The German Foreign Office learned in mid-July 1940 from sources said to be close to the Duke of Windsor that he had described himself as a firm supporter of a peaceful settlement with Germany, and thought that continued strong bombing would make Britain amenable to negotiations (Politisches Archiv des Auswärtigen Amtes, Berlin, R29571, Fiche-Nr. 191, Frame B002546).

CHAPTER 2. BERLIN, SUMMER AND AUTUMN 1940

1. Franz Halder, *Kriegstagebuch. Tägliche Aufzeichnungen des Chefs des Generalstabes des Heeres 1939-1942*, vol. 2: *Von der geplanten Landung in England bis zum Beginn des Ostfeldzuges (1.7.1940-21.6.1941)*, ed. Hans-Adolf Jacobsen, Stuttgart, 1963, p. 49 (31.7.40); trans. *The Halder War Diary, 1939-1942*, ed. and trans. Charles Burdick and Hans-Adolf Jacobsen, London, 1988, pp. 244-5.

2. David Stevenson, *Cataclysm. The First World War as Political Tragedy*, New York, 2004, p. 107; Norman Davies, *Europe. A History*, Oxford, 1996, p. 903.

3. Stephen Pope and Elizabeth-Anne Wheal, *The Macmillan Dictionary of the First World War*, London, 1995, p. 83.

4. In a speech on 31 May 1921: Eberhard Jäckel and Axel Kuhn (eds.), *Hitler. Sämtliche Aufzeichnungen 1905-1924*, Stuttgart, 1980, p. 426.

5. Halder, *Kriegstagebuch*, vol. 2, p. 33; Barry A. Leach, *German Strategy against Russia 1939-1941*, Oxford, 1973, p. 58.

6. Quoted in Vejas Gabriel Liulevicius, *War Land on the Eastern Front. Culture, National Identity and German Occupation in World War I*, Cambridge, 2000, p. 278.

7. Liulevicius, pp. 6-7.

8. Jäckel and Kuhn, p. 773; trans. Geoffrey Stoakes, *Hitler and the Quest for World Dominion*, Leamington Spa, 1986, p. 137.

9. Adolf Hitler, *Mein Kampf*, 876-880th reprint, Munich, 1943, pp. 741-3; trans. (slightly amended), Adolf Hitler, *Mein Kampf*, trans. Ralph Mannheim with an Introduction by D. C. Watt, paperback edn., London, 1973, pp. 597-8.

10. Eberhard Jäckel, *Hitlers Weltanschauung. Entwurf einer Herrschaft*, Tübingen, 1969, chs. 2-3.

11. See Ernst Piper, *Alfred Rosenberg. Hitlers Chefideologe*, Munich, 2005, pp. 49, 57-8. The 20,000 or so ethnic Germans from the Baltic, settled in

Germany after the war, particularly in and around Munich, had influence in rightist circles in the immediate postwar years disproportionate to their numbers. See Niall Ferguson, *The War of the World. History's Age of Hatred*, London, 2006, illustration 11 (between pp. 122 and 123), for an example of the association of Jewish leadership of the Bolshevik Revolution and 'Asiatic' methods of brutality. Such imagery fed into the press of the extreme Right in Germany at this time.

12. Hitler, *Mein Kampf*, pp. 741–3; trans. Mannheim (slightly amended), pp. 597–8.

13. *Hitler's Second Book. The Unpublished Sequel to Mein Kampf*, ed. Gerhard L. Weinberg, New York, 2003, p. 28.

14. *Hitler's Second Book*, p. 152.

15. Lew Besymenski, *Stalin und Hitler. Das Pokerspiel der Diktatoren*, Berlin, 2004, pp. 51–6.

16. Thilo Vogelsang, 'Neue Dokumente zur Geschichte der Reichswehr 1930–1933', *Vierteljahrshefte für Zeitgeschichte*, 2 (1954), pp. 434–5.

17. For the term, see Martin Broszat, 'Soziale Motivation und Führer-Bindung des Nationalsozialismus', *Vierteljahrshefte für Zeitgeschichte*, 18 (1970), p. 403.

18. See Jost Dülffer, 'Zum "decision-making process" in der deutschen Außenpolitik 1933–1939', in Manfred Funke (ed.), *Hitler, Deutschland und die Mächte: Materialen zur Außenpolitik des Dritten Reiches*, Düsseldorf, 1978, pp. 186–204.

19. *DGFP*, 1, doc. 19, p. 29.

20. Max Domarus (ed.), *Hitler. Reden und Proklamationen 1932–1945*, Wiesbaden, 1973, p. 1446.

21. Klaus-Jürgen Müller, *Das Heer und Hitler. Armee und nationalsozialistisches Regime 1933–1940*, Stuttgart, 1969, p. 208.

22. Domarus, p. 606.

23. See Adam Tooze, *The Wages of Destruction. The Making and Breaking of the Nazi Economy*, London, 2006, chs. 7–9, esp. pp. 206–7, 250–59, 285–9, 293–4.

24. See Timothy W. Mason, *Nazism, Fascism and the Working Class*, Cambridge, 1995, ch. 4, esp. pp. 128–9.

25. Hans-Henning Abendroth, 'Deutschlands Rolle im Spanischen Bürgerkrieg', in Funke, *Hitler, Deutschland und die Mächte*, 1978, pp. 477, 479.

26. 'Hitlers Denkschrift zum Vierjahresplan 1936', ed. Wilhelm Treue, *Vierteljahrshefte für Zeitgeschichte*, 3 (1955), p. 205.

27. *Die Tagebücher von Joseph Goebbels*, ed. Elke Fröhlich, part I, vol. 3/II, Munich, 2001, p. 389 (23.2.37); part I, vol. 4, Munich, 2000, p. 214 (10.7.37).

28. The emergence and conclusion of the pact are extensively surveyed in Anthony Read and David Fisher, *The Deadly Embrace. Hitler, Stalin and the Nazi–Soviet Pact 1939–1941*, London, 1988.

29. Carl J. Burckhardt, *Meine Danziger Mission 1937–1939*, Munich, 1962, p. 272; trans. Klaus Hildebrand, *The Foreign Policy of the Third Reich*, London, 1973, p. 88. For doubts about the authenticity of the remarks, see Paul Stauffer,

Zwischen Hofmannsthal und Hitler: Carl J. Burckhardt. Facetten einer ausser-gewöhnlichen Existenz, Zurich, 1991, pp. 178–201; and Ian Kershaw, *Hitler, 1936–1945. Nemesis*, London, 2000, pp. 898–9 n. 118.

30. See Kershaw, *Hitler, 1936–1945*, pp. 264–71, 290–91. For the number of new deadlines for the attack, see Milan Hauner, *Hitler. A Chronology of his Life and Time*, 2nd edn., Basingstoke/New York, 2005, p. 150.

31. On peace-feelers around this time, see Bernd Martin, 'Das "Dritte Reich" und die "Friedens"-Frage im Zweiten Weltkrieg', in Wolfgang Michalka (ed.), *Nationalsozialistische Außenpolitik*, Darmstadt, 1978, pp. 534–7; and esp. Ulrich Schlie, *Kein Friede mit Deutschland. Die geheimen Gespräche im Zweiten Weltkrieg 1939–1941*, Munich/Berlin, 1994, chs. 10, 12.

32. Nicolaus von Below, *Als Hitlers Adjutant 1937–1945*, Mainz, 1980, p. 242; Domarus, pp. 1540–59 for the speech, p. 1158 for the passage relating to Britain.

33. Winston S. Churchill, *The Second World War*, vol. 2: *Their Finest Hour*, London, 1949, pp. 229–30 for the British response.

34. Halder, *Kriegstagebuch*, vol. 2, p. 21 (13.7.40); trans. *The Halder War Diary*, p. 227.

35. Halder, *Kriegstagebuch*, vol. 2, pp. 30–34 (22.7.40); trans. *The Halder War Diary*, pp. 230–32.

36. Walter Warlimont, *Inside Hitler's Headquarters 1939–45*, Novato, Calif., n.d. (original English-language edn., London, 1964), pp. 111–12.

37. Albert Speer, *Erinnerungen*, Frankfurt am Main, 1969, p. 188.

38. Halder, *Kriegstagebuch*, vol. 2, p. 49; trans. *The Halder War Diary*, p. 244.

39. Tooze, pp. 402–3, p. 430, also emphasizes the strategic considerations involving Britain and the United States.

40. Halder, *Kriegstagebuch*, vol. 2, p. 33 (21.7.40).

41. Halder, *Kriegstagebuch*, vol. 2, pp. 46–7 (30.7.40).

42. Hitler still insisted on the correctness of his decision, for these reasons (and for posthumous justification), near the end of his life (*Hitlers politisches Testament. Die Bormann Diktate vom Februar und April 1945*, Hamburg, 1981, pp. 78–80).

43. *DRZW*) vol. 4, 1983, pp. 99–106, 109.

44. Quoted in *DRZW*, vol. 4, p. 110. See also Tooze, p. 420, and Heinz Magenheimer, *Hitler's War. Germany's Key Strategic Decisions 1940–1945*, London, 1998, pp. 63–4.

45. *DRZW*, vol. 4, p. 113.

46. *DRZW*, vol. 4, pp. 9–10. And see Kershaw, *Hitler, 1936–1945*, p. 307 and p. 924 n. 157, for evidence which counters the view of Robert Cecil, *Hitler's Decision to Invade Russia 1941*, London, 1975, p. 74, that there is no indication of the generals anticipating Hitler's wishes in planning the invasion of the Soviet Union, a point (correctly) asserted by Leach, p. 53.

47. A point also made by Leach, p. 73, whose understanding of a 'divided and

uncertain' military leadership is closer to the mark than Cecil's claim (p. 76) that the leaders of the armed forces were 'at one' in that they did not want an invasion of Russia.

48. A point also made by Magenheimer, pp. 44–5; Leach, p. 72, correctly points out, however, that the preparations continued unabated and that Hitler's verbal orders of 31 July were confirmed in late September 1940.

49. The naval leadership was not least anxious to emphasize that it had advanced an alternative which stood a good chance of success but had been spurned by Hitler's insistence upon the attack on Russia (Erich Raeder, *Mein Leben*, Tübingen/Neckar, 1957, pp. 246–8, and Kurt Assmann, *Deutsche Schicksalsjahre*, Wiesbaden, 1950, pp. 211–12). Raeder had already claimed his opposition to the Russian war, with reference to his audience with Hitler on 26 September, in his testimony at Nuremberg (*Der Prozeß gegen die Hauptkriegsverbrecher vor dem Internationalen Militärgerichtshof, Nürnberg, 14 November 1945–1. Oktober 1946*, 42 vols., Nuremberg, 1947–9, vol. 14, pp. 117–19). See also Michael Salewski, *Die deutsche Seekriegsleitung 1935–1945*, vol. 1, Frankfurt am Main, 1970, pp. 271–2.

50. The title of the early postwar classic by Friedrich Meinecke, *Die deutsche Katastrophe*, Wiesbaden, 1946.

51. See Andreas Hillgruber, *Hitlers Strategie. Politik und Kriegführung 1940–1941*, 3rd edn., Bonn, 1993, pp. 190–91; Lothar Gruchmann, 'Die "verpaßten strategischen Chancen" der Achsenmächte im Mittelmeerraum 1940/41', *Vierteljahrshefte für Zeitgeschichte*, 18 (1970), pp. 456–75; Gerhard Schreiber, 'Der Mittelmeerraum in Hitlers Strategie 1940. "Programm" und militärische Planung', *Militärgeschichtliche Mitteilungen*, 27/2 (1980), pp. 69–99; and Gerhard Schreiber's contribution to *DRZW*, vol. 3, 1984, p. 270.

52. Explicitly demonstrated by Gerhard Schreiber, 'Zur Kontinuität des Groß- und Weltmachtstrebens der deutschen Marineführung', *Militärgeschichtliche Mitteilungen*, 25/2 (1979), pp. 101–71.

53. On the twin strands of German imperialism, see Woodruff D. Smith, *The Ideological Origins of Nazi Imperialism*, New York/Oxford, 1986.

54. See Jost Dülffer, *Weimar, Hitler und die Marine. Reichspolitik und Flottenbau 1920–1939*, Düsseldorf, 1973, pp. 492 ff.

55. BA/MA, Freiburg, RM6/71, 'Gedanken des Oberbefehlshabers der Kriegsmarine zum Kriegsausbruch 3.9.1939'; quoted in Salewski, vol. 1, p. 91, and in English translation in Charles S. Thomas, *The German Navy in the Nazi Era*, London, 1990, p. 187.

56. See Hillgruber, *Hitlers Strategie*, pp. 242–55; Gerhard L. Weinberg, 'German Colonial Plans and Policies 1938–1942', in Waldemar Besson and Friedrich Frhr. Hiller v. Gaertringen (eds.), *Geschichte und Gegenwartsbewußtsein. Historische Betrachtungen und Untersuchungen*, Göttingen, 1963, pp. 462–91; Klaus Hildebrand, *Vom Reich zum Weltreich. Hitler, NSDAP und koloniale Frage 1919–1945*, Munich, 1969, pp. 652–700; Salewski, vol. 1, pp. 234–41; Gerhard

Schreiber, *Revisionismus und Weltmachtstreben. Marineführung und deutsch-italienische Beziehungen 1919 bis 1944*, Stuttgart, 1978, pp. 288-97; and *DRZW*, vol. 3, pp. 250-71.

57. Salewski, vol. 3, Frankfurt am Main, 1973, pp. 106-8; *DRZW*, vol. 3, pp. 254-5.

58. Salewski, vol. 3, pp. 108-14; *DRZW*, vol. 3, pp. 255-6. And see the two additional memoranda from this period (Salewski, vol. 3, pp. 114-18), and a further memorandum of 4 July 1940 (pp. 122-35) outlining the implications of the massive territorial expansion for the growth of the fleet.

59. BA/MA, RM6/83, printed in Schreiber, 'Zur Kontinuität', pp. 142-7; *DRZW*, vol. 3, pp. 257-8.

60. *Staatsmänner und Diplomaten bei Hitler. Vertrauliche Aufzeichnungen über die Unterredungen mit Vertretern des Auslandes 1939-1941*, ed. Andreas Hillgruber, paperback edn., Munich, 1969, p. 102 (Hitler's remarks to Serrano Suñer, at the time Minister of the Interior in Spain, shortly afterwards to become Foreign Minister, 17.9.40).

61. BA/MA, RM7/894, 'Studie Nordwest (Landung in England)', dated December 1939, considered possibilities of a landing in Great Britain, indicating beaches which might come into question, the difficulties of coastal lines, and other factors. Raeder reported the findings – based, he said, on analysis that had begun the previous November – to Hitler on 21 May 1940 (Karl Klee (ed.), *Dokumente zum Unternehmen 'Seelöwe'. Die geplante deutsche Landung in England 1940*, Göttingen, 1959, p. 239).

62. *Kriegstagebuch der Seekriegsleitung 1939-1945*, ed. Werner Rahn and Gerhard Schreiber, Herford/Bonn, 1989 (= *KTB der Seekriegsleitung*), vol. 10, part A (mimeographed reproduction from BA/MA, 7/13), p. 186 (18.6.40).

63. Hillgruber, *Hitlers Strategie*, pp. 157-8.

64. Hillgruber, *Hitlers Strategie*, pp. 169-71.

65. *KTB der Seekriegsleitung*, vol. 11, part A (= BA/MA, 7/14), p. 190 (19.7.40), pp. 219-24 (19.7.40). And see Salewski, vol. 1, pp. 58-9.

66. *KTB der Seekriegsleitung*, vol. 11, part A, p. 201 (18.7.40).

67. *KTB der Seekriegsleitung*, vol. 12, part A, (= BA/MA, 7/15), p. 3 (1.8.40).

68. *KTB der Seekriegsleitung*, vol. 12, part A, pp. 353-4 (30.8.40).

69. *KTB der Seekriegsleitung*, vol. 12, part A, pp. 354-6 (30.7.40), pp. 364-5 (31.7.40); *Lagevorträge des Oberbefehlshabers der Kriegsmarine vor Hitler 1939-1945*, ed. Gerhard Wagner, Munich, 1972, pp. 126-8 (31.7.40).

70. Karl Klee, *Das Unternehmen 'Seelöwe'. Die geplante deutsche Landung in England 1940*, Göttingen, 1958, p. 205.

71. Salewski, vol. 1, pp. 259-60.

72. Salewski, vol. 1, pp. 275-6.

73. *KTB der Seekriegsleitung*, vol. 11, part A, pp. 236-9 (21.7.40).

74. Salewski, vol. 3, pp. 137-44.

75. Schreiber, 'Der Mittelmeerraum', pp. 78-9.

76. *KTB d. OKW*, vol. 1, 1965, pp. 17–18, 31–2 (9.8.40, 14.8.40); Schreiber, 'Der Mittelmeerraum', pp. 78–9.

77. BA/MA, RM7/233, fols. 78–85: 'Kriegführung gegen England bei Ausfall der Unternehmung "Seelöwe"'; printed in *Lagevorträge*, pp. 138–41 (6.9.40). See also Schreiber, *Revisionismus*, pp. 281–2.

78. BA/MA, RM7/233, fols. 83–4.

79. On the destroyer deal, see Churchill, *The Second World War*, vol. 2, chapter 20; also John Lukacs, *The Duel. Hitler vs. Churchill*, Oxford, 1992, pp. 225–7; and Chapter 5 below.

80. *DRZW*, vol. 3, pp. 192–4; Schreiber, 'Der Mittelmeerraum', p. 80.

81. *Lagevorträge*, pp. 134–41 (6.9.40). Curiously, the passage on 'Problem S' is omitted in the translated *Fuehrer Conferences on Naval Affairs 1939–1945*, London, 1990, p. 135.

82. *Lagevorträge*, pp. 143–6 (26.9.40); Schreiber, 'Der Mittelmeerraum', p. 81; *DRZW*, vol. 3, pp. 199–201; Gruchmann, p. 463.

83. He nevertheless put the arguments for full cooperation with France less forcefully than they had been advanced within the Naval Warfare Executive. See BA/MA, RM8/1209, 'Die Bemühungen der Skl. um einen Ausgleich mit Frankreich und um die Sicherstellung des französischen Kolonialreiches in Afrika', draft analysis of Vice-Admiral Kurt Assmann. Compiled in 1944, this was intended to absolve the *Seekriegsleitung* (Naval Warfare Executive) from responsibility for the disastrous course of the war. It nonetheless points up the divergence in strategic preference. In the introduction (fol. 11), Assmann wrote: 'The problem of a French-German understanding and the upholding of the French colonial empire in north and west Africa was one of the fateful questions of this war. In dealing with this issue, the decisions and actions of the supreme German leadership were not in accord with the views of the Skl. The Skl. correctly foresaw the coming development, repeatedly warned against it, and tried to convey its view.'

84. *KTB d. Seekriegsleitung*, vol. 13, part A (= BA/MA, 7/16), p. 352 (26.9.40), 'Führer agrees in principle with the ideas of the head of the Naval Warfare Executive' ('Führer stimmt den Gedankengängen des Chefs Skl. grundsätzlich zu'). See also Raeder, pp. 246–8 and Assmann, pp. 211–12, though, in fact, Hitler's reported remarks to his naval adjutant were ambivalent – that Raeder's comments to him had been most valuable in that it served as a control on his own views, to see 'if he was right'.

85. *Lagevorträge*, pp. 143–4 (26.9.40).

86. Halder, *Kriegstagebuch*, vol. 2, p. 124 (3.10.40).

87. Hillgruber, *Hitlers Strategie*, pp. 178, 190; Wolfgang Michalka, *Ribbentrop und die deutsche Weltpolitik 1933–1940*, Munich, 1980, pp. 247–59.

88. Wolfgang Michalka, 'Vom Antikominternpakt zum euro-asiatischen Kontinentalblock. Ribbentrops Alternativkonzeption zu Hitlers außenpolitischen "Programm"', in Michalka, *Nationalsozialistische Außenpolitik*, pp. 490–91.

89. Andreas Hillgruber, 'Der Faktor Amerika in Hitlers Strategie 1938–1941', in Michalka, *Nationalsozialistische Außenpolitik*, p. 513.

90. Schreiber, 'Der Mittelmeerraum', p. 80; *DRZW*, vol. 3, p. 194.

91. Hillgruber, 'Amerika', pp. 512–13.

92. *Staatsmänner*, pp. 112–13.

93. Reports of the discussions in *Staatsmänner*, pp. 104–23; and *Ciano's Diplomatic Papers*, ed. Malcolm Muggeridge, London, 1948, pp. 395–9.

94. *Staatsmänner*, pp. 132–40; and see Paul Preston, 'Franco and Hitler. The Myth of Hendaye 1940', *Contemporary European History*, 1 (1992), pp. 1–16.

95. *Die Weizsäcker-Papiere 1933–1950*, ed. Leonidas E. Hill, Frankfurt am Main, 1974, p. 221 (21.10.40) – before Hitler's meeting with Franco. Hitler retrospectively asserted that he recognized the limited strategic value of Spanish intervention: the acquisition of Gibraltar, but also of much Atlantic coastline that would have needed defending (*Hitlers politisches Testament*, p. 60). For the extent of Spanish demands, see Elena Henández-Sandoica and Enrique Moradiellos, 'Spain and the Second World War, 1939–1945', in Neville Wylie (ed.), *European Neutrals and Non-Belligerents during the Second World War*, Cambridge, 2002, pp. 251–3.

96. *Staatsmänner*, pp. 142–9.

97. *Die Weizsäcker-Papiere*, pp. 220–21 (21.10.40).

98. Gerhard L. Weinberg, *A World at Arms. A Global History of World War II*, Cambridge, 1994, p. 206. Towards the end of his life (*Hitlers politisches Testament*, p. 73), Hitler regarded Germany's lenient treatment of Vichy France as 'complete nonsense' (*vollkommener Unsinn*).

99. Below, p. 250.

100. Halder, *Kriegstagebuch*, vol. 2, pp. 163–6 (4.11.40), quotation p. 165; *KTB d. OKW*, vol. 1, pp. 148–52 (4.11.40).

101. Warlimont, p. 120; Donald S. Detwiler, *Hitler, Franco und Gibraltar. Die Frage des spanischen Eintritts in den Zweiten Weltkrieg*, Wiesbaden, 1962, pp. 68–79; *DRZW*, vol. 3, pp. 205–7; Schreiber, 'Der Mittelmeerraum', pp. 84–5; Gruchmann, p. 466.

102. For the talks, see *Staatsmänner*, 165–93.

103. *Hitlers Weisungen für die Kriegführung. Dokumente des Oberkommandos der Wehrmacht*, ed. Walther Hubatsch, paperback edn., Munich, 1965, pp. 77–82.

104. *Heeresadjutant bei Hitler 1938–1943. Aufzeichnugen des Majors Engel*, ed. Hildegard von Kotze, Stuttgart, 1974, p. 91 (15.11.40).

105. *Lagevorträge*, pp. 151–5, 160–63 (14.11.40); Schreiber, 'Der Mittelmeerraum', pp. 86–7.

106. Schreiber, 'Der Mittelmeerraum', p. 87.

107. Below, p. 253.

108. *KTB d. OKW*, vol. 1, pp. 208–9 (5.12.40).

109. *KTB d. OKW*, vol. 1, p. 222 (10.12.40); *Hitlers Weisungen*, p. 90.

110. *KTB d. OKW*, vol. 1, p. 255 (9.1.41). On 28 January (p. 284), he accepted

that there was no possibility of renewing preparations to take Gibraltar, which he momentarily envisaged taking place in April, because troops were needed for 'Barbarossa'. Even in mid-February, he was exhorting Franco to reconsider his decision not to enter the war (Domarus, p. 1666).

111. *Hitlers Weisungen*, p. 96.

112. In the eyes of the navy leadership, the chance to exploit British weakness in the Mediterranean was still not exhausted in spring 1941, following the German landing in Crete and Rommel's successes in north Africa (*Lagevorträge*, pp. 240, 258–62 (6.6.41); Gruchmann, pp. 471–4). By this time, however, there was not a shadow of doubt about Hitler's priorities. Preparations for the imminent 'Barbarossa' took such precedence that, unlike autumn 1940, any strategic alternative existed purely in theory.

113. *KTB d. OKW*, vol. 1, p. 996 (17.12.40).

114. Hitler pointed this out to Mussolini during their meeting on 4 October 1940 (*Staatsmänner*, p. 115).

115. Paul Schmidt, *Statist auf diplomatischer Bühne 1923–45. Erlebnisse des Chefdolmetchers im Auswärtigen Amt mit den Staatsmännern Europas*, Bonn, 1953, pp. 516–17; *Heeresadjutant*, p. 88 (28.10.40).

116. By the end of 1940, in duress, Mussolini reversed his earlier objections to an increase in French strength in the Mediterranean and had come to favour an arrangement between Germany and France (Weinberg, *A World at Arms*, p. 214 n. a). But by then the strategic situation was different to that of the preceding October, when Hitler and Pétain had met. Most importantly, the decision to attack Russia had been confirmed. The Mediterranean was now for Hitler – though this had not always been the case – a sideshow.

117. This remained his view as the end of the Third Reich approached (*Hitlers politisches Testament*, pp. 78–80). Hitler, unlike others in the Nazi leadership, was never interested in increased trade with the Soviet Union as an alternative to military conquest. On this, see the interesting study by Heinrich Schwendemann, *Die wirtschaftliche Zusammenarbeit zwischen dem Deutschen Reich und der Sowjetunion von 1939 bis 1941. Alternative zu Hitlers Ostprogramm?*, Berlin, 1993, esp. pp. 355–7.

118. Warlimont, p. 115.

119. Warlimont, pp. 257–8, for Jodl's uncritical admiration of Hitler; see also Kershaw, *Hitler, 1936–1945*, p. 533.

120. Halder, *Kriegstagebuch*, vol. 2, p. 21 (13.7.40).

121. Alfred Kube, *Pour le mérite und Hakenkreuz. Hermann Göring im Dritten Reich*, Munich, 1986, pp. 336–7.

122. Warlimont, p. 118.

123. There is, therefore, a certain unreality to Magenheimer's conclusion, pp. 69–71 (quotation p. 70), that 'the critical omission on the German side . . . was not to have shifted the temporary strategic focus to the Mediterranean in the summer of 1940'.

124. Fedor von Bock, *The War Diary 1939–1945*, ed. Klaus Gerbet, Atglen, Pa., 1996, pp. 197–8 (1.2.41); *KTB d. OKW*, vol. 1, p. 300 (3.2.41).

CHAPTER 3. TOKYO, SUMMER AND AUTUMN 1940

1. Ian Nish, *Japanese Foreign Policy 1869–1942*, London, 1977, pp. 133–42; Akira Iriye, *The Origins of the Second World War in Asia and the Pacific*, London/New York, 1987, pp. 2–4; Zara Steiner, *The Lights that Failed. European International History 1919–1933*, Oxford, 2005, pp. 375–7, 708–10.

2. See Akira Iriye, *Across the Pacific. An Inner History of American-East Asian Relations*, New York, 1967, pp. 208–9; Roger D. Spotswood, 'Japan's Southward Advance as an Issue in Japanese-American Relations, 1940–1941', unpublished Ph.D. thesis, University of Washington, 1974, p. 20. Joyce C. Lebra, *Japan's Greater East Asia Co-Prosperity Sphere in World War II. Selected Readings and Documents*, Kuala Lumpur, 1975, pp. 3–54, provides extracts from contemporary writings illustrating differing concepts of Japanese economic dominance of the region.

3. For a detailed analysis of the background, from Japanese sources, Seki Hiroharu, 'The Manchurian Incident 1931', in James William Morley (ed.), *Japan Erupts. The London Naval Conference and the Manchurian Incident 1928–1932*, New York, 1984, pp. 139–230.

4. For an extensive analysis of the way the field army's expansionist aims propelled Japan towards war with China, see Shimada Toshihiko, 'Designs on North China 1933–1937', in James William Morley (ed.), *The China Quagmire. Japan's Expansion on the Asian Continent, 1933–1941*, New York, 1983, pp. 11–230.

5. Text in *Political Strategy Prior to the Outbreak of War (Part I)*, Office of the Chief of Military History, Department of the Army, Japanese Monographs, 144, appendix 1 (http://www.ibiblio.org/pha/monos/144/144appo1.html); Iriye, *Origins*, pp. 34–5; Herbert P. Bix, *Hirohito and the Making of Modern Japan*, London, 2001, pp. 308–12.

6. See Joseph C. Grew, *Ten Years in Japan*, New York, 1944, pp. 169–78, the account of the American ambassador, who was on the spot; also Iriye, *Origins*, p. 33; Bix, pp. 297–306; Andrew Gordon, *A Modern History of Japan from Tokugawa Times to the Present*, New York/Oxford, 2003, p. 198; and for a vivid description, John Toland, *The Rising Sun. The Decline and Fall of the Japanese Empire, 1936–1945*, New York, 1970, Modern Library edn., 2003, ch. 1.

7. Imai Seiichi, 'Cabinet, Emperor, and Senior Statesmen', in Dorothy Borg and Shumpei Okamoto (eds.), *Pearl Harbor as History. Japanese-American Relations 1931–1941*, New York, 1973, p. 66; Iriye, *Origins*, p. 34. Nish, pp. 215–16, brings out the way in which the Foreign Ministry was 'outpointed' by the military and started to play a less significant role. According to Robert J. C. Butow, *Tojo and the Coming of the War*, Princeton, 1961, p. 86, the Cabinet of Hirota Koki,

which entered office after the attempted coup of February 1936, 'can hardly be regarded as an unwilling tool of the imperial army and navy'.

8. Iriye, *Origins*, pp. 37–9.

9. See, for a detailed analysis, Hata Ikuhiko, 'The Marco Polo Bridge Incident, 1937', in Morley, *The China Quagmire*, pp. 243–86.

10. Bix, p. 320.

11. Quoted in Bix, p. 322.

12. Bix, pp. 325–6.

13. Iriye, *Origins*, p. 45.

14. Bix, p. 332.

15. Bix, pp. 334–5.

16. See Bix, pp. 340–41.

17. Iriye, *Across the Pacific*, pp. 178–9.

18. *Political Strategy Prior to the Outbreak of War (Part I)*, Japanese Monographs, 144, appendix 11 (http://www.ibiblio.org/pha/monos/144/144app11.html).

19. Bix, p. 345.

20. Bix, p. 346.

21. Iriye, *Origins*, p. 67.

22. Iriye, *Origins*, p. 68.

23. Akira Iriye, *Power and Culture. The Japanese-American War, 1941–1945*, Cambridge, Mass., 1981, p. 6.

24. Bix, p. 353.

25. David Bergamini, *Japan's Imperial Conspiracy*, New York, 1971, vol. 2, p. 908; Iriye, *Origins*, pp. 76–7; Spotswood, pp. 32–4.

26. John P. Fox, *Germany and the Far Eastern Crisis 1931–1938. A Study in Diplomacy and Ideology*, Oxford, 1982, ch. 10; Hartmut Bloß, 'Deutsche Chinapolitik im Dritten Reich', in Manfred Funke (ed.), *Hitler, Deutschland und die Mächte. Materialien zur Außenpolitik des Dritten Reichs*, Düsseldorf, 1978, pp. 419–23.

27. Sheffield University Library, Wolfson Microfilm 431, Diary of Marquis Kido Koichi (American translation of extracts for use in the Tokyo War Crimes Trials), doc. no. 1632BB (1), 22.8.39. For Kido, see Bix, pp. 370–1; and Toland, *The Rising Sun*, p. 79.

28. Iriye, *Origins*, p. 81; Nish, p. 231.

29. Iriye, *Origins*, pp. 83–4.

30. James William Morley (ed.), *The Fateful Choice. Japan's Advance into Southeast Asia, 1939–1941*, New York, 1980 (translated essays by Hosoya Chihiro on 'Northern Defence', Nagaoka Shinjiro on 'Economic Demands on the Dutch East Indies', Hata Ikuhiko on 'The Army's Move into Northern Indochina', Nagaoka Shinjiro on 'The Drive into Southern Indochina and Thailand' and Tsunoda Jun on 'The Navy's Role in the Southern Strategy', based upon Japanese documentation), p. 121.

31. Gordon, pp. 92–3; Misawa Shigeo and Minomiya Saburo, 'The Role of the Diet and Political Parties', in Borg and Okamoto, *Pearl Harbor as History*, pp. 321–4.

32. Shigeo and Saburo, pp. 324–6; Gordon, pp. 126–31, 162–73, 187–9.

33. Gordon, p. 333.

34. Gordon, p. 193.

35. Shigeo and Saburo, pp. 326–7.

36. Eugene Sathre, 'Communication and Conflict: Japanese Foreign Policy leading to the Pacific War', unpublished Ph.D. thesis, University of Minnesota, 1978, pp. 43–50.

37. The above all based upon Nobutaka Ike (ed.), *Japan's Decision for War. Records of the 1941 Policy Conferences*, Stanford, Calif., 1967, pp. xv–xix. See also Butow, pp. 149–50.

38. Ike, p. xviii; F. C. Jones, *Japan's New Order in East Asia. Its Rise and Fall, 1937–45*, Oxford, 1954, pp. 7–9.

39. Nazli Choucri, Robert C. North and Susumu Yamakage, *The Challenge of Japan before World War II and After*, London/New York, 1992, p. 165.

40. Bix, pp. 10–11; Jones, pp. 11–12.

41. Lesley Connors, *The Emperor's Adviser. Saionji Kinmochi and Pre-War Japanese Politics*, London, 1987, pp. 186–99.

42. Iriye, *Origins*, pp. 86–7, 99–100.

43. Yoshitake Oka, *Konoe Fumimaro. A Political Biography*, Tokyo, 1983, pp. 10–13. For a brief description of Konoe's early career and the development of his ideas, see also Seiichi, pp. 66–8.

44. Oka, pp. 36–8.

45. Toland, *The Rising Sun*, p. 73.

46. Oka, pp. 46–7; Murakami Hyoe and Thomas J. Harper (eds.), *Great Historical Figures of Japan*, Tokyo, 1978, p. 299.

47. Oka, pp. 75, 78.

48. Bix, pp. 344–6.

49. Oka, pp. 84–5. In a proclamation on 1 August 1940, Matsuoka Yosuke stated that 'our present foreign policy is to establish the Greater East Asia Co-Prosperity Sphere', which was 'the same as the New Order in East Asia Sphere or the Security Sphere, and its scope includes southern areas such as the Netherlands Indies and French Indo-China; the three nations of Japan, Manchuria and China are one link'. Achieving this would 'avoid all obstacles' to the 'completion of dealing with the China Incident' (Lebra, pp. 71–2).

50. Toland, *The Rising Sun*, p. 61.

51. Iriye, *Origins*, p. 106.

52. Quoted in Butow, pp. 141–2.

53. Cordell Hull, *The Memoirs of Cordell Hull*, New York, 1948, vol. 1, p. 902.

54. Grew, p. 328 (1.9.40). He swiftly came to see in Matsuoka, nevertheless, the

image of 'a nation determined to achieve its objectives at all cost' (Waldo H. Heinrichs, Jr., *American Ambassador. Joseph C. Grew and the Development of the United States Diplomatic Tradition*, Boston, 1966, pp. 243–5).

55. Oka, pp. 97–8.

56. Quoted in Bix, p. 374.

57. Iriye, *Origins*, p. 106.

58. Butow, pp. 143–7 (and pp. 115–19 for his earlier appointment as Vice-Minister of War under the first Konoe government); see also the pen-portrait of Tojo in Mark Weston, *Giants of Japan. The Lives of Japan's Greatest Men and Women*, New York/Tokyo/London, 1999, pp. 182–9.

59. James William Morley (ed.), *Deterrent Diplomacy. Japan, Germany, and the USSR 1935–1940*, New York, 1976 (translated essays by Ohata Tokushiro on 'The Anti-Comintern Pact, 1935–1939', Hata Ikuhiko on 'The Japanese-Soviet Confrontation, 1935–1939' and Hosoya Chihiro on 'The Tripartite Pact, 1939–1940', based upon Japanese documentation), pp. 229–30.

60. Morley, *Deterrent Diplomacy*, pp. 201–2; Morley, *The Fateful Choice*, pp. 136–7. On the American stance in June and July 1940, in the context of the dramatically altered circumstances following the German victory, see Heinrichs, *American Ambassador*, pp. 309–12.

61. Morley, *Deterrent Diplomacy*, pp. 206–7.

62. Herbert Feis, *The Road to Pearl Harbor. The Coming of the War between the United States and Japan*, Princeton, 1950, pp. 51–2, 66–71; Iriye, *Origins*, pp. 102–3; Spotswood, pp. 95–9.

63. Bergamini, vol. 2, p. 934.

64. Morley, *The Fateful Choice*, pp. 138–9.

65. Morley, *The Fateful Choice*, pp. 158–9.

66. Morley, *The Fateful Choice*, p. 159; Morley, *Deterrent Diplomacy*, pp. 206–7 (quotation p. 207).

67. Iriye, *Origins*, p. 102.

68. Morley, *The Fateful Choice*, pp. 245–6.

69. Morley, *The Fateful Choice*, pp. 241–2.

70. Morley, *The Fateful Choice*, pp. 243–4.

71. Morley, *The Fateful Choice*, p. 250.

72. Morley, *The Fateful Choice*, p. 249.

73. Morley, *The Fateful Choice*, p. 247.

74. Text in Morley, *Deterrent Diplomacy*, pp. 208–9; see also Iriye, p. 102; and Spotswood, pp. 99–104.

75. Morley, *The Fateful Choice*, pp. 247–8. See also, for the army's recognition of a 'golden opportunity', the remarks of Grew, p. 324 (1.8.40).

76. Morley, *The Fateful Choice*, pp. 250–51.

77. Morley, *The Fateful Choice*, pp. 251–2.

78. Sheffield University Library, Wolfson Microfilm 431, Diary of Marquis Kido Koichi, doc. no. 1632X, 8.7.40. And see Butow, p. 141 and Feis, pp. 76–83.

Manoeuvres behind the scenes, orchestrated by Kido, to install Konoe as next Prime Minister had begun as early as May (Tanaka Nobumasa (ed.), *Dokyumento Showa Tenno Dai Nikkan* [Documents of the Showa Emperor], vol. 2, Tokyo, 1988 [in Japanese], p. 113).

79. Kido Diary, doc. no. 1632X, 17.7.40.

80. Bix, pp. 178, 373; Tanaka, pp. 114–17; and Kido Diary, doc. no. 1632X, 17.7.40.

81. The army had been content to leave the selection of a Foreign Minister 'entirely to Prince Konoye' (Kido Diary, doc. no. 1632X, 8.7.40), though in the confidence that he would choose Matsuoka.

82. Oka, p. 98.

83. *DGFP*, 10, doc. 212, p. 278.

84. Text in Morley, *Deterrent Diplomacy*, pp. 218–19; and Spotswood, p. 109.

85. Morley, *Deterrent Diplomacy*, p. 220; see also Iriye, *Origins*, p. 107.

86. Morley, *Deterrent Diplomacy*, pp. 214–15. On 26 July Matsuoka told the American ambassador in Tokyo 'that history is based largely on the operation of blind forces which in a rapidly moving world cannot always be controlled' (Grew, p. 322).

87. Iriye, *Origins*, p. 107; Oka, p. 99; Bix, p. 375; Butow, pp. 148–9.

88. Text in *Political Strategy Prior to Outbreak of War (Part II)*, Japanese Monographs, 146, appendix 2 (http://www.ibiblio.org/pha/monos/146/146app 02.html).

89. Bix, p. 375; Butow, pp. 150–53.

90. Text in *Political Strategy Prior to the Outbreak of War (Part II)*, Japanese Monographs, 146, appendix 3 (http://www.ibiblio.org/pha/monos/146/ 146pp03.html).

91. Morley, *The Fateful Choice*, p. 141.

92. Morley, *The Fateful Choice*, pp. 254–7, 261.

93. Morley, *The Fateful Choice*, pp. 256–60.

94. Morley, *The Fateful Choice*, pp. 259–61.

95. Text in Morley, *Deterrent Diplomacy*, pp. 283–8, and see p. 221.

96. Grew, pp. 324–5 (1.8.40); see also his entry of 2.7.40, pp. 320–21.

97. Theo Sommer, *Deutschland und Japan zwischen den Mächten 1935–1940. Vom Antikominternpakt zum Dreimächtepakt*, Tübingen, 1962, pp. 384–5; Morley, *Deterrent Diplomacy*, p. 227. The 'destroyer deal' is more fully examined in Chapter 5 below.

98. Sommer, pp. 386–7; Morley, *Deterrent Diplomacy*, pp. 225–6.

99. *Matsuoka Yosuke. The Man and his Life*, Tokyo, 1974 [in Japanese], pp. 768–9.

100. Morley, *The Fateful Choice*, pp. 264–5. Matsuoka, and some in the army leadership, were initially suspicious that Yoshida's illness was no more than a 'diplomatic' one (*Matsuoka Yosuke*, pp. 768–9).

101. Morley, *The Fateful Choice*, pp. 229–30, 266–8; Oka, p. 104.

102. Morley, *Deterrent Diplomacy*, pp. 228–33.

103. Morley, *Deterrent Diplomacy*, pp. 232–7; Spotswood, pp. 127–9.

104. Michael Bloch, *Ribbentrop*, paperback edn., London, 1994, p. 303.

105. Sommer, p. 387.

106. Quoted in Morley, *Deterrent Diplomacy*, p. 233.

107. Quoted in Morley, *Deterrent Diplomacy*, p. 239.

108. Quoted in Morley, *Deterrent Diplomacy*, p. 241.

109. Butow, p. 163.

110. Quoted in Morley, *Deterrent Diplomacy*, p. 238.

111. Quoted in Morley, *Deterrent Diplomacy*, pp. 238–9.

112. Ike, pp. 4–13, for notes of the Conference.

113. Quoted in Morley, *Deterrent Diplomacy*, p. 248.

114. Bix, p. 382.

115. Oka, p. 105.

116. Fully examined in Sommer, pp. 394–426, and Morley, *Deterrent Diplomacy*, pp. 233–54.

117. Text in *Political Strategy Prior to the Outbreak of War (Part II)*, Japanese Monographs, 146, pp. 23–30 (http://www.ibiblio.org/pha/monos/146/146chap1.html). See also Feis, pp. 118–19. Butow, pp. 179–80, points out that no precise minutes were taken, as was normal in such conferences, and that the secretaries recorded the gist of what was said. Nevertheless, there seems no reason to doubt that the words cited represented the views of Konoe, Matsuoka and Tojo. Grew, p. 339 (2.10.40), recorded his impressions of extensive lack of enthusiasm for the pact.

118. Iriye, *Origins*, p. 116.

119. Text in Morley, *Deterrent Diplomacy*, pp. 298–9; and *DGFP*, 11, doc. 118, p. 204.

120. The United States regarded the pact as no more than confirmation of a relationship which had in practice long existed (Hull, vol. 1, p. 909).

121. Iriye, *Origins*, p. 117; Morley, *The Fateful Choice*, pp. 188–203.

122. Feis, pp. 105–9; William Carr, *Poland to Pearl Harbor. The Making of the Second World War*, London, 1985, pp. 109–10; Spotswood, pp. 157–63. The American ambassador in Tokyo, Joseph Grew, only became aware of the possibility of a deal between Japan and Germany as late as mid-September and remained largely in the dark until the Tripartite Pact was actually signed (Heinrichs, *American Ambassador*, p. 319).

123. Iriye, *Origins*, p. 117.

124. Carr, pp. 110–11.

125. That control over south-east Asia was the pivotal issue, with Japanese leaders determined to expand and control the area, and American policy-makers increasingly resolute in their resistance, is particularly emphasized by Iriye, *Across the Pacific*, p. 201, and Spotswood, pp. 13–18.

126. Morley, *The Fateful Choice*, p. 274; also quoted by Bergamini, vol. 2, p. 952;

and see Weston, p. 193. Yamamoto had told Prince Konoe in August 1940 that he had no expectation of success in a war that lasted longer than twelve months (Bergamini, vol. 2, p. 958).

127. Carr, pp. 107–8.

128. Iriye, *Origins*, p. 116.

129. Measured by gross national product, of the 'great powers' only Italy was weaker than Japan in 1940. Japan had also the smallest of the armed forces (apart from the United States, which was only just beginning to rearm), but spent almost as high a proportion of her national income on armaments as Germany (Mark Harrison (ed.), *The Economics of World War II. Six Great Powers in International Comparison*, Cambridge, 1998, pp. 10, 14, 21). Akira Hara, 'Japan: Guns before Rice' (pp. 224–67 of the same volume) brings out the important point (p. 225) that Japan's economy had been organized on a wartime basis since the beginning of the conflict with China in 1937.

130. Carr, p. 111.

CHAPTER 4. ROME, SUMMER AND AUTUMN 1940

1. Quoted in R. J. B. Bosworth, *Mussolini*, London, 2002, p. 369.

2. MacGregor Knox, *Common Destiny. Dictatorship, Foreign Policy, and War in Fascist Italy and Nazi Germany*, Cambridge, 2000, pp. 61, 67–9.

3. Stanley G. Payne, *A History of Fascism 1914–45*, London, 1995, p. 383; I. C. B. Dear and M. R. D. Foot (eds.), *The Oxford Companion to the Second World War*, Oxford/New York, 1995, p. 583.

4. In 1928 Hitler had written a lengthy tract – in the event left unpublished – setting out his policy renouncing claims on South Tyrol in the interests of an alliance with Italy. He had already, two years earlier, taken issue with those on the German nationalist Right using the issue of South Tyrol for anti-Italian agitation. See *Hitler's Second Book. The Unpublished Sequel to Mein Kampf*, ed. Gerhard L. Weinberg, New York, 2003, pp. xvi–xxi, and Ian Kershaw, *Hitler, 1889–1936: Hubris*, London, 1998, pp. 291–2.

5. Knox, *Common Destiny*, p. 96.

6. Denis Mack Smith, *Mussolini*, paperback edn., London, 1983, p. 235.

7. Alberto Aquarone, 'Public Opinion in Italy before the Outbreak of World War II', in Roland Sarti (ed.), *The Ax Within. Italian Fascism in Action*, New York, 1974, p. 212; Paul Corner, 'Everyday Fascism in the 1930s. Centre and Periphery in the Decline of Mussolini's Dictatorship', *Contemporary European History*, 15 (2006), pp. 215–18, pointing out the negative effect on the Duce cult of the alliance with Nazi Germany and the growing likelihood of war.

8. Quoted from MacGregor Knox, *Mussolini Unleashed 1939–1941. Politics and Strategy in Fascist Italy's Last War*, paperback edn., Cambridge, 1986, pp. 39–40.

9. *Ciano's Diary 1939–1943*, ed. Malcolm Muggeridge, London, 1947, pp. 45–6.

10. Ray Moseley, *Mussolini's Shadow. The Double Life of Count Galeazzo Ciano*, New Haven/London, 1999, p. 55.

11. Quoted in Knox, *Mussolini Unleashed*, p. 41.

12. *Ciano's Diary*, p. 90.

13. See Mario Toscano, *The Origins of the Pact of Steel*, Baltimore, 1967, chs. 4–5.

14. H. James Burgwyn, *Italian Foreign Policy in the Interwar Period 1918–1940*, Westport, Conn., 1997, p. 194.

15. Knox, *Mussolini Unleashed*, p. 42; Burgwyn, p. 194.

16. *DGFP*, 6, pp. 574–80; and see Gerhard L. Weinberg, *The Foreign Policy of Hitler's Germany. Starting World War II, 1937–1939*, Chicago/London, 1980, pp. 579–81 (and p. 579 n. 188 for the authenticity of the document, which had been called into question at the Nuremberg Trial and afterwards).

17. *Ciano's Diary*, p. 116.

18. *Ciano's Diary*, pp. 122–3.

19. Quotations in *Ciano's Diary*, pp. 123–5.

20. *Ciano's Diary*, pp. 126–30.

21. *Ciano's Diary*, p. 133.

22. *DGFP*, 7, doc. 271, p. 286 (25.8.39); Burgwyn, pp. 203–4.

23. *DGFP*, 7, doc. 317, p. 323; Burgwyn, pp. 204–5.

24. *Ciano's Diary*, pp. 134–6; Enno von Rintelen, *Mussolini als Bundesgenosse. Erinnerungen des deutschen Militärattachés in Rom 1936–1943*, Tübingen/Stuttgart, 1951, p. 71; Knox, *Mussolini Unleashed*, p. 43. On the concept of 'non-belligerency', see Neville Wylie (ed.), *European Neutrals and Non-Belligerents during the Second World War*, Cambridge, 2002, p. 4.

25. What follows relies on Knox, *Mussolini Unleashed*, pp. 16–19; and MacGregor Knox, *Hitler's Italian Allies. Royal Armed Forces, Fascist Regime, and the War of 1940–1943*, Cambridge, 2000, pp. 29–32.

26. Knox, *Mussolini Unleashed*, p. 10.

27. Denis Mack Smith, *Mussolini as a Military Leader*, Reading 1974, pp. 17, 28–9. Nor – what became harmful to accurate evaluation – was there an integrated intelligence service (which Mussolini saw as a threat to his own power) (MacGregor Knox, 'Fascist Italy Assesses its Enemies, 1935–1940', in Ernest R. May (ed.), *Knowing One's Enemies. Intelligence Assessment before the Two World Wars*, Princeton, 1983, pp. 347–72, at p. 372).

28. For the following, see Knox, *Mussolini Unleashed*, pp. 18–30; and Knox, *Common Destiny*, pp. 152–7.

29. Quoted in Knox, *Common Destiny*, p. 155; and Knox, *Mussolini Unleashed*, p. 10. Measured by gross national product, Italy was in economic terms by far the weakest of the major belligerent powers in 1940 and her military spending only a third as high as Germany's (Mark Harrison (ed.), *The Economics of World War II. Six Great Powers in International Comparison*, Cambridge, 1998, pp. 10, 21). In her contribution to this volume (pp. 177–223), Vera Zamagni, 'Italy: How

to Lose the War and Win the Peace', concludes that Italy's level of development did not allow the country to fight the war effectively, let alone to win it.

30. For the concept, in its application to Hitler's regime, see Peter Hüttenberger, 'Nationalsozialistische Polykratie', *Geschichte und Gesellschaft*, 2 (1976), pp. 417–42; and the summary in Ian Kershaw, *The Nazi Dictatorship. Problems and Perspectives of Interpretation*, 4th edn., London, 2000, pp. 58–9.

31. Payne, pp. 119, 122.

32. Payne, p. 117.

33. Adrian Lyttleton, *The Seizure of Power*, London, 1973, pp. 72–5, 175; Bosworth, *Mussolini*, pp. 154–5, 160–65.

34. Payne, pp. 116, 118–19.

35. Martin Broszat, *Der Staat Hitlers*, Munich, 1969, p. 262; Dieter Rebentisch, *Führerstaat und Verwaltung im Zweiten Weltkrieg*, Stuttgart, 1989, p. 422.

36. Maurizio Bach, *Die charismatischen Führerdiktaturen. Drittes Reich und italienischer Faschismus im Vergleich ihrer Herrschaftsstrukturen*, Baden-Baden, 1990, p. 111.

37. Payne, p. 221.

38. See Corner, esp. pp. 199, 206–17.

39. See Piero Melograni, 'The Cult of the Duce in Mussolini's Italy', *Journal of Contemporary History*, 11 (1976), pp. 221–37.

40. S. J. Woolf (ed.), *Fascism in Europe*, 2nd edn., London, 1981, p. 62.

41. Payne, pp. 219–20.

42. Knox, *Common Destiny*, p. 96; Burgwyn, p. 120; John Whittam, *Fascist Italy*, Manchester, 1995, p. 113.

43. Knox, *Common Destiny*, p. 96.

44. R. J. B. Bosworth, *Italy, the Least of the Great Powers. Italian Foreign Policy before the First World War*, Cambridge, 1979, esp. chs. 1, 2, 4, emphasizes the the broad consensus among the social and political elites behind Italy's pre-war great-power ambitions.

45. Bosworth, *Mussolini*, p. 255; Mack Smith, *Mussolini as a Military Leader*, p. 7.

46. Mack Smith, *Mussolini as a Military Leader*, pp. 5, 31.

47. Knox, *Mussolini Unleashed*, pp. 10, 18.

48. Bosworth, *Mussolini*, p. 347.

49. See Bosworth, *Mussolini*, p. 246.

50. Burgwyn, pp. 145–6.

51. Mack Smith, *Mussolini as a Military Leader*, p. 5.

52. *Ciano's Diary*, pp. 144–5.

53. Knox, *Mussolini Unleashed*, pp. 55–6.

54. *Ciano's Diary*, pp. 145–6, 151, 157 (quotation p. 157).

55. Knox, *Mussolini Unleashed*, p. 62.

56. Knox, *Mussolini Unleashed*, p. 79.

57. *Ciano's Diary*, p. 163.

58. *Ciano's Diplomatic Papers*, ed. Malcolm Muggeridge, London, 1948, pp. 314–15 (quotation p. 314).

59. Knox, *Mussolini Unleashed*, p. 61.

60. Knox, *Mussolini Unleashed*, p. 68; *DGFP*, 8, doc. 504, pp. 608–9 (letter of Mussolini to Hitler, written on 3.1.40, but sent, with minor amendments, on 5.1.40). Ciano thought Mussolini's letter 'a fine document, full of wisdom and restraint' (*Ciano's Diary*, p. 194).

61. *Ciano's Diary*, p. 164.

62. Knox, *Mussolini Unleashed*, pp. 71, 75.

63. Knox, *Mussolini Unleashed*, pp. 52–4, quotation p. 52.

64. *Ciano's Diary*, pp. 222–3.

65. *Ciano's Diplomatic Papers*, pp. 364–5; *Staatsmänner und Diplomaten bei Hitler. Vertrauliche Aufzeichnungen über die Unterredungen mit Vertretern des Auslandes 1939–1941*, ed. Andreas Hillgruber, paperback edn., Munich, 1969, pp. 52–3, 55, 57; *DGFP*, 9, doc. 1, pp. 1–16.

66. *Ciano's Diary*, pp. 224–5.

67. *Ciano's Diary*, pp. 225–6.

68. Knox, *Mussolini Unleashed*, p. 89; *DDI*, vol. 3, doc. 669, pp. 576–9; Burgwyn, p. 212. See also *Ciano's Diary*, p. 232.

69. *Ciano's Diary*, p. 231.

70. Knox, *Mussolini Unleashed*, pp. 90–91, 93–4.

71. *Ciano's Diary*, pp. 234, 235, 236 and 243, and see Knox, *Mussolini Unleashed*, p. 108.

72. *Ciano's Diary*, p. 221.

73. *Ciano's Diary*, p. 253. For the changing climate of opinion regarding war, see Denis Mack Smith, *Mussolini's Roman Empire*, London/New York, 1976, pp. 209–13.

74. Giuseppe Bottai, *Diario 1935–1944*, ed. Giordano Bruno Guerri, Milan, 1982, p. 192.

75. See Knox, *Common Destiny*, pp. 113–47, for a penetrating analysis of the elements of continuity and break in Mussolini's foreign policy. See also R. J. B. Bosworth, *The Italian Dictatorship. Problems and Perspectives in the Interpretation of Mussolini and Fascism*, London, 1998, pp. 99–101; and Stephen Corrado Azzi, 'The Historiography of Fascist Foreign Policy', *Historical Journal*, 36 (1993), pp. 187–203, at pp. 196–7, 199–200.

76. *Ciano's Diary*, pp. 249, 256.

77. *Ciano's Diary*, p. 250.

78. *Ciano's Diary*, p. 254.

79. *Ciano's Diary*, pp. 249, 250, 261.

80. *Ciano's Diary*, p. 261; Mack Smith, *Mussolini's Roman Empire*, p. 214; Knox, *Mussolini Unleashed*, pp. 104–5.

81. *Ciano's Diary*, p. 258; Knox, *Mussolini Unleashed*, pp. 104–5.

82. *Ciano's Diary*, p. 257.

83. Knox, *Mussolini Unleashed*, pp. 119, 121–3.

84. Moseley, p. 103.

85. Reynolds and Eleanor Packard, *Balcony Empire. Fascist Italy at War*, London, 1943, p. 82.

86. Quoted in Knox, *Mussolini Unleashed*, pp. 111–12.

87. *Ciano's Diary*, p. 255.

88. Max Domarus (ed.), *Hitler. Reden und Proklamationen 1932–1945*, Wiesbaden, 1973, p. 1518; *Ciano's Diary*, p. 257. Knox, *Mussolini Unleashed*, p. 117, has Hitler meeting Alfieri on 31 May at Bad Godesberg, but a Deutsches Nachrichtenbüro report mentions the meeting at the Felsennest the previous day.

89. Knox, *Mussolini Unleashed*, p. 116.

90. Pietro Badoglio, *Italy in the Second World War. Memories and Documents*, London/New York/Toronto, 1948, pp. 14–15.

91. Badoglio, pp. 15–16.

92. Elizabeth Wiskemann, *The Rome–Berlin Axis. A Study of the Relations between Hitler and Mussolini*, London, 1966, p. 255.

93. Knox, *Mussolini Unleashed*, p. 116; *DDI*, vol. 4, doc. 642, pp. 495–7; Badoglio, pp. 15–17.

94. *Ciano's Diary*, pp. 256–7.

95. *Ciano's Diary*, p. 259.

96. Packard and Packard, pp. 85–6.

97. Bottai, p. 193.

98. Badoglio, p. 20.

99. *Ciano's Diary*, p. 264. For the lack of enthusiasm of the crowd, see also Rintelen, p. 85.

100. Luigi Villari, *Italian Foreign Policy under Mussolini*, London, 1959, p. 255.

101. Winston S. Churchill, *The Second World War*, vol. 2: *Their Finest Hour*, London, 1949, p. 106.

102. Knox, *Mussolini Unleashed*, pp. 71–4.

103. Knox, *Mussolini Unleashed*, p. 82.

104. Knox, *Mussolini Unleashed*, p. 107.

105. See Rintelen, p. 93, who states that it would have been more expedient (for German war strategy) had Italy retained her 'non-belligerent' status and the Mediterranean remained out of the direct conflict.

106. Moseley, pp. 106–7.

107. *Ciano's Diary*, p. 266.

108. *Ciano's Diary*, p. 267. Ciano thought the Duce feared 'that the hour of peace is growing near and sees that unattainable dream of his life, glory on the field of battle, fading once again'.

109. *Ciano's Diary*, p. 268; Knox, *Mussolini Unleashed*, pp. 129–30.

110. *Ciano's Diary*, p. 269.

111. *Ciano's Diary*, pp. 270–71.

112. Bottai, p. 204.

113. *Ciano's Diary*, p. 278.

114. Mack Smith, *Mussolini*, p. 294.

115. Knox, *Mussolini Unleashed*, p. 138.

116. Mack Smith, *Mussolini*, p. 295.

117. Knox, *Mussolini Unleashed*, pp. 134–7, 155–65; William L. Langer and S. Everett Gleason, *The Undeclared War, 1940–1941*, New York, 1953.

118. *Ciano's Diary*, p. 87.

119. Mario Cervi, *The Hollow Legions. Mussolini's Blunder in Greece, 1940–1941*, London, 1972, pp. 7–10; also Mack Smith, *Mussolini*, p. 271. Ciano had written in his diary on 12 September 1939 that Mussolini had given 'instructions for an understanding with Greece, a country too poor for us to covet' (*Ciano's Diary*, p. 151).

120. Bottai, p. 191 (25.5.40).

121. Bottai, p. 224 (29.6.40).

122. Archivio Centrale, Rome, Carte Graziani, b. 42, Roatta Diary, 7.7.40.

123. *Ciano's Diplomatic Papers*, pp. 377–8; Knox, *Mussolini Unleashed*, pp. 139–42; Cervi, pp. 14–17; Ehrengard Schramm-von Thadden, *Griechenland und die Großmächte im Zweiten Weltkrieg*, Wiesbaden, 1955, pp. 48–51.

124. *DRZW*, vol. 3, 1984, p. 360. Roatta had nevertheless somehow gleaned information of Hitler's comment to Ciano that it was essential not to disturb the peace in the Balkans, from which the deduction was easily reached 'that we should do nothing against Yugoslavia' (Roatta Diary, 14.7.40).

125. *Ciano's Diary*, p. 281.

126. Knox, *Mussolini Unleashed*, pp. 166–7.

127. *Ciano's Diary*, pp. 281–2.

128. *Ciano's Diary*, p. 282.

129. Cervi, pp. 18–23; Knox, *Mussolini Unleashed*, pp. 167–71.

130. Cervi, p. 34; Moseley, p. 114.

131. *Ciano's Diary*, pp. 282–3.

132. *Ciano's Diary*, p. 283.

133. The anti-Italian feeling intensified when an old Greek cruiser, the *Helli*, was torpedoed on 15 August by a submarine that everyone presumed – correctly, as it turned out – to be Italian. The truth about the incident only emerged long after the war. It had been instigated, on his own initiative, by one of the Duce's particularly wild underlings, the notably arrogant and impetuous Fascist veteran Cesare Maria De Vecchi di Val Cismon, governor of the Italian islands in the Aegean (Cervi, pp. 29–32).

134. Quoted in Cervi, pp. 22–3; varying trans. in *DGFP*, 10, doc. 333, pp. 471–2.

135. *Ciano's Diplomatic Papers*, p. 381.

136. *DRZW*, vol. 3, p. 361; Knox, *Mussolini Unleashed*, p. 174.

137. Cervi, p. 23.

138. *Ciano's Diary*, p. 284.

139. Knox, *Mussolini Unleashed*, pp. 175–6.

140. *DDI*, vol. 5, p. 436; Knox, *Mussolini Unleashed*, pp. 176–7; *DRZW*, vol. 3, p. 365; Cervi, pp. 24, 42–3; Roatta Diary, 22.8.40.

141. *Ciano's Diary*, p. 285.

142. *Ciano's Diplomatic Papers*, p. 385.

143. Knox, *Mussolini Unleashed*, pp. 178–9.

144. Quoted in Cervi, p. 43; see also Knox, *Mussolini Unleashed*, p. 181.

145. Knox, *Mussolini Unleashed*, p. 186.

146. Quoted in Cervi, p. 45.

147. Ciano's phrase: *Ciano's Diary*, p. 291.

148. Enno von Rintelen, the German military attaché in Rome, had already indicated in early August that, though the offensive against England was in full preparation, its realization presented 'serious difficulties' (Roatta Diary, 7.8.40).

149. Cited in Knox, *Mussolini Unleashed*, p. 191.

150. *Ciano's Diplomatic Papers*, p. 391.

151. *Ciano's Diplomatic Papers*, p. 392; Schramm-von Thadden, p. 88; *DGFP*, 11, doc. 73, p. 121; *DRZW*, vol. 3, p. 369.

152. Moseley, p. 115, citing the comments of General Puntoni, the aide-de-camp to the King, that 'Ciano showed an impatience to give a lesson to Greece for its conduct which, he says, is ambiguous'.

153. Schramm-von Thadden, pp. 88–90; *DRZW*, vol. 3, p. 370; Knox, *Mussolini Unleashed*, p. 190.

154. Knox, *Mussolini Unleashed*, pp. 196–7.

155. Knox, *Mussolini Unleashed*, p. 197.

156. Knox, *Mussolini Unleashed*, p. 195.

157. Knox, *Mussolini Unleashed*, pp. 193–4; Renzo De Felice, *Mussolini l'alleato 1940–1945*, vol. 1, Turin, 1990, pp. 295–6; Cervi, pp. 56–7; *DRZW*, vol. 3, p. 372.

158. *Ciano's Diary*, p. 294.

159. The support lacked real warmth, however. When Ciano had presented, for a country that had scarcely been involved in any fighting, an embarrassingly long list of territorial demands at his meeting with Hitler on 7 July, Ribbentrop, no less, had told him that 'one must be moderate and not have eyes bigger than one's stomach'. Paul Schmidt, *Statist auf diplomatischer Bühne 1923–45. Erlebnisse des Chefdolmetschers im Auswärtigen Amt mit den Staatsmännern Europas*, Bonn, 1953, pp. 502–3; F. W. Deakin, *The Brutal Friendship. Mussolini, Hitler and the Fall of Italian Fascism*, London, 1962, p. 11.

160. *Ciano's Diplomatic Papers*, pp. 395–8; *Ciano's Diary*, p. 296.

161. *Ciano's Diary*, p. 296.

162. Schramm-von Thadden, pp. 88–9, 96. One tantalizing fragment of information passed from Soddu to Roatta suggests that Hitler and Mussolini might have agreed privately at the Brenner – though there is no mention in the official minutes of their meeting – that an Italian regiment should accompany the German military mission to Romania (Knox, *Mussolini Unleashed*, p. 202; De Felice,

p. 297). Knox surmises that the comment derived from a private tête-à-tête between Mussolini and Hitler. It seems unlikely, however, that Hitler gave any specific promise. And whether Soddu's information related to a comment made, or an Italian presumption deriving from a misunderstanding, cannot be determined. Ciano denied to Bottai that there had been any discussion at the Brenner of the German move into Romania (Bottai, p. 227).

163. De Felice (p. 297) dismisses the notion that Mussolini could have been taken completely by surprise at the German intervention in Romania, since the Italian Foreign Ministry had been informed of the positive German response to the Romanian 'request' to send troops. He accepts, however, that Mussolini might have been taken by surprise at the speed of the German action. But surely not just that; the manner in which he learned of the arrival of the German detachment could only have infuriated him.

164. *Ciano's Diary*, p. 297.

165. Bottai, p. 227.

166. Knox, *Mussolini Unleashed*, pp. 187, 203, 205–7; *DRZW*, vol. 3, pp. 374–5.

167. Knox, *Mussolini Unleashed*, pp. 207–8.

168. *Ciano's Diary*, p. 297. He told Bottai, however, that the military task would be harder than it would have been in August, when he was urging action, though he was still certain of success (Bottai, p. 227).

169. Churchill, *The Second World War*, vol 2, pp. 383–4; Knox, *Mussolini Unleashed*, pp. 152–3.

170. Knox, *Mussolini Unleashed*, pp. 208–9. A secondary motive was, perhaps, as De Felice, pp. 300–305, suggests, that victory over Greece would ensure him the bargaining power he would need were his fellow dictator to attempt to discuss peace terms with Vichy France at the cost of Italy's territorial claims, as seemed distinctly possible following Hitler's meetings with Laval and Pétain.

171. Knox, *Mussolini Unleashed*, p. 202; Martin van Creveld, *Hitler's Strategy 1940–1941. The Balkan Clue*, Cambridge, 1973, p. 34.

172. Knox, *Mussolini Unleashed*, p. 208.

173. Quoted in Knox, *Mussolini Unleashed*, p. 209; see also Schramm-von Thadden, p. 101; *DRZW*, vol. 3, pp. 376–7; and on the earlier planning, Cervi, pp. 36–7.

174. Cervi, pp. 61–2. A note from Mussolini to Graziani, soon after the Brenner meeting on 4 October, had nevertheless given a first indication that the occupation of the whole of the Greek mainland, not just Ciamuria, would be the objective of an invasion (Creveld, *Hitler's Strategy*, pp. 35–6).

175. Cervi, p. 62; Knox, *Mussolini Unleashed*, p. 210.

176. Schramm-von Thadden, p. 102; Cervi, p. 65; Mack Smith, *Mussolini as a Military Leader*, p. 31. Badoglio, p. 26, has Cavagnari and Pricolo in attendance, but this seems to be an error of memory.

177. Knox, *Mussolini Unleashed*, p. 211.

178. Text in *DDI*, vol. 5, doc. 728, pp. 699–705; reproduced in Schramm-von

Thadden, pp. 209-17; quotations above from the English translation in Cervi, pp. 311-20. See also the summary in Knox, *Mussolini Unleashed*, pp. 211-14 and the caustic comments on the meeting by Mack Smith, *Mussolini's Roman Empire*, pp. 232-3. The account by Sebastiano Visconti Prasca, *Io ho aggredito la Grecia*, 2nd edn., Milan, 1947, pp. 61-70, claimed that the stenograph of the meeting had been 'doctored' by Mussolini and was inaccurate (particularly regarding Visconti Prasca's own contribution), though it confirms the substance and dilettante nature of the discussion.

179. Visconti Prasca, pp. 68-70. The minutes of the meeting on 15 October do not support the statement of Walter Rauscher, *Hitler und Mussolini. Macht, Krieg und Terror*, Graz, 2001, p. 413, that Badoglio spoke out against an operation against Greece, but Mussolini did not want to listen.

180. *Ciano's Diary*, p. 298.

181. Knox, *Mussolini Unleashed*, pp. 214-17.

182. The following based on Knox, *Mussolini Unleashed*, pp. 217-19.

183. Schramm-von Thadden, p. 108.

184. See *Ciano's Diary*, p. 300; and Bottai, p. 229.

185. Quoted in Moseley, p. 117.

186. Quotations in Knox, *Mussolini Unleashed*, pp. 220-21.

187. *Ciano's Diary*, p. 300.

188. *Ciano's Diary*, p. 301.

189. *Heeresadjutant bei Hitler 1938-1943. Aufzeichnungen des Majors Engel*, ed. Hildegard von Kotze, Stuttgart, 1974, p. 88 (28.10.40); Schmidt, pp. 516-17. That Hitler was taken aback and angry about Mussolini's unilateral action against Greece is disputed by Creveld, *Hitler's Strategy*, pp. 39-51, and Martin van Creveld, '25 October 1940. A Historical Puzzle', *Journal of Contemporary History*, 6 (1971), pp. 87-96. But Knox, *Mussolini Unleashed*, p. 346 n. 84 and p. 350 n. 156, has some telling criticism of Creveld's argument.

190. See Ernst von Weizsäcker, *Erinnerungen*, Munich/Leipzig/Freiburg, 1950, pp. 302-3. According to Weizsäcker, State Secretary in the German Foreign Ministry, he had proposed sending an unequivocal warning to Mussolini not to widen the war without German agreement. Ribbentrop, wrote Weizsäcker, approved of this course of action, but Hitler had said that he did not want to restrain his fellow dictator and had indirectly, therefore, opened the way to Mussolini's foolhardy move. Hitler's later professed surprise was, in Weizsäcker's view, feigned. Weizsäcker accepted that Hitler had possibly not been prepared to believe in Mussolini's determination to carry out the attack.

191. Knox, *Mussolini Unleashed*, pp. 222-30; Cervi, pp. 87-92. See also Rintelen, pp. 108-10.

192. Schramm-von Thadden, p. 113, quoting Hitler's letter to Mussolini of 20 November 1940. Crete had been part of German strategic thinking on joint operations with Italy to force the British out of the eastern Mediterranean and north Africa. See Creveld, *Hitler's Strategy*, p. 37.

193. *Ciano's Diplomatic Papers*, p. 400.

194. The Italian record of the meeting is in *Ciano's Diplomatic Papers*, pp. 399–404, the German version in *Staatsmänner*, pp. 150–65. Perhaps in tacit acknowledgement of Hitler's acceptance of his Greek coup, Mussolini was less uncompromising about Vichy France than had been expected (De Felice, p. 307).

195. Mack Smith, *Mussolini*, p. 302; Knox, *Mussolini Unleashed*, p. 236; Bosworth, *Mussolini*, p. 375.

196. Churchill, *The Second World War*, vol. 2, p. 481.

197. Churchill, *The Second World War*, vol. 2, p. 544; Knox, *Mussolini Unleashed*, p. 256 (where the figure of captured Italians is given as 115,000); Lothar Gruchmann, *Der Zweite Weltkrieg*, Munich, 4th edn., 1975, p. 107, gives figures of 130,000 Italian prisoners and 470 tanks together with 1,300 artillery pieces lost between early December and early February. British losses were very small.

198. Before the Italian invasion, Britain had been very lukewarm about both the feasibility and the value of providing military aid to shore up Greece. See John S. Koliopoulos, *Greece and the British Connection 1935–1941*, Oxford, 1977, pp. 134–42. Once the attack had taken place, Britain was anxious to keep the Italo-Greek war going, but was keen to avoid Greece falling under German control. Greece and Crete were seen as important to the vital defence of Egypt. The British aid that could be spared from north Africa was, however, severely limited. See Martin van Creveld, 'Prelude to Disaster. The British Decision to Aid Greece, 1940–41', *Journal of Contemporary History*, 9 (1974), pp. 65–92. There was no major British military presence before a force was rushed from the Middle East at the end of March 1941 in the light of the crisis in Yugoslavia – a move later recognized as a strategic error which allowed the enemy to take the initiative in north Africa. The German attack on Yugoslavia and Greece began on 6 April. By the end of that month some 50,000 British and Commonwealth troops had been evacuated, and a further 7,000 were taken into captivity (Dear and Foot, pp. 102–6).

199. *DRZW*, vol. 3, pp. 421–2.

200. Creveld, *Hitler's Strategy*, pp. 134–5.

201. *The Testament of Adolf Hitler. The Hitler–Bormann Documents February–April 1945*, ed. François Genoud, London, 1961, pp. 65, 72–3, 81.

202. See Andreas Hillgruber, *Hitlers Strategie. Politik und Kriegführung 1940–1941*, 3rd edn., Bonn, 1993, p. 506 n. 26.

203. Rintelen, pp. 90, 92–3, 98–9, emphasizes from the German point of view the strategic mistake of not taking Malta.

204. Rintelen, p. 101.

205. James J. Sadkovich, 'The Italo-Greek War in Context. Italian Priorities and Axis Diplomacy', *Journal of Contemporary History*, 28 (1993), pp. 439–64, at p. 440, and see also p. 455.

206. *Fuehrer Conferences on Naval Affairs 1939–1945*, London, 1990, pp. 154–5.

207. James J. Sadkovich, 'Understanding Defeat. Reappraising Italy's Role in World War II', *Journal of Contemporary History*, 24 (1989), pp. 27–61, at p. 38.

208. Dear and Foot, pp. 504–8. The terrible conditions in Greece at the end of the German occupation, as the descent into civil war was beginning, are vividly described in Mark Mazower, *Inside Hitler's Greece. The Experience of Occupation, 1941–44*, New Haven/London, 1993, pp. 362–73.

209. See Creveld, *Hitler's Strategy*, p. 163.

210. Sadkovich, 'The Italo-Greek War', p. 446.

211. See Knox, *Mussolini Unleashed*, p. 209.

212. Badoglio, p. 29; also cited in Knox, *Mussolini Unleashed*, p. 236; and (with slightly differing translation) Cervi, pp. 149–50.

213. *Ciano's Diary*, p. 298; Knox, *Mussolini Unleashed*, pp. 215–16.

214. Churchill, *The Second World War*, vol. 2, p. 548. The assertion is nevertheless accepted by Brian R. Sullivan, ' "Where One Man, and Only One Man, Led". Italy's Path from Non-Alignment to Non-Belligerency to War, 1937–1940', in Wylie, p. 149.

215. Mack Smith, *Mussolini as a Military Leader*, p. 23, points out how recourse to the 'genius' of the Duce relieved senior officers of a sense of responsibility.

CHAPTER 5. WASHINGTON, DC,
SUMMER 1940–SPRING 1941

1. *The Public Papers and Addresses of Franklin D. Roosevelt*, ed. Samuel I. Rosenman, vol. 9, New York, 1940, p. 517.

2. *Public Opinion 1935–1946*, ed. Hadley Cantrill, Westport, Conn., 1951, p. 971.

3. *Public Opinion*, p. 973.

4. Yale University Library, Henry L. Stimson Diaries 1909–1945, Reel 6, entry for 19.12.40; William L. Langer and S. Everett Gleason, *The Undeclared War, 1940–1941*, New York, 1953, p. 243.

5. Quoted in John Morton Blum, *From the Morgenthau Diaries*, vol. 2: *Years of Urgency, 1938–1941*, Boston, 1965, p. 254 (from the diary entry of 14.5.41).

6. Stimson Diaries, Reel 6, entry for 22.4.41; Langer and Gleason, *The Undeclared War*, p. 442.

7. *Public Papers and Addresses*, vol. 8 (1939), p. 3; Joseph Alsop and Robert Kintner, *American White Paper. The Story of American Diplomacy and the Second World War*, London, 1940, p. 31; Robert Dallek, *Franklin D. Roosevelt and American Foreign Policy, 1932–1945*, New York, 1979, p. 179; Robert A. Divine, *The Reluctant Belligerent. American Entry into World War II*, New York, 1965, p. 56; David M. Kennedy, *Freedom from Fear. The American People in Depression and War, 1929–1945*, New York/Oxford, 1999, p. 427.

8. Quoted in Alsop and Kintner, p. 68.

9. Waldo H. Heinrichs, Jr., *Threshold of War. Franklin D. Roosevelt and American Entry into World War II*, New York/Oxford, 1988, p. 11.

10. Winston S. Churchill, *The Second World War*, vol. 2: *Their Finest Hour*, London, 1949, p. 503.

11. *Churchill and Roosevelt. The Complete Correspondence*, ed. Warren F. Kimball, Princeton, 1984, vol. 1, doc. C-84x, pp. 181–2 (3.5.41); Heinrichs, *Threshold of War*, p. 81.

12. Quoted in Kennedy, p. 496.

13. The title of chapter 3 of Warren F. Kimball, *Forged in War. Churchill, Roosevelt and the Second World War*, London, 1997.

14. Roosevelt's role in the New Deal was indispensable, to the point that his input was decisive to areas of success, while his lack of interest, for example in low-cost housing, and his indecision on industrial strategy helped to determine the inadequacies of the system (Tony Badger, *The New Deal. The Depression Years, 1933–40*, London, 1989, p. 9). Patrick Renshaw, *Franklin D. Roosevelt. Profiles in Power*, London, 2004, p. 107, points out the importance of Roosevelt's 'sheer force of personality' in the recovery of the nation's morale after 1933.

15. See Frank Freidel, *Franklin D. Roosevelt. A Rendezvous with Destiny*, Boston, 1990, p. 252. See also Renshaw, p. 120; and Badger, pp. 94–104.

16. Freidel, p. 287; Kennedy, pp. 347–9; Hugh Brogan, *The Pelican History of the United States of America*, Harmondsworth, 1986, p. 565. The Republicans won eighty seats in the House of Representatives and eight in the Senate. Though the Democrats still controlled both the House and the Senate, cross-party alignments meant that the anti-Roosevelt forces were substantially strengthened.

17. On American loans, and insistence on repayment, see Zara Steiner, *The Lights that Failed. European International History 1919–1933*, Oxford, 2005, pp. 38–9, 185, 188.

18. Divine, *The Reluctant Belligerent*, pp. 8–10; Kennedy, pp. 387–8.

19. Quoted in Kennedy, p. 386.

20. Freidel, p. 171.

21. Divine, *The Reluctant Belligerent*, pp. 17–22.

22. Kennedy, p. 393.

23. Kennedy, pp. 395–6. For American oil and the Abyssinian war, see Cordell Hull, *The Memoirs of Cordell Hull*, New York, 1948, vol. 1, pp. 422–42, esp. Hull's admission on p. 442 that, 'we had gone as far as we could', but although 'exports of oil from the United States to Italy were morally embargoed', the 'United States Government did not have legal authority to impose an oil embargo'. And see Robert A. Divine, *Roosevelt and World War II*, Baltimore, 1969, pp. 11–13.

24. Divine, *The Reluctant Belligerent*, p. 29.

25. Divine, *The Reluctant Belligerent*, pp. 31–3; Cordell Hull laid out the government's position, and defended it, in Hull, vol. 1, pp. 476–85.

26. Kennedy, pp. 398–9.

27. Eric Larrabee, *Commander in Chief. Franklin Delano Roosevelt, his Lieutenants, and their War*, London, 1987, pp. 32–3.

28. The passage containing the quotation is included in Divine, *Roosevelt and World War II*, p. 9; and also quoted in Brogan, p. 569.

29. Quoted in John T. Flynn, *The Roosevelt Myth*, New York, 1956, pp. 90–92.

30. Flynn, p. 92.

31. Divine, *The Reluctant Belligerent*, pp. 48–9.

32. Kennedy, p. 388.

33. For Hull's background and career, see Irwin F. Gellman, *Secret Affairs. Franklin Roosevelt, Cordell Hull, and Sumner Welles*, Baltimore/London, 1995, pp. 20–36.

34. Alsop and Kintner, pp. 14, 25.

35. David Reynolds, *The Creation of the Anglo-American Alliance 1937–1941. A Study in Competitive Co-operation*, Chapel Hill, NC, 1982, p. 27.

36. Quoted in Kennedy, p. 405. In a careful analysis of American public opinion at the time of the quarantine speech, Michael Leigh, *Mobilizing Consent. Public Opinion and American Foreign Policy, 1937–1947*, Westport, Conn., 1976, p. 48, concluded that, far from being constrained by popular attitudes, Roosevelt 'was able to project his own hesitancy on to the mass public', with the result that he 'deferred action even when popular isolationism was crumbling'.

37. Quoted in William R. Rock, *Chamberlain and Roosevelt. British Foreign Policy and the United States, 1937–1940*, Columbus, Ohio, 1988, p. 48.

38. Winston S. Churchill, *The Second World War*, vol. 1: *The Gathering Storm*, London, 1948, p. 229. The initiative had been prompted by Sumner Welles, and taken up by the President, but opposed by the Secretary of State, Cordell Hull. See Sumner Welles, *Seven Major Decisions*, London, 1951, pp. 29–44; and Rock, pp. 51–77.

39. Rock, p. 70.

40. *Foreign Relations of the United States. Diplomatic Papers 1938*, vol. 1, Washington, 1955, p. 688; also quoted in Rock, p. 124, and Divine, *The Reluctant Belligerent*, p. 54. See also Divine, *Roosevelt and World War II*, pp. 20–23, for the impact of the Czech crisis on Roosevelt.

41. Kennedy, p. 419.

42. Kennedy, pp. 416–17.

43. David Reynolds, *From Munich to Pearl Harbor. Roosevelt's America and the Origins of the Second World War*, Chicago, 2001, pp. 42–3.

44. Alsop and Kintner, pp. 25, 41. For Welles's personality and the development of his career, see Gellman, pp. 59–69.

45. Alsop and Kintner, pp. 28–9.

46. For the weight attached to the development of a strong air force, see Michael S. Sherry, *The Rise of American Air Power. The Creation of Armageddon*, New Haven/London, 1987, pp. 76–91.

47. Freidel, pp. 307–13.

48. Alsop and Kintner, pp. 57–9.

49. Divine, *The Reluctant Belligerent*, pp. 56–63.

50. Ian Kershaw, *Hitler, 1936–1945. Nemesis*, London, 2000, p. 189.

51. Quoted in William L. Langer and S. Everett Gleason, *The Challenge to Isolation, 1937–1940*, New York, 1952, pp. 160–61.

52. Freidel, p. 318.

53. *FDR's Fireside Chats*, ed. Russell D. Buhite and David W. Levy, New York, 1992, pp. 148–51.

54. Quoted in Alsop and Kintner, p. 31.

55. Quoted in Alsop and Kintner, pp. 85–6.

56. Alsop and Kintner, p. 86.

57. Alsop and Kintner, pp. 81–2, 90; Divine, *The Reluctant Belligerent*, p. 76.

58. Alsop and Kintner, p. 83.

59. Kennedy, p. 432.

60. Divine, *The Reluctant Belligerent*, p. 67.

61. Quoted in Reynolds, *From Munich to Pearl Harbor*, p. 65.

62. Divine, *The Reluctant Belligerent*, pp. 66–73.

63. Divine, *The Reluctant Belligerent*, p. 35.

64. Kennedy, p. 433; Freidel, p. 323.

65. Sumner Welles, *The Time for Decision*, London, 1944, pp. 61–118. Welles's original dispatch from London (12.3.40) conveyed less enthusiasm than his later published account. It indicated that Churchill had 'consumed a good many whiskeys' and was far from sober as he delivered a monologue – 'a cascade of oratory', though constituting merely a 'rehash' of views which he had already published – that lasted one hour and fifty minutes (http://www.fdrlibrary.marist.edu/psf/box6/a73g02.html).

66. P. M. H. Bell, *A Certain Eventuality ... Britain and the Fall of France*, London, 1974, p. 39.

67. Welles, *Time for Decision*, pp. 118–19.

68. *For the President: Personal and Secret. Correspondence between Franklin D. Roosevelt and William C. Bullitt*, ed. Orville H. Bullitt, London, 1973, p. 416.

69. Langer and Gleason, *Challenge*, p. 473. Dallek, p. 222, has even smaller numbers.

70. Langer and Gleason, *Challenge*, p. 462.

71. Freidel, p. 331.

72. Reynolds, *From Munich to Pearl Harbor*, p. 78.

73. Churchill, *The Second World War*, vol. 2, pp. 103–4; Winston S. Churchill, *Great War Speeches*, paperback edn., London, 1957, pp. 23–4; and quoted in Langer and Gleason, *Challenge*, p. 497.

74. Kennedy, p. 440.

75. Reynolds, *From Munich to Pearl Harbor*, p. 81.

76. John Lukacs, *Five Days in London. May 1940*, paperback edn., New Haven/London, 2001, pp. 75–6.

77. Alsop and Kintner, pp. 104–10.

78. James MacGregor Burns, *Roosevelt. The Soldier of Freedom 1940–1945*, London, 1971, p. 9.

79. Burns, p. 61.

80. Robert E. Sherwood, *The White House Papers of Harry L. Hopkins*, vol. 1, London, 1948, pp. 202–19, has a good description of Roosevelt's working environment. See also Burns, pp. 58–62; Alsop and Kintner, p. 23; and Larrabee, pp. 26–7.

81. Richard M. Pious, *The American Presidency*, New York, 1979, p. 31.

82. Larrabee, p. 42; Divine, *The Reluctant Belligerent*, p. 88.

83. Pious, pp. 53–5.

84. Pious, pp. 142, 154–5.

85. Kimball, *Forged in War*, pp. 18–19.

86. Heinrichs, *Threshold of War*, pp. 17, 19.

87. Stimson Diaries, Reel 6, entries for 7.11.40, 18.12.40.

88. Pious, pp. 240–42.

89. Langer and Gleason, *The Undeclared War*, p. 181.

90. Langer and Gleason, *Challenge*, p. 472.

91. Freidel, pp. 341–2.

92. Langer and Gleason, *Challenge*, p. 478; Freidel, p. 342; Blum, pp. 147–8.

93. Freidel, p. 324; Blum, p. 264.

94. Langer and Gleason, *The Undeclared War*, p. 181.

95. Langer and Gleason, *Challenge*, p. 674; quotation from Langer and Gleason, *The Undeclared War*, p. 181.

96. Langer and Gleason, *Challenge*, p. 478.

97. Sherwood, *White House Papers*, vol. 1, pp. 164–5; Freidel, p. 342.

98. Blum, p. 165; Flynn, pp. 221–2.

99. Burns, p. 39; Blum, p. 166.

100. Blum, p. 166; Larrabee, p. 45; Burns, p. 38.

101. Kimball, *Forged in War*, p. 53.

102. Heinrichs, *Threshold of War*, p. 18.

103. Larrabee, p. 45.

104. Larrabee, p. 98; Kennedy, pp. 430–31.

105. Larrabee, p. 121.

106. Quoted in Freidel, p. 339.

107. Blum, pp. 166–7.

108. Blum, p. 44.

109. Blum, p. 44; William Carr, *Poland to Pearl Harbor. The Making of the Second World War*, London, 1985, p. 48.

110. Heinrichs, *Threshold of War*, p. 20.

111. See Gellman, pp. 2, 226–34.

112. Sherwood, *White House Papers*, vol. 1, pp. 3–13; Larrabee, pp. 25–6; Kennedy, pp. 145–6, 161; Freidel, p. 347; quoted phrase, Burns, p. 60.

113. Heinrichs, *Threshold of War*, p. 20, for the above paragraph and for the quotation.

114. Divine, *The Reluctant Belligerent*, p. 99; Reynolds, *From Munich to Pearl Harbor*, p. 94.

115. Divine, *The Reluctant Belligerent*, pp. 86–8; Reynolds, *From Munich to Pearl Harbor*, pp. 92–4.

116. Langer and Gleason, *Challenge*, p. 479. This was the only, short-lived, period when opinion surveys indicated that a majority of Americans thought Germany would win the war. See the graph in Steven Casey, *Cautious Crusade. Franklin D. Roosevelt, American Public Opinion, and the War against Nazi Germany*, Oxford/New York, 2001, p. 26.

117. Quoted in Kimball, *Forged in War*, pp. 15, 35.

118. Kimball, *Forged in War*, pp. 13, 22–3; Freidel, p. 332; Reynolds, *Anglo-American Alliance*, p. 114. For Hopkins's disparagement of Roosevelt's 'vile' cocktails, see Sherwood, *White House Papers*, vol. 1, p. 113.

119. Kimball, *Forged in War*, p. 31.

120. Kimball, *Forged in War*, p. 36.

121. Quoted in Freidel, p. 333.

122. Churchill, *The Second World War*, vol. 2, pp. 22–3; *Churchill and Roosevelt*, vol. 1, C-9x (15.5.40), pp. 37–8.

123. Reynolds, *Anglo-American Alliance*, p. 98, citing a Foreign Office minute of 17.5.40.

124. Quoted in Reynolds, *Anglo-American Alliance*, p. 98 (italics in the original).

125. Reynolds, *Anglo-American Alliance*, p. 99. After Roosevelt had sent an encouraging message to Reynaud on 13 June, Churchill – echoed by Lord Beaverbrook, Minister of Aircraft Production – expected America's entry into the war 'in the near future'. Disillusionment of such unrealistic hopes soon followed (Christopher Hill, *Cabinet Decisions on Foreign Policy. The British Experience, October 1938–June 1941*, Cambridge, 1991, p. 168).

126. Freidel, p. 331. The Senate Foreign Relations Committee was forceful in voicing its opposition on 3 June to delivering material to other countries which might be required for national defence. Later in the month, Congress forbade the sale of army and navy supplies unless deemed non-essential for national defence (Dallek, pp. 227, 243).

127. Quoted in Langer and Gleason, *Challenge*, pp. 481–2; see also Hull, vol. 1, pp. 765–6; and Blum, p. 151.

128. Blum, pp. 150–52.

129. Freidel, p. 333.

130. Hull, vol. 1, p. 166; and see Blum, pp. 149–58.

131. Langer and Gleason, *Challenge*, p. 483.

132. Text in Langer and Gleason, *Challenge*, p. 485; and *Churchill and Roosevelt*, vol. 1, R-4x, 16.5.40, pp. 38–9; see also Churchill, *The Second World War*, vol. 2, p. 23; Kimball, *Forged in War*, p. 49; Reynolds, *Anglo-American Alliance*, p. 114.

133. Langer and Gleason, *Challenge*, p. 496.

134. Langer and Gleason, *Challenge*, pp. 489–90, 494.

135. Langer and Gleason, *Challenge*, pp. 486–7.

136. Langer and Gleason, *Challenge*, pp. 516–17.

137. Divine, *The Reluctant Belligerent*, p. 88.

138. Divine, *The Reluctant Belligerent*, p. 86. Putting this in perspective, Britain's defence outlay almost trebled between 1939 and 1940 and practically quadrupled from 1939 to 1941; German expenditure was less than double (from a high base) in 1939–40, and increased almost two-and-a-half fold from 1939 to 1941 (Jeremy Noakes and Geoffrey Pridham (eds.), *Nazism 1919–1945. A Documentary Reader*, vol. 2, Exeter, 1984, p. 298).

139. Churchill, *The Second World War*, vol. 2, pp. 50–51; *Churchill and Roosevelt*, vol. 1, C-10x, C-11x, C-17x, pp. 39–40, 49–51; Reynolds, *Anglo-American Alliance*, p. 115; Lukacs, *Five Days in London*, p. 73.

140. Quoted in Langer and Gleason, *Challenge*, p. 491.

141. Churchill, *The Second World War*, vol. 2, p. 205.

142. Langer and Gleason, *Challenge*, p. 744.

143. Freidel, p. 334.

144. Churchill, *The Second World War*, vol. 2, pp. 205–11; Joseph P. Lash, *Roosevelt and Churchill 1939–1941. The Partnership that Saved the West*, New York, 1976, p. 165; Langer and Gleason, *Challenge*, p. 573; Reynolds, *Anglo-American Alliance*, p. 119; Kennedy, p. 452.

145. Harold L. Ickes, *The Secret Diary of Harold L. Ickes*, vol. 3: *The Lowering Clouds 1939–1941*, New York, 1955, p. 233.

146. Reynolds, *Anglo-American Alliance*, pp. 119–20.

147. Freidel, pp. 342–3.

148. Flynn, pp. 214–15; Kennedy, pp. 456–7.

149. Sherwood, *White House Papers*, vol. 1, p. 174.

150. Lash, p. 206.

151. Churchill, *The Second World War*, vol. 2, pp. 117, 167.

152. Blum, p. 162.

153. Kimball, *Forged in War*, pp. 53–4.

154. Churchill, *The Second World War*, vol. 2, pp. 356–7; *Churchill and Roosevelt*, vol. 1, C-20x, pp. 56–7.

155. Langer and Gleason, *Challenge*, pp. 506–7.

156. Ickes, pp. 270–71, 293; Langer and Gleason, *Challenge*, pp. 745–6.

157. Sherwood, *White House Papers*, vol. 1, pp. 175–6.

158. *The Roosevelt Letters*, vol. 3: *[1928–1945]*, ed. Elliott Roosevelt, London, 1952, pp. 324–5; also printed in Langer and Gleason, *Challenge*, p. 745.

159. Langer and Gleason, *Challenge*, pp. 747–9.

160. Ickes, p. 283.

161. Langer and Gleason, *Challenge*, pp. 749–51; Burns, pp. 177–9; Ickes, pp. 292–3.

162. Churchill, *The Second World War*, vol. 2, pp. 358-60.

163. Langer and Gleason, *Challenge*, pp. 751-3.

164. Langer and Gleason, *Challenge*, pp. 753-7, quotation p. 757.

165. Langer and Gleason, *Challenge*, pp. 758-9; Churchill, *The Second World War*, vol. 2, pp. 360-61.

166. Dallek, p. 245; Langer and Gleason, *Challenge*, pp. 760-61; Divine, *Roosevelt and World War II*, p. 36.

167. Reynolds, *Anglo-American Alliance*, pp. 128-31.

168. Churchill, *The Second World War*, vol. 2, pp. 361-8; Langer and Gleason, *Challenge*, pp. 762-9.

169. Langer and Gleason, *Challenge*, p. 769; Blum, pp. 182-3.

170. Reynolds, *Anglo-American Alliance*, p. 131; Kennedy, p. 461.

171. *Ciano's Diary 1939-1943*, ed. Malcolm Muggeridge, London, 1947, p. 288; Langer and Gleason, *Challenge*, p. 775.

172. Franz Halder, *Kriegstagebuch. Tägliche Aufzeichnungen des Chefs des Generalstabes des Heeres 1939-1942*, vol. 2: *Von der geplanten Landung in England bis zum Beginn des Ostfeldzuges (1.7.1940-21.6.1941)*, ed. Hans-Adolf Jacobsen, Stuttgart, 1963, p. 75 (23.8.40), p. 98 (14.9.40); *Fuehrer Conferences on Naval Affairs 1939-1945*, London, 1990, p. 134; Andreas Hillgruber, *Hitlers Strategie. Politik und Kriegführung 1940-1941*, 3rd edn., Bonn, 1993, pp. 201-3.

173. Langer and Gleason, *The Undeclared War*, p. 24; Reynolds, *Anglo-American Alliance*, p. 132; Reynolds, *From Munich to Pearl Harbor*, p. 87.

174. Langer and Gleason, *Challenge*, pp. 770-76.

175. Quoted in Langer and Gleason, *Challenge*, p. 768. When, towards the end of the year, Halifax had reluctantly accepted the position as ambassador to Washington, Churchill thanked him 'for undertaking this heavy task', emphasizing the vital nature of American aid: 'If they do not help us wholeheartedly,' he wrote, 'there will only be miseries to share in this Island. If they give us the aid we deserve, you will have brought us inestimable blessings' (Borthwick Institute, University of York, Diary of Lord Halifax, A.7.8.7, Churchill letter appended to entry for 22.12.40).

176. Churchill, *Great War Speeches*, p. 59; Churchill, *The Second World War*, vol. 2, p. 362.

177. Churchill, *The Second World War*, vol. 2, p. 358.

178. Langer and Gleason, *Challenge*, p. 765; Gloria J. Barron, *Leadership in Crisis. FDR and the Path to Intervention*, Port Washington, NY/London, 1973, p. 69.

179. Langer and Gleason, *Challenge*, p. 776.

180. Kennedy, p. 466; Divine, *The Reluctant Belligerent*, p. 35.

181. Kennedy, p. 464; Dallek, p. 255.

182. Langer and Gleason, *The Undeclared War*, p. 212 (also for the quotation); and see Reynolds, *From Munich to Pearl Harbor*, pp. 102-3.

183. Reynolds, *Anglo-American Alliance*, p. 150 (also for the quotation). Churchill had to be pressed hard by Lothian to overcome his reluctance at 'putting all

our cards on the table' for Roosevelt (David Reynolds, *In Command of History. Churchill Fighting and Writing the Second World War*, London, 2004, p. 202).

184. Warren F. Kimball, *The Most Unsordid Act. Lend-Lease 1939–1941*, Baltimore, 1969, pp. 96–7.

185. Blum, pp. 199–200; Kimball, *The Most Unsordid Act*, pp. 100–101; Dallek, p. 253. U-boats accounted for 352,000 tons of shipping in October 1940, a record not subsequently matched. See Dan van der Vat, *The Atlantic Campaign. The Great Struggle at Sea 1939–1945*, London, 1988, p. 147.

186. Ickes, p. 367.

187. Reynolds, *Anglo-American Alliance*, p. 42.

188. Langer and Gleason, *The Undeclared War*, pp. 223–5; Kimball, *The Most Unsordid Act*, p. 99.

189. Sherwood, *White House Papers*, vol. 1, p. 221; Ickes, pp. 374–6.

190. Langer and Gleason, *The Undeclared War*, pp. 226–8 (also for the quotations); Kimball, *The Most Unsordid Act*, pp. 101–4; Blum, pp. 200–201.

191. Blum, pp. 202–4; Langer and Gleason, *The Undeclared War*, pp. 229–30; Kimball, *The Most Unsordid Act*, pp. 106–11.

192. Hull, vol. 1, pp. 872–3.

193. Churchill, *The Second World War*, vol. 2, p. 501. This was, even so, a belated recognition of the singular importance of the letter. Churchill had, in fact, dragged his feet over its drafting and then sending. His own emphasis had been placed on the need for American help in overcoming the growing crisis in shipping and transportation, rather than on finance, which Lothian had urged him to stress. Following Lothian's 'calculated indiscretion' about the state of British finances on his return to America, it was this aspect, rather than shipping, that caught the attention of Roosevelt. See Reynolds, *In Command of History*, p. 202.

194. Churchill, *The Second World War*, vol. 2, pp. 493–501, quotations pp. 500–501; *Churchill and Roosevelt*, vol. 1, C-43x, pp. 102–9.

195. Quoted in Langer and Gleason, *The Undeclared War*, p. 231; see also Blum, p. 204.

196. Blum, pp. 206–8; Langer and Gleason, *The Undeclared War*, pp. 233–5; Kimball, *The Most Unsordid Act*, pp. 112–15.

197. Sherwood, *White House Papers*, vol. 1, p. 223.

198. Kimball, *The Most Unsordid Act*, pp. 119–20, 124.

199. Kimball, *The Most Unsordid Act*, p. 115.

200. Stimson Diaries, Reel 6, entry for 13.12.40; Langer and Gleason, *The Undeclared War*, pp. 236–7.

201. Sherwood, *White House Papers*, vol. 1, p. 223; Kimball, *The Most Unsordid Act*, p. 117.

202. Blum, pp. 208–9.

203. Langer and Gleason, *The Undeclared War*, p. 238.

204. Kimball, *The Most Unsordid Act*, p. 123.

205. *Public Papers and Addresses*, vol. 9 (1940), pp. 604–15; Langer and

Gleason, *The Undeclared War*, pp. 239–41; Blum, p. 209; Sherwood, *White House Papers*, vol. 1, pp. 223–4; Kimball, *The Most Unsordid Act*, pp. 121–2; Dallek, p. 255.

206. Langer and Gleason, *Challenge*, p. 746; Kimball, *The Most Unsordid Act*, pp. 77, 123.

207. Sherwood, *White House Papers*, vol. 1, p. 224.

208. Langer and Gleason, *The Undeclared War*, pp. 241–4; Kennedy, p. 478.

209. Langer and Gleason, *The Undeclared War*, pp. 245–6.

210. *FDR's Fireside Chats*, p. 167.

211. *FDR's Fireside Chats*, pp. 164–73.

212. Reynolds, *From Munich to Pearl Harbor*, p. 108; Langer and Gleason, *The Undeclared War*, pp. 249–50, quoting the *New York Herald Tribune*, 30.12.40, the *Christian Science Monitor*, 30.12.40, and the *New York Times*, 31.12.40. For the 'fireside chats', reactions to them and Roosevelt's cautious handling of public opinion, see Casey, pp. 30–37.

213. Langer and Gleason, *The Undeclared War*, p. 253.

214. Langer and Gleason, *The Undeclared War*, p. 254, citing *New York Times*, 12.1.41. Opinion in December and January did not vary greatly in its ratio of roughly 2 : 1 of those in favour of helping Britain even at the risk of getting into the war, and those anxious to 'keep out of war ourselves' (Leigh, p. 78).

215. Langer and Gleason, *The Undeclared War*, pp. 253–4; Reynolds, *From Munich to Pearl Harbor*, pp. 108–9.

216. Blum, pp. 211–17; Kimball, *The Most Unsordid Act*, pp. 132–9.

217. *Public Opinion*, pp. 409–10.

218. Reynolds, *From Munich to Pearl Harbor*, p. 111.

219. Richard Norton Smith, *The Colonel. The Life and Legend of Robert R. McCormick 1880–1955*, Boston/New York, 1997, pp. 398–409.

220. Reynolds, *From Munich to Pearl Harbor*, pp. 110–14, and Kennedy, pp. 470–74, for brief summaries. The drafting, then progress through Congress, of the Lend-Lease bill is extensively covered in Langer and Gleason, *The Undeclared War*, pp. 254–84, and, especially, Kimball, *The Most Unsordid Act*, pp. 132–229.

221. Sherwood, *White House Papers*, vol. 1, pp. 265–7.

222. *Public Papers and Addresses*, vol. 10 (1941), pp. 61, 63.

223. Churchill, *The Second World War*, vol. 2, p. 501; Churchill, *Great War Speeches*, p. 101. See also Sherwood, *White House Papers*, vol. 1, p. 264. King George VI appears to have been less enamoured, while of course recognizing the importance of the new American commitment. Writing to Lord Halifax on 14 April 1941, the King said he 'did not feel too happy about the Lease of the Bases as the Americans wanted too much written & laid down. Everything was done in their interests, no give & take in certain circumstances . . . I do hope that the Americans will not try & bleed us white over the dollar asset question. As it is they are collecting the remaining gold in the world, which is of no use to them,

& they cannot wish to make us bankrupt. At least I hope they do not want to' (Borthwick Institute, University of York, Halifax Papers, A2.278.26.1).

224. Churchill, *Great War Speeches*, p. 105 (from his broadcast on 22.6.41).

225. Kimball, *The Most Unsordid Act*, pp. 9, 241; Divine, *The Reluctant Belligerent*, p. 106.

226. Hillgruber, *Hitlers Strategie*, pp. 400–401; *Die Tagebücher von Joseph Goebbels*, ed. Elke Fröhlich, part I, vol. 9, Munich, 1998, p. 186 (14.3.41); Langer and Gleason, *The Undeclared War*, p. 422.

227. Quoted in Freidel, p. 362.

228. Freidel, p. 323. Many others thought the same. See Wayne S. Cole, *Charles A. Lindbergh and the Battle against American Intervention in World War II*, New York/London, 1974, pp. 146–7.

229. Sherwood, *White House Papers*, vol. 1, pp. 267–8.

230. Reynolds, *From Munich to Pearl Harbor*, pp. 114–16.

231. Stimson Diaries, Reel 6, entry for 29.12.40; Kimball, *The Most Unsordid Act*, p. 129.

232. Sherwood, *White House Papers*, vol. 1, p. 271. And see Freidel, p. 366 for Roosevelt's belief that victory could only follow engagement of a huge American expeditionary force with the German enemy. Roosevelt talked during the spring and summer of 1941 of organizing a 75,000-man American expeditionary force for use outside the western hemisphere (Casey, p. 15).

233. A sign of the relative weighting attached by the administration to the dangers from across the Atlantic and in the Pacific is that, in his public addresses, Roosevelt made only four references to Japan in the eleven months before Pearl Harbor, whereas he attacked Hitler and Nazism more than 150 times over the same period (Casey, pp. 39–40).

234. Heinrichs, *Threshold of War*, p. 38.

235. Langer and Gleason, *The Undeclared War*, pp. 221–2; Heinrichs, *Threshold of War*, p. 38.

236. Sherwood, *White House Papers*, vol. 1, pp. 271–3; Langer and Gleason, *The Undeclared War*, pp. 285–9; Reynolds, *Anglo-American Alliance*, pp. 182–5; Reynolds, *From Munich to Pearl Harbor*, pp. 117–18; Kennedy, pp. 479–82.

237. Sherwood, *White House Papers*, vol. 1, p. 270; quotation from Langer and Gleason, *The Undeclared War*, p. 289.

238. Quoted in Kimball, *Forged in War*, p. 84. See also Heinrichs, *Threshold of War*, p. 81; and Freidel, p. 368 for Churchill's disappointment in Roosevelt around this time.

239. Freidel, p. 368.

240. Blum, p. 251.

241. See Heinrichs, *Threshold of War*, p. 85 for the rising support for escorting in April and May.

242. Roosevelt was pressing in May for action to take over the Azores, and also the Cape Verde Islands, to forestall what he imagined might be a German move

into Spain and Portugal 'at any moment'. He wanted a landing force of 50,000 men ready within a month. But when he was told of the difficulties in finding sufficient numbers of vessels for the action within such a short space of time, he 'let himself be argued out of the thing' (Sheffield University Library, Wolfson Microfilm 575, The Presidential Diaries of Henry Morgenthau 1938–45 [Microform], Frame 0931, 22.5.41).

243. Freidel, pp. 369–70; Reynolds, *From Munich to Pearl Harbor*, pp. 125–7; Reynolds, *Anglo-American Alliance*, p. 198; Heinrichs, *Threshold of War*, p. 46. See also Ickes, p. 466, for the reported comment by Roosevelt that 'things are coming to a head: Germany will be making a blunder soon', causing Ickes to infer that the President was anticipating an incident that would justify a declaration of war or, at least, escorts for convoys. Roosevelt implied around seven times in the first half of 1941 that a German retaliation in the Atlantic would be welcome in giving him justification for a more belligerent approach (Casey, pp. 14–15).

244. See Barron, pp. 91–4.

245. *For the President*, p. 512.

246. Lash, pp. 309–10.

247. *Churchill and Roosevelt*, C84x, p. 182; Reynolds, *Anglo-American Alliance*, p. 199.

248. Ickes, pp. 512–13; Sherwood, *White House Papers*, vol. 1, p. 293.

249. Quoted in Blum, p. 253; and see Langer and Gleason, *The Undeclared War*, pp. 455–6.

250. Quoted in Larrabee, p. 55. Morgenthau confided to his diary on 17 May: 'I gathered that he [Roosevelt] wanted to be pushed into the war rather than lead us into it' (Morgenthau Diaries, Frame 0929, 17.5.41). See also Dallek, p. 265; and Divine, *Roosevelt and World War II*, p. 42.

251. Sherwood, *White House Papers*, vol. 1, p. 298; Larrabee, p. 56; Burns, pp. 99–101; Reynolds, *Anglo-American Alliance*, pp. 202–3. Stimson had no doubt that Hull had toned down the speech. He said he 'felt rather depressed and tired and for that reason I was rather inclined to be disappointed with the President's speech, which he nevertheless thought was a good one' (Stimson Diaries, Reel 6, entries for 27–28.5.41).

252. *FDR's Fireside Chats*, pp. 184, 187; Sherwood, *White House Papers*, vol. 1, pp. 296–8.

253. Langer and Gleason, *The Undeclared War*, p. 463; Larrabee, p. 60; Burns, p. 101.

254. Langer and Gleason, *The Undeclared War*, pp. 457, 463; Ickes, pp. 526–7; Sherwood, *White House Papers*, vol. 1, p. 299.

255. Larrabee, p. 62.

256. Barron, p. 98, citing an interview with Benjamin V. Cohen.

257. Langer and Gleason, *The Undeclared War*, pp. 337, 342; Welles, *Time for Decision*, pp. 135–6.

258. Langer and Gleason, *The Undeclared War*, p. 528; Reynolds, *From Munich*

to Pearl Harbor, p. 132; Dallek, p. 268. Stimson noted in his diary, reflecting still prevalent misinterpretations of a German ultimatum preceding war: 'The dominating news over all is the fact that Russia and Germany are at the point of war in a negotiation in which Germany is bringing every bit of her gigantic pressure to bear on Russia to get some enormous advantages at the threat of war and at present, from all the dispatches, it seems to be nip and tuck whether Russia will fight or surrender. Of course I think the chances are that she will surrender' (Stimson Diaries, Reel 6, 17.6.41).

259. Sherwood, *White House Papers*, vol. 1, p. 299; Ickes, p. 552; Freidel, p. 372; Lash, p. 339; Dallek, pp. 267–8; Thomas A. Bailey and Paul B. Ryan, *Hitler vs. Roosevelt. The Undeclared Naval War*, New York, 1979, pp. 138–43.

260. Churchill, *Great War Speeches*, p. 102; Winston S. Churchill, *The Second World War*, vol. 3: *The Grand Alliance*, London, 1950, p. 210; *Churchill and Roosevelt*, p. 178.

261. Freidel, p. 369.

262. Heavily critical of Roosevelt, claiming – as is a commonplace revisionist argument – that he was actively seeking to take America into war, is Charles Callan Tansill, *Back Door to War. The Roosevelt Foreign Policy*, Chicago, 1952. A similar approach informed the argument of one of Roosevelt's contemporary critics, Charles A. Beard, *President Roosevelt and the Coming of War 1941. A Study in Appearance and Realities*, New Haven, 1948. Flynn, though his critique is largely directed at domestic policy, also claims that, while preaching peace, Roosevelt 'had made up his mind to go into the war as early as October 1940' (p. 295) – the date of his express promise not to send American troops into a foreign war. A different line of attack, that Roosevelt 'shut so many doors to peace' through parochialism and simplistic idealism, is adopted, along with a highly generous view of the motives of the German and Japanese military, in Frederick W. Marks III, *Wind over Sand. The Diplomacy of Franklin Roosevelt*, Athens, Ga., 1988 (quotation p. 288). Bitter divides in interpretation of his foreign policy have peppered the historiography and still not wholly subsided.

263. Van der Vat, pp. 196–201; David Stafford, *Roosevelt and Churchill. Men of Secrets*, paperback edn., London, 2000, p. 60. For the sharp rise in losses again in 1942, when the German navy changed the cipher, see Ronald Lewin, *Ultra Goes to War. The Secret Story*, paperback edn., London, 2001, pp. 209–10.

CHAPTER 6. MOSCOW, SPRING–SUMMER 1941

1. Anastas Ivanovich Mikoyan, *Tak bylo* [That's How It Was], Moscow, 1999, p. 390. Also quoted in Dmitri Volkogonov, *Stalin. Triumph and Tragedy*, New York, 1991, p. 410, and see p. 607 n. 11. Edvard Radzinsky, *Stalin*, New York, 1996, p. 468, quotes a similar obscenity, derived from the unpublished memoirs of Y. Chadaev, chief administrative assistant to the Council of People's

Commissars (who was not, however, present, as Mikoyan was, when Stalin made the comment). See also Simon Sebag Montefiore, *Stalin. The Court of the Red Tsar*, London, 2003, pp. 330, 331 n. (referring to variants of the same comment); and Roy Medvedev and Zhores Medvedev, *The Unknown Stalin. His Life, Death, and Legacy*, Woodstock/New York, 2004, p. 242 ('screwed up'), from Khrushchev's memoirs (Russian version; the English version, *Khrushchev Remembers*, ed. Strobe Talbott, London, 1971, p. 591, sanitizes it, in the 1956 denuciation speech, to 'All that which Lenin created we have lost forever'). Khrushchev was not there at the time, and apparently heard the comment from Beria. Sergo Beria, *Beria. My Father*, London, 2000, p. 70, has: 'Lenin left us a state and we have turned it into shit.' This account, however, has the Defence Commissar, Semion Konstantinovich Timoshenko, present, though Stalin made the comment once he and his associates had left the generals. Apart from Mikoyan, the only direct witness to the comment who left a record of it was Vyacheslav Molotov in *Molotov Remembers: Inside Kremlin Politics. Conversations with Felix Chuev*, Chicago, 1993, p. 39 ('we blew it'). I am grateful to the late Dr Derek Watson (University of Birmingham) for advice on the textual references to Stalin's utterance.

2. Montefiore, p. 34.

3. Volkogonov, p. 410 includes Andrei Zhdanov, a member of the Politburo, Leningrad party boss and close associate of Stalin, and Marshal Kliment Voroshilov (the former Defence Commissar). Whether Zhdanov had returned from holiday at Sochi, a Black Sea resort, where he had gone to recuperate from illness just before the Germans invaded (*Molotov Remembers*, p. 25; and Mikoyan, p. 380) is unclear. Neither Molotov nor Mikoyan indicated his presence at the meeting. Mikoyan's memoirs (p. 390) make no mention of Voroshilov going to the Defence Commissariat, and refer only to Molotov, Malenkov, Beria and himself, alongside Stalin.

4. *Molotov Remembers*, p. 39. For a character sketch of the man who, after the war, remained so obedient to Stalin that he was prepared to believe the Politburo's ludicrous charges of treason against his Jewish wife, rather than her own assertions of innocence, see Roy Medvedev, *All Stalin's Men*, Oxford, 1983, pp. 82–112; and for a full study of his career, Derek Watson, *Molotov. A Biography*, London, 2005.

5. Quoted in Medvedev and Medvedev, p. 237; also (with varied translation) in David E. Murphy, *What Stalin Knew. The Enigma of Barbarossa*, New Haven/London, 2005, p. xv.

6. For the lavish birthday tributes in December 1939, see Robert C. Tucker, *Stalin in Power. The Revolution from Above, 1928–1941*, New York, 1990, pp. 607–9. In fact, it has been established that Stalin was born not, as he himself always claimed, on 21 December 1879, but on 6 December 1878 (Robert Service, *Stalin. A Biography*, London, 2004, p. 15).

7. Quoted in Tucker, p. 119.

8. See J. Arch Getty, 'The Politics of Repression Revisited', in J. Arch Getty and

Roberta T. Manning (eds.), *Stalinist Terror. New Perspectives*, Cambridge, 1993, pp. 43–9.

9. Tucker, p. 444.

10. Moshe Lewin, *The Making of the Soviet System. Essays in the Social History of Interwar Russia*, New York, 1985, pp. 308–9.

11. Quoted in Montefiore, p. 197.

12. Moshe Lewin, *The Soviet Century*, London, 2005, pp. 100–104.

13. Lewin, *The Soviet Century*, pp. 100, 106–7.

14. Roger R. Reese, 'The Red Army and the Great Purges' in Getty and Manning, pp. 199, 210.

15. Reese, p. 213; Bernd Bonwetsch, 'Stalin, the Red Army, and the "Great Patriotic War"', in Ian Kershaw and Moshe Lewin (eds.), *Stalinism and Nazism. Dictatorships in Comparison*, Cambridge, 1997, p. 187.

16. Lew Besymenski, *Stalin und Hitler. Das Pokerspiel der Diktatoren*, Berlin, 2004, p. 96; slightly differing figures in Volkogonov, p. 368, and Gabriel Gorodetsky, *Grand Delusion. Stalin and the German Invasion of Russia*, New Haven/London, 1999, p. 115.

17. Montefiore, p. 29.

18. Richard Overy, *The Dictators. Hitler's Germany and Stalin's Russia*, London, 2004, p. 469; Montefiore, p. 197.

19. Tucker, pp. 433–4.

20. Besymenski, p. 96.

21. Besymenski, pp. 97–8.

22. Volkogonov, p. 369; Lewin, *The Soviet Century*, p. 110.

23. Gregor Suny, 'Stalin and his Stalinism. Power and Authority in the Soviet Union', in Kershaw and Lewin, pp. 26–7.

24. Quoted in Overy, *Dictators*, p. 64.

25. Tucker, p. 439.

26. Overy, *Dictators*, p. 65.

27. Montefiore, p. 29; Evan Mawdsley, *The Stalin Years. The Soviet Union, 1929–1953*, Manchester, 1998, p. 17.

28. Watson, p. 146.

29. Lewin, *The Soviet Century*, pp. 86–7.

30. Quoted in Service, p. 383. For the growth in bureaucracy, see Moshe Lewin, 'Bureaucracy and the Stalinist State', in Kershaw and Lewin, pp. 62–6.

31. Tucker, p. 595; Geoffrey Roberts, *Unholy Alliance. Stalin's Pact with Hitler*, London, 1989, pp. 128–9; Watson, pp. 153–7.

32. Albert L. Weeks, *Stalin's Other War. Soviet Grand Strategy 1939–1941*, Lanham, Md., 2002, p. 108.

33. Roberts, *Unholy Alliance*, p. 34.

34. A. J. P. Taylor, *The Origins of the Second World War*, Harmondsworth, 1964, p. 76.

35. Roberts, *Unholy Alliance*, p. 35; Heinrich Schwendemann, *Die wirtschaftliche*

Zusammenarbeit zwischen dem Deutschen Reich und der Sowjetunion von 1939 bis 1941. Alternative zu Hitlers Ostprogramm?, Berlin, 1993, p. 23.

36. Besymenski, pp. 51–6 (Soviet report on the cooperation, 1928).

37. Roberts, *Unholy Alliance*, p. 41.

38. Quoted in Besymenski, p. 67.

39. Quoted in Roberts, *Unholy Alliance*, p. 57.

40. Quoted in Besymenski, pp. 21–2. See also Roberts, *Unholy Alliance*, p. 100, and Barton Whaley, *Codeword Barbarossa*, Cambridge, Mass., 1973, p. 200, for further references, in 1935–6, by Soviet leaders to Hitler's professed aggressive aims towards the Soviet Union in *Mein Kampf*.

41. Roberts, *Unholy Alliance*, pp. 43–4.

42. David M. Glantz, *The Military Strategy of the Soviet Union. A History*, London, 1992, pp. 58, 60.

43. Quoted in Roberts, *Unholy Alliance*, p. 109.

44. Glantz, *Military Strategy*, pp. 69–70. G. Zhukov, *Reminiscences and Reflections*, Moscow, 1985, vol. 1, p. 209, states that 'up to 40 divisions were massed in regions adjacent to the western border'.

45. Besymenski, pp. 98–101, 116–18; Roberts, *Unholy Alliance*, pp. 87–92.

46. Text of the foreign policy section of Stalin's speech in Besymenski, pp. 134–42; 'chestnuts' quotation, p. 142, and quoted in Roberts, *Unholy Alliance*, p. 116 and Watson, p. 152. Both Roberts (p. 118) and Watson (p. 313 n. 55) point out that the literal translation of what Stalin said was 'to rake the fire with someone else's hands'.

47. Roberts, *Unholy Alliance*, p. 130. The USSR was prepared to commit 70 per cent of the specified armed forces directly deployed by Britain and France in the event of a German attack on the west. In the event of a German attack against the USSR, Britain and France would immediately deploy 70 per cent of specified Soviet forces (Zhukov, vol. 1, pp. 212–16).

48. Roberts, *Unholy Alliance*, p. 134.

49. For a full account of the failure of Britain and France to make common cause with the Soviet Union against the threat of Hitler, and the strong anti-Communism that lay behind the half-hearted diplomacy, see Michael Jabara Carley, *1939. The Alliance that Never Was and the Coming of World War II*, Chicago, 1999.

50. Ivan Maisky, *Who Helped Hitler?*, London, 1964, p. 133.

51. The background to and conclusion of the pact is well described by Anthony Read and David Fisher, *The Deadly Embrace. Hitler, Stalin and the Nazi–Soviet Pact 1939–1941*, London, 1988, chs. 13–23. The relevant diplomatic documents (from German files) were conveniently brought together in *Nazi–Soviet Relations 1939–1941*, ed. Raymond James Sontag and James Stuart Beddie, New York, 1948, pp. 1–78. The closer economic relations since spring 1939 are dealt with by Schwendemann, pp. 44–54.

52. See Besymenski, pp. 67–88; and Roberts, *Unholy Alliance*, pp. 101–8.

53. Besymenski, pp. 186–92.

54. Quoted in Roberts, *Unholy Alliance*, p. 139.

55. Carley, pp. 196–8.

56. Besymenski, pp. 238–9; Gerhard L. Weinberg, *The Foreign Policy of Hitler's Germany. Starting World War II, 1937–1939*, Chicago/London, 1980, p. 604; Volkogonov, p. 353.

57. See Gustav Hilger and Alfred G. Meyer, *The Incompatible Allies. A Memoir of German–Soviet Relations 1918–1941*, New York, 1953, pp. 293–301.

58. Ian Kershaw, *Hitler, 1936–1945. Nemesis*, London, 2000, p. 205.

59. *Khrushchev Remembers*, p. 128.

60. Quoted in Montefiore, p. 275.

61. Volkogonov, p. 352; and see Montefiore, p. 272.

62. *Nazi–Soviet Relations*, pp. 131–2 (memorandum on the German-Soviet Commercial Agreement of 11 February 1940); Alexander Werth, *Russia at War, 1941–1945*, paperback edn., New York, 1984, p. 113; Roberts, *Unholy Alliance*, pp. 175–8; Schwendemann, p. 143.

63. Quoted in Roberts, *Unholy Alliance*, p. 185.

64. Gorodetsky, pp. 5, 14.

65. *Khrushchev Remembers*, p. 166.

66. Roberts, *Unholy Alliance*, p. 186.

67. Besymenski, pp. 279–81.

68. Roberts, *Unholy Alliance*, p. 195. The Soviet unease was plainly expressed by Molotov in a memorandum for the German government delivered on 21 September 1940 (*Nazi–Soviet Relations*, pp. 189–94).

69. The official German accounts of the meetings are in *DGFP*, 11, docs. 325–9, 339.

70. Besymenski, pp. 315–18.

71. Stalin interrupted Molotov's report on the talks with anti-German comments, berated the Nazi leaders and stated that 'the chief principle of their policy is perfidy' (quoted in Watson, p. 186).

72. *1941 god. Dokumenty* [The Year 1941. Documents], ed. A. N. Iakovlev, V. P. Naumov et al., Moscow, 1998, vol. 1, docs. 41–2, 44, 53, 58, 93 (all from July and August 1940); also Gorodetsky, p. 38.

73. Besymenski, pp. 97–8.

74. Gorodetsky, p. 118.

75. Gorodetsky, p. 120.

76. Seweryn Bialer (ed.), *Stalin and his Generals*, London, 1970, pp. 35–6; Albert Seaton, *Stalin as Warlord*, London, 1976, pp. 87–9; Adam Ulam, *Stalin. The Man and his Era*, Boston, 1989, p. 530; Mikoyan, p. 382.

77. Besymenski, p. 368.

78. Seaton, p. 91.

79. *Khrushchev Remembers*, pp. 158–60, 163–4.

80. Besymenski, pp. 282–98 (Timoshenko's report of 7 December 1940). David M. Glantz, *Stumbling Colossus. The Red Army on the Eve of World War,*

Lawrence, Kan., 1998, p. 89, refers to the report as the joint work of Voroshilov and Timoshenko on 8 May 1940. This date was, however, that of the handover of responsibility to Timoshenko, not of the report itself. Timoshenko received the background material from the Red Army's central administration at that time. But there is no indication that Voroshilov assisted in compiling the report which was eventually submitted by Timoshenko on 7 December 1940.

81. Bonwetsch, p. 186; Besymenski, p. 98; Louis Rotundo, 'Stalin and the Outbreak of War in 1941', *Journal of Contemporary History*, 24 (1989), p. 280; Glantz, *Military Strategy*, p. 92; Glantz, *Stumbling Colossus*, p. 107; and see Zhukov, vol. 1, pp. 228, 244-5.

82. Mark von Hagen, 'Soviet Soldiers and Officers on the Eve of the German Invasion. Toward a Description of Social Psychology and Political Attitudes', in Robert W. Thurston and Bernd Bonwetsch (eds.), *The People's War. Responses to World War II in the Soviet Union*, Urbana/Chicago, 2000, pp. 191-9.

83. John Erickson, *The Road to Stalingrad. Stalin's War with Germany*, vol. 1, London, paperback edn., 1998, pp. 62-4. See also Zhukov, vol. 1, pp. 233-43 for the deficiencies in rearmament, communications and defence.

84. Jacques Sapir, 'The Economics of War in the Soviet Union during World War II', in Kershaw and Lewin, p. 216. The Red Army's weaknesses and inadequacy for battlefield combat on the eve of 'Barbarossa' are fully outlined in David M. Glantz, 'The Red Army in 1941', in David M. Glantz (ed.), *The Initial Period of War on the Eastern Front, 22 June-August 1941*, London, 1993, pp. 1-39; and David M. Glantz, *Barbarossa. Hitler's Invasion of Russia 1941*, Stroud, 2001, pp. 22-8.

85. Gorodetsky, pp. 116-17; Sapir, pp. 210-11; Glantz, *Military Strategy*, pp. 65-6.

86. John Erickson, 'Threat Identification and Strategic Appraisal by the Soviet Union 1930-1941', in E. R. May (ed.), *Knowing One's Enemies. Intelligence Assessment between the Two World Wars*, Princeton, 1983, pp. 416-18; Whaley, pp. 175, 181, 199, 223, 228, 242; Roberts, *Unholy Alliance*, pp. 187, 213; Glantz, *Military Strategy*, pp. 61-2. The Red Army's General Staff continued to work on the assumption that the Wehrmacht would take ten to fifteen days to mobilize and deploy, ruling out, therefore, a surprise attack (Glantz, *Stumbling Colossus*, p. 96).

87. Gorodetsky, p. 126. The continuity of strategic thinking, also under Zhukov, is also stressed by Glantz, *Military Strategy*, pp. 87-8. Zhukov later remarked (Zhukov, vol. 1, p. 245): 'Military strategy was chiefly based on the correct assertion that an aggressor can only be defeated by offensive operations.'

88. Besymenski, pp. 355-63. See also Glantz, *Military Strategy*, pp. 70-75; and Glantz, *Stumbling Colossus*, pp. 90-92.

89. Quoted in Glantz, *Stumbling Colossus*, p. 93 and Besymenski, p. 364. Zhukov, vol. 1, p. 250, recalled Stalin saying: 'Nazi Germany will not be able to wage a major lengthy war without those vital resources.'

90. Besymenski, pp. 364-5; *1941 god*, vol. 1, docs. 95, 134; Evan Mawdsley,

'Crossing the Rubicon. Soviet Plans for Offensive War in 1940–1941', *International History Review*, 25 (2003), pp. 821–3; Gorodetsky, pp. 122–4; Jacob Kipp, 'Soviet War Planning', in Glanz, *Initial Period of War*, pp. 46–7; Glantz, *Military Strategy*, pp. 78–81.

91. Gorodetsky, p. 127. For the proceedings of the conference, see Erickson, *Road to Stalingrad*, pp. 40–46.

92. Gorodetsky, pp. 128–9; Mawdsley, 'Crossing the Rubicon', pp. 825–7; Erickson, *Road to Stalingrad*, pp. 50–5; Glantz, *Military Strategy*, pp. 81–6; Zhukov, vol. 1, pp. 221–5.

93. Mawdsley, 'Crossing the Rubicon', pp. 827–32; *1941 god*, vol. 1, doc. 315; extracts in Besymenski, pp. 365–7; Zhukov, vol. 1, p. 250.

94. Mawdsley, 'Crossing the Rubicon', pp. 827–9; Besymenski, p. 368; Glantz, *Stumbling Colossus*, pp. 100–102, 108. Those units that did exist found themselves short of equipment, weaponry and ammunition, lacking transport and hampered by poor communications (Catherine Merridale, *Ivan's War. The Red Army 1939–1945*, London, 2005, pp. 87–90).

95. Besymenski, pp. 368–70.

96. Richard Overy, *Russia's War*, London, 1997, pp. 64–5. See also Rotundo, p. 282; Glantz, *Military Strategy*, pp. 75, 79; and Glantz, *Stumbling Colossus*, p. 88: 'Given the scarcity of resources, although primacy was accorded to the erection of defences along the new border, neither set was fully prepared or manned in June 1941.' See also Zhukov, vol. 1, pp. 251–3.

97. Mikoyan, p. 377.

98. Winston S. Churchill, *The Second World War*, vol. 4: *The Hinge of Fate*, London, 1951, p. 443.

99. Gorodetsky, pp. 113–14; Roberts, *Unholy Alliance*, p. 205.

100. Quoted in Gorodetsky, p. 174.

101. Gorodetsky, pp. 173, 176 (and *passim* in ch. 8); Zhukov, vol. 1, p. 268, where the wording varies slightly from Gorodetsky's quotation of the Russian version of Zhukov's memoirs; also Whaley, pp. 62–3. For similar sentiments attributed to Stalin, see Mikoyan, p. 377: 'It would be a great advantage for Churchill if we entered the war, but for us it is useful to stay on the sidelines for a little longer.'

102. Winston S. Churchill, *The Second World War*, vol. 3: *The Grand Alliance*, London, 1950, pp. 316, 322–3.

103. For Soviet intelligence agencies, see Whaley, pp. 192–200, and the more recent extensive survey in Murphy, esp. pp. 62–116.

104. Gorodetsky, p. 130.

105. *Khrushchev Remembers*, p. 340.

106. Gorodetsky, p. 54. See Glantz, *Stumbling Colossus*, pp. 233–57, for the distrust of both civilian and military intelligence – a distrust aided and abetted by the tone of the reports passed to Stalin, which frequently placed the emphasis upon misinformation.

107. See Whaley, pp. 170–77, 180–81; Read and Fisher, pp. 594–601; Glantz, *Barbarossa*, p. 31.

108. Whaley, p. 242.

109. *1941 god*, vol. 1, doc. 204; and see Gorodetsky, p. 124.

110. Quoted in Gorodetsky, p. 125; *1941 god*, vol. 1, doc. 227. See also Whaley, p. 34.

111. *1941 god*, vol. 1, doc. 301.

112. *1941 god*, vol. 1, doc. 308. At the end of May 1941, Stalin was still prepared to believe that Hitler was ignorant about the contraventions of Soviet airspace, and that the Wehrmacht was operating on its own initiative. See Gorodetsky, p. 225. And see below for Stalin's initial reaction to the attack on the Soviet Union, that it had been carried out without Hitler's knowledge.

113. *1941 god*, vol. 1, doc. 321.

114. *1941 god*, vol. 1, doc. 340.

115. For example, *1941 god*, vol. 2, doc. 376. On 24 April a communication from the German naval attaché in Moscow to the naval High Command mentioned rumours allegedly emanating from the British ambassador accurately predicting 22 June as the day of the outbreak of war (*Nazi–Soviet Relations*, p. 330).

116. *1941 god*, vol. 2, doc. 377.

117. *1941 god*, vol. 2, doc. 394.

118. *1941 god*, vol. 2, doc. 421 and doc. 592 for a calendar of twenty-five important reports from 'Starshina' and 'Corsican' between 6 September 1940 and 16 June 1941 (German trans. in Gerd R. Ueberschär and Lev A. Bezymenskij (eds.), *Der deutsche Angriff auf die Sowjetunion 1941. Die Kontroverse um die Präventivkriegsthese*, Darmstadt, 1998, pp. 199–212). The calendar was put together, on Stalin's bidding, on 20 June 1941. It was passed to Merkulov, the head of external security, only after the German invasion had taken place (Gorodetsky, p. 297).

119. *1941 god*, vol. 2, doc. 443. For Sorge's activities in the weeks preceding the German invasion, see Robert Whymant, *Stalin's Spy. Richard Sorge and the Tokyo Espionage Ring*, London/New York, 1996, chs. 11–12; and Murphy, pp. 84–90.

120. See, for example, the reports printed in *Sekrety Gitlera no stole u Stalina* [Hitler's Secrets on Stalin's Desk], Moscow, 1995, docs. 3–4, 6–7, 15–16. 18; and Gorodetsky, pp. 130–36.

121. Most of the eighty-four warnings assembled by Whaley (chs. 3–5) came through foreign channels. But some of the best information, as we have noted, was provided by Soviet agents. Stalin even thought that Dekanozov, the Soviet ambassador in Berlin, was being duped by British agents and passing on their disinformation (Mikoyan, p. 377).

122. *1941 god*, vol. 1, doc. 327. See also Murphy, pp. 156–8; Rotundo, p. 290; and Glantz, *Stumbling Colossus*, pp. 241–2. The report included information on the date and character of the German attack which turned out to be almost wholly

accurate predictions, but had already been damaged in presentation by Golikov's disclaimer that they had mainly derived from Anglo-American sources. For Golikov's way of presenting intelligence to Stalin, see Zhukov, vol. 1, pp. 272–3; Erickson, *Road to Stalingrad*, pp. 88–9; Whaley, pp. 194–6; and Murphy, pp. 141–61.

123. See Whaley, p. 227, for the *general* failure of intelligence systems to interpret German intentions correctly; also Waldo, Heinrichs, Jr., *Threshold of War. Franklin D. Roosevelt and American Entry into World War II*, New York/Oxford, 1988, pp. 24–6.

124. Zhukov, vol. 1, pp. 265–6; Whaley, pp. 172–5, 181; Murphy, pp. 173–84.

125. Gorodetsky, pp. 156–7, 164–5; Roberts, *Unholy Alliance*, p. 217.

126. *Molotov Remembers*, p. 22. Stalin spoke on similar lines to Zhukov on 14 June on hearing intelligence reports on the war-readiness of the advanced German divisions: 'You can't believe everything intelligence says' (Zhukov, vol. 1, pp. 275–6). Zhukov was adamant (p. 274) that the Defence Commissariat was not privy to the non-military intelligence reports sent to Stalin.

127. Medvedev and Medvedev, p. 229.

128. *DGFP*, 12, doc. 468; *Nazi–Soviet Relations*, pp. 335–6. And see Gorodetsky, p. 211.

129. Isaac Deutscher, *Stalin. A Political Biography*, revised edn., London, 1988, p. 444.

130. Besymenski, p. 379.

131. Besymenski, pp. 374–5.

132. *1941 god*, vol. 2, doc. 437; Besymenski, pp. 380–86, 391–3; extracts from notes made by Georgi Dimitrov in Ueberschär and Bezymenskij, pp. 184–5.

133. See Besymenski, pp. 394–7; Gorodetsky, p. 208 and p. 365 n. 36; Montefiore, p. 311 n.; Overy, *Russia's War*, pp. 68–9; R. W. Davies, *Soviet History in the Yeltsin Era*, London, 1997, pp. 56–8; and Geoffrey Roberts, *The Soviet Union and the Origins of the Second World War. Russo-German Relations and the Road to War, 1933–1941*, London, 1995, p. 144. The relevant historiography, Russian and German, which poses the 'preventive war' hypothesis is well surveyed – and its findings roundly dismissed – in Ueberschär and Bezymenskij, especially the contributions by Gerd R. Ueberschär, 'Hitlers Überfall auf die Sowjetunion 1941 und Stalins Absichten. Die Bewertung in der deutschen Geschichtsschreibung und die neuere "Präventivkriegsthese"' (pp. 48–69) and Alexander I. Boroznjak, 'Ein russischer Historikerstreit? Zur sowjetischen und russischen Historiographie über den deutschen Angriff auf die Sowjetunion' (pp. 116–28). The case for an intended pre-emptive offensive by the Red Army, forestalled by Hitler's launch of 'Barbarossa', has recently been strongly advanced by Weeks, esp. chs. 5 and 8, and Heinz Magenheimer, *Hitler's War. Germany's Key Strategic Decisions 1940–1945*, London, 1998, pp. 51–7, while Constantine Pleshakov, *Stalin's Folly. The Secret History of the German Invasion of Russia, June 1941*, London, 2005, sees (p. 77) the 15 May strategic plan as the blueprint for an

attack that Stalin intended to carry out in 1942. The balanced appraisal of 'traditionalist' and 'revisionist' interpretations by Mawdsley, 'Crossing the Rubicon', pp. 864–5, judiciously concludes that, while offensive war – as a *counter*-offensive, that is – constituted an intrinsic part of Soviet military planning in 1940–41, there were no plans to stage an offensive pre-emptive strike in 1941. See in addition also now the sensible comments of Geoffrey Roberts, *Stalin's Wars. From World War to Cold War, 1939–1953*, New Haven/London, 2006, pp. 76–9.

134. See Mawdsley, 'Crossing the Rubicon', pp. 850–51; Besymenski, pp. 438–40. Colonel I. T. Starinov, a commander in the Western Army Group, later recalled the discrepancy between the claims in Stalin's speech and the awareness of military leaders that 'rearming was just beginning' (though, he said, they did not speak of this, even among themselves). See Bialer, p. 223.

135. *DGFP*, 12, doc. 593.

136. Besymenski, p. 387. Gorodetsky, p. 208, suggests that the speech was deliberately leaked abroad, though gives no indication that it reached Berlin. Medvedev and Medvedev, p. 232, also presume that the speech was meant as disinformation, though again provide no evidence of knowledge of its genuine content in Berlin. The brilliant British journalist Alexander Werth, based at the time in Moscow, gleaned information about the speech, but only some weeks later, once the Soviet Union was involved in the war. What he heard, however (see Werth, pp. 122–3), did not accord with the surviving notes of the speech, indicating, in contrast to what Stalin actually said, that he pointed to the weaknesses, rather than strength, of the Red Army. Erickson, *Road to Stalingrad*, p. 82, on the other hand, correctly contrasts the false impression gained abroad with the real content of the speech.

137. Glantz, *Stumbling Colossus*, pp. 242–4.

138. *1941 god*, vol. 2, doc. 473; Ueberschär and Bezymenskij, pp. 186–93. Analyses in Besymenski, pp. 435–53 and Mawdsley, 'Crossing the Rubicon', pp. 833–62.

139. Mawdsley, 'Crossing the Rubicon', pp. 834–7.

140. Glantz, *Military Strategy*, p. 87, points out that the plan of 15 May 'sits comfortably within the context of previous Soviet strategic planning and, in particular, the experiences of the January war games'. He also pertinently remarks (p. 89) that the plan 'established limited objectives well short of the destruction of the German state', amounting to 'a clear example of justifiable preventative war involving the conduct of a strategic offensive operation with definite limited aims'.

141. Mawdsley, 'Crossing the Rubicon', p. 839.

142. See Glantz, *Stumbling Colossus*, pp. 244–5.

143. Quoted in Mawdsley, 'Crossing the Rubicon', pp. 852–3. Mawdsley concludes that Stalin was almost certainly shown the plan (which Glantz, *Stumbling Colossus*, p. 95, and Roberts, *Stalin's Wars*, p. 76, doubt) but did not approve it (a point that 'revisionist' historians, rejecting Zhukov's testimony as tendentious and self-serving, dispute).

144. Quoted in Mawdsley, 'Crossing the Rubicon', p. 853.

145. *1941 god*, vol. 2, doc. 560 (Mikoyan to the Council of People's Commissars, the Central Committee and Stalin, 16 June 1941); Schwendemann, p. 354 (and pp. 315–52 for a full analysis of economic relations in the months running up to the invasion, in which extensive German industrial exports to the Soviet Union were also made). And see Werth, p. 114. A German memorandum of 15 May 1941 on trading relations, listing the huge amounts of grain, petrol, cotton and metals delivered that year by the Soviet Union (with high figures for April), commented that 'the status of Soviet raw materials still presents a favourable picture' (*Nazi–Soviet Relations*, pp. 339–41).

146. Erickson, *Road to Stalingrad*, p. 91.

147. Quoted in Besymenski, p. 444.

148. Mawdsley, 'Crossing the Rubicon', pp. 861–2. Glantz, *Military Strategy*, p. 88, concludes that Zhukov's plan was flawed in a number of important respects, that it could not have been executed before mid-July at the earliest – too late to pre-empt the Germans – and that Stalin's decision to ignore the proposal 'seems to have been prudent'.

149. *DGFP*, 12, doc. 505.

150. Erickson, *Road to Stalingrad*, p. 78; Deutscher, pp. 443–4.

151. Quoted in Gorodetsky, p. 214.

152. Quoted in Hilger and Meyer, p. 328 and Gorodetsky, p. 206. Schulenburg's official report is in *DGFP*, 12, doc. 423, and *Nazi–Soviet Relations*, pp. 330–32.

153. Gorodetsky, pp. 206–7, 221; Besymenski, pp. 425–8.

154. F. H. Hinsley, *British Intelligence in the Second World War*, London, 1993, pp. 106–9; also F. H. Hinsley, 'British Intelligence and Barbarossa', in John Erickson and David Dilks (eds.), *Barbarossa. The Axis and the Allies*, Edinburgh, 1994, pp. 63–6.

155. See Gorodetsky, pp. 266–7.

156. *Khrushchev Remembers*, p. 133.

157. Gorodetsky, pp. 263–5, 267–74; Roberts, *Unholy Alliance*, p. 218; and Roberts, *The Soviet Union and the Origins of the Second World War*, p. 144.

158. Quoted in Gorodetsky, p. 224.

159. Quoted in Gorodetsky, p. 279, from the Russian edition of Zhukov's memoirs. The English version, *Reminiscences and Reflections*, vol. 1, p. 275, only contains part of the quotation. Medvedev and Medvedev, p. 233, place Stalin's comment on 15 June, though Zhukov's memoirs make plain that it was uttered on the previous day. For the belated emergency defence measures, see Zhukov, vol. 1, pp. 259, 264; Gorodetsky, p. 280; also Glantz, *Stumbling Colossus*, p. 246.

160. Glantz, *Stumbling Colossus*, pp. 102–7.

161. Medvedev and Medvedev, pp. 233–4, 238–9.

162. Volkogonov, p. 393; Glantz, *Stumbling Colossus*, p. 251.

163. Gorodetsky, p. 307.

164. Gorodetsky, p. 275.

165. *1941 god*, vol. 2, doc. 513.

166. *1941 god*, vol. 2, doc. 514. And see Whymant, pp. 164–7.

167. Whymant, p. 184.

168. Murphy, p. 87 (who comments further (p. 88) that Sorge's reports had been dismissed as 'German disinformation' by Stalin as early as 1936).

169. *1941 god*, vol. 2, doc. 543.

170. *1941 god*, vol. 2, doc. 544.

171. *1941 god*, vol. 2, doc. 570; *Sekrety Gitlera*, doc. 72.

172. *1941 god*, vol. 2, doc. 581.

173. Erickson, *Road to Stalingrad*, p. 93; Whaley, pp. 99–103; Read and Fisher, p. 609.

174. *1941 god*, vol. 2, doc. 590.

175. Medvedev and Medvedev, p. 239.

176. *Sekrety Gitlera*, docs. 73–7.

177. *Molotov Remembers*, p. 31. For the *Tass* communiqué, see Whaley, pp. 207–8.

178. Roberts, *Unholy Alliance*, p. 218.

179. Gorodetsky, p. 289.

180. Hinsley, *British Intelligence in the Second World War*, pp. 109–11; Hinsley, 'British Intelligence and Barbarossa', pp. 69–70; Erickson, *Road to Stalingrad*, p. 93; Whaley, pp. 230–34.

181. Gorodetsky, pp. 301–3.

182. *1941 god*, vol. 2, doc. 599.

183. Besymenski, p. 421.

184. Quoted in Besymenski, p. 409.

185. Zhukov, vol. 1, pp. 277–8, 280 (quotation p. 277); *Khrushchev Remembers*, p. 167; Mikoyan, p. 388; Medvedev and Medvedev, p. 240; Glantz, *Barbarossa*, p. 31 and (for the text of the directive) p. 242; Glantz, *Stumbling Colossus*, pp. 252–4; Murphy, pp. 213–15.

186. The preceding account is based on Zhukov, vol. 1, pp. 281–2; Volkogonov, pp. 402–4; Montefiore, pp. 321–4; Radzinsky, pp. 458–9; Gorodetsky, pp. 311–13; Service, pp. 437–8; Tucker, p. 625; Ulam, pp. 538–9; Read and Fisher, pp. 5–6, 635–7, 639–42; Watson, p. 189; and Overy, *Russia's War*, pp. 73–4.

187. Montefiore, p. 324.

188. Volkogonov, p. 407; text of the directive in Glantz, *Barbarossa*, p. 242 and Amnon Sella, '"Barbarossa". Surprise Attack and Communication', *Journal of Contemporary History*, 13 (1978), p. 571. See Zhukov, vol. 1, p. 282: 'it [the directive] proved plainly unrealistic – and was therefore never carried out.'

189. Mawdsley, 'Crossing the Rubicon', p. 863; text of the directive in Glantz, *Barbarossa*, pp. 242–3. And see Sella, pp. 559–73 for the confusion, incoherence and lack of coordination in the Soviet response to the surprise attack.

190. Mikoyan, p. 388.

191. Quoted in Watson, pp. 189–90.

192. Quoted in Radzinsky, p. 462. For the response to the radio address, see Sella, p. 575.
193. 'Iz vospominanii upravliyushchego delami sovnarkoma SSSR Ya. E. Chadaev' ['From the Memoirs of the Head of Sovnarkom USSR – Yakov Ermolae-vich Chadaev'], *Otechestvennaya Istoriya*, 2 (2005), pp. 8–10; also Zhukov, vol. 1, pp. 305, 309.
194. Volkogonov, pp. 421–2; Bonwetsch, p. 196.
195. Mikoyan, pp. 390–2; Stepan A. Mikoyan, 'Barbarossa and the Soviet Leadership', in Erickson and Dilks, pp. 127–8; Volkogonov, pp. 409–12; Monte-fiore, pp. 329–34; Radzinsky, pp. 468–72; Medvedev and Medvedev, pp. 241–5; Service, pp. 441–3. Stalin's unscheduled absence from his duties lasted only two days. It was simply not the case, as his full list of appointments detailed in his appointments book demonstrates, that 'for ten days the Soviet Union was leaderless', as is asserted by Jonathan Lewis and Phillip Whitehead, *Stalin. A Time for Judgement*, London, 1991, p. 89.
196. *1941 god*, vol. 2, doc. 651. This is a memorandum presented by Sudoplatov to the Soviet Council of Ministers on 7 August 1953, after Stalin's death and in the context of moves to discredit Beria. In his published memoirs many years later (Pavel Sudoplatov and Anatoli Sudoplatov, *Special Tasks: The Memoirs of an Unwanted Witness. A Soviet Spymaster*, Boston, 1994, pp. 145–8), Sudoplatov suggests the meeting was intended to spread disinformation 'intended to weaken German resolve' by implying that the *Blitzkrieg* had failed and a prolonged war was inevitable. Overy, *Russia's War*, p. 96, accepts the disinformation argument, though he places the Stamenov meeting in October, not in July. If it *was* meant as disinformation, it is strange that – to go from the lack of evidence on the German side – nothing reached the enemy. And in the context of the massive German advances and conquests during July the disinformation claim sounds implausible. Nor is the story undermined by being part of an anti-Beria campaign in 1953. The peace-feelers were, in fact, mentioned by two other sources. See Volkogonov, pp. 412–13 and Radzinsky, p. 474.
197. Montefiore, p. 346.
198. John Barber, 'The Moscow Crisis of October 1941', in Julian Cooper, Maureen Perrie and E. A. Rees (eds.), *Soviet History, 1917–53. Essays in Honour of R. W. Davies*, Basingstoke, 1995, pp. 201–5.
199. Werth, pp. 232, 236–7. See also the vivid account in Rodric Braithwaite, *Moscow 1941. A City and its People at War*, London, 2006, pp. 242–59, 271–6.
200. Barber, pp. 209–11; Mikhail M. Gorinov, 'Muscovites' Moods, 22 June 1941 to May 1942', in Thurston and Bonwetsch, pp. 122–5; Roy A. Medvedev, *On Stalin and Stalinism*, Oxford, 1979, pp. 128–32; Nikolai Tolstoy, *Stalin's Secret War*, London, 1981, p. 241; and Overy, *Russia's War*, pp. 95–8. Mikoyan, pp. 417–22, outlines the measures to evacuate the government and prepare to detonate installations within Moscow, but misleadingly claims (p. 420) that calm prevailed and that there was no panic in the city's population.

201. Radzinsky, p. 482.

202. Barber, p. 206; Volkogonov, pp. 433–4; Montefiore, pp. 349–50; Radzinsky, pp. 482–3.

203. BBC interview with Nikolai Vasilievich Ponomariov, *c.* 1998, typescript, fols. 29–35. See also the 'heroic' depiction of Stalin during these days in A. T. Rybin, *Next to Stalin. Notes of a Bodyguard*, Toronto, 1996, pp. 31–4.

204. Watson, p. 193.

205. A point emphasized by Schwendemann, pp. 354–63.

206. *Molotov Remembers*, pp. 21–32.

207. *Khrushchev Remembers*, pp. 587–92.

208. Gorodetsky, p. 323 (also p. 239).

209. *Die Tagebücher von Joseph Goebbels*, ed. Elke Fröhlich, part I, vol. 4, Munich, 2000, p. 214 (10.7.37).

210. This is the presumption of the counter-factual assessment by Valentin Falin, *Zweite Front. Die Interessenkonflikte in der Anti-Hitler-Koalition*, Munich, 1995, pp. 100–103.

211. Had they followed Soviet proposals for a full-scale military pact in 1939, however, Britain and France would have committed themselves to direct military intervention in the event of a German attack on Poland, presuming the Poles, Romanians and Lithuanians would have permitted the Red Army to pass through their territories to engage in the conflict (Zhukov, vol. 1, p. 214).

212. Roberts, *Unholy Alliance*, p. 225.

213. Glantz, *Barbarossa*, p. 31; Overy, *Russia's War*, p. 71.

214. See Rotundo, pp. 295–6.

215. Volkogonov, p. 470.

216. Quoted in Mawdsley, 'Crossing the Rubicon', p. 864.

217. Glantz, *Barbarossa*, p. 30; Whaley, pp. 217–18. Tolstoy, pp. 224–30, finds Stalin's emphasis on avoidance of provocation so unpersuasive as an explanation of his stance in spring 1941 that he posits the hypothesis that Hitler himself sent a personal assurance to lull the Soviet leader's suspicions, suggesting that conspiratorial elements in the German High Command were pressing for aggression that he opposed. There is, however, no evidence for this hypothesis. Nothing exists in either German or Russian archives to lend authentication to the text of two purported letters from Hitler to Stalin, of 31 December 1940 and 14 May 1941. These (printed in Murphy, pp. 256–8, apparently based upon their publication in a Russian *novel* of 1997) are almost certainly forgeries. Despite major question marks over the provenance of the alleged documents, Murphy (pp. 185–91) seems prepared to offer them some credence. John Lukacs, *June 1941. Hitler and Stalin*, New Haven/London, 2006, pp. 150–58, is, however, wisely dismissive of the letters.

218. The threat of such an attack had been sharply reduced by the Neutrality Pact of 13 April 1941. Though, as the deliberations by the Japanese government following the German invasion would show, there was no guarantee that Japan

would adhere to the pact, from the Soviet perspective 'the treaty held promise of a certain gain in time' (Zhukov, vol. 1, p. 257).

219. For the lamentable failings of German intelligence – which did little more than uphold existing prejudice about the weakness of the Red Army – see David Kahn, *Hitler's Spies. German Military Intelligence in World War II*, New York, 2000, pp. 445–61. See also Whaley, p. 33. There appears to have been no attempt made by Soviet military intelligence to spread disinformation to advertise the strength of the Red Army.

220. Erickson, *Road to Stalingrad*, pp. 69–73, 81, 86; Glantz, *Military Strategy*, pp. 63, 98, 101–2; Glantz, *Stumbling Colossus*, p. 97. See also Zhukov, vol. 1, p. 249.

221. Medvedev and Medvedev, p. 245.

222. Zhukov, vol. 1, p. 250, immediately adding that Stalin's conjecture that the Germans would strike in the south, not the north, had proved incorrect. Zhukov (pp. 300–301) nevertheless admitted the military's part of the responsibility for the tactical and strategic errors made on the eve of the invasion and immediately thereafter. See also Roberts, *Stalin's Wars*, pp. 74, 80, and the comments on the failings of Soviet intelligence in Glantz, *Stumbling Colossus*, pp. 254–7. The *general* failure of the intelligence services of the major powers to anticipate 'Barbarossa' is emphasized by Whaley, p. 227.

CHAPTER 7. WASHINGTON, DC, SUMMER–AUTUMN 1941

1. Robert E. Sherwood, *The White House Papers of Harry L. Hopkins*, London, 1948, vol. 1, pp. 304–5; Frank Freidel, *Franklin D. Roosevelt. A Rendezvous with Destiny*, Boston, 1990, p. 373.

2. Winston S. Churchill, *The Second World War*, vol. 3: *The Grand Alliance*, London, 1950, pp. 330–33. The 'token assistance' which Churchill was prepared in practice to offer the Soviet Union, despite his forthright expressions of vocal support, is emphasized by Sheila Lawlor, 'Britain and the Russian Entry into the War', in Richard Langhorne (ed.), *Diplomacy and Intelligence during the Second World War*, Cambridge, 1985, pp. 171–4.

3. William L. Langer and S. Everett Gleason, *The Undeclared War, 1940–1941*, New York, 1953, p. 537. This was essentially the view in the State Department. When Roosevelt decided to aid the Soviet Union, he did so (as has been said) 'with only hope and intuition to guide him' (Warren F. Kimball, *The Juggler. Franklin Roosevelt as Wartime Statesman*, Princeton, 1991, pp. 27, 40).

4. On MAGIC, see I. C. B. Dear and M. R. D. Foot (eds.), *The Oxford Companion to the Second World War*, Oxford/New York, 1995, pp. 706–9.

5. *The Roosevelt Letters*, vol. 3: *[1928–1945]*, ed. Elliott Roosevelt, London, 1952, p. 375.

6. Quoted in Herbert Feis, *The Road to Pearl Harbor. The Coming of the War between the United States and Japan*, Princeton, 1950, p. 227.

7. Waldo H. Heinrichs, Jr., *Threshold of War. Franklin D. Roosevelt and American Entry into World War II*, New York/Oxford, 1988, pp. 104–5, 174, 206.

8. Thomas A. Bailey and Paul B. Ryan, *Hitler vs. Roosevelt. The Undeclared Naval War*, New York, 1979, pp. 263–4.

9. Winston S. Churchill, *Great War Speeches*, paperback edn., London, 1957, p. 109.

10. Quoted in Langer and Gleason, *The Undeclared War*, p. 541.

11. Quoted in Robert A. Divine, *The Reluctant Belligerent. American Entry into World War II*, New York, 1965, p. 123.

12. Langer and Gleason, *The Undeclared War*, p. 541.

13. Sherwood, *White House Papers*, vol. 1, pp. 303–4.

14. Quoted in Langer and Gleason, *The Undeclared War*, p. 538; and James McGregor Burns, *Roosevelt. The Soldier of Freedom 1940–1945*, London, 1971, p. 104.

15. Sherwood, *White House Papers*, vol. 1, p. 309.

16. Yale University Library, Henry L. Stimson Diaries 1909–1945, Reel 6, entry for 2.7.41; also in Henry L. Stimson and McGeorge Bundy, *On Active Service in Peace and War*, New York, 1948, p. 371.

17. Quoted in Langer and Gleason, *The Undeclared War*, p. 538.

18. Harold L. Ickes, *The Secret Diary of Harold L. Ickes*, vol. 3: *The Lowering Clouds 1939–1941*, New York, 1955, pp. 557–8.

19. Quoted in Langer and Gleason, *The Undeclared War*, p. 542.

20. Langer and Gleason, *The Undeclared War*, pp. 542–6.

21. Sherwood, *White House Papers*, vol. 1, p. 309.

22. Joseph E. Davies, *Mission to Moscow*, New York, 1941, p. 488.

23. Davies, pp. 494–5, 497; also printed in Sherwood, *White House Papers*, vol. 1, pp. 306–9.

24. Langer and Gleason, *The Undeclared War*, pp. 560–61; Burns, pp. 114–15.

25. Quotations from Ickes, vol. 3, pp. 592–3.

26. Quoted in Langer and Gleason, *The Undeclared War*, p. 561.

27. Langer and Gleason, *The Undeclared War*, pp. 545, 558–63; Freidel, p. 374. Nor was the initial help from Britain, which dispatched the first Arctic convoy to the Soviet Union in August 1941, of great value. The materials shipped to aid the Soviet fight against Hitler's forces began, however, to play a significant role in 1942.

28. Sherwood, *White House Papers*, vol. 1, p. 319.

29. Kimball, *The Juggler*, pp. 22, 31–4, 36.

30. Sherwood, *White House Papers*, vol. 1, pp. 313–22; Churchill, *The Second World War*, vol. 3, pp. 377–8, for Hopkins's talks in London.

31. Sherwood, *White House Papers*, vol. 1, pp. 324–49, for the Moscow visit; p. 325, for the hat.

32. Sherwood, *White House Papers*, vol. 1, p. 329.

33. Sherwood, *White House Papers*, vol. 1, p. 337.

34. Sherwood, *White House Papers*, vol. 1, pp. 335–42, 347.

35. Sherwood, *White House Papers*, vol. 1, pp. 342–4.

36. Sherwood, *White House Papers*, vol. 1, p. 350; Churchill, *The Second World War*, vol. 3, p. 381.

37. Divine, *The Reluctant Belligerent*, p. 129.

38. Freidel, p. 375.

39. Heinrichs, *Threshold of War*, pp. 174–5; Churchill, *The Second World War*, vol. 3, pp. 417–19, for the British contribution.

40. Sherwood, *White House Papers*, vol. 1, p. 396.

41. Ickes, vol. 3, p. 620.

42. Freidel, p. 376.

43. Langer and Gleason, *The Undeclared War*, pp. 818–19; Sherwood, *White House Papers*, vol. 1, pp. 399–400; Freidel, p. 376. When the Lend-Lease bill had first come before Congress early in 1941, it had already prompted opposition from those unwilling to see aid extended to the Soviet Union (Warren F. Kimball, *The Most Unsordid Act. Lend-Lease 1939–1941*, Baltimore, 1969, p. 189).

44. Langer and Gleason, *The Undeclared War*, p. 560; Freidel, p. 376.

45. Quoted in Langer and Gleason, *The Undeclared War*, p. 544.

46. Langer and Gleason, *The Undeclared War*, p. 738; David M. Kennedy, *Freedom from Fear. The American People in Depression and War, 1929–1945*, New York/Oxford, 1999, pp. 486–7; David Reynolds, *The Creation of the Anglo-American Alliance 1937–1941. A Study in Competitive Co-operation*, Chapel Hill, NC, 1982, p. 212; Mark A. Stoler, *Allies and Adversaries. The Joint Chiefs of Staff, the Grand Alliance, and U.S. Strategy in World War II*, Chapel Hill, NC/London, 2000, pp. 47, 49, 50, 55; substantial extracts from the text in Sherwood, *White House Papers*, vol. 1, pp. 413–23.

47. Quoted in Langer and Gleason, *The Undeclared War*, p. 544.

48. *The Roosevelt Letters*, vol. 3, p. 378.

49. Langer and Gleason, *The Undeclared War*, pp. 539, 579.

50. Burns, p. 104; Stimson Diaries, Reel 6, entries for 6–7 July 1941, indicate Knox's disappointment and frustration at Roosevelt's lack of boldness.

51. Heinrichs, *Threshold of War*, p. 110; Freidel, p. 383.

52. Quoted in Burns, p. 105.

53. Joseph P. Lash, *Roosevelt and Churchill 1939–1941. The Partnership that Saved the West*, New York, 1976, pp. 341–2.

54. Langer and Gleason, *The Undeclared War*, p. 576; Ickes, vol. 3, p. 571.

55. Bailey and Ryan, p. 155.

56. *The Churchill War Papers*, vol. 3: *The Ever-Widening War, 1941*, ed. Martin Gilbert, London, 2000, p. 914 (9.7.41); Langer and Gleason, *The Undeclared War*, p. 578.

57. Reynolds, *Anglo-American Alliance*, p. 208.

58. Burns, p. 105. In the Far East, too, the imposition of oil sanctions makes it possible to view July 1941 as a turning point in American strategic thinking and diplomacy. See David Reynolds, *From Munich to Pearl Harbor. Roosevelt's America and the Origins of the Second World War*, Chicago, 2001, p. 143.

59. Ickes, vol. 3, p. 571; Bailey and Ryan, p. 156.

60. Langer and Gleason, *The Undeclared War*, p. 577.

61. Langer and Gleason, *The Undeclared War*, p. 578. See Lash, p. 343, for the muted isolationist protest.

62. Sherwood, *White House Papers*, vol. 1, p. 367.

63. Sherwood, *White House Papers*, vol. 1, pp. 367–9; Langer and Gleason, *The Undeclared War*, pp. 570–74; Divine, *The Reluctant Belligerent*, pp. 129–31.

64. Sherwood, *White House Papers*, vol. 1, p. 368.

65. Stimson and Bundy, p. 377; Langer and Gleason, *The Undeclared War*, p. 574.

66. Quoted in Sherwood, *White House Papers*, vol. 1, p. 368.

67. Quoted in Reynolds, *Anglo-American Alliance*, p. 169.

68. Both quotations in Lash, p. 391.

69. See Lash, p. 392.

70. Extensive coverage of the conference in Sherwood, *White House Papers*, vol. 1, pp. 350–66; Churchill, *The Second World War*, vol. 3, pp. 385–400; Langer and Gleason, *The Undeclared War*, pp. 663–92; Lash, pp. 393–400; Heinrichs, *Threshold of War*, pp. 148–61; and, especially, Theodore A. Wilson, *The First Summit. Roosevelt and Churchill at Placentia Bay 1941*, London, 1970.

71. Langer and Gleason, *The Undeclared War*, pp. 670–77; Wilson, pp. 112–13, 117, 119, 163–6, 215, 241–4.

72. Freidel, p. 386.

73. Churchill, *The Second World War*, vol. 3, pp. 388–9; Sherwood, *White House Papers*, vol. 1, p. 356; Wilson, pp. 88, 160–63; Heinrichs, *Threshold of War*, p. 157.

74. Wilson, p. 144.

75. Wilson, p. 145.

76. Reynolds, *Anglo-American Alliance*, p. 216; Freidel, p. 392; Divine, *The Reluctant Belligerent*, p. 143.

77. Heinrichs, *Threshold of War*, p. 164.

78. Robert Dallek, *Franklin D. Roosevelt and American Foreign Policy, 1932–1945*, New York, 1979, p. 286.

79. Reynolds, *Anglo-American Alliance*, p. 217.

80. Quoted in Reynolds, *Anglo-American Alliance*, pp. 214–15 (where it is pointed out that some of Churchill's Cabinet colleagues were sceptical of his positive account); and Dallek, p. 285.

81. Text in Churchill, *The Second World War*, vol. 3, pp. 393–4; Langer and Gleason, *The Undeclared War*, pp. 687–8; and Wilson, p. 206.

82. See Wilson, pp. 174, 260–62.

83. Churchill, *The Second World War*, vol. 3, pp. 384, 394 (for the quotation); Wilson, pp. 108–11 for a description of the service.

84. Quoted in Wilson, p. 111.

85. Wilson, p. 203.

86. Freidel, p. 385.

87. Wilson, pp. 210–11; text in Churchill, *The Second World War*, vol. 3, pp. 395–6.

88. Wilson, p. 203; Heinrichs, *Threshold of War*, p. 159.

89. Wilson, pp. 212, 214.

90. See Wilson, pp. 223–4 and 231–4, 266–7, for reactions in the United States.

91. Sherwood, *White House Papers*, vol. 1, p. 369.

92. Freidel, p. 389.

93. Sherwood, *White House Papers*, vol. 1, p. 374.

94. Bailey and Ryan, pp. 168–73.

95. Bailey and Ryan, pp. 173–4.

96. *The Public Papers and Addresses of Franklin D. Roosevelt*, ed. Samuel I. Rosenman, vol. 10 (1941), New York, 1950, pp. 374–83; Bailey and Ryan, pp. 175–6.

97. Bailey and Ryan, pp. 171, 173, 175.

98. Sherwood, *White House Papers*, vol. 1, pp. 371–3 (quotation p. 373). Stimson told Hopkins that he had not been consulted about the speech, but took the view that 'unless the President was prepared to say something good and strong, it were better for him not to speak at all'. When he heard it, he thought Roosevelt's speech 'the most decisive one which he has made' (Stimson Diaries, Reel 7, entries for 9–10.9.41). In his memoirs, Cordell Hull mentions his agreement on the evening of the 10th that the President 'should make it emphatically plain that our naval vessels in the Atlantic would fire on any Axis submarines or surface warships seeking to intercept shipping in our defensive waters', though does not refer to his intervention the next day in the hope of toning down the speech (Cordell Hull, *The Memoirs of Cordell Hull*, New York, 1948, vol. 2, p. 1047).

99. Lash, p. 417.

100. *Public Papers and Addresses*, vol. 10, pp. 384–92; *FDR's Fireside Chats*, ed. Russell D. Buhite and David W. Levy, New York, 1992, pp. 189–96.

101. *FDR's Fireside Chats*, pp. 188–9.

102. Langer and Gleason, *The Undeclared War*, pp. 742, 746.

103. Langer and Gleason, *The Undeclared War*, p. 746.

104. Heinrichs, *Threshold of War*, p. 168.

105. Langer and Gleason, *The Undeclared War*, p. 747; Lash, p. 419.

106. Bailey and Ryan, pp. 177 n. and 182 n.

107. Quoted in Langer and Gleason, *The Undeclared War*, p. 747.

108. Quoted in Langer and Gleason, *The Undeclared War*, p. 747.

109. Langer and Gleason, *The Undeclared War*, p. 749.

110. *FDR's Fireside Chats*, p. 196.

111. Even so, Roosevelt's short-circuiting of Congress through executive action resting upon the presentation of misleading information, even in a good cause, has been interpreted as establishing a harmful precedent for later action in Vietnam (Lash, pp. 420–21).

112. Quoted in Langer and Gleason, *The Undeclared War*, p. 749.

113. Quoted in Dallek, p. 289. Robert Divine's comment, 'the public reaction [to the introduction of escorting] was so favourable that Roosevelt could have begun convoys months earlier with solid public support', takes insufficient account of the fundamental contradiction in American public opinion (and the President's perception of this), even though figures from Gallup polls reflecting it are presented on the same page (Divine, *The Reluctant Belligerent*, p. 144).

114. Langer and Gleason, *The Undeclared War*, p. 751.

115. Bailey and Ryan, pp. 188–91.

116. Bailey and Ryan, pp. 191–2, 195–6.

117. Bailey and Ryan, pp. 196–7.

118. Reynolds, *Anglo-American Alliance*, p. 219; Nicholas John Cull, *Selling War. The British Propaganda Campaign against American 'Neutrality' in World War II*, New York/Oxford, 1995, pp. 170–73.

119. *Public Papers and Addresses*, vol. 10, pp. 438–45.

120. *Public Papers and Addresses*, vol. 10, pp. 444–5.

121. Quoted in Dallek, p. 289.

122. Freidel, p. 394; Bailey and Ryan, p. 208; Divine, *The Reluctant Belligerent*, p. 146.

123. Hull, vol. 2, p. 943.

124. The Senate's leading spokesmen on foreign affairs had told Roosevelt that, while in their view there was a majority in favour of revision, there would be prolonged debate and isolationist filibustering (Lash, p. 426).

125. Hull, vol. 2, pp. 1046–7.

126. Sherwood, *White House Papers*, vol. 1, p. 380.

127. Langer and Gleason, *The Undeclared War*, p. 752.

128. Langer and Gleason, *The Undeclared War*, pp. 752–6; Sherwood, *White House Papers*, vol. 1, p. 381.

129. Divine, *The Reluctant Belligerent*, p. 146.

130. Sherwood, *White House Papers*, vol. 1, p. 383.

131. Langer and Gleason, *The Undeclared War*, p. 757.

132. Langer and Gleason, *The Undeclared War*, p. 758; Divine, *The Reluctant Belligerent*, p. 147.

133. See Dallek, p. 292.

134. Quoted in Bailey and Ryan, p. 209.

135. See Reynolds, *Anglo-American Alliance*, p. 218.

136. Some of the following points are presented in Bailey and Ryan, pp. 260–63; Reynolds, *Anglo-American Alliance*, p. 218; and Reynolds, *From Munich to Pearl Harbor*, p. 157.

137. This was explicitly stated in a memorandum by Admiral Stark in late September, relating to the issue of whether to press for a revision of the neutrality legislation. But Stark, who had consistently pressed for direct American involvement in the war, was of the opinion that 'the United States should enter the war against Germany as soon as possible, even if hostilities with Japan must be accepted' (quoted in Sherwood, *White House Papers*, vol. 1, p. 381). Roosevelt, as we have seen, had not been ready to follow such a course of action.

138. Quoted in Dallek, p. 289; and Reynolds, *Anglo-American Alliance*, p. 353 n. 114.

139. Reynolds, *Anglo-American Alliance*, pp. 219-20.

140. Langer and Gleason, *The Undeclared War*, p. 923; Kennedy, pp. 487-8.

141. Kennedy, p. 487.

142. Quoted in Sherwood, *White House Papers*, vol. 1, p. 415.

143. In autumn 1941, Roosevelt still thought, it seems, that he could possibly avoid sending troops to fight in Europe if the Soviet Union could hold out, and saw provision of aid to Russia as a vehicle to help prevent the use of American ground forces. The army, however, took the view that the Soviet Union and Great Britain would be incapable of defeating Germany without American deployment of troops. Aid to both countries was, from this perspective, aimed at sustaining military resistance until American rearmament was complete. In the event, lend-lease to the Soviet Union equipped approximately 101 army divisions and meant that American deployment in Europe was smaller than that envisaged in the Victory Program (Stoler, pp. 55-8, and 285 n. 64).

144. Quoted in Sherwood, *White House Papers*, vol. 1, p. 419.

CHAPTER 8. TOKYO, AUTUMN 1941

1. Nobutaka Ike (ed.), *Japan's Decision for War. Records of the 1941 Policy Conferences*, Stanford, Calif., 1967, p. 72.

2. The deliberations about the northern option can be followed in the essay by Hosoya Chihiro, 'Northern Defence', in James William Morley (ed.), *The Fateful Choice. Japan's Advance into Southeast Asia, 1939-1941*, New York, 1980, pp. 94-112. The emergence of the navy's stance on the southern advance is explored in the essay in the same volume by Tsunoda Jun, 'The Navy's Role in the Southern Strategy', esp. pp. 287-95.

3. Figures in Herbert P. Bix, *Hirohito and the Making of Modern Japan*, London, 2001, p. 400.

4. Akira Iriye, *The Origins of the Second World War in Asia and the Pacific*, London/New York, 1987, p. 148; James William Morley (ed.), *The Final Confrontation. Japan's Negotiations with the United States, 1941*, Columbia, NY, 1994 (translated essays of Tsunoda Jun, based upon Japanese documentation), p. 159.

5. David Reynolds, *The Creation of the Anglo-American Alliance 1937–1941. A Study in Competitive Co-operation*, Chapel Hill, NC, 1982, pp. 234–6; William Carr, *Poland to Pearl Harbor. The Making of the Second World War*, London, 1985, p. 153; Iriye, *Origins*, pp. 149–50.

6. Iriye, *Origins*, p. 147.

7. Iriye, *Origins*, pp. 148–9.

8. Bix, p. 401.

9. Sheffield University Library, Wolfson Microfilm 431, Diary of Marquis Kido Koichi, doc. no. 1632W (63) 31.7.41, (63) 2.8.41, (66) 7.8.41; Carr, pp. 154–5.

10. Herbert Feis, *The Road to Pearl Harbor. The Coming of the War between the United States and Japan*, Princeton, 1950, remarks (p. 244): 'From now on the oil gauge and the clock stood side by side. Each fall in the level brought the hour of decision closer.' Using a similar analogy (p. 270), he comments: 'Time had become the meter of strategy for both governments. But one did not mind its passing, while the other was crazed by the tick of the clock.'

11. Morley, *The Final Confrontation*, p. 157; *Foreign Relations of the United States. Japan 1931–41*, vol. 2 [= *Japan II*], Washington, 1943, pp. 549–50.

12. Sheffield University Library, Wolfson Microfilm 437, copied from National Archives, Washington, Record Group 243: Records of the United States Strategic Bombing Survey, File 1d (10), Memoirs of Prince Konoye [Konoe] [=Konoe Memoirs] March 1942, fols. 29–30.

13. Quoted in Morley, *The Final Confrontation*, p. 179.

14. Yoshitake Oka, *Konoe Fumimaro. A Political Biography*, Tokyo, 1983, pp. 139–40.

15. John Toland, *The Rising Sun. The Decline and Fall of the Japanese Empire, 1936–1945*, New York, 1970, Modern Library edn., 2003, p. 100; Ike, p. 151 and n. 35; Feis, p. 282.

16. Bix, pp. 403–4; Morley, *The Final Confrontation*, p. 181.

17. Morley, *The Final Confrontation*, pp. 180–81.

18. Konoe Memoirs, fols. 30–31; Oka, p. 139; Robert J. C. Butow, *Tojo and the Coming of the War*, Princeton, 1961, pp. 243–4; Roger D. Spotswood, 'Japan's Southward Advance as an Issue in Japanese-American Relations, 1940–1941', unpublished Ph.D. thesis, University of Washington, 1974, pp. 398–401.

19. Quotations in Morley, *The Final Confrontation*, p. 180.

20. Iriye, *Origins*, p. 157; Morley, *The Final Confrontation*, p. 181. For Nomura's appearance and character, Cordell Hull, *The Memoirs of Cordell Hull*, New York, 1948, vol. 2, p. 987; Toland, *The Rising Sun*, p. 67; Gordon W. Prange, *At Dawn We Slept. The Untold Story of Pearl Harbor*, London, 1982, p. 6.

21. *Foreign Relations of the United States. Diplomatic Papers 1941*, vol. 4: *The Far East*, Washington, 1956 [= *FRUS, 1941*], p. 359; also quoted in Carr, pp. 154–5. Hull, vol. 2, pp. 1014–15, indicates the Secretary of State's conviction, following the invasion of southern Indochina, that war between Japan and the United States was now a likely eventuality.

22. Morley, *The Final Confrontation*, p. 182.

23. Iriye, *Origins*, p. 156.

24. Toland, *The Rising Sun*, p. 91. For the different emphases in strategy towards Japan between Churchill and Roosevelt, see Waldo H. Heinrichs, Jr., *Threshold of War. Franklin D. Roosevelt and American Entry into World War II*, New York/Oxford, 1988, pp. 152–5; and Feis, pp. 256–7.

25. Konoe Memoirs, fol. 33; *The 'MAGIC' Background of Pearl Harbor*, vol. 3, Washington, 1977, appendix, pp. A38–9; Hull, vol. 2, pp. 1019–20; Morley, *The Final Confrontation*, pp. 183–4; Reynolds, *Anglo-American Alliance*, p. 239 (for the shift in Roosevelt's position on return from Placentia Bay, on the advice of the State Department).

26. *Japan II*, p. 565; also quoted in Toland, *The Rising Sun*, p. 93; Grew's subsequent dispatch is in *FRUS, 1941*, vol. 4, pp. 382–3. See also Joseph C. Grew, *Ten Years in Japan*, New York, 1944, pp. 416–21; Hull, vol. 2, p. 1025; Waldo H. Heinrichs, Jr., *American Ambassador. Joseph C. Grew and the Development of the United States Diplomatic Tradition*, Boston, 1966, pp. 309–12, 337–43; and Morley, *The Final Confrontation*, pp. 186–7.

27. Ike, pp. 124–5.

28. Konoe Memoirs, fol. 35.

29. William L. Langer and S. Everett Gleason, *The Undeclared War, 1940–1941*, New York, 1953, pp. 700–701; Oka, p. 141; Morley, *The Final Confrontation*, p. 185.

30. Hull, vol. 2, p. 1024; Langer and Gleason, *The Undeclared War*, p. 701; Morley, *The Final Confrontation*, pp. 185–8; Oka, pp. 141–2.

31. Morley, *The Final Confrontation*, pp. 165, 169, 364–6 (appendix 6); Ike, pp. 135–6; Iriye, *Origins*, p. 159.

32. Morley, *The Final Confrontation*, p. 365.

33. Morley, *The Final Confrontation*, p. 366.

34. Morley, *The Final Confrontation*, p. 169.

35. Ike, pp. 129–33; Morley, *The Final Confrontation*, pp. 267–74.

36. Bix, p. 410.

37. Sheffield University Library, Wolfson Microfilm 431, Diary of Marquis Kido Koichi, doc. no. 1632W (67), 5.9.41; Oka, pp. 145–6.

38. Bix, pp. 412–13; Morley, *The Final Confrontation*, p. 174; Konoe Memoirs, fols. 40–41.

39. Bix, p. 410. Bix argues that the Emperor faced 'the most important decision of his entire life', that he 'clearly had options at this moment', that a withdrawal from Indochina and loss of the chance of seizing the Dutch East Indies would have met with the approval of at least some of the navy's top leadership, and that, consequently, Hirohito freely and willingly chose the route to war.

40. Kido Diary, doc. no. 1632W (68), 6.9.41; Bix, p. 413; Toland, *The Rising Sun*, p. 98.

41. The following (except where otherwise referenced) all from Ike, pp. 138–51.

42. Morley, *The Final Confrontation*, p. 172.

43. Kido Diary, doc. no. 1632W (68), 6.9.41; Konoe Memoirs, fol. 41; Bix, p. 414; Morley, *The Final Confrontation*, p. 176; Toland, *The Rising Sun*, p. 99; Oka, pp. 146–7.

44. Quoted Morley, *The Final Confrontation*, pp. 170–71.

45. Toland, *The Rising Sun*, p. 103.

46. Konoe Memoirs, fol. 42; *Japan II*, pp. 604–6; Grew, pp. 425–8 (6.9.41); Oka, pp. 148–9; Toland, *The Rising Sun*, pp. 100–102 (partly on the basis of an interview with Konoe's (unnamed) mistress); Hull, vol. 2, pp. 1028–31; Heinrichs, *American Ambassador*, p. 346; Langer and Gleason, *The Undeclared War*, p. 716; Heinrichs, *Threshold of War*, pp. 185–6. David Bergamini, *Japan's Imperial Conspiracy*, New York, 1971, vol. 2, p. 1019, has Baron Ito's daughter serving the food and drink. Feis, p. 271, refers to the 'daughter of the house'. Konoe recalled the talk lasting one and a half hours; Grew (p. 425) notes that 'the conversation lasted for three hours'. Hull was anxious that Grew maintained caution in his dealings with Japanese leaders. He cabled the ambassador on 9 September: 'While the [State] Department perceives no objections to your carrying on conversations paralleling those here with a view to obtaining further elucidation of the intent of the Japanese Government, it is felt that, as the subject is a matter in which the President has a close and active interest, any definitive discussions concerned with the reaching of an agreement on principle should continue to be conducted here' (*FRUS, 1941*, p. 434). For the 'Four Principles', see Hull, vol. 2, pp. 994–5.

47. Konoe Memoirs, fol. 36; Langer and Gleason, *The Undeclared War*, pp. 704–5; Morley, *The Final Confrontation*, pp. 189, 194; Carr, p. 156.

48. *The 'MAGIC' Background of Pearl Harbor*, vol. 3, appendix, pp. A88–90; Iriye, *Origins*, p. 163; Ike, p. 169.

49. Ike, pp. 170–71. Grew expressed his pessimism when he met Toyoda on 22 September (Grew, pp. 432–4).

50. Iriye, *Origins*, p. 163.

51. See Ike, pp. 155–6. The timing had been laid down in the 'Reference Materials for Answering Questions at the Imperial Conference on September 6 Regarding "The Essentials for Carrying Out the Empire's Policies"', prepared after consultation between the government and the Supreme Command (Ike, pp. 152–63).

52. Kido Diary, doc. no. 1632W (71), 26.9.41; Oka, pp. 150–1; Ike, pp. 176–8; Toland, *The Rising Sun*, p. 105; Morley, *The Final Confrontation*, p. 209.

53. *FRUS, 1941*, pp. 494–7; *Japan II*, pp. 656–61; Hull, vol. 2, p. 1033; Konoe Memoirs, fol. 47; Heinrichs, *American Ambassador*, p. 350.

54. Ike, pp. 179–80.

55. Morley, *The Final Confrontation*, p. 210.

56. Quoted in Morley, *The Final Confrontation*, p. 213.

57. Morley, *The Final Confrontation*, pp. 213–17; Iriye, *Origins*, pp. 164–5.

58. Konoe Memoirs, fols. 49–50; Morley, *The Final Confrontation*, pp. 222–5;

Toland, *The Rising Sun*, pp. 109–11; Oka, pp. 154–6. And see Tojo's postwar testimony at the International Military Tribunal for the Far East on the meeting (differing in some detail): *Political Strategy Prior to the Outbreak of War (Part III)*, Japanese Monographs, 147, Office of the Chief of Military History, Department of the Army, appendix 6 (http://www.ibiblio.org/pha/monos/147/147appo6.html).

59. Konoe Memoirs, fols. 50–51; Toland, *The Rising Sun*, pp. 111–12; Oka, pp. 155–6.

60. Quoted in Morley, *The Final Confrontation*, p. 227; Bix, p. 417; Oka, p. 156; Toland, *The Rising Sun*, pp. 112–13.

61. Iriye, *Origins*, pp. 165–6.

62. Oka, pp. 156–7.

63. Konoe Memoirs, fols. 85–6.

64. Konoe Memoirs, fols. 52–3; Kido Diary, doc. no.1632W (79–82, quotation 80); Morley, *The Final Confrontation*, pp. 230–45; Butow, pp. 285–301, 308; Toland, *The Rising Sun*, pp. 113–18; Bix, pp. 418–19; Oka, pp. 157–9; Feis, pp. 285–6.

65. Takashi Ito, Tadamitsu Hirohashi and Norio Katashima (eds.), *The Secret Documents of Prime Minister Tojo. Records of the Words and Deeds of General Hideki Tojo* [in Japanese], Tokyo, n.d., p. 478.

66. Morley, *The Final Confrontation*, p. 239.

67. Kido Diary, doc. no. 1632W (81), 17.10.41; Butow, pp. 301–2; Feis, pp. 286–7; Morley, *The Final Confrontation*, pp. 241, 243–4; Toland, *The Rising Sun*, p. 118.

68. Butow, pp. 302–5; Morley, *The Final Confrontation*, pp. 246–7.

69. Iriye, *Origins*, pp. 168–70.

70. Langer and Gleason, *The Undeclared War*, pp. 842–3; Carr, p. 161; Robert Dallek, *Franklin D. Roosevelt and American Foreign Policy, 1932–1945*, New York, 1979, pp. 304–5.

71. Hull, vol. 2, p. 1054. Ambassador Grew in Tokyo, on the other hand, was initially not unduly pessimistic. He was persuaded that Tojo could control the army and make it accept a settlement (Grew, p. 460 (20.10.41); Heinrichs, *American Ambassador*, p. 354). Nor was the State Department's estimate of the Tojo Cabinet, written on 18 October 1941 by Maxwell M. Hamilton, Chief of the Division of Far Eastern Affairs, totally negative. 'It is not believed', Hamilton wrote, 'that the new cabinet will reject a negotiated solution of Japan's international relations, but at the same time will take every measure possible to insure that, if such negotiated solutions are not forthcoming or are not successful, the opportunity for a solution by force will not be lost through lack of preparation or deployment of forces' (*FRUS, 1941*, pp. 522–3). This was similar to the view which Grew came to advance (Grew, pp. 469–70 (3–4.11.41)), that Japan was obviously preparing 'to implement an alternative program in the event the peace program fails'.

72. Langer and Gleason, *The Undeclared War*, pp. 845–6 (memorandum of the Joint Board of the Army and Navy, 5.11.41). See also Carr, p. 161.

73. Morley, *The Final Confrontation*, p. 249.

74. Quoted in Morley, *The Final Confrontation*, p. 247.

75. Morley, *The Final Confrontation*, pp. 248–9.

76. Quoted in Morley, *The Final Confrontation*, p. 249.

77. Quoted in Morley, *The Final Confrontation*, p. 252.

78. Quoted in Morley, *The Final Confrontation*, p. 250.

79. Ike, p. 195.

80. Ike, p. 188.

81. Ike, p. 191. This was prescient. The flaws in Japanese planning and the increasing gaps as the war lengthened between estimated and real availability of *matériel* and shipping are exposed in Morley, *The Final Confrontation*, pp. 267–303.

82. Ike, pp. 191–2, 195. Tojo testified after the war that it would have taken between four and seven years to produce the minimal requirement of synthetic oil. During this time, Japan would have had to rely upon her stock supplies, which could not have lasted for such a period (*Political Strategy Prior to the Outbreak of War (Part III)*, Japanese Monographs, 147, appendix 7 (http://www.ibiblio.org/pha/monos/147/147app07.html)).

83. Ike, p. 198.

84. Ike, pp. 197–8.

85. Ike, pp. 198–9.

86. All the quotations from contributions to the Conference that follow, unless otherwise referenced, are from the text in Ike, pp. 199–207.

87. Morley, *The Final Confrontation*, pp. 255–8; Toland, *The Rising Sun*, p. 124.

88. Text in Morley, *The Final Confrontation*, pp. 368–9 (appendix 9).

89. Text in Morley, *The Final Confrontation*, p. 370 (appendix 9); and Langer and Gleason, *The Undeclared War*, p. 878.

90. Quoted in Morley, *The Final Confrontation*, pp. 263–4.

91. Morley, *The Final Confrontation*, pp. 264–5. Looking back from 1945, Togo – defending his actions, but with some justice – pointed to the impossible odds with which he had to contend in attempting at this late juncture to avoid war (Sheffield University Library, Translation of Japanese Documents [prepared for the Tokyo War Crimes Trial], Wolfson Microfilm 306, Togo Memoirs, April–August 1945, fol. 1).

92. Bix, p. 424.

93. Morley, *The Final Confrontation*, p. 266; Toland, *The Rising Sun*, p. 130.

94. All the above quotations from contributions to the Conference, unless otherwise referenced, are from Ike, pp. 208–39.

95. Iriye, *Origins*, pp. 177–8.

96. Grew, pp. 468–9 (his report to Washington, 3.11.41; almost identical wording in his diary entry, 4.11.41); *Japan II*, pp. 703–4.

97. Toland, *The Rising Sun*, pp. 129, 136.

98. Hull, vol. 2, p. 1062.

99. Toland, *The Rising Sun*, pp. 129–30.

100. Morley, *The Final Confrontation*, p. 285; and see Bergamini, vol. 2, pp. 1020–22. Yamamoto – ironically, an opponent of war against the United States – had, in fact, conceived his brilliant plan of attack as early as November 1940 and had brought it to the attention of the Emperor, who was interested in it. In January 1941 Hirohito had ordered research on the plan to be undertaken, which concluded 'that the attack would be extremely hazardous but would have a reasonable chance of success' (Bergamini, vol. 2, pp. 954–5 and n. 1). Word must have leaked out (see Prange, p. 31), since Grew reported to Washington already on 27 January 1941: 'There is a lot of talk around town to the effect that the Japanese, in case of a break with the United States, are planning to go all out in a surprise attack on Pearl Harbor' (Grew, p. 368). See also Hull, vol. 2, p. 984; *FRUS, 1941*, p. 17. For a pen-picture of Yamamoto, see Mark Weston, *Giants of Japan. The Lives of Japan's Greatest Men and Women*, New York/Tokyo/London, 1999, pp. 190–200.

101. Iriye, *Origins*, pp. 170–71.

102. Quoted in Feis, p. 296; and (with slightly varied translation) Bergamini, vol. 2, p. 1041.

103. Bix, p. 423; Morley, *The Final Confrontation*, p. 265.

104. Bix, pp. 421–2.

105. Examples in Toland, *The Rising Sun*, pp. 132–5. The note to p. 133 indicates that there is no evidence of intentional mistranslation. See also Butow, p. 335 and n. 38, which indicates 'that the distortions did not essentially do violence to the reality of Japan's intentions'.

106. Hull, vol. 2, pp. 1056–7, 1060.

107. See Grew, pp. 468–9 (3.11.41) for the difference in tone from that of the State Department in Washington; and Morley, *The Final Confrontation*, pp. 310–11.

108. Langer and Gleason, *The Undeclared War*, pp. 855–66; *Japan II*, pp. 729–37; Hull, vol. 2, pp. 1058–62; Feis, pp. 303–5.

109. Feis, pp. 307–8; Langer and Gleason, *The Undeclared War*, pp. 863–4; Ike, p. 251 (Togo's report to the Liaison Conference of 20.11.41); Hull, vol. 2, pp. 1063–4; Morley, *The Final Confrontation*, pp. 301–5.

110. Hull, vol. 2, pp. 1069–71 (quotation p. 1070); and Butow, pp. 336–8. Langer and Gleason, *The Undeclared War*, p. 880, are critical of 'the depth of Mr. Hull's indignation over Japanese-sponsored suggestions which in many respects resembled ideas current in the State Department itself'. Spotswood (pp. 450–51) defends Hull's judgement, particularly in the light of the rapid growth of the numbers of Japanese troops in Indochina.

111. *FRUS, 1941*, pp. 635–6 (final draft pp. 661–4); Langer and Gleason, *The Undeclared War*, pp. 881–2.

112. Langer and Gleason, *The Undeclared War*, p. 872.

113. Hull, vol. 2, pp. 1072–3.

114. *FRUS, 1941*, pp. 640, 650–51, 655–6, 659–61, 666; Heinrichs, *Threshold of War*, pp. 209–11.

115. *The 'MAGIC' Background of Pearl Harbor*, vol. 4, Washington, 1978, appendix, p. A89. The President told his close advisers on 25 November that 'we were likely to be attacked perhaps next Monday [1 December], for the Japanese are notorious for making an attack without warning, and the question was what we should do'. A difficult issue, he felt, was 'how we should manoeuver them into the position of firing the first shot without allowing too much danger to ourselves' (Yale University Library, Henry L. Stimson Diaries 1909–1945, Reel 7, entry for 25.11.41).

116. *FRUS, 1941*, pp. 660–61; Stimson Diaries, Reel 7, entry for 26.11.41.

117. *FRUS, 1941*, p. 665.

118. Hull, vol. 2, p. 1081.

119. Hull, vol. 2, pp. 1074–6, 1082; Toland, *The Rising Sun*, pp. 140–3; Morley, *The Final Confrontation*, pp. 305–7, 309; Carr, p. 163; Heinrichs, *Threshold of War*, pp. 208–12; Stimson Diaries, Reel 7, entry for 27.11.41.

120. *Japan II*, pp. 766–70; text also in Langer and Gleason, *The Undeclared War*, pp. 896–7; and *Political Strategy Prior to the Outbreak of War (Part III)*, Japanese Monographs, 147, appendix 9 (http://www.ibiblio.org/pha/monos/147/147app09.html). They were far tougher than the proposals advanced six months earlier, on 21 June (see *Japan II*, pp. 483–5)– themselves described as 'an uncompromising restatement of the principles of international relations so frequently enunciated by Secretary Hull' (Langer and Gleason, *The Undeclared War*, p. 632).

121. Morley, *The Final Confrontation*, pp. 313–15, 317–18; Langer and Gleason, *The Undeclared War*, pp. 893, 898; Hull, vol. 2, pp. 1081–4; Carr, pp. 163–4; Bix, p. 428.

122. Quoted in Toland, *The Rising Sun*, p. 143.

123. Quoted in Morley, *The Final Confrontation*, p. 313.

124. See Tojo's postwar testimony to the International Military Tribunal for the Far East, where he stated the view at the time that the United States' proposal was an ultimatum, and that 'all were dumbfounded at the severity' of the demands (*Political Strategy Prior to the Outbreak of War (Part IV)*, Japanese Monographs, 150, appendix 3 (http://www.ibiblio.org/pha/monos/150/150app03.html)). Togo, in a cable to Nomura and Kurusu on 28 November, spoke of 'this humiliating proposal', which had been 'quite unexpected and extremely regrettable' (*The 'MAGIC' Background of Pearl Harbor*, vol. 4, pp. 84–6 and appendix, pp. A118). Nomura had, two days earlier, stated that he and Kurusu were 'dumbfounded' when Hull confronted them with the Ten Points (vol. 4, appendix, p. A102–3).

125. Toland, *The Rising Sun*, p. 145.

126. Morley, *The Final Confrontation*, pp. 315–17; Ike, pp. 256–7.

127. Quoted in Morley, *The Final Confrontation*, p. 320.

128. Bix, p. 430; Toland, *The Rising Sun*, pp. 176–9; Morley, *The Final Confrontation*, pp. 324–6.

129. *Political Strategy Prior to the Outbreak of War (Part IV)*, Japanese Monographs, 150, appendix 4 (http://www.ibiblio.org/pha/monos/150/150appo4.html).

130. Bix, pp. 430–31; Iriye, *Origins*, p. 182; Ike, pp. 262–3 (where the fleet departure time is mistakenly given as 6.00 p.m.); Morley, *The Final Confrontation*, p. 332; Prange, p. 390; Bergamini, vol. 2, pp. 1057–9.

131. Ike, p. 261 and n. 46; Morley, *The Final Confrontation*, p. 327; Toland, *The Rising Sun*, p. 179.

132. Quoted in Bix, pp. 430–31.

133. Bix, p. 431.

134. Ike, p. 271.

135. Ike, p. 279.

136. Ike, p. 282.

137. Ike, pp. 282–3; Bix, p. 433.

138. Butow, p. 363; Toland, *The Rising Sun*, p. 182.

139. Toland, *The Rising Sun*, p. 183; Morley, *The Final Confrontation*, p. 323.

140. Morley, *The Final Confrontation*, p. 344; *The 'MAGIC' Background of Pearl Harbor*, vol. 4, appendix, pp. A130–34.

141. Morley, *The Final Confrontation*, p. 329.

142. Morley, *The Final Confrontation*, p. 338.

143. Robert E. Sherwood, *The White House Papers of Harry L. Hopkins*, London, 1948, vol. 1, p. 430; also quoted in Morley, *The Final Confrontation*, p. 344; Toland, *The Rising Sun*, p. 194.

144. Toland, *The Rising Sun*, pp. 193–4, 198–9; Bix, p. 436.

145. Morley, *The Final Confrontation*, p. 344; Iriye, *Origins*, p. 183.

146. A 'prophetic' survey undertaken the previous July had, in fact, raised the possibility of exactly such a carrier-led air attack, and pointed to the need to strengthen defences at Pearl Harbor (Prange, pp. 185–8). The subsequently devised Joint Army-Navy Hawaiian Defense Plan for the protection of Pearl Harbor against a surprise attack from the air was, however, a very good one (Toland, *The Rising Sun*, p. 195). No one seemed to recall the warning passed on by Grew the previous January (Grew, p. 368).

147. Langer and Gleason, *The Undeclared War*, pp. 926–7 (and p. 911); Iriye, *Origins*, p. 183; Morley, *The Final Confrontation*, p. 345; Heinrichs, *Threshold of War*, p. 216.

148. Toland, *The Rising Sun*, pp. 201–2; Morley, *The Final Confrontation*, pp. 334–5, 344–5.

149. Morley, *The Final Confrontation*, p. 338.

150. I. C. B. Dear and M. R. D. Foot (eds.), *The Oxford Companion to the Second World War*, Oxford/New York, 1995, p. 872; Toland, *The Rising Sun*,

pp. 221, 235; Dallek, p. 311; Gerhard L. Weinberg, *A World at Arms. A Global History of World War II*, Cambridge, 1994, pp. 260–61.

151. Letter to Sasakawa Ryochi, 24 January [1941], appended as a last folio to the Konoe Memoirs.

152. It was such that conspiracy theories – essentially, that the American administration knew of the forthcoming attack, but deliberately avoided proper security precautions and let the devastating assault take place as the event necessary to justify the United States entering the war – rapidly surfaced and have never entirely been put to rest. They were always wildly far-fetched, and the thorough analyses by Prange of the military build-up to Pearl Harbor on both the American and Japanese sides (see here particularly the remarks in his concluding chapter, pp. 725–38), and of American intelligence by Roberta Wohlstetter, *Pearl Harbor. Warning and Decision*, Stanford, Calif., 1962, esp. pp. 382–96, have pointed unmistakably to a catalogue of errors and misjudgements, not Machiavellian plotting, behind the extraordinary events. This is underpinned by the more recent study of Richard J. Aldrich, *Intelligence and the War against Japan. Britain, America and the Politics of Secret Service*, Cambridge, 2000. This dispatches (pp. 68–84) a further strand of conspiracy theory: that Churchill received clear intelligence about Pearl Harbor, but deliberately withheld it from Roosevelt.

153. Toland, *The Rising Sun*, p. 227. When Kido, in the royal palace, heard the 'great news', he 'felt that the Gods had come to our aid' (Kido Diary, doc. no. 1632W (90), 8.12.41).

154. Bix, pp. 436–7; text of the Imperial Rescript on the Declaration of War, in *Political Strategy Prior to the Outbreak of War (Part IV)*, Japanese Monographs, 150, appendix 7 (http://www.ibiblio.org/pha/monos/150/150app07.html).

155. Hull, vol. 2, pp. 1095–7 (quotation p. 1096); Morley, *The Final Confrontation*, p. 338; *The 'MAGIC' Background of Pearl Harbor*, vol. 4, p. 101; Toland, *The Rising Sun*, pp. 224–5. Nomura's description is in *Political Strategy Prior to the Outbreak of War (Part IV)*, Japanese Monographs, 150, appendix 6 (http://www.ibiblio.org/pha/monos/150/150app06.html).

156. Frank Freidel, *Franklin D. Roosevelt. A Rendezvous with Destiny*, Boston, 1990, p. 407; Bergamini, vol. 2, p. 1096; Carr, p. 166.

157. Langer and Gleason, *The Undeclared War*, pp. 938–9.

158. Nazli Choucri, Robert C. North and Susumu Yamakage, *The Challenge of Japan before World War II and After*, London/New York, 1992, pp. 37–8, 40–43, 118–20, 132–7.

159. See Paul W. Schroeder, *The Axis Alliance and Japanese-American Relations 1941*, Ithaca, NY, 1958, pp. 203–8. Carr, p. 157, poses the same question, to which he then offers a cogent answer: 'No American president, especially one as sensitive to public opinion as Roosevelt, could possibly have carried through a *volte-face* on this scale in the teeth of an outraged public . . . Also, any hint of surrender to Japan would have had a demoralizing effect on the enemies of the Axis.'

160. See on this the pertinent comments of Feis, pp. 274–5, that Konoe 'was a

prisoner, willing or unwilling, of the terms precisely prescribed in conferences over which he presided', and 'it is unlikely that he could have got around them or that he would have in some desperate act discarded them. The whole of his political career speaks to the contrary.'

161. See, for instance, Toland, *The Rising Sun*, notes to pp. 141 and 145; and Morley, *The Final Confrontation*, p. 319.

162. See Langer and Gleason, *The Undeclared War*, p. 721.

163. See Iriye, *Origins*, pp. 178–9.

CHAPTER 9. BERLIN, AUTUMN 1941

1. Sebastian Haffner, *Von Bismarck zu Hitler. Ein Rückblick*, paperback edn., Munich, 1989, p. 293. See also Enrico Syring, 'Hitlers Kriegserklärung an Amerika vom 11. Dezember 1941', in Wolfgang Michalka (ed.), *Der Zweite Welt-krieg. Analysen, Grundzüge, Forschungsbilanz*, Munich/Zurich, 1989, p. 683.

2. Max Domarus (ed.), *Hitler. Reden und Proklamationen 1932–1945*, Wiesbaden, 1973, p. 1809.

3. Text in Domarus, p. 1808 n. 543; and *DGFP*, 13, doc. 577, pp. 1004–5; see also Paul Schmidt, *Statist auf diplomatischer Bühne 1923–45. Erlebnisse des Chefdolmetschers im Auswärtigen Amt mit den Staatsmännern Europas*, Bonn, 1953, p. 554.

4. *Meldungen aus dem Reich. Auswahl aus den geheimen Lageberichten des Sicherheitsdienstes der SS 1939–1944*, ed. Heinz Boberach, Neuwied/Berlin, 1965, p. 198.

5. Harry W. Flannery, *Assignment to Berlin*, London, 1942, p. 291.

6. *Mein Tagebuch. Geschichten vom Überleben 1939–1947*, ed. Heinrich Breloer, Cologne, 1984, p. 64.

7. 'Inside Germany Report' for December 1941, cited in Philipp Gassert, *Amerika im Dritten Reich. Ideologie, Propaganda und Volksmeinung 1933–1945*, Stuttgart, 1997, p. 321.

8. Wilm Hosenfeld, *'Ich versuche jeden zu retten'. Das Leben eines deutschen Offiziers in Briefen und Tagebüchern*, ed. Thomas Vogel, Munich, 2004, p. 561.

9. *Die Tagebücher von Joseph Goebbels*, ed. Elke Fröhlich, part II, vol. 2, Munich, 1996, p. 453 (8.12.41).

10. Nicolaus von Below, *Als Hitlers Adjutant 1937–1945*, Mainz, 1980, p. 296.

11. Karl Dönitz, *Memoirs. Ten Years and Twenty Days*, New York, 1997, p. 195.

12. Walter Warlimont, *Inside Hitler's Headquarters 1939–45*, Presidio edn., Novato, Calif., n.d., p. 208.

13. Warlimont, p. 203.

14. Warlimont, p. 50.

15. *The Ribbentrop Memoirs*, London, 1954, p. 160.

16. Ernst von Weizsäcker, *Erinnerungen*, Munich/Leipzig/Freiburg, 1950, p. 328.

17. Even as late as 24 February 1945, Hitler still spoke of the 'vast territory' of the United States, 'ample to absorb the energies of all their people', as the model which he hoped to emulate for Germany in Europe, 'to ensure for her complete economic independence inside a territory of a size compatible with her population', adding that 'a great people has need of broad acres' (*The Testament of Adolf Hitler. The Hitler–Bormann Documents, February–April 1945*, ed. François Genoud, London, 1961, p. 88). For textual problems with this source, see Ian Kershaw, *Hitler, 1936–1945. Nemesis*, London, 2000, n. 121, pp. 1024–5.

18. *Hitler: Reden, Schriften, Anordnungen. Februar 1925 bis Januar 1933*, ed. Institut für Zeitgeschichte, vol. 3, part 1, Munich, 1994, p. 161 (18.10.28).

19. *Hitler: Reden, Schriften, Anordnungen*, vol. 4, part 1, p. 417 (25.6.31).

20. The preceding paragraph draws on the informative analysis in Gassert, pp. 87–103.

21. Gassert, pp. 34–6.

22. Eberhard Jäckel and Axel Kuhn (eds.), *Hitler. Sämtliche Aufzeichnungen 1905–1924*, Stuttgart, 1980, pp. 96–7, 99.

23. Adolf Hitler, *Mein Kampf*, 876–880th printing, Munich, 1943, pp. 722–3; trans. Ralph Mannheim with an Introduction by D. C. Watt, paperback edn., London, 1973, pp. 582–3.

24. Dietrich Aigner, 'Hitler und die Weltherrschaft', in Wolfgang Michalka (ed.), *Nationalsozialistische Außenpolitik*, Darmstadt, 1978, p. 62.

25. See Gassert, pp. 95–6; and Gerhard L. Weinberg, *The Foreign Policy of Hitler's Germany. Diplomatic Revolution in Europe 1933–36*, Chicago/London, 1970, p. 21; Gerhard L. Weinberg, 'Hitler's Image of the United States', *American Historical Review*, 69 (1964), p. 1009.

26. *Hitler's Second Book. The Unpublished Sequel to Mein Kampf*, ed. Gerhard L. Weinberg, New York, 2003, p. 112.

27. *Hitler's Second Book*, pp. 116–17.

28. Hitler's alleged remarks about the United States in tainted and discredited sources, Edouard Calic, *Unmasked. Two Confidential Interviews with Hitler in 1931*, London, 1971, and Hermann Rauschning, *Hitler Speaks*, London, 1939, cannot be regarded as authentic statements.

29. Ernst Hanfstaengl, *Hitler. The Missing Years*, paperback edn., New York, 1994, p. 188.

30. Gassert, pp. 93–4; Andreas Hillgruber, 'Der Faktor Amerika in Hitlers Strategie 1938–1941', *Aus Politik und Zeitgeschichte. Beilage zur Wochenzeitung 'Das Parlament'*, 11 May 1966, p. 4; Weinberg, 'Hitler's Image', pp. 1010–12.

31. Weinberg, *Diplomatic Revolution*, pp. 133–58, esp. pp. 145, 149, 157.

32. See Gassert, pp. 183–246, for an extensive survey of these features of German depictions of the United States.

33. *Akten der Reichskanzlei. Die Regierung Hitler*, ed. Karl-Heinz Minuth, vol. 1, Boppard am Rhein, 1983, p. 317; and see Gassert, pp. 183–4.

34. *IMT*, vol. 25, pp. 402–13, doc. 386-PS; trans. Jeremy Noakes and Geoffrey

Pridham (eds.), *Nazism 1919–1945. A Documentary Reader*, vol. 3, Exeter, 1988, pp. 680–87.

35. *DGFP*, 1, doc. 423, p. 656; Hillgruber, 'Amerika', p. 7. For the 'quarantine speech', chiefly targeting Japan, see Robert Dallek, *Franklin D. Roosevelt and American Foreign Policy, 1932–1945*, New York, 1979, p. 148.

36. Gassert, pp. 246–59.

37. Frank Freidel, *Franklin D. Roosevelt. A Rendezvous with Destiny*, Boston, 1990, p. 314; Gassert, pp. 258–9.

38. Saul Friedländer, *Prelude to Downfall. Hitler and the United States, 1939–1941*, New York, 1967, pp. 8–9.

39. Adam Tooze, *The Wages of Destruction. The Making and Breaking of the Nazi Economy*, London, 2006, p. 283.

40. Wilhelm Treue (ed.), 'Rede Hitlers vor der deutschen Presse (10. November 1938)', *Vierteljahrshefte für Zeitgeschichte*, 6 (1958), p. 191.

41. *DGFP*, 4, doc. 158, p. 192; Friedländer, *Prelude to Downfall*, p. 9.

42. Domarus, p. 1058; trans. Noakes and Pridham, vol. 3, p. 1049. And see Tooze, pp. 283–4.

43. See Dallek, p. 181 for Roosevelt's remarks, made in private, but leaked to the press; and Gassert, p. 261 for the German propaganda response.

44. William L. Langer and S. Everett Gleason, *The Challenge to Isolation, 1937–1940*, New York, 1952, pp. 84–5; Cordell Hull *The Memoirs of Cordell Hull*, New York, 1948, vol. 1, p. 621.

45. Below, p. 161.

46. Langer and Gleason, *Challenge*, p. 87.

47. Domarus, pp. 1166–79, for the parts of the speech given over to the 'answer' to Roosevelt.

48. *Die Tagebücher von Joseph Goebbels*, ed. Elke Fröhlich, part I, vol. 6, Munich, 1998, p. 332 (29.4.39). See Gassert, pp. 263–6 for the positive impact of the speech within Germany.

49. William L. Shirer, *Berlin Diary, 1934–1941*, paperback edn., London, 1970, p. 133. Shirer was correct in presuming that Hitler's comments would go down well with isolationists. See Langer and Gleason, *Challenge*, p. 89.

50. Friedländer, *Prelude to Downfall*, pp. 50–51; Gassert, pp. 271–7.

51. Friedländer, *Prelude to Downfall*, pp. 61, 65.

52. *KTB d. OKW*, vol. 1, 1965, p. 108E; Hillgruber, 'Amerika', p. 8.

53. *DGFP*, 8, doc. 172, p. 180 (1.10.39); doc. 405, pp. 470–71 (1.12.39); Hillgruber, 'Amerika', p. 9.

54. *DGFP*, 7, doc. 378, p. 377 (28.8.39); Hillgruber, 'Amerika', p. 9.

55. Below, p. 200.

56. Franz Halder, *Kriegstagebuch. Tägliche Aufzeichnungen des Chefs des Generalstabes des Heeres 1939–1942*, vol. 1: *Vom Polenfeldzug bis zum Ende der Westoffensive (14.8.1939–30.6.1940)*, ed. Hans-Adolf Jacobsen, Stuttgart, 1962, pp. 86–90.

57. *DGFP*, 9, doc. 192, p. 277; Hillgruber, 'Amerika', p. 9.

58. Quoted in Langer and Gleason, *Challenge*, p. 516.

59. *DGFP*, 10, doc. 199, pp. 259–60; Hillgruber, 'Amerika', p. 12.

60. Wolfgang Michalka, 'From the Anti-Comintern Pact to the Euro-Asiatic Bloc. Ribbentrop's Alternative Concept of Hitler's Foreign Policy Programme', in H. W. Koch (ed.), *Aspects of the Third Reich*, London, 1985, pp. 281–2.

61. Friedländer, *Prelude to Downfall*, p. 125.

62. Gassert, p. 281.

63. Gassert, pp. 284–6.

64. *Fuehrer Conferences on Naval Affairs 1939–1945*, London, 1990, p. 162.

65. *DGFP*, 11, doc. 633, pp. 1061–2.

66. Friedländer, p. 172.

67. Domarus, p. 1661.

68. *KTB d. OKW*, vol. 1, pp. 257–8; also quoted in Andreas Hillgruber, *Hitlers Strategie. Politik und Kriegführung 1940–1941*, 3rd edn., Bonn, 1993, p. 364.

69. *Fuehrer Conferences*, p. 172.

70. Quoted in Friedländer, *Prelude to Downfall*, p. 175.

71. Quoted in Friedländer, *Prelude to Downfall*, p. 175 n. 1.

72. *Heeresadjutant bei Hitler 1938–1943. Aufzeichnungen des Majors Engel*, ed. Hildegard von Kotze, Stuttgart, 1974, p. 99 (24.3.41).

73. Friedländer, *Prelude to Downfall*, p. 203.

74. *Fuehrer Conferences*, p. 199 (22.5.41); Friedländer, *Prelude to Downfall*, pp. 205–8; Thomas A. Bailey and Paul B. Ryan, *Hitler vs. Roosevelt. The Undeclared Naval War*, New York, 1979, pp. 122–9.

75. Bailey and Ryan, pp. 129–32, 138–44.

76. *Fuehrer Conferences*, p. 218 (6.6.41).

77. Bailey and Ryan, pp. 148–9.

78. *Fuehrer Conferences*, pp. 219–20 (21.6.41).

79. *Hitlers Weisungen für die Kriegführung. Dokumente des Oberkommandos der Wehrmacht*, ed. Walther Hubatsch, paperback edn., Munich, 1965, p. 121.

80. *DGFP*, 12, doc. 78, pp. 144–5.

81. See Friedländer, *Prelude to Downfall*, pp. 196, 202.

82. *DGFP*, 12, doc. 281, p. 382.

83. *DGFP*, 12, doc. 222, pp. 388–92.

84. *DGFP*, 12, doc. 266, pp. 455–6.

85. *DGFP*, 12, doc. 496, pp. 777–80; *Ciano's Diary 1939–1943*, ed. Malcolm Muggeridge, London, 1947, p. 341 (12.5.41).

86. *DGFP*, 12, doc. 596, pp. 967–70.

87. *KTB d. OKW*, vol. 1, p. 996.

88. Quoted in Friedländer, *Prelude to Downfall*, p. 255.

89. *Fuehrer Conferences*, p. 221 (9.7.41).

90. *Fuehrer Conferences*, p. 222 (25.7.41).

91. Franz Halder, *Kriegstagebuch. Tägliche Aufzeichnungen des Chefs des Gen-*

eralstabes des Heeres 1939–1942, vol. 3: *Der Rußlandfeldzug bis zum Marsch auf Stalingrad (22.6.1941–24.9.1942)*, ed. Hans-Adolf Jacobsen, Stuttgart, 1964, p. 38.

92. *Hitlers Weisungen*, pp. 159–62.

93. *Fuehrer Conferences*, p. 199; Hillgruber, 'Amerika', p. 18.

94. See Eberhard Jäckel, *Hitler in History*, Hanover/London, 1984, p. 72.

95. *Staatsmänner und Diplomaten bei Hitler. Vertrauliche Aufzeichnungen über die Unterredungen mit Vertretern des Auslandes 1939–1941*, ed. Andreas Hillgruber, paperback edn., Munich, 1969, pp. 292–303; and see Hillgruber, 'Amerika', p. 17.

96. *Die Tagebücher von Joseph Goebbels*, part II, vol. 1, Munich, 1996, p. 263 (19.8.41).

97. Halder, *Kriegstagebuch*, vol. 3, p. 170 (11 Aug. 1941); trans. *The Halder War Diary, 1939–1942*, ed. Charles Burdick and Hans-Adolf Jacobsen, London, 1988, p. 506.

98. See Kershaw, *Hitler, 1936–1945*, London, 2000, pp. 407–18.

99. *Die Tagebücher von Joseph Goebbels*, part II, vol. 1, pp. 236–7 (15.8.41). And for German propaganda about the Atlantic Charter, see Friedländer, pp. 268–9; Gassert, pp. 312–13.

100. *DGFP*, 13, doc. 209, p. 323; Friedländer, p. 267.

101. David Kahn, *Hitler's Spies. German Military Intelligence in World War II*, New York, 2000, pp. 80–83.

102. Friedländer, *Prelude to Downfall*, pp. 266–7, citing Bötticher's telegram of 14 August 1941.

103. For Churchill's critics at this point, see John Charmley, *Churchill: The End of Glory. A Political Biography*, London, 1993, pp. 448–9.

104. *Die Tagebücher von Joseph Goebbels*, part II, vol. 1, p. 263 (19.8.41).

105. *Fuehrer Conferences*, pp. 228–9 (22.8.41).

106. Friedländer, *Prelude to Downfall*, pp. 275–81.

107. *Die Tagebücher von Joseph Goebbels*, part II, vol. 1, pp. 367–8, 370–71, 375–6 (6–8.9.41), quotation p. 376.

108. *Die Tagebücher von Joseph Goebbels*, part II, vol. 1, pp. 407–8 (13.9.41).

109. *Die Tagebücher von Joseph Goebbels*, part II, vol. 1, p. 417 (14.9.41).

110. *Fuehrer Conferences*, pp. 231–3 (17.9.41). Ernst von Weizsäcker, State Secretary in the Foreign Office, had noted in his diary on 19 September the utmost caution to be exercised towards the United States, even though Roosevelt had eight days earlier declared that American ships would shoot on sight (*Die Weizsäcker-Papiere 1933–1950*, ed. Leonidas E. Hill, Frankfurt am Main, 1974, p. 270).

111. Halder, *Kriegstagebuch*, vol. 3, p. 219 (10.9.41); Jäckel, *Hitler in History*, p. 75; *Die Weizsäcker-Papiere*, p. 268 (6.9.41).

112. *DGFP*, 13, doc. 316, p. 505; Jäckel, *Hitler in History*, p. 75.

113. Friedländer, *Prelude to Downfall*, p. 280.

114. *Die Tagebücher von Joseph Goebbels*, part II, vol. 2, Munich, 1966, pp. 136, 149 (18, 21. 10.41), quotation p. 136.

115. *Die Tagebücher von Joseph Goebbels*, part II, vol. 2, pp. 140, 145 (19–20.10.41); Bailey and Ryan, p. 202.

116. *Die Tagebücher von Joseph Goebbels*, part II, vol. 2, pp. 216 (quotation), 223 (1–2.11.41).

117. Domarus, p. 1778.

118. *Fuehrer Conferences*, p. 239 (13.11.41); see also Friedländer, *Prelude to Downfall*, p. 294.

119. William Carr, *Poland to Pearl Harbor. The Making of the Second World War*, London, 1985, p. 143.

120. Dr Henry Picker, *Hitlers Tischgespräche im Führerhauptquartier 1941–1942*, ed. Percy Ernst Schramm, Stuttgart, 1963, p. 145 (10.9.41); *Staatsmänner*, p. 319 (conversation with Ciano, 25.10.41); Hillgruber, 'Amerika', pp. 4, 18.

121. *Die Weizsäcker-Papiere*, p. 274 (21.10.41); Weizsäcker, *Erinnerungen*, p. 326.

122. *Die Tagebücher von Joseph Goebbels*, part II, vol. 2, p. 180 (26.10.41).

123. *DGFP*, 13, doc. 434, p. 717; Jäckel, *Hitler in History*, p. 75.

124. *Die Tagebücher von Joseph Goebbels*, part II, vol. 2, p. 240 (6.11.41).

125. Jäckel, *Hitler in History*, p. 75. See also *DGFP*, 13, p. 745 n. 3.

126. *DGFP*, 13, doc. 480, p. 799; cited also in Jäckel, *Hitler in History*, p. 76, with slightly varying translation; see also Friedländer, *Prelude to Downfall*, p. 306; and Gerhard Krebs, 'Deutschland und Pearl Harbor', *Historische Zeitschrift*, 253 (1991), pp. 341–2. Krebs (pp. 327–47) offers a thorough account of the Japanese efforts to secure a guarantee of German assistance.

127. *DGFP*, 13, doc. 487, pp. 806–7; Jäckel, *Hitler in History*, p. 76; Friedländer, p. 306; Klaus Hildebrand, *Das vergangene Reich. Deutsche Außenpolitik von Bismarck bis Hitler*, Stuttgart, 1995, pp. 762–3. Unsurprisingly, Ott interpreted Ribbentrop's answer as approval to support for Japan in circumstances not covered by the Tripartite Pact, namely Japanese aggression. This prompted great relief in the Japanese leadership (Krebs, p. 342).

128. *DGFP*, 13, doc. 492, p. 813; Jäckel, *Hitler in History*, p. 77.

129. *Staatsmänner*, pp. 256–7 (4.4.41).

130. Nobutaka Ike (ed.), *Japan's Decision for War. Records of the 1941 Policy Conferences*, Stanford, Calif., 1967, pp. 241–2 (12.11.41).

131. *Die Weizsäcker-Papiere*, p. 277 (23.11.41).

132. *Die Tagebücher von Joseph Goebbels*, part II, vol. 2, p. 308 (18.11.41).

133. Possibly preparation for Hitler's involvement for three days, from 27 to 29 November, in a series of talks with foreign dignitories in Berlin to celebrate the extension of the Anti-Comintern Pact of 1936 delayed matters. See Milan Hauner, *Hitler. A Chronology of his Life and Time*, 2nd edn., Basingstoke/New York, 2005, p. 171.

134. *DGFP*, 13, doc. 506, pp. 847–8; Michael Bloch, *Ribbentrop*, paperback edn., London, 1994, p. 346.

135. *The 'MAGIC' Background of Pearl Harbor*, vol. 4, Washington, 1978, appendix, p. A383; *DGFP*, 13, doc. 512, p. 870, n. 4; Jäckel, *Hitler in History*, p. 79. See Krebs, pp. 346–7, and Syring, pp. 688–9, for the question of the authenticity of the evidence on Hitler's quoted words. Krebs, p. 369, cites Oshima's telegram of 29 November to Tokyo as stating: 'I have found to be confirmed that he [Hitler] will support Japan with all his might if a conflict should arise in Japanese-American relations.'

136. *IMT*, vol. 31, doc. 2898-PS, p. 268. Friedländer, p. 306, mistakenly gives the date as 10 November, and places Ott's conversation with Tojo.

137. *Nazi Conspiracy and Aggression*, United States Government, vol. 6, Washington, 1946, doc. 3598-PS; also quoted in John Toland, *Adolf Hitler*, London, 1977, p. 694.

138. *The 'MAGIC' Background of Pearl Harbor*, vol. 4, appendix, pp. A387–8; Jäckel, *Hitler in History*, p. 80. See also Carl Boyd, *Hitler's Japanese Confidant. General Oshima Hiroshi and MAGIC Intelligence, 1941–1945*, Lawrence, Kan., 1992, p. 36. Syring, p. 689 (and see p. 695 n. 57), leaves open the question, disputed by historians, whether the date was 1 or 2 December. Little hinges on the point.

139. Krebs, pp. 352–3; Jäckel, *Hitler in History*, pp. 80–81; Bloch, p. 346.

140. *Ciano's Diary*, pp. 405–6 (3, 5.12.41).

141. *DGFP*, 13, doc. 546, pp. 958–9; Jäckel, *Hitler in History*, p. 81; Krebs, pp. 352–3.

142. *Die Weizsäcker-Papiere*, p. 279 (6.12.41).

143. Weizsäcker, *Erinnerungen*, p. 327; *Die Tagebücher von Joseph Goebbels*, part II, vol. 2, p. 468 (10.12.41).

144. *Die Weizsäcker-Papiere*, pp. 278–9 (6.12.41).

145. Halder, *Kriegstagebuch*, vol. 3, p. 332 (7.12.41); trans. *Halder War Diary*, p. 582.

146. *Die Tagebücher von Joseph Goebbels*, part II, vol. 2, p. 439 (6.12.41).

147. Friedländer, *Prelude to Downfall*, p. 307.

148. Weizsäcker, *Erinnerungen*, p. 328. Jodl's own surprise was, he thought, shared by Hitler (*IMT*, vol. 15, p. 397).

149. Schmidt, p. 553.

150. *Ciano's Diary*, p. 407 (8.12.41).

151. *Die Weizsäcker-Papiere*, pp. 279–80 (8.12.41).

152. *Die Tagebücher von Joseph Goebbels*, part II, vol. 2, p. 453 (8.12.41).

153. Institut für Zeitgeschichte, Munich, ED 100, Diary of Walther Hewel (8.12.41); also quoted in David Irving, *Hitler's War*, London, 1977, p. 352.

154. Franz von Papen, *Memoirs*, London, 1952, p. 484.

155. *Generalfeldmarschall Keitel: Verbrecher oder Offizier? Erinnerungen, Briefe, Dokumente des Chefs OKW*, ed. Walter Görlitz, Göttingen, 1961, p. 285. Otto Dietrich, *12 Jahre mit Hitler*, Munich, 1955, p. 85, also recalled the immediate change in Hitler's demeanour when given the news of Pearl Harbor.

156. Warlimont, pp. 207–8.

157. *Die Tagebücher von Joseph Goebbels*, part II, vol. 2, pp. 469 (10.12.41).

158. Below, p. 296.

159. Unpublished notes and tape-recording of an interview of Wolfgang Brocke by Hans Mommsen, 25.4.97. I am most grateful to Professor Mommsen for access to this material.

160. *Generalfeldmarschall Keitel*, p. 285.

161. Gerhard Weinberg, *A World at Arms. A Global History of World War II*, Cambridge, 1994, p. 262; Jäckel, *Hitler in History*, p. 82; Friedländer, p. 308.

162. *Die Tagebücher von Joseph Goebbels*, part II, vol. 2, pp. 464–5 (10.12.41).

163. *Nazi Conspiracy and Aggression*, Washington, 1948, supplement B, p. 1199; with slightly different wording, also in *IMT*, vol. 10, p. 298; and *The Ribbentrop Memoirs*, p. 160.

164. See Domarus, pp. 1806–7.

165. *Die Tagebücher von Joseph Goebbels*, part II, vol. 2, p. 494 (13.12.41).

166. Domarus, p. 1807.

167. Friedländer, *Prelude to Downfall*, p. 308.

168. *Die Tagebücher von Joseph Goebbels*, part II, vol. 2, p. 476 (11.12.41).

169. *Die Tagebücher von Joseph Goebbels*, part II, vol. 2, p. 468 (10.12.41).

170. *Nazi Conspiracy and Aggression*, supplement B, p. 1199; the same sentiments in slightly different wording in *The Ribbentrop Memoirs*, p. 160.

171. *The Ribbentrop Memoirs*, pp. 160, 167.

172. *DGFP*, 13, doc. 569, p. 994; Friedländer, p. 308.

173. *DGFP*, 13, doc. 562, p. 982; Jäckel, *Hitler in History*, p. 82.

174. Domarus, pp. 1809–10.

175. A point made by Jäckel, *Hitler in History*, p. 86.

176. Syring, p. 691.

177. Jäckel, *Hitler in History*, p. 83; Syring, p. 688.

178. See Syring, p. 692; Gassert, p. 317.

179. Weizsäcker, *Erinnerungen*, p. 328.

180. *Die Weizsäcker-Papiere*, p. 280 (10.12.41).

181. See *Die Tagebücher von Joseph Goebbels*, part II, vol. 2, pp. 433, 439 (5–6.12.41).

182. *Die Tagebücher von Joseph Goebbels*, part II, vol. 2, p. 468 (10.12.41).

183. Hillgruber, *Hitlers Strategie*, p. 554.

184. Dönitz, pp. 202–6. Even so, Dönitz lamented how few U-boats were placed at his disposal as the needs of submarine warfare in the Mediterranean and to protect Norway made competing claims.

185. Kahn, pp. 83–4.

186. See Hitler's comments to Oshima on 3 Jan. 1942, that if Japan and Germany act together so that 'England loses India, an entire world collapses. India is the heart of the English Empire' (quoted in Hildebrand, *Das vergangene Reich*, p. 764).

187. Hildebrand, *Das vergangene Reich*, p. 762.

188. Hull, vol. 2, pp. 1099–100.

189. Freidel, p. 408.

190. Dallek, p. 312.

191. Freidel, p. 407.

192. David M. Kennedy, *Freedom from Fear. The American People in Depression and War, 1929–1945*, New York/Oxford, 1999, pp. 565–9.

193. Weinberg, *A World at Arms*, p. 330.

194. This differs from the implication in Kennedy, p. 524, that 'in the absence of such a legal declaration, Roosevelt might well have found it impossible to resist demands to place the maximum American effort in the Pacific, against the formally recognized Japanese enemy, rather than in the Atlantic, in a nondeclared war against the Germans'.

195. Kennedy, p. 543; I. C. B. Dear and M. R. D. Foot (eds.), *The Oxford Companion to the Second World War*, Oxford/New York, 1995, p. 860.

196. Richard Overy, *Why the Allies Won*, London, 1995, p. 15, writes that 'on the face of things, no rational man in early 1942 would have guessed at the eventual outcome of the war'. 'On the face of things', that may have been the case. But Churchill, to go from his later account, recognized that, after Pearl Harbor and with the United States drawn into the conflict, 'we had won the war . . . Hitler's fate was sealed. Mussolini's fate was sealed. As for the Japanese, they would be ground to powder. All the rest was merely the proper application of overwhelming force' (Winston S. Churchill, *The Second World War*, vol. 3: *The Grand Alliance*, London, 1950, p. 539).

197. *Staatsmänner*, p. 329 (Hitler's meeting with the Danish Foreign Minister, Erik Scavenius, 27.11.41). He repeated similar sentiments to his own entourage on 27.1.42 (Picker, p. 171). Both are quoted by Hillgruber, 'Amerika', p. 20.

CHAPTER 10. BERLIN/EAST PRUSSIA, SUMMER–AUTUMN 1941

1. *Die Tagebücher von Joseph Goebbels*, ed. Elke Fröhlich, part II, vol. 2, Munich, 1996, pp. 498–9 (13.12.41).

2. Helmut Krausnick and Hans-Heinrich Wilhelm, *Die Truppe des Weltanschauungskrieges. Die Einsatzgruppen der Sicherheitspolizei und des SD 1938–1942*, Stuttgart, 1981, p. 619.

3. *Dimension des Völkermords. Die Zahl der jüdischen Opfer des Nationalsozialismus*, ed. Wolfgang Benz, Munich, 1991, p. 17.

4. Jeremy Noakes and Geoffrey Pridham (eds.), *Nazism 1919–1945. A Documentary Reader*, vol. 3, Exeter, 1988, p. 1130; Mark Roseman, *The Villa, the Lake, the Meeting. Wannsee and the Final Solution*, London, 2002, pp. 111–12. The target figure included Jews in England, as well as in neutral countries such as Switzerland, Turkey, Sweden, Ireland and Spain.

5. Donald Bloxham, 'The Armenian Genocide of 1915–16. Cumulative Radicaliz-

ation and the Development of a Destruction Policy', *Past and Present*, 181 (2003), pp. 141–3, 146, 186–91; Norman M. Naimark, *Fires of Hatred. Ethnic Cleansing in Twentieth-Century Europe*, Cambridge, Mass./London, 2001, pp. 18–36.

6. Also pointed out by Robert S. Wistrich, *Hitler and the Holocaust*, New York, 2001, p. 238.

7. Naimark, p. 35.

8. Michael Mann, *The Dark Side of Democracy. Explaining Ethnic Cleansing*, Cambridge, 2005, pp. 140, 145; Bloxham, p. 152. And see Naimark, pp. 28–30.

9. Max Domarus (ed.), *Hitler. Reden und Proklamationen 1932–1945*, Wiesbaden, 1973, p. 1058; trans. Noakes and Pridham, vol. 3, p. 1049.

10. Werner Maser (ed.), *Hitlers Briefe und Notizen. Sein Weltbild in handschriftlichen Dokumenten*, Düsseldorf, 1973, pp. 360–61; trans. *Nazi Conspiracy and Aggression*, United States Government, Washington, 1946–8, vol. 6, p. 260.

11. Eberhard Jäckel and Axel Kuhn (eds.), *Hitler. Sämtliche Aufzeichnungen 1905–1924*, Stuttgart, 1980, pp. 89–90; trans. Noakes and Pridham, vol. 1, Exeter, 1983, pp. 12–14.

12. Adolf Hitler, *Mein Kampf*, 876–880th reprint, Munich, 1943, p. 772; trans. Ralph Mannheim, *Hitler's Mein Kampf*, with an Introduction by D. C. Watt, London, 1973, p. 620.

13. *IMT*, vol. 28, pp. 538–9.

14. On the development of Eichmann's career, see David Cesarani, *Eichmann. His Life and Crimes*, London, 2004, chs. 1–3.

15. See, especially, Michael Wildt, *Generation des Unbedingten. Das Führungskorps des Reichssicherheitshauptamtes*, Hamburg, 2002, specifically on career opportunities, pp. 163–89.

16. Otto Dov Kulka, 'Die deutsche Geschichtsschreibung über den Nationalsozialismus und die "Endlösung". Tendenzen und Entwicklungsphasen 1924–1984', *Historische Zeitschrift*, 240 (1985), pp. 628–9; and Otto Dov Kulka, 'Critique of Judaism in European Thought. On the Historical Meaning of Modern Antisemitism', *Jerusalem Quarterly*, 52 (1989), pp. 128–9. See also Saul Friedländer. *Nazi Germany and the Jews. The Years of Persecution, 1933–39*, London, 1977, pp. 84, 87–90, for the notion of 'redemptive antisemitism'.

17. *IMT*, vol. 29, pp. 145–6; trans. Noakes and Pridham, vol. 3, pp. 1199–1200.

18. *Die Tagebücher von Joseph Goebbels*, part II, vol. 3, Munich, 1994, p. 561 (27.3.42).

19. This is not, however, to support the controversial claims of Daniel Jonah Goldhagen, *Hitler's Willing Executioners. Ordinary Germans and the Holocaust*, New York, 1996, p. 77, emphasizing Germany's specific path to genocide by asserting that 'eliminationist antisemitism' had throughout the nineteenth and early twentieth centuries been 'extremely widespread in all social classes and sectors of German society, for it was deeply embedded in German cultural and political life and conversation, as well as integrated into the moral structure of society'.

20. Ian Kershaw, *Hitler, 1889–1936. Hubris*, London, 1998, pp. 33–5.

21. Léon Poliakov, *The History of Anti-Semitism*, vol. 4: *Suicidal Europe, 1870–1933*, Oxford, 1977, pp. 52–7.

22. Thomas Nipperdey, *Deutsche Geschichte 1866–1918*, vol. 2: *Machtstaat vor der Demokratie*, Munich, 1992, p. 295.

23. Nipperdey, pp. 299, 305; George Mosse, *The Crisis of German Ideology. Intellectual Origins of the Third Reich*, London, 1966, pp. 93–7, 112. Hitler's claim to have studied Fritsch was made in a letter he wrote to the antisemitic author on 28 November 1930. He said he was convinced that Fritsch's book had paved the way for the Nazi antisemitic movement (*Hitler: Reden, Schriften, Anordnungen. Februar 1925 bis Januar 1933*, ed. Institut für Zeitgeschichte, vol. 4, part 1, Munich/London/New York/Paris, 1994, p. 133).

24. See Nipperdey, pp. 290, 303, and his balanced account, pp. 289–311.

25. Jäckel and Kuhn, p. 89.

26. Otto Dov Kulka, 'Richard Wagner und die Anfänge des modernen Anti-semitismus', *Bulletin des Leo Baeck Instituts*, 4 (1961), pp. 281–300, locates an early manifestation of messianic, redemptive antisemitism as the basis of a revolutionary ideology in Wagner's writings.

27. Ulrich Herbert, '"Generation der Sachlichkeit". Die völkische Studenten-bewegung der frühen zwanziger Jahre in Deutschland', in Werner Johe and Uwe Lohalm (eds.), *Zivilisation und Barbarei*, Hamburg, 1991, pp. 115–44; and, extensively, in Wildt, *Generation des Unbedingten*.

28. Peter Gay, 'In Deutschland zu Hause ... Die Juden der Weimarer Zeit', in Arnold Paucker (ed.), *Die Juden im Nationalsozialistischen Deutschland 1933–1943*, Tübingen, 1986, pp. 31–43.

29. *Adolf Hitler. Monologe im Führerhauptquartier*, ed. Werner Jochmann, Hamburg, 1980, p. 108.

30. See Martin Broszat, 'Soziale Motivation und Führer-Bindung des National-sozialismus', *Vierteljahrshefte für Zeitgeschichte*, 18 (1970), p. 403.

31. For the term, see Kershaw, *Hitler, 1889–1936*, pp. 529–30.

32. See Karl A. Schleunes, *The Twisted Road to Auschwitz. Nazi Policy toward German Jews 1933–1939*, Urbana, Ill., 1970.

33. Otto Dov Kulka and Eberhard Jäckel (eds.), *Die Juden in den geheimen NS-Stimmungsberichten 1933–1945*, Düsseldorf, 2004, pp. 372–3 (from the SD's report on German Jewry for 1938).

34. Michael Wildt, *Die Judenpolitik des SD 1935 bis 1938. Eine Dokumentation*, Munich, 1995, pp. 32–3.

35. Avraham Barkai, *Vom Boykott zur 'Entjudung'. Der wirtschaftliche Exist-enzkampf der Juden im Dritten Reich 1933–1943*, Frankfurt am Main, 1988, p. 156.

36. Peter Longerich (ed.), *Die Ermordung der europäischen Juden. Eine umfas-sende Dokumentation des Holocaust 1941–1945*, Munich/Zurich, 1989, p. 45; Noakes and Pridham, vol. 3, p. 566.

37. See the reports from the regime's own agencies in Kulka and Jäckel, pp. 304–78; a thorough analysis has been conducted by Martin Korb, 'Deutsche Reaktionen auf die Novemberpogrome im Spiegel amtlicher Berichte', unpubl. Magisterarbeit, Technische Universität Berlin, 2004.

38. Kulka and Jäckel, pp. 367–8, 372–3.

39. Główna Komisa Badania Zbrodni Hitlerowskich w Polsce [Archive of the Central Commission for the Investigation of Hitlerite Crimes in Poland, Ministry of Justice, Poland], Process Artura Greisera, vol. 27, fol. 167.

40. Christopher R. Browning, with contributions by Jürgen Matthäus, The Origins of the Final Solution. The Evolution of Nazi Jewish Policy, September 1939–March 1942, Lincoln, Nebr., 2004, pp. 26–7.

41. Browning, The Origins of the Final Solution, pp. 36–43.

42. Browning, The Origins of the Final Solution, p. 47.

43. Quoted in Browning, The Origins of the Final Solution, p. 45.

44. Browning, The Origins of the Final Solution, p. 62.

45. Browning, The Origins of the Final Solution, p. 71.

46. Magnus Brechten, 'Madagaskar für die Juden'. Antisemitische Idee und politische Praxis 1885–1945, Munich, 1997, p. 16.

47. Browning, The Origins of the Final Solution, p. 57.

48. Helmut Krausnick, 'Denkschrift Himmlers über die Behandlung der Fremdvölkischen im Osten (Mai 1940)', Vierteljahrshefte für Zeitgeschichte, 5 (1957), p. 197; trans. Noakes and Pridham, vol. 3, p. 932.

49. Browning, The Origins of the Final Solution, p. 72.

50. Das Diensttagebuch des deutschen Generalgouverneurs in Polen 1939–1945, ed. Werner Präg and Wolfgang Jacobmeyer, Stuttgart, 1975, p. 252; and quoted in Browning, The Origins of the Final Solution, p. 84.

51. Browning, The Origins of the Final Solution, p. 83.

52. Browning, The Origins of the Final Solution, p. 45.

53. Browning, The Origins of the Final Solution, p. 88.

54. Helmut Heiber, 'Der Generalplan Ost', Vierteljahrshefte für Zeitgeschichte, 6 (1958), pp. 281–325.

55. Heeresadjutant bei Hitler 1938–1943. Aufzeichnungen des Majors Engel, ed. Hildegard von Kotze, Stuttgart, 1974, pp. 94–5.

56. Quoted in Peter Longerich, Politik der Vernichtung. Eine Gesamtdarstellung der nationalsozialistischen Judenverfolgung, Munich/Zurich, 1998, p. 287; also in Götz Aly, 'Endlösung'. Völkerverschiebung und der Mord an den europäischen Juden, Frankfurt am Main, 1995, p. 269; and Browning, The Origins of the Final Solution, pp. 103–4. See also Édouard Husson, 'Nous pouvons vivre sans les Juifs': Novembre 1941. Quand et comment ils décidèrent de la solution finale, Paris, 2005, pp. 71–3. I am indebted to M. Husson for providing me with a copy of Dannecker's memorandum from the Centre de Documentation Juive Contemporaine (Paris), reference DCL1–2, V-59.

57. Aly, pp. 195–201.

58. Aly, p. 200.

59. Aly, p. 268; Longerich, *Politik der Vernichtung*, p. 287.

60. Aly, pp. 270–71; Browning, *The Origins of the Final Solution*, p. 104.

61. *Diensttagebuch*, pp. 332–3, 336–7.

62. *Die Tagebücher von Joseph Goebbels*, part I, vol. 9, Munich, 1998, p. 192 (18.3.41).

63. See Ian Kershaw, *Hitler, 1936–1945. Nemesis*, London, 2000, pp. 353–60, for a summary of the developments mentioned in this paragraph.

64. *KTB d. OKW*, vol. 1: 1. *August 1940–31. Dezember 1941*, 1965, p. 341.

65. Aly, p. 270.

66. Heinz Höhne, *The Order of the Death's Head. The Story of Hitler's SS*, London, 1969, p. 330.

67. See Kershaw, *Hitler, 1936–1945*, pp. 243–7.

68. Kershaw, *Hitler, 1936–1945*, p. 251.

69. Domarus, p. 1663.

70. Quoted in Omer Bartov, *The Eastern Front 1941–45. German Troops and the Barbarisation of Warfare*, New York, 1986, pp. 116–17.

71. Jürgen Matthäus, 'Operation Barbarossa and the Onset of the Holocaust, June–December 1941', in Browning, *The Origins of the Final Solution*, p. 244.

72. Longerich, *Ermordung*, pp. 116–18; Krausnick and Wilhelm, p. 164.

73. Matthäus in Browning, *The Origins of the Final Solution*, pp. 258–9.

74. Matthäus in Browning, *The Origins of the Final Solution*, pp. 253–5; Richard Breitman, *The Architect of Genocide. Himmler and the Final Solution*, London, 1991, p. 168.

75. Longerich, *Politik der Vernichtung*, pp. 345–8.

76. Krausnick and Wilhelm, p. 163.

77. See Matthäus in Browning, *The Origins of the Final Solution*, pp. 268–77.

78. Krausnick and Wilhelm, p. 196.

79. See Browning, *The Origins of the Final Solution*, pp. 313, 317.

80. *Der Dienstkalender Heinrich Himmlers 1941/42*, ed. Peter Witte et al., Hamburg, 1999, pp. 184–5.

81. *'Führer-Erlasse' 1939–1945*, ed. Martin Moll, Stuttgart, 1997, pp. 188–9 (17.7.41).

82. *IMT*, vol. 38, pp. 86–94, doc. 221-L.

83. *Dienstkalender*, p. 185.

84. Christopher R. Browning, *The Path to Genocide. Essays on Launching the Final Solution*, Cambridge, 1992, pp. 105–6; Breitman, pp. 181–4; Yehoshua Büchler, 'Kommandostab Reichsführer-SS. Himmler's Personal Murder Brigades in 1941', *Holocaust and Genocide Studies*, 1/1 (1986), pp. 11–25; Longerich, *Politik der Vernichtung*, pp. 362–6.

85. Matthäus in Browning, *The Origins of the Final Solution*, p. 279.

86. Quoted in Longerich, *Politik der Vernichtung*, p. 367; Christian Gerlach, *Kalkulierte Morde. Die deutsche Wirtschafts- und Vernichtungspolitik in Weiß-*

rußland 1941 bis 1944, Hamburg, 1999, p. 560; and Matthäus in Browning, *The Origins of the Final Solution*, p. 281.

87. See Raul Hilberg, 'The Kommandostab Revisited', *Yad Vashem Studies*, 34 (2006), pp. 360–62.

88. Gerlach, *Kalkulierte Morde*, pp. 560–66; Matthäus in Browning, *The Origins of the Final Solution*, pp. 281–2.

89. *Adolf Hitler. Monologe*, p. 106 (25.10.41).

90. Gerald Fleming, *Hitler and the Final Solution*, paperback edn., Berkeley/Los Angeles, 1994, pp. 73–4.

91. Gerlach, *Kalkulierte Morde*, pp. 573–4.

92. Alfred Streim, *Die Behandlung sowjetischer Kriegsgefangener im 'Fall Barbarossa'*, Heidelberg/Karlsruhe, 1981, pp. 85–6.

93. Gerlach, *Kalkulierte Morde*, pp. 567–9.

94. Matthäus in Browning, *The Origins of the Final Solution*, p. 283, and p. 504 n. 212; Breitman, pp. 195–6; Longerich, *Politik der Vernichtung*, pp. 372–3.

95. Gerlach, *Kalkulierte Morde*, pp. 572–3 and n. 435.

96. See Streim, pp. 89–93.

97. Roseman, p. 101; Aly, pp. 302–3 and n. 10.

98. In East Galicia alone, a further half a million Jews fell under Nazi control (Browning, *The Origins of the Final Solution*, p. 347).

99. Institut für Zeitgeschichte, Munich, ED 100, Diary of Walther Hewel (10 July 1941); also quoted in David Irving, *Hitler's War*, London, 1977, p. 291; and Kershaw, *Hitler, 1936–1945*, p. 470.

100. *Staatsmänner und Diplomaten bei Hitler. Vertrauliche Aufzeichnungen über die Unterredungen mit Vertretern des Auslandes 1939–1941*, ed. Andreas Hillgruber, paperback edn., Munich, 1969, p. 310; also quoted in Kershaw, *Hitler, 1936–1945*, p. 470; and Browning, *The Origins of the Final Solution*, p. 315.

101. Quoted in Aly, p. 285, and see pp. 301–6 for the convincing suggestion that the figures provided at the Wannsee Conference in January 1942 mainly reflect the planning perspectives of June and July 1941.

102. Aly, pp. 273, 328; Kershaw, *Hitler, 1936–1945*, p. 471.

103. Quoted in Browning, *The Origins of the Final Solution*, p. 318.

104. Kershaw, *Hitler, 1936–1945*, pp. 473–4 and plate 45.

105. Browning, *The Origins of the Final Solution*, p. 319.

106. Aly, p. 338; Browning, *The Origins of the Final Solution*, pp. 321–2.

107. Longerich, *Ermordung*, p. 157.

108. Longerich, *Ermordung*, pp. 74–5.

109. Ian Kershaw, 'Improvised Genocide? The Emergence of the "Final Solution" in the "Warthegau"', *Transactions of the Royal Historical Society*, 6th series, 2 (1992), pp. 62–71.

110. Browning, *The Origins of the Final Solution*, p. 329.

111. Browning, *The Origins of the Final Solution*, pp. 375–7, for the city of origin of the deportations.

112. Browning, *The Origins of the Final Solution*, pp. 342–3, 346, 351.

113. Browning, *The Origins of the Final Solution*, p. 372.

114. Christian Gerlach, 'Die Wannsee-Konferenz, das Schicksal der deutschen Juden und Hitlers politische Grundsatzentscheidung, alle Juden Europas zu ermorden', *Werkstattgeschichte*, 18 (1997), p. 17; Longerich, *Politik der Vernichtung*, p. 464.

115. This is the plausible claim in the fine, short study by Husson, pp. 145–55.

116. *Adolf Hitler. Monologe*, pp. 125–6, 130–31.

117. Domarus, pp. 1772–3, 1781.

118. *Adolf Hitler. Monologe*, p. 148.

119. Roseman, pp. 56–60.

120. *Die Tagebücher von Joseph Goebbels*, part II, vol. 2, p. 498 (13.12.41).

121. *Diensttagebuch*, pp. 457–8; trans. Noakes and Pridham, vol. 3, pp. 1126–7; and Browning, *The Origins of the Final Solution*, pp. 408–9. See also Bogdan Musial, *Deutsche Zivilverwaltung und Judenverfolgung im Generalgouvernement*, Wiesbaden, 1999, pp. 218–20.

122. Cesarani, p. 114. At his Jerusalem trial, Eichmann recalled, he said, that there had been talk at the conference of 'killing and eliminating and exterminating' (Longerich, *Ermordung*, p. 93). See Roseman, pp. 68–79 for the most plausible interpretation of the deliberately opaque written record of the meeting.

123. The civil administration in the General Government was already anticipating the 'final solution' in its organizational preparations (Musial, pp. 220–22).

124. Roseman, p. 77.

125. It is far more convincing to see this as an extension of the murderous programme, rather than as the outcome of a fundamental decision to carry out the 'final solution' taken as late as June 1942 (see Florent Brayard, *La 'solution finale de la question juive'. La technique, le temps et les catégories de la décision*, Paris, 2005, esp. pp. 16–18, 30–38).

126. The title of Richard Breitman's impressive book was *The Architect of Genocide. Himmler and the Final Solution*.

127. Eberhard Jäckel, 'From Barbarossa to Wannsee. The Role of Reinhard Heydrich', unpublished essay kindly made available by the author.

128. Berlin Document Centre, SS-HO, 933, Himmler to Gottlob Berger, 28.7.42.

129. Fleming, pp. 106–12.

130. *Hitlers politisches Testament. Die Bormann Diktate von Februar und April 1945*, Hamburg, 1981, pp. 69–70. These last recorded monologues by Hitler survive in a somewhat dubious form (see Kershaw, *Hitler, 1936–1945*, pp. 1024–5 n. 121). Despite necessary caveats, the comments have an authentic ring of Hitler about them.

List of Works Cited

1941 god. Dokumenty [The Year 1941. Documents], ed. A. N. Iakovlev, V. P. Naumov et al., 2 vols., Moscow, 1998.

Abendroth, Hans-Henning, 'Deutschlands Rolle im Spanischen Bürgerkrieg', in Manfred Funke (ed.), *Hitler, Deutschland und die Mächte. Materialien zur Außenpolitik des Dritten Reichs*, Düsseldorf, 1978.

Adolf Hitler. Monologe im Führerhauptquartier, ed. Werner Jochmann, Hamburg, 1980.

Aigner, Dietrich, 'Hitler und die Weltherrschaft', in Wolfgang Michalka (ed.), *Nationalsozialistische Außenpolitik*, Darmstadt, 1978.

Akira, Hara, 'Japan: Guns before Rice', in Mark Harrison (ed.), *The Economics of World War II. Six Great Powers in International Comparison*, Cambridge, 1998.

Akten der Reichskanzlei. Die Regierung Hitler, ed. Karl-Heinz Minuth, vol. 1, Boppard am Rhein, 1983.

Aldrich, Richard J., *Intelligence and the War against Japan. Britain, America and the Politics of Secret Service*, Cambridge, 2000.

Allison, Graham T., *The Essence of Decision. Explaining the Cuban Missile Crisis*, Boston, 1971.

Alsop, Joseph, and Kintner, Robert, *American White Paper. The Story of American Diplomacy and the Second World War*, London, 1940.

Aly, Götz, *'Endlösung'. Völkerverschiebung und der Mord an den europäischen Juden*, Frankfurt am Main, 1995.

Aquarone, Alberto, 'Public Opinion in Italy before the Outbreak of World War II', in Roland Sarti (ed.), *The Ax Within. Italian Fascism in Action*, New York, 1974.

Assmann, Kurt, *Deutsche Schicksalsjahre*, Wiesbaden, 1950.

Avon, Earl of, *The Eden Memoirs. The Reckoning*, London, 1965.

Azzi, Stephen Corrado, 'The Historiography of Fascist Foreign Policy', *Historical Journal*, 36 (1993).

Bach, Maurizio, *Die charismatischen Führerdiktaturen. Drittes Reich und italienischer Faschismus im Vergleich ihrer Herrschaftsstrukturen*, Baden-Baden, 1990.

Badger, Tony, *The New Deal. The Depression Years, 1933–40*, London, 1989.

Badoglio, Pietro, *Italy in the Second World War. Memories and Documents*, London/New York/Toronto, 1948.

Bailey, Thomas A., and Ryan, Paul B., *Hitler vs. Roosevelt. The Undeclared Naval War*, New York, 1979.

Barber, John, 'The Moscow Crisis of October 1941', in Julian Cooper, Maureen Perrie and E. A. Rees (eds.), *Soviet History, 1917–53. Essays in Honour of R. W. Davies*, Basingstoke, 1995.

Barkai, Avraham, *Vom Boykott zur 'Entjudung'. Der wirtschaftliche Existenzkampf der Juden im Dritten Reich 1933–1943*, Frankfurt am Main, 1988.

Barron, Gloria J., *Leadership in Crisis. FDR and the Path to Intervention*, Port Washington, NY/London, 1973.

Bartov, Omer, *The Eastern Front 1941–45. German Troops and the Barbarisation of Warfare*, New York, 1986.

Bastianini, Giuseppe, *Volevo fermare Mussolini. Memorie di un diplomatico fascista*, Milan, 2005; orig. edn., *Uomini, cose, fatti. Memorie di un ambasciatore*, Milan, 1959.

Beard, Charles A., *President Roosevelt and the Coming of War 1941. A Study in Appearance and Realities*, New Haven, 1948.

Bell, P. M. H., *A Certain Eventuality . . . Britain and the Fall of France*, London, 1974.

von Below, Nicolaus, *Als Hitlers Adjutant 1937–1945*, Mainz, 1980.

Bergamini, David, *Japan's Imperial Conspiracy*, 2 vols., New York, 1971.

Beria, Sergo, *Beria. My Father*, London, 2000.

Besymenski, Lew, *Stalin und Hitler. Das Pokerspiel der Diktatoren*, Berlin, 2004.

Bialer, Seweryn (ed.), *Stalin and his Generals*, London, 1970.

Bix, Herbert P., *Hirohito and the Making of Modern Japan*, London, 2001.

Bloch, Michael, *Ribbentrop*, paperback edn., London, 1994.

Bloß, Hartmut, 'Deutsche Chinapolitik im Dritten Reich', in Manfred Funke (ed.), *Hitler, Deutschland und die Mächte. Materialien zur Außenpolitik des Dritten Reichs*, Düsseldorf, 1978.

Bloxham, Donald, 'The Armenian Genocide of 1915–16. Cumulative Radicalization and the Development of a Destruction Policy', *Past and Present*, 181 (2003).

Blum, John Morton, *From the Morgenthau Diaries*, vol. 2: *Years of Urgency, 1938–1941*, Boston, 1965.

von Bock, Fedor, *The War Diary 1939–1945*, ed. Klaus Gerbet, Atglen, Pa., 1996.

Bonwetsch, Bernd, 'Stalin, the Red Army, and the "Great Patriotic War"', in Ian Kershaw and Moshe Lewin (eds.), *Stalinism and Nazism. Dictatorships in Comparison*, Cambridge, 1997.

Boroznjak, Alexander I., 'Ein russischer Historikerstreit? Zur sowjetischen und russischen Historiographie über den deutschen Angriff auf die Sowjetunion', in Gerd R. Ueberschär and Lev A. Bezymenskij (eds.), *Der deutsche Angriff auf die Sowjetunion 1941. Die Kontroverse um die Präventivkriegsthese*, Darmstadt, 1998.

Bosworth, R. J. B., *Italy, the Least of the Great Powers. Italian Foreign Policy before the First World War*, Cambridge, 1979.

—— *The Italian Dictatorship. Problems and Perspectives in the Interpretation of Mussolini and Fascism*, London, 1998.

—— *Mussolini*, London, 2002.

Bottai, Giuseppe, *Diario 1935–1944*, ed. Giordano Bruno Guerri, Milan, 1982.

Boyd, Carl, *Hitler's Japanese Confidant. General Oshima Hiroshi and MAGIC Intelligence, 1941–1945*, Lawrence, Kan., 1992.

Braithwaite, Rodric, *Moscow 1941. A City and its People at War*, London, 2006.

Brayard, Florent, *La 'solution finale de la question juive'. La technique, le temps et les catégories de la décision*, Paris, 2005.

Brechten, Magnus, *'Madagaskar für die Juden'. Antisemitische Idee und politische Praxis 1885–1945*, Munich, 1997.

Breitman, Richard, *The Architect of Genocide. Himmler and the Final Solution*, London, 1991.

Brogan, Hugh, *The Pelican History of the United States of America*, Harmondsworth, 1986.

Broszat, Martin, *Der Staat Hitlers*, Munich, 1969.

—— 'Soziale Motivation und Führer-Bindung des Nationalsozialismus', *Vierteljahrshefte für Zeitgeschichte*, 18 (1970).

Browning, Christopher R., *The Path to Genocide. Essays on Launching the Final Solution*, Cambridge, 1992.

—— with contributions by Jürgen Matthäus, *The Origins of the Final Solution. The Evolution of Nazi Jewish Policy, September 1939–March 1942*, Lincoln, Nebr., 2004.

Büchler, Yehoshua, 'Kommandostab Reichsführer-SS. Himmler's Personal Murder Brigades in 1941', *Holocaust and Genocide Studies*, 1/1 (1986).

Burckhardt, Carl J., *Meine Danziger Mission 1937–1939*, Munich, 1962.

Burgdorff, Stephan, and Wiegrefe, Klaus (eds.), *Der Erste Weltkrieg. Die Urkatastrophe des 20. Jahrhunderts*, Munich, 2004.

Burgwyn, H. James, *Italian Foreign Policy in the Interwar Period 1918–1940*, Westport, Conn., 1997.

Burns, James MacGregor, *Roosevelt. The Soldier of Freedom 1940–1945*, London, 1971.

Butow, Robert J. C., *Tojo and the Coming of the War*, Princeton, 1961.

Calder, Angus, *The People's War*, London, 1969.

Calic, Edouard, *Unmasked. Two Confidential Interviews with Hitler in 1931*, London, 1971.

Carley, Michael Jabara, *1939. The Alliance that Never Was and the Coming of World War II*, Chicago, 1999.

Carr, William, *Poland to Pearl Harbor. The Making of the Second World War*, London, 1985.

Casey, Steven, *Cautious Crusade. Franklin D. Roosevelt, American Public Opinion, and the War against Nazi Germany*, Oxford/New York, 2001.

'Cato', *Guilty Men*, London, 1940.

Cecil, Robert, *Hitler's Decision to Invade Russia 1941*, London, 1975.

Cervi, Mario, *The Hollow Legions. Mussolini's Blunder in Greece, 1940–1941*, London, 1972.

Cesarani, David, *Eichmann. His Life and Crimes*, London, 2004.

Charmley, John, *Churchill: The End of Glory. A Political Biography*, London, 1993.

Chihiro, Hosoya, 'The Tripartite Pact, 1939–1940', in James William Morley (ed.), *Deterrent Diplomacy. Japan, Germany, and the USSR 1935–1940*, New York, 1976.

—— 'Northern Defence', in James William Morley (ed.), *The Fateful Choice. Japan's Advance into Southeast Asia, 1939–1941*, New York, 1980.

Chips. The Diaries of Sir Henry Channon, ed. Robert Rhodes James, London, 1967.

Choucri, Nazli, North, Robert C., and Yamakage, Susumu, *The Challenge of Japan before World War II and After*, London/New York, 1992.

Churchill, Winston S., *The Second World War*, vol. 1: *The Gathering Storm*, London, 1948.

—— *The Second World War*, vol. 2: *Their Finest Hour*, London, 1949.

—— *The Second World War*, vol. 3: *The Grand Alliance*, London, 1950.

—— *The Second World War*, vol. 4: *The Hinge of Fate*, London, 1951.

—— *Great War Speeches*, paperback edn., London, 1957.

Churchill and Roosevelt. The Complete Correspondence, ed. Warren F. Kimball, 3 vols., Princeton, 1984.

The Churchill War Papers, vol. 2: *Never Surrender, May 1940–December 1940*, ed. Martin Gilbert, London, 1995.

The Churchill War Papers, vol. 3: *The Ever-Widening War, 1941*, ed. Martin Gilbert, London, 2000.

Ciano's Diary 1939–1943, ed. Malcolm Muggeridge, London, 1947.

Ciano's Diplomatic Papers, ed. Malcolm Muggeridge, London, 1948.

Clarke, Peter, *Hope and Glory. Britain 1900–1990*, London, 1996.

Cole, Wayne S., *Charles A. Lindbergh and the Battle against American Intervention in World War II*, New York/London, 1974.

Colville, John, *The Fringes of Power. Downing Street Diaries 1939–1955*, London, 1985.

Connors, Lesley, *The Emperor's Adviser. Saionji Kinmochi and Pre-War Japanese Politics*, London, 1987.

Corner, Paul, 'Everyday Fascism in the 1930s. Centre and Periphery in the Decline of Mussolini's Dictatorship', *Contemporary European History*, 15 (2006).

Costello, John, *Ten Days that Saved the West*, London, 1991.

van Creveld, Martin, '25 October 1940. A Historical Puzzle', *Journal of Contemporary History*, 6 (1971).

—— *Hitler's Strategy 1940–1941. The Balkan Clue*, Cambridge, 1973.

—— 'Prelude to Disaster. The British Decision to Aid Greece, 1940–41', *Journal of Contemporary History*, 9 (1974).

Crowson, N. J., *Facing Fascism. The Conservative Party and the European Dictators 1935–40*, London, 1997.

Cull, Nicholas John, *Selling War. The British Propaganda Campaign against American 'Neutrality' in World War II*, New York/Oxford, 1995.

Dallek, Robert, *Franklin D. Roosevelt and American Foreign Policy, 1932–1945*, New York, 1979.

Davies, Joseph E., *Mission to Moscow*, New York, 1941.

Davies, Norman, *Europe. A History*, Oxford, 1996.

Davies, R. W., *Soviet History in the Yeltsin Era*, London, 1997.

Deakin, F. W., *The Brutal Friendship. Mussolini, Hitler and the Fall of Italian Fascism*, London, 1962.

Dear, I. C. B., and Foot, M. R. D. (eds.), *The Oxford Companion to the Second World War*, Oxford/New York, 1995.

Detwiler, Donald S., *Hitler, Franco und Gibraltar. Die Frage des spanischen Eintritts in den Zweiten Weltkrieg*, Wiesbaden, 1962.

Das Deutsche Reich und der Zweiten Weltkrieg, ed. Militärgeschichtliches Forschungsamt, vol. 4, Stuttgart, 1983.

—— vol. 3, ed. Militärgeschichtliches Forschungsamt, Stuttgart, 1984.

Deutscher, Isaac, *Stalin. A Political Biography*, revised edn., London, 1988.

The Diaries of Sir Alexander Cadogan 1938–1945, ed. David Dilks, London, 1971.

Der Dienstkalender Heinrich Himmlers 1941/42, ed. Peter Witte et al., Hamburg, 1999.

Das Diensttagebuch des deutschen Generalgouverneurs in Polen 1939–1945, ed. Werner Präg and Wolfgang Jacobmeyer, Stuttgart, 1975.

Dietrich, Otto, *12 Jahre mit Hitler*, Munich, 1955.

Dilks, David, 'The Twilight War and the Fall of France. Chamberlain and Churchill in 1940', *Transactions of the Royal Historical Society*, 5th series, 28 (1978).

Dimension des Völkermords. Die Zahl der jüdischen Opfer des Nationalsozialismus, ed. Wolfgang Benz, Munich, 1991.

The Diplomatic Diaries of Oliver Harvey 1937–1940, ed. John Harvey, London, 1970.

Divine, Robert A., *The Reluctant Belligerent. American Entry into World War II*, New York, 1965.

—— *Roosevelt and World War II*, Baltimore, 1969.

I documenti diplomatici italiani, 9th series, 1939–1943, Rome, 1954–60.

Documents on German Foreign Policy, 1918–1945. Series D (1937–1945), London, 1957–66.

Domarus, Max (ed.), *Hitler. Reden und Proklamationen 1932–1945*, Wiesbaden, 1973.

Dönitz, Karl, *Memoirs. Ten Years and Twenty Days*, New York, 1997.

Dülffer, Jost, *Weimar, Hitler und die Marine. Reichspolitik und Flottenbau 1920–1939*, Düsseldorf, 1973.

—— 'Zum "decision-making process" in der deutschen Außenpolitik 1933–1939', in Manfred Funke (ed.), *Hitler, Deutschland und die Mächte*, Düsseldorf, 1978.

Erickson, John, 'Threat Identification and Strategic Appraisal by the Soviet Union 1930–1941', in E. R. May (ed.), *Knowing One's Enemies. Intelligence Assessment before the Two World Wars*, Princeton, 1983.

—— *The Road to Stalingrad. Stalin's War with Germany*, vol. 1, paperback edn., London, 1998.

Esnouf, Guy Nicholas, 'British Government War Aims and Attitudes towards a Negotiated Peace, September 1939 to July 1940', unpublished Ph.D. thesis, King's College London, 1988.

Falin, Valentin, *Zweite Front. Die Interessenkonflikte in der Anti-Hitler-Koalition*, Munich, 1995.

FDR's Fireside Chats, ed. Russell D. Buhite and David W. Levy, New York, 1992.

Feiling, Keith, *The Life of Neville Chamberlain*, London, 1946.

Feis, Herbert, *The Road to Pearl Harbor. The Coming of the War between the United States and Japan*, Princeton, 1950.

Felice, Renzo de, *Mussolini l'alleato 1940–1945*, vol. 1, Turin, 1990.

Ferguson, Niall, *The War of the World. History's Age of Hatred*, London, 2006.

Flannery, Harry W., *Assignment to Berlin*, London, 1942.

Fleming, Gerald, *Hitler and the Final Solution*, paperback edn., Berkeley/Los Angeles, 1994.

Flynn, John T., *The Roosevelt Myth*, New York, 1956.

Foreign Relations of the United States. Diplomatic Papers 1938, vol. 1, Washington, 1955.

Foreign Relations of the United States. Diplomatic Papers 1941, vol. 4: *The Far East*, Washington, 1956.

Foreign Relations of the United States. Japan 1931–41, vol. 2, Washington, 1943.

For the President: Personal and Secret. Correspondence between Franklin D. Roosevelt and William C. Bullitt, ed. Orville H. Bullitt, London, 1973.

Fox, John P., *Germany and the Far Eastern Crisis 1931–1938. A Study in Diplomacy and Ideology*, Oxford, 1982.

Freidel, Frank, *Franklin D. Roosevelt. A Rendezvous with Destiny*, Boston, 1990.

Friedländer, Saul, *Prelude to Downfall. Hitler and the United States, 1939–1941*, New York, 1967.

——*Nazi Germany and the Jews. The Years of Persecution, 1933–39*, London, 1997.

Fuehrer Conferences on Naval Affairs 1939–1945, London, 1990.

'*Führer-Erlasse*' *1939–1945*, ed. Martin Moll, Stuttgart, 1997.

Gardiner, Juliet, *Wartime Britain 1939–1945*, London, 2004.

Gassert, Philipp, *Amerika im Dritten Reich. Ideologie, Propaganda und Volksmeinung 1933–1945*, Stuttgart, 1997.

Gay, Peter, 'In Deutschland zu Hause . . . Die Juden der Weimarer Zeit', in Arnold Paucker (ed.), *Die Juden im Nationalsozialistischen Deutschland 1933–1943*, Tübingen, 1986.

Gellman, Irwin F., *Secret Affairs. Franklin Roosevelt, Cordell Hull, and Sumner Welles*, Baltimore/London, 1995.

Generalfeldmarschall Keitel: Verbrecher oder Offizier? Erinnerungen, Briefe, Dokumente des Chefs OKW, ed. Walter Görlitz, Göttingen, 1961.

Gerlach, Christian, 'Die Wannsee-Konferenz, das Schicksal der deutschen Juden und Hitlers politische Grundsatzentscheidung, alle Juden Europas zu ermordern', *Werkstattgeschichte*, 18 (1997).

—— *Kalkulierte Morde. Die deutsche Wirtschafts- und Vernichtungspolitik in Weißrußland 1941 bis 1944*, Hamburg, 1999.

Getty, J. Arch, 'The Politics of Repression Revisited', in J. Arch Getty and Roberta T. Manning (eds.), *Stalinist Terror. New Perspectives*, Cambridge, 1993.

Gibbs, N. H., *Grand Strategy*, vol. 1: *Rearmanent Policy*, London, 1976.

Gilbert, Martin, *Winston S. Churchill*, vol. 5: 1922–1939, London, 1976.

—— *Winston S. Churchill 1939–1941*, vol. 6: *Finest Hour*, paperback edn., London, 1983.

Glantz, David M., *The Military Strategy of the Soviet Union. A History*, London, 1992.

—— 'The Red Army in 1941', in David M. Glantz (ed.), *The Initial Period of War on the Eastern Front, 22 June–August 1941*, London, 1993.

—— *Stumbling Colossus. The Red Army on the Eve of World War*, Lawrence, Kan., 1998.

—— *Barbarossa. Hitler's Invasion of Russia 1941*, Stroud, 2001.

Goldhagen, Daniel Jonah, *Hitler's Willing Executioners. Ordinary Germans and the Holocaust*, New York, 1996.

Gordon, Andrew, *A Modern History of Japan from Tokugawa Times to the Present*, New York/Oxford, 2003.

Gorinov, Mikhail M., '"Muscovites' Moods, 22 June 1941 to May 1942', in W. Thurston and Bernd Bonwetsch (eds.), *The People's War. Responses to World War II in the Soviet Union*, Urbana/Chicago, 2000.

Gorodetsky, Gabriel, *Grand Delusion. Stalin and the German Invasion of Russia*, New Haven/London, 1999.

Grew, Joseph C., *Ten Years in Japan*, New York, 1944.

Gruchmann, Lothar, 'Die "verpaßten strategischen Chancen" der Achsenmächte im Mittelmeerraum 1940/41', *Vierteljahrshefte für Zeitgeschichte*, 18 (1970).

—— *Der Zweite Weltkrieg*, Munich, 4th edn., 1975.

Haffner, Sebastian, *Von Bismarck zu Hitler. Ein Rückblick*, paperback edn., Munich, 1989.

von Hagen, Mark, 'Soviet Soldiers and Officers on the Eve of the German Invasion. Toward a Description of Social Psychology and Political Attitudes', in Robert W. Thurston and Bernd Bonwetsch (eds.), *The People's War. Responses to World War II in the Soviet Union*, Urbana/Chicago, 2000.

Halder, Franz, *Kriegstagebuch. Tägliche Aufzeichnungen des Chefs des Generalstabes des Heeres 1939–1942*, vol. 1: *Vom Polenfeldzug bis zum Ende der Westoffensive (14.8.1939–30.6.1940)*, ed. Hans-Adolf Jacobsen, Stuttgart, 1962.

—— *Kriegstagebuch. Tägliche Aufzeichnungen des Chefs des Generalstabes des Heeres 1939–1942*, vol. 2: *Von der geplanten Landung in England bis zum Beginn des Ostfeldzuges (1.7.1940–21.6.1941)*, ed. Hans-Adolf Jacobsen, Stuttgart, 1963.

—— *Kriegstagebuch. Tägliche Aufzeichnungen des Chefs des Generalstabes des Heeres 1939–1942*, vol. 3: *Der Rußlandfeldzug bis zum Marsch auf Stalingrad (22.6.1941–24.9.1942)*, ed. Hans-Adolf Jacobsen, Stuttgart, 1964.

The Halder War Diary, 1939–1942, ed. and trans. Charles Burdick and Hans-Adolf Jacobsen, London, 1988.

Hanfstaengl, Ernst, *Hitler. The Missing Years*, paperback edn., New York, 1994.

Harrison, Mark (ed.), *The Economics of World War II. Six Great Powers in International Comparison*, Cambridge, 1998.

Hauner, Milan, *Hitler. A Chronology of his Life and Time*, 2nd edn., Basingstoke/New York, 2005.

Heeresadjutant bei Hitler 1938–1943. Aufzeichnungen des Majors Engel, ed. Hildegard von Kotze, Stuttgart, 1974.

Heiber, Helmut, 'Der Generalplan Ost', *Vierteljahrshefte für Zeitgeschichte*, 6 (1958).

Heinrichs, Waldo H., Jr., *American Ambassador. Joseph C. Grew and the Development of the United States Diplomatic Tradition*, Boston, 1966.

—— *Threshold of War. Franklin D. Roosevelt and American Entry into World War II*, New York/Oxford, 1988.

Hénandez-Sandoica, Elena, and Moradiellos, Enrique, 'Spain and the Second World War, 1939–1945', in Neville Wylie (ed.), *European Neutrals and Non-Belligerents during the Second World War*, Cambridge, 2002.

Herbert, Ulrich, '"Generation der Sachlichkeit". Die völkische Studentenbewegung der frühen zwanziger Jahre in Deutschland', in Werner Johe and Uwe Lohalm (eds.), *Zivilisation und Barbarei*, Hamburg, 1991.

Higgins, Patrick, 'The Political Beliefs of R. A. Butler' (unpublished paper).

Hilberg, Raul, 'The Kommandostab Revisited', *Yad Vashem Studies*, 34 (2006).

Hildebrand, Klaus, *Vom Reich zum Weltreich. Hitler, NSDAP und koloniale Frage 1919–1945*, Munich, 1969.

—— *The Foreign Policy of the Third Reich*, London, 1973.

—— *Das vergangene Reich. Deutsche Außenpolitik von Bismarck bis Hitler*, Stuttgart, 1995.

Hilger, Gustav, and Meyer, Alfred G., *The Incompatible Allies. A Memoir of German–Soviet Relations 1918–1941*, New York, 1953.

Hill, Christopher, *Cabinet Decisions on Foreign Policy. The British Experience, October 1938–June 1941*, Cambridge, 1991.

Hillgruber, Andreas, 'Der Faktor Amerika in Hitlers Strategie 1938–1941', *Aus Politik und Zeitgeschichte. Beilage zur Wochenzeitung 'Das Parlament'*, 11 May 1966, reprinted in Wolfgang Michalka (ed.), *Nationalsozialistische Außenpolitik*, Darmstadt, 1978.

—— *Hitlers Strategie. Politik und Kriegführung 1940–1941*, 3rd edn., Bonn, 1993.

Hinsley, F. H., *British Intelligence in the Second World War*, London, 1993.

—— 'British Intelligence and Barbarossa', in John Erickson and David Dilks (eds.), *Barbarossa. The Axis and the Allies*, Edinburgh, 1994.

Hiroharu, Seki, 'The Manchurian Incident 1931', in James William Morley (ed.), *Japan Erupts. The London Naval Conference and the Manchurian Incident 1928–1932*, New York, 1984.

Hitler, Adolf, *Mein Kampf*, 876–880th reprint, Munich, 1943.

—— *Mein Kampf*, trans. Ralph Mannheim, with an Introduction by D. C. Watt, paperback edn., London, 1973.

Hitler: Reden, Schriften, Anordnungen. Februar 1925 bis Januar 1933, ed. Institut für Zeitgeschichte, 5 vols. in 12 parts, Munich/London/New York/Paris, 1992–8.

'Hitlers Denkschrift zum Vierjahresplan 1936', ed. Wilhelm Treue, *Vierteljahrshefte für Zeitgeschichte*, 3 (1955).

Hitlers politisches Testament. Die Bormann Diktate vom Februar und April 1945, Hamburg, 1981.

Hitler's Second Book. The Unpublished Sequel to Mein Kampf, ed. Gerhard L. Weinberg, New York, 2003.

Hitlers Weisungen für die Kriegführung. Dokumente des Oberkommandos der Wehrmacht, ed. Walther Hubatsch, paperback edn., Munich, 1965.

Höhne, Heinz, *The Order of the Death's Head. The Story of Hitler's SS*, London, 1969.

Hosenfeld, Wilm, *'Ich versuche jeden zu retten'. Das Leben eines deutschen Offiziers in Briefen und Tagebüchern*, ed. Thomas Vogel, Munich, 2004.

Hull, Cordell, *The Memoirs of Cordell Hull*, 2 vols., New York, 1948.

Husson, Édouard, *'Nous pouvons vivre sans les Juifs': Novembre 1941. Quand et comment ils décidèrent de la solution finale*, Paris, 2005.

Hüttenberger, Peter, 'Nationalsozialistische Polykratie', *Geschichte und Gesellschaft*, 2 (1976).

Hyoe, Murakami, and Harper, Thomas J. (eds.), *Great Historical Figures of Japan*, Tokyo, 1978.

Ickes, Harold L., *The Secret Diary of Harold L. Ickes*, vol. 3: *The Lowering Clouds 1939–1941*, New York, 1955.

Ike, Nobutaka (ed.), *Japan's Decision for War. Records of the 1941 Policy Conferences*, Stanford, Calif., 1967.

Ikuhiko, Hata, 'The Japanese-Soviet Confrontation, 1935–1939', in James William Morley (ed.), *Deterrent Diplomacy. Japan, Germany, and the USSR 1935–1940*, New York, 1976.

—— 'The Army's Move into Northern Indochina', in James William Morley (ed.), *The Fateful Choice. Japan's Advance into Southeast Asia, 1939–1941*, New York, 1980.

—— 'The Marco Polo Bridge Incident, 1937', in James William Morley (ed.), *The China Quagmire. Japan's Expansion on the Asian Continent, 1933–1941*, New York, 1983.

Iriye, Akira, *Across the Pacific. An Inner History of American-East Asian Relations*, New York, 1967.

—— *Power and Culture. The Japanese-American War, 1941–1945*, Cambridge, Mass., 1981.

—— *The Origins of the Second World War in Asia and the Pacific*, London/New York, 1987.

The Ironside Diaries, 1937–1940, ed. Roderick Macleod and Denis Kelly, London, 1962.

Irving, David, *Hitler's War*, London, 1977.

—— *Churchill's War*, vol. 1: *The Struggle for Power*, Bullsbrook, Australia, 1987.

Ito, Takashi, Hirohashi, Tadamitsu, and Katashima, Norio (eds.), *The Secret Documents of Prime Minister Tojo: Records of the Words and Deeds of General Hideki Tojo* [in Japanese], Tokyo, n.d.

'Iz vospominanii upravliyushchego delami sovnarkoma SSSR Ya. E. Chadaev' ['From the Memoirs of the Head of Sovnarkom USSR – Yakov Ermolaevich Chadaev'], *Otechestvennaya Istoriya*, 2 (2005).

Jäckel, Eberhard, *Hitlers Weltanschauung. Entwurf einer Herrschaft*, Tübingen, 1969.

—— *Hitler in History*, Hanover/London, 1984.

—— 'From Barbarossa to Wannsee. The Role of Reinhard Heydrich', unpublished essay.

—— and Kuhn, Axel (eds.), *Hitler. Sämtliche Aufzeichnungen 1905–1924*, Stuttgart, 1980.

Jenkins, Roy, *Churchill*, London, 2001.

Jones, F. C., *Japan's New Order in East Asia. Its Rise and Fall, 1937–45*, Oxford, 1954.

Jones, Thomas, *A Diary with Letters 1931–1950*, London, 1954.

Judt, Tony, *Postwar. A History of Europe since 1945*, London, 2005.

Jun, Tsunoda, 'The Navy's Role in the Southern Strategy', in James William Morley (ed.), *The Fateful Choice. Japan's Advance into Southeast Asia, 1939–1941*, New York, 1980.

Kahn, David, *Hitler's Spies. German Military Intelligence in World War II*, New York, 2000.

Kennedy, David M., *Freedom from Fear. The American People in Depression and War, 1929–1945*, New York/Oxford, 1999.

Kershaw, Ian, 'Improvised Genocide? The Emergence of the "Final Solution" in the "Warthegau"', *Transactions of the Royal Historical Society*, 6th series, 2 (1992).

—— *Hitler, 1889–1936. Hubris*, London, 1998.

—— *Hitler, 1936–1945. Nemesis*, London, 2000.

—— *The Nazi Dictatorship. Problems and Perspectives of Interpretation*, 4th edn., London, 2000.

—— *Making Friends with Hitler. Lord Londonderry and Britain's Road to War*, London, 2004.

Khrushchev Remembers, ed. Strobe Talbott, London, 1971.

Kimball, Warren F., *The Most Unsordid Act. Lend-Lease 1939–1941*, Baltimore, 1969.

—— *The Juggler. Franklin Roosevelt as Wartime Statesman*, Princeton, 1991.

—— *Forged in War. Churchill, Roosevelt and the Second World War*, London, 1997.

Kipp, Jacob, 'Soviet War Planning', in David M. Glantz (ed.), *The Initial Period of War on the Eastern Front, 22 June–August 1941*, London, 1993.

Klee, Karl, *Das Unternehmen 'Seelöwe'. Die geplante deutsche Landung in England 1940*, Göttingen, 1958.

—— (ed.), *Dokumente zum Unternehmen 'Seelöwe'. Die geplante deutsche Landung in England 1940*, Göttingen, 1959.

Knight, Jonathan, 'Churchill and the Approach to Mussolini and Hitler in May 1940. A Note', *British Journal of International Studies*, 3 (1977).

Knox, MacGregor, 'Fascist Italy Assesses its Enemies, 1935–1940', in Ernest R. May (ed.), *Knowing One's Enemies. Intelligence Assessment before the Two World Wars*, Princeton, 1983.

—— *Mussolini Unleashed 1939–1941. Politics and Strategy in Fascist Italy's Last War*, paperback edn.. Cambridge, 1986.

—— *Common Destiny. Dictatorship, Foreign Policy, and War in Fascist Italy and Nazi Germany*, Cambridge, 2000.

—— *Hitler's Italian Allies. Royal Armed Forces, Fascist Regime, and the War of 1940–1943*, Cambridge, 2000.

Koliopoulos, John S., *Greece and the British Connection 1935–1941*, Oxford, 1977.

Korb, Martin, 'Deutsche Reaktionen auf die Novemberpogrome im Spiegel amtlicher Berichte', unpublished Magisterarbeit, Technische Universität Berlin, 2004.

Krausnick, Helmut, 'Denkschrift Himmlers über die Behandlung der Fremdvölkischen im Osten (Mai 1940)', *Vierteljahrshefte für Zeitgeschichte*, 5 (1957).

—— and Wilhelm, Hans-Heinrich, *Die Truppe des Weltanschauungskrieges. Die Einsatzgruppen der Sicherheitspolizei und des SD 1938–1942*, Stuttgart, 1981.

Krebs, Gerhard, 'Deutschland und Pearl Harbor', *Historische Zeitschrift*, 253 (1991).

Kriegstagebuch des Oberkommandos der Wehrmacht (Wehrmachtführungsstab), ed. Percy Ernst Schramm, 4 vols., Frankfurt am Main, 1961–5.

Kriegstagebuch der Seekriegsleitung 1939–1945, ed. Werner Rahn and Gerhard Schreiber, Herford/Bonn, 1989.

Kube, Alfred, *Pour le mérite und Hakenkreuz. Hermann Göring im Dritten Reich*, Munich, 1986.

Kulka, Otto Dov, 'Richard Wagner und die Anfänge des modernen Antisemitismus', *Bulletin des Leo Baeck Instituts*, 4 (1961).

—— 'Die deutsche Geschichtsschreibung über den Nationalsozialismus und die "Endlösung". Tendenzen und Entwicklungsphasen 1924–1984', *Historische Zeitschrift*, 240 (1985).

—— 'Critique of Judaism in European Thought. On the Historical Meaning of Modern Antisemitism', *Jerusalem Quarterly*, 52 (1989).

—— and Jäckel, Eberhard (eds.), *Die Juden in den geheimen NS-Stimmungsberichten 1933–1945*, Düsseldorf, 2004.

Kuper, Leo, *Genocide. Its Political Use in the Twentieth Century*, Harmondsworth, 1981.

Lagevorträge des Oberbefehlshabers der Kriegsmarine vor Hitler 1939–1945, ed. Gerhard Wagner, Munich, 1972.

Langer, William L., and Gleason, S. Everett, *The Challenge to Isolation, 1937–1940*, New York, 1952.

—— *The Undeclared War, 1940–1941*, New York, 1953.

Larrabee, Eric, *Commander in Chief. Franklin Delano Roosevelt, his Lieutenants, and their War*, London, 1987.

Lash, Joseph P., *Roosevelt and Churchill 1939–1941. The Partnership that Saved the West*, New York, 1976.

Lawlor, Sheila, 'Britain and the Russian Entry into the War', in Richard Langhorne (ed.), *Diplomacy and Intelligence during the Second World War*, Cambridge, 1985.

Leach, Barry A., *German Strategy against Russia 1939–1941*, Oxford, 1973.

Lebra, Joyce C., *Japan's Greater East Asia Co-Prosperity Sphere in World War II. Selected Readings and Documents*, Kuala Lumpur, 1975.

Leigh, Michael, *Mobilizing Consent. Public Opinion and American Policy 1937–1947*, Westport, Conn., 1976.

Lewin, Moshe, *The Making of the Soviet System. Essays in the Social History of Interwar Russia*, New York, 1985.

—— 'Bureaucracy and the Stalinist State', in Ian Kershaw and Moshe Lewin (eds.), *Stalinism and Nazism. Dictatorships in Comparison*, Cambridge, 1997.

—— *The Soviet Century*, London, 2005.

Lewin, Ronald, *Ultra Goes to War. The Secret Story*, paperback edn., London, 2001.

Lewis, Jonathan, and Whitehead, Phillip, *Stalin. A Time for Judgement*, London, 1991.

Liulevicius, Vejas Gabriel, *War Land on the Eastern Front. Culture, National Identity and German Occupation in World War I*, Cambridge, 2000.

Longerich, Peter (ed.), *Die Ermordung der europäischen Juden. Eine umfassende Dokumentation des Holocaust 1941–1945*, Munich/Zurich, 1989.

—— *Politik der Vernichtung. Eine Gesamtdarstellung der nationalsozialistischen Judenverfolgung*, Munich/Zurich, 1998.

Lukacs, John, *The Duel. Hitler vs. Churchill*, Oxford, 1992.

—— *Five Days in London. May 1940*, paperback edn., New Haven/London, 2001.

—— *June 1941. Hitler and Stalin*, New Haven/London, 2006.

Lyttleton, Adrian, *The Seizure of Power*, London, 1973.

Mack Smith, Denis, *Mussolini as a Military Leader*, Reading, 1974.

—— *Mussolini's Roman Empire*, London/New York, 1976.

—— *Mussolini*, paperback edn., London, 1983.

Magenheimer, Heinz, *Hitler's War. Germany's Key Strategic Decisions 1940–1945*, London, 1998.

The 'MAGIC' Background of Pearl Harbor, 8 vols., Washington, 1977–8.

Maisky, Ivan, *Who Helped Hitler?*, London, 1964.

Mann, Michael, *The Dark Side of Democracy. Explaining Ethnic Cleansing*, Cambridge, 2005.

Marks, Frederick W., III, *Wind over Sand. The Diplomacy of Franklin Roosevelt*, Athens, Ga., 1988.

Martin, Bernd, 'Das "Dritte Reich" und die "Friedens"-Frage im Zweiten Weltkrieg', in Wolfgang Michalka (ed.), *Nationalsozialistische Außenpolitik*, Darmstadt, 1978.

Maser, Werner (ed.), *Hitlers Briefe und Notizen. Sein Weltbild in handschriftlichen Dokumenten*, Düsseldorf, 1973.

Mason, Timothy W., *Nazism, Fascism and the Working Class*, Cambridge, 1995.

Matsuoka Yosuke. The Man and his Life, Tokyo, 1974 [in Japanese].

Matthäus, Jürgen, 'Operation Barbarossa and the Onset of the Holocaust, June–December 1941', in Christopher Browning, *The Origins of the Final Solution. The Evolution of Nazi Jewish Policy, September 1939–March 1942*, Lincoln, Nebr., 2004.

Mawdsley, Evan, *The Stalin Years. The Soviet Union, 1929–1953*, Manchester, 1998.

—— 'Crossing the Rubicon. Soviet Plans for Offensive War in 1940–1941', *International History Review*, 25 (2003).

Mazower, Mark, *Inside Hitler's Greece. The Experience of Occupation, 1941–44*, New Haven/London, 1993.

Medvedev, Roy, *On Stalin and Stalinism*, Oxford, 1979.

—— *All Stalin's Men*, Oxford, 1983.

—— and Medvedev, Zhores, *The Unknown Stalin. His Life, Death, and Legacy*, Woodstock/New York, 2004.

Meinecke, Friedrich, *Die deutsche Katastrophe*, Wiesbaden, 1946.

Mein Tagebuch. Geschichten vom Überleben 1939–1947, ed. Heinrich Breloer, Cologne, 1984.

Meldungen aus dem Reich. Auswahl aus den geheimen Lageberichten des Sicher-heitsdienstes der SS 1939–1944, ed. Heinz Boberach, Neuwied/Berlin, 1965.

Melograni, Piero, 'The Cult of the Duce in Mussolini's Italy', *Journal of Contemporary History*, 11 (1976).

The Memoirs of General the Lord Ismay, London, 1960.

Merridale, Catherine, *Ivan's War. The Red Army 1939–1945*, London, 2005.

Michalka, Wolfgang, 'Vom Antikominternpakt zum euro-asiatischen Konti-nentalblock. Ribbentrops Alternativkonzeption zu Hitlers außenpolitischen "Programm"', in Wolfgang Michalka (ed.), *Nationalsozialistische Außen-politik*, Darmstadt, 1978.

—— *Ribbentrop und die deutsche Weltpolitik 1933–1940*, Munich, 1980.

—— 'From the Anti-Comintern Pact to the Euro-Asiatic Bloc. Ribbentrop's Alternative Concept of Hitler's Foreign Policy Programme', in H. W. Koch (ed.), *Aspects of the Third Reich*, London, 1985.

Mikoyan, Anastas Ivanovich, *Tak bylo*, Moscow, 1999.

Mikoyan, Stepan A., 'Barbarossa and the Soviet Leadership', in John Erickson and David Dilks (eds.), *Barbarossa. The Axis and the Allies*, Edinburgh, 1994.

Molotov Remembers: Inside Kremlin Politics. Conversations with Felix Chuev, Chicago, 1993.

Montefiore, Simon Sebag, *Stalin. The Court of the Red Tsar*, London, 2003.

Morley, James William (ed.), *Deterrent Diplomacy. Japan, Germany, and the USSR 1935–1940*, New York, 1976.

—— (ed.), *The Fateful Choice. Japan's Advance into Southeast Asia, 1939–1941*, New York, 1980.

—— (ed.), *The China Quagmire. Japan's Expansion on the Asian Continent, 1933–1941*, New York, 1983.

—— (ed.), *Japan Erupts. The London Naval Conference and the Manchurian Incident 1928–1932*, New York, 1984.

—— (ed.), *The Final Confrontation. Japan's Negotiations with the United States, 1941*, Columbia, NY, 1994.

Moseley, Ray, *Mussolini's Shadow. The Double Life of Count Galeazzo Ciano*, New Haven/London, 1999.

Mosse, George, *The Crisis of German Ideology. Intellectual Origins of the Third Reich*, London, 1966.

Mowat, Charles Loch, *Britain between the Wars, 1918–1940*, London, 1956.

Müller, Klaus-Jürgen, *Das Heer und Hitler. Armee und nationalsozialistisches Regime 1933–1940*, Stuttgart, 1969.

Murphy, David E., *What Stalin Knew. The Enigma of Barbarossa*, New Haven/London, 2005.

Musial, Bogdan, *Deutsche Zivilverwaltung und Judenverfolgung im Generalgouvernement*, Wiesbaden, 1999.

Naimark, Norman M., *Fires of Hatred. Ethnic Cleansing in Twentieth-Century Europe*, Cambridge, Mass./London, 2001.

Nazi Conspiracy and Aggression, United States Government, 11 vols., Washington, 1946–8.

Nazi–Soviet Relations 1939–1941, ed. Raymond James Sontag and James Stuart Beddie, New York, 1948.

Nicolson, Harold, *Diaries and Letters 1930–1964*, ed. Stanley Olson, New York, 1980.

Nipperdey, Thomas, *Deutsche Geschichte 1866–1918*, vol. 2: *Machtstaat vor der Demokratie*, Munich, 1992.

Nish, Ian, *Japanese Foreign Policy 1869–1942*, London, 1977.

Noakes, Jeremy, and Pridham, Geoffrey (eds.), *Nazism 1919–1945. A Documentary Reader*, 4 vols., Exeter, 1983–98.

Nobumasa, Tanaka (ed.), *Dokyumento Showa Tenno Dai Nikkan* [Documents of the Showa Emperor], vol. 2, Tokyo, 1988 [in Japanese].

Oka, Yoshitake, *Konoe Fumimaro. A Political Biography*, Tokyo, 1983.

Overy, R. J., *War and Economy in the Third Reich*, Oxford, 1994.

—— *Why the Allies Won*, London, 1995.

—— *Russia's War*, London, 1997.

—— *The Dictators. Hitler's Germany and Stalin's Russia*, London, 2004.

Packard, Reynolds, and Packard, Eleanor, *Balcony Empire. Fascist Italy at War*, London, 1943.

von Papen, Franz, *Memoirs*, London, 1952.

Parker, R. A. C., *Chamberlain and Appeasement. British Policy and the Coming of the Second World War*, London, 1993.

—— *Churchill and Appeasement*, London, 2000.

Payne, Stanley G., *A History of Fascism 1914–45*, London, 1995.

Picker, Dr Henry, *Hitlers Tischgespräche im Führerhauptquartier 1941–1942*, ed. Percy Ernst Schramm, Stuttgart, 1963.

Pious, Richard M., *The American Presidency*, New York, 1979.

Piper, Ernst, *Alfred Rosenberg. Hitlers Chefideologe*, Munich, 2005.

Pleshakov, Constantine, *Stalin's Folly. The Secret History of the German Invasion of Russia, June 1941*, London, 2005.

Poliakov, Léon, *The History of Anti-Semitism*, vol. 4: *Suicidal Europe, 1870–1933*, Oxford, 1977.

Political Strategy Prior to the Outbreak of War (Parts III–IV), Office of the Chief of Military History, Department of the Army, Japanese Monographs, 144–50, n.d.

Pope, Stephen, and Wheal, Elizabeth-Anne, *The Macmillan Dictionary of the First World War*, London, 1995.

Prange, Gordon W., *At Dawn We Slept. The Untold Story of Pearl Harbor*, London, 1982.

Preston, Paul, 'Franco and Hitler. The Myth of Hendaye 1940', *Contemporary European History*, 1 (1992).

Der Prozeß gegen die Hauptkriegsverbrecher vor dem Internationalen Militärgerichtshof, Nürnberg, 14. November 1945–1. Oktober 1946, 42 vols., Nuremberg, 1947–9.

Public Opinion 1935–1946, ed. Hadley Cantril, Westport, Conn., 1951.

The Public Papers and Addresses of Franklin D. Roosevelt, ed. Samuel I. Rosenman, 13 vols., New York, 1938–50.

Radzinsky, Edvard, *Stalin*, New York, 1996.

Raeder, Erich, *Mein Leben*, Tübingen/Neckar, 1957.

Rauscher, Walter, *Hitler und Mussolini. Macht, Krieg und Terror*, Graz, 2001.

Rauschning, Hermann, *Hitler Speaks*, London, 1939.

Read, Anthony, and Fisher, David, *The Deadly Embrace. Hitler, Stalin and the Nazi–Soviet Pact 1939–1941*, London, 1988.

Rebentisch, Dieter, *Führerstaat und Verwaltung im Zweiten Weltkrieg*, Stuttgart, 1989.

Reese, Roger R., 'The Red Army and the Great Purges', in J. Arch Getty and Roberta T. Manning (eds.), *Stalinist Terror. New Perspectives*, Cambridge, 1993.

Renshaw, Patrick, *Franklin D. Roosevelt. Profiles in Power*, London, 2004.

Reynaud, Paul, *In the Thick of the Fight 1930–1945*, London, 1955.

Reynolds, David, *The Creation of the Anglo-American Alliance 1937–1941. A Study in Competitive Co-operation*, Chapel Hill, NC, 1982.

—— 'Churchill and the British "Decision" to Fight on in 1940. Right Policy, Wrong Reasons', in Richard Langhorne (ed.), *Diplomacy and Intelligence during the Second World War*, Cambridge, 1985.

—— 'Churchill the Appeaser? Between Hitler, Roosevelt and Stalin in World War Two', in Michael Dockrill and Brian McKercher (eds.), *Diplomacy and World Power. Studies in British Foreign Policy, 1890–1950*, Cambridge, 1996.

—— *From Munich to Pearl Harbor. Roosevelt's America and the Origins of the Second World War*, Chicago, 2001.

—— *In Command of History. Churchill Fighting and Writing the Second World War*, London, 2004.

The Ribbentrop Memoirs, London, 1954.

von Rintelen, Enno, *Mussolini als Bundesgenosse. Erinnerungen des deutschen Militärattachés in Rom 1936–1943*, Tübingen/Stuttgart, 1951.

Roberts, Andrew, 'The Holy Fox'. *The Life of Lord Halifax*, paperback edn., London, 1997.

Roberts, Geoffrey, *Unholy Alliance. Stalin's Pact with Hitler*, London, 1989.

—— *The Soviet Union and the Origins of the Second World War. Russo-German Relations and the Road to War, 1933–1941*, London, 1995.

—— *Stalin's Wars. From World War to Cold War, 1939–1953*, New Haven/London, 2006.

Rock, William R., *Chamberlain and Roosevelt. British Foreign Policy and the United States, 1937–1940*, Columbus, Ohio, 1988.

The Roosevelt Letters, vol. 3: [1928–1945], ed. Elliott Roosevelt, London, 1952.

Roseman, Mark, *The Villa, the Lake, the Meeting. Wannsee and the Final Solution*, London, 2002.

Rotundo, Louis, 'Stalin and the Outbreak of War in 1941', *Journal of Contemporary History*, 24 (1989).

Rybin, A. T., *Next to Stalin. Notes of a Bodyguard*, Toronto, 1996.

Sadkovich, James J., 'Understanding Defeat. Reappraising Italy's Role in World War II', *Journal of Contemporary History*, 24 (1989).

—— 'The Italo-Greek War in Context. Italian Priorities and Axis Diplomacy', *Journal of Contemporary History*, 28 (1993).

Salewski, Michael, *Die deutsche Seekriegsleitung 1935–1945*, vol. 1, Frankfurt am Main, 1970.

—— *Die deutsche Seekriegsleitung 1935–1945*, vol. 3, Frankfurt am Main, 1973.

Sapir, Jacques, 'The Economics of War in the Soviet Union during World War II', in Ian Kershaw and Moshe Lewin (eds.), *Stalinism and Nazism. Dictatorships in Comparison*, Cambridge, 1997.

Sathre, Eugene, 'Communication and Conflict: Japanese Foreign Policy leading to the Pacific War', unpublished Ph.D. thesis, University of Minnesota, 1978.

Schleunes, Karl A., *The Twisted Road to Auschwitz. Nazi Policy toward German Jews 1933–1939*, Urbana, Ill., 1970.

Schlie, Ulrich, *Kein Friede mit Deutschland. Die geheimen Gespräche im Zweiten Weltkrieg 1939–1941*, Munich/Berlin, 1994.

Schmidt, Paul, *Statist auf diplomatischer Bühne 1923–45. Erlebnisse des Chefdolmetschers im Auswärtigen Amt mit den Staatsmännern Europas*, Bonn, 1953.

Schramm-von Thadden, Ehrengard, *Griechenland und die Großmächte im Zweiten Weltkrieg*, Wiesbaden, 1955.

Schreiber, Gerhard, *Revisionismus und Weltmachtstreben. Marineführung und deutsch-italienische Beziehungen 1919 bis 1944*, Stuttgart, 1978.

—— 'Zur Kontinuität des Groß- und Weltmachtstrebens der deutschen Marine-führung', *Militärgeschichtliche Mitteilungen*, 25/2 (1979).

—— 'Der Mittelmeerraum in Hitlers Strategie 1940. "Programm" und militär-ische Planung', *Militärgeschichtliche Mitteilungen*, 27/2 (1980).

Schroeder, Christa, *Er war mein Chef. Aus dem Nachlaß der Sekretärin von Adolf Hitler*, ed. Anton Joachimsthaler, Munich/Vienna, 1985.

Schroeder, Paul W., *The Axis Alliance and Japanese-American Relations 1941*, Ithaca, NY, 1958.

Schwendemann, Heinrich, *Die wirtschaftliche Zusammenarbeit zwischen dem Deutschen Reich und der Sowjetunion von 1939 bis 1941. Alternative zu Hitlers Ostprogramm?*, Berlin, 1993.

Seaton, Albert, *Stalin as Warlord*, London, 1976.

The Second World War Diary of Hugh Dalton, 1940–1945, ed. Ben Pimlott, London, 1988.

Seiichi, Imai, 'Cabinet, Emperor, and Senior Statesmen', in Dorothy Borg and Shumpei Okamoto (eds.), *Pearl Harbor as History. Japanese-American Relations 1931–1941*, New York, 1973.

Sekrety Gitlera no stole u Stalina [Hitler's Secrets on Stalin's Desk], Moscow, 1995.

Sella, Amnon, ' "Barbarossa". Surprise Attack and Communication', *Journal of Contemporary History*, 13 (1978).

Service, Robert, *Stalin. A Biography*, London, 2004.

Sherry, Michael S., *The Rise of American Air Power. The Creation of Armaged-don*, New Haven/London, 1987.

Sherwood, Robert E., *The White House Papers of Harry L. Hopkins*, 2 vols., London, 1948.

Shigeo, Misawa, and Saburo, Minomiya, 'The Role of the Diet and Political Parties', in Dorothy Borg and Shumpei Okamoto (eds.), *Pearl Harbor as History. Japanese-American Relations 1931–1941*, New York, 1973.

Shinjiro, Nagaoka, 'Economic Demands on the Dutch East Indies', in James William Morley (ed.), *The Fateful Choice. Japan's Advance into Southeast Asia, 1939–1941*, New York, 1980.

—— 'The Drive into Southern Indochina and Thailand', in James William Morley (ed.), *The Fateful Choice. Japan's Advance into Southeast Asia, 1939–1941*, New York, 1980.

Shirer, William L., *Berlin Diary, 1934–1941*, paperback edn., London, 1970.

Smith, Richard Norton, *The Colonel. The Life and Legend of Robert R. McCormick 1880–1955*, Boston/New York, 1997.

Smith, Woodruff D., *The Ideological Origins of Nazi Imperialism*, New York/Oxford, 1986.

Sommer, Theo, *Deutschland und Japan zwischen den Mächten 1935–1940. Vom Antikominternpakt zum Dreimächtepakt*, Tübingen, 1962.

Speer, Albert, *Erinnerungen*, Frankfurt am Main, 1969.

Spotswood, Roger D., 'Japan's Southward Advance as an Issue in Japanese-American Relations, 1940–1941', unpublished Ph.D. thesis, University of Washington, 1974.

Staatsmänner und Diplomaten bei Hitler. Vertrauliche Aufzeichnungen über die Unterredungen mit Vertretern des Auslandes 1939–1941, ed. Andreas Hillgruber, paperback edn., Munich, 1969.

Stafford, David, *Roosevelt and Churchill. Men of Secrets*, paperback edn., London, 2000.

Stauffer, Paul, *Zwischen Hofmannsthal und Hitler: Carl J. Burckhardt. Facetten einer aussergewöhnlichen Existenz*, Zurich, 1991.

Steiner, Zara, *The Lights that Failed. European International History 1919–1933*, Oxford, 2005.

Stevenson, David, *Cataclysm. The First World War as Political Tragedy*, New York, 2004.

Stimson, Henry L., and Bundy, McGeorge, *On Active Service in Peace and War*, New York, 1948.

Stoakes, Geoffrey, *Hitler and the Quest for World Dominion*, Leamington Spa, 1986.

Stoler, Mark A., *Allies and Adversaries. The Joint Chiefs of Staff, the Grand Alliance, and U.S. Strategy in World War II*, Chapel Hill, NC/London, 2000.

Streim, Alfred, *Die Behandlung sowjetischer Kriegsgefangener im 'Fall Barbarossa'*, Heidelberg/Karlsruhe, 1981.

Sudoplatov, Pavel, and Sudoplatov, Anatoli, *Special Tasks: The Memoirs of an Unwanted Witness. A Soviet Spymaster*, Boston, 1994.

Sullivan, Brian R., "Where One Man, and Only One Man, Led'. Italy's Path from Non-Alignment to Non-Belligerency to War, 1937–1940', in Neville Wylie (ed.), *European Neutrals and Non-Belligerents during the Second World War*, Cambridge, 2002.

Suny, Gregor, 'Stalin and his Stalinism. Power and Authority in the Soviet Union', in Ian Kershaw and Moshe Lewin (eds.), *Stalinism and Nazism. Dictatorships in Comparison*, Cambridge, 1997.

Syring, Enrico, 'Hitlers Kriegserklärung an Amerika vom 11. Dezember 1941', in Wolfgang Michalka (ed.), *Der Zweite Weltkrieg. Analysen, Grundzüge, Forschungsbilanz*, Munich/Zurich, 1989.

Die Tagebücher von Joseph Goebbels, ed. Elke Fröhlich, part I: *Aufzeichnungen*, 9 vols.; part II: *Diktate 1941–1945*, 15 vols., Munich, 1993–2005.

Tansill, Charles Callan, *Back Door to War. The Roosevelt Foreign Policy*, Chicago, 1952.

Taylor, A. J. P., *The Origins of the Second World War*, Harmondsworth, 1964.

—— *English History 1914–1945*, Harmondsworth, 1970.

The Testament of Adolf Hitler. The Hitler–Bormann Documents, February–April 1945, ed. François Genoud, London, 1961.

Thomas, Charles S., *The German Navy in the Nazi Era*, London, 1990.

Tokushiro, Ohata, 'The Anti-Comintern Pact, 1935–1939', in James William Morley (ed.), *Deterrent Diplomacy. Japan, Germany, and the USSR 1935–1940*, New York, 1976.

Toland, John, *The Rising Sun. The Decline and Fall of the Japanese Empire, 1936–1945*, New York, 1970, Modern Library edn., 2003.

—— *Adolf Hitler*, London, 1977.

Tolstoy, Nicolai, *Stalin's Secret War*, London, 1981.

Tooze, Adam, *The Wages of Destruction. The Making and Breaking of the Nazi Economy*, London, 2006.

Toshihiko, Shimada, 'Designs on North China 1933–1937', in James William Morley (ed.), *The China Quagmire. Japan's Expansion on the Asian Continent, 1933–1941*, New York, 1983.

Toscano, Mario, *The Origins of the Pact of Steel*, Baltimore, 1967.

Treue, Wilhelm (ed.), 'Rede Hitlers vor der deutschen Presse (10. November 1938)', *Vierteljahrshefte für Zeitgeschichte*, 6 (1958).

Trial of the Major War Criminals before the International Military Tribunal, 14 November 1945–1 October 1946, 42 vols., Nuremberg, 1947–9.

Tucker, Robert C., *Stalin in Power. The Revolution from Above, 1928–1941*, New York, 1990.

Ueberschär, Gerd R., and Bezymenskij, Lev A. (eds.), *Der deutsche Angriff auf die Sowjetunion 1941. Die Kontroverse um die Präventivkriegsthese*, Darmstadt, 1998.

—— 'Hitlers Überfall auf die Sowjetunion 1941 und Stalins Absichten. Die Bewertung in der deutschen Geschichtsschreibung und die neuere "Präventivkriegsthese"', in Gerd R. Ueberschär and Lev A. Bezymenskij (eds.), *Der deutsche Angriff auf die Sowjetunion 1941. Die Kontroverse um die Präventivkriegsthese*, Darmstadt, 1998.

Ulam, Adam, *Stalin. The Man and his Era*, Boston, 1989.

van der Vat, Dan, *The Atlantic Campaign. The Great Struggle at Sea 1939–1945*, London, 1988.

Villari, Luigi, *Italian Foreign Policy under Mussolini*, London, 1959.

Visconti Prasca, Sebastiano, *Io ho aggredito la Grecia*, 2nd edn., Milan, 1947.

Vogelsang, Thilo, 'Neue Dokumente zur Geschichte der Reichswehr 1930–1933', *Vierteljahrshefte für Zeitgeschichte*, 2 (1954).

Volkogonov, Dmitri, *Stalin. Triumph and Tragedy*, New York, 1991.

Warlimont, Walter, *Inside Hitler's Headquarters 1939–45*, Novato, Calif., n.d. (original English-language edn., London, 1964).

Watson, Derek, *Molotov. A Biography*, London, 2005.

Weeks, Albert L., *Stalin's Other War. Soviet Grand Strategy 1939–1941*, Lanham, Md., 2002.

Wehler, Hans-Ulrich, 'Die Urkatastrophe. Der Erste Weltkrieg als Auftakt und Vorbild für den Zweiten Weltkrieg', *Der Spiegel*, 8 (16 Feb. 2004).

Weinberg, Gerhard L., 'German Colonial Plans and Policies 1938–1942', in

Waldemar Besson and Friedrich Frhr. Hiller v. Gaertringen (eds.), *Geschichte und Gegenwartsbewußtsein. Historische Betrachtungen und Untersuchungen*, Göttingen, 1963.

—— 'Hitler's Image of the United States', *American Historical Review*, 69 (1964).

—— *The Foreign Policy of Hitler's Germany. Diplomatic Revolution in Europe 1933–36*, Chicago/London, 1970.

—— *The Foreign Policy of Hitler's Germany. Starting World War II, 1937–1939*, Chicago/London, 1980.

—— *A World at Arms. A Global History of World War II*, Cambridge, 1994.

Weizsäcker, Ernst von, *Erinnerungen*, Munich/Leipzig/Freiburg, 1950.

Die Weizsäcker-Papiere 1933–1950, ed. Leonidas E. Hill, Frankfurt am Main, 1974.

Welles, Sumner, *The Time for Decision*, London, 1944.

—— *Seven Major Decisions*, London, 1951.

Werth, Alexander, *Russia at War, 1941–1945*, paperback edn., New York, 1984.

Weston, Mark, *Giants of Japan. The Lives of Japan's Greatest Men and Women*, New York/Tokyo/London, 1999.

Whaley, Barton, *Codeword Barbarossa*, Cambridge, Mass., 1973.

Whittam, John, *Fascist Italy*, Manchester, 1995.

Whymant, Robert, *Stalin's Spy. Richard Sorge and the Tokyo Espionage Ring*, London/New York, 1996.

Wildt, Michael, *Die Judenpolitik des SD 1935 bis 1938. Eine Dokumentation*, Munich, 1995.

—— *Generation des Unbedingten. Das Führungskorps des Reichssicherheitshauptamtes*, Hamburg, 2002.

Wilson, Theodore A., *The First Summit. Roosevelt and Churchill at Placentia Bay 1941*, London, 1970.

Wiskemann, Elizabeth, *The Rome–Berlin Axis. A Study of the Relations between Hitler and Mussolini*, London, 1966.

Wistrich, Robert S., *Hitler and the Holocaust*, New York, 2001.

Wohlstetter, Roberta, *Pearl Harbor. Warning and Decision*, Stanford, Calif., 1962.

Woodward, Llewellyn, *British Foreign Policy in the Second World War*, vol. 1, London, 1970.

Woolf, S. J. (ed.), *Fascism in Europe*, 2nd edn., London, 1981.

Wright, Jonathan, *Gustav Stresemann, Weimar's Greatest Statesman*, Oxford, 2002.

Wylie, Neville (ed.), *European Neutrals and Non-Belligerents during the Second World War*, Cambridge, 2002.

Zamagni, Vera, 'Italy: How to Lose the War and Win the Peace', in Mark Harrison (ed.), *The Economics of World War II. Six Great Powers in International Comparison*, Cambridge, 1998.

Zhukov, G., *Reminiscences and Reflections*, 2 vols., Moscow, 1985.

Index

and nature of governments 471–8
in Nazi regime 59–61, 71, 476–7
pressures on 481
significance of personalities 481–3
in United States 202–3, 479–80
use of intelligence 480
decisions, and alternatives 6, 471–83
Germany 70, 85–90, 423–30
Great Britain 50–52
Italy 28–9, 149, 157–9
Japan 375–81
Soviet Union 291–7
United States 240–42, 310–11, 323–4
Dekanozov, Vladimir, Soviet ambassador to Berlin 272, 282, 285–6, 538n
Denmark, German invasion of 20, 23, 64, 150
Dieckhoff, Hans Heinrich, German ambassador in Washington 391, 397
Dimitrov, Georgi, Comintern 285
disarmament, policy of 16
Disarmament Conference (1932–3) 61, 189
Djibouti, French Somaliland 149, 160
Dollfuss, Engelbert, Austrian Chancellor 133
Dönitz, Admiral Karl 384, 409
Dooman, Eugene H., US embassy in Tokyo 347
Dowding, Air Chief Marshal Hugh 25
Dreyfus, Alfred 438
Dunkirk
evacuation of 38, 42, 45, 46, 198, 493n
retreat to 20, 24, 28, 32
Durazzo, port of 171, 174
Dutch East Indies 91, 100, 111, 124
Japanese ambitions in 112, 117, 363
Japanese attack on 366

Earle, George, Governor of Pennsylvania 189
East Africa 77
economy, world 13–14, 58, 77
see also individual countries; Wall Street
Eden, Anthony 16, 17
Edison, Charles, US Naval Secretary 203
Edward VIII, King (Duke of Windsor) 21, 51, 495n
Egypt 13, 77
British forces in 172, 176
Italian offensive against 130, 161–2, 168, 170, 172, 179
Eichmann, Adolf 435, 444
and deportation of Jews 445, 447, 459
and Wannsee Conference 467
Elizabeth, Queen 23
Epirus, Greece 165, 170, 172–3
Erbach-Schönberg, Prince Viktor zu, German ambassador in Athens 165
Eritrea 134
Estonia 55, 259, 260, 267

Far East
ABCD powers 333–4, 368, 379
European and American interests in 4, 5, 14, 15–16, 91
Japanese ambitions in 9, 15–16
and Washington Nine Power Treaty (1922) 15
see also China; Indochina; Japan; Philippines
Farinacci, Roberto, Fascist leader in Cremona 142
Fascist party (Italy) 131–2, 142, 177
Fascist Grand Council 135, 142, 145, 181
relationship to state 141–3, 182
splits in 177, 180–81
and support for war 151, 152

Helli incident 514*n*
Italian invasion 5, 83, 86, 130, 162–82
Greek forces, underestimation of 171, 172, 173, 174–5, 182
Greenland 235, 399
Greenwood, Arthur, Minister without Portfolio in War Cabinet 25, 36, 37, 39, 49
Greer, USS, encounter with U-boat (U-625) 319–23
Greiser, Arthur, head of Gau Wartheland 444–5, 446, 462–3
Grew, Joseph C., American ambassador in Tokyo 109, 118–19, 338, 554*n*
and Japanese decision for war 366, 367
meeting with Konoe 347–8
and proposed meeting of Konoe and Roosevelt 348
Guadacanal, battle of 429
Guadalajara, Italian defeat at (1937) 134
Guilty Men 12
Guzzoni, General Alfredo, Italian commander in Albania 162–3

Hainan Island 100
Halder, Colonel-General Franz, chief of German army General Staff 54, 67, 68, 84, 87
and invasion of Soviet Union 273, 405, 406–7
and Japanese entry into war 416
Halifax, Lord, British Foreign Secretary 12, 18, 23, 24, 49
and American occupation of Iceland 313
and appeal to Roosevelt 30–31, 36, 45, 219
and approach to Mussolini 30, 31–2, 34, 35–40, 43–4

broadcast speech on intention to fight on 66
meeting with Bastianini 32–3, 36, 50, 490*n*
relations with Churchill 491*n*, 494*n*
on Roosevelt's *Greer* speech 323, 326
search for alternatives to fighting 47, 48, 49, 482
Hanfstaengl, Ernst 389
Hara Yoshimichi, president of Japanese Privy Council 331, 343, 345, 365, 371–2
Harnack, Arvid (the 'Corsican'), German communist agent 272–4
Harvey, Oliver, British embassy in Paris 493*n*
Hata Shunroku, Japanese Army Minister 91, 111
Haushofer, Karl 57
Hess, Rudolf 57, 281–2
Heydrich, Reinhard
as architect of 'final solution' 467–8
and deportations 461
and gas chambers 462–3, 465
and 'Jewish Question' 443, 444, 447, 448–9, 451, 460
and Soviet Jews 453, 454
and Wannsee Conference 467, 469
Higashikuni, Prince 354
Hillmann, Sidney, Amalgamated Clothing Workers 228
Himmler, Heinrich, head of SS 59–60, 437, 445
as architect of 'final solution' 467–8
and deportations of Jews 445, 446–7, 448–9
and elimination of Jews 451, 454–5, 462–3
and gas chambers 463–4
and Soviet Jews 452, 456–8

Kan'in Kotohito, Prince, chief of
    Japanese imperial staff 97
Katowice, deportation of Jews from
    445
Kaya Okinori, Japanese Finance
    Minister 358, 360–61, 364–5
Kearny, USS, torpedo attack on
    324–5, 326, 327, 328, 411
Keitel, Field Marshal Wilhelm 83, 87,
    385, 418
Kelly, Edward J., mayor of Chicago
    214
Kennedy, John F. 231
Kennedy, Joseph, US ambassador in
    London 199, 210
Kenya 37
Khrushchev, Nikita 258, 260, 264,
    281, 291
Kido Koichi, Marquis, Japanese Lord
    Privy Seal 101, 114, 343, 354, 355
    and alliance with Axis powers 121
    and negotiations with America 349
Kiev 247, 282–3
King, Admiral Ernest J., US Atlantic
    Fleet 204
King, W. L. Mackenzie, Canadian
    Prime Minister 218, 311
Kirov, Sergei, Leningrad party boss
    245
Kirponos, Lieutenant-General 280
Knox, Frank, US Secretary of the
    Navy 124, 203–4, 215, 216, 373
    and aid for Britain 224
    and Atlantic convoys 311–12
    on German invasion of Soviet
        Union 303–4
Knudsen, William, General Motors
    228
Kondo Bobutake, vice-chief of
    Japanese navy staff 121
Konoe Fumimaro, Prince, Japanese
    Prime Minister 97, 98, 99,
    106–8, 340

and alliance with Axis powers
    122–3
and 'Essentials' plan for war 341–2,
    343–4
first administration (1937–9) 106,
    108
and 'Four Pillars Conference'
    115–16
meeting with Grew 347–8
and negotiations with America 333,
    351–4
opposition to war with America
    334, 376–7, 378
proposal for meeting with
    Roosevelt 335–9, 345
second administration (1940–41)
    109–11, 114–16; resignation
    353–4
Korea, Japanese occupation 92, 93
Krüger, Friedrich-Wilhelm, SS chief
    465
Kube, Wilhelm, Commissar of
    Belorussia 464
Kurusu Saburo, Japanese special
    envoy to Washington 366, 367,
    368, 374, 378
Kvaternik, Marshal Sladko, Croatian
    minister 459–60

Lagarde, Paul de 446
Lammers, Hans Heinrich, head of the
    Reich Chancellery 455
Lateran Pacts (1929) 141
Latvia 55, 259, 260, 267
League of Nations 15, 17, 57
    German withdrawal from 16, 61
    and Italian invasion of Abyssinia
        134, 144
    Japanese withdrawal from 16, 95,
        109
    and Mukden Incident 94
    Soviet membership of 253, 254
    United States and 15, 94, 189

Stalin, Joseph – *cont.*
  relations with Britain 270–71,
    281–2
  rise of 244–5
  and war: expectation of 250; hope
    for American intervention 311;
    need to delay 258, 269, 276,
    281–2, 294–5
  see also Non-Aggression Pact
    (Hitler–Stalin); Red Army; Soviet
    Union
Stalingrad, battle of 429
Stamenov, Ivan, Bulgarian
  ambassador to Moscow 289
Starace, Achille, Fascist Party
  Secretary 142
Stark, Admiral Harold R., US head of
  naval operations 124, 204, 226,
    234
  and Atlantic convoys 304
  and destroyer deal 215, 218
  and occupation of Iceland 312
  and Pearl Harbor 373
Stimson, Henry L., US Secretary of
  War 124, 184, 203, 204, 373
  advice to Roosevelt 185–6, 202,
    206
  and aid for Britain 224
  and defence production 226, 228,
    233–4
  on German invasion of Soviet
    Union 303–4
  and negotiations with Japan 367
  support for intervention 185, 204
  and war with Germany 427
Stresa, Conference of (1935) 133
Stresemann, Gustav, German Foreign
  Minister 15, 57
Sudan 77
Sudoplatov, General Pavel 288–9
Suez Canal
  German intentions for 73, 77, 83, 86
  Italy and 33, 75, 76, 79, 130, 161

Sugiyama Gen, chief of Japanese army
  General Staff 336, 340
  and decision for war 363, 365,
    371
  and 'Essentials' plan for war 342,
    344–5
  and negotiations with America 349,
    357, 360, 363
Sugiyama Gen, Japanese Army
  Minister 97
Suzuki, General Teiichi 345, 351,
    358
  and decision for war 360, 361,
    364–5
Switzerland, Ticino Italian enclave
    163
Syria 79

Taiwan, Japanese occupation 92
Takamatsu, Prince 97–8, 370
Tanaka Shin'chi, Japanese army
  Operations Division 336, 362
Taranto, Italian fleet at 174, 176, 180
Tass, communiqué on British press
  reports 284–5
Texas, USS 400
Thailand 117
Tientsin, blockade of 100
Tilsit, shooting of Jews 453
Timoshenko, Marshal S. K.
  on deficiencies of Red Army 264–5,
    266
  and German invasion 287
  on prospects for war 267–8
  and suggestion of pre-emptive strike
    278–80
  war plans 276, 282–3
Togo Shigenori, Japanese Foreign
  Minister
  appointment 356
  and decision for war 370, 371
  wish to avoid war 359, 360, 361,
    362–4, 378